SERIES

(ex·ploring)

1. Investigating in a systematic way: examining. 2. Searching into or ranging over for the purpose of discovery.

Microsoft®

Microsoft 365® 2021 Word

Series Editor **Mary Anne Poatsy**

Hogan

Content Development: Barbara Stover
Content Management: Ellen Thibault
Content Production: Rudrani Mukherjee
Product Management: Marcus Scherer
Product Marketing: Wayne Stevens
Rights and Permissions: Jenell Forschler

Please contact https://support.pearson.com/getsupport/s/ with any queries on this content

Cover Image by Zedspider/Shutterstock and Hallojulie/Shutterstock

Library of Congress Cataloging-in-Publication Data
Names: Hogan, Lynn, author. | Poatsy, Mary Anne, editor.
Title: Microsoft 365. Word 2021 / series editor, Mary Anne Poatsy ; Hogan,
  [Word author].
Other titles: Word 2021
Description: Boston : Pearson, [2023] | Series: Exploring series | Includes
  bibliographical references and index.
Identifiers: LCCN 2021038347 | ISBN 9780137602438 (paperback)
Subjects: LCSH: Microsoft Word. | Word processing.
Classification: LCC Z52.5.M52 H634 2023 | DDC 005.52—dc23
LC record available at https://lccn.loc.gov/2021038347

3 2022

Print Rental
ISBN 10:   0-13-760243-X
ISBN 13: 978-0-13-760243-8

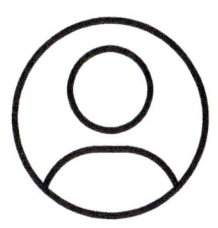

Pearson's Commitment to Diversity, Equity, and Inclusion

Pearson is dedicated to creating bias-free content that reflects the diversity, depth, and breadth of all learners' lived experiences.

We embrace the many dimensions of diversity, including but not limited to race, ethnicity, gender, sex, sexual orientation, socioeconomic status, ability, age, and religious or political beliefs.

Education is a powerful force for equity and change in our world. It has the potential to deliver opportunities that improve lives and enable economic mobility. As we work with authors to create content for every product and service, we acknowledge our responsibility to demonstrate inclusivity and incorporate diverse scholarship so that everyone can achieve their potential through learning. As the world's leading learning company, we have a duty to help drive change and live up to our purpose to help more people create a better life for themselves and to create a better world.

Our ambition is to purposefully contribute to a world where:

- Everyone has an equitable and lifelong opportunity to succeed through learning.
- Our educational content accurately reflects the histories and lived experiences of the learners we serve.

- Our educational products and services are inclusive and represent the rich diversity of learners.
- Our educational content prompts deeper discussions with students and motivates them to expand their own learning (and worldview).

Accessibility

We are also committed to providing products that are fully accessible to all learners. As per Pearson's guidelines for accessible educational Web media, we test and retest the capabilities of our products against the highest standards for every release, following the WCAG guidelines in developing new products for copyright year 2022 and beyond.

 You can learn more about Pearson's commitment to accessibility at **https://www.pearson.com/us/accessibility.html**

Contact Us

While we work hard to present unbiased, fully accessible content, we want to hear from you about any concerns or needs with this Pearson product so that we can investigate and address them.

 Please contact us with concerns about any potential bias at **https://www.pearson.com/report-bias.html**

 For accessibility-related issues, such as using assistive technology with Pearson products, alternative text requests, or accessibility documentation, email the Pearson Disability Support team at **disability.support@pearson.com**

  Pearson

Dedications

For my husband, Ted, who unselfishly continues to take on more than his share to support me throughout the process; and for my children, Laura, Carolyn, and Ted, whose encouragement and love have been inspiring.
Mary Anne Poatsy

For my father, Lawrence Conwill, a lifelong educator and administrator who has inspired so many both in and out of a classroom. His legacy in education and his love of family can never be truly matched but are something I will always aspire to and admire in him. He is my hero.
Lynn Hogan

About the Authors

Mary Anne Poatsy, Series Editor, Common Features, Windows, and Teams Author

Mary Anne is a senior faculty member at Montgomery County Community College, teaching various computer application and concepts courses in face-to-face and online environments. She holds a B.A. in Psychology and Education from Mount Holyoke College and an M.B.A. in Finance from Northwestern University's Kellogg Graduate School of Management.

Mary Anne has more than 25 years of educational experience. She has taught at Gwynedd Mercy College, Bucks County Community College, and Muhlenberg College. She also engages in corporate training. Before teaching, she was Vice President at Shearson Lehman in the Municipal Bond Investment Banking Department.

Dr. Lynn Hogan, Word Author

Dr. Lynn Hogan currently teaches at the University of North Alabama, providing instruction in the area of computer applications. Prior to her current assignment, she taught for more than 25 years at the community college level, serving in academic administration and teaching applications, programming, and concepts courses in both online and classroom environments. She has served as an author for several Pearson publications over the past 14 years, including *Exploring* 2010, 2013, and 2016. She also contributed Word chapters for the first edition of *Your Office* and developed and wrote *Practical Computing*. She received an M.B.A. from the University of North Alabama and a Ph.D. from the University of Alabama.

Lynn has two daughters and resides with her husband, Paul, in Alabama. Her interests include creative writing, photography, traveling, and helping manage a family horse farm.

Brief Contents

Contents

Microsoft Office 2021

Microsoft Office Word 2021

Acknowledgments

It takes the dedication of many individuals to publish a product like the *Exploring Series*. In addition to the team of talented and knowledgeable authors, others deserve to be recognized for their hard work to ensure the *Exploring Series* consistently exceeds the expectations of our users. In particular, we'd like to thank Jenifer Niles, Manager Higher Ed Content Strategy, Ellen Thibault, Senior Content Manager, and Marcus Scherer, Product Manager, who have provided constant support and encouragement throughout the project. In addition, a heartfelt thanks to our Developmental Editor, Barbara Stover. We could not have done this without her kind support, stellar management and organizational skills, and eagle eye for details! We would also like to extend our appreciation to the Media and Production team, especially Heather Darby, Digital Content Specialist, Becca Golden, Product Management Analyst, and Rudrani Mukherjee, Content Producer, for all their hard work and steadfast commitment.

There are so many other people whom we do not meet at Pearson and elsewhere who have helped to design and illustrate the book, compose pages, produce media, and secure permissions. We thank them all!

Last, but not least, the *Exploring* team would like to acknowledge and thank all the reviewers who helped us throughout the years by providing us with their invaluable comments, suggestions, and constructive criticism that help us continue to improve the *Exploring Series* with each new edition and update.

The Exploring Series and You

The *Exploring Series* keeps students at the forefront of project and content creation by focusing on the skills, functionality, and concepts of Microsoft 365 that are needed to succeed in a cloud-based world. Students are challenged to think "beyond the point and click" and to learn to adapt as productivity tools and apps continually update and change.

The goal of the *Exploring Series* is to provide more than the steps to accomplish a task—but to explain the skills in real-life context so students understand not just *how* to apply a skill but *when* and *why* to use the skill. The visual design presents the theory content on *White* pages and the Hands-On Exercises on *Yellow* pages. Students can easily jump between the pages using *visual step icons* if they want to try a Hands-On Exercise or need a reminder of the *why* from the theory pages. With this understanding, students know which application, function, or feature to use to achieve specific goals and to critically solve problems in academic work and future career roles.

In this 2021 edition, the *Exploring Series* continues to keep pace with Microsoft 365 application updates through constant content review and semester updates to the eText. And with a greater emphasis on Mac compatibility and critical thinking, all students will be able to work effectively and attain the skills needed to succeed no matter which device they are working on.

The most effective way to use the *Exploring Series* is through **MyLab IT**, where students and instructors have the teaching and learning platform that empowers learning. By combining trusted author content with digital tools and a flexible platform, MyLab IT personalizes the learning experience and improves results for each student. The *Exploring Series* MyLab IT 2021 delivers trusted content and resources through an expansive course materials library, including updated easy-to-use Ready-to-Assign modules that promote student success. Through an authentic learning experience, students become sharp critical thinkers and proficient in Microsoft Office, developing essential skills employers seek.

New and Updated Content

NEW Content: All content for Excel, Word, and PowerPoint has been revised and updated for Microsoft 2021 Office Applications with many new scenarios and projects.

NEW Windows *and* macOS chapter teaches the fundamentals of operating systems and file management.

NEW Microsoft Teams chapter covers the essential functionality and collaboration tools of this popular application used in businesses and online academic courses.

Updated Common Features chapter presents the most commonly used features that are similar across most Microsoft 365 applications and is especially helpful for those new to Microsoft 365 applications.

More Focus on Mac: Mac usage is growing, and Microsoft continues to improve cross-system compatibility of the Office applications. All of the content has been created, updated, and tested to work as seamlessly as possible, whether the student is working in Windows or macOS. Each chapter includes *Mac How To* boxes, *Mac Tip* boxes, and *Mac Troubleshooting* tips.

NEW Critical Thinking questions throughout each chapter (formerly Quick Concept Checks) ensure students are really understanding the "why" and not just the skills.

NEW *Cumulative* chapter projects (formerly chapter Capstone exercises) assess students' understanding of all the skills taught in the chapter. Available as Grader projects.

Series Hallmarks

- **Pedagogical approach** of *how* to apply a skill and *when* and *why* to use the skill delivered through theory and hands-on content and a visual design. **Case Studies** present a scenario for the chapter, creating a story that ties the Hands-On Exercises together and gives context to the skills being introduced.

- **Hands-On Exercise Videos** are tied to each Hands-On Exercise and walk students through the steps of the exercise while weaving in conceptual information related to the Case Study and the objectives as a whole.

An **Outcomes focus** allows students and instructors to know the higher-level learning goals and how those are achieved through discreet objectives and skills.

- **Outcomes** presented at the beginning of each chapter identify the learning goals for students and instructors.

- **Objective Mapping** enables students to follow a directed path from the objectives list through the exercises at the end of the chapter.

   Objectives List: Provides a simple list of key chapter objectives including page numbers for easy navigation.

   Step Icons: Appear in the white theory pages to reference the step numbers in the yellow pages with Hands-On Exercises so students can easily find conceptual help when needed as they work hands-on.

   Critical Thinking questions (Formerly Quick Concept Questions): Provided at the end of each white theory section, these cover the most essential concepts required to complete the Hands-On Exercises successfully. Page numbers are included for easy reference to help students locate the answers.

   Chapter Objectives Review: Located near the end of the chapter and reviews all important concepts covered in the chapter. Designed in an easy-to-read bulleted format.

   MOS Certification Guide for instructors and students to direct anyone interested in prepping for the MOS exam to the specific locations to find all content required for the test.

End-of-Chapter Exercises offer instructors several options for assessment. Each chapter has approximately 9–11 exercises ranging from multiple choice questions to open-ended projects.

   Multiple Choice, Key Terms Matching, Practice Exercises, Mid-Level Exercises, Running Case, Disaster Recovery, and Cumulative Exercises are at the end of all chapters.

   Application Capstone exercises are included in the book to allow instructors to test students on the contents of a single application.

The Exploring Series MyLab IT

The *Exploring Series* MyLab IT 2021 is the easiest and most accessible in its history. MyLab IT provides everything instructors and students need—the instruction, practice, training, and assessment all in one location. The fully integrated **eText, Grader Projects**, and **Simulations** combine to offer the highest-quality, in-depth content and the best technology available.

With *Ready-to-Assign Modules* and LMS Integration, course setup has never been easier. The LMS integration gives users seamless access to MyLab IT with single sign-on, grade sync, and asset-level deep linking.

NEW Gradebook: The all-new MyLab IT Gradebook provides a modern and streamlined experience for instructors and students alike. Dynamic search and advanced filtering allow users to quickly and easily see the most relevant assignment results without drilling into subfolders or manually creating complex custom reports.

Updated Ready-to-Assign Modules make course setup a snap. The modules are based on research and instructor best practices and can be easily customized to meet your course requirements.

Critical Thinking Modules pair a Grader Project with a critical thinking objective-based quiz that requires students to first complete a hands-on Grader Project and then answer a series of objective-based critical thinking questions. These are offered both at the chapter level for regular practice and at the application level where students can earn a critical thinking badge.

MyLab IT eText

NEW Pearson eText available through MyLab IT provides a visually appealing design, enhanced note taking and mobile functionality, linking between White and Yellow pages, and direct links to videos and interactive study tools that engage students and improve learning.

Continued eText Semester Updates: The *Exploring Series* provides a market-leading approach to keeping pace with Microsoft® 365® updates. The Microsoft 365 updates are reviewed regularly by the authors and updated in the eText each semester so students don't get confused and can continue to work projects without frustration.

MyLab IT Grader Projects

The *Exploring Series* includes a wide variety of live-in-the-application, autograded Grader projects for homework and assessment. The Grader Projects enable students to gain real-world context as they work live in the Office applications, applying an understanding of both how and why to perform certain skills to complete a project.

- **Final Solution Image.** Homework Graders include a final solution image allowing students to visualize what their solution should look like.

- **Critical Thinking** is encouraged by incorporating the scenario and the "why" in the instructions so that students think critically about the steps they are performing.

- **Learning Aids.** The Grader report includes a video to help students learn and remediate for steps done incorrectly.

NEW Hands-On-Exercise Grader Projects: The *Hands-On Exercise* Grader Projects now follow the skills in the textbook projects so students can work live in the application to demonstrate their understanding.

New Microsoft *Office for the web* Grader Projects are available in MyLab IT for Chapters 1–4 of Word, Excel, and PowerPoint specifically for students using the Web versions of these applications.

Enhanced Mac Compatibility in Grader Projects: All Graders are tested for Mac compatibility, provide 100% Mac compatibility where possible, and are identified in the course. This excludes Access projects as well as any that use functionality not available in Mac Office.

Autograded Integrated Grader Projects: Based on the discipline-specific topics, these integrated projects use Word, Excel, PowerPoint, and Access in meaningful ways so students can experience the interconnectedness of these applications in Microsoft 365.

Application Capstone Graders for each Application (Word, Excel, PowerPoint, and Access) cover all the skills from the chapter and allow students to earn an application-specific badge.

MyLab IT Simulations

The *Exploring Series* includes realistic Microsoft application simulations to help students feel like they are working in the actual applications where they can explore and practice skills and get feedback and assistance through integrated learning aids:

> **Read** (via the eText)
>
> **Watch** (via an author-created hands-on video)
>
> **Practice** (via a guided simulation) whenever they get stuck

These are conveniently accessible directly *within the simulation training* so that students do not have to leave the graded assignment to access these helpful resources. Available for all the Hands-On Exercises *training* versions.

- **One-to-One Content Match.** Simulations are authored by the *Exploring Series* author team to ensure one-to-one content matching the Hands-On Exercises.

- **Student Action Visualization** (video) is included for the training simulations to provide a playback of the exact student actions to help students with remediation and instructors to provide guidance.

- **Virtual Keyboard** that enables students to complete keyboard actions entirely on screen. There is also an enhanced focus on Mac compatibility with even more Mac-compatible Grader projects.

Badging and Employability Skills

- **High-demand Office skills** needed to succeed in work and to prepare for Microsoft Office Certification exams (MOS) are taught throughout.
  - **MOS Objective Appendix** provides a clear map of where to find each objective in the textbook content.
  - **Practice Exam Grader Projects** are available in MyLab IT.

- **Digital Badges** are available for students in Introductory and Advanced Microsoft Word, Excel, Access, and PowerPoint.
  - Digital credential issued to students upon successful completion (90%+ score) of an *Application Capstone Badging Grader* project.
  - MyLab IT badges provide verification of proficiency with the applicable skills and help distinguish students within the job pool. Badges can be placed in a LinkedIn profile, posted on social media (Facebook, Twitter), and/or included in a résumé.

- **Critical Thinking Badges** provide verification that learners have demonstrated the ability to not only complete a real project, but also to analyze and problem-solve using Microsoft Office 365 applications. Students prove this by completing an objective quiz that requires them to critically think about the project, interpret data, and explain why they performed the actions they did. Critical Thinking is an essential skill sought after by employers.

Resources

Instructor Teaching Resources	
Supplements Available to Instructors at www.pearsonhighered.com/ exploring	**Features of the Supplement**
Instructor's Manual	Available for each chapter and includes:
	• List of all Chapter Resources, File Names, and Where to Find
	• Chapter Overview
	• Class Run-Down
	• Key Terms
	• Discussion Questions
	• Practice Projects & Applications
	• Teaching Notes
	• Additional Web Resources
	• Projects and Exercises with File Names
	• Solutions to Multiple Choice, Key Terms Matching, and Critical Thinking
Solutions Files, Annotated Solution Files, Scorecards	• Available for all exercises with definitive solutions
	• Annotated Solution Files in PDF feature callouts to enable easy grading
	• Scorecards for easy scoring for hand-grading all exercises with definitive solutions and scoring by step adding to 100 points
Test Bank	Approximately 75–100 total questions per chapter, made up of multiple-choice, true/false, and matching
	Questions include these annotations:
	• Correct Answer
	• Difficulty Level
	• Learning Objective
	Alternative versions of the Test Bank are available for the following LMS: Blackboard CE/Vista, Blackboard, Desire2Learn, Moodle, Sakai, and Canvas

Computerized TestGen	TestGen allows instructors to: • Customize, save, and generate classroom tests • Edit, add, or delete questions from the Test Item Files • Analyze test results • Organize a database of tests and student results
PowerPoint Presentations	PowerPoint presentations for each chapter cover key topics, feature key images from the text, and include detailed speaker notes in addition to the slide content. PowerPoint presentations meet accessibility standards for students with disabilities. Features include, but are not limited to: • Keyboard and Screen Reader access • Alternative text for images • High color contrast between background and foreground colors
Outcome and Objective Maps	• Available for each chapter to help determine what to assign • Includes every exercise and identifies which outcomes, objectives, and skills are included from the chapter
MOS Mapping, MOS Online Appendix	• Based on the most current MOS Objectives • Includes a full mapping of where each objective is covered in the materials • For any content not covered in the textbook, additional material is available in the Online Appendix document
Transition Guide	A detailed spreadsheet that provides a clear mapping of content from Exploring Microsoft Office 2019 to Exploring Microsoft Office 365, 2021 Edition
Sample Syllabus	Syllabus templates set up for 8-week, 12-week, and 16-week courses
Answer Keys for Multiple Choice, Key Terms Matching, and Critical Thinking	Answer keys for each objective, matching, or short-answer question type from each chapter

Student Resources

Supplements Available to Students at www.pearsonhighered.com/exploring	**Features of the Supplement**
Student Data Files	All data files needed for the following exercises, organized by chapter: • Hands-On Exercises • Practice Exercises • Mid-Level Exercises • Running Case • Disaster Recovery Case • Cumulative Exercise
MOS Certification Material	• Based on the most current MOS Objectives • Includes a full mapping of where each objective is covered in the materials • For any content not covered in the textbook, additional material is available in the Online Appendix document

Operating Systems and File Management

LEARNING OUTCOMES

You will explore the Windows and macOS desktop environments and work with open windows.

You will organize files and folders using File Explorer and Finder.

OBJECTIVES & SKILLS: After you read this chapter, you will be able to:

Operating System Fundamentals

There are two types of software on your computer: application software and system software. ***Application software*** consists of programs you use for email, gaming, social networking, and digital photo management. Application software also includes productivity software such as word processing, spreadsheet, and presentation applications. ***System software*** is the essential software the computer needs to function. System software includes the operating system and utility programs, and helps to run application software, manage your files, and manage system resources and other computer activities.

In this section, you will learn about the desktop features of the Windows and macOS operating systems. You will also learn how to work with windows and how to organize and group your tasks into different desktops.

Work with Windows and MacOS

CHAPTER 1

Dean Drobot/Shutterstock

Navigate the Desktop

Windows is Microsoft's operating system and is available for desktops, laptops, and tablet computers. *macOS* is Apple's operating system that is used on Apple desktop and laptop computers. Windows 10 has been the operating system from Microsoft since 2015; and Windows 11 is the newest release. Big Sur is the latest version of macOS. A separate operating system, iOS, is used on Apple iPads and iPhones. This section will focus on Windows and macOS.

Explore the Windows Desktop

Once you sign into Windows, the first thing you will see is the *desktop*, the main workspace for the operating system. The key features of the Windows desktop are discussed in Table 1.1. Figure 1.1 displays the Windows 11 desktop.

For a little variety, you can customize the desktop with a different background or color theme. You can choose to display a slide show of favorite photos or a static image. To change the desktop background, right-click an empty area of the desktop and click Personalize. Alternatively, from the Start menu, click Settings, click Personalization, and then select Background from the Personalization menu. You can also select a color or picture to display on the lock screen. A lock screen is a security feature that displays when a computer has been idle for a while to prevent unauthorized users from accessing the device.

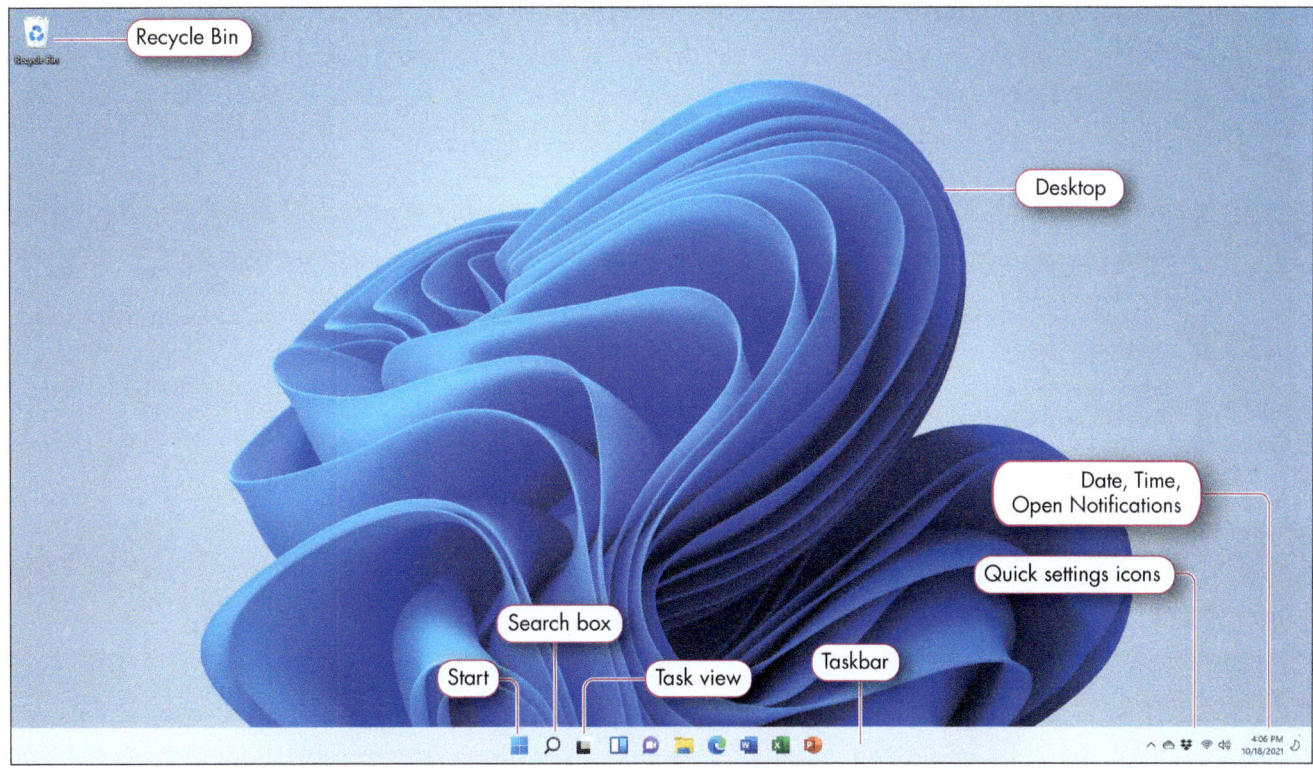

FIGURE 1.1 Windows 11 Desktop Features

TABLE 1.1 Windows Desktop Features

Quick settings	Provides quick access to settings and notifications from apps, new email, and other updates; quick settings is customizable.
Desktop background	Enables you to personalize your workspace by choosing a built-in image or an image of your own. The desktop background is also known as the *wallpaper*.
Notification area	Includes a clock and calendar, as well as access to notifications.
Windows	Displays open folders or applications. Active windows can be minimized so they remain available but not seen, maximized to take up the full screen, or closed. All windows include a title bar.
Recycle Bin	Provides temporary storage for files deleted from the C: drive on your computer. To permanently delete files, right-click the Recycle Bin and choose Empty Recycle Bin.
Search	Searches for documents, applications, and other information.
Start	Opens the Start menu when clicked. Right-click to access the Power User Menu, which contains options for the computer system and disk management.
Taskbar	Contains shortcuts to applications, date and time, Search, and Task view.

Explore the macOS Desktop

The operating system that runs on Apple desktop and laptop computers is macOS. Like Windows the main workspace for macOS is the desktop and displays when you power on a Mac. The key features to the macOS desktop are outlined in Table 1.2. The Menu Bar displays at the top of the macOS desktop and provides access to many features of the operating system, open applications, and notifications as are shown in Figure 1.2.

TABLE 1.2 macOS Desktop Features

Desktop background	Enables you to personalize your space with your own image or a built-in image.
Menu Bar	Contains the Apple menu and menu options for the active application on the left side of the Menu Bar. The right side of the Menu Bar contains Status menus (such as Wi-Fi and Battery), Spotlight, Ask Siri, Control Center, and Notification Center.
Apple Menu	Provides access to System Preferences, recent documents, and to shut down the computer. Denoted by the Apple icon.
Apps Menu	Displays the name of the active application in bold, followed by other menus for that application, such as File, Edit, Format, and Help.
Notification Center	Displays alerts of upcoming appointments, weather, and other real-time events.
Spotlight	Searches for files or applications.
Control Center	Provides access to features such as AirDrop, Screen and Keyboard Brightness, Sound and Music controls.
The Dock	Contains shortcuts to applications, files, and folders. You can use the Dock to quickly open programs and switch between open programs.
Trash	Provides temporary storage for files deleted from the hard drive. You can recover deleted files from Trash. You can empty Trash to permanently delete all files in Trash.

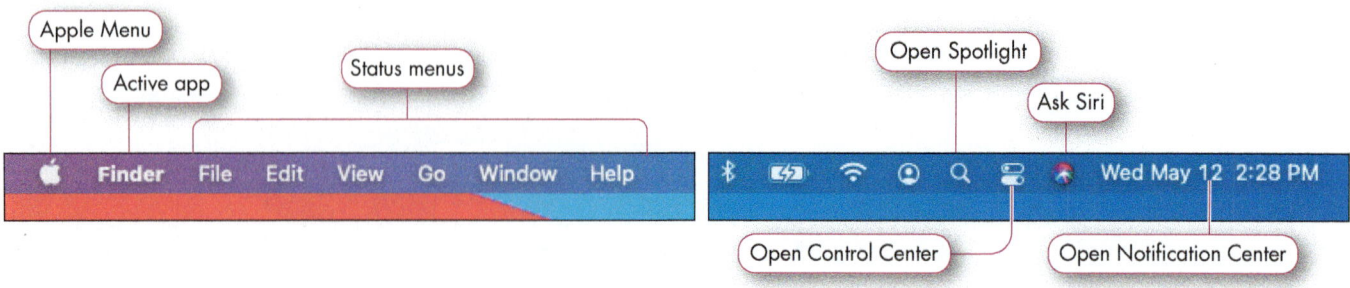

FIGURE 1.2 macOS Menu Bar

Use the Taskbar

At the bottom of the Windows desktop is the *taskbar* (refer to Figure 1.1). The taskbar is used to access applications and other desktop features. Application icons display in the middle of the taskbar when the application is open or when an application icon is pinned to the taskbar for easy access. You can also access notifications and use Search to search for documents, apps, and webpages.

You can *pin*, or add, frequently used apps or websites to the taskbar for faster access. If the program that you want to pin is open, right-click the program icon on the taskbar, and then click Pin to taskbar. Alternatively, locate the program from the Start menu, right-click the program name, click More, and then select Pin to taskbar. A short grey line displays under the open program icons. Although several windows can be open at one time, only one is active. A longer blue line displays under the active program icon and the background of the active program icon is shaded (see Figure 1.3).

FIGURE 1.3 Taskbar with Active, Pinned, and Open Program Icons

Figure 1.4 shows two windows on the Windows desktop, with corresponding taskbar program icons. You can move from one open program to another by clicking the program's icon on the taskbar. Right-click a program icon to display the Jump List. A *Jump List* is a list of program-specific shortcuts to recently opened files, the program name, an option to pin or unpin an item, and to close any windows in that application.

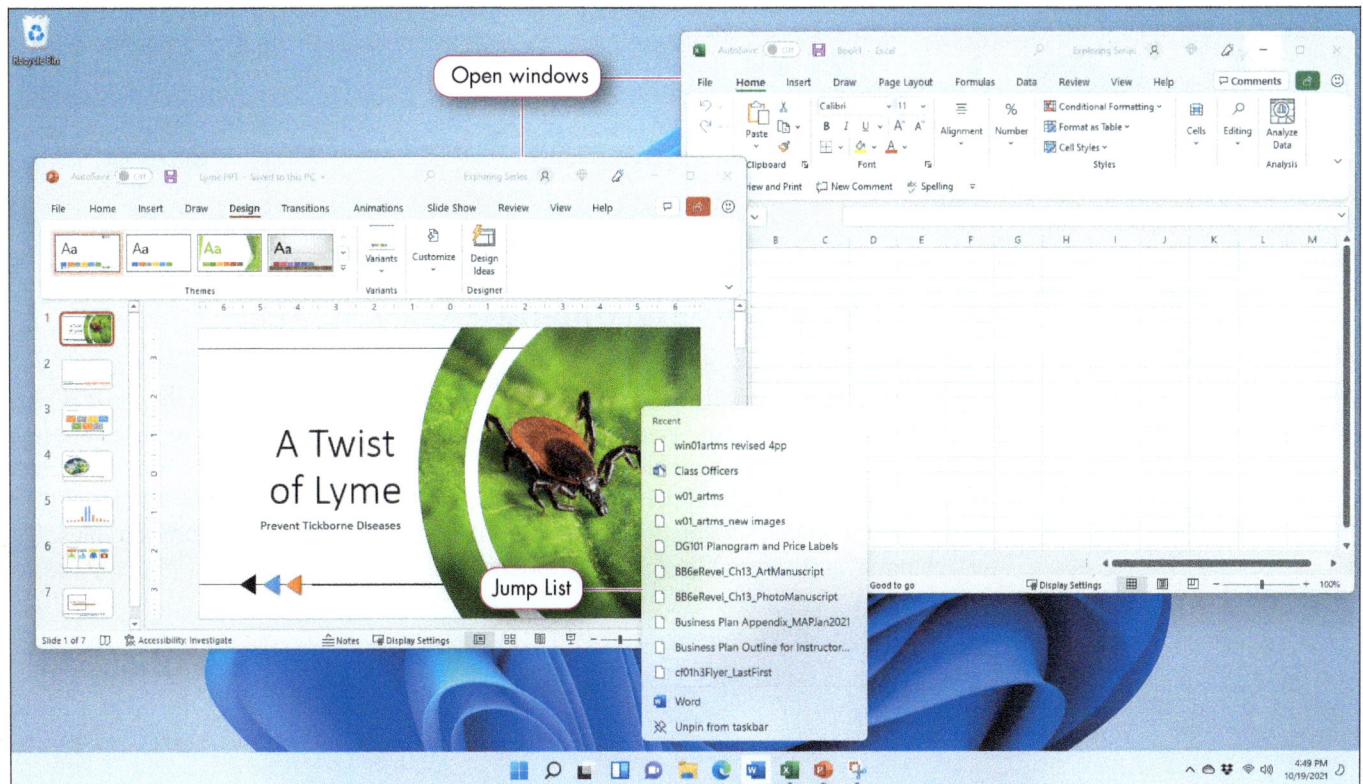

FIGURE 1.4 Desktop with Open Windows

On the right side of the taskbar are system icons, including clock and calendar, volume, Internet access, and access to OneDrive. In Windows 11, clicking on the grouped Wi-Fi and sound icons displays a Quick Settings menu where you can adjust what system icons display on the taskbar, as well as modify volume and brightness settings.

In Windows 11, notification alerts display next to the date and time. To display the notifications, click on the date and time. The notifications display above a calendar, where they can be managed, cleared, or acted upon. In Windows 10, the Action Center is opened by clicking on the chat icon on the right side of the taskbar.

FIGURE 1.5 The macOS Dock

Use the Windows Start Menu

The Windows **Start menu** provides main access to all programs and features on your computer. Click Start on the taskbar or press the Windows key to open the Start menu. As shown in Figure 1.6, the Windows 11 Start Menu has two areas: the top area displays pinned apps. The Recommended section on the bottom of the Start menu displays recently used files. You can access all installed apps by clicking All apps. Clicking More in the Recommended section displays additional recently used applications and files. The Search box is at the very top of the Start Menu.

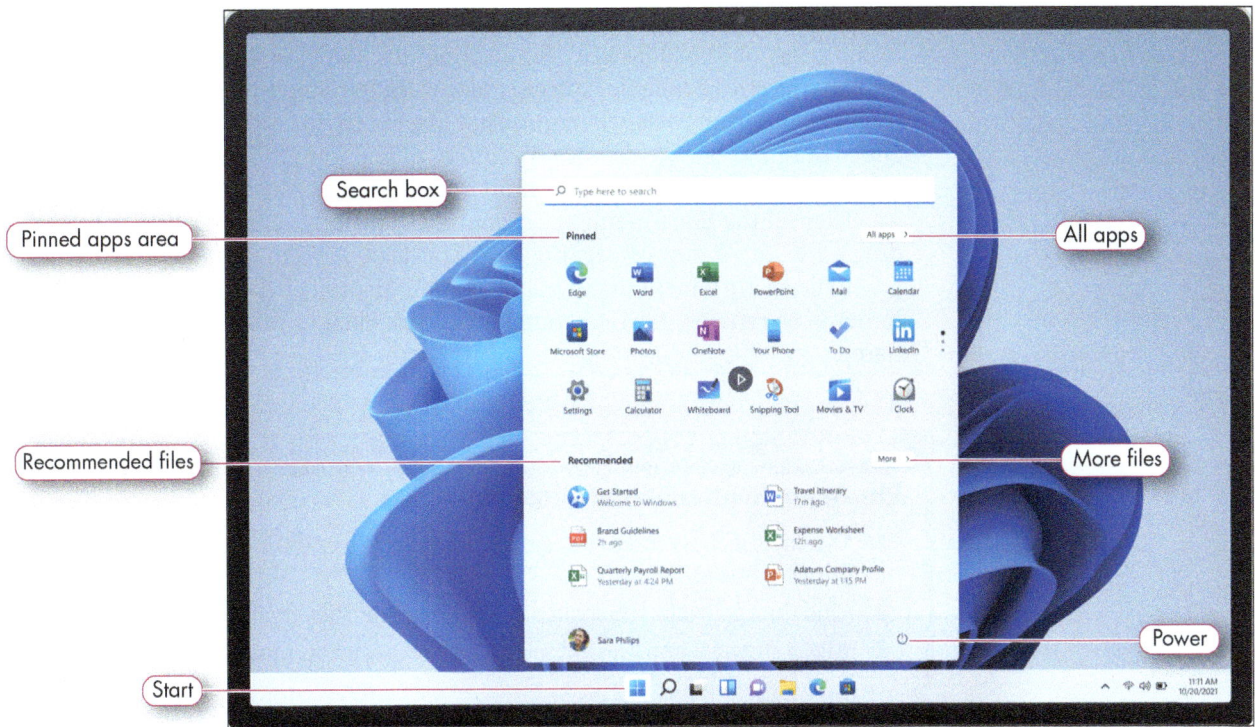

FIGURE 1.6 Windows 11 Start Menu

Figure 1.7 shows the Windows 10 Start menu, which has two areas. The left side of the Windows 10 Start menu displays a list of all apps installed on your computer. In addition, it provides access to Documents (File Explorer), Pictures, Settings, and Power controls. You can also access your account settings. These features are discussed later in this chapter.

The right side of the Windows 10 Start menu provides access to your most frequently used programs and folders. Shortcuts to a program or folder is represented by a *tile* that you can pin to the Start menu. Click or tap a tile on the Start menu to launch a program or open a folder. You can add and remove, resize, and move tiles on the Start menu as well as group tiles and name the groups.

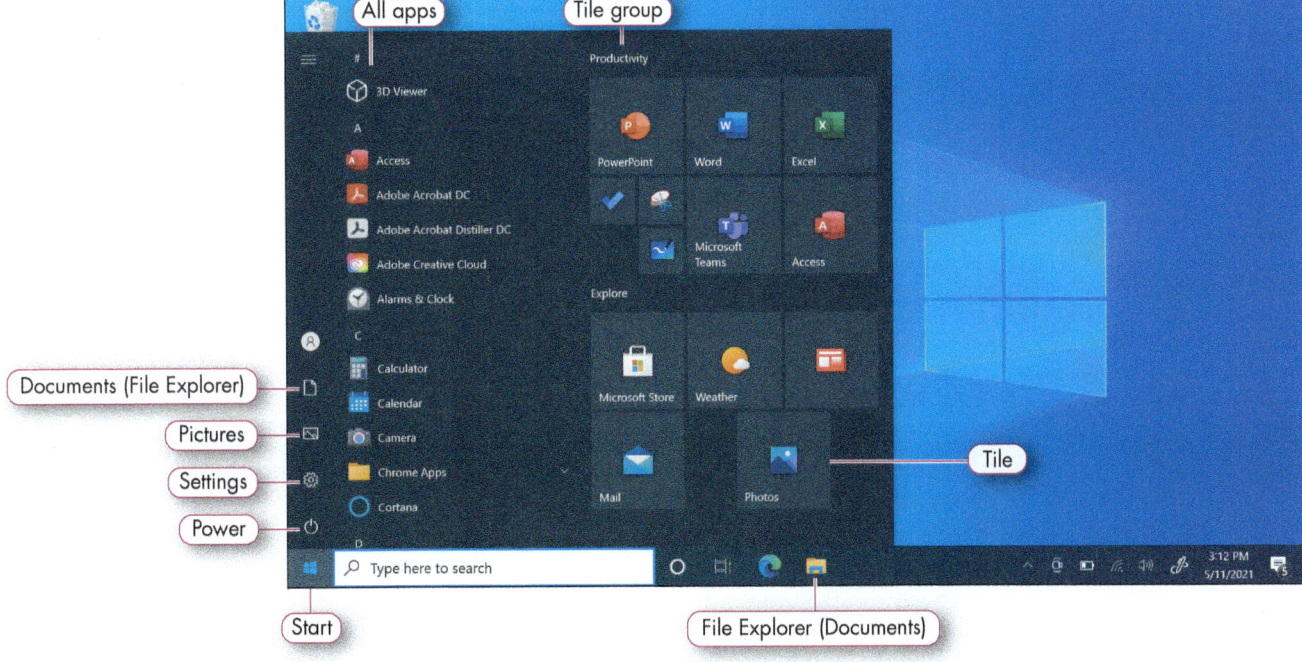

FIGURE 1.7 Windows 10 Start Menu

To resize a tile on the Start menu, right-click a tile, point to Resize, and then select from the list of available sizes: Small, Medium, Wide, or Large. Note that some tiles may not have all sizes available. You may also want to remove tiles from the Start menu. These might be programs or applications that display on the Start menu by default or tiles you added but now want to remove. To unpin an app from the Start menu, right-click the tile you want to remove and select Unpin from Start to remove the tile.

Tiles on the Start menu are organized in groups, as shown in Figure 1.7. Click and drag a tile into a new or existing group or drag a group to a new location. You can also give a tile group a meaningful name. Point to the top of the tile or group of tiles you want to name or rename if a new name is needed, click in the box that displays, and enter a name.

HOW TO

Pin an application to the Start menu:

1. Display the Start menu by clicking Start on the taskbar or by pressing Windows on your keyboard.
2. Find the application that you want to pin to the Start menu.
3. Right-click the app tile and select Pin to Start. (You may also choose Pin to taskbar.)

MAC TIP: USE THE LAUNCHPAD
All applications installed on a Mac are found in the Applications folder in Finder. Apps downloaded from the App Store or that are part of macOS can be found in Launchpad. Launchpad is a convenient place to find, organize, and open apps. Click Launchpad on the Dock to open it, then click any app's icon in Launchpad to open the application. You can also type the app name in the Search box and press Return to open the app. To better organize apps within Launchpad, drag the app icon to any location within Launchpad. You can further organize your applications by grouping them into folders. To create a folder in Launchpad, find two apps you want in the same folder and drag one app icon onto the other. The folder will be assigned a name based on the perceived commonality of the apps. However, you can rename any folder by clicking the folder's name and typing a new name. To remove an app from a folder, drag the app away. You cannot remove an app directly from Launchpad. Instead, the app must be removed from the Applications folder in Finder. To close Launchpad, click anywhere in the desktop.

Work with Open Windows

In both Windows and macOS, each application, file, or folder that you use displays as a window. When only one window is open, there is little management that needs to happen to facilitate your workspace beyond opening, closing, maximizing or minimizing the window. When more than one window is open, you can modify how they display to work most efficiently. You can move, resize, and close windows as well as arrange windows automatically, even snapping them quickly to the desktop borders.

Resize and Close Windows

All windows share common elements to help you to manage the size and position of any window on the desktop. At the top of each window is a *title bar* that displays the name of the opened folder, file, or program. Controls on the right side of the title bar in Windows and on the left side of the title bar in macOS enable you to minimize, maximize (or restore down), or close any open window (see Figure 1.8).

To Minimize:

- In Windows, clicking the horizontal line hides a window from view but does not close it. You can click on the taskbar icon to view the window again.

- In macOS, clicking the yellow button minimizes a window so it no longer displays on the desktop, but the file remains open and accessible from the Dock.

To Maximize/Restore down:

- In Windows, when a window is open, but less than full size, clicking the small box, brings a window to full size. When a window is full size, Restore Down, represented by two overlapping boxes, displays. Clicking Restore Down returns a window to the size it was before the window was maximized.

- In macOS, click the green button to size a window to full screen mode.

To Close:

- In Windows, clicking the X closes a window. When you close a window, you remove the file or program from the computer's random access memory (RAM). RAM is temporary (or volatile) storage, meaning files stored in RAM are not permanently saved. To save a file so you can access it later, the file must be saved to a permanent storage device such as the computer's hard drive or a flash drive or to OneDrive or other Web-based storage. If you have not saved a file or any changes that you have made to a previously saved file that you are closing, Windows 10 will prompt you to save it. If the file is saved to OneDrive, AutoSave is enabled by default so that the file changes are automatically saved periodically. You can turn AutoSave off if you want to maintain control of when to save changes.

- In macOS, clicking the red button closes the window but does not close the application. If there are unsaved changes to a file, a black dot displays in the center of the Close button, and you will be asked to save the file before continuing to close.

TIP: RIBBON DISPLAY OPTIONS

Ribbon Display Options enables you to auto-hide the ribbon, show only the ribbon tabs, or to show the ribbon tabs and commands all the time. Collapse the Ribbon displays at the lower right corner of the ribbon (see Figure 1.8). Click this to show only tabs, and then double-click any tab to display the full ribbon.

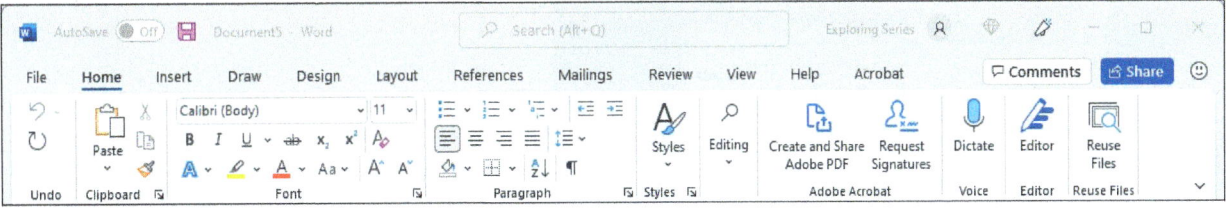
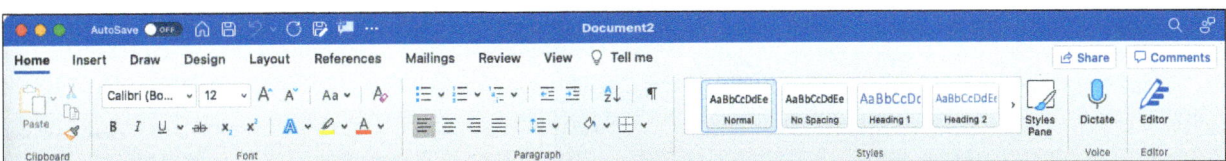

FIGURE 1.8 Resize and Close Window Controls for Windows (Top) and macOS (Bottom)

Snap and Move Windows

Working with multiple open windows at the same time sometimes requires moving or resizing windows so you can see the contents of each window. *Snap assist* is a feature in Windows to "snap" windows to either side or in any of the corners of the screen. Drag any window to the edge of the screen until an outline of the expanded window displays indicating where the windows will snap to once the mouse button is released. When you release the mouse button, thumbnails of all other open windows display (see Figure 1.9), giving you the option of selecting which window should display on the other side of the screen. If you want to display a third or fourth window, press Windows plus an arrow key, to snap windows into corners. Windows 11 offers *Snap layouts* so you have more options on how to arrange open windows. To use Snap layouts, point to a window's maximize control, choose a layout, and click on a zone in that layout to snap that window into place.

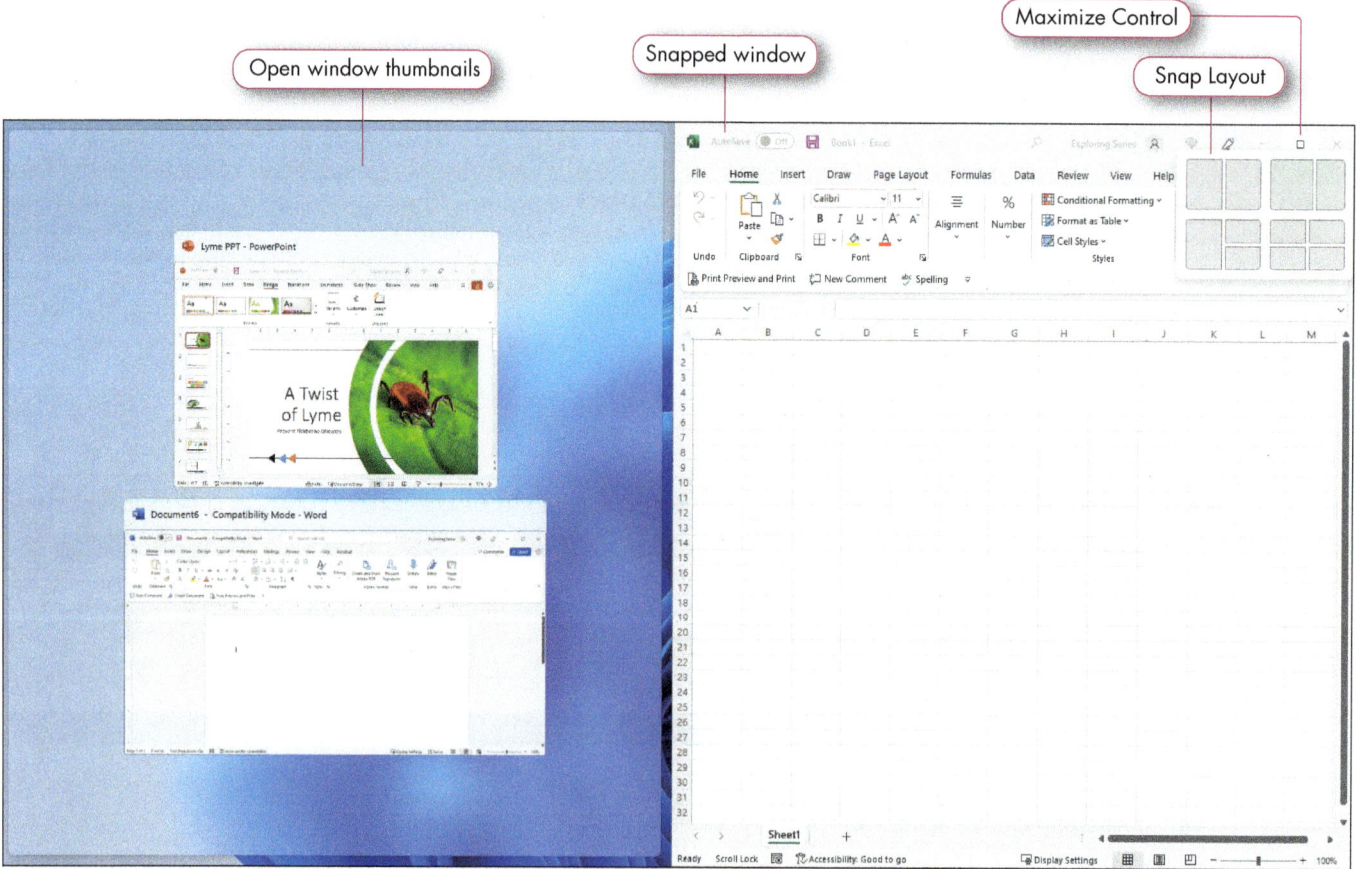

FIGURE 1.9 Snap Assist

Instead of using Snap assist or Snap layout, you can freely position windows on your display. To do so, first restore down a window if it is maximized, and then drag the window to the new location.

Use Task View

As explained earlier, the desktop is the main workspace where you can view all open programs and files. While you can easily view a few open windows on your desktop, if you are working on multiple projects at the same time, it may be difficult to organize and view many open windows or files that are visible onscreen or opened but minimized and offscreen. **Task view** enables you to quickly see all open windows at the same time (see Figure 1.10). In Windows 10, Task view also shows a timeline of your activities on all the devices connected to your Microsoft account for the past 30 days. In addition to accessing any files you have recently used, the timeline enables you to quickly resume work on a document or view a webpage that you may not have used in a while.

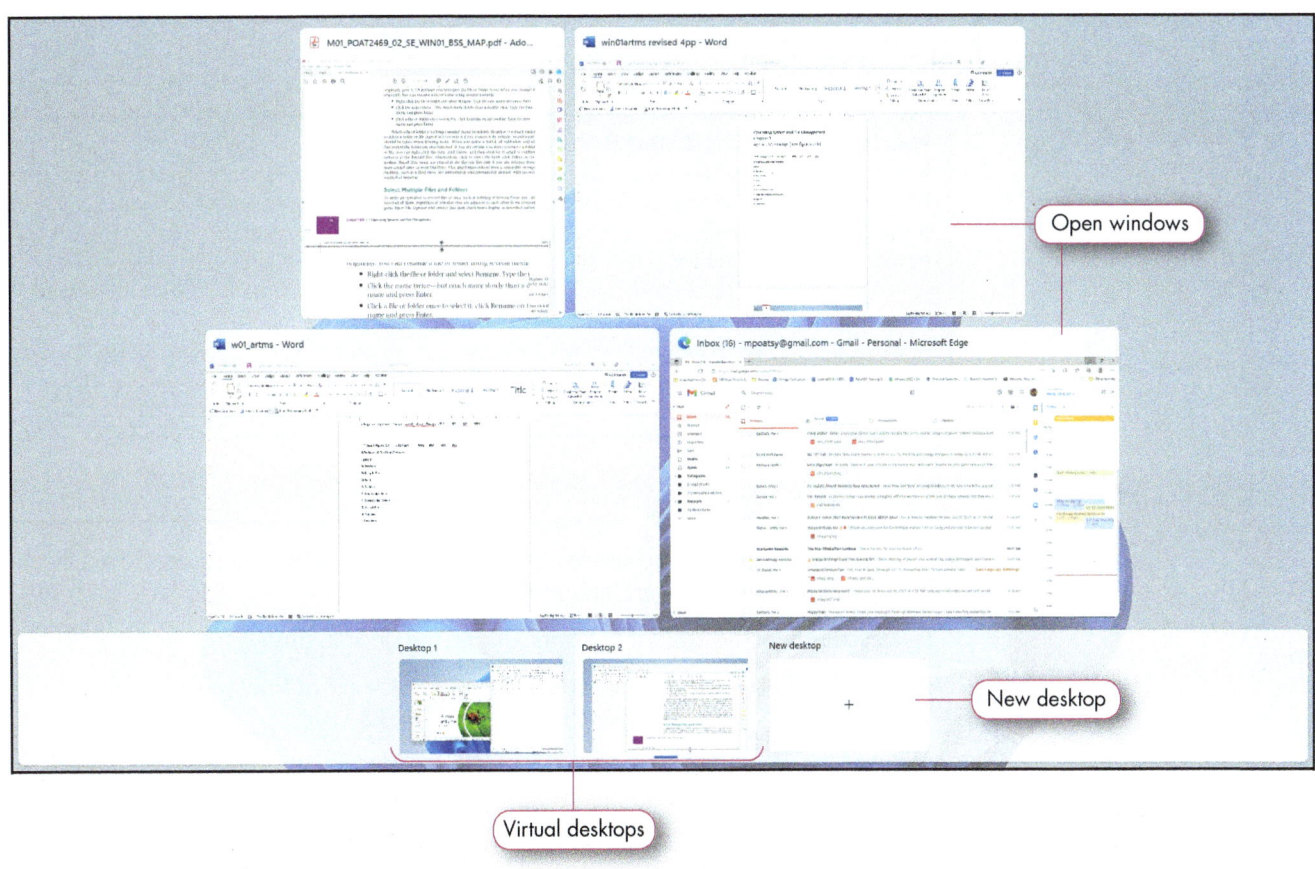

FIGURE 1.10 Task View

> **TIP: CYCLE THROUGH OPEN WINDOWS**
> In Windows, you can use the keyboard to cycle through all open windows. Press and hold Alt and repeatedly press Tab. Release Alt when the window that you want to display is selected. On a Mac, use command+tab to cycle through open windows.

Create a Virtual Desktop

Another feature of Task view is virtual desktops (refer to Figure 1.10). A ***virtual desktop*** is a way to organize and access groups of windows for different purposes on separate desktops. For example, when you do your schoolwork, you might have your school's learning management system (such as Blackboard or Desire to Learn), your school's email account, and MyLab IT open. When you are not working on schoolwork, you might have several social media accounts open, perhaps a video game, and maybe Netflix or YouTube running. Using Task view you can group these applications into virtual desktops, so that you can quickly switch between your "school" desktop and your "entertainment" desktop. While in Task view right-click a desktop thumbnail to give the desktop a meaningful name. To delete a virtual desktop, point to the top right corner of the desktop thumbnail, and click Close.

HOW TO

Create a new virtual desktop and move applications between desktops:

1. Click Task view then click New desktop. A thumbnail preview of the new desktop (Desktop 2) displays alongside the current desktop (in this case, Desktop 1).

2. Drag or right-click and select a thumbnail of the window you want to move from the Task view of one desktop to another desktop.

3. Right-click a thumbnail preview of any open application in Task view alternatively, and select an option to snap the window, move the window to a different desktop, or display the window on all desktops.

MAC TIP: MISSION CONTROL

Mission Control is like Task view. It offers a view of all open windows, desktop spaces, and any apps in full screen or split view. You can find Mission Control in the Applications Folder in Finder. Or you can swipe up with three fingers on the trackpad or double-tap the mouse with two fingers. There is also a Mission Control key in the top row of keys on an Apple keyboard.

When Mission Control opens, the Spaces bar displays at the top of the window and contains thumbnails of each desktop space. Any open windows display in the main area of the Mission Control window. To add a space (a new desktop), click the plus sign on the right of the Spaces bar. You can move between desktop spaces by clicking the thumbnails in the Spaces bar, or by swiping left or right with three or four fingers on your trackpad or swiping left or right with two fingers on the mouse.

Critical Thinking

1. Describe the features in both Windows and macOS that provide access to applications such as Word and PowerPoint. ***p. 4***

2. Describe how the taskbar in Windows and the Dock in macOS are similar. ***p. 5***

3. Explain what a virtual desktop is and give an example of how you would use virtual desktops for school, work, or entertainment. ***p. 12***

File Management

One of the main functions of the operating system is *file management*, which provides an organizational structure to your computer's contents. You can view and organize your files using File Explorer in Windows and Finder in macOS.

In this section, you will learn how to manage your files and folders. You will learn how to create, open, rename, and delete folders, so that you can better organize your files and how to move or copy files between different folders. Lastly, you will learn how to compress and extract files and folders.

Find and Organize Files

File Explorer is a Windows app that you can use to create folders and manage folders and files across various storage locations: your PC, online storage, and external storage devices such as a flash drive or backup drive. Similarly, macOS organizes files and folders with the *Finder* app. Often, related files are organized together into folders. A folder structure can occur across several levels, so you can create folders within other folders—called subfolders. The most common analogy for File Explorer and Finder is that of a filing cabinet in which related documents and files are grouped and organized by folders—sometimes multiple layers of folders located within a single drawer (in this case, a storage location). Files can be opened, moved, renamed, or deleted through either of these file management systems.

Understand the File Explorer Interface

To open File Explorer, click the File Explorer icon on the taskbar or from the Start menu. As shown in Figure 1.11 and further described in Table 1.3, there are various functional areas of the Windows 11 File Explorer interface.

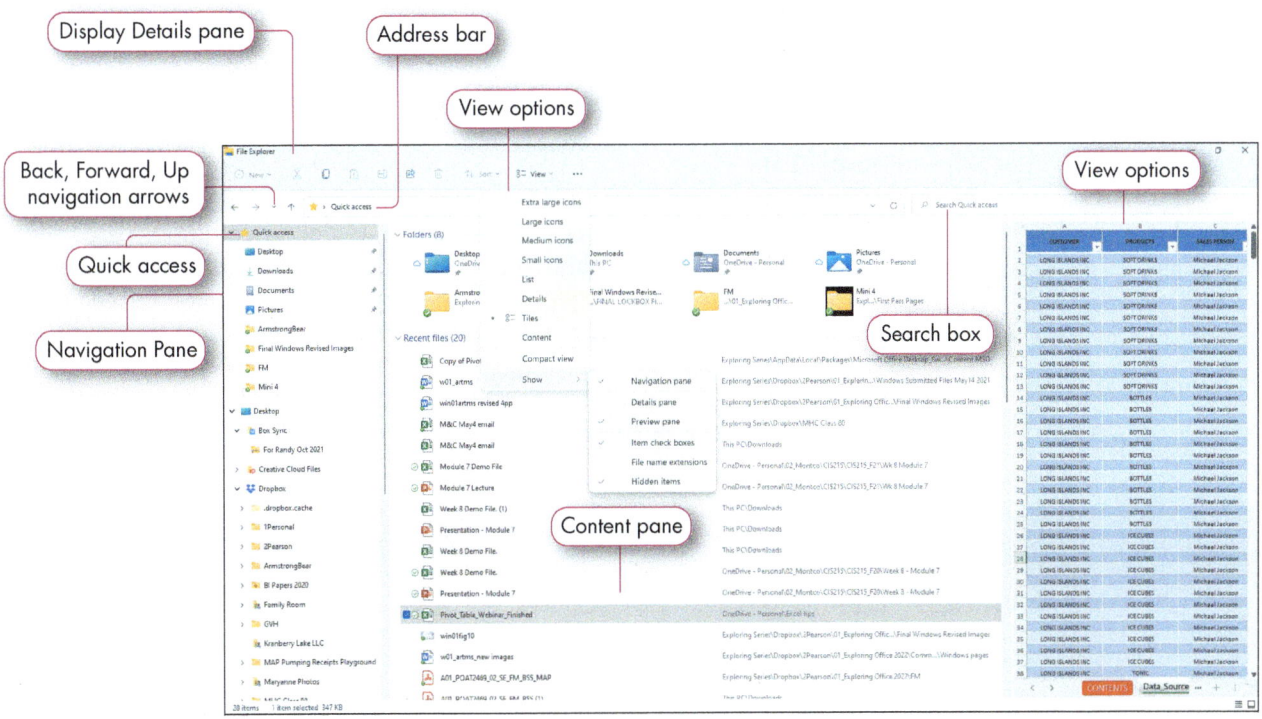

FIGURE 1.11 Windows 11 File Explorer

TABLE 1.3   File Explorer Interface

Component	Description
Toolbar/Ribbon	In Windows 11, the controls to sort and view files and folders displays in a toobar at the top of the File Explorer interface. In Windows 10, the ribbon includes Home, Share and View tabs. In both versions, contextual tabs or commands that are relevant to some selected files will display. For example, if you are working with a picture file, the toolbar or ribbon contains commands to modify pictures.
Back, Forward, and Up navigation arrows	The navigation arrows are used to visit previously opened folders. Use the Up command to open the parent folder for the current location.
Address bar	The Address bar enables you to navigate to other folders within File Explorer.
Search box	The Search box is used to find files and folders by typing descriptive text in the Search box. Windows immediately begins a search after you type the first character, further narrowing results as you type. You can search the entire contents of File Explorer or conduct a more directed search by first selecting a folder or drive.
Navigation Pane	The Navigation Pane contains Quick access, OneDrive, This PC, and Network. Click the arrow next to any of these content groups in the Navigation Pane to display contents and to manage files housed within a selected folder. Click any folder in the Navigation Pane to display the contained files.
Quick access	Quick access, as its name implies, provides immediate access to those files and folders that you use most often.
Content pane	The Content pane shows the contents of the currently selected folder or storage location. Files and folders can display in a variety of layouts that either show detailed information about the specific file or folder or just file or folder names with small, medium, or large icons. The icon is associated with the type of file or folder. For example, all Word documents are identified by a W in a blue box icon.
Details pane	The Details pane displays the properties of the file or folder. Common properties include information such as the author's name and the date the file was last modified. The Details pane does not display by default but displays after you click the View tab and click the Details pane in the Panes group.
Preview pane	The Preview pane provides a snapshot of a selected file's contents (but not the contents of a selected folder). You can see file contents before opening the file. This pane does not display by default but is displayed after clicking the View tab and then clicking Preview pane in the Panes group.

Explore the Finder Interface in macOS

The Finder is the organizational file management system in macOS. It opens when you log into your Mac and stays open as you work. If Finder has been closed, click Finder on the Dock or select New Finder Window from File on the Menu Bar to reopen it. Like File Explorer, files, folders, apps, and downloads are managed through Finder (see Figure 1.12).

On the left side of the Finder window, the Sidebar contains shortcuts to all programs installed on the computer, recently used files, as well as commonly used storage areas such as Documents, iCloud, and Network locations. It also contains colored tags that can be used to further categorize files and folders. In the main portion of the Finder window, you can see all the files stored in any selected folder. At the top of the Finder window are controls that change how files are displayed in the Finder window as well as other means to manipulate files and folders. To the left of the Finder window is a preview pane that can be turned on or off through View on the Finder menu.

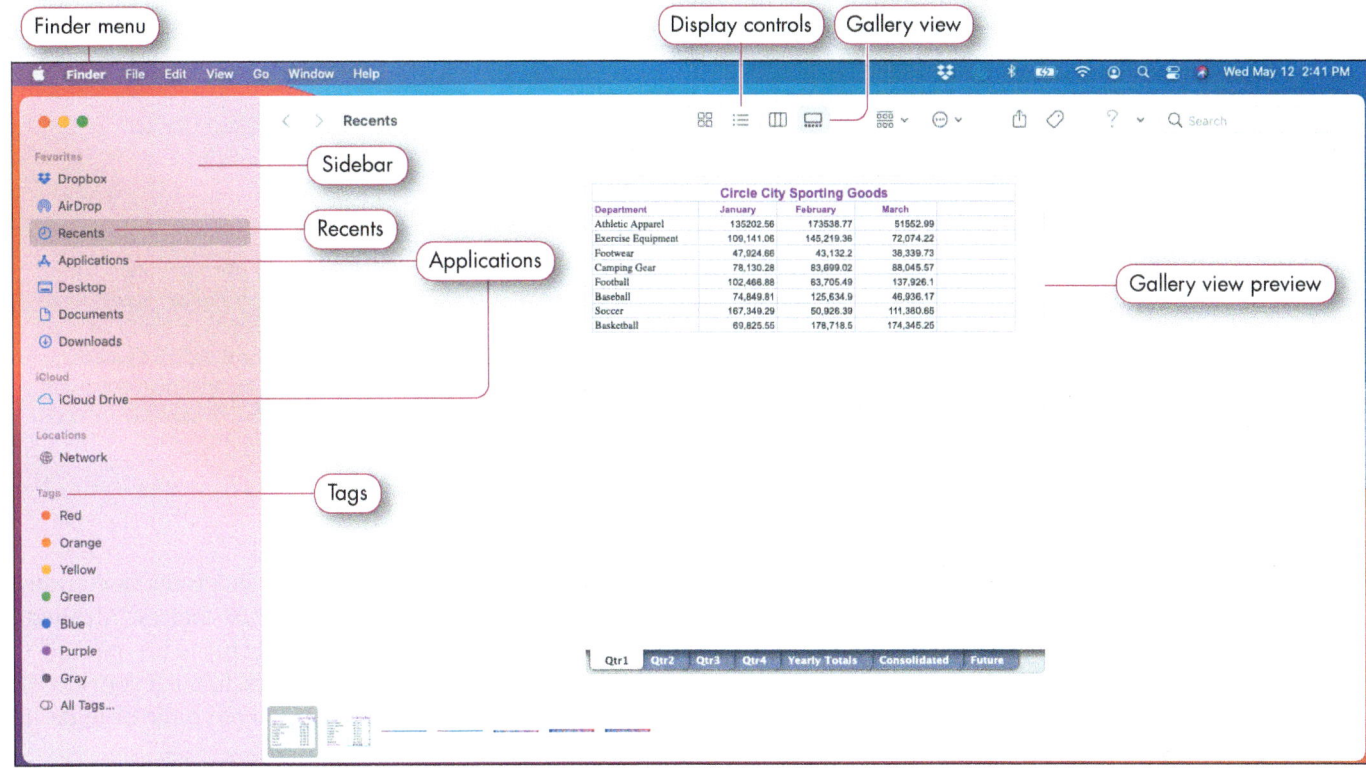

FIGURE 1.12 macOS Finder Window

> **MAC TIP: USE GALLERY VIEW TO PREVIEW A FILE**
> Before opening a file in Finder, you can preview the contents using Gallery view. Using Gallery view, you can scroll through a large document or presentation and view individual worksheets of an Excel workbook. You can even play videos in Gallery view. Quick Look is another convenient way to preview files with the same interactivity that Gallery view provides. To use Quick Look, click on a file in Finder and press Space to display a preview (refer to Figure 1.12).

Navigate File Explorer

The Navigation Pane enables you to move between folder and storage locations in File Explorer. The Navigation Pane consists of four main areas: Quick access, OneDrive, This PC, and Network. **OneDrive** is Microsoft's cloud storage system. Saving files to OneDrive saves them to a Web-based location (OneDrive.com) and syncs them across all Windows devices. Sign in with your Microsoft account to access your files from any Internet-connected computer or mobile device. Changes you make will sync with the cloud, keeping your files up-to-date everywhere. Use File Explorer to access your OneDrive and to create new folders and organize existing folders.

Files stored to This PC are saved onto the hard drive and are accessible only when working on that device. Documents, Music, Pictures, Videos and Downloads are standard folders in the This PC area of File Explorer. Clicking on Network in the Navigation Pane displays all networked devices such as gaming and entertainment systems, printers, and other networked computers. Clicking the arrow next to each of these main storage areas or folders in the Navigation Pane expands or collapses the folder to show or hide the folders and documents within each group. When you select a file or folder, the location of that file or folder is displayed in the Address bar (refer to Figure 1.11).

The Address bar displays the current location of a selected file or folder as a series of links and arrows. Next to the Address bar are the Back, Forward, and Up navigation arrows. The arrows enable you to move up or down the links in the location shown in the Address bar. Alternatively, you can click on any of the links in the Address bar to jump directly to that location within File Explorer. You can use the Address bar to navigate to a particular location (e.g., to Documents or Quick access), or you can click any of the arrows between the folder links to view the subfolders. You can also use the Address bar to move files and folders to different locations.

Use and Modify Quick Access

When you launch File Explorer, it opens to **Quick access** by default. Quick access contains shortcuts to your most recently used files and most frequently used folders. Although certain folders such as Downloads, Desktop, Documents, and Pictures are pinned to Quick access by default, you can unpin any of those, and pin others, to meet your needs. A pushpin icon identifies a pinned folder (refer to Figure 1.11). To pin a file or folder to Quick access, do one of the following:

- Right-click the file or folder and select Pin to Quick access.
- Alternatively, you can select the item to pin and then click Pin to Quick access in the Clipboard group on the Home tab.

Eventually, a pinned file or folder may no longer need to be readily available and therefore can be removed from Quick access. Removing a file or folder does not delete it; the file or folder still remains in its permanent storage location. To unpin a file or folder from Quick access, right-click the pinned file or folder and select Unpin from Quick access from the shortcut menu.

Use File Explorer Views

Like all the Office applications, File Explorer includes ways to customize how files display. The Details layout lists the files and folders with relevant information such as Date modified, Type, and Size. The List layout shows the file names without added detail, whereas Tiles and Content layouts show file thumbnails (small pictures describing file contents) and varying levels of file details. You can display additional detail, such as who the file or folder is shared with and its availability by displaying the Details pane. To show a preview of a file, open the Preview pane. You can change the width of a pane by positioning the pointer on the border that separates the panes to display a double-headed arrow, then dragging the border left or right.

Other useful features in File Explorer enable you to display file name extensions and item check boxes. Each file that displays in the Content pane has a corresponding icon that indicates the application that is associated with that file type, or a folder icon with the name of the folder. In Windows 11, if you want the file extension to display (such as .docx, .jpg, or .pdf) click the View arrow on the toolbar, point to Show, then choose File name extensions. In Windows 10, select the File name extensions check box in the Show/hide group on the View tab. Displaying item check boxes will add a check box next to each file name in the Content pane. Clicking a check box to select individual files and folders is useful when selecting and moving files. The process to display item check boxes is similar to that used to display file name extensions described above.

TIP: CUSTOMIZE DETAILS LAYOUT

The Details layout in File Explorer provides a wealth of information about all your files. Activate Details view by clicking the View arrow on the Windows 11 File Explorer toobar or by clicking Details in the Layout group on the File Explorer View tab in Windows 10. Details view can be customized to best fit how you search for and locate files. By default, File Explorer shows the file name, date modified, file type, and file size. You can add additional columns to reflect other file properties such as file tags or authors. To add a column in Details view, click Add columns in the Current View group on the View tab and select Tag or any other column you want displayed. You can reorder columns by clicking the column heading and dragging the column to the new location. It may be helpful to organize your files alphabetically by file name, chronologically by date modified, or by file type. You can sort columns by clicking the column heading.

Search for Files in File Explorer

Occasionally, even the most organized person will need to search for a file or folder. You can search just the contents of a specific folder by navigating to that folder in File Explorer and then entering the search terms in the Search box. Or you can search an entire drive for a broader search. You can then further sort the search results by file type or date modified to continue to locate the specific file or folder. This is more efficient than using the Search box on the taskbar because your search is limited to the contents of that specific folder or storage area. For a comprehensive search, use the Search box on the taskbar and select Documents to exclude Web and App contents from the results.

When you type a term in the File Explorer Search box, a list of files that meet the search requirements displays immediately under the Search box. You can click a file from that list to open it. If you need further search refinements, press Enter after typing in the search terms to display the search results. Search options in the Windows 11 toolbar or the Windows 10 Search Tools tab displays features that enable you to:

- Refine your search results by Date, Kind, Size, or Other properties.
- Revise the search location to include subfolders, the entire PC or another location.
- Save a search if you tend to conduct the same search repeatedly.

TIP: SEARCH BY FILE EXTENSION

To search for all files of a particular file type or application, enter the file extension in the Search box. For example, to search for all .mp3 files on your computer, type .mp3 in the Search box.

Work with Folders and Files

As you work with software to create a file, such as when you type a report using Microsoft Word, you should save the file so that you can retrieve it later. It is often beneficial, as has been discussed earlier, to group related files into folders. Folders help to keep related files together. By creating an appropriate folder structure, you can find and retrieve files more efficiently.

Create a Folder

A folder helps to organize and group related files together. You can create a folder in a couple of different ways. You can use File Explorer to create a folder structure, providing descriptive names and placing the folders in a well-organized hierarchy.

Create a folder in File Explorer:

1. Open File Explorer and click OneDrive or any other location such as the hard drive or flash drive, in the Navigation Pane where you want the folder to reside.
2. Click New on the File Explorer toolbar in Windows 11. In Windows 10, click the Home tab and click New folder in the New group.
3. Type the new folder name and press Enter.
4. Repeat the process to create additional folders.

Undoubtedly, you will occasionally find that you have just created a file but have no appropriate folder in which to save the file. For example, you might have just finished the slide show for your speech class but have not yet created a speech folder for your assignments. You can create a folder from within the software application at the time you are saving a file. Click the File tab and click Save As to display the Save As screen and navigate to the location where you want to store your file. Click New Folder, type the new folder name, and click OK. Click to open the new folder. After entering the file name, click Save.

Open, Rename, and Delete Folders and Files

Once files are saved to locations such as OneDrive or Documents, you can use File Explorer to open, rename, and delete files. Using the Navigation Pane or Search box, you can locate and select a file that you want to open. For example, you might want to open the speech slide show so that you can practice before giving a presentation to the class. Open File Explorer and navigate to the folder that contains the file. The file will display in the Content pane. To preview the contents of a file before opening, enable the Preview pane, and then click the file name in the Content pane. Double-click the file. The program that is associated with the file will open the file. For example, Microsoft PowerPoint will launch and a presentation will display when you double-click a file associated with a PowerPoint extension.

At times, you may want to give a different name to a file or folder than the one you originally gave it. Or perhaps you mistyped the file or folder name when you created it originally. You can rename a file or folder using several methods:

- Right-click the file or folder and select Rename. Type the new name and press Enter.
- Click the name twice—but much more slowly than a double-click. Type the new name and press Enter.
- Click a file or folder once to select it, click Rename on the toolbar. Type the new name and press Enter.

When a file or folder is no longer needed, it can be deleted. However, it is much easier to delete a folder or file than it is to recover it if you remove it by mistake, so extra care should be taken when deleting items. When you delete a folder, all subfolders and all files within the folder are also removed. If you are certain you want to remove a folder or file, you can right-click the item, click Delete, and then click Yes if asked to confirm removal to the Recycle Bin. Alternatively, click to select the item, click Delete on the toolbar. Recall that items are placed in the Recycle Bin only if you are deleting them from a hard drive or from OneDrive. Files and folders deleted from a removable storage medium, such as a flash drive, are immediately and permanently deleted, with no easy method of retrieval.

Select Multiple Files and Folders

To apply an operation to several files at once, such as deleting or moving them, you can select all of them, regardless of whether they are adjacent to each other in the Content pane. Open File Explorer and ensure that item check boxes display as described earlier.

As you move the pointer along the left side of files and folders, a check box displays. Click the check box to select the file. If you want to select all items in the folder quickly, click the check box that displays in the Name column heading.

Alternately, you can select files and folders without using the check boxes. Locate the files you want to select in the Content pane and do one of the following:

- To select adjacent files, select the first file, press and hold Shift, and then click the last file. All consecutive files will be highlighted, indicating that they are selected. At that point, you can delete, copy, or move the selected files at the same time.

- To select files or folders that are not adjacent, click the first item. Press and hold Ctrl while you click the files or folders you want, releasing Ctrl only when you have finished selecting the files or folders. At that point, you can delete, copy, or move the selected files at the same time.

- To select all items in a folder or disk drive, use File Explorer to navigate to the folder. Open the folder, press and hold Ctrl, and then press A on the keyboard. You can also click the Home tab, and in the Select group click *Select all* to select all items. At that point, you can delete, copy, or move the selected files at the same time.

Copy and Move Files and Folders

Sometimes you want to relocate a file or folder. For example, after downloading files from an email or the Internet, you want to move them from the Downloads folder to another more memorable location. You can move or copy a folder or file to another location on the same drive or to another drive. When you copy or move a folder, you affect both the folder and any files that it contains. If you want to make a copy of an important file or folder as a backup, you can copy it to an external drive or to OneDrive. To move or copy a file or folder, right-click the item(s) and select either Cut (to move) or Copy on the shortcut menu. Then, in the Navigation Pane, locate the destination drive or folder, right-click the destination drive or folder, and click Paste. Alternately, to move files or folders you can select the items using the check boxes and drag the item(s) from the Content pane to another folder in the Navigation Pane. To copy items, press and hold Ctrl while dragging.

Compress a Folder

You may have an extremely large file, such as a video file, that you want to email or upload to the Internet. Or, you might have several pictures to share that you do not want to send as individual attachments. In these situations, you can compress (zip) a file or zip multiple files together into a single compressed folder. A ***compressed (zipped) folder*** or file has a smaller file size and facilitates sharing or uploading. Use Zip in File Explorer to create a compressed (zipped) folder. When compressing a file or folder, the compressed folder is created in the same location and takes on the same name as the file or folder that is being compressed. However, if you are compressing a group of files that are not in a folder, it may be best to first put them in a folder and give that folder a meaningful name. Otherwise, the zipped folder will take the name of one of the files in the group. Of course, you can always rename a zipped folder, using the same methods described previously for renaming a file or folder. The zipped file or folder does not replace the original files.

To compress (zip) a file or folder, open File Explorer, and in the Content pane select the file, group of files, or folder that you want to compress. Right-click one of the selected items and click Compress to ZIP file. A compressed folder is created and placed in the same folder location along with the original files or folder. Alternatively, click See more on the File Explorer toolbar and then select Compress to ZIP file.

Once a compressed folder is created, you can add additional files to the folder without having to undo and redo the zipping process. Just drag new files into the compressed folder.

Compress Files and Folders:

1. Open a Finder window. Choose to display the files as icons, a list, or columns for easier access.

2. Select the files you want to compress by holding shift. If the files are not contiguously arranged, hold command while selecting the individual files.

3. Click File, and then choose Compress. When you compress a single file or a folder of files, the compressed file retains the original file or folder name. When you compress multiple items at once, the compressed file is named Archive.zip.

Extract Files from a Compressed Folder

You might have received or downloaded a compressed file or folder, such as the data files from this book, and need to unzip the folder and extract the files. To unzip (extract) files or folders from a compressed folder, open File Explorer and select the compressed folder. Click Extract all. The individual files, by default, are saved to the same location as the zipped folder. Click Browse to navigate to a new location if you want to change where the individual files are to be stored. Click Extract. Extracting files does not remove the compressed folder from your computer. The compressed folder will remain until you delete it. If you are extracting files from a folder you have downloaded from the Web, you should ensure your files are saved in a meaningful location. Otherwise, they may end up in the Downloads folder.

Critical Thinking

4. Discuss the importance of organizing files and folders using File Explorer or Finder. *p. 13*

5. Describe why it might be more efficient to use the Search box in File Explorer than Search on the taskbar to look for a file. *p. 17*

6. Explain at least two circumstances in which file compression would be useful, and the process to compress and extract compressed files. *p. 19*

Chapter Objectives Review

After reading this chapter, you have accomplished the following objectives:

1. Navigate the desktop.

- **Explore the Windows desktop:** The Windows desktop is the main workspace for the Windows operating system. The taskbar and Start are at the bottom of the desktop.

- **Explore the macOS desktop:** The macOS desktop is the main working area for computers running the macOS operating system. The Menu Bar displays at the top of the desktop, and the Dock displays at the bottom of the desktop.

- **Use the taskbar:** At the bottom of the Windows 11 desktop is the taskbar. The taskbar displays open application icons that include Search, Task view, and File Explorer. At the far right are system icons such as Wi-Fi and Sound and the Date and Clock. Click on the Wi-Fi and Sound icons to open quick settings. Click on the Date and clock icons to open Notifications. You can pin application icons to the taskbar for easier access to programs you use most often.

- **Use the Windows Start menu:** The Start menu provides the main access to all programs and features on your computer. Shortcuts to programs or folders can be pinned to the Start menu.

2. Work with windows.

- **Resize and close windows:** The title bar displays at the top of each open window. The title bar features the name of the opened folder, file, or program. Controls are found on the title bar that are used to manage the ribbon display as well as to minimize, maximize/restore down, and close any open window.

- **Snap and move windows:** Working with multiple open windows at the same time sometimes requires moving or resizing windows so you can see the contents of each window. Snap assist is used to "snap" windows to either side or in any corner of the screen. Snap layout enables you to choose the configuration of open windows.

- **Use Task view:** Task view is used to see all windows on the desktop at the same time. In Windows 10, Task view also shows the most recently opened files and apps for the past 30 days. A timeline enables you to scroll through the recently used files and apps.

- **Create a virtual desktop:** If you are working on several projects and want to keep opened windows organized by project, you can create individual virtual desktops for each project by clicking Task view on the taskbar.

3. Find and organize files.

- **Understand the File Explorer interface:** File Explorer is a Windows app that manages files and folders across various storage locations. File Explorer has a Search box to search through large folders for specific content and the Navigation Pane that is the main organizational system in File Explorer. Quick access houses those files and folders that have been most recently used.

- **Explore the Finder interface in macOS:** Finder is the file management system in macOS. Finder has a Sidebar that features the organizational structure for all programs, files, and storage areas in the computer. It also contains colored tags that can be used to further categorize items. You can change how you view files by using the display controls in the Finder window.

- **Navigate File Explorer:** The left side of File Explorer is the Navigation Pane that lists files and folders stored on the computer within each storage area such as OneDrive, Documents, Downloads, and so on. The contents of a storage folder or area display in the central area of File Explorer and, if selected, the Preview pane shows the contents of the selected file. The Address bar shows the current location and path to the main storage area for any file.

- **Use and modify Quick access:** Quick access is the default view of File Explorer. It shows all recently saved files and folders. Files or folders can be pinned or unpinned to Quick access.

- **Use File Explorer views:** You can choose how files display in File Explorer. Details layout lists files and folders with relevant information such as Date modified, Type, and Size. List layout shows files names without additional details. Tiles and Content layouts show file thumbnails and are useful layouts especially for picture files.

- **Search for files in File Explorer:** Enter a search term in the Search box to search for files containing specific content. The Search box in File Explorer can help narrow down your search by searching only in a specific folder or storage location.

4. Work with files and folders.

- **Create a folder:** Folders help to organize and group related files together. Folders can be created as a file is being saved or can be created ahead of time using the New command in File Explorer.

- **Open, rename, and delete folders and files:** Files and folders can be renamed, grouped, and deleted to keep the organizational structure relevant, and can be copied and moved, as needed. You can open files and folders from File Explorer, or you can open a file directly within the file's associated application. Files and folders are given a name as they are being saved, but any item can be renamed. Once a file or folder is no longer useful, it can be deleted. Items saved in OneDrive or on any hard drive are moved to the Recycle Bin when they are deleted. The Recycle Bin holds deleted items. Items in the Recycle Bin are permanently deleted when the Recycle Bin is emptied. Items deleted from other storage areas such as a flash drive are not sent to the Recycle Bin and are permanently deleted.

- **Select multiple files and folders:** To apply an operation such as deleting or moving to several files at once, you can use the Item check boxes in the Contents pane of File Explorer. Alternatively, you can select individual files by pressing Shift while selecting contiguous files and pressing Ctrl (or command on macOS) while selecting files that are not located together.
- **Copy and move files and folders:** When you copy or move a folder, you affect both the folder and any files that it contains. You can move or copy a folder or file to another location on the same drive or to another drive.
- **Compress a folder:** To upload or share multiple files, either you need to send each file individually, which is a time-consuming process, or you can group the related files into a folder and then "zip" the folder up by compressing it. A compressed (zipped) folder has a smaller file size and facilitates uploading and sharing multiple files. The zipped file or folder does not replace the original files.
- **Extract files from a compressed folder:** You might download a compressed folder of pictures that someone sent you. Before viewing the pictures, you need to uncompress the folder. File Explorer contains Extract, which will "unzip" the compressed folder, enabling access to the files within the folder. In the extraction process, you can designate the location of the extracted files and the name of the folder containing the extracted files.

Key Terms Matching

Match the key terms with their definitions. Write the key term letter by the appropriate numbered definition.

a. Application software
b. Compressed (zipped) folder
c. Desktop
d. Dock
e. File Explorer
f. File management
g. Finder

h. Jump List
i. macOS
j. OneDrive
k. Pin
l. Quick access
m. Search
n. Snap layouts

o. Start menu
p. Task view
q. Taskbar
r. Tile
s. Title bar
t. Virtual desktop

1. _____ The operating system that runs on Apple desktops and laptops. **p. 3**

2. _____ The primary working area of an operating system. **p. 13**

3. _____ A feature of macOS desktop used to access frequently used apps, files, and folders. **p. 6**

4. _____ Microsoft's cloud storage system. **p. 15**

5. _____ A folder that uses less drive space and can be transferred or shared with other users more quickly. **p. 19**

6. _____ A component of File Explorer that contains shortcuts to the most frequently used folders. **p. 5**

7. _____ The main access to all programs and features on your computer. **p. 3**

8. _____ A feature at the top of a window that displays the file name and options to manipulate the display of a window. **p. 8**

9. _____ The means of providing an organizational structure to file and folders. **p. 13**

10. _____ A macOS app that is used to manage apps, folders, and files across various storage locations. **p. 13**

11. _____ A list of program-specific shortcuts to recently opened files and other commands related to that application. **p. 16**

12. _____ Located on the Windows 11 taskbar, provides a convenient way to search your computer or the Web. **p. 5**

13. _____ Programs that are used for tasks such as email, gaming, and productivity. **p. 2**

14. _____ The horizontal bar at the bottom of the desktop that displays open applications, Notification area, the Search box, and pinned apps or programs. **p. 6**

15. _____ Prearranged alternatives for how open windows can be displayed on a screen. **p. 10**

16. _____ To add a tile to the Start menu or an icon to the taskbar. **p. 5**

17. _____ A block icon on the Windows 10 Start menu that is a shortcut to a program or app. **p. 5**

18. _____ A way to organize and access groups of windows for different purposes. **p. 12**

19. _____ The Windows app that is used to create folders and manage files and folders across various storage locations. **p. 13**

20. _____ A feature on the taskbar that enables the user to view thumbnail previews of all open tasks in one glance. **p. 11**

Multiple Choice

1. Where does a file deleted from OneDrive end up?
   (a) Downloads folder
   (b) Permanently deleted
   (c) Recycle Bin
   (d) Trash

2. Which of the following best describes Snap assist?
   (a) Minimize all open apps simultaneously so that the Start menu displays.
   (b) Auto-arrange all open apps so that they are of uniform size.
   (c) Manually reposition all open apps so that you can see the content of each.
   (d) Fix an app window(s) to either side or the corners of the screen.

3. Which of the following represent the file management systems on Windows and macOS?
   (a) Finder and Dock
   (b) File Explorer and Dock
   (c) Dock and taskbar
   (d) File Explorer and Finder

4. What are the rectangular icons on the Windows 10 Start menu called?
   (a) Gadgets
   (b) Tiles
   (c) Thumbnails
   (d) Boxes

5. What feature is used to organize and access groups of open windows for different purposes, such as schoolwork and entertainment?
   (a) Windows Defender
   (b) Windows Desktop
   (c) Virtual Desktop
   (d) Task Manager

6. Which of the following best describes Snap layouts?
   (a) Adds files to the computer
   (b) Prearranged settings for how open windows display
   (c) Contains shortcuts to the most frequently used folders
   (d) Used to switch between open desktops

7. Which term describes the process of adding a tile to the Start menu or an icon to the taskbar?
   (a) Snapping
   (b) Snipping
   (c) Pinning
   (d) Tacking

8. Which of the following is a method of switching between open desktops?
   (a) Ctrl+Tab
   (b) Task view
   (c) Snap layouts
   (d) Right-click the desktop

9. What is the result when you restore down a window?
   (a) Keep it open, but remove it from view.
   (b) Make the window smaller, but keep it displayed on the desktop.
   (c) Move the window from Quick access to Documents.
   (d) Minimize the window's width but leave its height unchanged.

10. What happens when you enter search keywords in the Search box of File Explorer and the OneDrive option is selected?
    (a) The search is limited to that specific location.
    (b) The search cannot be further narrowed.
    (c) The search is automatically expanded to include every folder on the hard drive.
    (d) The search is limited to the selected location but can be expanded if you like.

Microsoft Teams

You will explore Microsoft Teams and its many features to communicate and collaborate with others in a virtual environment.

OBJECTIVES & SKILLS: After you read this chapter, you will be able to:

Introduction to Microsoft Teams

Microsoft Teams is a Microsoft application that facilitates communication and collaboration among groups of people who are participating from different locations. Using the many features of Microsoft Teams, the virtual meeting can provide an engaging, interactive, and supportive group experience similar to or even better than the experience offered in a face-to-face meeting.

In this section, you will learn about the basic components of Microsoft Teams. You will also learn how they are used to communicate with team members.

Dean Drobot/Shutterstock

Collaborate and Communicate Virtually

Apply Microsoft Teams Basics

Using Microsoft Teams, you can have the same experience in a virtual meeting as you could in an in-person meeting. Team members can have conversations and chat with each other as well as engage with each other in live meetings in big or small groups using some of the interactive features that will be discussed later in the chapter.

Explore the Microsoft Teams Interface

When you sign in to Microsoft Teams, you first select the team in which you want to participate. A *team* is a collection of people, conversations, files, and tools—all in one place. You can be a member of many teams. On the left menu of Microsoft Teams, you can access all your activity, chats, teams, meetings, calls, and files, as shown in Figure 1.1. You can also add or access other apps that can help enhance the team experience. Select Teams from the left menu to create a team.

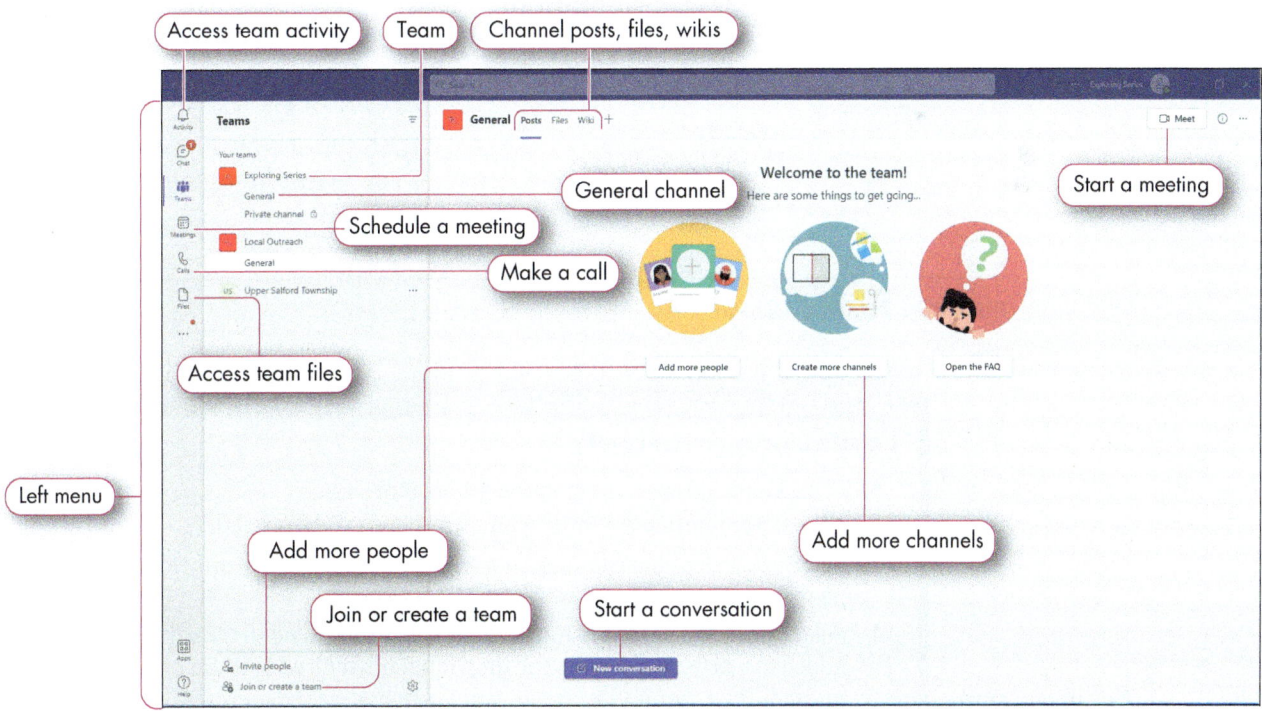

FIGURE 1.1 Microsoft Teams Interface

Create a Channel

A ***channel*** is a section within a team that relates to a specific department, project, or topic. Every team has a General channel that includes all team members by default, but additional channels can be created to focus conversations, tasks, or files around a specific purpose or work group. To create additional channels, click More options (...) next to the team name in the main pane, and select Add channel (see Figure 1.2). A channel can be open to all team members, or it can be private for just a selected group. Most channels are open so that everyone on the team can review and participate in team conversations and share files between themselves. A private channel focuses conversations among specific team members.

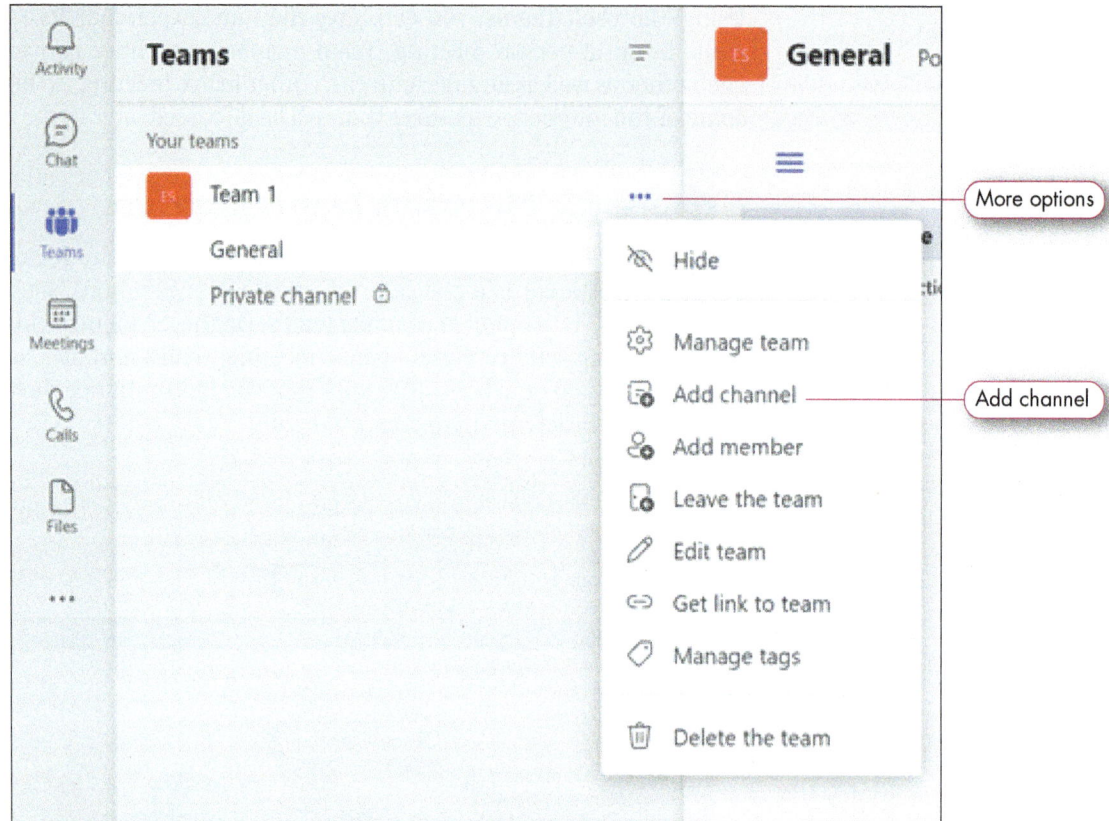

FIGURE 1.2 Create a Channel

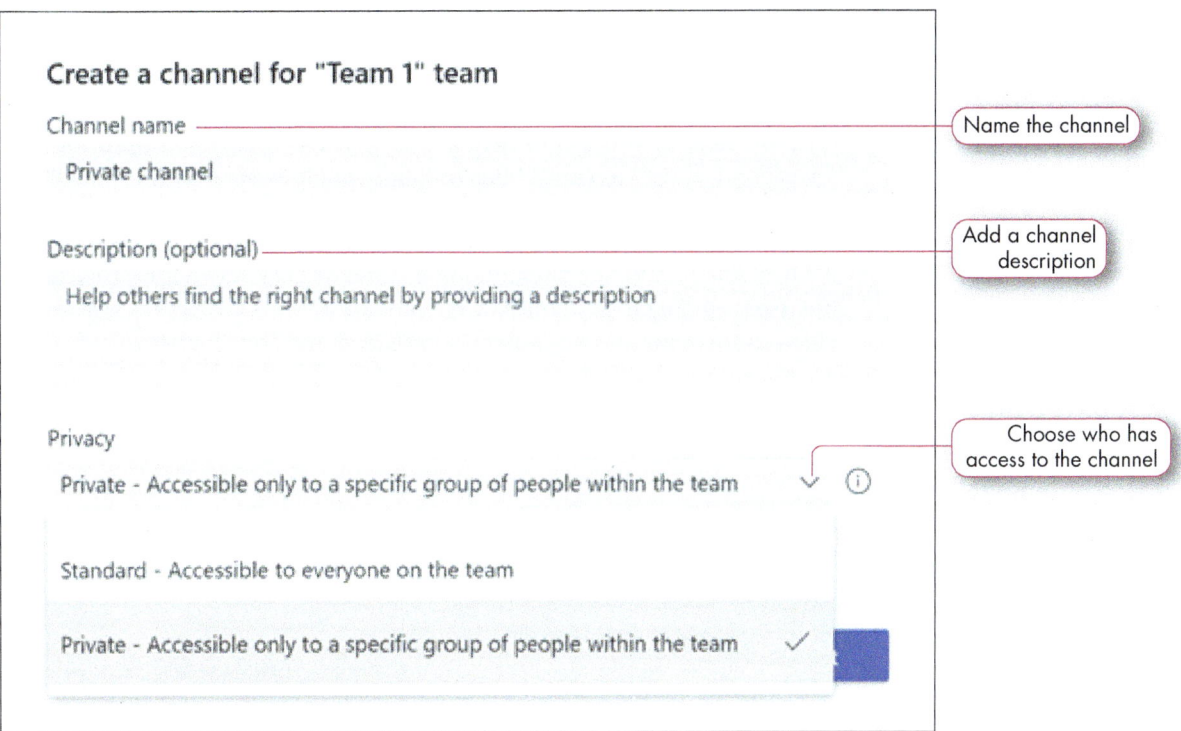

FIGURE 1.3 Create a Private Channel

Check Team Activity

The *activity feed* is a summary of all activity within a team (see Figure 1.4). You can use the Filter at the top right corner of the feed to show specific types of messages such as unread messages and replies. You can also view those messages that include @mentions and emoticon reactions such as likes or hearts. When a red circle displays next to Activity, you have a notification—such as an @mention or a reply—in your feed. After two weeks, notifications expire and no longer show in your feed. You can view just your own activities by selecting the Feed arrow and choosing My Activity.

FIGURE 1.4 Channel Activity Feed

TIP: USING SEARCH TO CHECK NOTIFICATIONS

Another way to check your activity feed is to use the Search box at the top of Microsoft Teams. Type /unread to view your unread channel notifications. Type /mentions to view all your @mentions.

Use Apps

Although you can do quite a bit within Microsoft Teams, adding an **app** enables you to incorporate even more functionality. For example, you can add a weather app, the YouTube app, or an app to help create polls. You can add apps for Word, Excel, and PowerPoint as well as other Microsoft apps such as Forms and OneNote. There are apps that relate to education, productivity, images and videos, project management, and more. To add an app for the entire team to use, click Apps at the bottom of the left menu of Microsoft Teams; then search for the app or click More apps to access the Apps store and use the categories to narrow down your options. To access any apps that have been added to the team already, click More added apps on the left menu of Microsoft Teams (see Figure 1.5).

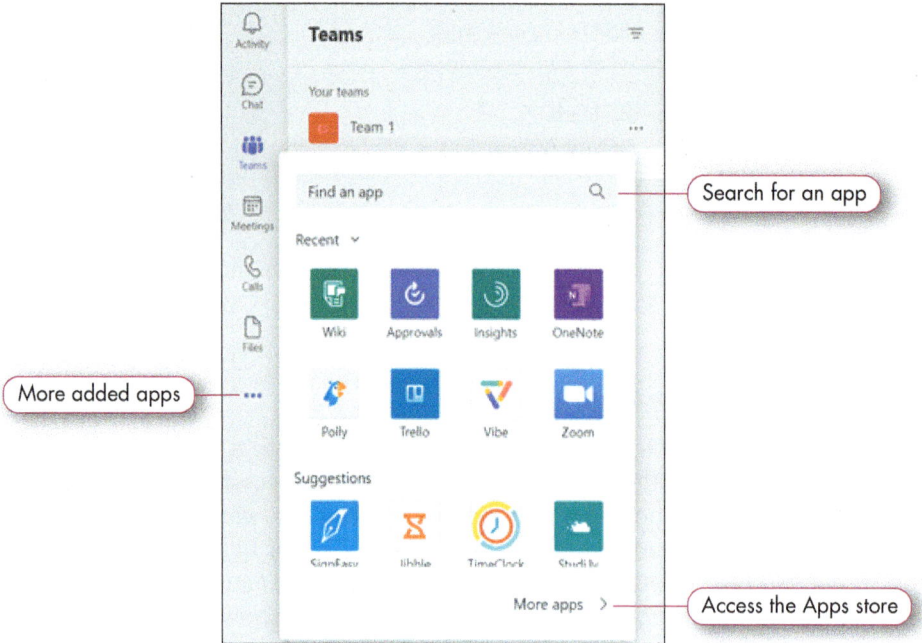

FIGURE 1.5 Add Apps to a Team

You can use apps while working within a channel as well as within a conversation. For example, if you and a team member are chatting about planning an event, you may want to add a weather app in the conversation so that you can monitor the conditions for the event date. If a new app is required in a conversation, click Messaging extensions to find and add the new app (see Figure 1.6). If an app will be used often by all channel members, then add an app to the channel. To add an app in a channel, click Add a tab from the top menu and select the app you want to add. Added apps display at the bottom of a conversation so you can select an app to incorporate it into any conversation.

Some apps, such as Trello, YouTube, or RSS feeds, are called **connectors** and may offer frequently updated content. To get notifications delivered to your channel for these types of apps, add a connector by clicking More options next to the channel name and select Connectors. Click Add next to the connector name. You may be directed to click Add again.

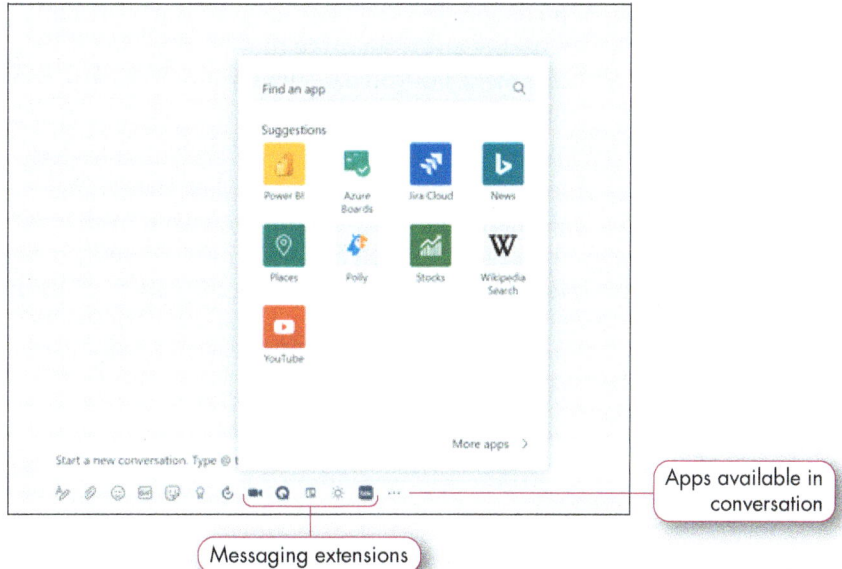

FIGURE 1.6 Add an App to a Conversation

Use the Command Box

At the top of the Microsoft Teams interface is the command box. The ***command box*** enables you to search for and access almost anything in your team. You can search for messages, people, and files. In addition, use the command box to launch apps or take quick actions. When you enter the forward slash (/) into the command box, a list of quick actions displays. Some of those actions are listed in Table 1.1.

TABLE 1.1	Command Box Commands
Command	**Description**
/activity	View a list of members; choose a member to see their activity
/away, /busy, /available, /brb	Change your status to away, busy, available, or brb (be right back)
/unread	See your unread activity
/chat	Send a quick message to a team member
/whatsnew	See what is new in Microsoft Teams

Communicate with Microsoft Teams

There are several ways to communicate with Microsoft Teams. You can converse with the entire team, a channel, a small group, or an individual. You can start a chat or conversation while you are working in any activity or place in Microsoft Teams.

Chat

A ***chat*** is like a text or instant message (IM) because you type short messages that are then delivered almost instantly to the person with whom you are chatting. Chats are used for brief or private conversations with another person or with a small group but can also be directed to the entire channel or team.

- To start a chat within a channel, select New conversation at the bottom of the channel page and enter your message. Select Format beneath the message box for access to formatting tools, such as Bold and Highlight. You can also include an image, access an app, or even start a meeting. Click Send when you finish entering and formatting the message. The message will be sent to all channel members, but you can direct your message to someone specific by using @ mention (described later).

- To start a chat within a team, click Chat from the left menu of Microsoft Teams to display the Chat page, and click New chat from the top of the Chat pane. Enter the name or names of those you want to chat with, then enter and format your message in the text box. Alternatively, you can begin a message to the entire team by starting a message at the bottom of the page. Click Send when you finish entering and formatting the message. At the top of each chat page, you can access the chat history, share files, create meeting notes, and use a whiteboard (see Figure 1.7).

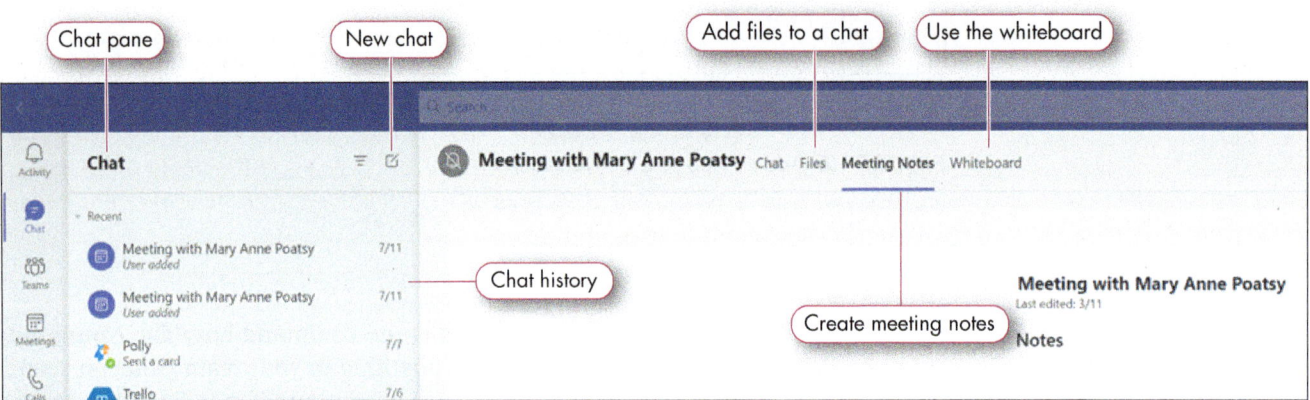

FIGURE 1.7 Chat Page

You can view who is in the chat or add more people by clicking View and add participants in the top right corner of the chat page. (see Figure 1.8).

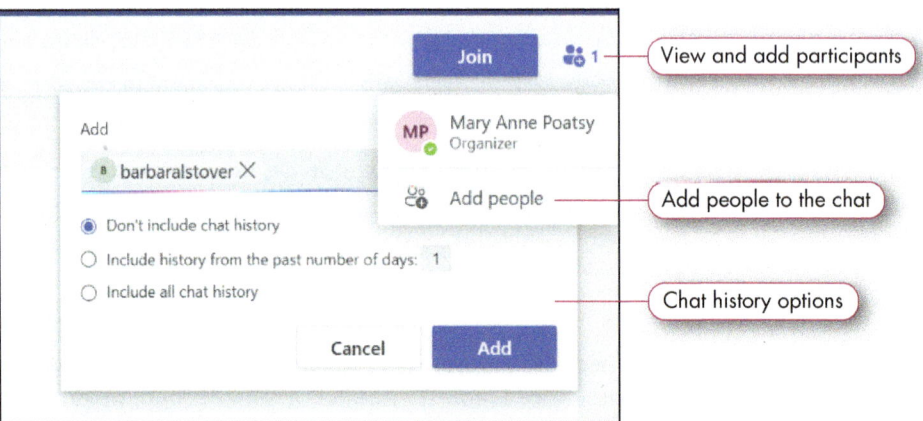

FIGURE 1.8 Adding Members to a Group Chat

If you no longer want to participate in a group chat, you can choose to leave by selecting Chat from the left menu of Microsoft Teams, selecting More options next to the chat you want to leave, and selecting Leave. Similarly, you can remove people from a group chat by clicking Add or view participants and selecting the X next to the name of the chat member you want to remove. Anyone removed from a chat can view the chat history but will no longer be able to participate in any further conversations between those in the chat group.

Use @mention

Sometimes in a chat or conversation, you can direct part of the conversation specifically to a person by using **@mention**. For example, if you and a colleague are planning an event for the new product launch your channel is working on but you need the advice of Venice Conley, the product manager, use @VeniceConley to bring her into the conversation. Typing the @ sign before typing the person's name will notify that person. Responding to the notification will place the person in the conversation where they were mentioned so they do not have to read through a lengthy stream. You can also use @mention to post messages to an entire team or channel by entering @ and the team or channel name.

Make Audio Calls

With Microsoft Teams, you can make audio calls just like using your phone. You can start a one-on-one conversation or create a group call with anyone on your team. If the person you want to call is in your group, you can use the stored phone information to place the call. Select Calls from the left menu of Microsoft Teams, type in the team member's name, and click Call (see Figure 1.9). If connecting with more than one member, enter all the names and then select Call. You can view and filter calls by Incoming, Missed, and Voicemail in Call History. You can select any caller from the History list to place a call.

You can create a speed dial group for those you call frequently to quickly initiate a call or meeting. Select More options next to Speed dial and click Add a contact to this group. Type a name in the Add to contacts dialog box, and then click Add. The contact will display in the Speed dial pane of the Calls window.

> **TIP: CONFIGURE YOUR CALLS SETTINGS**
> You can modify your call answering rules and choose your ringtone. You can also opt to have your calls forwarded to a different number. Next to your profile photo, select *Settings and more* (the three dots), click Settings, select General, and then click Calls.

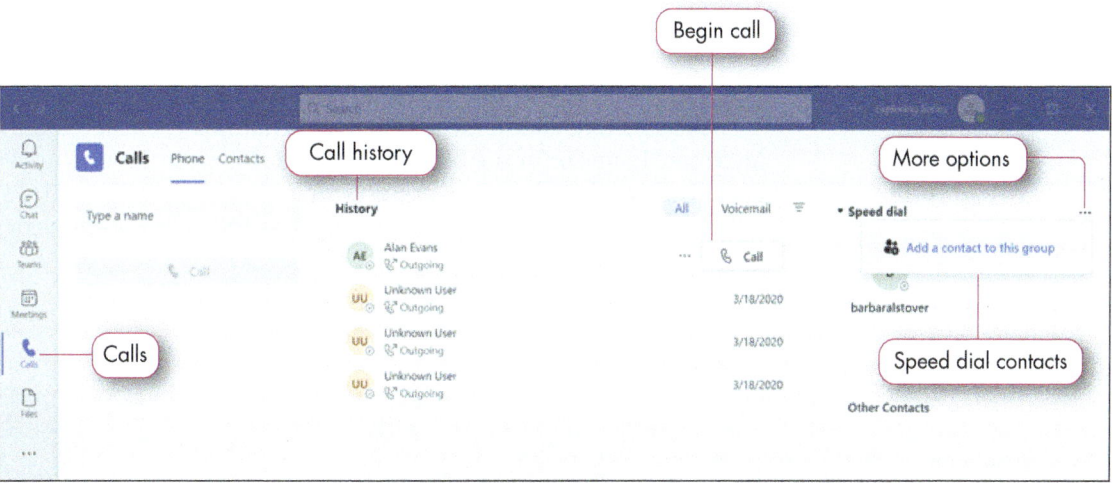

FIGURE 1.9 Calls

Share Files

As you are working in your team or channel, you may want to share files with other team members. You can also work collaboratively on a shared file with your team or channel. Each channel has a Files tab that holds all files shared with the channel members. You can share files that have already been created, or you can create a new file. All files that have been created and saved in a channel are automatically made available in the Microsoft Teams Files folder that you can access from the left Microsoft Teams menu.

If you have a file that has been previously created and stored outside Microsoft Teams, you can upload the file into your Files list. Ensure you are in the appropriate channel and then click Upload. You can also drag and drop a file from File Explorer into the main window area. Any file you upload will be accessible by any member of the channel.

You can attach a file to a channel conversation by clicking Attach in the Conversation tools and navigating to the file that is stored in Microsoft Teams, OneDrive, or any storage location on your computer (see Figure 1.10).

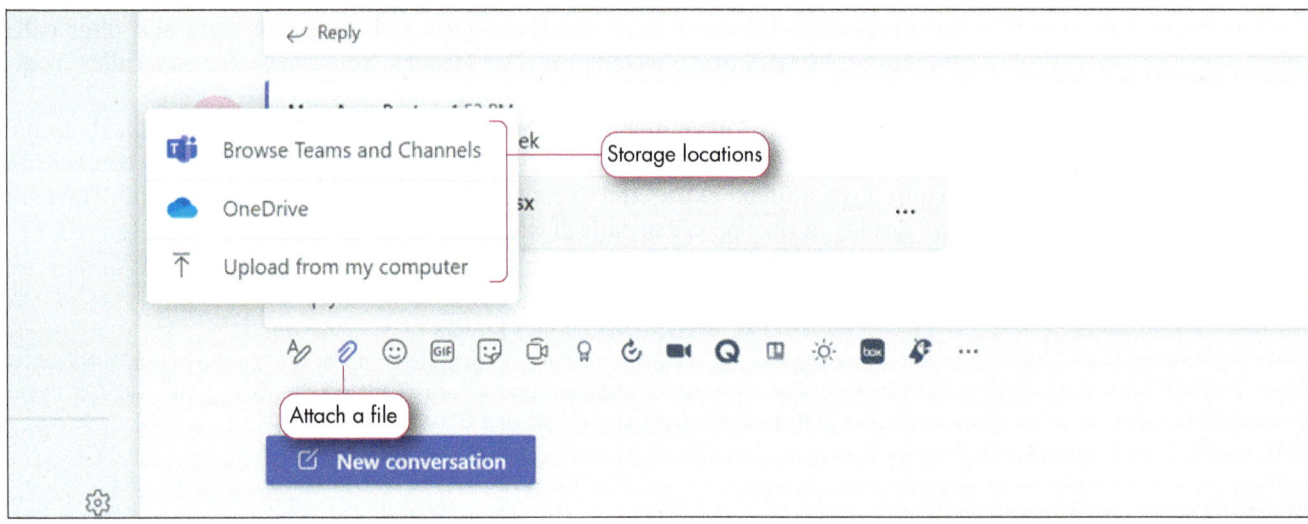

FIGURE 1.10 Attach a File in a Conversation

Alternatively, once a file is stored in a channel, you can choose to open and edit it in Microsoft Teams or in the browser with an Office for the web application. You can also copy a link to the file to share, or download the file (see Figure 1.11). If this is a file that will be accessed often, you can make the file a tab in the channel for easier access.

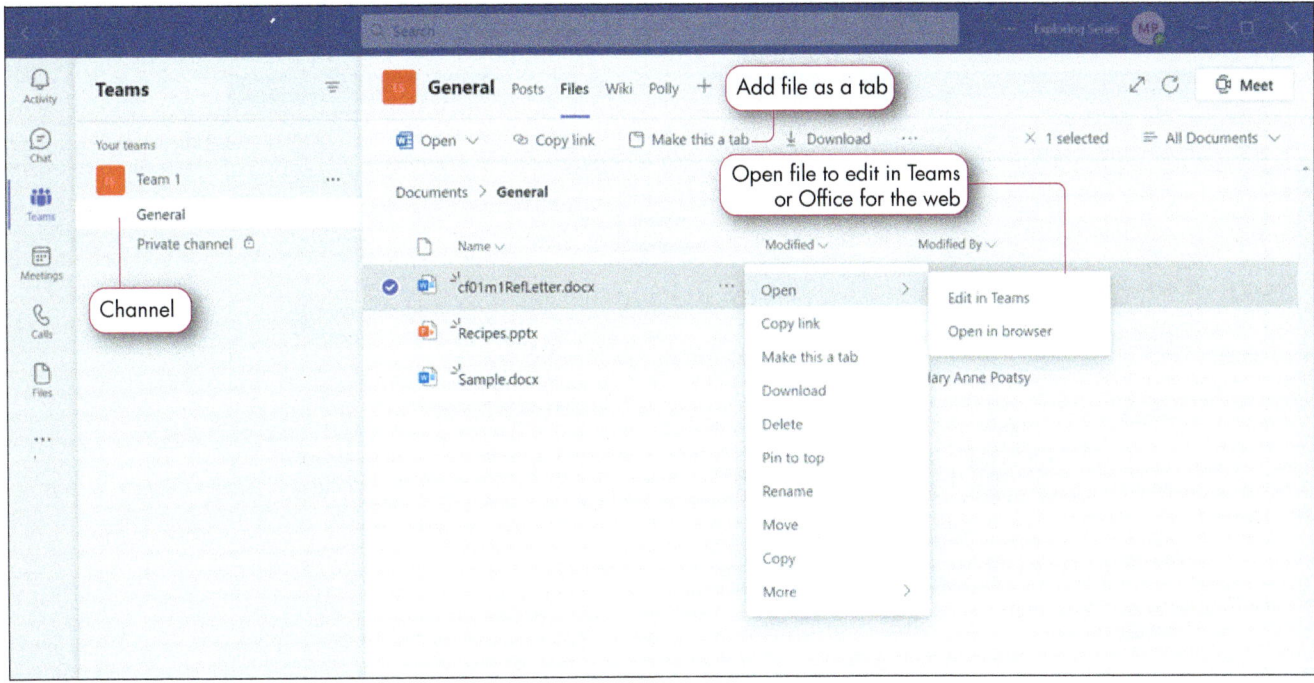

FIGURE 1.11 Different Options for Files in a Channel

> **TIP: ACCESS ALL FILES**
> Each channel has a Files tab that houses files shared among channel members. If you have multiple channels and teams and want to see all files posted to every channel or team of which you are a member, select Files from the left menu of Microsoft Teams. That will give you access to all files rather than files for a specific channel.

You can begin a new Word, Excel, or PowerPoint document in Microsoft Teams. Select New and then choose the type of file you want to create. Enter a name for the new file and click Create. The file will open in Microsoft Teams using the online application. You can give permission to all or specific channel members to edit the file. Anyone with editing privileges can work simultaneously in the file. While working on a file in Microsoft Teams, you can begin a conversation with any channel member by selecting Conversation at the top of the application ribbon. You can also leave comments within the document (see Figure 1.12). Use @mention in the comment or conversation to direct your chat to specific channel members.

HOW TO

Open and collaborate on a file in a Microsoft Teams channel:

1. Select More options next to the file in a team conversation or on the Files tab.
2. Choose if you want to edit the file in Microsoft Teams, on your desktop, or online.
3. Edit the file. Colored flags show who is working on it with you.
4. Select Start conversation to add a message about the file.
5. Type your message or @mention someone and select Send.

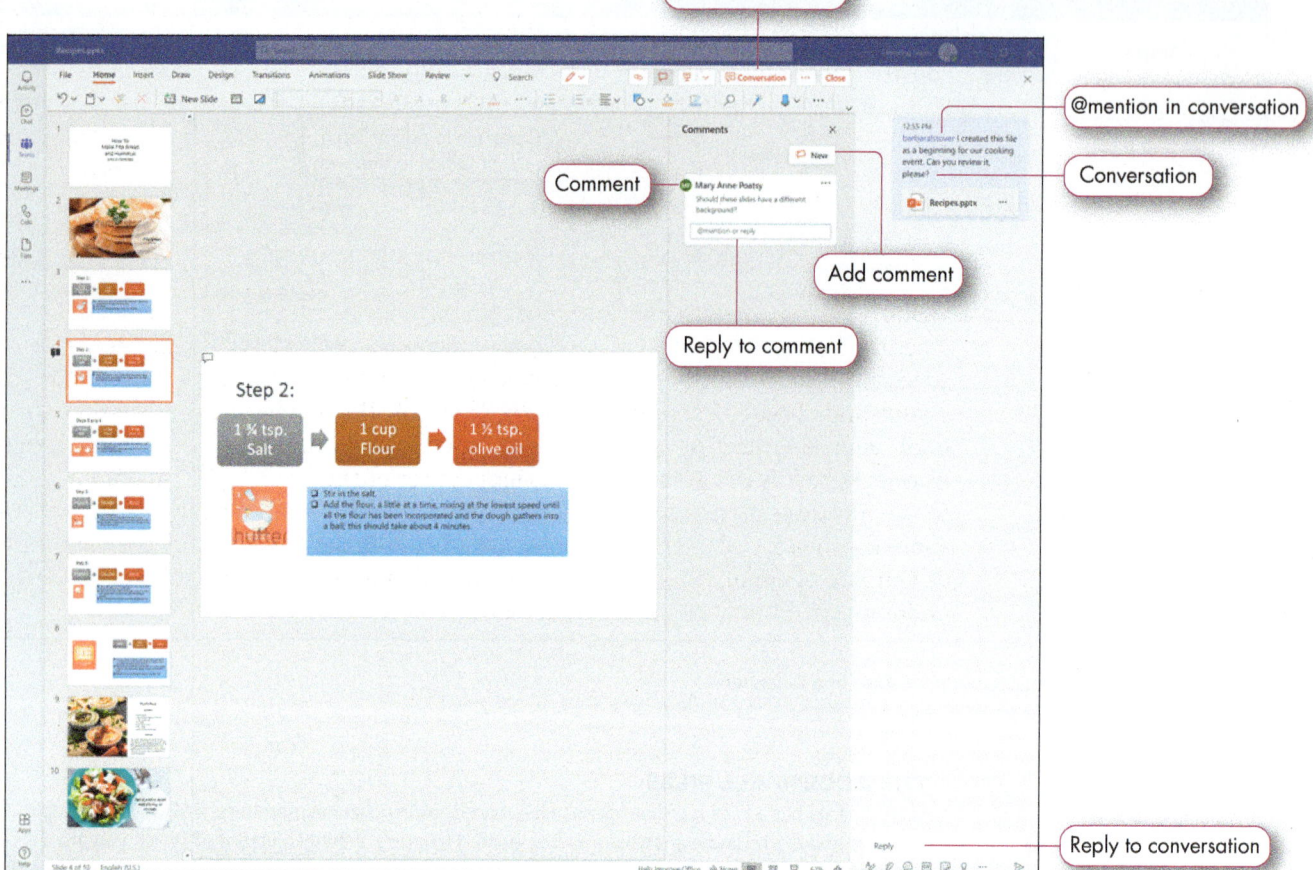

FIGURE 1.12 Collaborating on a PowerPoint Presentation

TIP: USE THE DESKTOP APPLICATION

When you create a file in Microsoft Teams, it opens in Microsoft Teams and uses the online application, which does not have all the features the desktop version has. If you prefer to work in the desktop application, select Open in Desktop App at the top of the window or download the file for later use.

Critical Thinking

1. Explain the difference between a team and a channel. *pp. 27–28*

2. Describe different ways you can communicate with team members. *pp. 31–36*

3. Describe the different ways files can be shared within Microsoft Teams. *pp. 34–36*

Use Virtual Team Meetings

With Microsoft Teams, you can create a Microsoft Teams *meeting* so that you can get together with others and share audio, video, and screen content. These features enable members of a group to collaborate on a project without everyone having to be in the same place.

In this section, you will learn how to set up and attend a virtual Microsoft Teams meeting. You will also learn how to share content, use the whiteboard, and initiate breakout rooms during a Microsoft Teams meeting.

Conduct Virtual Meetings

It is often difficult to gather many people together in the same room due to time or travel constraints. Although conversations can happen via text, email, or phone calls, being able to see the people with whom you are meeting adds an extra layer of connectedness. Although virtual meetings are not a substitute for in-person meetings, they are often easier and more efficient and so can make the workday more productive.

Create a Meeting

When you want to use video or audio to get together with others, you can create a meeting. To ensure everyone is available, meetings are often scheduled in advance. To schedule a meeting in Microsoft Teams, click Meetings from the left menu of Microsoft Teams and choose Schedule a meeting. Then title the meeting and choose the day and time when the meeting will occur (see Figure 1.13). Alternatively, you can use Meet now or Schedule meeting in the top right corner of the Teams window. To invite others to the meeting, copy the invitation and paste it into an email, chat, or other means to share the invite. Depending on whether Microsoft Teams is connected to a calendar such as Outlook or Gmail, there may also be an option to schedule, share, or adjust meeting options such as adding a reminder directly from the calendar.

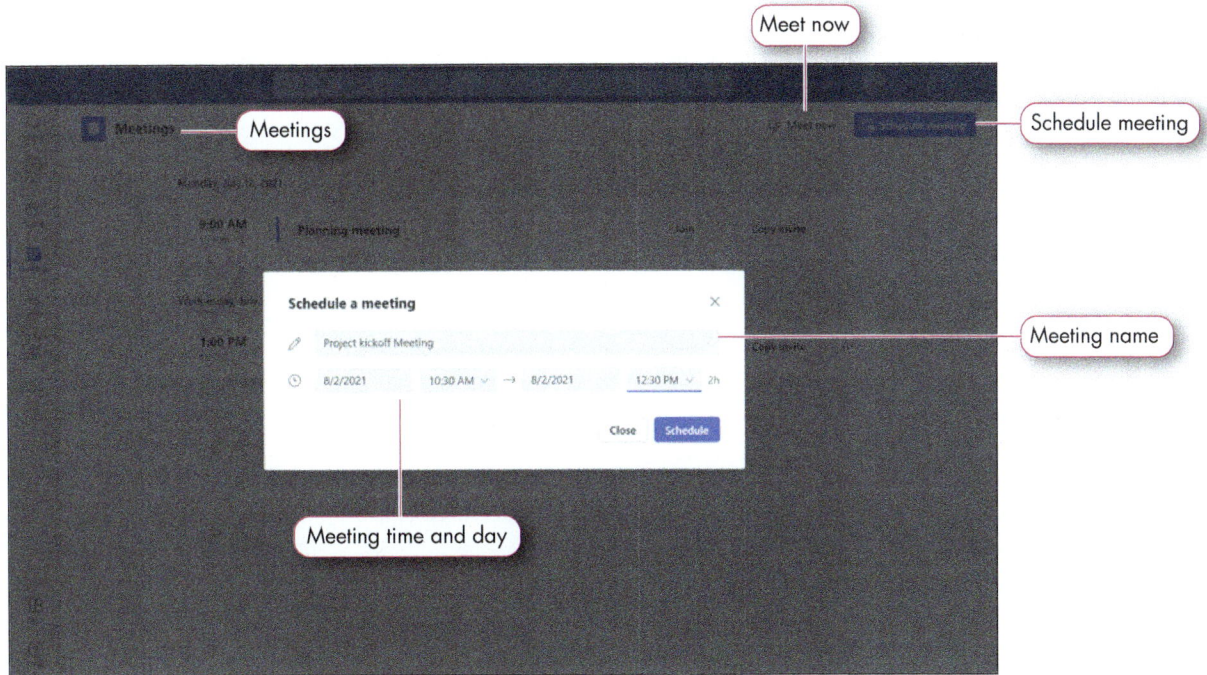

FIGURE 1.13 Scheduling a Microsoft Teams Meeting

TIP: SCHEDULING A MICROSOFT TEAMS MEETING FROM GOOGLE CALENDAR

If you use the Google calendar, you can use the Microsoft Teams add-on to schedule Microsoft Teams meetings directly from the Google calendar. To add the Microsoft Teams add-on for Google Workspace, open the Google Calendar and ensure that the right panel displays. Click the plus sign to Get Add-ons, and search for Microsoft Teams. When the add-on is installed, the Microsoft Teams icon displays in the right panel. Depending on the browser you use to view the Google Calendar, you can schedule the meeting directly in the calendar or by clicking the Microsoft Teams icon in the right panel.

Join a Scheduled Meeting

Once a meeting has been scheduled, you can join a meeting in several ways. You can open Meetings in Microsoft Teams and click Join on the meeting listed. Alternatively, you can click Join from the meeting notification on your Outlook or other calendar. Lastly, if you were sent a link to the meeting, select Click here to join the meeting (see Figure 1.14).

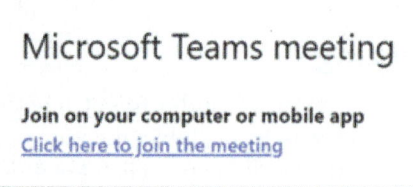

Microsoft Teams meeting

Join on your computer or mobile app
Click here to join the meeting

FIGURE 1.14 Join a Microsoft Teams Meeting

Start a Meeting from a Chat or Conversation

If you are chatting with team members and determine that a virtual meeting is necessary at that moment, you can choose Meet from the chat or conversation or by selecting Meet from the top right corner of the General windows (see Figure 1.15). Alternatively, you can also choose Meetings from the left menu of Microsoft Teams and select Meet now (refer to Figure 1.13). After you have adjusted your audio and video settings (described in more detail next), click Join to be connected to the meeting. If you initiated the meeting, then you have the option of adding participants from the channel or team. To add participants outside the channel, you can get a meeting link and share it through email.

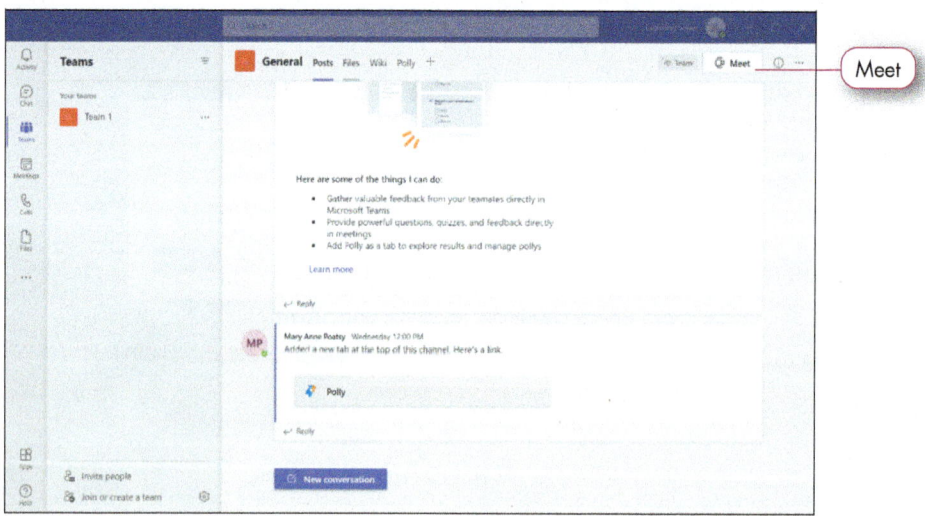

FIGURE 1.15 Meet Within a Channel

Adjust Meeting Settings

Before you join a meeting, a window displays with a preview of what your video will display. You can adjust the audio and video device settings as well as background effects from the preview window. You can also adjust your settings once the meeting has started (see Figure 1.16) by selecting More actions. Applying background effects is useful when you use the camera for video meetings and you want to hide your background to avoid displaying distracting or unsightly environments. You can use a background filter to blur the background so everything behind you is subtly concealed. If you would prefer, you can replace your background with an image. You can choose an image provided

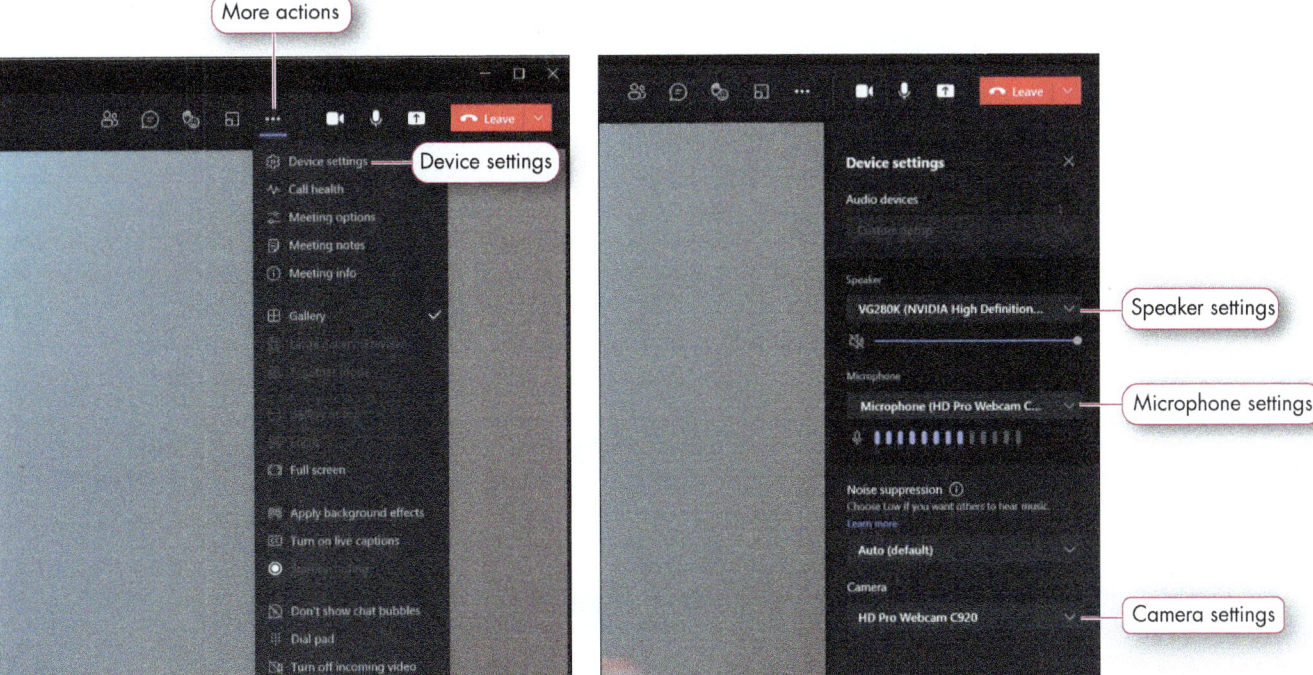

FIGURE 1.16 Meeting and Device Settings

in Microsoft Teams or select your own. Once you choose a background effect, the new background will remain for all future video meetings until you turn it off or change it. If you want to change your background effect during a meeting, you are given the option to preview the effect before applying it. During the preview, your video will turn off and participants will see your initials or static image.

HOW TO

Join a Microsoft Teams meeting:

1. Select Join from your Calendar or email invite.
2. Turn on your camera, select Background effects, and check your microphone. It may have been muted automatically when you entered the meeting.
3. Select a custom background or select Blur.
4. Choose your audio settings.
5. Select Join now.

TIP: VIRTUAL MEETING ETIQUETTE

It is proper etiquette to join a meeting with your microphone muted. If the meeting features one person speaking at a time, then it is also helpful to mute all participants, leaving only the speaker with an active microphone. To mute all participants during a meeting, right-click a participant tile and select Mute All Participants. When a muted participant wants to make a comment, they can unmute themselves for the time they are speaking. This practice limits unnecessary background noise, which can be distracting to others in the meeting. If you plan to participate with video, check your background in the video preview before joining. Choose to use a background effect if you feel your background is inappropriate or distracting.

Record and Share a Meeting

The host of any Microsoft Teams meeting can opt to record the audio, video, and screen-sharing activity. In some instances, recording a meeting may seem superfluous, but often having a recording available can be helpful later. One of the most obvious reasons to record a meeting is so those who are unable to make the meeting can review the recording and get up to speed quickly. Similarly, even though you are attending the meeting, you can become distracted or lose focus on the conversation. Being able to review the meeting later will help fill in the blanks about the parts of the conversation you missed. Additionally, ideas are tossed around and built upon in fluid fashion throughout a discussion. While the main idea may be remembered, some of the smaller details that were interspersed throughout the discussion may be lost. Reviewing the discussion later will help capture and solidify the larger idea as well as all the details. Lastly, in some meetings, recordings help to keep everyone accountable for what they say and how they act. Reviewing a recorded meeting can be a great way to improve communication skills. To record a meeting, click More actions in the Meeting controls and then select Start recording (see Figure 1.17).

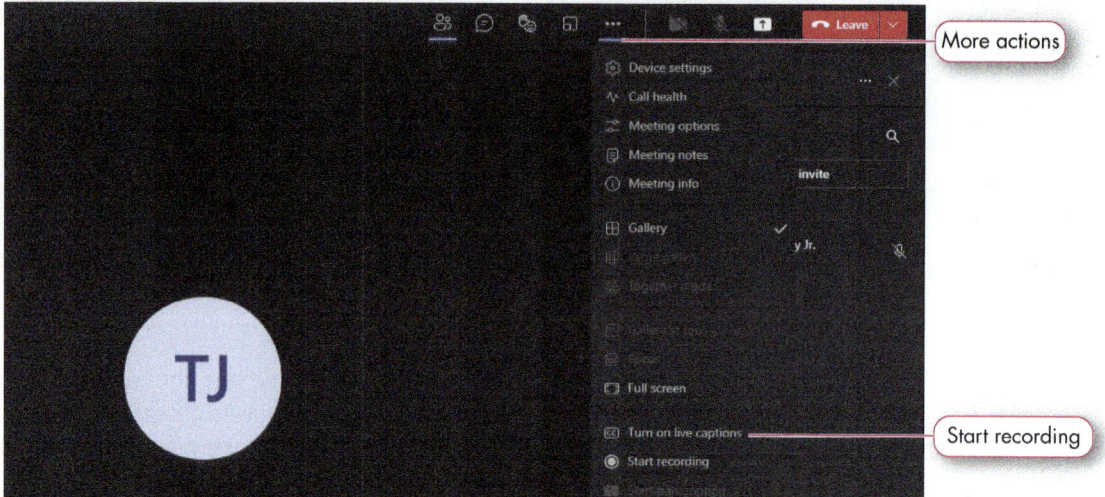

FIGURE 1.17 Record a Microsoft Teams Meeting

> **TIP: RECORDING NOTIFICATION**
> All participants are alerted when a Microsoft Teams meeting is recorded and participants who are uncomfortable with joining a recorded meeting are given the option of not joining. Regardless, it is good form to alert everyone that the meeting is being recorded before the meeting starts and ask if anyone has objections. In some places, you legally need to get everyone's permission before you can record them, so make sure you know the rules before you record!

The recording will stop when the meeting is ended. But if you want to record only a portion of the meeting and stop the recording before the meeting is ended, click More actions in the Meeting controls and select Stop recording and transcription. If a recording is stopped during a meeting and needs to be resumed before the meeting ends, a new separate recording will be made. When the recording is complete, it is then saved to OneDrive or SharePoint, depending on the type of meeting.

Meeting recordings can be found in the chat or channel conversations. Additionally, recordings are stored in the Recordings folder in the OneDrive directory of the person who started the meeting. You can share the recording like you would any other document by sharing the recording directly from Microsoft Teams or by sending a link to the recording.

Collaborate in Virtual Meetings

If you and your team members were sitting together in a meeting, you might view a common file such as a PowerPoint presentation, Word document, or Excel workbook. In those instances, the common file might be projected on a screen for everyone to view, or perhaps copies of the file might be passed around to everyone in the room. Sometimes a big group may break into smaller groups for more focused discussions. Those same experiences can take place even if team members are in different locations using virtual meetings in Microsoft Teams.

Share Content

In a Microsoft Teams meeting, you can share content from your device for all participants to view. This content can be your entire screen, a window, access to PowerPoint Live, or a whiteboard. Table 1.2 describes how each sharing option is used. To share content, click Share Content in the Meeting controls. Thumbnails will display of your desktop and each open window. Click the desktop or the window you want to share. The default is to give the presenter permission to share content from their computer. Other participants can share their content but the presenter must give permission for another participant to share. In the sharing controls, select Give Control, and select the name of the person to give control to. Control can be given back to the presenter when the participant stops sharing, or the meeting initiator can choose Take back control from the sharing controls. A participant can also request control from the person sharing. The person sharing can approve or deny the request. To end your control of the screen, select Release control to stop showing your screen to other participants.

TABLE 1.2	Share Content in Microsoft Teams	
Shared Content	**What Is Shared**	**Situations to Use**
Desktop	Shows entire screen. All notifications and other desktop activity will display.	Good when you want to share multiple windows seamlessly.
Window	Shows the contents of a single window. This prevents notifications and other distracting desktop activities from displaying during a meeting.	Enables the presenter to have other windows open while presenting.
PowerPoint Live	Displays a PowerPoint file in PowerPoint Live so others can interact with the presentation.	Others can move through at their own pace.
Whiteboard	Displays a blank screen for brainstorming activities.	Enables meeting participants to add their own input to a common area.

> **MAC TIP: SHARE CONTENT**
> Before sharing content, you need to grant permission to Microsoft Teams to record the computer's screen. The first time you try to share content, you will be prompted to grant permission. Select Open System Preferences. Without the prompt, click the Apple Menu, select System Preferences, and then select Security & Privacy. Under Screen Recording, make sure the Microsoft Teams check box is selected.

Share a PowerPoint Presentation

You can choose to run a PowerPoint presentation from an open window, or you can share the slides from the PowerPoint window, in the shared content pane. Sharing from the PowerPoint window enables *PowerPoint Live* where the meeting participants view the presentation at their preferred pace, such as when an attendee wants to spend more time on a slide after the presenter has moved on to another slide.

When the presentation is shared in a PowerPoint window, the presentation displays on the presenter's screen in Presenter view as shown in Figure 1.18. If you choose to turn off Presenter view, click More options below the main slide display and select Hide presenter view. The participants see the current slide but can also move around to different slides without affecting anyone else's view. As a participant, to get back to the slide that is currently being presented, click Sync to Presenter.

> **TIP: KEEP PARTICIPANTS FOCUSED**
> To keep everyone focused on the presentation and to disable participants from moving about the presentation at their own pace, select the eye icon next to Stop presenting.

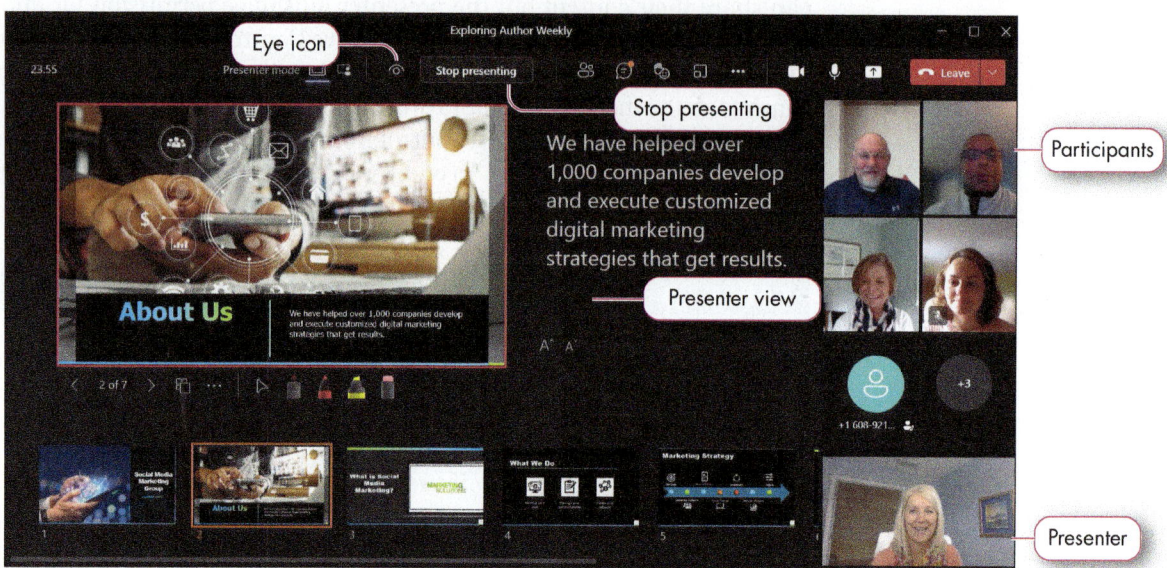

FIGURE 1.18 Presenter View in PowerPoint Live

Use the Whiteboard

At times in a virtual meeting, you might want team participants to share their thoughts and ideas in real time. Using the **whiteboard** in Microsoft Teams enables meeting participants to work collaboratively on a shared canvas. To start the whiteboard, click Share and click Microsoft Whiteboard in the Whiteboard section of the shared content pane. Once the whiteboard has been started, all meeting participants can use the pens, text boxes, and notes to add to the canvas.

> **TIP: WHITEBOARD IS NOT PART OF MICROSOFT TEAMS RECORDING**
> If you share a whiteboard during a recorded Microsoft Teams meeting, the whiteboard will not be part of the recording. However, after a Microsoft Teams meeting, the whiteboard will be made available to all participants in the channel chat. The whiteboard can also be saved and uploaded for additional distribution.

Use Breakout Rooms

Participants can be divided into small groups called **breakout rooms** to facilitate discussions and teamwork. You can assign individuals manually to breakout rooms, or they can be assigned automatically. To create a breakout room, when all participants have joined, select Breakout Rooms from the Meeting controls, and select how many rooms you want to create and how you want to assign people to the rooms. Select Automatically for a random placement of participants or, if you want to assign people to specific rooms, choose Manually (see Figure 1.19). When assigning people manually, point to each name to display check boxes, choose the individual by selecting the check box next to each name, select Assign, and then choose a room from the list. Repeat this process until all participants have been assigned to rooms. You can view the people assigned to each room by expanding the arrow next to each room name. Use Room options to enable attendees to pop in and out of breakout rooms to the main meeting to ask questions and then return to their breakout room.

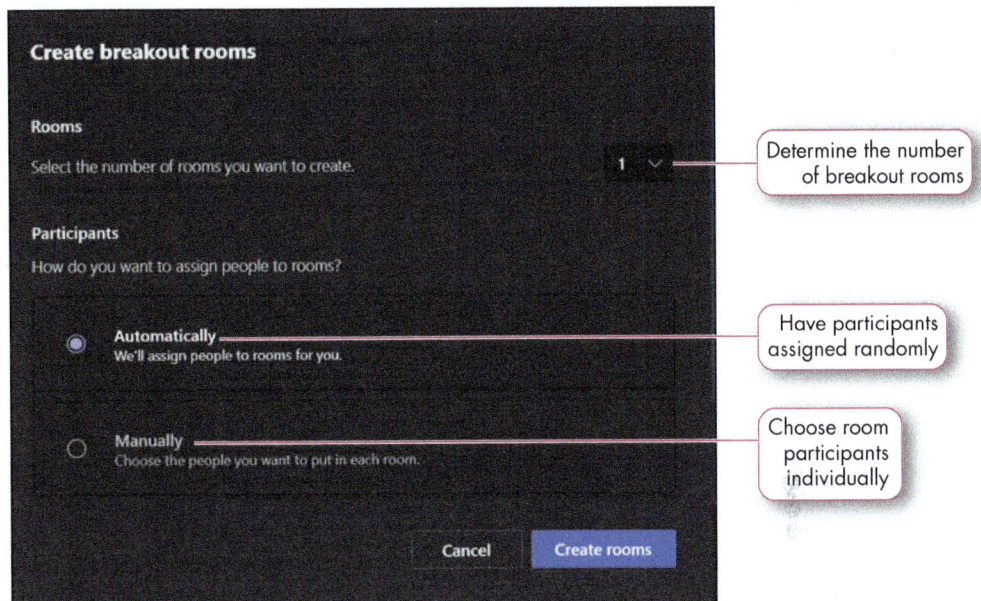

FIGURE 1.19 Create Breakout Rooms

To start all breakout rooms at the same time, select Open Rooms. To start rooms individually, select More Options next to each room and select Open Room. Breakout rooms can be recorded just like main meetings. To start recording breakout room sessions, select More options in the Meeting controls, and then select Start recording. If you want to send a message to each breakout room, select More Options, and then select Make an announcement. Type your announcement and select Send. Participants will receive a notification in their meeting chat to check for the announcement. As the meeting presenter, you can choose to pop in and out of breakout rooms by selecting Join from More options to participate and then selecting Return to go back to the main meeting.

Content can be shared in breakout rooms, but participants must first be given permission to share their screens. Once breakout rooms have been started, as the meeting presenter, join each room and click More options; then under Who can present, select Everyone to enable all members of the breakout room to share their screens or select individual participants. Members then can share their desktop or a window or enable the whiteboard.

To close breakout rooms, you can close them all at once by selecting Close rooms, or you can close rooms individually. Alternatively, you can set a time limit for the breakout rooms to control the length of any discussion. A timer keeps everyone on track and aware of the time remaining. When time is up, breakout rooms will close automatically, returning everyone to the main meeting. All files, notes, and recordings are available after the room has closed through the room's chat feature.

Critical Thinking

4. Describe the benefits of participating in a virtual meeting. ***pp. 37–43***

5. Explain why a whiteboard may be used in a meeting. ***p. 42***

6. Explain why breakout rooms are used in a meeting. ***p. 42***

Chapter Objectives Review

After reading this chapter, you have accomplished the following objectives:

1. **Apply Microsoft Teams basics.**
   - **Explore the Microsoft Teams interface:** The Microsoft Teams interface is where you create a team, channel, view all activity, set up meetings and calls, and access files. A team is a collection of people, conversations, files, and tools.
   - **Create a channel:** A channel is a section of a team that relates to a specific department, topic, or project. Every team has a General channel by default. Additional channels can be created and opened to all team members or set up for a select group.
   - **Check team activity:** The Activity Feed is a summary of all activity within a team. You can filter the feed to show specific types of messages.
   - **Use apps:** An app is an application that adds more functionality to Microsoft Teams. Apps can be added to a team or channel and into a conversation. There are many types of apps that can be added. A connector is a type of app that offers frequently updated content such as an RSS app or YouTube app.
   - **Use the command box:** The command box is where you search for and access anything within a team such as messages, people, and files.

2. **Communicate with Microsoft Teams.**
   - **Chat:** A chat is like a text or IM (instant message). Chats can be used for brief or private conversations with another person or small group but can also be directed to an entire team. Chats can contain files and apps.
   - **Use @mention:** An @mention directs a part of a chat or conversation specifically to a person or a group. When an @mention is used, the receiver will get a notification indicating they have been mentioned in a chat or conversation.
   - **Make audio calls:** Audio calls can be made through Microsoft Teams, just like calls placed by phone. Audio calls can be between two or more people.
   - **Share files:** Files can be shared while working in a team or channel or while in a chat or conversation. Shared files can be distributed so each member has their own copy or can be worked on collaboratively by team or channel members. Previously created files can be uploaded, or new files can be created in Microsoft Teams using the online versions of Word, Excel, and PowerPoint.

3. **Conduct virtual meetings.**
   - **Create a meeting:** Meetings are used when audio, video, and sharing screen content are required. You can schedule a meeting in advance or right when it is needed.
   - **Join a scheduled meeting:** Once a meeting has been scheduled, participants can join by clicking on a calendar notification that was sent out when the meeting was created or by clicking on a link in an email.
   - **Start a meeting from a chat or conversation:** You can start a meeting directly from a chat or conversation.
   - **Adjust meeting settings:** It is important to adjust your audio and video settings before joining a meeting, but they can also be adjusted while you are in a meeting. In addition, if you are uncomfortable displaying the background environment from where you are joining the meeting, you can adjust the background by blurring or by choosing an image provided by Microsoft or one of your own.
   - **Record and share a meeting:** Meetings can be recorded to capture the audio, video, and screen-sharing activity and shared afterward. The recording is automatically stopped when the meeting has ended, but it can be stopped at any point during a meeting. If you want to resume recording, if it has been ended before the meeting has ended, you can start recording again, but it will be a separate recording rather than a continuation of the first.

4. **Collaborate in virtual meetings.**
   - **Share content:** Content from the presenter's or other participants' computers can be shared using what displays on the desktop, in a window, directly in PowerPoint, or with a whiteboard. Control is by default given to the presenter, but the presenter can give control to and take back control from a participant, or a participant can request control and then give control back.
   - **Share a PowerPoint presentation:** If a PowerPoint presentation is being used during the meeting, the presenter can share the presentation by sharing the desktop or window in which the presentation is displaying. In these instances, the participants can only follow along in the exact order and pace as the presenter. If the presenter chooses to share PowerPoint

content by choosing the PowerPoint sharing option, the presentation displays in PowerPoint Live and enables participants to move through the presentation at their own pace without affecting the experience of any other participant.

- **Use the whiteboard:** Another sharing option is a whiteboard. A whiteboard is a collaborative canvas in which all participants can enter their input using pens in the app that are controlled by a stylus or mouse, text boxes, and notes. Whiteboard content is not recorded in a recorded meeting, but it can be saved and distributed separately. Whiteboards are also available in a chat or conversation for impromptu collaboration.

- **Use breakout rooms:** Sometimes there is a benefit to break a large group into smaller groups during a meeting for more focused and personalized conversations. The same can occur in Microsoft Teams by creating breakout rooms. Participants can be manually selected and assigned to breakout rooms or automatically assigned once the number of rooms is chosen. While in breakout rooms, participants can be given permission to share content, including whiteboards. Timers can be placed to automatically close rooms after a specified amount of time, returning all participants to the main meeting area. The presenter can pop in and out of breakout rooms and send chats to all rooms or individual rooms as well.

Key Terms Matching

Match the key terms with their definitions. Write the key term letter by the appropriate numbered definition.

a. @mention   **f.** Chat   **k.** PowerPoint Live

b. Activity feed   **g.** Command box   **l.** Team

c. App   **h.** Connector   **m.** Whiteboard

d. Breakout room   **i.** Meeting

e. Channel   **j.** Microsoft Teams

1. _____ A feature that enables users to work collaboratively on a shared canvas. **p. 42**

2. _____ A feature that enables meeting participants to be divided into smaller groups. **p. 42**

3. _____ Enables meeting participants to view a PowerPoint presentation at their own pace. **p. 41**

4. _____ To get together in real time with others and share audio, video, and screen content. **p. 36**

5. _____ A section within a team that relates to a specific department, project, or topic. **p. 28**

6. _____ An application that adds additional functionality to Microsoft Teams. **p. 30**

7. _____ Software that facilitates communication and collaboration in real time between groups of individuals in different locations. **p. 26**

8. _____ Used to search for and access almost anything within a team. **p. 31**

9. _____ A summary of all activities within a channel. **p. 29**

10. _____ Directs a chat or conversation to a specific individual, group, or channel. **p. 33**

11. _____ A collection of people, conversations, files, and tools. **p. 27**

12. _____ A form of communication like a text or instant message. **p. 31**

13. _____ A type of app that offers frequently updated content. **p. 30**

Multiple Choice

1. Which of the following is a section of a team that relates to a particular project?

   (a) Breakout room

   (b) Chat

   (c) Channel

   (d) Activity

2. Which would you choose to find all forms of communication within a team?

   (a) Activity feed

   (b) Chat

   (c) Communications app

   (d) Channel activity

3. When is an @mention used?

   (a) To start a meeting with a team or channel member

   (b) To direct part of a conversation to a team or channel member

   (c) To begin an audio call to a team or channel member

   (d) To add a team or channel member to an app feed

4. Which of the following cannot be done to a channel file?

   (a) Edit the file in Microsoft Teams

   (b) Open the file in a browser

   (c) Make the file a tab

   (d) Upload the file to a whiteboard

5. Which of the following is *not* considered good etiquette when participating in a Microsoft Teams meeting?

   (a) Blur your background

   (b) Keep your microphone on at all times

   (c) Turn off your video when you are not presenting

   (d) Customize your display name

6. Which sharing option enables you to share content from your entire screen?

   (a) Window

   (b) Desktop

   (c) Whiteboard

   (d) Computer

7. Which feature available in a Microsoft Teams meeting acts like a shared canvas?

   (a) PowerPoint Live

   (b) Wiki

   (c) Live Canvas

   (d) Whiteboard

8. Which of the following separates participants into smaller groups in a meeting?

   (a) Breakout room

   (b) Chat

   (c) Channel

   (d) Activity room

9. Which sharing feature in a meeting lets participants follow a presentation at their own pace?

   (a) Desktop with PowerPoint displaying

   (b) Window with PowerPoint displaying

   (c) PowerPoint Live

   (d) PowerPoint Participant View

10. Which of the following would be considered a connector app?

    (a) Microsoft Word

    (b) YouTube

    (c) Microsoft Excel

    (d) OneNote

Microsoft 365 Common Features

LEARNING OUTCOME You will apply skills common to Microsoft 365 applications to create and format documents and edit content.

OBJECTIVES & SKILLS: After you read this chapter, you will be able to:

CASE STUDY | Spotted Begonia Art Gallery

You are an administrative assistant for Spotted Begonia, a local art gallery. The gallery does a lot of community outreach to help local artists develop a network of clients and supporters. Local schools are invited to bring students to the gallery for enrichment programs.

As the administrative assistant for Spotted Begonia, you are responsible for overseeing the production of documents, spreadsheets, newspaper articles, and presentations that will be used to increase public awareness of the gallery. Other clerical assistants who are familiar with Microsoft 365 will prepare the promotional materials, and you will proofread, make necessary corrections, adjust page layouts, save and print documents, and identify appropriate templates to simplify tasks. Your experience with Microsoft 365 is limited, but your knowledge of certain fundamental tasks that are common to Word, Excel, and PowerPoint will help you accomplish your oversight task. You are excited to get started with your work!

Take the First Step

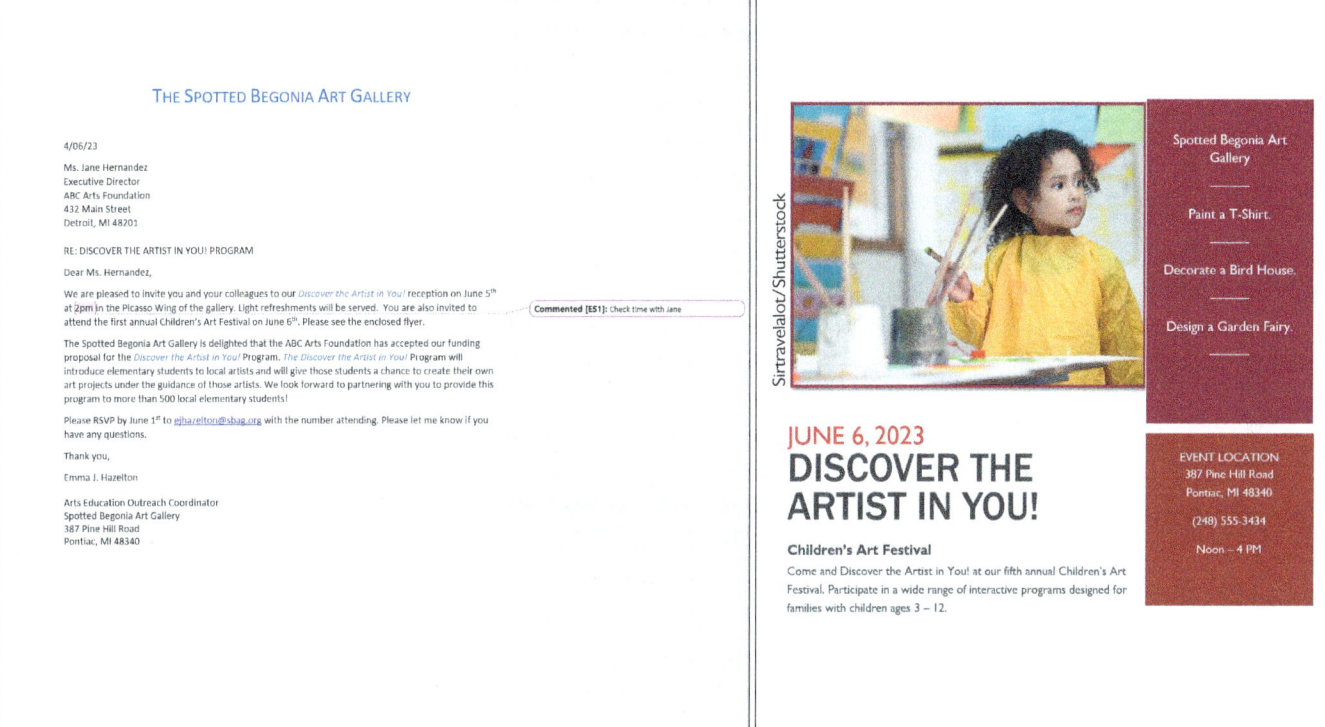

FIGURE 1.1 Spotted Begonia Art Gallery Documents

CASE STUDY | Spotted Begonia Art Gallery

Starting Files	Files to Be Submitted	MyLab IT HOE Grader
cf01h1Letter.docx cf01h2Art.jpg Seasonal Event Flyer Template	cf01h1Letter_LastFirst.docx cf01h3Flyer_LastFirst.docx	

MyLab IT Grader: This project is available as a Hands-On Exercise project in MyLab IT.

Work with Microsoft 365 Files

Organizations around the world rely heavily on Microsoft 365 applications to produce documents, spreadsheets, presentations, and databases. **Microsoft 365** includes a set of software applications, each one specializing in a specific type of output. Microsoft 365 is purchased as a monthly or annual subscription and is fully installed on your PC, tablet, and phone. With Microsoft 365, you receive periodic updates of new features and security measures. Microsoft 365 also includes access to OneDrive storage. Office 2021 is a one-time purchase and is fully installed on your PC. Periodic upgrades are not available. There are also Office on the web applications that are freely available, but offer limited capabilities. Microsoft 365 and Office 2021 have Mac-compatible versions.

All versions of Microsoft 365 include Word, Excel, and PowerPoint as well as some other applications. Some versions of Microsoft 365 also include Access. Microsoft 365 for Mac and Office 2021 for Mac include Word, Excel, and PowerPoint, but not Access. Access is not supported by Mac operating systems. **Microsoft Word** (Word) is a word processing application, used to produce all sorts of documents, including memos, newsletters, reports, and brochures. **Microsoft Excel** (Excel) is a financial spreadsheet program, used to organize and analyze records, financial transactions, and business information in the form of worksheets. **Microsoft PowerPoint** (PowerPoint) is presentation software, used to create dynamic presentations to inform and persuade audiences. Finally, **Microsoft Access** (Access) is a database program, used to record and link data, query databases, and create forms and reports. The choice of which software application to use really depends on what type of output you are producing. Table 1.1 describes the major tasks of the four primary applications in Microsoft 365.

TABLE 1.1	Microsoft 365 Applications
Microsoft 365 Application	**Application Characteristics**
Word	Word processing software used with text and graphics to create, edit, and format documents.
Excel	Spreadsheet software used to store quantitative data and to perform accurate and rapid calculations, what-if analyses, and charting, with results ranging from simple budgets to sophisticated financial and statistical analyses.
PowerPoint	Presentation graphics software used to create slide shows for presentation by a speaker or delivered online, to be published as part of a website, or to run as a stand-alone application on a computer kiosk.
Access	Relational database software used to store data and convert it into information. Database software is used primarily for decision making by businesses that compile data from multiple records stored in tables to produce informative reports.

These programs are designed to work together, so you can integrate components created in one application into a file created by another application. For example, you could integrate a chart created in Excel into a Word document or a PowerPoint presentation, or you could export a table created in Access into Excel for further analysis. You could also start a presentation outline in Word and use it as the foundation for a PowerPoint presentation.

Microsoft 365 applications share common features. Such commonality gives a similar feel to each software application so that learning and working with each application is easier. This chapter focuses on many common features that the Microsoft 365 applications share. Although Word is primarily used to illustrate many examples, you are encouraged to open and explore Excel and PowerPoint (and to some degree, Access) to examine the same features in those applications.

Most of the content in this chapter and book is for the Windows-based Microsoft 365 applications. Although the Microsoft 365 apps have Mac-compatible versions, there are some differences. When there are significant differences to point out, TIP boxes and Troubleshooting boxes will provide the necessary information to help out.

In this section, you will learn how to open an application, and open and save a file. You will also learn to identify interface components common to Microsoft 365 applications, such as using and customizing the ribbon, the File tab, and the Quick Access Toolbar. You will experience Live Preview.

Work with Files

When working with a Microsoft 365 application, you can begin by opening an existing file that has already been saved to a device or an external storage medium, or you can begin work on a new file or template. When you are finished with a file, you should save it, so you can retrieve it at another time. The File tab is located at the far left of the ribbon. The *File tab* is where you do things "to" a file, whereas the other tabs on the ribbon enable you to do things "in" a file. The options on the File tab are used to manage your files and access the data about them—creating; saving; printing; sharing; inspecting for accessibility, compatibility, and other document issues; and accessing other setting options.

STEP 1 ## Open a Saved File

After opening a Microsoft 365 application, select New blank document (workbook, presentation, database, etc.) to start a new blank file. You can also create a new file from within an application or choose a template by selecting New from the File tab. You will learn about using templates later in this chapter.

Often you will want to work on an existing file that has been saved to a storage location. This may be an email attachment that you have downloaded to a storage device, a file that has been shared with you in OneDrive, or a file you have previously created. To open an existing file, use File Explorer to navigate to the folder or drive where the document is stored, and then double-click the file name to open the file. The associated application and the file will open. Alternatively, if the application is already open, from the File tab, click Open, and then navigate to the file location and open the file (see Figure 1.2).

> **MAC TIP: USE FINDER**
> To open an existing file, use Finder to navigate to the folder or drive where the document is stored and double-click the file name to open the file.

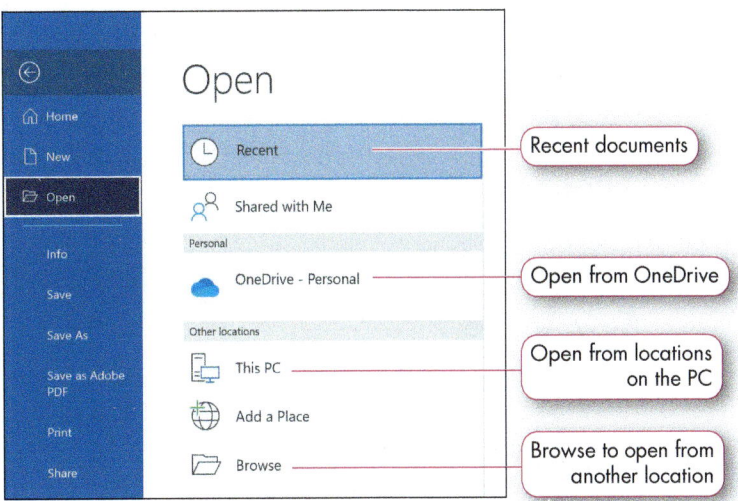

FIGURE 1.2 Open a Previously Saved Document

A Recent documents list with links to your most recently used files is available when you select Home or Open from the File tab. The Recent documents list simplifies the task of reopening files, as shown in Figure 1.3. The Recent list changes to reflect only the most recently opened files, so if it has been quite some time since you worked with a particular file, or if you have worked on several other files in between and you do not see your file listed, you can click More documents (or workbooks, presentations, etc.).

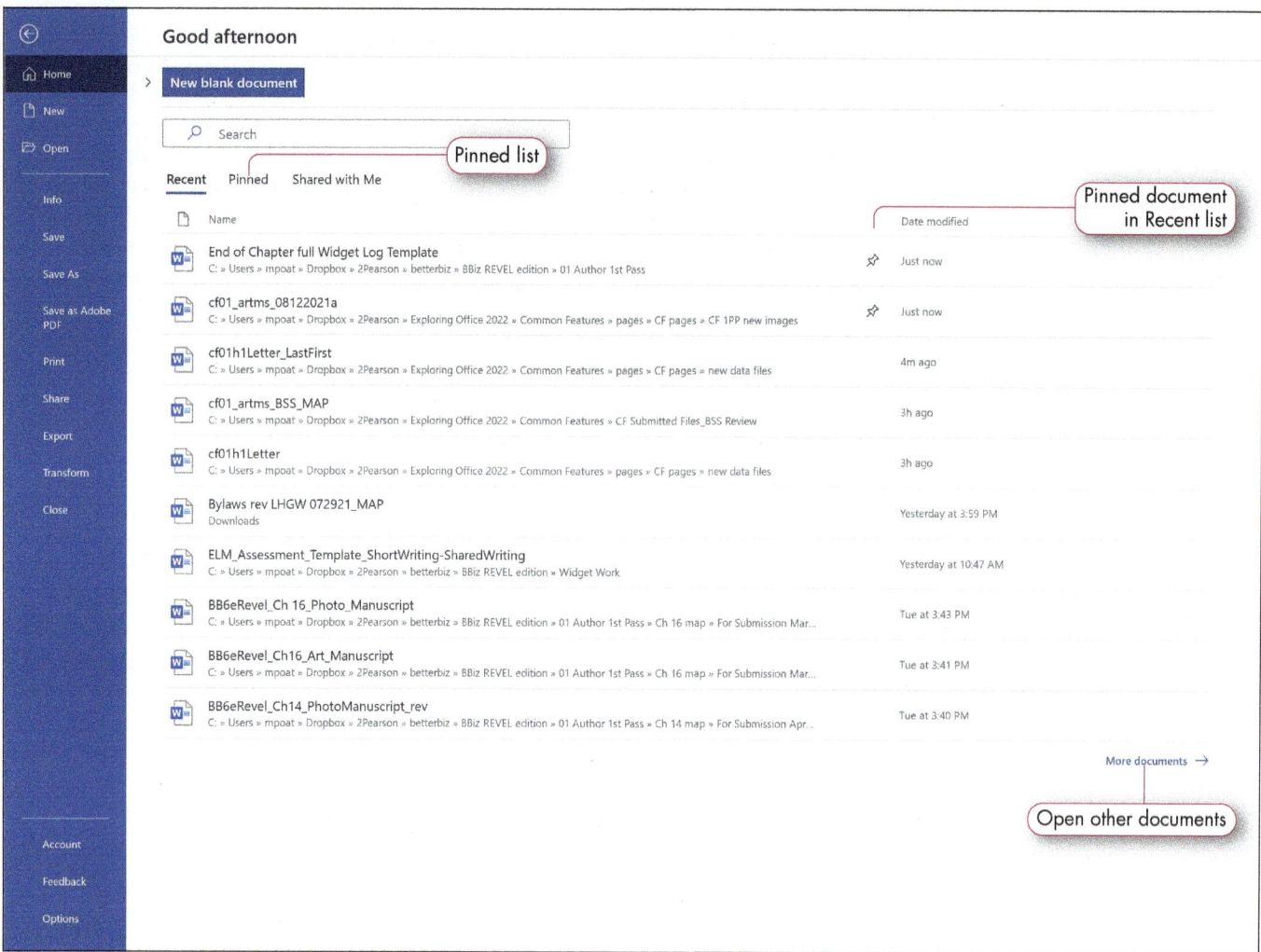

FIGURE 1.3 Recent Documents List

> **TIP: KEEPING FILES ON THE RECENT DOCUMENTS LIST**
> The Recent list displays a limited list of the most recently opened files. However, you might want to keep a particular file in the list regardless of how recently it was opened. *Pin this item to the list* icon displays to the right of each file when you point to or select the file. Select the icon to pin the file to the list. The pushpin of the "permanent" file will display indicating that it is a pinned item (refer to Figure 1.3). Once pinned, you will always have access to the file from the Pinned list. Later, if you want to remove the file from the list, click the pushpin icon. The file will remain on the Recent documents list while it is being used but will be bumped off the list when other, more recently opened files take its place.

Save a File

Saving a file enables you to open it for additional updates or reference later. Files are saved to a storage medium such as a hard drive, flash drive, or to OneDrive and usually to a folder within one of these storage mediums.

The first time you save a file, use Save As to indicate where the file will be saved and assign a file name. It is best to save the file in an appropriately named folder so you have less difficulty finding it later. Thereafter, you can continue to save the file with the same name and location using Save. You can access Save by clicking the File tab or by clicking Save on the left side of the document title bar. If the file is saved in OneDrive, any changes to the file will be automatically saved if AutoSave is turned on. You do not have to actively save the document. AutoSave is on the left side of the document title bar. If you want more control over when changes to your document are saved to OneDrive, you have the option to turn AutoSave off (or back on).

There are instances where you will want to rename the file or save it to a different location. For example, you might reuse a budget saved as an Excel worksheet, modifying it for another year, and want to keep a copy of both the old and revised budgets. In this instance, you would save the new budget workbook with a new name, and perhaps save it in a different folder. To do so, use Save As, and continue with the same procedure to save a new file: navigate to the new storage location and change the file name. Figure 1.4 shows a typical Save As window that enables you to select a location before saving the file. Notice that OneDrive is listed as well as This PC. To navigate to a location other than This PC or OneDrive, use Browse.

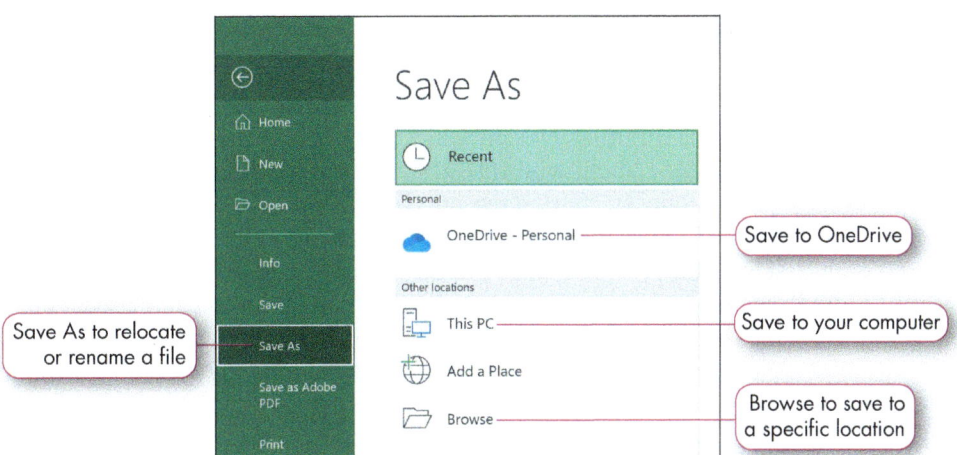

FIGURE 1.4 Save As Window

Use Common Interface Components

When you open any Microsoft 365 application, you will first notice the title bar and ribbon (see Figure 1.5) at the top of the document. These features enable you to identify the document, provide simple access to frequently used commands, and controls the window in which the document displays. The **title bar** identifies the current file name and the application in which you are working. It also includes control buttons on the right that enable you to minimize, restore down, or close the application window, and controls on the left to Save or AutoSave. The **Quick Access Toolbar (QAT)**, provides one-click access to commonly executed tasks such as check spelling or print. The QAT is hidden by default, but can be displayed by selecting the Ribbon Display Options arrow at the far right side of the ribbon and choosing Show Quick Access Toolbar. Located just below the title bar is the ribbon. The **ribbon** is the command center containing tabs, groups, and commands. If you are working with a large project, you can maximize your workspace by temporarily hiding the ribbon. There are several methods that can be used to hide and then redisplay the ribbon:

- Double-click any tab name to collapse; click any tab name to expand.
- Click the Ribbon Display Options arrow at the far-right side of the ribbon. These controls enable you not only to collapse or expand the ribbon but also to choose whether you want to see the tabs or no tabs at all.

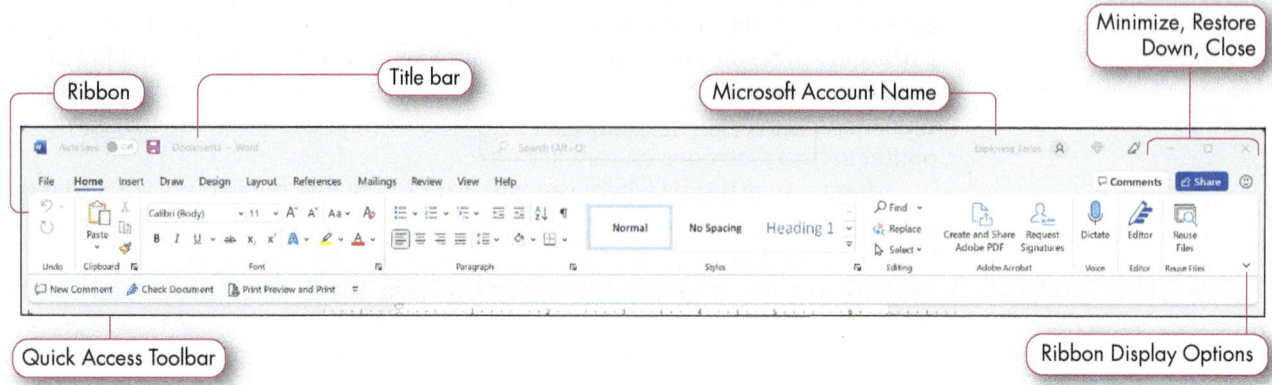

FIGURE 1.5 The Title Bar, Quick Access Toolbar, and Document and Ribbon Controls

STEP 2 ▶ **Use the Ribbon**

The main organizational grouping on the ribbon is ***tabs***. The tab name indicates the type of commands located on the tab. On each tab, the ribbon displays several task-oriented groups. A ***group*** is a subset of a tab that organizes similar commands together. A ***command*** is a button or icon within a group that you select to perform a task (see Figure 1.6). The ribbon, with the tabs and groups of commands, is designed to provide efficient functionality. For that reason, the Home tab displays when you first open a file in a Microsoft 365 application and contains groups with the most commonly used commands for that program. For example, because you often want to change the way text is displayed, the Home tab includes a Font group, with commands related to modifying text. Similarly, other tabs contain groups of related actions, or commands, many of which are unique to each Microsoft 365 application. The active tab shown in Figure 1.6 is the Home tab.

> **MAC TIP: GROUP NAMES**
> Microsoft 365 for Mac may not display group names on the ribbon by default. To display group names on the ribbon, click the application name menu (Word, Excel, PowerPoint) and select Preferences. Click View and click to select Show group titles in the Ribbon section of the View dialog box.

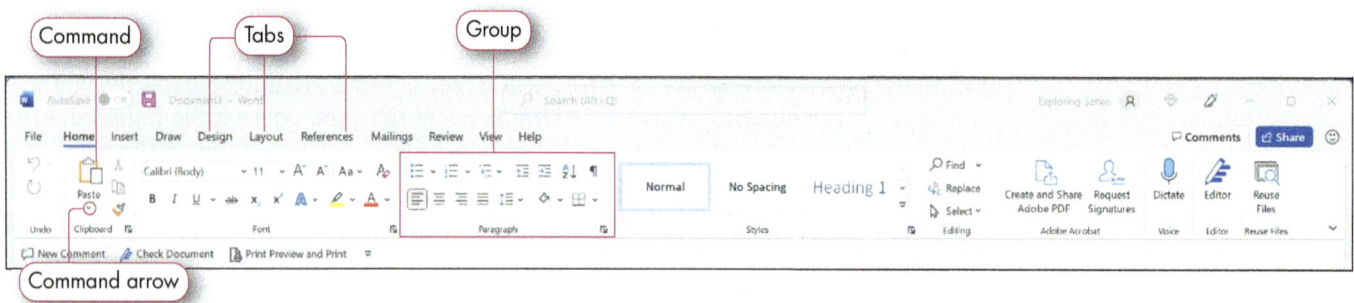

FIGURE 1.6 The Ribbon

As shown in Figure 1.6, some ribbon commands, such as Paste in the Clipboard group, contain two parts: the main command and an arrow. The arrow may be below or to the right of the main command, depending on the command, window size, or screen resolution. When selected, the arrow displays additional commands or options associated with the main command. For example, selecting the Paste arrow enables you to access the Paste Options commands, and the Font Color arrow displays a set of colors from which to choose. Instructions in the *Exploring Series* use the command name to instruct you to click the main command to perform the default action, such as click Paste. Instructions include the word *arrow* when you need to select the arrow to access an additional option, such as click the Paste arrow.

You can work with objects such as images, shapes, charts, and tables in any Microsoft 365 application. When you include such objects in a project, they are considered separate components that you can manage independently. To work with an object, you must first select it. When an object is selected, the ribbon is modified to include one or more *contextual tabs* that contain groups of commands related to the selected object. When the object is no longer selected, the contextual tab no longer displays.

Word, PowerPoint, Excel, and Access all share a similar ribbon structure. Although the specific tabs, groups, and commands vary among the programs, the way in which you use the ribbon and the descriptive nature of tab titles is the same, regardless of which program you are using. For example, if you want to insert a chart in Excel, a header in Word, or a shape in PowerPoint, those commands are found on the Insert tab in those programs. The first thing you should do as you begin to work with a Microsoft 365 application is to study the ribbon. Look at all tabs and their contents. That way, you will have a good idea of where to find specific commands, and how the ribbon with which you are currently working differs from one that you might have used in another application.

STEP 3 ▸ Use a Dialog Box and Gallery

Some commands and features do not display on the ribbon because they are not as commonly used. For example, you might want to apply a special effect such as Small caps or apply character spacing to some text. Because these effects are not found on the ribbon, they will most likely be found in a *dialog box* (in this case, the Font dialog box). When you open a dialog box, you gain access to more precise or less frequently used commands. Dialog boxes are accessed by clicking a *Dialog Box Launcher* found in the lower right corner of some ribbon groups. Figure 1.7 shows the Dialog Box Launcher in the Font group and the Font dialog box.

> **MAC TIP: DIALOG BOX LAUNCHERS**
> Dialog Box Launchers are not available in Microsoft 365 for Mac. Instead, click a menu option such as Format, Edit, or Insert for additional options.

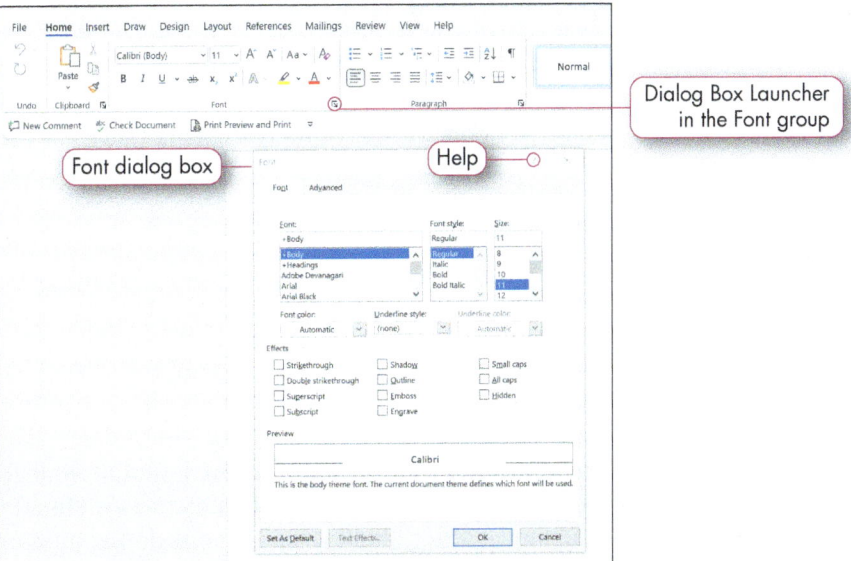

FIGURE 1.7 The Font Dialog Box in Word

Similarly, some formatting and design options are too numerous to include in the ribbon's limited space. For example, the Styles group displays on the Home tab of the Word ribbon. Because there are more styles than can easily display at once, the Styles group can be expanded to display a gallery with additional styles. A ***gallery*** displays additional formatting and design options. Galleries in Excel and PowerPoint provide additional choices of chart styles and slide themes, respectively. Figure 1.8 shows an example of the PowerPoint Themes gallery. From the ribbon, you can display a gallery by clicking More, which is located at the bottom right of the group's scroll bar found in some ribbon selections.

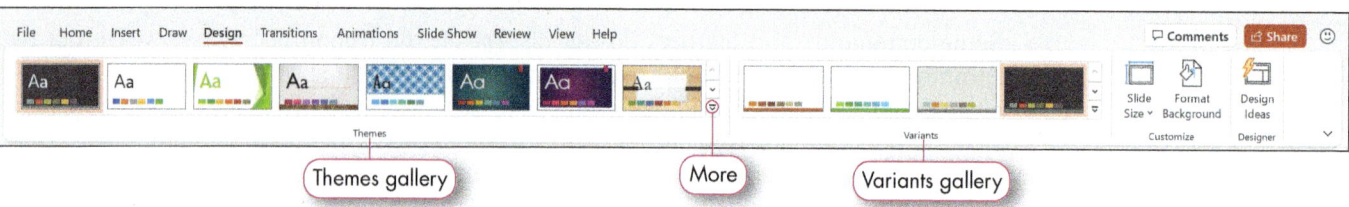

FIGURE 1.8 Themes and Variants Galleries in PowerPoint

When editing a document, worksheet, or presentation, it is helpful to see the results of formatting changes before you make final selections. The feature that displays a preview of the results of a format selection is called ***Live Preview***. For example, you might consider modifying the color of an image in a document or worksheet. As you place the pointer over a color selection in a ribbon gallery or group, the selected image will temporarily display the color to which you are pointing. Similarly, you can get a preview of how theme designs would display on PowerPoint slides by pointing to specific themes in the PowerPoint Themes group and noting the effect on a displayed slide. When you click the item, the selection is applied. Live Preview is available in various ribbon selections among the Microsoft 365 applications.

Customize the Ribbon

Although the ribbon is designed to put the tasks you need most in an easily accessible location, there may be tasks that are specific to your job or hobby that are on various tabs, or not displayed on the ribbon at all. In this case, you can personalize the ribbon by creating your own tabs and grouping together the commands you want to use. To add a command to a tab, you must first add a custom group. You can create as many new tabs and custom groups with as many commands as you need. You can also create a custom group on any of the default tabs and add commands to the new group or hide any commands you use less often (see Figure 1.9). Keep in mind that when you customize the ribbon, the customization applies only to the application in which you are working at the time. If you want a new tab with the same set of commands in both Word and PowerPoint, for example, the new tab would need to be created in each application.

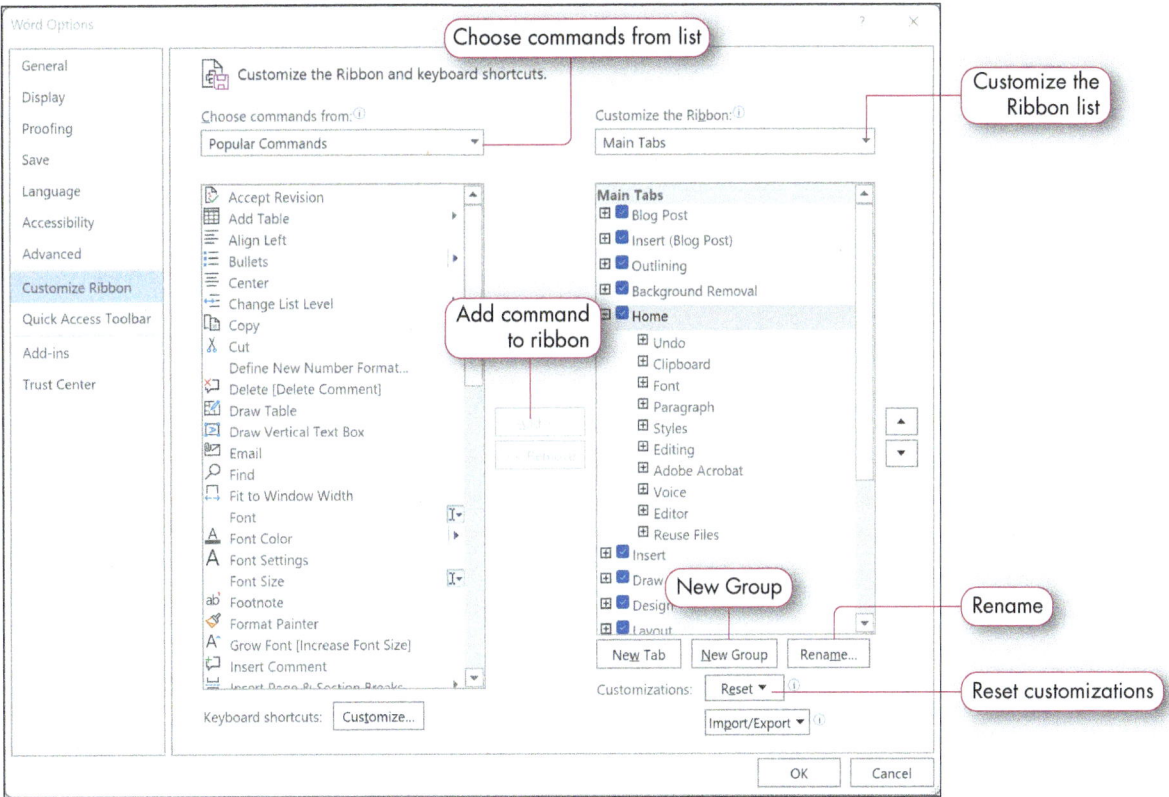

FIGURE 1.9 Customize the Ribbon in Word

There are several ways to access the Customize the Ribbon options:

- Right-click in an empty space in the ribbon and select Customize the Ribbon on the shortcut menu.
- Click the File tab, select Options, and then select Customize Ribbon.
- Display the QAT, click the Customize Quick Access Toolbar button, select More Commands, and then select Customize Ribbon.

The left side of the Customize the Ribbon window displays popular commands associated with the active application, but all available commands can be displayed by selecting All Commands in the *Choose commands from* list. On the right side of the Customize the Ribbon window is a list of the Main Tabs and Groups in the active application. You can also access the contextual tabs by selecting the arrow in the Customize the Ribbon list and selecting Tool Tabs.

HOW TO
Customize the ribbon by adding a command to an existing tab:

1. Click the File tab, click Options, and then select Customize Ribbon. (Alternatively, follow the other steps above to access the Customize the Ribbon window.)
2. Click the tab name that you want to add a group to under the Customize the Ribbon list. Ensure a blue background displays behind the tab name. Note that checking or unchecking the tab is not selecting the tab for this feature.
3. Click New Group. New Group (Custom) displays as a group on the selected tab.
4. Click Rename and give the new group a meaningful name.
5. Click the command to be added under the Choose commands from list.
6. Click Add.
7. Repeat as necessary, click OK when you have made all your selections.

Customize the ribbon:

1. Click the Word menu (or whichever application you are working in) and select Preferences.

2. Click Ribbon & Toolbar in the Authoring and Proofing Tools (or in Excel, Authoring).

3. Click the plus sign at the bottom of the Main Tabs box and select New Group.

4. Click the Settings icon and click Rename. Give the new group a meaningful name. Click Save.

5. Click the command to be added under the Choose commands from list.

6. Click Add.

7. Repeat as necessary, click OK when you have made all your selections.

To revert all tabs or to reset a selected tab to original settings, click Reset, and then click Reset all customizations or Reset only selected Ribbon tab (refer to Figure 1.9).

STEP 4 ▶ ## Use and Customize the Quick Access Toolbar

Recall that the Quick Access Toolbar (QAT), when displayed, is located at the bottom-left corner of the ribbon (refer to Figure 1.5), and provides one-click access to commonly executed tasks. You can customize the QAT to include commands you frequently use (see Figure 1.10). One command you may want to add is Quick Print. Rather than clicking the File tab, selecting Print, and then selecting various print options, you can add Quick Print to the QAT so that with one click you can print your document with the default Print settings. Other convenient commands can be added, such as Editor to check the spelling of a Word document.

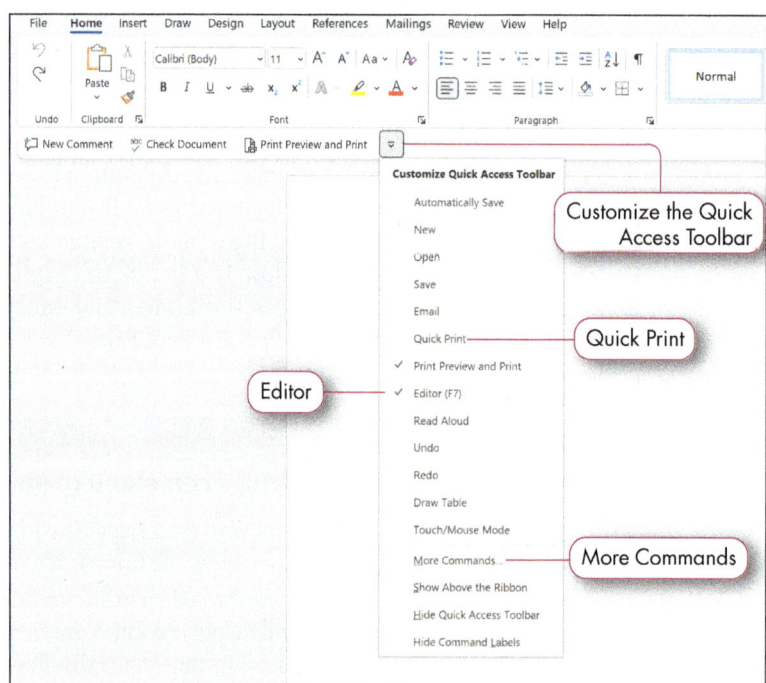

FIGURE 1.10 Customize the Quick Access Toolbar

You customize the QAT by selecting the Customize Quick Access Toolbar arrow on the right side of the displayed QAT commands or by right-clicking an empty area on the QAT, and then selecting or deselecting the options from the displayed list of commands.

Alternatively, you can right-click any command on the ribbon and select Add to Quick Access Toolbar from the shortcut menu.

To remove a command from the QAT, right-click the command and select Remove from Quick Access Toolbar. If you want to move the QAT to display above the ribbon, select Customize Quick Access Toolbar and click *Show Above the Ribbon*.

STEP 5 ### Use a Shortcut Menu

In Microsoft 365, you can usually accomplish the same task in several ways. Although the ribbon and QAT provide efficient access to commands, in some situations you might find it more convenient to access the same commands from a shortcut menu. A ***shortcut menu*** is a context-sensitive menu that displays commands and options relevant to the active object. Shortcut menus are accessed by selecting text or an object or by placing the insertion point in a document and pressing the right mouse button or pressing the right side of a trackpad. (On a Mac, press control when you tap the mouse or use a two-finger tap on a trackpad.) The shortcut menu will always include options to cut, copy, and paste. In addition, a shortcut menu features tasks that are specifically related to the document content where the insertion point is placed. For example, if the insertion point is on a selected word or group of words, the shortcut menu would include tasks such as to find a synonym or add a comment. If the active object is a picture, the shortcut menu includes options to group objects, provide a caption, or wrap text. As shown in Figure 1.11, when right-clicking a slide thumbnail in PowerPoint, the shortcut menu displays options to add a new slide, duplicate or delete slides, or change the slide layout.

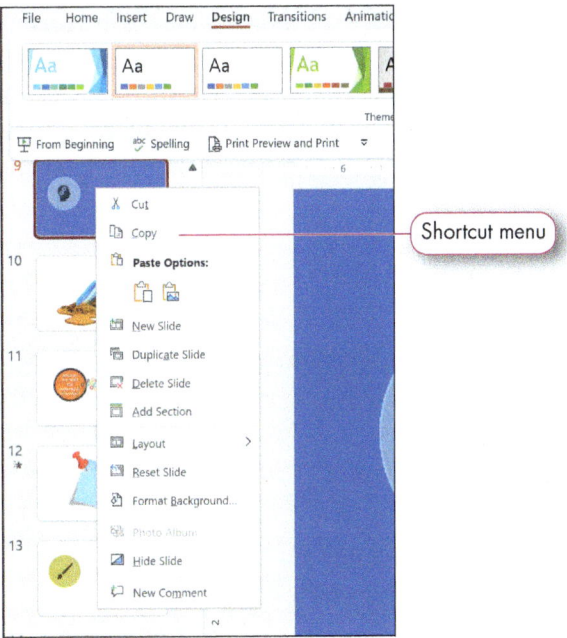

FIGURE 1.11 A Shortcut Menu in PowerPoint

Use Keyboard Shortcuts

Another way to simplify initiating commands is to use ***keyboard shortcuts***. Keyboard shortcuts are created by pressing combinations of two or more keys to initiate a software command. Keyboard shortcuts are viewed as being more efficient because you do not have to take your fingers off the keyboard. Some of the most common keyboard shortcuts in Microsoft 365 include Ctrl+C (Copy), Ctrl+X (Cut), Ctrl+V (Paste), and

Ctrl+Z (Undo). Pressing Ctrl+Home moves the insertion point to the beginning of a Word document, to cell A1 in Excel, or to the first PowerPoint slide. To move to the end of those files, press Ctrl+End. There are many other keyboard shortcuts. To discover a keyboard shortcut for a command, point to a command icon on the ribbon to display the ScreenTip. If a keyboard shortcut exists, it will display in the ScreenTip. Many similar keyboard shortcuts exist for Microsoft 365 for Mac applications. When instructed to press Ctrl plus another key on a PC, on a Mac press the command key rather than the Ctrl key, such as command+C for Copy.

> **TIP: USING KEYTIPS**
> Another way to use shortcuts, especially those that do not have a keyboard shortcut, is to press Alt to display KeyTips. You can use KeyTips to do tasks quickly without using the mouse by pressing a few keys—no matter where you are in a Microsoft 365 program. You can use every command on the ribbon by using an access key—usually by pressing two to four keys sequentially. To stop displaying KeyTips, press Alt again.

STEP 6 ▸ Use the Search Box

On the title bar is the **Search box** (see Figure 1.12). Enter words and phrases in the Search box to find help and information about a command or task you want to perform. Alternatively, use Search for a shortcut to a command or, in some instances (like Bold), to complete the action for you. Search can also help you research or define a term you entered. Perhaps you want to find an instance of a word in your document and replace it with another word but cannot locate the Find and Replace commands on the ribbon. As shown in Figure 1.12, you can type *find* in the Search box and a list of commands related to the skill will display in the Actions section, including Find & Select and Replace. Find & Select gives options for the Find command. If you click Replace, the Find and Replace dialog box opens without you having to locate the command on the ribbon. If there is a single action that relates to the search term, Best Action will display. Clicking that option will initiate the command without having to first go to the ribbon.

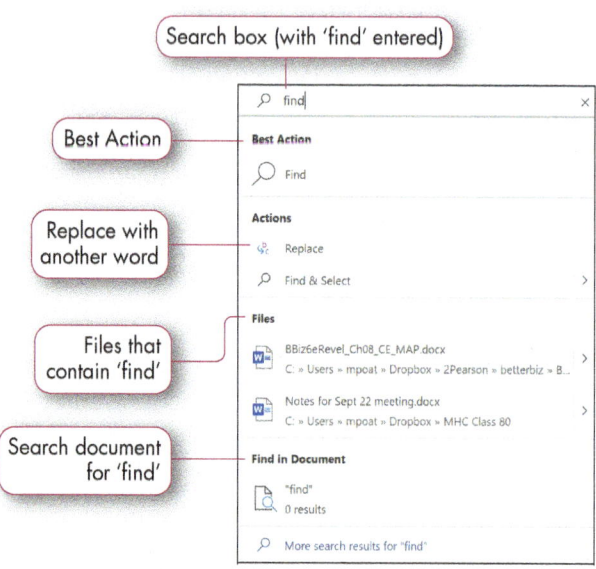

FIGURE 1.12 The Search Box

The Search box provides results for the search term beyond applicable actions such as Get Help on, Definition, and Find in Document. It will also list some files that contain the search term. Should you want to read about the feature instead of applying it, you can click *Get Help on "find,"* which will open the Help pane with results for the feature.

Use the Help Tab

If you are looking for additional help or training on certain features in any Microsoft 365 application, you can access this support on the Help tab (see Figure 1.13). The Help command opens the Help pane with a list of tutorials on a variety of application-specific topics. Show Training displays application-specific training videos in the Help pane. Besides Help and Show Training, the Help tab also includes means to contact Microsoft support and to share your feedback. If you are using Microsoft 365, you receive periodic updates with new features as they are released. To learn more about these features, or simply to discover what a new or previous update includes, use What's New. What's New brings you to a webpage that discusses all the newly added features organized by release date. You can also access What's New by clicking Account from the File tab.

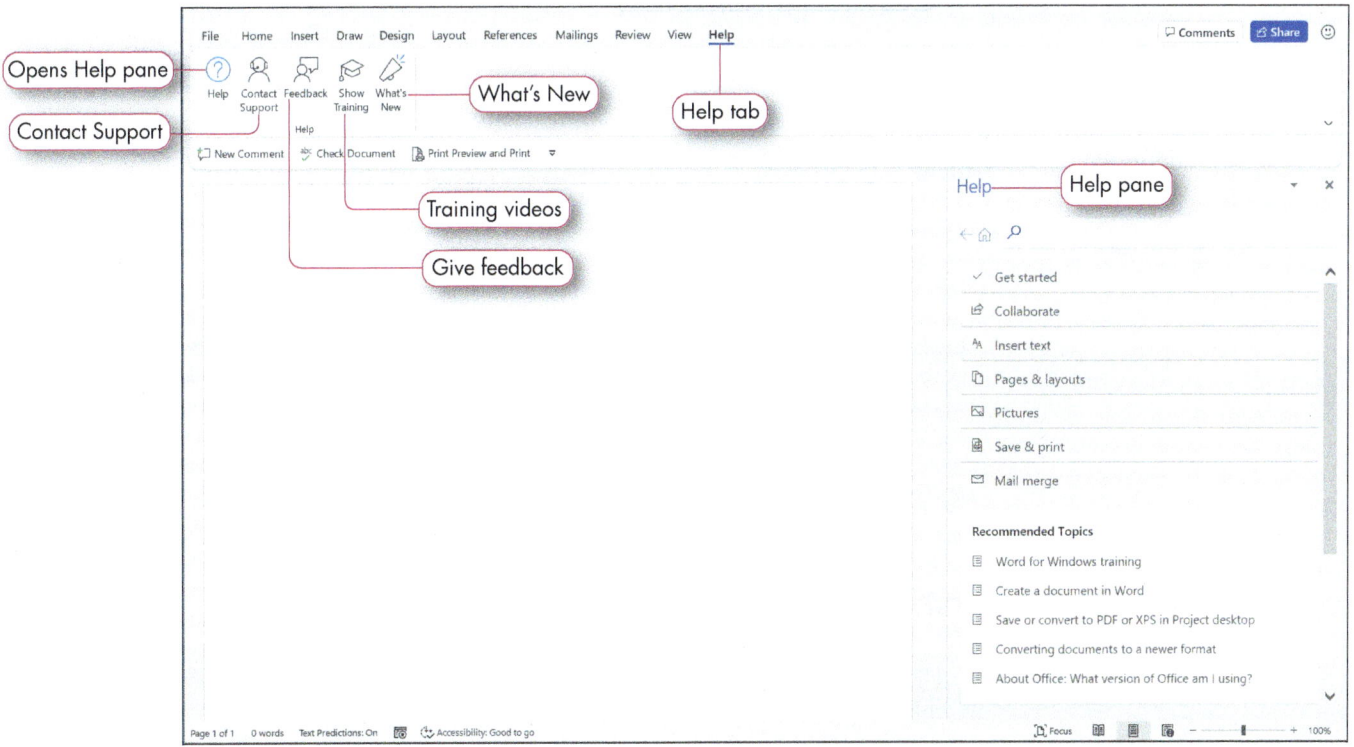

FIGURE 1.13 Help Tab

Use ScreenTips

There may be some commands on the ribbon that you are unfamiliar with, or you would like assurance that you are selecting the correct command. For quick summary information on the name and purpose of a command, point to the command until a **ScreenTip** displays, with the name and a brief description of the command. If applicable, a keyboard shortcut is also included. Enhanced ScreenTips include more detailed information about the command as well as a link to *Tell me more* for additional information on that command. The Enhanced ScreenTip shown for **Format Painter** in Figure 1.14 provides a short description of the command in addition to the steps that discuss how to use Format Painter. Use Format Painter to copy all applied formatting from one set of text to another.

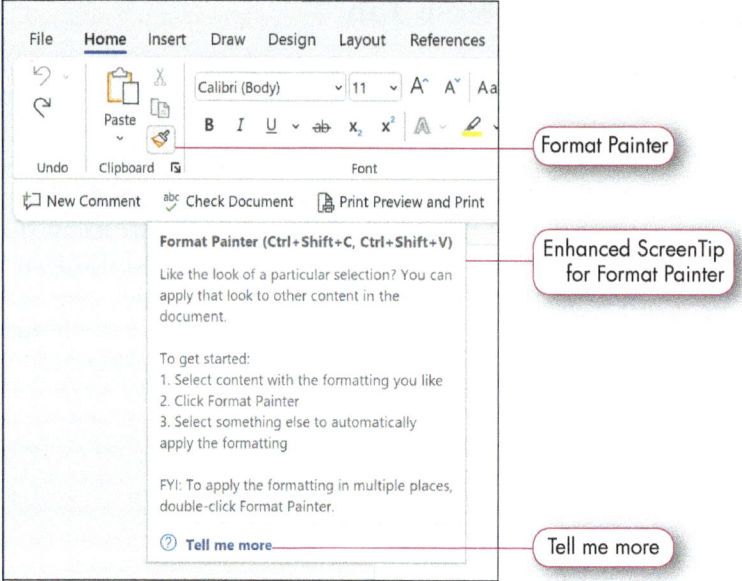

FIGURE 1.14 ScreenTip

> **TIP: COPY FORMAT WITH FORMAT PAINTER**
> Use Format Painter to quickly apply the same formatting, such as color, font style, and size to other text. Format Painter can also be used to copy border styles to shapes. Format Painter is available in Word, Excel, and PowerPoint, and can be extremely useful when applying multiple formats to other text. Using Format Painter also ensures consistency in appearance between sets of text. To copy formatting to one location, single-click Format Painter, and then click or drag to select where you want the format applied. To copy formatting to multiple locations, double-click Format Painter. Press Esc or click Format Painter again to turn off the command.

Critical Thinking

1. Describe when you would use Save and when you would use Save As when saving a document. *p. 52*

2. Explain how the ribbon is organized. *p. 54*

3. Describe the Microsoft 365 application features that are available to assist you in getting help with a task. *p. 61*

Hands-On Exercises

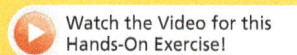

Watch the Video for this Hands-On Exercise!

Skills covered: Open a
Saved File • Save a File • Use the
Ribbon • Use a Dialog Box and
Gallery • Use and Customize the
Quick Access Toolbar • Use a
Shortcut Menu • Use the Search
Box • Use ScreenTips

1 Work with Microsoft 365 Files

The Spotted Begonia Art Gallery just hired several new clerical assistants to help you develop materials for the various activities coming up throughout the year. A coworker sent you a letter and asked for your assistance in making a few minor formatting changes. The letter is an invitation to the *Discover the Artist in You!* program's Children's Art Festival. To begin, you will open Word and open an existing document. You will use the shortcut menu to make simple changes to the document. Finally, you will use the Search box to apply a style to the first line of text.

STEP 1 OPEN A SAVED FILE AND SAVE A FILE

You start Microsoft Word and open a letter that was sent by your coworker. You rename the file to preserve the original and to save the changes you will make later. Refer to Figure 1.15 as you complete Step 1.

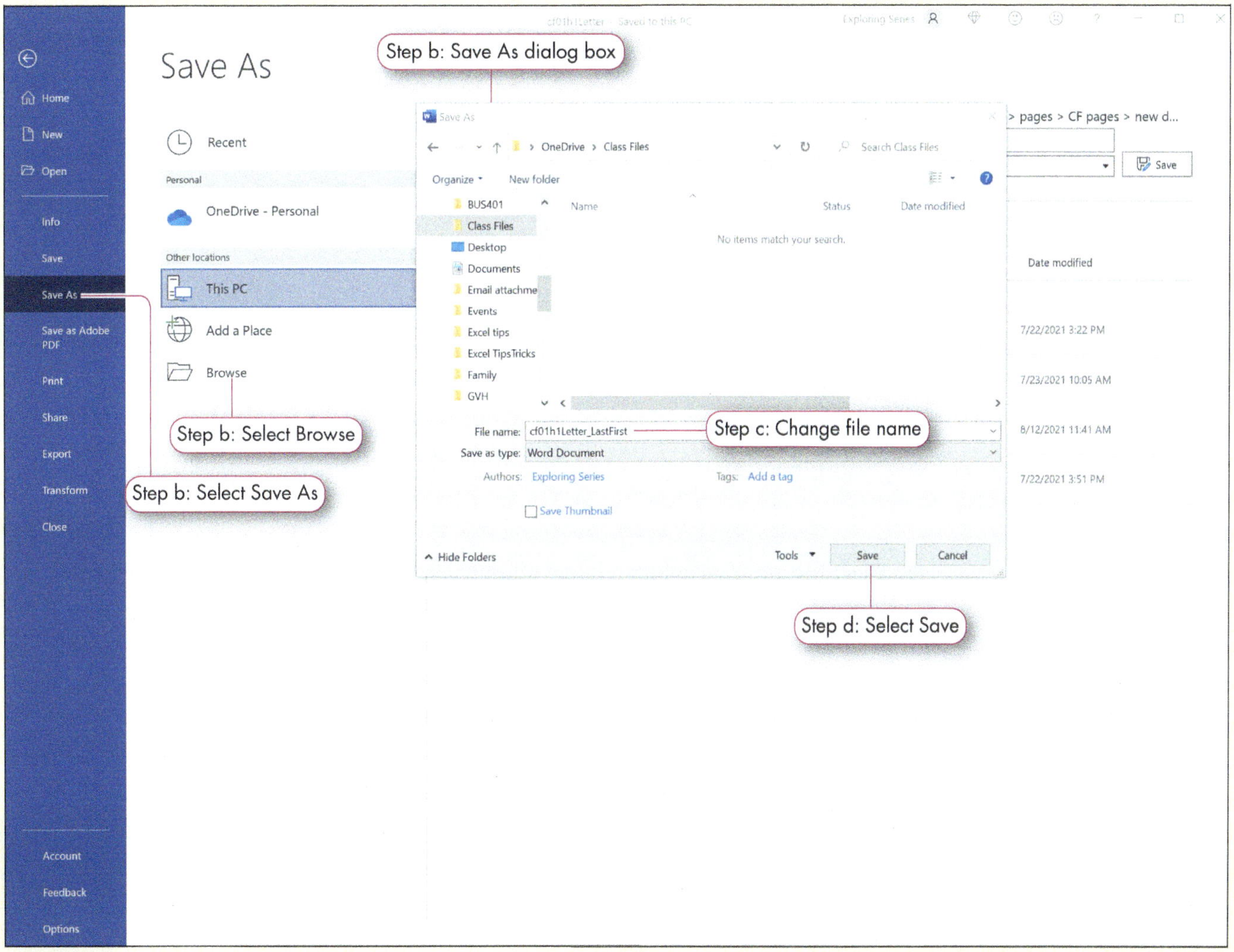

FIGURE 1.15 The Save As Dialog Box

    a. Open the Word document *cf01h1Letter.docx*.

    The event invitation letter opens.

b. Click the **File tab**, click **Save As**, and then click **Browse** to display the Save As dialog box.

Because you will change the name of an existing file, you use the Save As command to give the file a new name. (On a Mac, click the File menu and click Save As.)

c. Navigate to the location where you are saving your files. Click in the **File name box** (on a Mac, click in the Save As box) and type **cf01h1Letter_LastFirst**.

You save the document with a different name to preserve the original file.

When you save files, use your last and first names. For example, as the Common Features author, I would name my document "cf01h1Letter_PoatsyMaryAnne.docx."

d. Click **Save**.

> **TROUBLESHOOTING:** If you make any major mistakes in this exercise, you can close the file, open *cf01h1Letter.docx* again, and then start this exercise over.

The file is now saved as cf01h1Letter_LastFirst.docx. Check the title bar of the document to confirm that the file has been saved with the correct name.

USE THE RIBBON

You want to modify the letter, so you use ribbon commands to make the changes. Refer to Figure 1.16 as you complete Step 2.

FIGURE 1.16 Use Ribbon Commands to Modify Text

a. Place the insertion point in the left margin just before the first line of text *The Spotted Begonia Art Gallery* so an angled right-pointing arrow displays and click.

This is an efficient way of selecting an entire line of text. Alternatively, you can drag the pointer across the text while holding down the left mouse button to select the text. You will learn more about selecting text later in this chapter.

b. Click the **Font Color arrow** in the Font group on the Home tab and select **Blue** in the Standard Colors section. With the text still selected, click the **Font Size arrow** in the Font group and select **22**.

You have changed the color and size of the art gallery's name.

c. Click **Center** in the Paragraph group.

The name of the gallery is centered horizontally at the top of the letter.

d. Click **File** and click **Save**.

Because the file has already been saved, and the name and location are not changing, you use the Save command to save the changes.

USE A DIALOG BOX AND GALLERY

Some of the modifications you want to make to the letter require using tasks that are in dialog boxes and galleries. You will use a Dialog Box Launcher and More to expand the galleries to access the needed commands and features. Refer to Figure 1.17 as you complete Step 3.

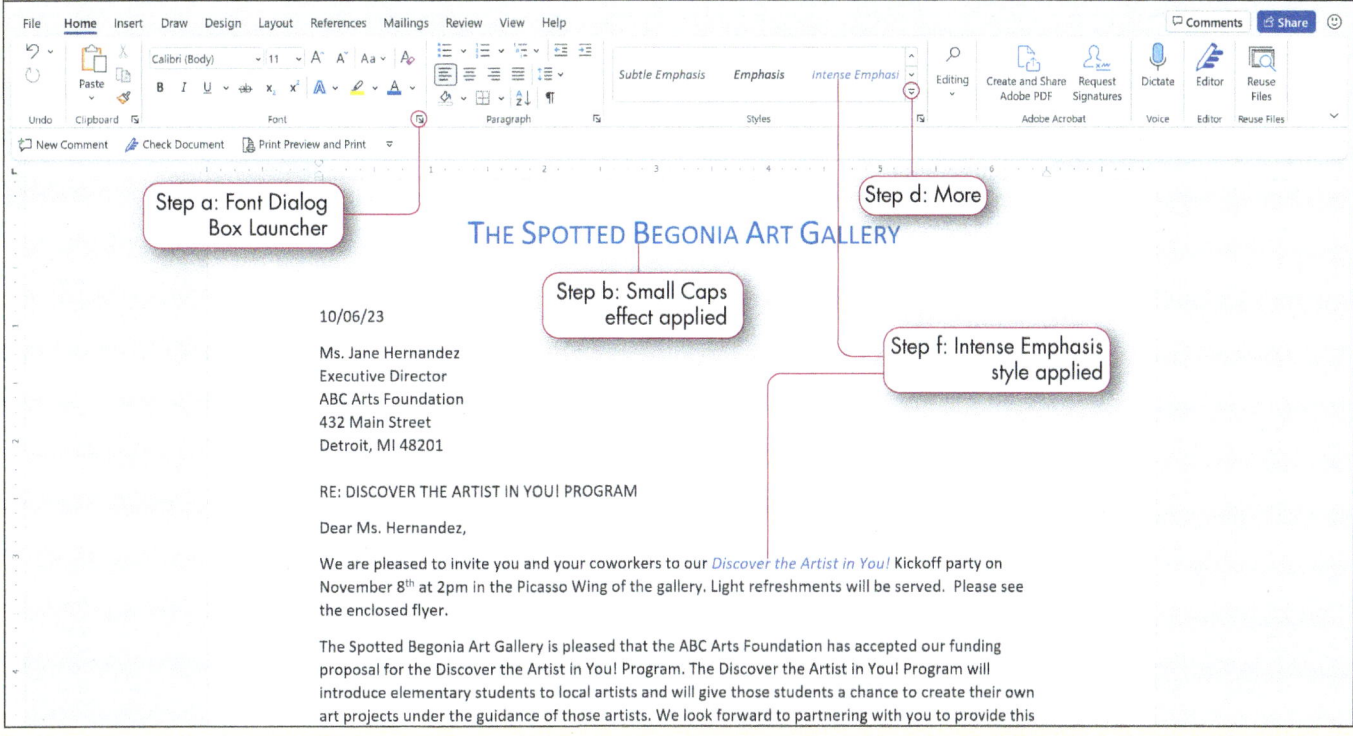

FIGURE 1.17 Use a Dialog Box and Gallery

a. Select the text **The Spotted Begonia Art Gallery**, if it is not already selected. Click the **Dialog Box Launcher** in the Font group.

   The Font dialog box displays.

> **MAC TROUBLESHOOTING:** Microsoft 365 for Mac does not have Dialog Box Launchers. Instead, click the Format menu and click Font.

b. Click the **Small caps check box** in the Effects section to select it and click **OK**.

   The Small caps text effect is applied to the selected text.

c. Place the insertion point immediately to the left of the text *Discover the Artist in You!* in the first sentence of the paragraph beginning *We are pleased*. Hold the left mouse button down and drag the pointer to select the text up to and including the exclamation point.

> **TROUBLESHOOTING:** Be sure the file you are working on is displayed as a full window. Otherwise, you may need to use the vertical scroll bar to bring the paragraph into view.

d. Click **More** in the Styles group to display the Styles gallery. (On a Mac, click the right gallery arrow or click the down arrow to view more options.)

e. Point to Heading 1 style.

   Notice that Live Preview shows how the effect will look on the selected text.

f. Click **Intense Emphasis**.

   The Intense Emphasis style is applied to the program name.

g. Click **File** and click **Save**.

You notice a problem with the date of the reception and add a note to double-check the date. You also anticipate checking the spelling on the letter before sending it out. Because you use Editor often to check spelling and grammar, you decide to add the command to the QAT. Finally, you realize that you could save the document more efficiently by using Save on the title bar. Refer to Figure 1.18 as you complete Step 4.

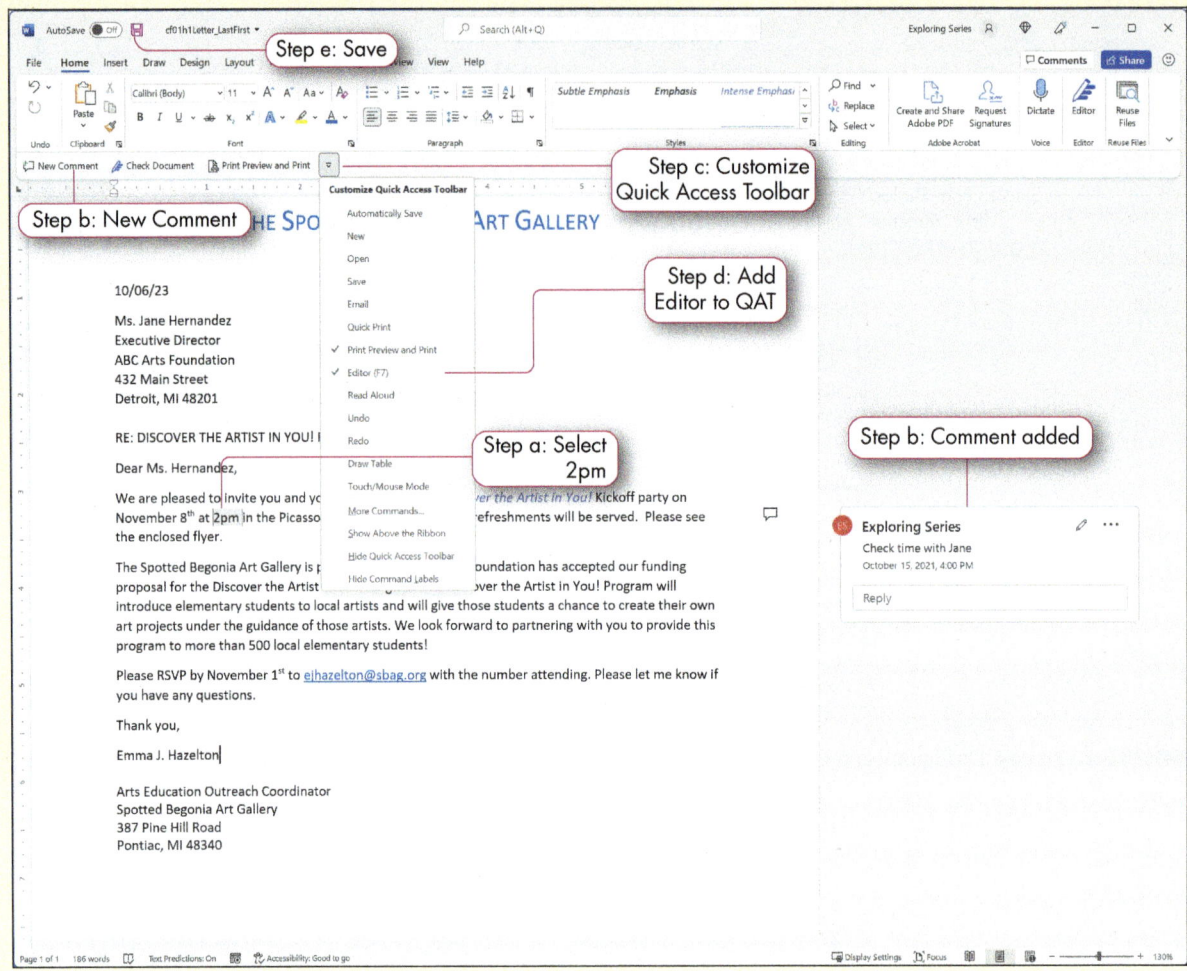

FIGURE 1.18 Customize the Quick Access Toolbar

a. Scroll down so the first paragraph beginning with *We are pleased* is visible. Select **2pm**.

b. Click **New Comment** on the QAT. Type **Check time with Jane** in the Start a conversation box. Click the **Post arrow**.

A comment box displays on the right side of the document. You add and post a comment.

> **TROUBLESHOOTING:** If you are working in Windows 11, the QAT may not be visible. To display the QAT, click Ribbon Display Options and click Show Quick Action Toolbar.

c. Click **Customize Quick Access Toolbar** on the right side of the QAT.

A list of commands that can be added to the QAT displays.

d. Click **Editor** to select it.

> **TROUBLESHOOTING:** If Editor is already selected, do not uncheck it. Skip to Step e.

The Editor icon displays on the QAT so you can check for spelling, grammar, and writing issues. You will run the document through the Editor when you are finished formatting the letter as the final check.

e. Click **Save** on the title bar.

The letter inviting Ms. Hernandez also extends the invitation to her coworkers and other associates. One of your team members suggested that you use a different word for coworkers, so you use a shortcut menu to find a synonym. Refer to Figure 1.19 as you complete Step 5.

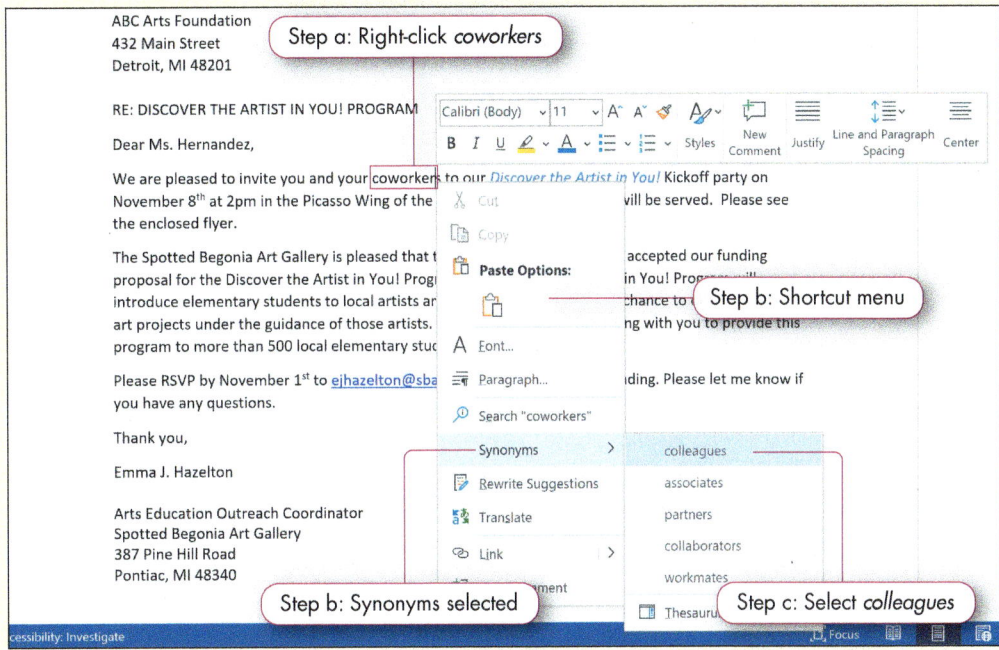

FIGURE 1.19 Use the Shortcut Menu to Find a Synonym

a. Right-click the word **coworkers** in the first sentence of the letter that starts with *We are pleased.*

A shortcut menu displays.

> **MAC TROUBLESHOOTING:** To open a shortcut menu, use control+click.

b. Select **Synonyms** on the shortcut menu.

A list of alternate words for *coworkers* displays.

c. Select **colleagues** from the list.

The synonym *colleagues* replaces the word *coworkers.*

d. Click **Save** on the title bar.

STEP 6 ▶ USE THE SEARCH BOX AND SCREENTIPS

You want to apply the Intense Effect style you used to format *Discover the Artist in You!* to other instances of the program name in the second paragraph. You think there is a more efficient way of applying the same format to other text, but you do not know how to complete the task. Therefore, you use the Search box to search for the command and then you apply the change. Refer to Figure 1.20 as you complete Step 6.

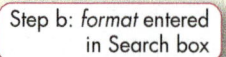

Step b: *format* entered in Search box

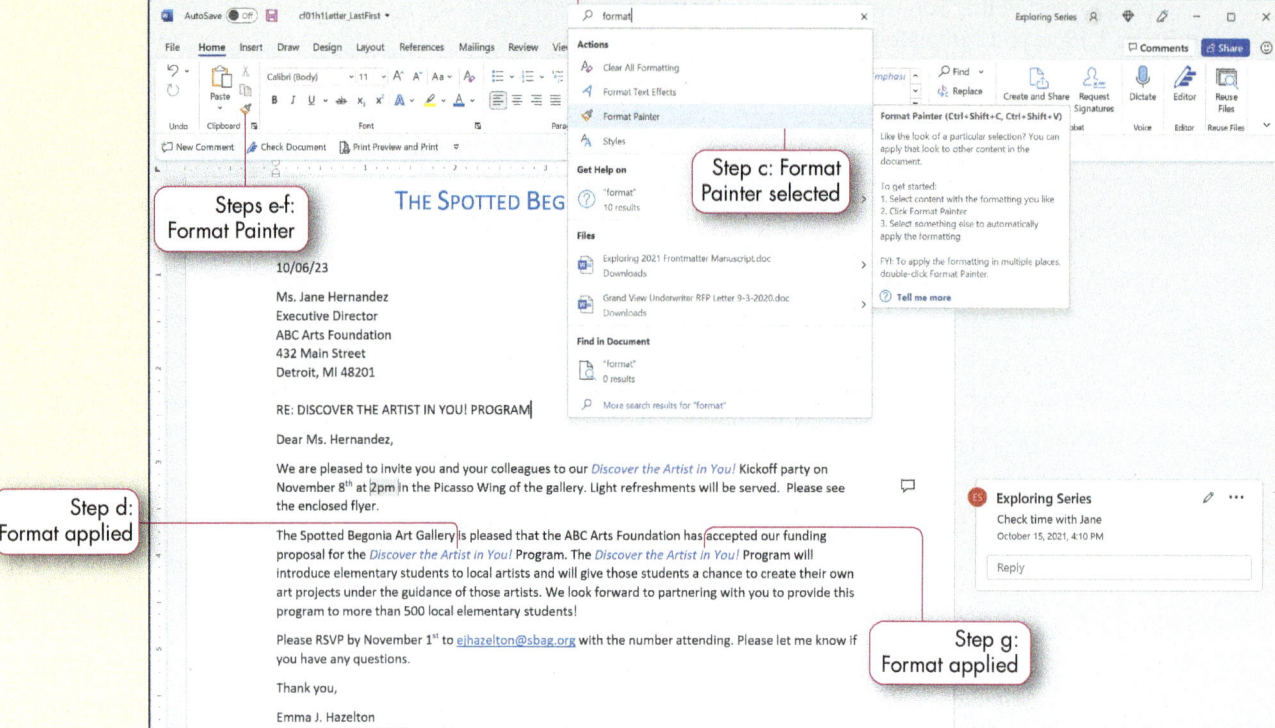

Step c: Format Painter selected

Steps e-f: Format Painter

Step d: Format applied

Step g: Format applied

FIGURE 1.20 Use the Search Box

a. Click anywhere in the text **Discover the Artist in You!** in the first sentence of the letter that starts with *We are pleased*.

b. Click the **Search box** and type **format**. (On a Mac, the Search box may display as Tell me.)

The Search box displays a list of options related to apply format.

c. Select **Format Painter** from the list of Actions in the Search results.

Notice that the Format Painter command in the Clipboard group is selected and a paint-brush is added to the insertion point 📇.

d. Drag the pointer over the first instance of **Discover the Artist in You!** in the second line of the second paragraph beginning with *The Spotted Begonia*.

The Intense Emphasis style was applied to the selected text.

> **TROUBLESHOOTING:** If the format is not applied to the text, select the text as described in Step a, double-click Format Painter, and apply the format to both instances of Discover the Artist in You! noted in Steps d and g.

e. Point to **Format Painter** in the Clipboard group and read the ScreenTip.

You notice that to apply formatting to more than one selection, you must double-click Format Painter, but because you want to apply the format to only one more instance of the text, you will single-click the command.

f. Click **Format Painter** in the Clipboard group.

g. Drag the pointer over the second instance of **Discover the Artist in You!** in the second paragraph beginning with *The Spotted Begonia*.

You used the Format Painter to copy the formatting applied to text to other text.

> **TROUBLESHOOTING:** Press Esc on the keyboard to turn off Format Painter if you double-clicked Format Painter in Step f.

h. Save and close the document. You will submit this file to your instructor at the end of the last Hands-On Exercise.

Format File Content

In the process of creating a document, worksheet, or presentation, you will most likely make some formatting changes. You might center a title or format budget worksheet totals as currency. You can change the font so that characters are larger or in a different style. You might even want to bold text to add emphasis. Sometimes, it may be more efficient to start with a document that has formatting already applied or apply a group of coordinated fonts, font styles, and colors. You might also want to add, delete, or reposition text. Inserting and formatting images can add interest to a document or illustrate content. Finally, no document is finished until all spelling and grammar have been checked and all errors removed.

In this section, you will explore themes and templates. You will learn to use the Mini Toolbar to quickly make formatting changes. You will learn how to select and edit text as well as check your grammar and spelling. You will learn how to move, copy, and paste text and how to insert pictures. And, finally, you will learn how to resize and format pictures and graphics.

Use Templates and Apply Themes

Rather than starting from a blank file, you can get a head start on formatting and even content suggestions by beginning with a template. A ***template*** is a predesigned file that incorporates formatting elements and layouts and may include content that can be modified. You can enhance your documents whether you start with a blank file or a preformatted template by applying a theme. A ***theme*** is a collection of design choices that includes colors, fonts, and special effects used to give a consistent look to a document, workbook, or presentation. There are high-quality templates and themes incorporated into Word, Excel, Access, and PowerPoint. These are designed to make it faster and simpler to create professional-looking documents.

STEP 1 ▸ Open a Template

When you launch any Microsoft 365 program and click New, the screen displays thumbnail images of a sampling of templates for that application (see Figure 1.21). Alternatively, if you are already working in an application, click the File tab and select New to view the variety of available templates.

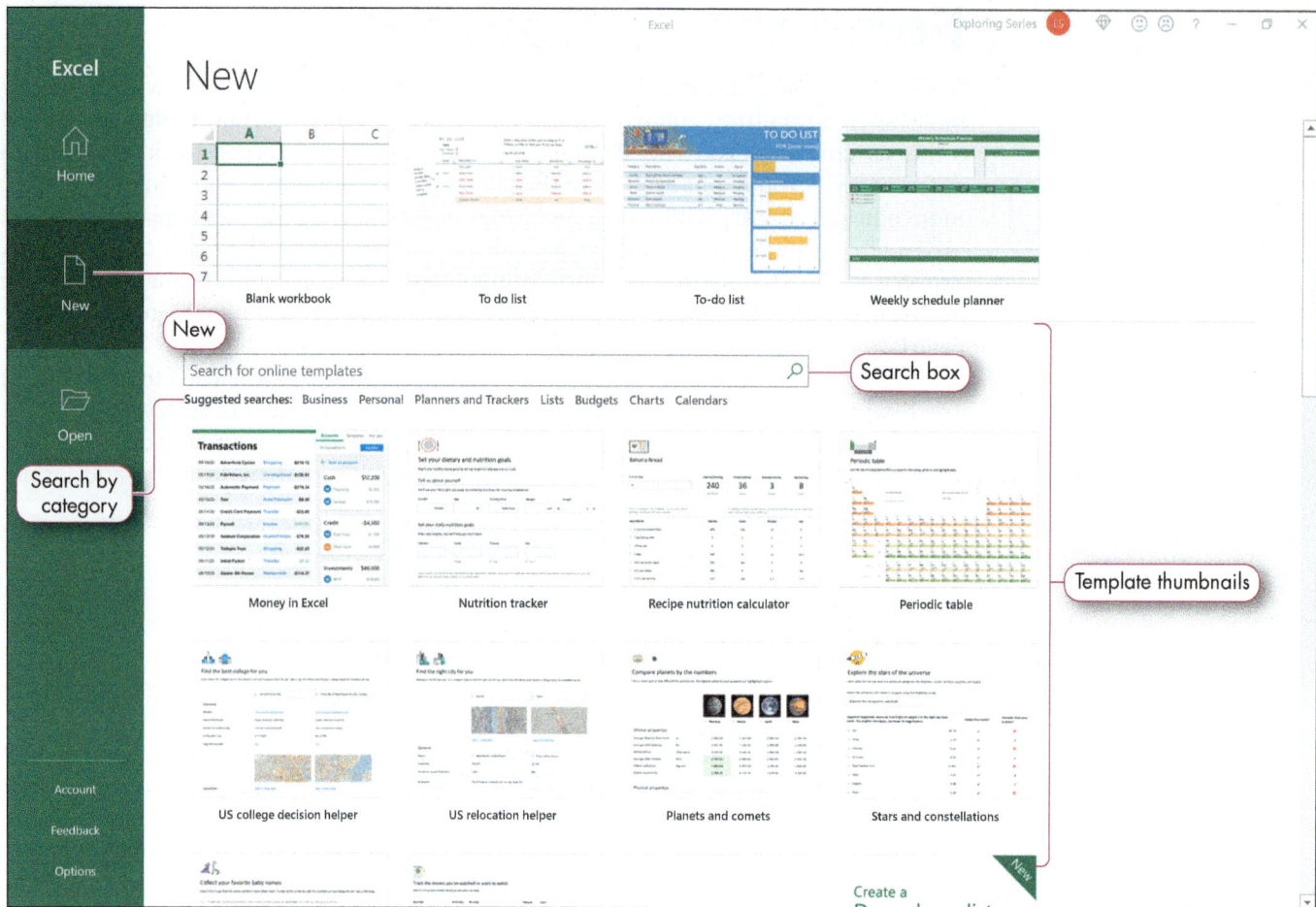

FIGURE 1.21 Templates in Excel

One benefit of starting with a template is that with only a few simple changes you can have a well-formatted document that represents your specific needs. Starting with a template can be much more efficient than if you designed it yourself from a blank file. Templates in Excel often use complex formulas and formatting to achieve a dynamic workbook that automatically adjusts with only a few inputs. In Excel, you can find useful templates to help create a mortgage amortization table or a nutrition tracker. Using a résumé template in Word, for example, greatly simplifies potentially complex formatting, enabling you to concentrate on just inputting your personal experiences. PowerPoint templates can include single element slides (such as organization charts) but also include comprehensive presentations on topics such as Business Plans or the backbone of a Black History Month presentation.

Templates are grouped by topic, such as Education, Business, or Holiday, with other groups more specific to each application. You can search for other templates that are available online. When you select a template, you can view more information about the template, including author information, a general overview about the template, and additional views (if applicable).

Search for and use a template:

1. Open the Microsoft 365 application with which you will be working and click New. Or, if the application is already open, click File and click New. (On a Mac, click the File menu and click New from Template.)

2. Type a search term in the *Search for online templates box* or click one of the Suggested searches listed under the Search box.

3. Scroll through the template options or, after selecting a search term, use the list at the right to narrow your search further.

4. Select a template and review its information in the window that opens.

5. Click Create to open the template in the application.

STEP 2 ## Apply a Theme

Applying a theme enables you to visually coordinate various page elements. Themes are different for each of the Microsoft 365 applications. In Word, a theme is a set of coordinating fonts, colors, and special effects, such as shadowing or glows, that are combined into a package to provide a stylish appearance (see Figure 1.22). In PowerPoint, a theme is a file that includes the formatting elements such as a background, a color scheme, and slide layouts that position content placeholders. Themes in Excel are like those in Word in that they are a set of coordinating fonts, colors, and special effects. Themes also affect any SmartArt or charts in a document, workbook, or presentation. Access also has a set of themes that coordinate the appearance of fonts and colors for objects such as Forms and Reports. In Word and PowerPoint, themes are accessed from the Design tab. In Excel, they are accessed from the Page Layout tab. In Access, themes can be applied to forms and reports and are accessed from the respective object's Design tab. In any application, themes can be modified with different fonts, colors, or effects, or you can design your own theme and set it as a default.

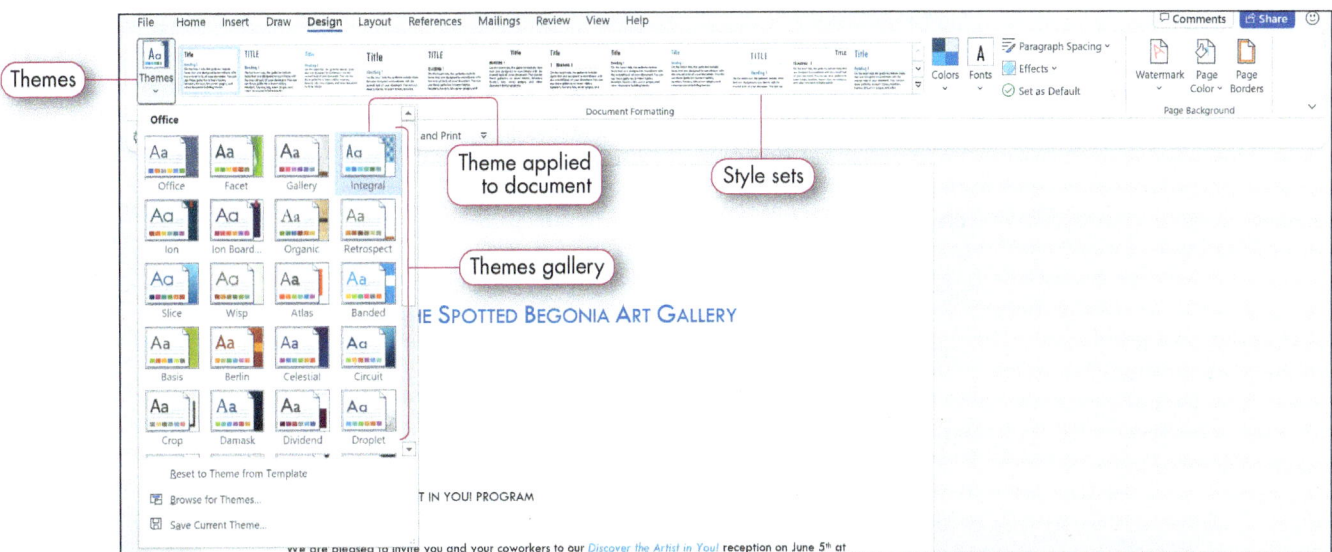

FIGURE 1.22 Themes in Word

Modify, Relocate, and Review Text

Formatting and modifying text in documents, worksheets, or presentations is an essential function when using Microsoft 365 applications. Centering a title, formatting cells, or changing the font color or size are tasks that occur frequently. In all Microsoft 365 applications, the Home tab provides tools for editing text.

STEP 3 ## Select Text

Before making any changes to existing text or numbers, you must first select the characters. A common way to select text or numbers is to place the pointer before the first character of the text you want to select, press the left mouse button, and then drag to highlight the intended selection. Note that in Word and PowerPoint when the pointer is used to select text in this manner, it takes on the shape of the letter I, and is referred to as the Text Select pointer I.

Sometimes it can be difficult to precisely select a small amount of text, such as a few letters or a punctuation mark. Other times, the task can be overwhelmingly large, such as when selecting an entire multi-page document. Or, you might want to select a single word, sentence, or paragraph. In these situations, you should use one of the shortcuts to select large or small blocks of text. The shortcuts shown in Table 1.2 are primarily applicable to text in Word and PowerPoint. When working with Excel, you will more often need to select multiple cells. To select multiple cells, drag the selection when the pointer displays as a large white plus sign ⊕.

Once you have selected the text, besides applying formatting, you can delete or simply type to replace the text.

TABLE 1.2 Shortcut Selection in Word and PowerPoint	
Item Selected	**Action**
One word	Double-click the word.
One line of text	Place the pointer at the left of the line, in the margin area. When the pointer changes to an angled right-pointing arrow, click to select the line.
One sentence	Press and hold Ctrl and click in the sentence to select it. (On a Mac, press and hold command.)
One paragraph	Triple-click in the paragraph.
One character to the left of the insertion point	Press and hold Shift and press the left arrow on the keyboard.
One character to the right of the insertion point	Press and hold Shift and press the right arrow on the keyboard.
Entire document	Press and hold Ctrl and press A on the keyboard. (On a Mac, press and hold control and press A.)

Format Text

At times, you will want to make the font size larger or smaller, change the font color, or apply other font attributes, for example, to emphasize key information such as titles, headers, dates, and times. Because formatting text is commonplace, formatting commands are found in convenient places within each Microsoft 365 application.

You can find the most common formatting commands in the Font group on the Home tab. As noted earlier, Word, Excel, and PowerPoint all share very similar Font groups that provide access to tasks related to changing the font, size, and color. Remember that you can place the pointer over any command icon to view a summary of the command's purpose.

If the font change that you plan to make is not included as a choice on the Home tab, that option may be available in the Font dialog box. If you are making many formatting choices at once, using the Font dialog box may be more efficient. Depending on the application, the contents of the Font dialog box vary slightly, but the purpose is consistent—providing access to choices related to modifying characters (see Figure 1.23).

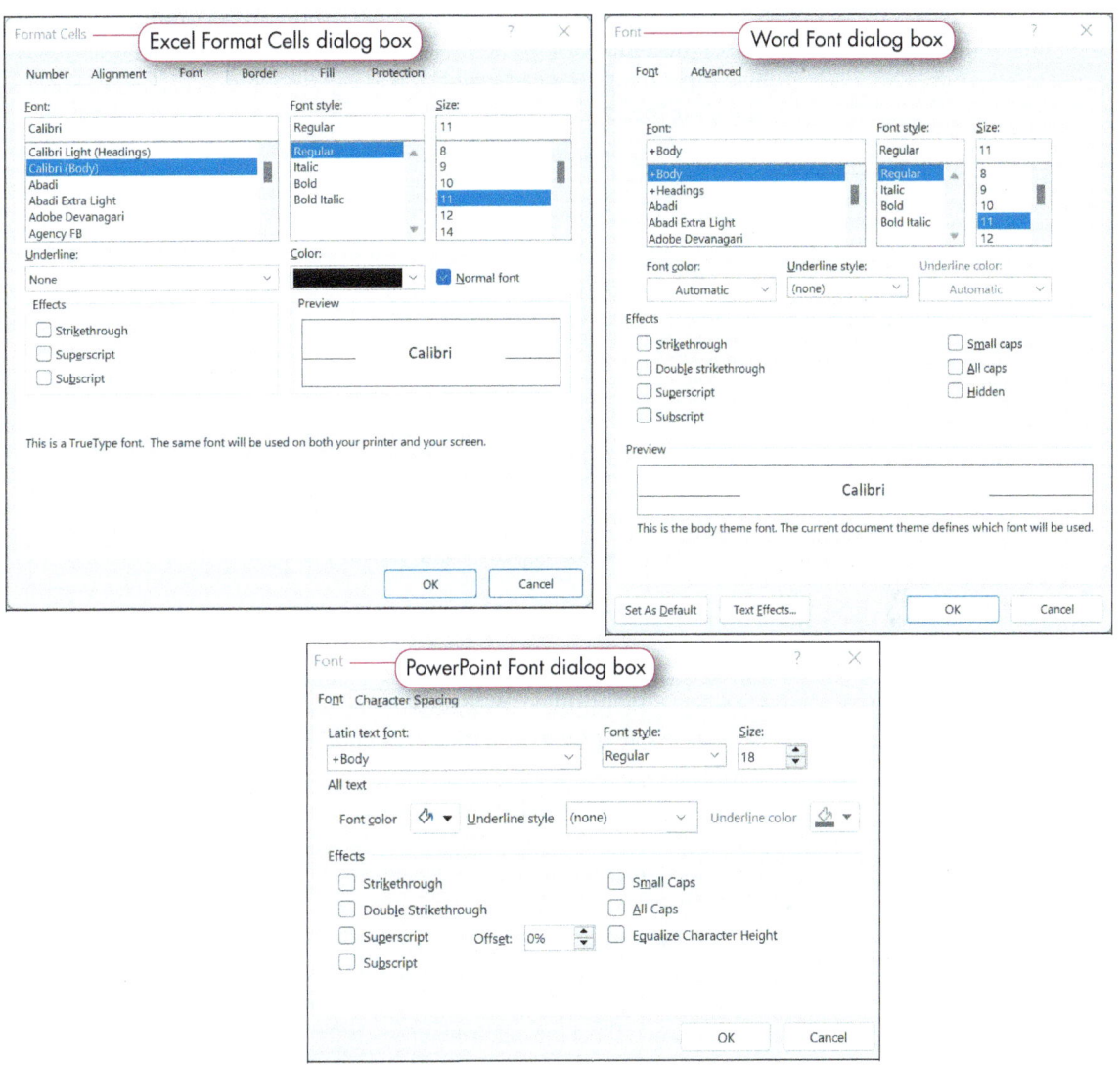

FIGURE 1.23 The Font Dialog Boxes

The way characters display onscreen or print in documents, including qualities such as size, spacing, and shape, is determined by the font. When you open a Blank document, you are opening the Normal template with the Office theme and the Normal style. The Office theme with Normal Style includes the following default settings: Calibri font, 11-point font size, and black font color. These settings remain in effect unless you change them. Some formatting commands, such as Bold and Italic, are called ***toggle commands*** that you can turn on and off. Once you have applied bold formatting to text, the Bold command is highlighted on the ribbon when that text is selected. To undo bold formatting, select the bold formatted text and click Bold again. The highlighting of the Bold command is removed as well.

Use the Mini Toolbar

You have learned that you can always use commands on the Home tab to change selected text within a document, worksheet, or presentation. Although selecting commands on the ribbon is simple enough, the ***Mini Toolbar*** provides another convenient way to accomplish some of the same formatting changes. When you select or right-click any amount of text within a worksheet, document, or presentation, the Mini Toolbar displays (see Figure 1.24) along with the shortcut menu. The Mini Toolbar provides access to the most common formatting selections as well as access to styles and list options. Unlike the QAT, you cannot add or remove options from the Mini Toolbar. To temporarily remove the Mini Toolbar from view, press Esc. You can permanently disable the Mini Toolbar so that it does not display in any open file when text is selected by selecting Options on the File tab. Ensure the General tab is selected and deselect *Show Mini Toolbar on selection* in the User Interface options section.

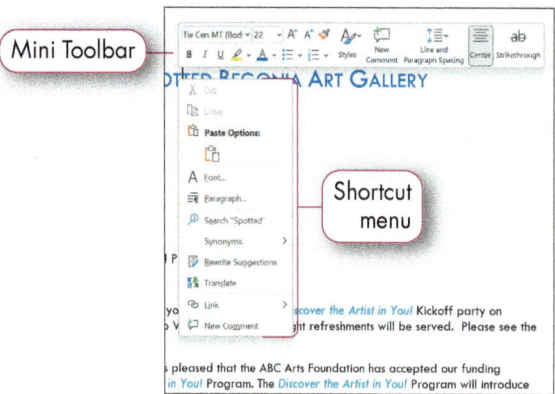

FIGURE 1.24 The Mini Toolbar and Shortcut Menu

STEP 4 ▸ Cut, Copy, and Paste Text

On occasion, you may want to relocate a section of text from one area of a Word document to another. Or suppose that you have included text on a PowerPoint slide that you believe would be more appropriate on a different slide. Or perhaps an Excel formula should be copied from one cell to another because both cells should show totals in a similar manner. In all these instances, you would use the cut, copy, and paste features found in the Clipboard group on the Home tab. The **Clipboard** is an area of memory reserved to temporarily hold selections that have been cut or copied and enables you to paste the selections to another location.

To **cut** means to remove a selection from the original location and place it in the Clipboard. To **copy** means to duplicate a selection from the original location and place a copy in the Clipboard. To **paste** means to place a cut or copied selection into another location in a file. Only the most recent item you have copied or cut will be available in the Clipboard. However, clicking the Dialog Box Launcher in the Clipboard group activates the Office Clipboard. Once the Office Clipboard is activated, cut and copied items remain in the Office Clipboard even after they have been pasted to another location.

HOW TO

Cut or copy text, and paste to a new location:

1. Select the text you want to cut or copy.
2. Click the appropriate command in the Clipboard group either to cut or copy the selection.
3. Click the location where you want the cut or copied text to be placed. The location can be in the current file or in another open file within most Microsoft 365 applications.
4. Click Paste in the Clipboard group on the Home tab.

You can paste the same item multiple times because it will remain in the Office Clipboard until you power down your computer or until the Clipboard exceeds 24 items. However, it is advisable to complete the paste process soon after you have cut or copied text.

In addition to using the commands in the Clipboard group, you can also cut, copy, and paste by using the Mini Toolbar, a shortcut menu (right-clicking), or by keyboard shortcuts. These methods are listed in Table 1.3.

TABLE 1.3	Cut, Copy, and Paste Options
Command	**Actions**
Cut	• Click Cut in Clipboard group. • Right-click selection and select Cut. • Press Ctrl+X. (On a Mac, press command+X.)
Copy	• Click Copy in Clipboard group. • Right-click selection and select Copy. • Press Ctrl+C. (On a Mac, press command+C.)
Paste	• Click in destination location and click Paste in Clipboard group. • Click in destination location and press Ctrl+V. (On a Mac, press command+V.) • Right-click in destination location and select one of the choices under Paste Options in the shortcut menu. • Click Clipboard Dialog Box Launcher to open Clipboard pane. Click in destination location. With the Clipboard pane open, click the arrow beside the intended selection and select Paste.

TIP: USE PASTE OPTIONS

When you paste text, you may not want to paste the text with all its formatting. In some instances, you may want to paste only the text, unformatted, so that special effects such as hyperlinks are not copied. In other instances, you might want to paste and match the formatting in the destination location or keep the current formatting in the new location. Paste Options commands are displayed when you click the Paste arrow or use the shortcut menu. Paste Options are different in each application, but in general, they include pasting contents without any formatting applied, pasting contents using the source formats, or pasting contents using the destination formats. In Excel, Paste Options also include pasting values to replace formulas, and transposing columns and rows to rows and columns. There are also options related to pasting pictures.

Use the Office Clipboard

Regardless of which Microsoft 365 application you are using, you can view the results of cut or copied selections in the Office Clipboard by clicking the Dialog Box Launcher in the Clipboard group, as shown in Figure 1.25.

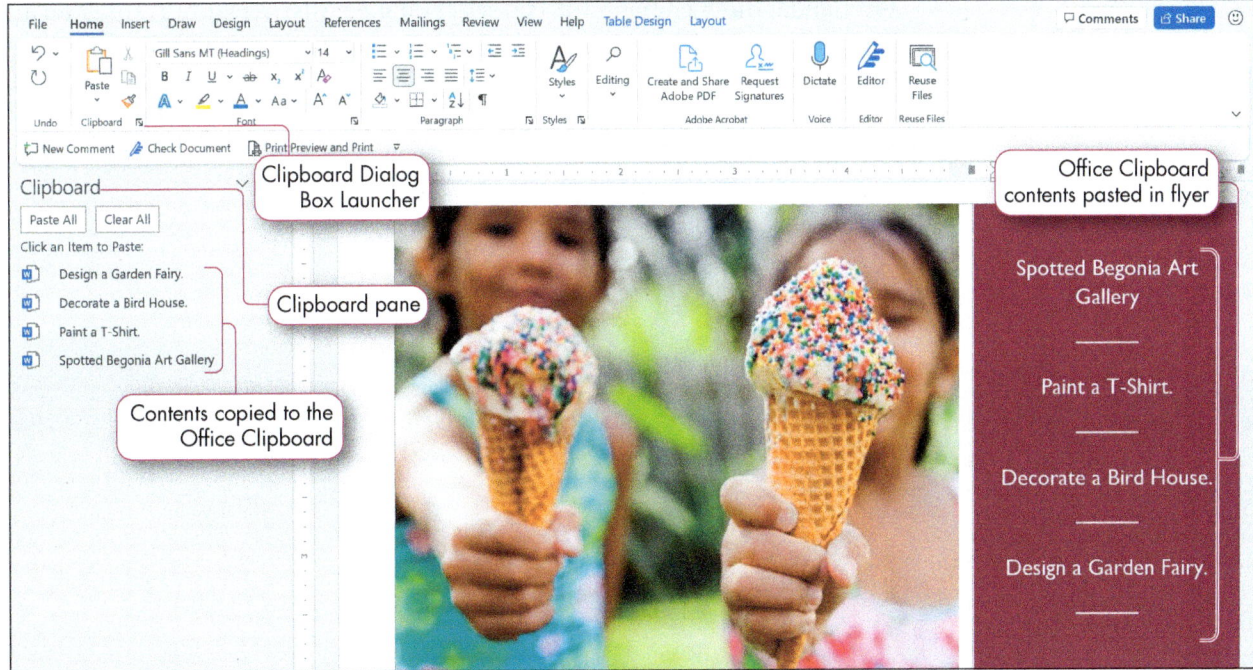

FIGURE 1.25 The Office Clipboard

Unless you specify otherwise when beginning a paste operation, the item that was most recently added to the Clipboard is pasted. If you know you will be cutting or copying and then pasting several items, rather than doing each individually, you can cut or copy all the items to the Office Clipboard and then paste each or all Office Clipboard items to the new location. This is especially helpful if you are pasting the Clipboard items to a different file. Just open the new file, display the Clipboard pane, and select the item in the list to paste into the document. The Office Clipboard also stores graphics that have been cut or copied. You can delete items from the Office Clipboard by clicking the arrow next to the selection in the Clipboard pane and selecting Delete. You can remove all items from the Office Clipboard by clicking Clear All. The Options button at the bottom of the Clipboard pane enables you to control when and where the Office Clipboard is displayed. Close the Clipboard pane by clicking the Close button in the top-right corner of the pane or by clicking the arrow in the title bar of the Clipboard pane and selecting Close.

STEP 5 ▶ Check Spelling and Grammar

As you create or edit a file, and certainly as you finalize a file, you should make sure no spelling or grammatical errors exist. It is important that you carefully review your document for any spelling or punctuation errors as well as any poor word choices before you send it along to someone else to read. Word, Excel, and PowerPoint all provide standard tools for proofreading, including a spelling and grammar checker and a thesaurus.

Word and PowerPoint automatically check your spelling and grammar as you type. If a word is unrecognized, it is flagged as misspelled or grammatically incorrect. Misspellings are identified with a red wavy underline, and grammatical or word-usage errors (such as using *bear* instead of *bare*) have a blue double underline. Excel does not check spelling as you type, so it is important to run the spelling checker in Excel. Excel's spelling checker will review charts, PivotTables, and textual data entered in cells.

Although spelling and grammar may be checked along the way, it can be more efficient to check the file for spelling and grammar errors when you are finished with the document. Editor is found on the Home tab in the Editor group and on the Review tab in the Proofing group in Word. In Excel and PowerPoint, Spelling is on the Review tab in the Proofing group. When Editor is selected in Word, the Editor pane opens on the right. For each error, you are offered one or more suggestions as a correction. You can select a suggestion and click Change, or if it is an error that is made more than one time throughout the document, you can select Change All (see Figure 1.26). If an appropriate suggestion is not made, you can always enter a correction manually.

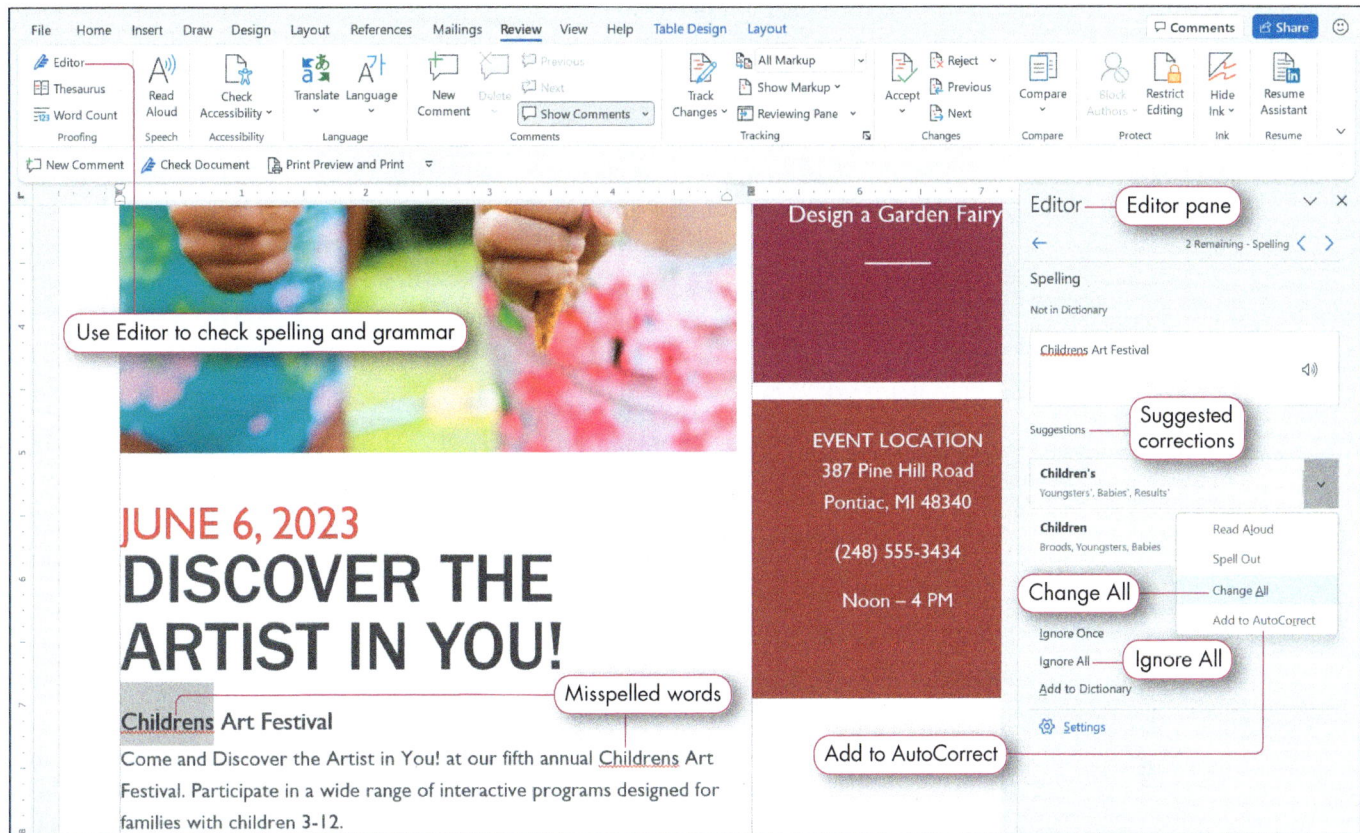

FIGURE 1.26 Using the Editor Pane to Correct Spelling

It is important to understand that the spelling and grammar check is not always correct, so you still need to proof a document thoroughly and review the errors carefully. For example, you might have a word that is truly misspelled in its context, but perhaps is still a valid word in the dictionary. Spell check might not pick it up as a misspelled word, but a careful read through would probably pick it up. There are times when the spelling and grammar check will indicate a word is misspelled and it really is not. This often happens with names or proper nouns or with new technical terms that may not be in the application's dictionary. In these instances, you can choose to Ignore, Ignore All, or Add to Dictionary. Choosing Ignore will skip the word without changing it. If you know there are multiple instances of that word throughout the document, you can choose Ignore All, and it will skip all instances of the word. Finally, if it is a word that is spelled correctly and that you use it often, you can choose Add to Dictionary so it will not be flagged as an error in future spelling checks.

If you right-click a word or phrase that is identified as a potential error, you will see a shortcut menu similar to that shown in Figure 1.27. The top of the shortcut menu will identify the type of error, whether it is spelling or grammar. A pane opens next to the shortcut menu with a list of options to correct the misspelling. These would be the same options that would display in the Editor pane if you ran the spell check command from the ribbon. Click on any option to insert it into the document. Similarly, you have the choices to Add to Dictionary or Ignore All. Each alternative also has options to Read Aloud or Add to AutoCorrect.

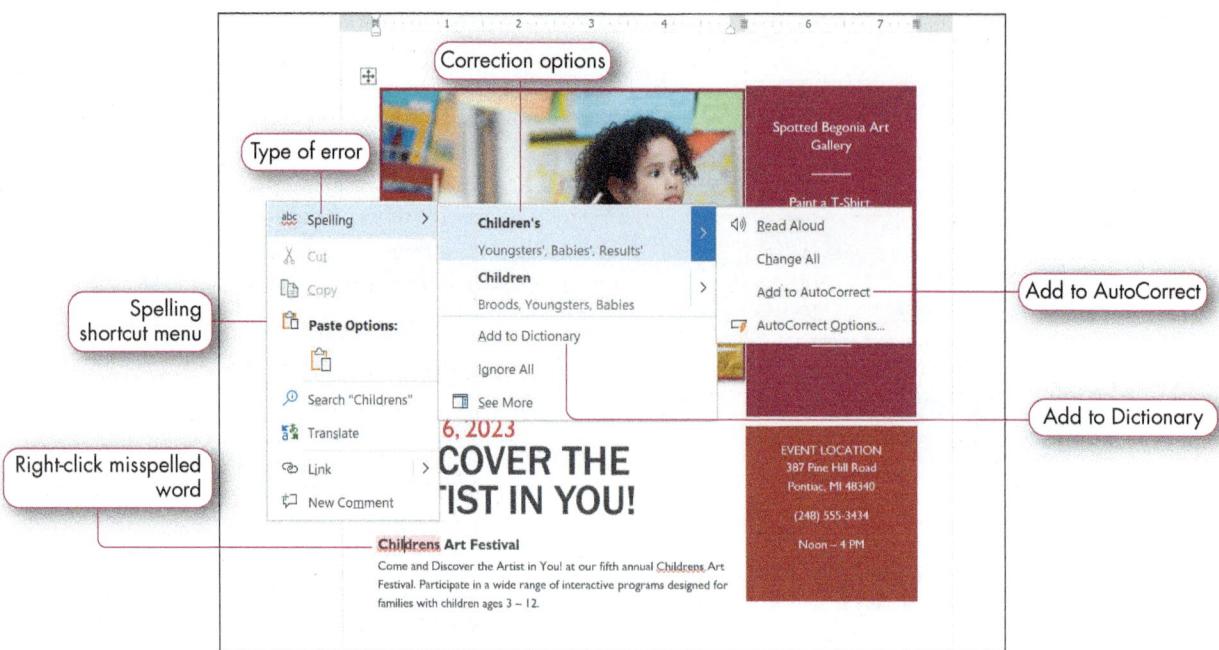

FIGURE 1.27 Spell Check Shortcut Menu Options

You can use AutoCorrect to correct common typing errors, misspelled words, and capitalization errors as well as to insert symbols (see Figure 1.28). There is a standard list of common errors and suggested replacements that is used in Excel, Word, and PowerPoint. So, if you type a word that is found in the Replace column, it will automatically be replaced with the word in the With column. For example, if you typed *accross* it would automatically correct to *across*. If you typed (tm) it would automatically change to the trademark symbol ™. You can add or delete terms and manage AutoCorrect by selecting Options from the File tab, and then in the Options dialog box, select Proofing and click AutoCorrect Options.

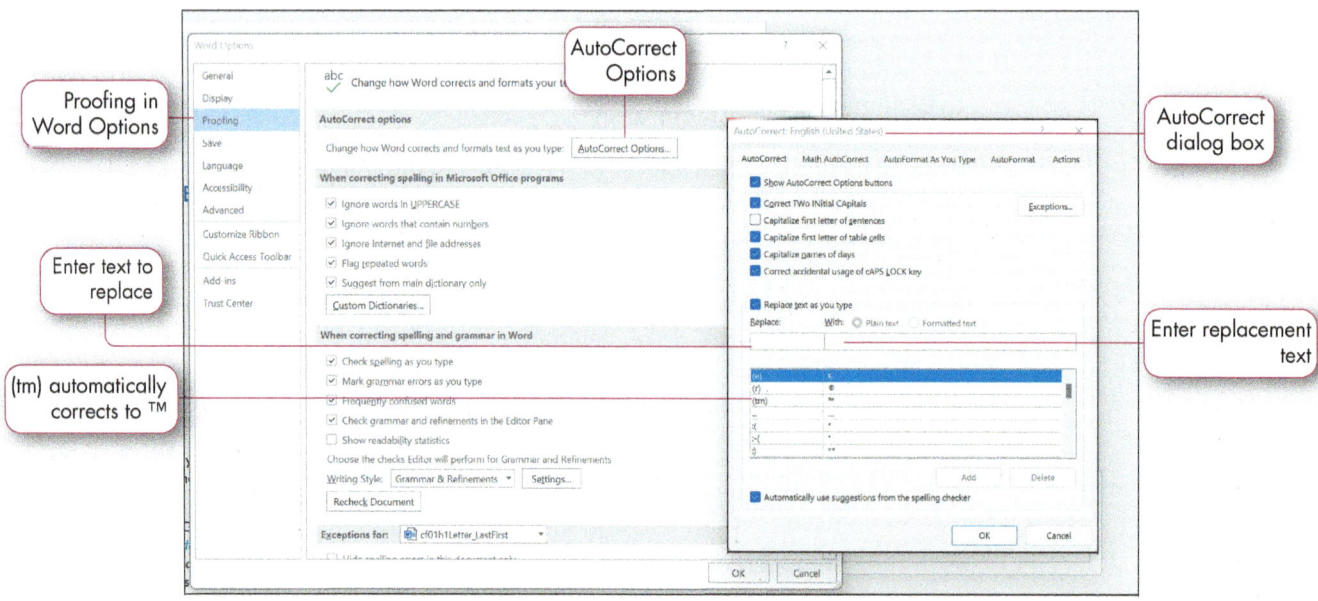

FIGURE 1.28 Proofing and AutoCorrect

Work with Pictures

Documents, worksheets, and presentations can include much more than just words and numbers. You can add energy and additional description to a project by including pictures and other graphic elements. A *picture* is just that—a digital photo. A picture can also be considered an object. Objects are also shapes, icons, SmartArt, tables, and charts. While each of these types of objects have definitive differences, they are all handled basically the same when it comes to inserting and resizing. For the purposes of simplicity, the following discussion focuses on pictures, but the same information can be applied to any object you include in your document, worksheet, or presentation.

STEP 6 ## Insert a Picture

In Word, Excel, and PowerPoint, you can insert pictures from your own library of digital photos you have saved on your hard drive, OneDrive, or another storage medium. If you want a wider variety of pictures to choose from, you can choose from the library of stock images available in the Microsoft 365 program you are using, or you can search for an online picture using Bing. Stock Images include a wide assortment of photographs, icons, cutout people, stickers, and illustrations. Pictures, Stock Images, and Online Pictures are found on the Insert tab. To insert any of these options, click in the file where the picture, stock image or online picture is to be placed, click the Picture arrow from the Illustrations group on the Insert tab and select the appropriate option. Click Insert.

When the picture is inserted into a document, the Picture Format tab displays. You can use these tools to modify the picture as needed. When any object is inserted or selected, a Format tab features commands appropriate to the particular object. For example, if a table is inserted, the Table Format tab will display.

TIP: CREATIVE COMMONS LICENSE

The Bing search filters are set to use the Creative Commons license system so the results display images that have been given a Creative Commons license. These are images and drawings that can be used more freely than images found directly on websites. Because there are different levels of Creative Commons licenses, you should read the Creative Commons license for each image you use to avoid copyright infringement.

Modify a Picture

Once you add a picture to your document, you may want to resize or adjust it. Before you make any changes to a picture, you must first select it. When the picture is selected, eight sizing handles display on the corners and in the middle of each edge (see Figure 1.29). To adjust the size while maintaining the proportions, point to a corner sizing handle and drag the pointer on an angle upward or downward to increase or decrease the size, respectively. If you use one of the center edge sizing handles, you will stretch or shrink the picture out of proportion. In addition to the sizing handles, a rotation handle displays at the top of the selected image. Use this to turn the image. For more precise controls, use the Size and Rotate commands on the Picture Format tab. The Picture Format tab includes additional options for modifying a picture. You can apply a picture style or effect as well as add a picture border from selections in the Picture Styles group. Click More in the Picture Styles group to view a gallery of picture styles. As you point to a style, the style is shown in Live Preview, but the style is not applied until you select it. As shown in Figure 1.29, options in the Adjust group simplify changing a color scheme, applying creative artistic effects, and even adjusting the brightness, contrast, and sharpness of an image.

If a picture contains areas that are not necessary, you can crop it, which is the process of trimming edges that you do not want to display. Crop is located on the Picture Format tab (see Figure 1.29). Even though cropping enables you to adjust the amount of a picture that displays, it does not actually delete the portions that are cropped out. Therefore, you can later recover parts of the picture, if necessary. Cropping a picture also does not reduce the file size of the picture. If you want to permanently remove the cropped portions of a figure and reduce the file size, you must compress the picture. Compress Pictures is found in the Adjust group on the Picture Format tab (see Figure 1.29). Lastly, when a picture is selected, Layout Options displays in the top right corner of the picture. These options control how text flows or wraps around the picture. The same options are available by clicking Wrap Text in the Arrange group on the Picture Format tab.

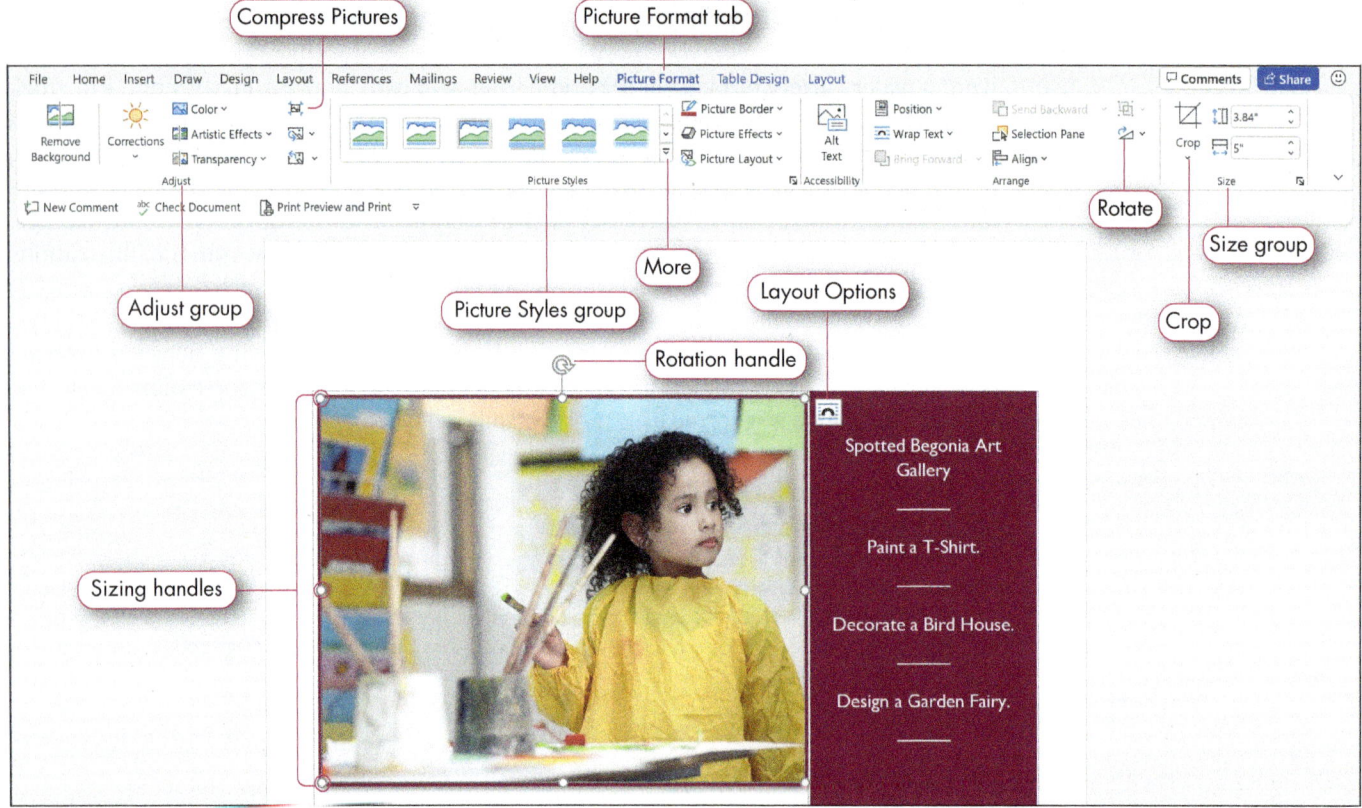

FIGURE 1.29 Formatting a Picture

Critical Thinking _____

4. Discuss the differences between themes and templates. *p. 69*

5. Discuss several ways text can be modified. *p. 72*

6. Explain how the Clipboard is used when removing or relocating text. *p. 75*

7. Explain how to review a file for spelling and grammar issues. *p. 76*

8. Explain why it is important to use the corner sizing handles of a picture when resizing. *p. 79*

Hands-On Exercises

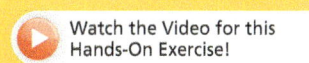
Watch the Video for this Hands-On Exercise!

Skills covered: Open a Template • Apply a Theme • Select Text • Use the Mini Toolbar • Format Text • Cut, Copy, and Paste Text • Check Spelling and Grammar • Insert a Picture • Modify a Picture

2 Format File Content

As the administrative assistant for the Spotted Begonia Art Gallery, you want to create a flyer to announce the *Discover the Artist in You!* Children's Art Festival. You decide to use a template to help you get started more quickly and to take advantage of having a professionally formatted document without knowing much about Word. You will modify the flyer created with the template by adding and formatting your own content and changing out the photo.

STEP 1 OPEN A TEMPLATE

To facilitate making a nice-looking flyer, you review the templates that are available in Microsoft Word. You search for flyers and finally choose one that is appropriate for the event, knowing that you will be able to replace the photo with your own. Refer to Figure 1.30 as you complete Step 1.

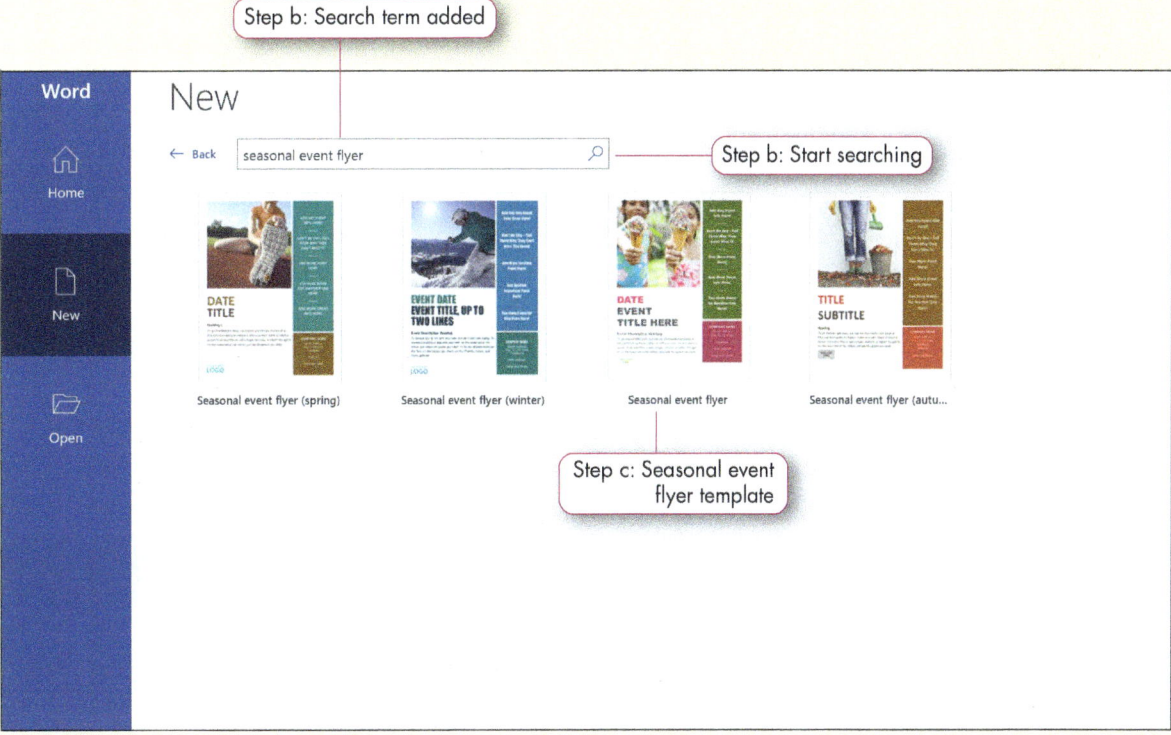

FIGURE 1.30 Search for a Template

a. Ensure Word is open. Click **File** and click **New**. (On a Mac, click the File tab, select New from Template.)

b. Type the search term **seasonal event flyer** in the *Search for online templates* box to search for event flyer templates. Click **Start searching**.

Your search results in a selection of event flyer templates.

c. Locate the Seasonal event flyer template as shown in Figure 1.30 and click to select it.

The template displays in a preview.

> **TROUBLESHOOTING:** Do not choose the template that has Office Add-in Ready. If you do not find the template, you may access the template from the student data files – *cf01h2Flyer.dotx* – and skip to Step e.

d. Click **Create** to open the flyer template.

The flyer template that you selected opens in Word.

e. Click the **File tab** and select **Save As**.

Because this is the first time you save the flyer file, you use Save As to indicate the file name and the location where the file will be saved.

f. Click **Browse** to navigate to where you save your files. Save the document as **cf01h2Flyer_LastFirst**.

> **TROUBLESHOOTING:** If you selected Save on the QAT, the Save this file window displays. Enter cf01h2Flyer_LastFirst in the File Name box and navigate to the location where you save your files. Click Save.

APPLY A THEME

You want to change the theme of the template for a different font effect and color scheme that better match the Spotted Begonia Art Gallery's branding. Refer to Figure 1.31 as you complete Step 2.

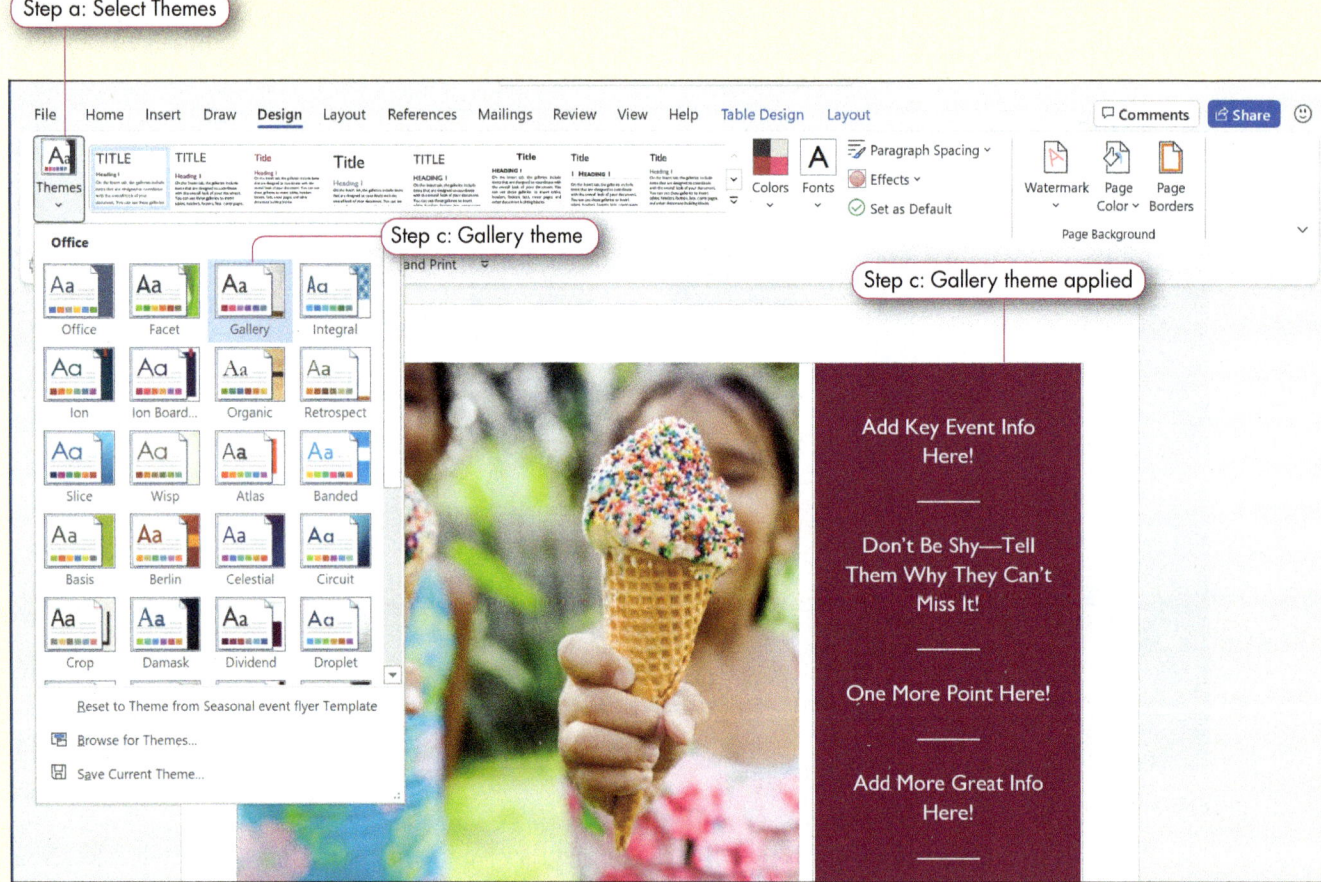

FIGURE 1.31 Apply a Theme

a. Click the **Design tab** and click **Themes** in the Document Formatting group.

The Themes gallery displays.

b. Point to a few themes and notice how the template changes with each different theme.

c. Click **Gallery**.

The Gallery theme is applied, changing the color of the banners and modifying the font and font size.

d. Save the document.

You will replace the template text to create the flyer, adding information such as a title, date, and description. After adding the text to the document, you will modify the formatting of the organization name in the flyer. Refer to Figure 1.32 as you complete Step 3.

FIGURE 1.32 Edit Placeholder Text

a. Scroll so the **Date placeholder** is visible in the main body of the template. Click **Date** and then type **June 6, 2023** in the placeholder.

b. Click the **Event Title Here placeholder** and type **Discover the Artist in You!** in the placeholder.

c. Press **Enter** and continue typing **Spotted Begonia Art Gallery**.

d. Click the **Event Description Heading placeholder** and type **Childrens Art Festival**. (Ignore the misspelling for now.)

e. Select each text placeholder in the bottom box of the right table column and replace the content in each text placeholder with the content from the right column below.

Placeholder	Text Typed Entry
Company Name	**Event Location**
Street Address City ST Zip Code	**387 Pine Hill Road Pontiac, MI 48340**
Telephone	**(248) 555-3434**
Web Address	**Noon – 4 PM**
Dates and Times	**Delete this text**

You modify the placeholders to customize the flyer.

f. Select the title text **Discover the Artist in You!**. Click the **Font arrow** on the Mini Toolbar. Select **Franklin Gothic Medium**.

> **TROUBLESHOOTING:** If the Mini Toolbar does not display after selecting the text, right-click the selected text to display the Mini Toolbar. Alternatively, click the Font arrow in the Font group on the Home tab and select Franklin Gothic Medium.

The font is changed.

g. Select the text **June 6, 2023**. Click the **Font Size arrow** on the Mini Toolbar. (On a Mac, select the Font Size arrow in the Font group on the Home tab.) Select **26** on the Font Size menu.

The font size is reduced in size so the title of the event is more prominent.

h. Save the document.

STEP 4 ▶ CUT, COPY, AND PASTE TEXT

You add descriptive text about the event. You then decide to move some of the text to the banner panel on the right. You also copy the sponsor's name to the top of the banner. Finally, you delete some unwanted placeholders. Refer to Figure 1.33 as you complete Step 4.

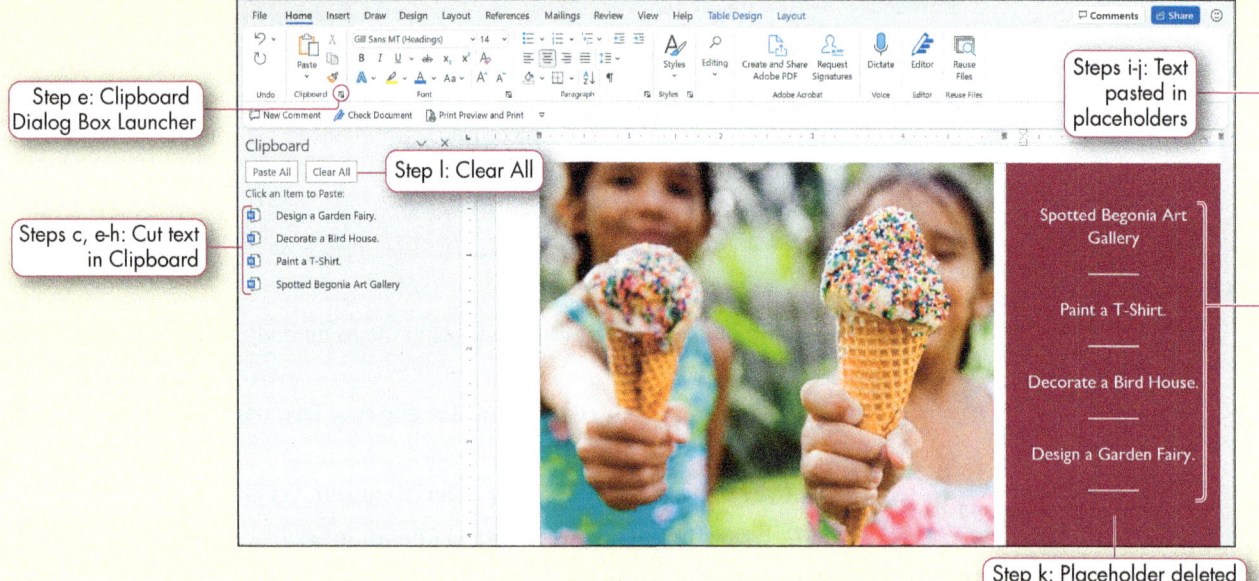

FIGURE 1.33 Use the Clipboard Commands

a. Click anywhere in the **placeholder text** below Childrens Art Festival that begins with *To get started* and press **Delete**. Enter the following text and ignore any intentional misspellings. They will be corrected later.

Come and Discover the Artist in You! at our fifth annual Childrens Art Festival. Participate in a wide range of interactive programs designed for families with children ages 3–12. Paint a T-Shirt. Decorate a Bird House. Design a Garden Fairy.

b. Click the **YOUR LOGO HERE placeholder** and press **Delete**.

The Spotted Begonia Art Gallery does not have a logo so you delete the option to include one.

c. Select the text **Spotted Begonia Art Gallery**. Right-click the selected text and click **Cut** from the shortcut menu.

d. Scroll to the top of the flyer. Click the **Add Key Event Info Here! placeholder** in the right column. Click the **Home tab** and click **Paste** in the Clipboard group to paste the previously cut text.

The text is now moved to the banner.

e. Click the **Dialog Box Launcher** in the Clipboard group.

The cut text displays in the Clipboard pane.

> **MAC TROUBLESHOOTING:** Skip Step e. For Step f, select Paint a T-Shirt and press command+X. Select the text Don't be Shy… and press command+V. Repeat for Steps g and h, using command+X to cut the indicated text and command+V to paste the text in the two placeholders below Paint a T-Shirt. Skip to Step k.

f. Scroll to the paragraph at the bottom of the flyer beginning with *Come and Discover*. Select the text **Paint a T-Shirt.** (include the period) and press **Ctrl+X**. (On a Mac, press command+X or click Cut from the Clipboard group.)

Notice that the cut text selection is in the Clipboard.

g. Select the text **Decorate a Bird House.** from the text you entered in Step a and press **Ctrl+X**.

h. Select the text **Design a Garden Fairy.** from the text you entered in Step a and press **Ctrl+X**.

You cut the three phrases individually because you will be pasting each phrase in separate locations. The Clipboard displays the three cut selections of text.

i. Scroll to the top of the flyer. Select the **Don't Be Shy… placeholder text** and click **Paint a T-Shirt.** from the Clipboard.

The text in the Clipboard is pasted in a new location.

j. Repeat Step i, replacing *One More Point Here!* placeholder text with **Decorate a Bird House.** and *Add More Great Info Here* placeholder text with **Design a Garden Fairy.**

k. Select the last **placeholder text** in the banner and press **Delete**.

l. Click **Clear All** in the Clipboard pane and close the Clipboard. Save the document.

CHECK SPELLING AND GRAMMAR

Because this flyer will be seen by the public, it is important to check the spelling and grammar in your document. Refer to Figure 1.34 as you complete Step 5.

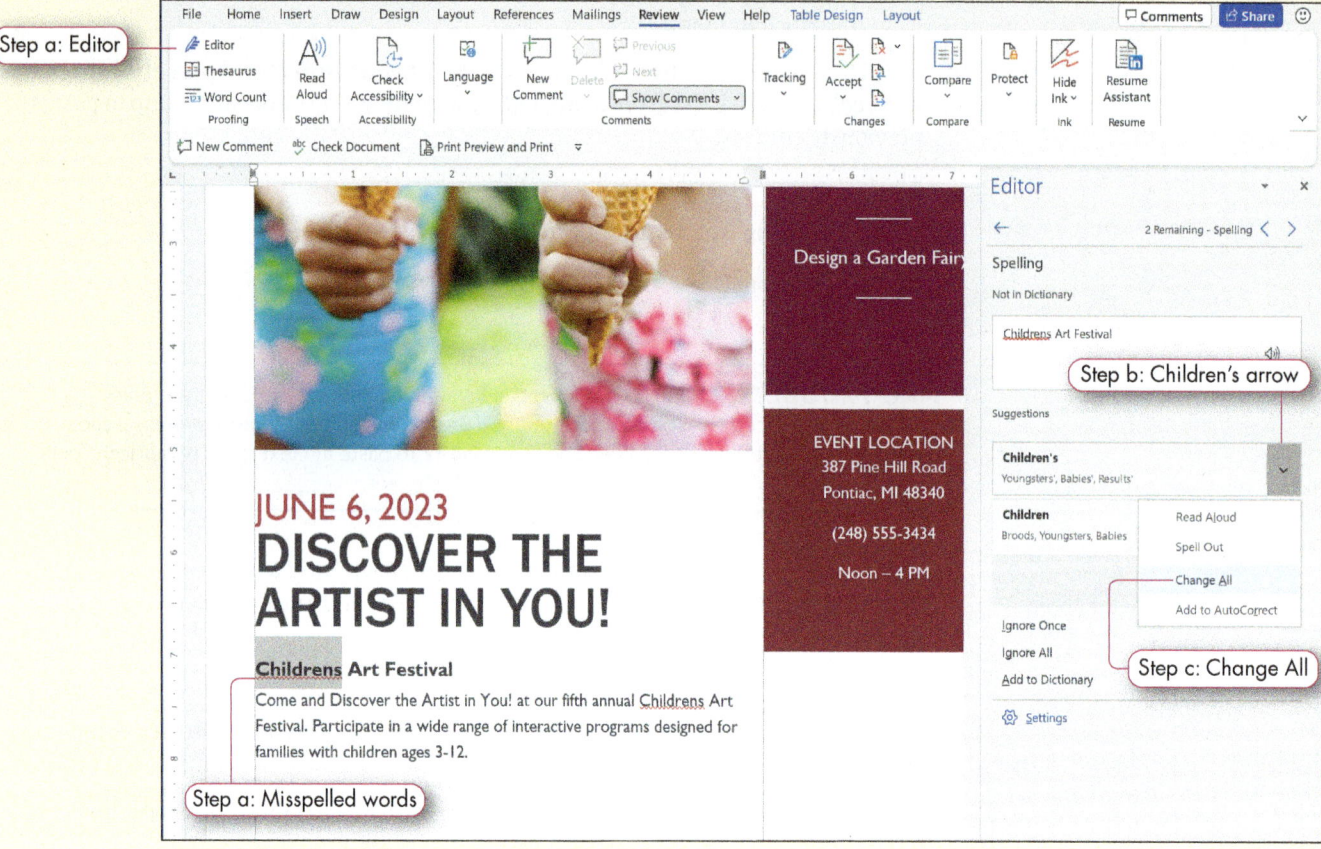

FIGURE 1.34 Check Spelling and Grammar

a. Place the insertion point before the date in the flyer. Click the **Review tab** and click **Editor** in the Proofing group.

The Editor pane opens and two spelling errors are identified.

b. Click **Spelling** in the Corrections box and click the **arrow** to the right of Children's in the Editor pane.

c. Select **Change All** to accept the suggested change to *Children's* in the Spelling pane for all instances. Make any other changes as needed. Close the Editor pane.

The spelling and grammar check is complete.

d. Save the document.

You want to change the template image to an image that better reflects the children's event being held at the gallery. You use an image the art gallery director has provided you. You want to make the picture stand out better, so you decide to add a border frame around the image. Refer to Figure 1.35 as you complete Step 6.

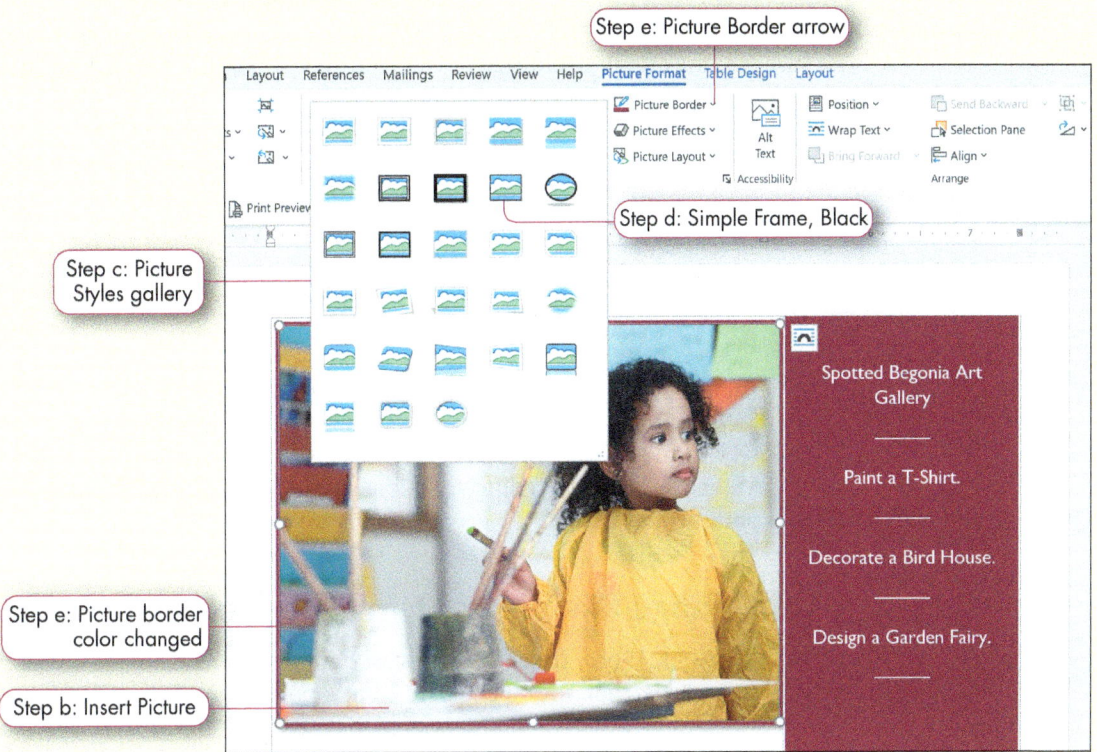

FIGURE 1.35 Insert and Modify Picture

a. Scroll to the top of the flyer. Right-click the **image** and select **Change Picture** from the shortcut menu and then select **From a File**.

You will change out the image with a different one that is saved to your computer.

b. Navigate to your student data files and select *cf01h2Art.jpg*. Click **Insert**.

The new image is placed in the document. The Picture Format tab displays on the ribbon and sizing handles display around the image. The Table Design and Layout tabs also display because the flyer template uses a table to place the elements. Selecting the picture also selects the table.

c. Click the **Picture Format tab** and click **More** in the Picture Styles group.

A gallery of Picture Styles displays.

d. Point to a few different Picture Styles to see the effects in Live Preview and use the ScreenTips to locate and select **Simple Frame, Black**. Keep the image selected.

A black border is applied around the picture.

e. Click the **Picture Border arrow** in the Picture Styles group and select **Pink, Accent 2, Darker 50%** under Theme Colors.

The border color is changed to coordinate with the colors on the flyer.

f. Save the document. Keep the document open if you plan to continue with the next Hands-On Exercise. If not, close the document and exit Word.

Modify File Layout and Properties

When working with a document, before you send or print it, you will want to view the final product to make sure that your margins and page layout are as they should be. Moreover, you might want to add some details in a header or footer, or in document properties to help identify the author and contents of the document to help in later searches. Although you can always print a document using the default printer settings, you may want to change printer settings or page layout settings before printing.

In this section, you will explore how to view and edit document properties. You will learn about views and how to change a document view. In addition, you will learn how to modify the page layout, including page orientation and margins as well as how to add headers and footers. Finally, you will explore Print Preview and the various printing options available to you.

STEP 1 | Change File Views

As you prepare or read a document, you may find that you want to change the way you view it. A section of your document may be easier to view when you can see it magnified, or you might want to display more of your document than what is showing onscreen. You can also select a different *view*, the way a file displays onscreen, to make working on your project easier.

Change File Views Using the Ribbon

Views for Word, Excel, and PowerPoint are available on the View tab. Each application has views that are specific to that application. PowerPoint and Excel each have a Normal view, which is the typical view used to create and view presentation slides and workbooks. Word's Print Layout view is like Normal view in that it is the view used to create documents. Print Layout view is useful when you want to see both the document text and features such as margins and page breaks. Table 1.4 outlines the other views in each application. Access does not have a View tab, but rather incorporates unique views that are visible when working with any Access object.

TABLE 1.4	Application Views	
Application	**View**	**Description**
Word	Print Layout	The default view used when creating documents.
	Read Mode	All editing commands are hidden. Arrows on the left and right sides of the screen are used to move through the pages of the document.
	Web Layout	All page breaks are removed. Use this view to see how a document will display as a webpage.
	Outline View	If Style Headings are used in a document, the document is organized by level. Otherwise, the document will display with each paragraph as a separate bullet.
	Draft View	A pared-down version of Print Layout view.
Excel	Normal	The default view used when creating worksheets.
	Page Break Preview	Displays a worksheet with dashed lines that indicate automatic page breaks. Used to adjust page breaks manually.
	Page Layout	Displays the worksheet headers and margins.
	Custom Views	Create custom views.
PowerPoint	Normal	The default view used when creating presentations.
	Outline View	Displays a presentation as an outline using titles and main text from each slide.
	Slide Sorter	Displays presentation slides in thumbnail form, making it easier to sort and organize slide sequence.
	Notes Page	Makes the Notes pane, which is located under the Slide pane, visible. You can type notes that apply to the current slide. Notes do not display during a presentation.
	Reading View	Displays the presentation in full screen like Slide Show.

Change File Views Using the Status Bar

The *status bar*, located at the bottom of the program window, displays information relevant to the application and file on which you are working as well as some commands. On the left side of the status bar is application- and file-specific information. When you work with Word, the status bar informs you of the number of pages and words in an open document. Excel shows the status of the file and a Macro recording command. The PowerPoint status bar shows the slide number and total number of slides in the presentation. Word and PowerPoint also display a proofing icon that looks like an opened book. An X in the icon indicates there are proofing errors that need to be fixed and a check in the icon indicates that no proofing errors exist (see Figure 1.36). Clicking the icon will start the spelling and grammar check.

> **TIP: KEEP ACCESSIBILITY CHECKER RUNNING IN THE BACKGROUND**
> You can choose to keep the Accessibility checker running in the background while you work. When it is running, the status of accessibility inspection results also displays on the status bar (see Figure 1.36). To configure the Accessibility checker to run in the background, click the Review tab and click the Check Accessibility arrow in the Accessibility group. Choose Check Accessibility to open the Accessibility pane. Click the checkbox to select *Keep accessibility checker running while I work.*

The right side of the status bar includes the means for changing the view and for changing the zoom size of onscreen file contents. As shown in Figure 1.36, the view buttons on the status bar of each application enable you to change the view of the open file. These views correspond to the most commonly used views in each application.

Other pertinent document features display on the right side of the status bar for each application. The Excel status bar displays summary information, such as average and sum, of selected cells. On the Word status bar, a Focus Mode option eliminates distracting window elements from view. The PowerPoint status bar provides access to slide notes.

FIGURE 1.36 Application Information, Views and Zoom Slider on the Status Bar

The *Zoom slider* is a horizontal bar on the right side of the status bar that enables you to increase or decrease the size of the document onscreen. You can drag the tab along the slider in either direction to increase or decrease the magnification of the file (refer to Figure 1.36). Be aware, however, that changing the size of text onscreen does not change the font size when the file is printed or saved.

STEP 2 Change the Page Layout

When you prepare a document or worksheet, you are concerned with the way the project displays onscreen and possibly in print. The Layout tab in Word and the Page Layout tab in Excel provide access to a full range of options such as margin settings and page orientation. PowerPoint does not have a Page Layout tab because its primary purpose is displaying contents onscreen rather than in print.

Because a document or workbook is most often designed to be printed, you may want to adjust margins and change the page orientation, or to center a worksheet vertically or horizontally on a page for the best display. In addition, perhaps the text in a Word document should be aligned in columns. You will find these and other common page settings in the Page Setup group on the Layout tab in Word or the Page Layout tab in Excel. For less common settings, such as determining whether headers should print on odd or even pages, use the Page Setup dialog box.

Change Margins

A ***margin*** is the area of blank space that displays to the left, right, top, and bottom of a document or worksheet. Margins display when you are in Print Layout view (Word) or Page Layout view (Excel), or when previewing a document or workbook to print from the File tab. You make margin adjustments by clicking Margins in the Page Setup group on the Layout or Page Layout tabs (see Figure 1.37). There are Normal, Wide, and Narrow default margin settings for Word and Excel. Word also includes Moderate and Mirrored margins. If you want more customized margin settings, use the Custom Margins option at the bottom of the Margins gallery to display the Page Setup dialog box.

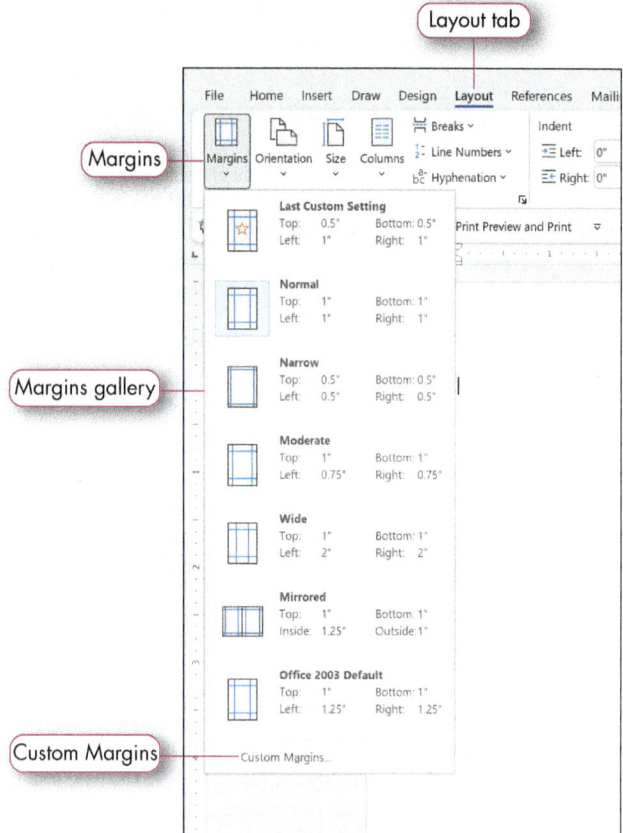

FIGURE 1.37 Page Margins in Word

Change Page Orientation

Documents, worksheets, and presentation slides can be displayed or printed in different ***page orientations*** that determine the layout of a page. A page in portrait orientation is taller than it is wide. A page in landscape orientation is wider than it is tall. Word documents are usually displayed in portrait orientation, whereas Excel worksheets are often more suited to landscape orientation. In PowerPoint, you can change the orientation of slides as well as notes and handouts. Page Orientation settings for Word and Excel are found in the Page Setup group on the Layout or Page Layout tabs, respectively. Orientation is also an option on the Print page on the File tab.

Use the Page Setup Dialog Box

As noted previously, the Page Setup group contains Margins and Orientation settings as well as other commonly used page options for Word and Excel. Some are unique to Excel, and others are more applicable to Word. Other less common settings are available in the Page Setup dialog box only, displayed when you click the Dialog Box Launcher in the Page Setup group. The Page Setup dialog box includes options for customizing margins, selecting page orientation, centering horizontally or vertically, printing gridlines, and creating headers and footers. Figure 1.38 shows both the Excel and Word Page Setup dialog boxes.

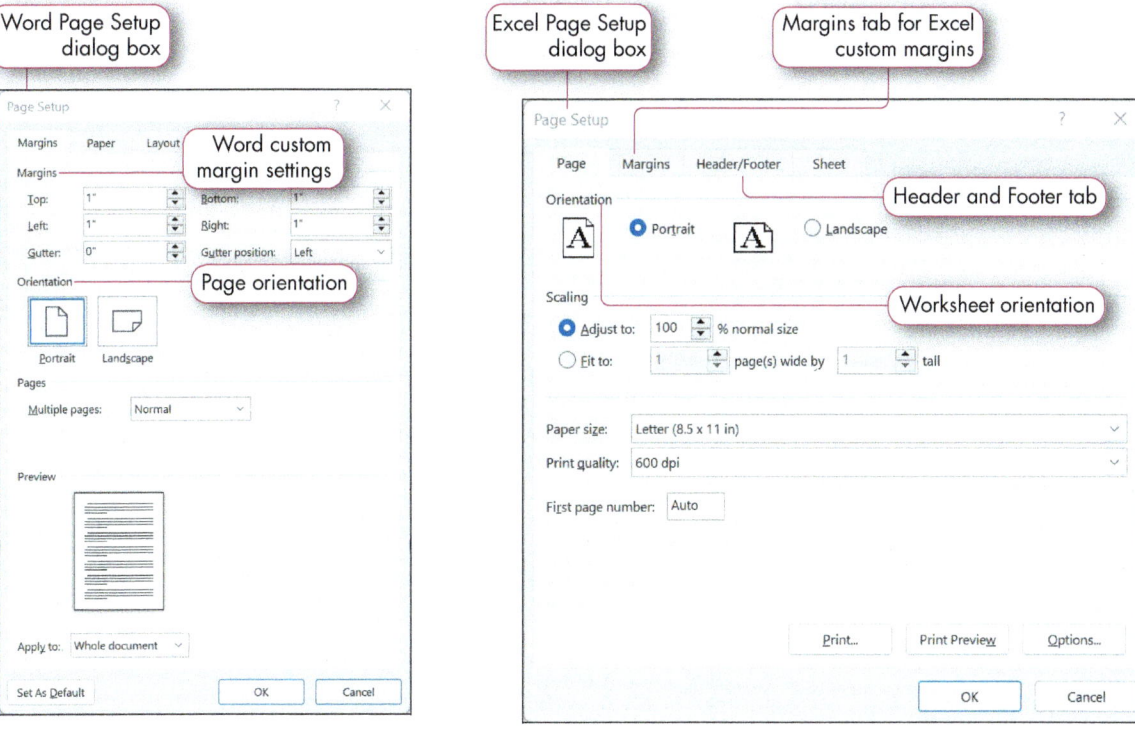

FIGURE 1.38 Page Setup Dialog Boxes in Word and Excel

Although PowerPoint slides are generally set to landscape orientation, you can change to portrait orientation by accessing the Slide Size controls in the Customize group on the Design tab and selecting Custom Slide Size. When choosing to print Notes Pages, Outline, or Handouts, the page orientation can be changed by clicking the File tab and selecting Print.

STEP 3 ## Create Headers and Footers

The purpose of including a header or footer is to add identifying information to the file and give it a professional appearance. A **header** is a section in the top margin of a file. A **footer** is a section in the bottom margin of a file. Generally, page numbers, dates, author's name, or file name are included in Word documents or PowerPoint presentations. Excel worksheets might include the name of a worksheet tab as well. Company logos are often displayed in a header or footer. Contents in a header or footer will appear on each page of the document, so you only have to specify the content once, after which it displays automatically on all pages. Although you can type the text yourself at the top or bottom of every page, it is time-consuming and allows for the possibility of making a mistake.

Header and footer commands are found on the Insert tab in each application. In Word, you can choose from a predefined gallery of headers and footers as shown in Figure 1.39. To create your own unformatted header or footer, select Edit Header (or Edit Footer) at the bottom of the gallery. You can only add footers to PowerPoint slides (see Figure 1.39). You can apply footers to an individual slide or to all slides. To add date and time or a slide number, select each option to apply. Check the Footer option to add in your own content. In PowerPoint, the location of a footer will depend on the template or theme applied to the presentation. For some templates and themes, the footer will display on the side of the slide rather than at the bottom. Headers and footers are available for PowerPoint Notes and Handouts. Select the Notes and Handouts tab in the Header and Footer dialog box and enter in the content similarly to how you would enter footer information on slides. In Excel, headers and footers are separated into left, center, and right sections. You can type your own contents or use a predefined header or footer element, such as date, file name, or sheet name.

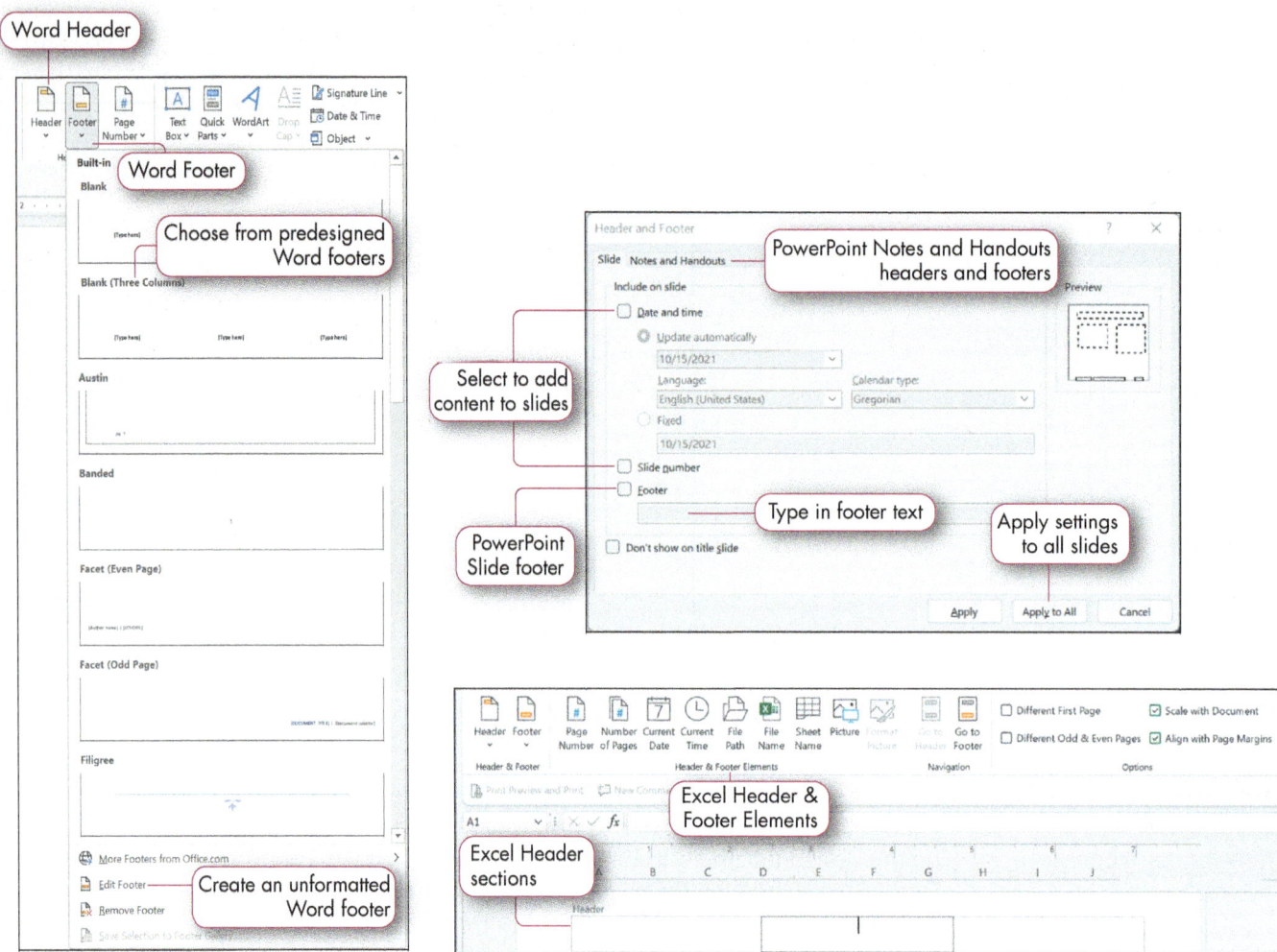

FIGURE 1.39 Insert Footer Options

After entering a header or a footer, it can be formatted like any other text. It can be formatted in any font or font size. In Word or Excel, when you want to leave the header and footer area and return to the document, click Close Header and Footer or double-click in the body of the document.

Configure File Properties and Print a File

Recall that the File tab provides a collection of commands related to a file. Earlier in this chapter, you used the File tab to open and save a file and a template and to customize ribbon settings. Selecting Info on the File tab, you can also view or specify settings related to the properties of a file. The File tab also includes options for customizing program settings, signing in to your Microsoft 365 account, and exiting the application. In addition, you can access print, share, export, and close file options from the File tab.

Once selected, any option from the File tab fills the entire application window, hiding the file with which you are working. You can return to the file by clicking the Back arrow in the top-left corner or pressing Esc on the keyboard.

STEP 4 ▶ View and Edit File Properties

The Info page is where you can protect, inspect, and manage your document as well as manage specific document properties. A file's properties include the author, file size, permissions, and date modified. It is helpful to include information that identifies a document, such as the author and title. You can also add one or more tags (see Figure 1.40). A **_tag_** is a data element or metadata that is added as a document property. Like a keyword, you can search for a file based on tags you assign a document. For example, suppose you apply a tag of *Picasso* to all documents you create that are associated with that artist. Later, you can use that keyword as a search term, locating all associated documents. Statistical information related to the current document such as file size, number of pages, and total words are located on the Info page.

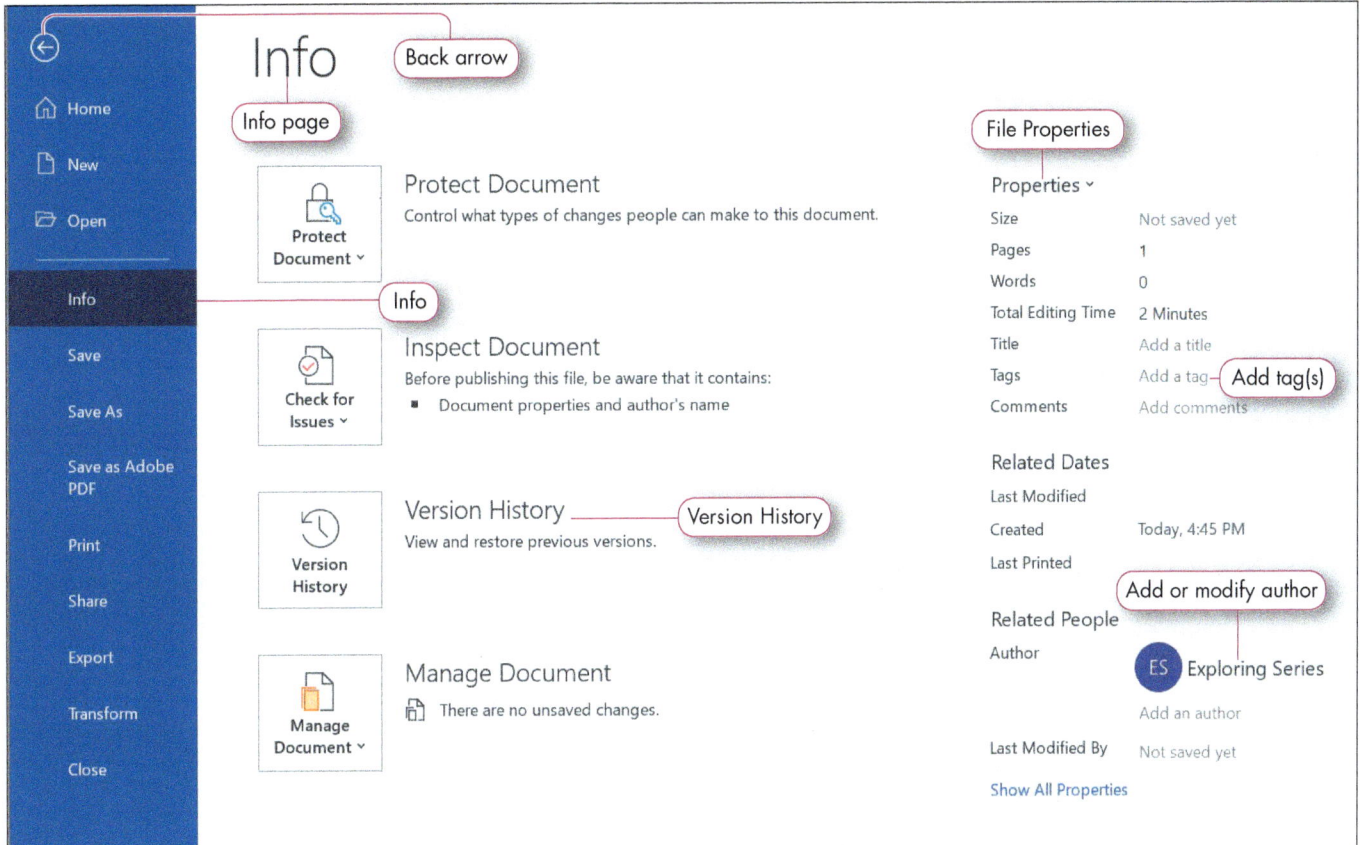

FIGURE 1.40 The File Tab and Info Page

TIP: VERSION HISTORY
If your file is saved to OneDrive and you have AutoSave turned on, you can revert back to an earlier version of the file. On the Info page of the File tab, click Version History (refer to Figure 1.40). The past versions of the file display with the time each version was saved. Click on any instance to restore the document to that version.

STEP 5 ## Preview and Print a File

It is a good habit to look at how your document or worksheet will display before you print it. When you select Print from the File tab, the file previews on the right, with print settings located in the center of the print preview. Figure 1.41 shows a typical print preview. You can select from various print options, including the number of copies and the specific pages to print. Other options in the Print view vary depending on the application in which you are working. For example, PowerPoint's Print view includes options for printing slides and handouts in various configurations and colors, whereas Excel's focuses on worksheet selections and Word's includes document options. Regardless of the Microsoft 365 application, you can access Settings options, including page orientation (landscape or portrait), margins, and paper size.

If you determine that the page setup is correct and that there are no further print settings to select, click Print. Note that you can add Quick Print and Print Preview and Print options to the Quick Access Toolbar for convenience.

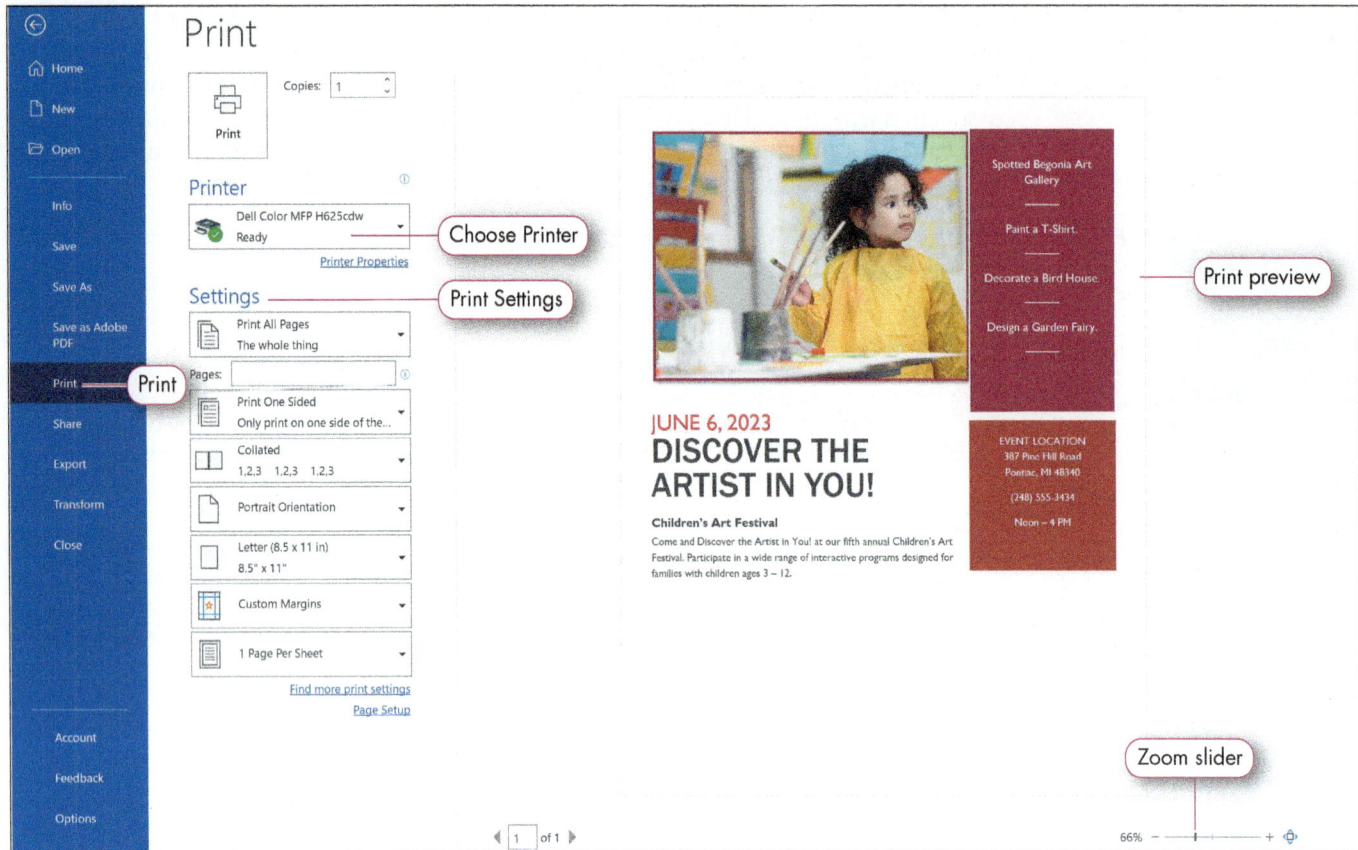

FIGURE 1.41 Print Preview in Word

TIP: CHANGING THE SIZE OF PRINT PREVIEW

Sometimes the preview image of your document shows only a part of the document page or shows a smaller image of the document page. You can change the size of the print preview by using the Zoom slider in the bottom-right corner of the preview (refer to Figure 1.41).

Critical Thinking

9. Discuss why you would need to change the view of a document. ***p. 88***

10. Discuss the various ways you can change a page layout. ***p. 89***

11. Explain what functions and features are included on the File tab. ***p. 92***

12. Discuss some file properties and explain why they are helpful. ***p. 92***

Hands-On Exercises

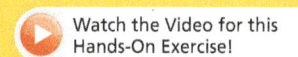

Skills covered: Change File Views Using the Ribbon • Change File Views Using the Status Bar • Change Margins • Change Page Orientation • Create Headers and Footers • View and Edit File Properties • Preview a File • Change Print Settings

3 Modify File Layout and Properties

You continue to work on the flyer for the Children's Art Festival. You will review and add document properties, and prepare the document to print and distribute by changing the page setup. You will also add a footer with Spotted Begonia's information. As the administrative assistant for the Spotted Begonia Art Gallery, you must be able to search for and find documents previously created. You know that by adding tags to your flyer you will more easily find it later. Finally, you will explore printing options.

STEP 1 CHANGE FILE VIEWS

To get a better perspective on how your flyer would look if posted to the gallery's website, you explore the Web Layout view available in Word. Refer to Figure 1.42 as you complete Step 1.

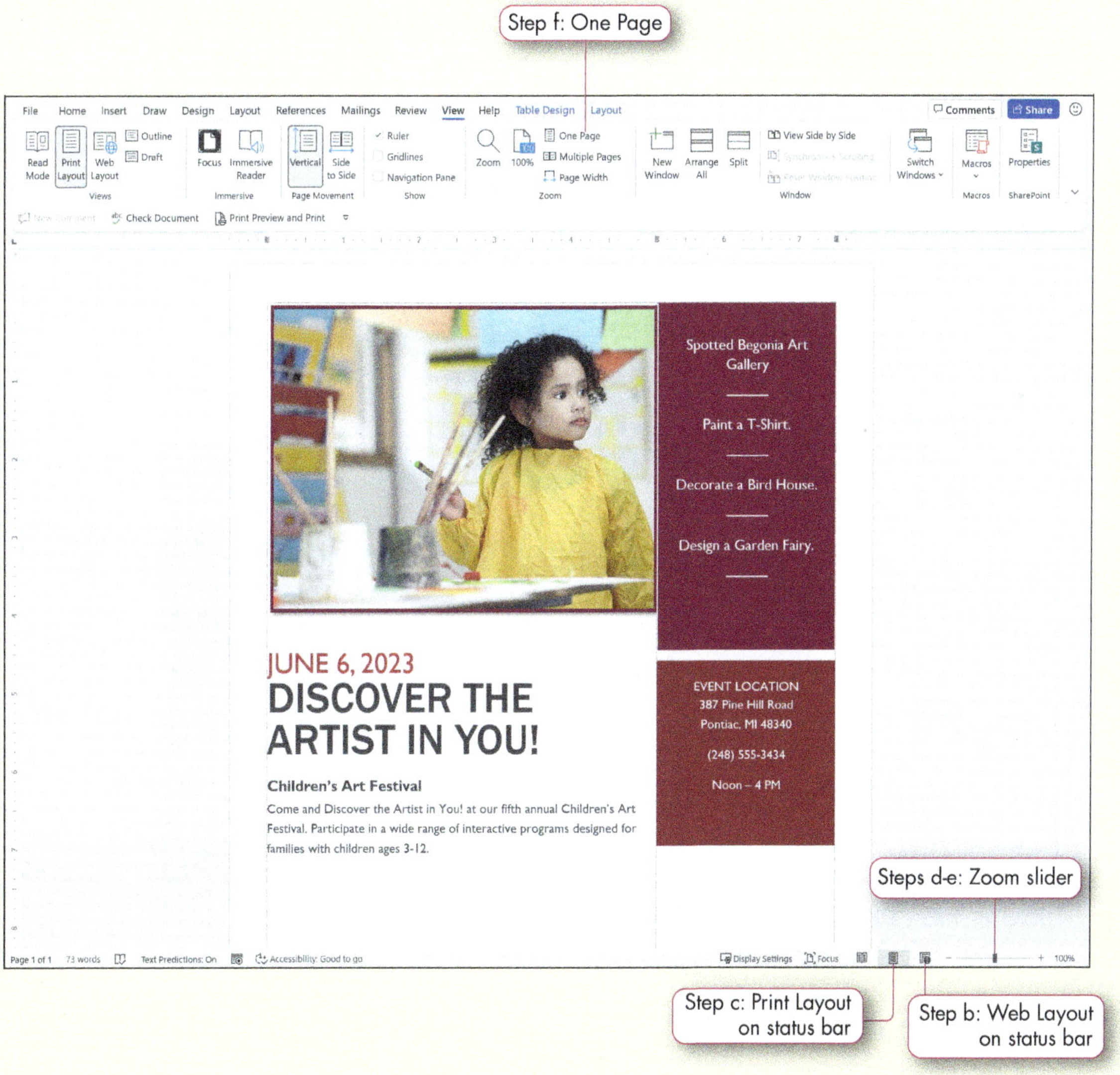

Step f: One Page

Steps d-e: Zoom slider

Step c: Print Layout on status bar

Step b: Web Layout on status bar

FIGURE 1.42 The Flyer in Print Layout View

a. Open *cf01h2Flyer_LastFirst.docx* if you closed it at the end of Hands-On Exercise 2, and save it as **cf01h3Flyer_LastFirst**, changing h2 to h3.

b. Click the **View tab** and click **Web Layout** in the Views group. Observe the changes to the view.

The view is changed to Web Layout and simulates how the document would display on the Web. It is not well formatted for the Web. Changes would need to be made before uploading as a webpage.

c. Click **Print Layout** on the status bar. Observe the changes to the view.

The document has returned to Print Layout view.

d. Drag the **Zoom slider** to the left so you can see the full page of the flyer.

e. Drag the **Zoom slider** to the right to zoom in on the image.

f. Click the **View tab** and click **One Page** in the Zoom group.

The entire flyer is displayed.

STEP 2 CHANGE THE PAGE LAYOUT

You show the flyer to the program director. You both wonder whether changing the orientation and margin settings will make the flyer look better when it is printed. You change the orientation setting, but ultimately revert to portrait orientation. You modify the margins in portrait orientation to improve the spacing around the edges of the page. Refer to Figure 1.43 as you complete Step 2.

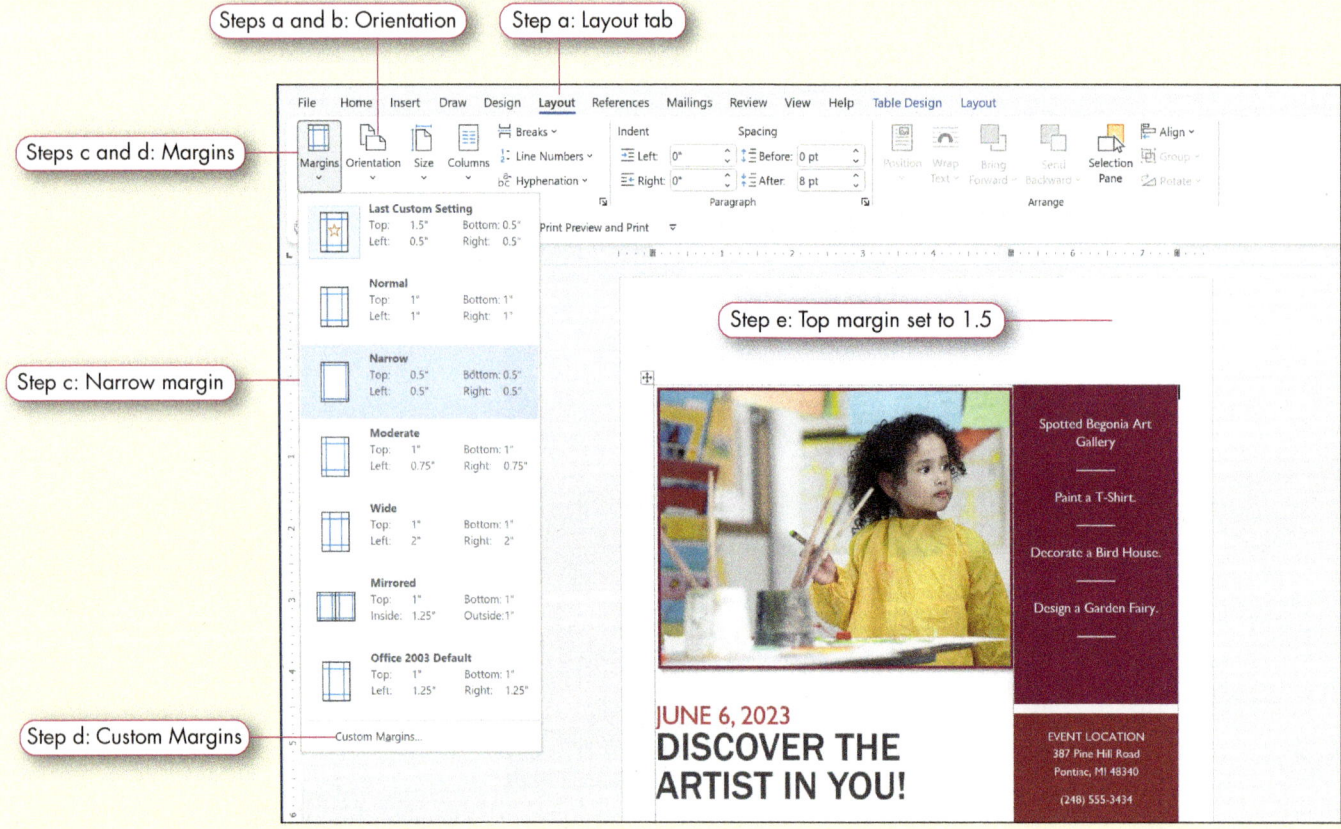

FIGURE 1.43 Change Margins and Orientation

a. Click the **Layout tab** and click **Orientation** in the Page Setup group. Select **Landscape.**

The document is now wider than it is tall.

b. Click **Orientation** and select **Portrait**.

The document returns to portrait orientation.

c. Click **Margins** in the Page Setup group. Select **Narrow**.

The document margins were changed to narrow. The narrow margin allows for better spacing horizontally, but you would like the flyer to be centered vertically on the page.

d. Click **Margins** and select **Custom Margins**.

The Page Setup dialog box opens.

e. Change the Top margin to **1.5"**. Click OK.

f. Click the **View tab** and click **One Page** in the Zoom group.

The document looks well balanced on the page.

> **TROUBLESHOOTING:** A new page with duplicate content is created when the margins are changed. You can ignore the second page and continue making changes to the first page.

g. Save the document.

CREATE HEADERS AND FOOTERS

You decide to add the gallery's name and website URL to the flyer as a footer so anyone who is looking for more information on the Spotted Begonia Art Gallery can access the website. Refer to Figure 1.44 as you complete Step 3.

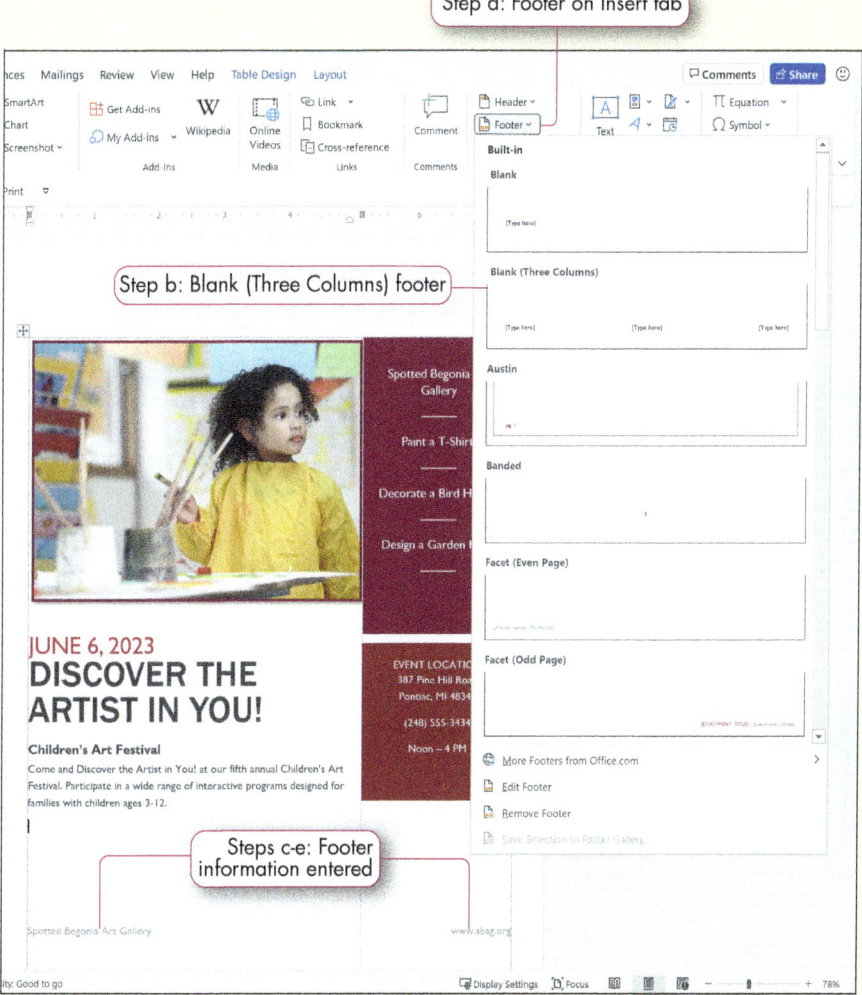

FIGURE 1.44 Insert a Footer

a. Click the **Insert tab** and click **Footer** in the Header & Footer group.

A footer gallery displays.

b. Click the **Blank (Three Columns) footer**.

You select a footer with three areas to add your own information.

c. Click **[Type here]** on the left side of the footer. Type **Spotted Begonia Art Gallery**.

d. Click **[Type here]** on the center of the footer. Press **Delete**.

e. Click **[Type here]** on the right side of the footer. Type **www.sbag.org**.

f. Click **Close Header and Footer** in the Close group.

The footer information is entered.

g. Save the document.

STEP 4 VIEW AND EDIT FILE PROPERTIES

You add document properties, which will help you locate the file in the future when performing a search of your files. Refer to Figure 1.45 as you complete Step 4.

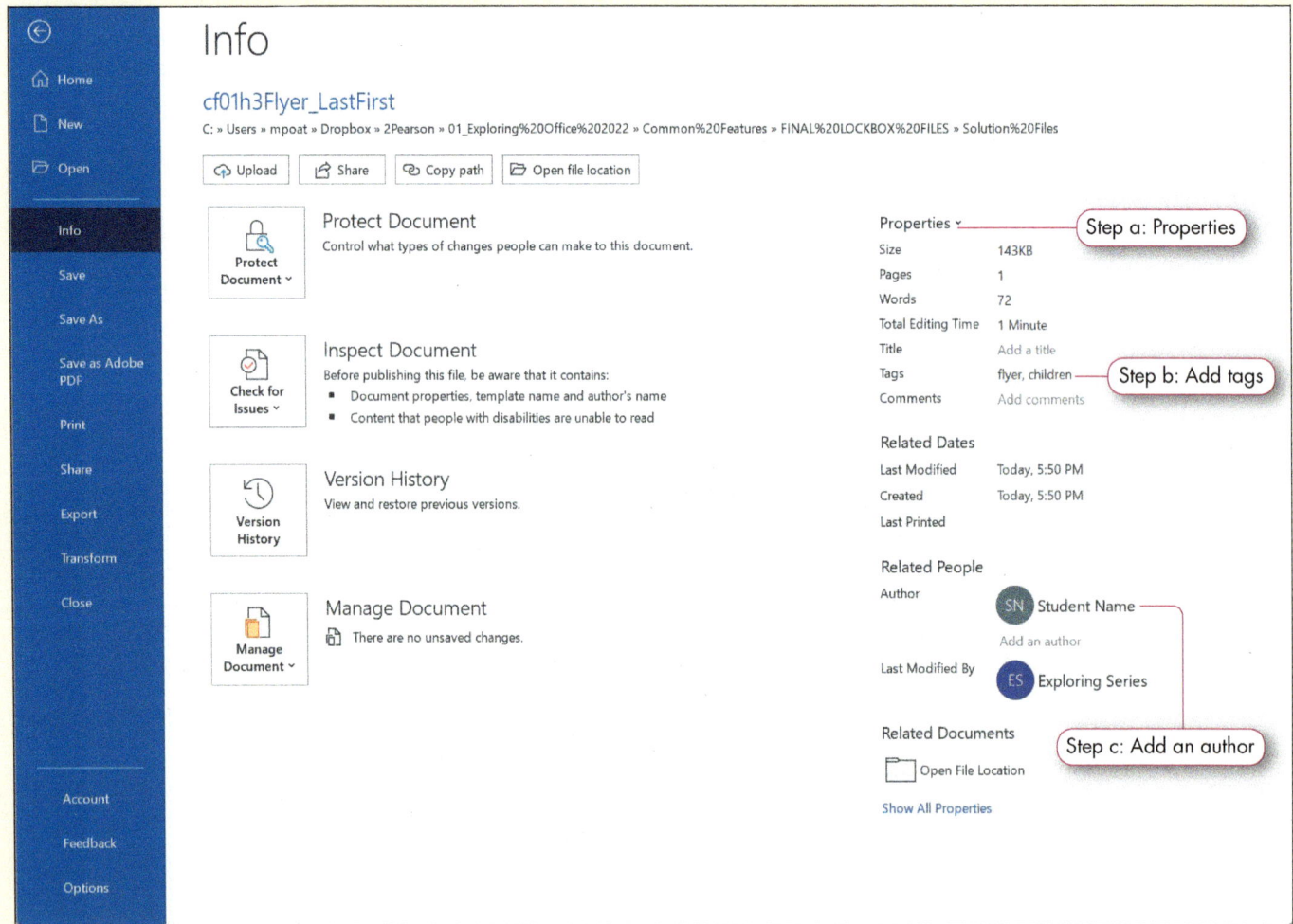

FIGURE 1.45 Enter Document Properties

a. Click the **File tab** and click **Info** on the File tab. Locate Properties at the top of the right section of the Info page.

b. Click the **Add a tag box** and type **flyer, children**.

> **MAC TROUBLESHOOTING:** On a Mac, to add a tag, click the File menu and select Properties. Click the Summary tab and enter text in the Keywords box.

You added tag properties to the flyer.

c. Click the **Add an Author box** and type your first and last names. (On a Mac, replace name in the Author box with your first and last names.)

You added an Author property to the flyer.

d. Click **Save** in the File tab.

STEP 5 **PREVIEW AND PRINT A FILE**

You have reviewed and almost finalized the flyer. You want to look at how it will display when printed. You also want to look over Print Settings to ensure they are correct. Refer to Figure 1.46 as you complete Step 5.

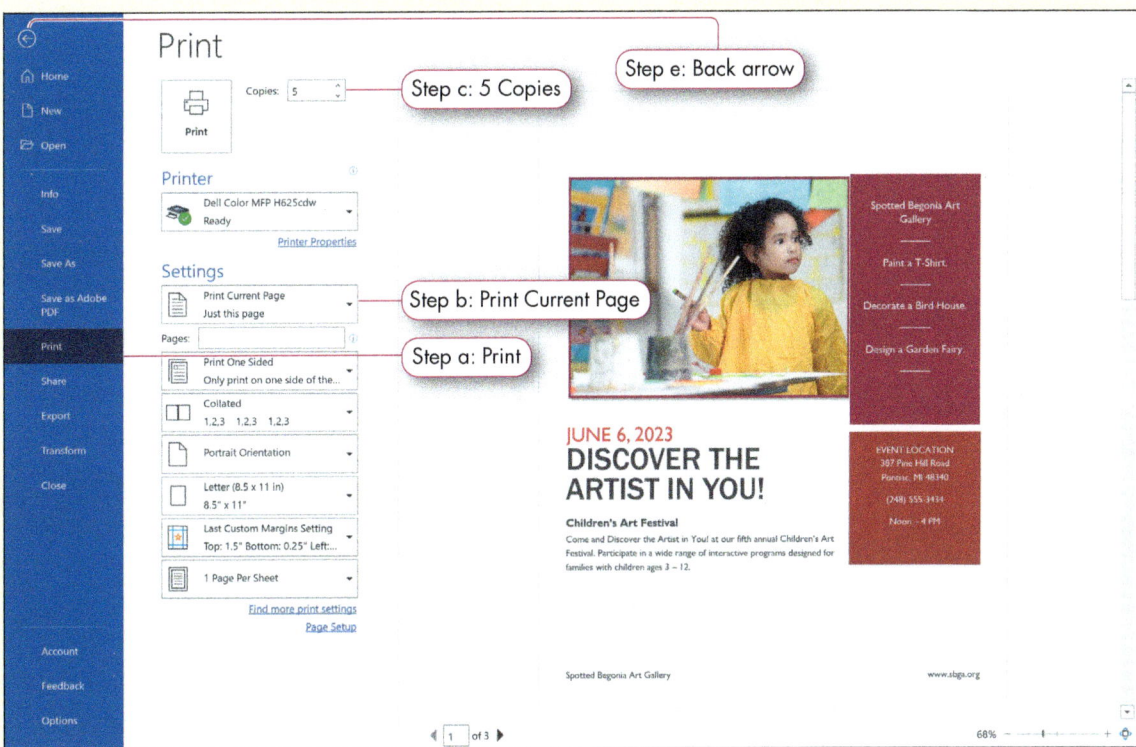

FIGURE 1.46 Print Preview

a. Click the **File tab** and click **Print**.

It is always a good idea before printing to use Print Preview to check how a file will look when printed.

b. Click **Print All Pages arrow** under Settings and select **Print Current Page**.

When the margins were changed an extra page was created. You only want to print the current page.

c. Select the **1** in the Copies box and type or use the up arrow to display **5**.

You increase the number of copies to print so you can distribute them to the other members of the art gallery for their review.

d. Review the margin and orientation settings.

The orientation and custom margins settings match what was done previously. Even though you will not print the document now, the print settings will be preserved when you save the document.

e. Click the **Back arrow.** (On a Mac, click Cancel.)

f. Save and close the file. Exit Word. Based on your instructor's directions, submit the following:
cf01h 1Letter_LastFirst.docx
cf01h3Flyer_LastFirst.docx

Chapter Objectives Review

After reading this chapter, you have accomplished the following objectives:

1. Work with files.

- You can create a document as a blank document or from a template.
- **Open a saved file:** You can open an existing file using the Open dialog box. Recently saved files can be accessed using the Recent documents list.
- **Save a file:** Saving a file enables you to open it later for additional updates or reference. Files are saved to a storage medium such as a hard drive, flash drive, or to OneDrive.

2. Use common interface components.

- **Use the ribbon:** The ribbon, the long bar located just beneath the title bar containing tabs, groups, and commands, is the command center of Microsoft 365 applications.
- **Use a dialog box and gallery:** Some commands are not on the ribbon. To access these commands, you can open a dialog box with a Dialog Box Launcher. A gallery displays additional formatting and design options for a command. Galleries are accessed by clicking More at the bottom of a gallery scroll bar.
- **Customize the ribbon:** You can personalize the ribbon by creating your own tabs and custom groups with commands you want to use. You can create a custom group and add to any of the default tabs.
- **Use and customize the Quick Access Toolbar:** The Quick Access Toolbar, provides one-click access to commonly executed tasks. The QAT is hidden by default, but can be displayed using Ribbon Display Options. You can customize the QAT by adding or deleting commands.
- **Use a shortcut menu:** When you right-click selected text or objects, a context-sensitive menu displays with commands and options relating to the selected text or object.
- **Use keyboard shortcuts:** Keyboard shortcuts are keyboard equivalents for software commands. Universal keyboard shortcuts in Microsoft 365 include Ctrl+C (Copy), Ctrl+X (Cut), Ctrl+V (Paste), and Ctrl+Z (Undo). Not all commands have a keyboard shortcut. If one exists, it will display in the command ScreenTip.
- **Use the Search box:** The Search box on the title bar links to online resources and technical support, and also provides quick access to commands.
- **Use the Help tab:** The Help tab includes resources for written and video tutorials and training, a means to contact Microsoft Support, and a way to share feedback. What's New displays a webpage that discusses all newly added features organized by release date.
- **Use ScreenTips:** A ScreenTip describes a command and provides a keyboard shortcut, if applicable. Enhanced ScreenTips have more descriptive content and a link to access more information for that command.

3. Use templates and apply themes.

- **Open a template:** Templates are a convenient way to save time when designing a document. A gallery of template options displays when you start any application. You can also access a template when you start a new document, worksheet, presentation, or database.
- **Apply a theme:** Themes are collections of design choices that include colors, fonts, and special effects used to give a consistent look to a document, workbook, or presentation.

4. Modify, relocate, and review text.

- **Select text:** Text can be selected by a variety of methods. You can drag to highlight text and select individual words or groups of text with shortcuts.
- **Format text:** You can change the font, font color, size, and many other attributes.
- **Use the Mini Toolbar:** The Mini Toolbar provides instant access to common formatting commands after text is selected.
- **Cut, copy, and paste text:** To cut means to remove a selection from the original location and place it in the Clipboard. To copy means to duplicate a selection from the original location and place a copy in the Clipboard. To paste means to place a cut or copied selection into another location.
- **Use the Office Clipboard:** When you cut or copy selections, they are placed in the Clipboard and can be pasted individually. When the Office Clipboard is opened, you can paste the same item multiple times; it will remain in the Office Clipboard until you exit all Microsoft 365 applications or until the Office Clipboard exceeds 24 items.
- **Check spelling and grammar:** As you type, Microsoft 365 applications check and mark spelling and grammar errors (Word and PowerPoint only) for later correction. The Thesaurus enables you to search for synonyms. Use AutoCorrect to correct common typing errors and misspelled words and to insert symbols. Spelling (PowerPoint and Excel) and Editor (Word) commands are on the ribbon.

5. Work with pictures.

- **Insert a picture:** You can insert pictures from your own library of digital photos saved on your hard drive, OneDrive, or another storage medium, or you can initiate a Bing search for online pictures directly inside the Microsoft 365 program you are using.
- **Modify a picture:** To resize a picture, drag a corner-sizing handle; never resize a picture by dragging a center sizing handle. You can apply a picture style or effect as well as add a picture border from selections in the Picture Styles group.

6. Change file views.

- **Change file views using the ribbon:** The View tab offers views specific to the individual application. A view is how a file will be seen onscreen.
- **Change file views using the status bar:** In addition to information relevant to the open file, the Status bar provides access to View and Zoom level options.

7. Change the page layout.

- **Change margins:** A margin is the area of blank space that displays to the left, right, top, and bottom of a document or worksheet.
- **Change page orientation:** Documents and worksheets can be displayed in different page orientations. Portrait orientation is taller than it is wide; landscape orientation is wider than it is tall.
- **Use the Page Setup dialog box:** The Page Setup dialog box includes options for customizing margins, selecting page orientation, centering horizontally or vertically, printing gridlines, and creating headers and footers.
- **Create headers and footers:** A header displays at the top of each page. A footer displays at the bottom of each page.

8. Configure file properties and print a file.

- **View and edit file properties:** Information that identifies a document, such as the author, title, or tags, can be added to the document's properties. Those data elements are saved with the document as metadata, but do not appear in the document as it displays onscreen or is printed.
- **Preview and print a file:** It is important to preview your file before printing. Print options can be set in the File tab and include page orientation, the number of copies, and the specific pages to print. When all settings are established, print a file using Print on the File tab or from the QAT if Quick Print or Print Preview and Print are added.

Key Terms Matching

Match the key terms with their definitions. Write the key term letter by the appropriate numbered definition.

a. Clipboard

b. Command

c. Dialog box

d. File tab

e. Footer

f. Format Painter

g. Group

h. Header

i. Margin

j. Microsoft 365

k. Mini Toolbar

l. Quick Access Toolbar

m. Ribbon

n. Search box

o. Shortcut menu

p. Status bar

q. Tag

r. Template

s. Theme

t. Title bar

1. _____ A productivity software suite including a set of software applications, each one specializing in a type of output. **p. 50**

2. _____ The long bar located just beneath the title bar containing tabs, groups, and commands. **p. 53**

3. _____ A button within a group on the ribbon that performs a specific task. **p. 54**

4. _____ A collection of design choices that includes colors, fonts, and special effects used to give a consistent look to a document, workbook, or presentation. **p. 69**

5. _____ A data element or metadata that is added as a document property. **p. 93**

6. _____ A component of every Microsoft 365 program where tasks related to doing things "to" a file are located, such as save, open, and print. **p. 51**

7. _____ A tool that displays near selected text that contains formatting commands. **p. 73**

8. _____ A feature of a window that identifies the file name, contains controls to manipulate window display, and houses the Quick Access Toolbar. **p. 53**

9. _____ A feature in a document that consists of one or more lines at the bottom of each page. **p. 91**

10. _____ A predesigned file that incorporates formatting elements, such as a theme and layouts, and may include content that can be modified. **p. 69**

11. _____ A feature that enables you to obtain help and information about a command or task you want to perform and also presents you with a shortcut directly to that command. **p. 60**

12. _____ A tool that copies all formatting from one area to another. **p. 62**

13. _____ Stores up to 24 cut or copied selections for use later in your computing session. **p. 74**

14. _____ A task-oriented section of a ribbon tab that contains related commands. **p. 54**

15. _____ A window that contains commands and features related to a ribbon group that are not displayed on the ribbon. **p. 55**

16. _____ Provides handy access to commonly executed tasks, such as saving a file and undoing recent actions. **p. 53**

17. _____ The long bar at the bottom of the screen that houses the Zoom slider and various view buttons. **p. 89**

18. _____ The area of blank space that displays to the left, right, top, and bottom of a document or worksheet. **p. 90**

19. _____ A context-sensitive menu that displays commands and options relevant to the active object. **p. 59**

20. _____ A feature in a document that consists of one or more lines at the top of each page. **p. 91**

Multiple Choice

1. In Word or PowerPoint, which of the following is a quick way to select an entire paragraph?
   (a) Place the pointer at the left of the line, in the margin area, and click.
   (b) Triple-click inside the paragraph.
   (c) Double-click at the beginning of the paragraph.
   (d) Press Ctrl+C inside the paragraph.

2. Which action would you take when you want to copy the format of a selection but not the content?
   (a) Double-click Copy in the Clipboard group.
   (b) Right-click the selection and click Copy.
   (c) Click Copy Format in the Clipboard group.
   (d) Click Format Painter in the Clipboard group.

3. Which of the following displays when an object, such as a picture, is selected?
   (a) Shortcut menu
   (b) Dialog box
   (c) Contextual tab(s)
   (d) Mini toolbar

4. What does a red wavy underline in a document or presentation mean?
   (a) A word is misspelled or not recognized by the Microsoft 365 dictionary.
   (b) A grammatical mistake exists.
   (c) An apparent formatting error was made.
   (d) A word has been replaced with a synonym.

5. Which of the following is *true* about headers and footers?
   (a) They can be inserted from the Layout tab.
   (b) Headers and footers only appear on the last page of a document.
   (c) Headers appear at the top of every page in a document.
   (d) Only page numbers can be included in a header or footer.

6. You can get help when working with a Microsoft 365 application in which one of the following areas?
   (a) Search box
   (b) Status tab
   (c) Mini Toolbar
   (d) Quick Access Toolbar

7. To access commands that are not on the ribbon, you need to open which of the following?
   (a) Gallery
   (b) Dialog box
   (c) Shortcut menu
   (d) Mini Toolbar

8. Which of the following should you use to create a document without knowing much about the software?
   (a) Theme
   (b) Live Preview
   (c) Template
   (d) Design Style

9. Which is the preferred method for resizing a picture so that it keeps its proportions?
   (a) Use the rotation handle
   (b) Use a corner-sizing handle
   (c) Use a side-sizing handle
   (d) Use the controls in the Adjust group

10. Which of the following does not describe a tag in a Word document?
    (a) A data element
    (b) Document metadata
    (c) Keyword
    (d) Document title

MyLab IT Grader
Office for the web project available in **MyLab IT**.

1 Designing Webpages

You have been asked to make a presentation at the next chamber of commerce meeting. With the chamber's continued emphasis on growing the local economy, many small businesses are interested in establishing a Web presence. The business owners would like to know more about how webpages are designed. In preparation for the presentation, you will proofread and edit your PowerPoint file. You decide to insert an image to enhance your presentation. Refer to Figure 1.47 as you complete this exercise.

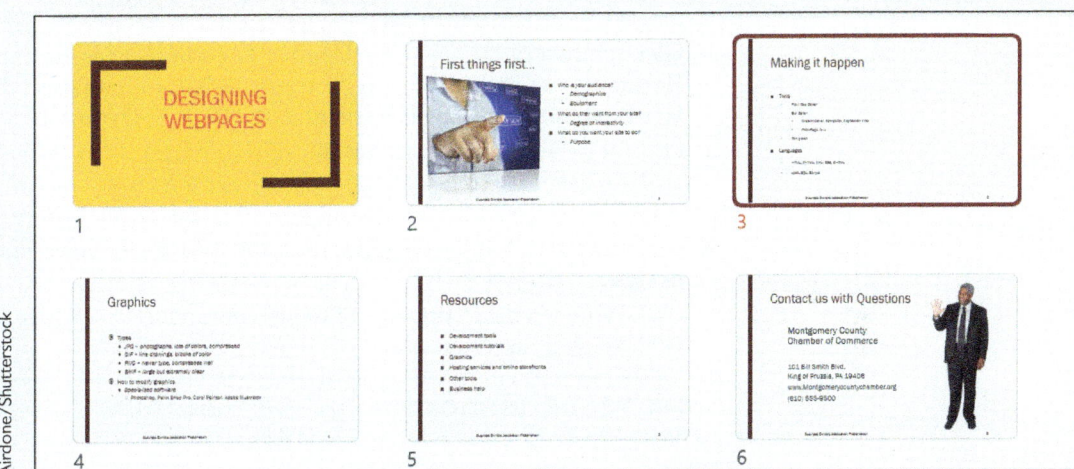

Airdone/Shutterstock

FIGURE 1.47 Designing Webpages Presentation

a. Open the PowerPoint presentation *cf01p1Design.pptx*.

b. Click the **File tab**, click **Save As**, and then save the file as **cf01p1Design_LastFirst**.

c. Click the **Design tab** and click **More** in the Themes group. Scroll through the themes to find and select **Crop theme**. Select the **last Variant** in the Variants group. Close the Design Ideas pane if it opens.

d. Click **Slide 1** in the Slides pane on the left. Double-click to select **Designing Webpages** in the slide title placeholder. Use the Mini Toolbar to click the **Font Color arrow**. Select **Red, Accent 6** in the Theme Colors group. Click **Bold** on the Mini Toolbar.

e. Click **Slide 3** in the Slides pane. Click the **Pictures icon** in the left content placeholder. Browse to the student data files, locate and select *cf01p1Website.jpg*, and then click **Insert**. Close the Design Ideas pane if it opens.

f. Ensure the picture is selected. Click the **Picture Format tab** and click **More** in the Picture Styles group to open the Pictures Style Gallery. Use the ScreenTips to locate and select the **Reflected Perspective Right**. Click the **Height box** in the Size group and type **4**. Press **Enter**. Place the pointer over the image to display a 4-headed arrow ⊹ and drag to position the image so it is centered vertically in the open space.

g. Click the **Home tab** and click the **Dialog Box Launcher** in the Clipboard group. If there is content in the Clipboard, click Clear All to remove all previously cut or copied items from the Clipboard. Click **Slide 7** and select all the placeholder content. Right-click the selected text and click **Cut** from the shortcut menu.

> **MAC TROUBLESHOOTING:** Select the text and press command+X. Click Slide 4 and press control+V. Repeat for Step h. Skip to Step j.

h. Click **Slide 5** and select all the placeholder content. Press **Ctrl+X**. (On a Mac, press command+X.)

i. Click **Slide 4** and click the **content placeholder**. Click **Paste All** in the Clipboard. Close the Clipboard.

j. Click **Slide Sorter** on the status bar. Click **Slide 5** and press **Delete**. Click **Slide 6** and press **Delete**. Drag **Slide 2** to the right of **Slide 5**. Click the **View tab** and click **Normal**.

k. Click **Slide 6** in the Slides pane. Click the **Insert tab**, click **Pictures** in the Images group, select **Stock Images**, and then click **Cutout People**. Type **Stanley** in the Images search box. Select the picture where the man is waving his hand in a hello gesture and click **Insert**. Resize and position the image so it displays attractively on the slide.

l. Click **Slide 1**. Click the **Insert tab** and click **Header & Footer** in the Text group. Click the **Slide number check box** to select it. Click the **Footer check box** to select it and type **Business Owners Association Presentation**. Click **Don't show on title slide check box** to select it. Click **Apply to All**.

m. Click the **Insert tab** and click **Header & Footer** in the Text group. Click the **Notes and Handouts tab** in the Header & Footer dialog box. Click to select the **Header check box** and type **Designing Webpages Presentation**. Click **Apply to All**.

n. Click the **Review tab** and click **Spelling** in the Proofing group. In the Spelling pane, click **Change** or **Ignore** to make changes as needed. The words *KompoZer* and *Nvu* are not misspelled, so you should ignore them when they are flagged. Click **OK** when you have finished checking spelling.

o. Click the **File tab** and click **Info**. Click the **Add a Tag box** and type **business, BOA, Web design**.

p. Click **Print**. Click the **Full Page Slides arrow** and select **6 Slides Horizontal** to see a preview of all the slides as a handout.

> **MAC TROUBLESHOOTING:** Click the File menu, click Print, and then click Show Details. In the Print dialog box, click the Layout arrow and select Handouts (6 slides per page).

q. Click the **Portrait Orientation arrow** and select **Landscape Orientation**. Click **Save**.

r. Close the file. Exit PowerPoint. Based on your instructor's directions, submit: cf01p1Design_LastFirst.pptx

2 Upscale Bakery

You have always been interested in baking and have worked in the field for several years. You now have an opportunity to devote yourself full time to your career as the CEO of a company dedicated to baking cupcakes and pastries. One of the first steps in getting the business off the ground is developing a business plan so that you can request financial support. You will use Word to develop your business plan. Refer to Figure 1.48 as you complete this exercise.

FIGURE 1.48 Upscale Bakery Business Plan

a. Open the Word document *cf01p2Bakery.docx*. Click the **File tab**, click **Save As**, and save the file as **cf01p2Bakery_LastFirst**.

b. Click the **Design tab**, click **Themes**, and then select **Slice**.

c. Select the paragraphs beginning with *Our Staff* and ending with *(Nutritionist)*. Click the **Home tab** and click **Cut** in the Clipboard group. Click to the left of *Our Products* and click **Paste**.

d. Select the text **Your name** in the first bullet in the *Our Staff* section and replace it with your first and last names. Select the entire bullet list in the *Our Staff* section. On the Mini Toolbar, click the **Font Size arrow** and select **11**. Keep the text selected.

e. Click **Format Painter** in the Clipboard group. Drag the Format Painter pointer across all four *Our Products* bullets to change the bullets' font size to **11 pt**.

f. Click the **Search box** and type **footer**. Click **Add a Footer**, scroll to locate the **Facet (Odd Page) footer**, and click to add it to the page. Keep the footer open.

g. Click the **Title control box** in the footer and type **UpscaleBakery.com**. Click the **Subtitle control box** in the footer and type **401-555-8234**. Click **Close Header and Footer** in the Close group on the Header & Footer tab.

h. Select the title text **Upscale Bakery and Catering**. Right-click the selected text and click **Bold** from the Mini Toolbar.

i. Triple-click any word in the last line of the document to select the words *Insert and position picture here*, and press **Ctrl+X**. Click the **Insert tab**, click **Pictures** in the Illustrations group, and click **Stock Images**.

j. Click in the **Image search box**, type **cupcakes**. Select any **cupcake image** and click **Insert**. Do not deselect the image.

> **TROUBLESHOOTING:** If you are unable to find a cupcake image in Stock Images, you can use *cf01p2Cupcake.jpg* from the student data files.

k. Ensure the Picture Format tab is active, and in the Picture Styles group, use the ScreenTips to locate and select the **Drop Shadow Rectangle**.

l. Click the **Dialog Box Launcher** in the Size group and ensure that Lock aspect ratio is selected. Click **OK**. Click the **Shape width box** in the Size group and change the width to **2.5**.

m. Click outside the picture.

n. Press **Ctrl+Home**. Click **Customize Quick Access Toolbar** and select **Editor** (ignore if present). Click **Check Document** on the QAT. Correct the spelling error (ignore the suggestion to change *Sughand*) and click **OK**.

o. Click the **View tab** and select **Draft** in the Views group. Click **Print Layout** in the Views group and click **One Page** in the Zoom group.

p. Click the **Layout tab** and click **Margins** in the Page Setup group. Change to **Moderate Margins**.

q. Click the **File tab** and click **Info**. In the Properties section, click the **Add a tag box** and type **business plan**. Click **Add an author** and add your first and last name to the Author property. Right-click the **current author** (it should say Exploring Series) and click **Remove Person**.

r. Click **Print** in the File tab. Change the number of copies to **2**.

s. Click **Save** in the File tab. Close the file. Exit Word. Based on your instructor's directions, submit:

cf01p2Bakery_LastFirst.docx

Mid-Level Exercises

1 Reference Letter

MyLab IT Grader

You are an instructor at a local community college. A student asked you to provide her with a letter of reference for a job application. You have used Word to prepare the letter, but now you want to make a few changes before it is finalized.

a. Open the Word document *cf01m1RefLetter.docx* and save it as **cf01m1RefLetter_LastFirst**.

b. Change the theme to **Gallery**. Point to Colors in the Document Formatting group and read the ScreenTip. Click **Colors** and select **Red**.

c. Insert a **Blank footer**. Type **410 Wellington Parkway, Huntsville, AL 35611**. Center the footer. Close the footer.

d. Place the insertion point at the end of Professor Smith's name in the signature line. Press **Enter** twice. Search for an icon from Stock Images using the keyword **college**. Select either version of the building icon. Right-click the icon, click **Fill** from the Mini Toolbar and select **Dark Red, Accent 1**. Click **Center** in the Paragraph group on the Home tab.

e. Press **Ctrl+Home**. Select all the text in the letter, starting with the date and ending with *Professor Smith*. Using the Mini Toolbar, change the font to **Cambria** and the font size to **12**.

f. Right-click the word **considerate** in the second paragraph starting with *Stacy is an* and click **Synonyms** from the shortcut menu. Replace *considerate* with **thoughtful**.

g. Triple-click any word in the last paragraph—beginning with *In my opinion*—to select all the text in that paragraph. Use cut and paste to move the selected text before the second paragraph—beginning with *Stacy is an intelligent*.

h. Use Editor to correct all spelling and grammar errors. Make any spelling changes that are suggested. Stacy's last name is spelled correctly. Review the Conciseness suggestions. Ignore the suggestion to change *a valuable asset*. Accept all other suggestions.

i. Change the margins to **Narrow**.

j. Customize the QAT to add **Print Preview and Print**. (On a Mac, add Print.) Preview the document as it will display when printed.

k. Click **Info** on the File tab. Add the tag **reference** to the Properties for the file.

l. Save and close the file. Exit Word. Based on your instructor's directions, submit: cf01m1RefLetter_LastFirst.docx

2 Medical Monitoring

MyLab IT Grader

You are enrolled in a health informatics study program in which you learn to manage databases related to health fields. For a class project, your instructor requires that you monitor your blood pressure, recording your findings in an Excel worksheet. You have recorded the week's data and will now make a few changes before printing the worksheet for submission.

a. Open the Excel workbook *cf01m2Tracker.xlsx* and save it as **cf01m2Tracker_LastFirst**.

b. Change the theme to **Crop**.

c. Click in **cell I1** (to the right of *Name*) and type your first and last names. Press **Enter**.

d. Select cells **H1, I1, J1**, and **K1**. Cut the selected cells and paste to **cell C2**. Click **cell A1**.

e. Press **Ctrl+A**. (On a Mac, press command+A.) Change the font of the worksheet to **Arial**.

f. Add **Spelling** to the QAT and check the spelling for the worksheet. Correct any errors that are found.

g. Select cells **E22, F22**, and **G22**. Click the **Borders arrow** in the Font group on the Home tab and select **Top and Double Bottom Border**.

h. Click **cell A1** and insert an **Online Picture** of your choice related to blood pressure. Resize the image to **1"** Height and ensure the image is in cell A1. Apply the **Drop Shadow Rectangle Picture Style** to the image.

i. Insert a footer in the center section using the **Page Number** header and footer element. Use the **File Name** header and footer element in the right section of the footer. Click in a cell on the worksheet.

j. Insert a header in the right section using the **Current Date** header and footer element.

k. Change the orientation to **Landscape**. Change the margins so Left and Right are **1.5"** and Top and Bottom are **1"**. Center the worksheet both vertically and horizontally. Close the dialog box.

l. Add **blood pressure** as a tag and adjust print settings to print two copies. You will not actually print two copies unless directed by your instructor.

m. Save and close the file. Exit Excel. Based on your instructor's directions, submit: cf01m2Tracker_LastFirst.xlsx

Running Case

New Castle County Technical Services

New Castle County Technical Services (NCCTS) provides technical support for companies in the greater New Castle County, Delaware, area. The company has been in operation since 2011 and has grown to become one of the leading technical service companies in the area. NCCTS has prided itself on providing great service at reasonable costs, but as you begin to review the budget for next year and the rates your competitors are charging, you are realizing that it may be time to increase some of your rates. You have prepared a worksheet with suggested rates and will include those rates in a memo to the CFO. You will format the worksheet, copy the data to the Clipboard, and use the Clipboard to paste the information into a memo. You will then modify the formatting of the memo, check the spelling, and ensure the document is ready for distribution before sending it on to the CFO.

a. Open the Excel workbook *cf01r1NCCTSRates.xlsx* and save it as **cf01r1NCCTSRates_LastFirst**.

b. Select **cells A4:C4**. Click **More** in the Styles group on the Home tab and select the cell style **Heading 2**.

c. Select **cells A5:C5**. Press **Ctrl** (or command on a Mac) and select cells **A7:C7**. Change the font color to **Red** in Standard Colors.

d. Select **cells A5:C10** and increase the font size to **12**.

e. Select cells **A4:C10**. Open the **Office Clipboard**. Clear the Office Clipboard if items display. Click **Copy** in the Clipboard group. Keep Excel open.

f. Open the Word document *cf01r1NCCTSMemo.docx* and save it as **cf01r1NCCTSMemo_LastFirst**.

g. Change *Your Name* in the From: line to your own name.

h. Press **Ctrl+Home**. Insert image *cf01r1Logo.jpg*. Resize the height to **1"**.

i. Change the document theme to **Retrospect**.

j. Place the insertion point in the blank line above the paragraph beginning with *Please*.

k. Open **Clipboard** and click the item in the Clipboard that was copied from the NCCTS Rates workbook. **Paste** the content. Clear and close the Clipboard. (On a Mac, click the Paste arrow.)

l. Check the spelling. Correct all grammar and spelling mistakes.

m. Increase left and right margins to **1.5"**.

n. Insert a footer and click **Edit Footer**. Click **Document Info** in the Insert group on the Header & Footer tab. Click **File Name**. Click **Close Header and Footer**.

o. Enter **2022**, **rates** as tags.

p. Save and close the files. Exit Word and Excel. Based on your instructor's directions, submit: cf01r1NCCTSMemo_LastFirst.docx

Disaster Recovery

Résumé Enhancement

You are applying for a new position and you have asked a friend to look at your résumé. She has a better eye for details than you do, so you want her to let you know about any content or formatting errors. She has left some instructions pointing out where you can improve the résumé. Open the Word document *cf01d1Resume.docx* and save it as **cf01d1Resume_LastFirst**. Add your name, address, phone number, and email address in the placeholders at the top of the document. Change the theme of the résumé to Office. Bold all the job titles and dates held in the Experience section and the university and location in the Education section. Italicize all company names and locations. Italicize the major and date in the Education section. Use Format Painter to copy the formatting of the bullets in the Software Intern description and apply them to the bullets in the other job description. Change the margins to Narrow. Add résumé as a tag. Check the spelling and grammar. Save and close the file. Exit Word. Based on your instructor's directions, submit: cf01d1Resume_LastFirst.docx

Cumulative Exercise

As a nutritionist, you have been asked to create a presentation about healthy eating and to provide recipes for easy-to-make dishes. You decided to talk about making pita bread and hummus as a part of a healthy lunch when paired with a salad. You have most of the presentation done. You just need to add a few images and format some text.

Open and Save Files

You will open, review, and save a PowerPoint presentation.

1. Open the PowerPoint presentation *cf01c1Recipes.pptx* and save it as **cf01c1Recipes_LastFirst**.

Apply a Theme and Change the View

You applied the Retrospect theme when you started creating the presentation, but you think a different theme will be better now that the slides are built out more. You change the view to see all the slides and notice that a slide is out of order. So, you change a slide's location.

2. Apply the **Office theme** to the presentation.
3. Change to **Slide Sorter view**. Drag **Slide 2** to become **Slide 5**.
4. Return to **Normal view**.

Select Text, Move Text, and Format Text

You make some changes to the placement of text and modify the format of text.

5. Click **Slide 3** and click the text box in slide title area that says *Makes 10 – 12*. **Cut** and **paste** it on the slide title area of **Slide 2**.
6. Select the text in the box for Step 1 on Slide 3 and change the font size to **12**.
7. Select **Hummus** on Slide 5 and apply **bold** and change the font color to **Orange, Accent 2, Darker 50%.**
8. Click **Slide 3,** change *frothy* in the third paragraph of Step 1 to the synonym **foamy**.

Insert and Modify a Picture

You want to add a picture to Slide 2 and modify the size. You also add a style to all the images that show the process of making pita bread to give them a more distinct appearance. Lastly, you modify the size of the image on another slide to be more consistent with the image on Slide 2.

9. Click **Slide 2** and insert the picture *cf01c1Pita.jpg* from your data files.

10. Drag the picture so the top left corner is just under the colored title bar at the top of the slide. Resize the picture width to **8.8"**.
11. Apply the **Center Shadow Rectangle Picture Style** to all 7 images on Slides 3 and 4.
12. Click **Slide 6** and use the bottom right sizing handle to enlarge the image so it fills the entire slide.

Use the Search Box

You notice the images on a slide are not aligned with each other. You use the Search box to help with the alignment. You also need help to change a list of ingredients to SmartArt. You know that there is a way to convert text to SmartArt, but you cannot remember where it is. You use the Search box to help you with this function, too.

13. Click **Slide 3**, press **Ctrl** (or command on a Mac) and select all three images. Type **Align** in the Search box. Click **Align Objects** and select **Align Bottom**.
14. Select the list of ingredients on **Slide 2**. Use the Search box to search **SmartArt**.
15. Select **Convert to SmartArt Graphic** from the search results. Click **More SmartArt Graphics** and select **Lined List**.

Insert Header and Footer

You want to give the audience printed handouts of your presentation, so you add a header and footer to the handouts, with page numbers and information to identify you and the topic.

16. Add **slide numbers** to all slides and **page numbers** to all handouts.
17. Add **your email address** as a footer in all handouts.
18. Add **Creating a Healthy Meal** as a header in all handouts.

Customize the Quick Access Toolbar and Check Spelling

You know to review the presentation for spelling errors. Because you regularly check spelling, you add a button on the QAT. You also add a button to preview and print your presentation for added convenience. You then check the presentation for spelling errors.

19. Add **Spelling** to the QAT.
20. Add **Print Preview and Print** to the QAT. (On a Mac, add Print.)
21. Check the spelling of the presentation. Make any changes necessary.

Use Print Preview, Change Print Layout, and Adjust Document Properties

You want to print handouts of the presentation so that 2 slides will display on one page.

22. Click the **Print Preview and Print command** on the QAT to preview the document as it will display when printed.

23. Change Full Page Slides to **2 Slides**.

> **MAC TROUBLESHOOTING:** Click the File menu and click Print. Click Show Details. Click Layout and choose Handouts (3 slides per page).

24. Change the Page Orientation of the handouts to **Portrait**.

25. Adjust the print settings to print **two** copies. You will not actually print two copies unless directed by your instructor.

26. Change document properties to add **recipes, pita, hummus** as tags and add your name as another author.

27. Save and close the file. Exit PowerPoint. Based on your instructor's directions, submit: cf01c1Recipes_LastFirst.pptx

Introduction to Word

LEARNING OUTCOME

You will develop a document using features of Microsoft Word.

OBJECTIVES & SKILLS: After you read this chapter, you will be able to:

CASE STUDY | Middleton Community Career Center

You are employed part-time with the Middleton Community Career Center (MCCC), an organization designed to assist those in the community who are dealing with financial and other hardships, with special emphasis on improving their employment situation. Services include job training, GED tutoring, access to interview-appropriate clothing, workplace skills training, and small scholarships. Local partnerships with domestic violence centers and employment services assist in providing training and affording safe housing for people in the program. The center's primary goal is to provide avenues for those accepted to MCCC to become productive members of the local workforce, gaining confidence and independence in the process.

Because you are familiar with Word, your responsibility is the preparation of class material that introduces documents typically used in a job search. Through workplace readiness classes, MCCC staff encourage acquisition of good interview skills and the use of Word in developing such documents as a cover letter and a résumé. Using templates where available, you will design a sample résumé and cover letter for use in a workplace readiness class led by a local college professor. Because such documents might be submitted online or otherwise shared with others, the documents you develop should vary in format as well as file type. You want students to be aware of a range of possibilities, all available within the Word environment. You will ensure that documents used in the workplace readiness class are formatted attractively and are accessible to those with visual impairments. They will also be well documented as the property of MCCC and searchable using tags.

Organize a Document

NDAB Creativity/Shutterstock

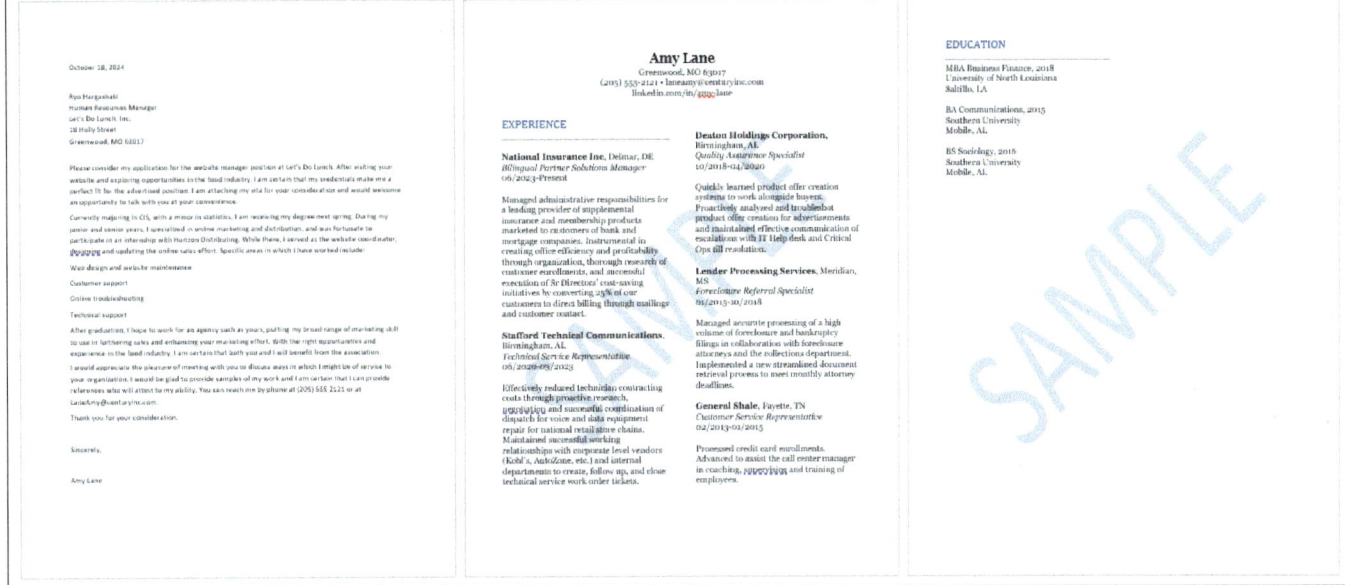

FIGURE 1.1 Middleton Community Career Center Documents

CASE STUDY | Middleton Community Career Center

Starting Files	Files to Be Submitted	MyLab IT HOE Grader
w01h1Letter	w01h3ItalianVita_LastFirst	
Blank document	w01h3Job_LastFirst	
w01h2Vita	w01h3Job_LastFirst.pdf	

MyLab IT Grader: This project is available as a Hands-On Exercise project in MyLab IT.

Document Basics

Word processing software is one of the most commonly used types of software in homes, schools, and businesses. You can create letters, reports, research papers, newsletters, brochures, and all sorts of documents with word processing software. You can even create and send email, produce webpages, post to social media sites, and update blogs. People around the world—students, office assistants, managers, and professionals in all fields—use word processing programs such as ***Microsoft Word*** for a variety of tasks. Figure 1.2 shows examples of documents created in Word. If a project requires collaboration online or between offices, Word facilitates sharing documents, tracking changes, viewing comments, and efficiently producing a document to which several authors can contribute. By using Word to develop a research paper, you can create citations, a bibliography, a table of contents, a cover page, an index, and other reference pages. To enhance a document, you can change colors, add interesting styles of text, insert graphics, and use tables to present data. With emphasis on saving documents to OneDrive, Word enables you to share these documents with others or access them from any device. Word is a comprehensive word processing solution, to say the least.

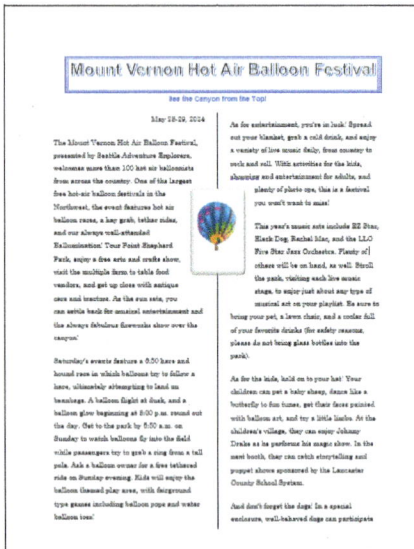
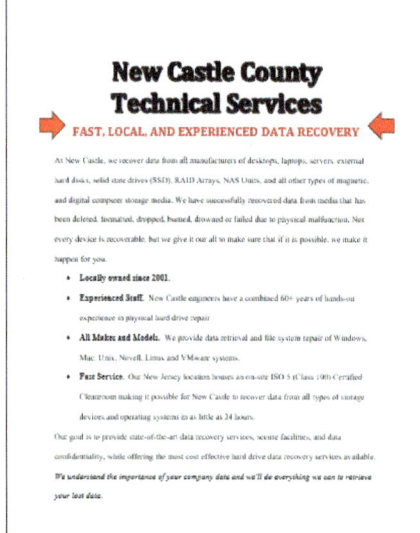
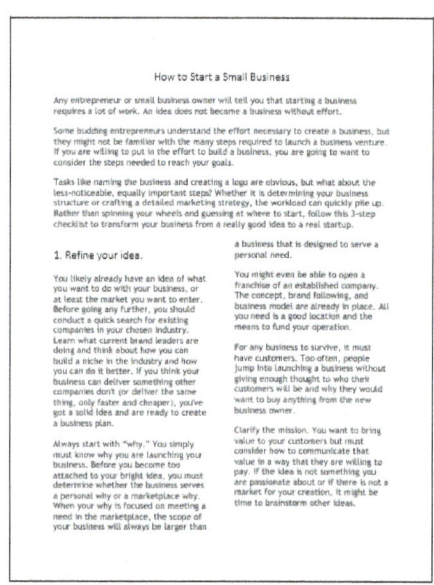

FIGURE 1.2 Sample Word Processing Documents

Communicating through the written word is an important, in fact, vital, task for any business or organization. Word processing software, such as Word, simplifies the technical task of preparing documents, but a word processor does not replace the writer. Be careful when phrasing a document so you are sure it is appropriate for the intended audience. Always remember that once you distribute a document, either on paper or electronically, you cannot retract the words. Therefore, you should always check a document carefully to be sure it conveys your message in the best way possible. Also, be sure to closely proofread every document you create because you cannot depend completely on a word processor to identify all spelling and grammatical errors. Although several word processors, including Word, provide predesigned documents (called templates) that include basic layouts for various tasks, it is ultimately up to you to compose well-worded documents. The role of business communication, including the written word, in the success or failure of a business cannot be overemphasized.

In this section, you will explore Word's interface, learn how to create a document, explore the use of templates, find and replace document content, and perform basic editing operations. Using Word options, you will explore ways to customize Word to suit your preferences and you will work with the AutoCorrect feature.

Begin and Edit a Document

When you open Word, your screen will be similar to Figure 1.3, although it may vary a bit depending upon your version of Word. You can create a blank document, or you can select from several types of templates. In addition, you can open a previously created document, perhaps selecting from the list of recent files, and then edit and print a document as you want.

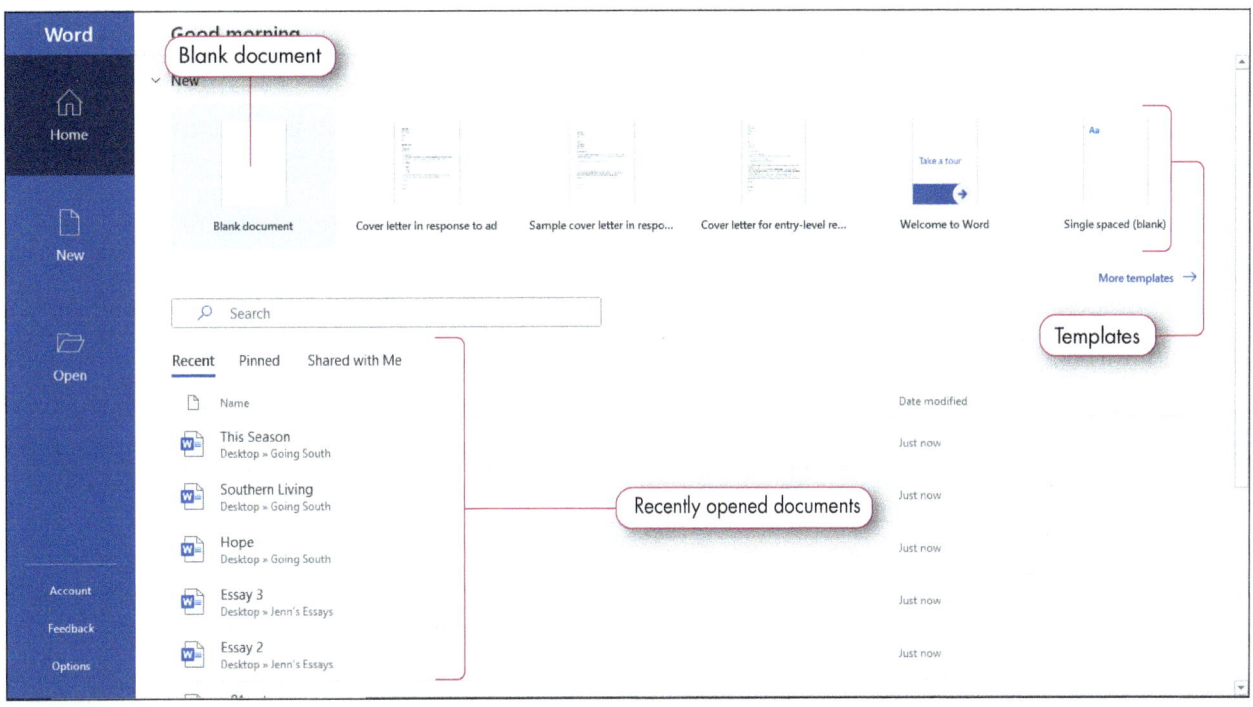

FIGURE 1.3 Word Document Options

STEP 1 ▶ Create a Document

To create a blank document, click Blank document when Word opens (refer to Figure 1.3). As you type text, the **_word wrap_** feature automatically pushes words to the next line when you reach the right margin, creating what is known as a soft return. The location of automatically generated soft returns changes as text is inserted or deleted, or as page features or settings, such as objects or margins, are added or changed. Such soft returns cannot be deleted.

Although word wrap is convenient, you may occasionally want to control when one line ends and another begins, such as at the end of a paragraph or a major section. Or perhaps you are typing several lines of an address or bulleted lines. In those cases, you can indicate that a line should end before text reaches the right margin. To do so, you can either insert a hard return or a soft return. When you press Enter, Word inserts a hard return. As a hard return is entered, a new paragraph begins, with any associated paragraph spacing separating the two paragraphs. In the case of multiple address lines, bulleted text, or text associated with objects such as SmartArt, however, you might want to avoid the paragraph space that results from a hard return. You can insert a manual soft return, or line break, when you press Shift+Enter at the end of any line of text. A new line begins after the soft return, but without any associated paragraph spacing. Manual soft returns, as opposed to the automatic soft returns generated by Word when the right margin is reached, are considered characters and can be deleted. Hard returns are also nonprinting characters that can be removed.

Actions such as a hard return, manual soft return, and even a tab or space are included in a document as nonprinting characters that are only visible when you make a point to display them. To show nonprinting characters, click Show/Hide on the Home tab (see Figure 1.4). The display of nonprinting characters enables you to troubleshoot a document and modify its appearance before printing or distributing. For example, if lines in a document end awkwardly, some not even extending to the right margin, you can check for the presence of poorly placed, or perhaps unnecessary, hard returns. Deleting the hard returns might realign the document so that lines end in better fashion. Just as you delete any other character by pressing Backspace or Delete, you can delete a nonprinting character. To turn off the display of nonprinting characters, click Show/Hide again.

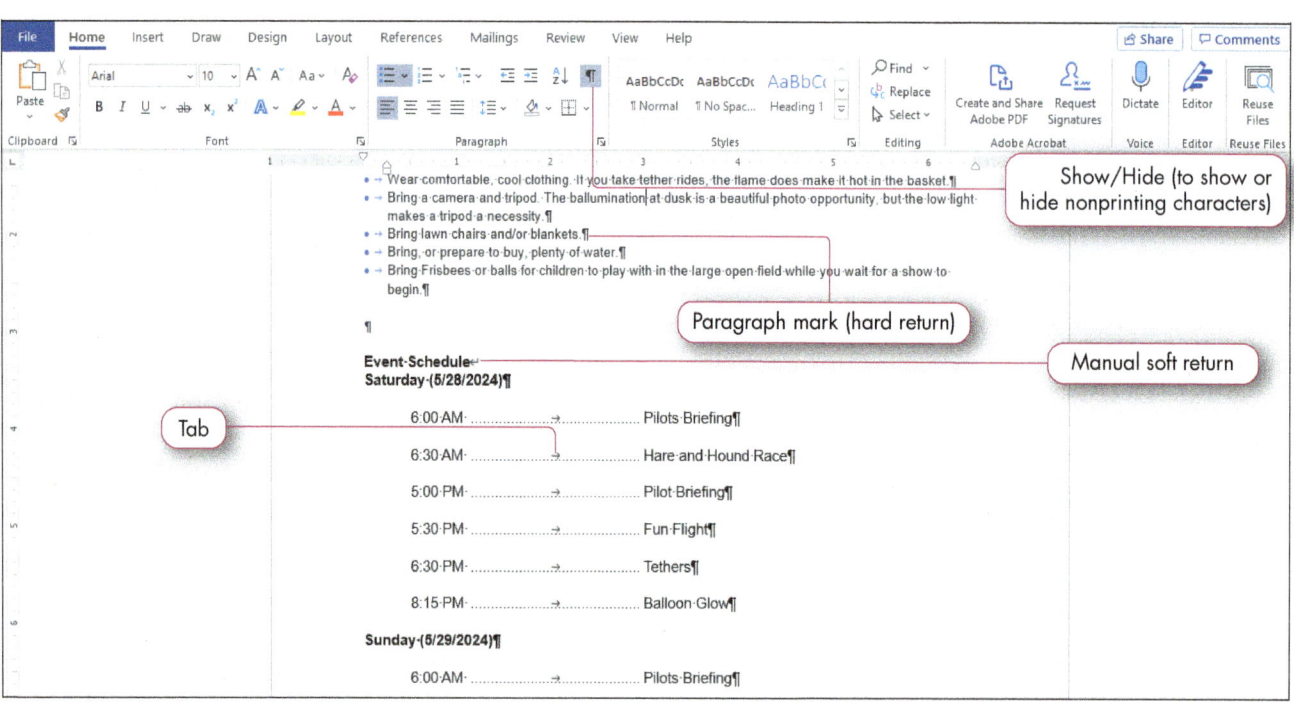

FIGURE 1.4 Display Nonprinting Characters

As you work with Word, you must understand that Word's definition of a paragraph and your definition are not likely to be the same. You would probably define a paragraph as a related set of sentences, which is correct in a literary sense. When the subject or direction of thought changes, a new paragraph begins. However, Word defines a paragraph as text that ends in a hard return. Even a blank line, created by pressing Enter, is considered a paragraph. Therefore, as a Word student, you will consider every line that ends in a hard return a paragraph. When you press Enter, a paragraph mark is displayed in the document if you choose to show nonprinting characters (refer to Figure 1.4).

Reuse Text

You might find occasion to reuse text from a previously created document. For example, a memo to employees describing new insurance benefits might borrow all wording from another document describing the same benefits to company retirees. Word facilitates the addition of all text from a saved document to any location within a document that is being developed. Reusing text can save development time, as existing text is inserted without the need to type it again and can also avoid introducing typing errors that are likely to occur if text is typed.

Inserting text from a previously saved document into one that is currently open incorporates all text from the saved document, unlike the copy and paste procedure that is often used to acquire only a portion of text from another document. Text that is copied and pasted must be drawn from a currently open document, whereas text that is reused is retrieved from a saved document without the need to first open it. If the intention is to include all text from a saved file into one that is being created, you will find that inserting text is an efficient way to accomplish that.

HOW TO

Insert text from another document:

1. Position the insertion point where the text is to be placed.
2. Click the Insert tab. Click the Object arrow (see Figure 1.5).
3. Click Text from File.
4. Navigate to the location of the source document and double-click the file name.

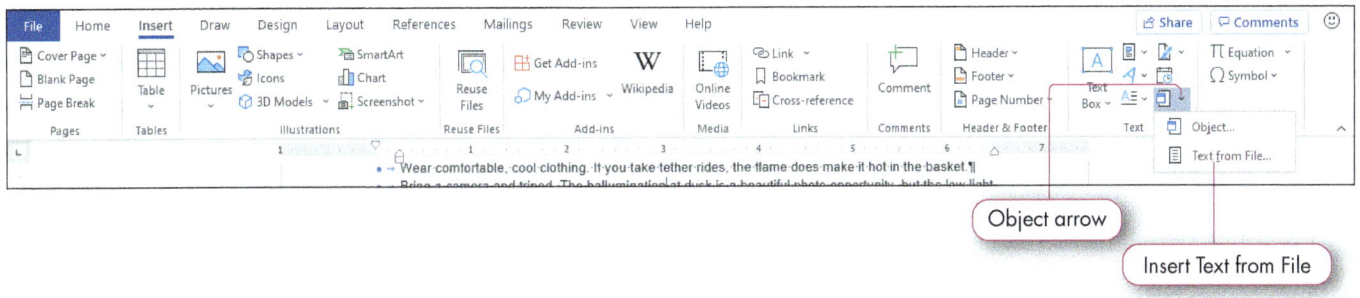

FIGURE 1.5 Insert Text from Another File

Use a Template

Developing a new document related to a specific scenario or with precise or elaborate formatting can be difficult. With that in mind, the developers of Word have included a library of *templates* from which you can select a predesigned document. You can then modify the document to suit your needs. Various types of templates are displayed when you first open Word, or when you click the File tab and click New. In addition to local templates—those that are available offline with a typical Word installation—Microsoft provides many more online. All online templates are displayed or searchable within Word when you begin the process of creating a new document, as shown in Figure 1.6. Microsoft continually updates content in the template library, so you are assured of having access to all the latest templates each time you open Word.

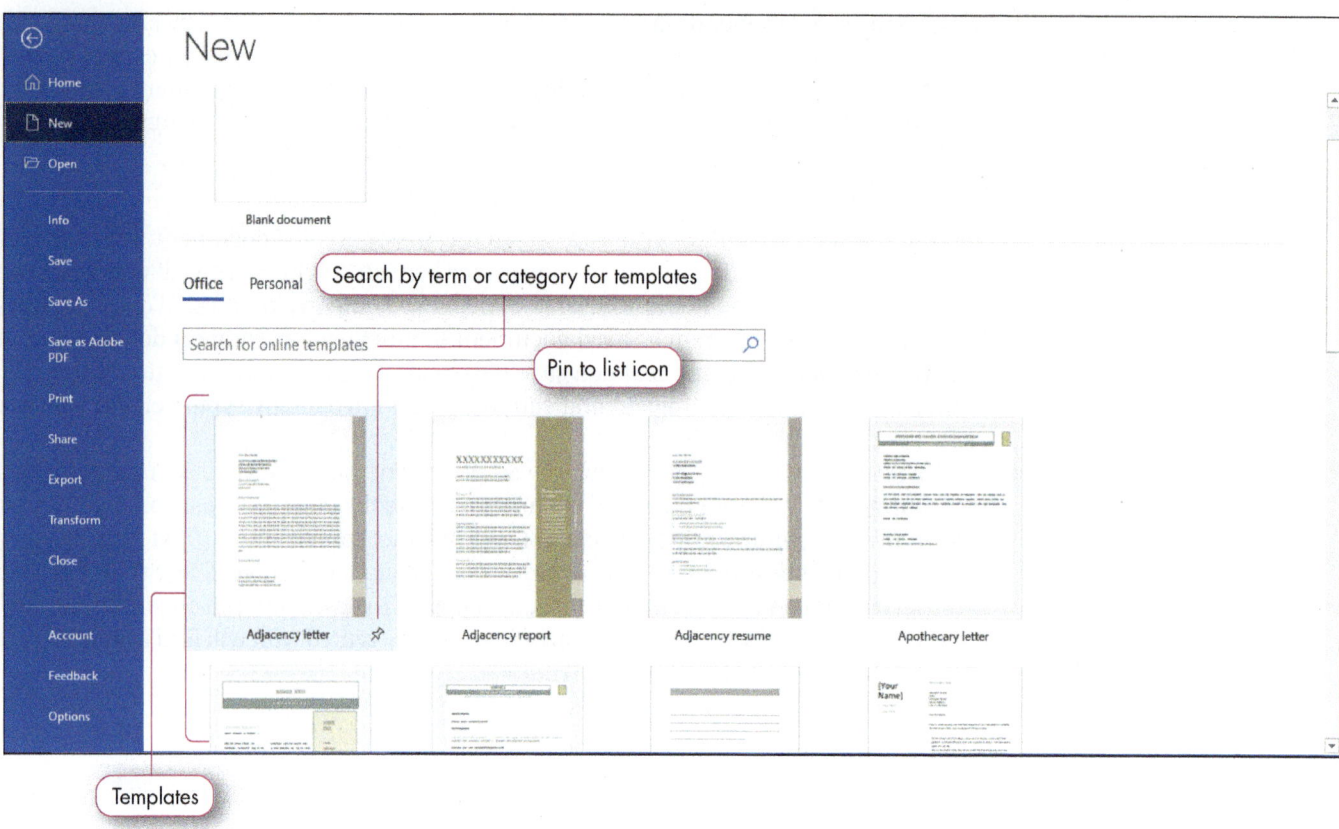

FIGURE 1.6 Work with Templates

Some templates are likely to become your favorites. Because you will want quick access to those templates, you can pin them to the top of the templates menu so they will always be available. Having pinned a template, you can also unpin it when it is no longer necessary. To pin a template, either right-click a favorite template and then pin it to the list or point to a template and click the horizontal Pin to list icon (refer to Figure 1.6). Unpin a template by completing the same steps but choosing to unpin.

STEP 2 Add Text and Navigate a Document

The *insertion point* indicates where the text you type will be placed. It is shown as a blinking vertical line in a Word document. It is important to remain aware of the location of the insertion point and to know how to move it to control where text is typed. Most often, you will move the insertion point by moving the pointer and clicking the location you want. You can also position the insertion point in other ways, including the use of arrow keys on the keyboard or by using shortcuts such as Ctrl+Home (to move to the beginning of the document) and Ctrl+End (to move to the end). (On a Mac, use the keyboard shortcuts command+fn+left arrow or command+fn+right arrow to move to the top or end of a document, respectively.) In addition, you can tap a touchscreen with a finger or stylus to reposition the insertion point.

If a document contains more text than will display onscreen at one time, click the horizontal or vertical scroll arrows (or drag a scroll bar) to view different parts of the document. An alternative is to press the Page Up or Page Down keys. Then, when the text you want to see displays, position the insertion point and continue editing the document. Be aware that using the scroll bar or scroll arrows to move the display does not reposition the insertion point. It merely enables you to see different parts of the document, leaving the insertion point where it was last positioned. Only when you click or tap in the document, or use a keyboard shortcut, is the insertion point moved.

Find and Replace Document Content

A typical document is a work in progress. As you develop a document, you might find that a word or phrase should be replaced. Perhaps the text is overused, or you might have consistently misspelled a name or term. In those instances, you can choose to find and replace a few or all occurrences of the text. In addition to identifying words or characters to be replaced, Word's Replace feature enables you to replace numbers, punctuation, and even to specify whether capitalization should be considered in results of a find operation.

HOW TO

Find and replace text in a document:

1. Click the Home tab and click Replace in the Editing group.
2. Type the text you want to find in the Find what box.
3. Type the text you want to replace it with in the Replace with box.
4. Click More, optionally, to specify additional search requirements, such as matching case or ignoring punctuation.
5. Click Replace All if you want to immediately replace all occurrences throughout the document. Or click Find Next if you want to stop at each occurrence, and then click Find Next to review each instance of the searched-for item in the document. At any occurrence, you can replace the item when you click Replace.

MAC HOW TO

Find and replace text in a document:

1. Click Edit on the menu bar (or click the magnifying glass arrow in the top right of the document and move to Step 3).
2. Click Find.
3. Click Replace.
4. Type the word or phrase sought and type the replacement in the Find and Replace Pane.
5. Click Find (to stop at each occurrence, clicking Replace to change any item), or click Replace All (to replace all occurrences). Click OK.

> **TIP: USING REPLACE ALL**
> Use caution when selecting the Replace All option during a Find and Replace operation. You might find unanticipated matches that should not be changed, but the global Replace All operation will change all without stopping for your consideration. Conversely, the Find Next option enables you to consider each replacement before invoking it. You should only use the Replace All option if you are absolutely certain that nothing will be unintentionally replaced.

Occasionally, it might be necessary to locate a word or phrase, regardless of whether you plan to change or replace it. Perhaps you are searching for a particular term, or the mention of a specific name, so that it can be modified. Other times, you are searching through a lengthy document for a certain text occurrence, with no intention of changing anything. Word's Navigation Pane enables you to search for text, with results displayed wherever they occur in the document. It is not typically used to replace text but is instead a practical tool for finding text that you may not intend to change. It serves as a quick way to identify and perhaps move to a specific location.

The Navigation Pane is displayed on the left side of the Word document, enabling you to type a search term, with results subsequently shown. To display the Navigation Pane, click Find in the Editing group on the Home tab, or click the View tab and select Navigation Pane in the Show group. (On a Mac, click View on the menu bar, point to Sidebar, and then click Navigation. Also, you can press shift+command+H.)

The Navigation Pane includes three tabs, Headings, Pages, and Results (see Figure 1.7). Each tab shows results of a search in a different way. The Headings tab displays a list of all text formatted with a Heading style, including only those document sections that contain the searched text. The Pages tab includes a thumbnail preview of each page in the document that includes a search result, and the Results tab shows a list of text that matches the search term or phrase, with each find highlighted in the document on the right. Figure 1.7 shows the Results tab.

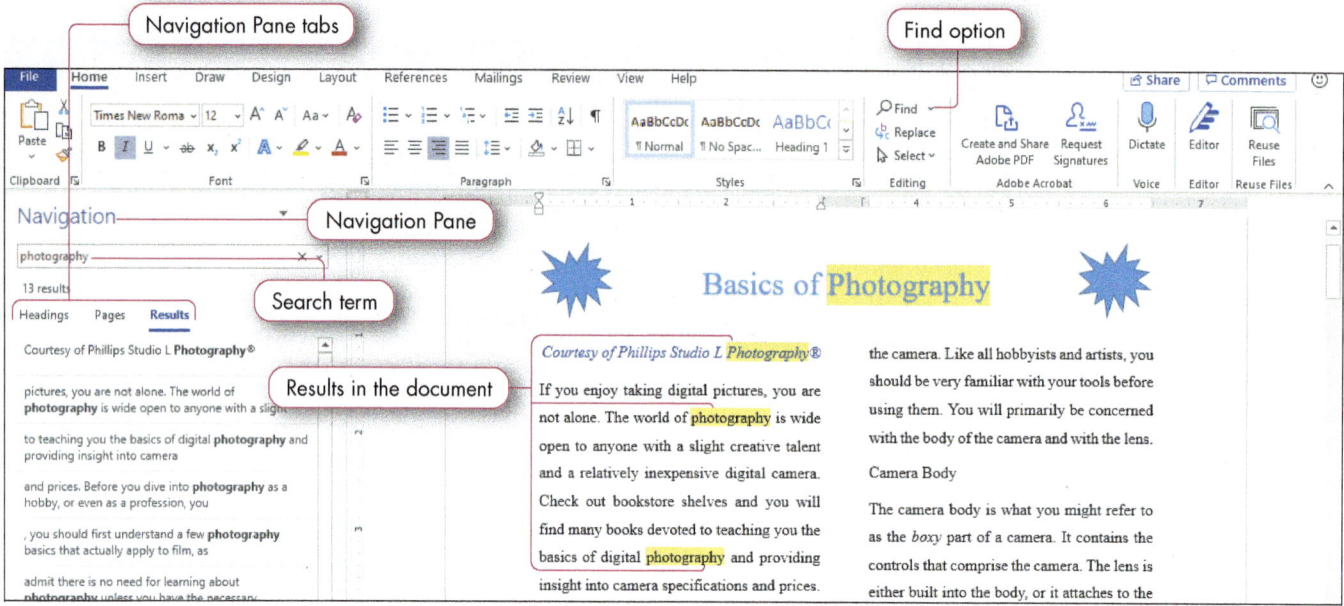

FIGURE 1.7 Display the Navigation Pane

STEP 4 › Review Spelling and Grammar

It is important to create a document free of spelling and grammatical errors. One of the easiest ways to lose credibility with readers is to allow such errors to occur. Choose words that are appropriate and that best convey your intentions in writing or editing a document. Word provides tools on the Review tab that simplify the tasks of reviewing a document for errors, identifying proper wording, and providing insight into unfamiliar words.

A word considered by Word to be misspelled is underlined with a red wavy line. A possible grammatical mistake or word usage error is underlined in blue. Stylistic issues, which are not actually mistakes but are constructs that could possibly be rephrased for clarity or simplicity, are indicated with a dashed blue underline. Various types of errors are shown in Figure 1.8. To correct possible grammatical or word usage errors in a document, right-click an underlined error and select the correct option from one or more choices that may be displayed. You can instead choose to ignore the concern or add a flagged word to the Office dictionary so it will be recognized as a valid term.

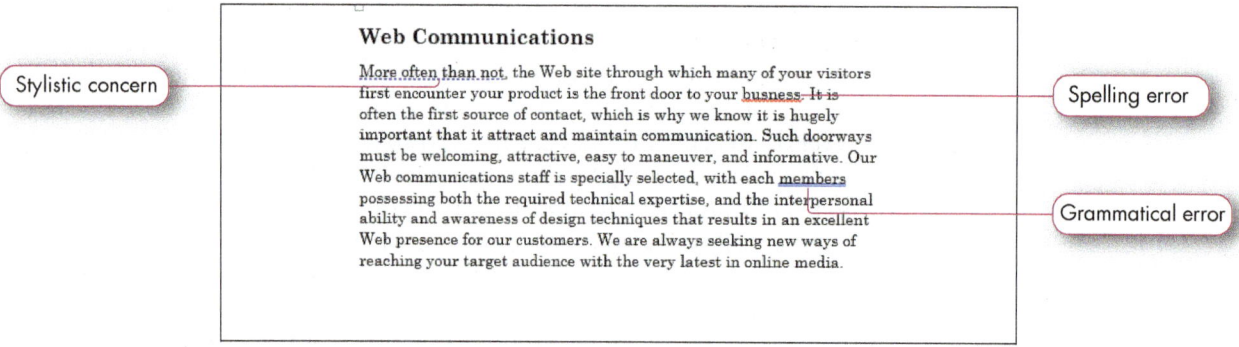

FIGURE 1.8 Spelling and Word Usage Errors

Correcting each error individually by right-clicking can become time-consuming, especially if there are many mistakes. In that case, Word can check an entire document, displaying results in the Editor pane. To check an entire document for spelling, grammatical, and writing concerns, use the Review tab to check the document, as shown in Figure 1.9. Choose a correction or refinement type in the Editor pane to step through each occurrence of that type of issue.

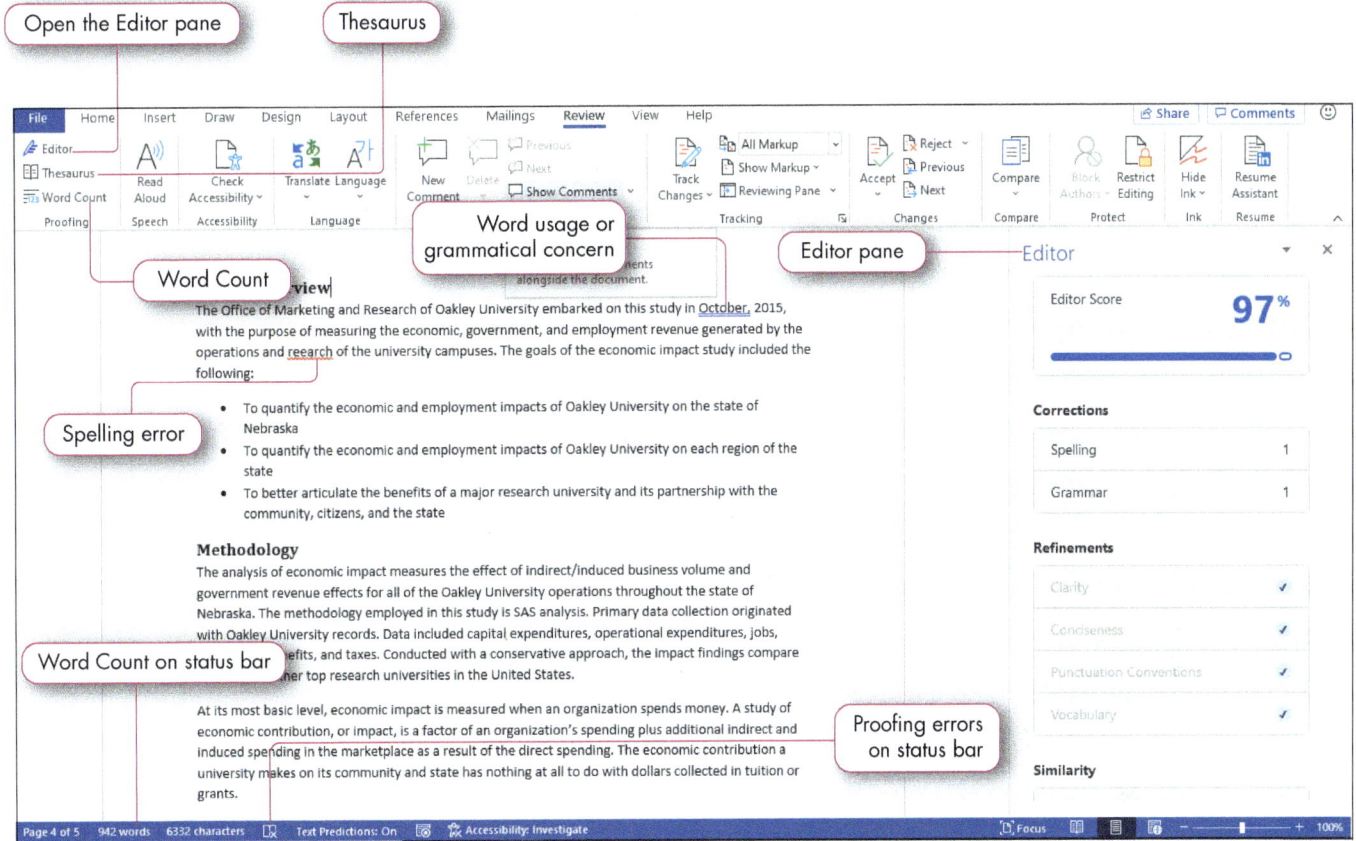

FIGURE 1.9 Options for Proofing a Document

As an alternative to identifying errors, click Proofing errors on the status bar (refer to Figure 1.9) to display the Editor pane. By default, Word automatically checks the entire open document for spelling, grammatical, and word usage errors, displaying an *x* on the status bar if errors are found. Click the Proofing errors icon and choose a category of error or refinement in the Editor pane to step through flagged concerns, one at a time. If, instead, you see a check mark on the Proofing errors icon, the document appears to be error free. The document in Figure 1.9 contains at least one error, as indicated by the Proofing errors icon on the status bar.

Never depend completely on Word to catch all errors; always proofread a document yourself. For example, typing the word *fee* when you meant to type *free* is not an error that Word would typically catch, because *fee* is not actually misspelled and might not be flagged as a word usage error, depending upon the sentence context.

Words do not always come easily. Occasionally, you might want to find a synonym (a word with the same meaning as another) for a particular word. Word provides a handy ***thesaurus*** for just such an occasion. In addition to providing synonyms, Word's thesaurus also includes antonyms (words with the opposite meaning) for a selected word, if any are available. To identify a synonym, select a word in a document and choose Thesaurus on the Review tab (refer to Figure 1.9). Point to a synonym and click the arrow that displays to insert the word. You can also right-click a selected word and point to Synonyms on the shortcut menu. Select a synonym from a subsequent list of words or click Thesaurus to open the Thesaurus pane for more options.

You can identify a synonym for a word that is not in the current document. In that case, open the thesaurus, type the word for which you want a synonym in the Thesaurus pane, and begin a search. The Thesaurus pane is shown in Figure 1.10. Select from the list presented.

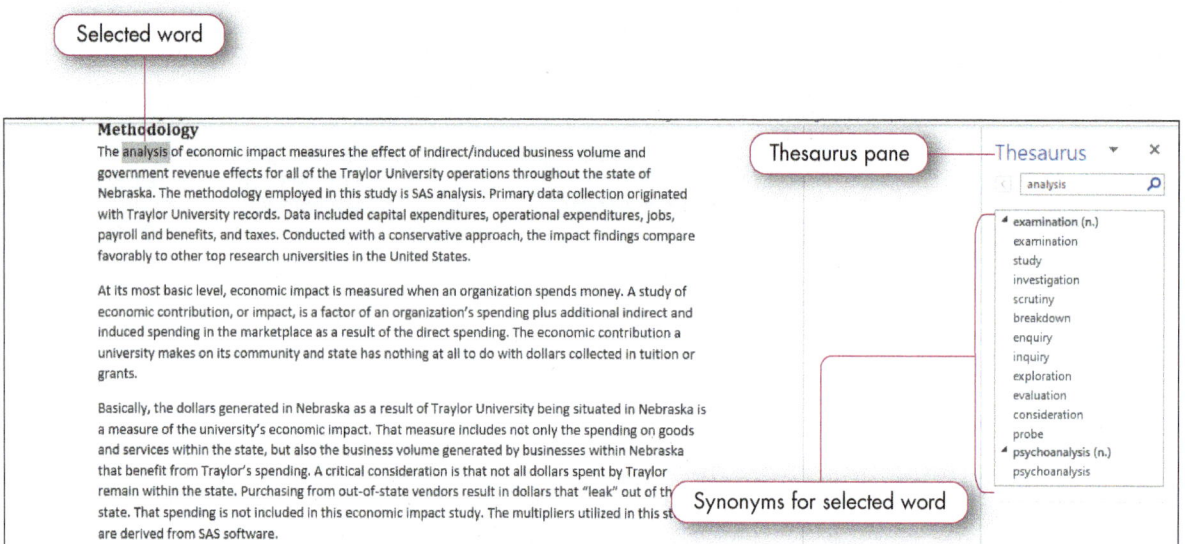

FIGURE 1.10 Thesaurus Pane

TIP: COUNTING WORDS

Occasionally, you might need to know how many words are included in a document, or in a selected portion of a document. For example, your English instructor might require a minimum word count for an essay. The status bar provides a running total of the number of words typed in a document thus far, or the total number of words for a completed document. You can also find Word Count on the Review tab in the Proofing group (refer to Figure 1.9). You can also display character count on the status bar when you right-click the status bar and ensure that Character Count (with spaces) is selected.

Especially when editing or collaborating on a document created by someone else, you might come across a word with which you are unfamiliar. Select Search in the Research group on the References tab to peruse additional information related to a selected word (see Figure 1.11). You can also right-click a selected word to show related information. The Search pane displays links, a definition, and even videos if available, related to a selected term.

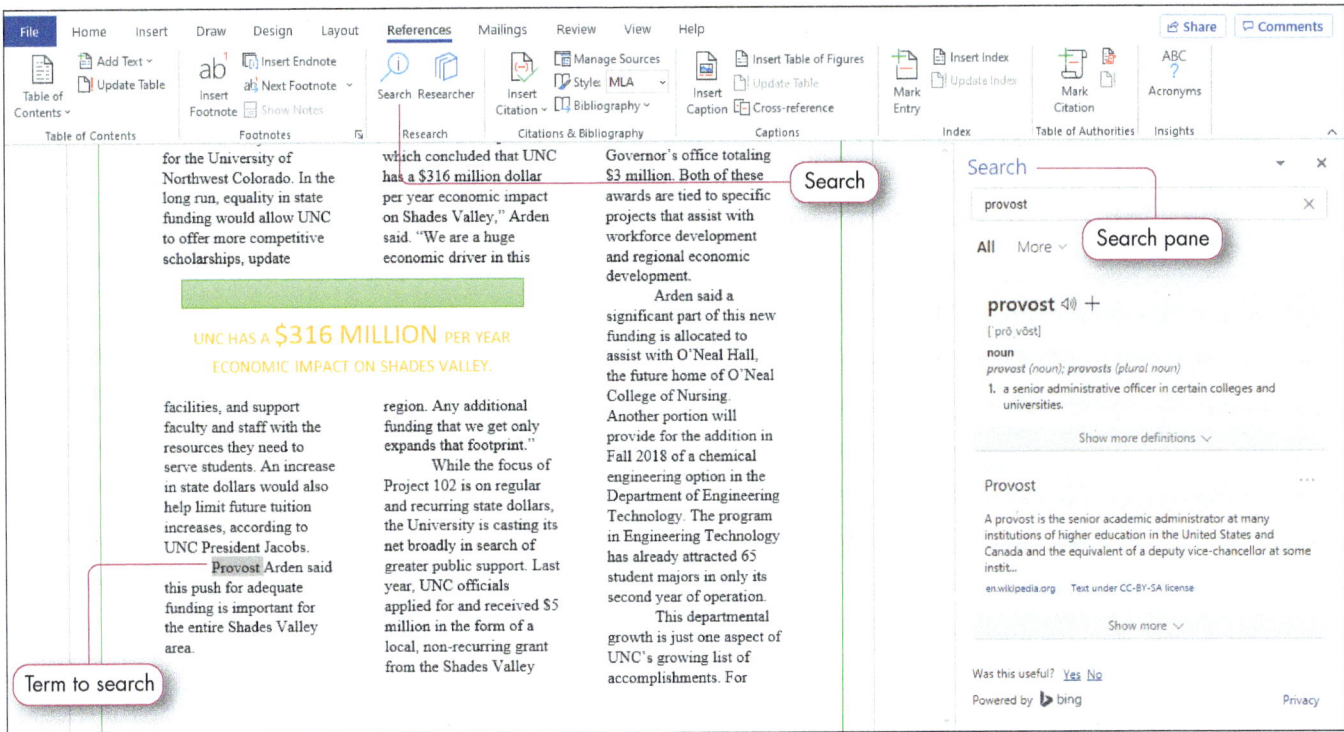

FIGURE 1.11 Use Search

Customize Word

As installed, Word is immediately useful. However, you might find options that you would prefer to customize so that your Word installation is personalized and effective for your specific use. You might want to change the default location to which documents are saved, or maybe you prefer a particular theme or background. These and other options are available for customization when you select Word Options.

Explore Word Options

By default, certain Word settings are determined and in place when you begin a Word document. For example, unless you specify otherwise, Word will automatically check spelling as you type. Similarly, the Mini Toolbar will automatically display when text is selected, although it will not show on a Mac. Although those and other settings are most likely what you will prefer, there may be occasions when you want to change them. When you change Word Options, you change them for all documents—not just the currently open file. To modify Word Options, click the File tab and select Options. Then choose from categories of options, as shown in Figure 1.12.

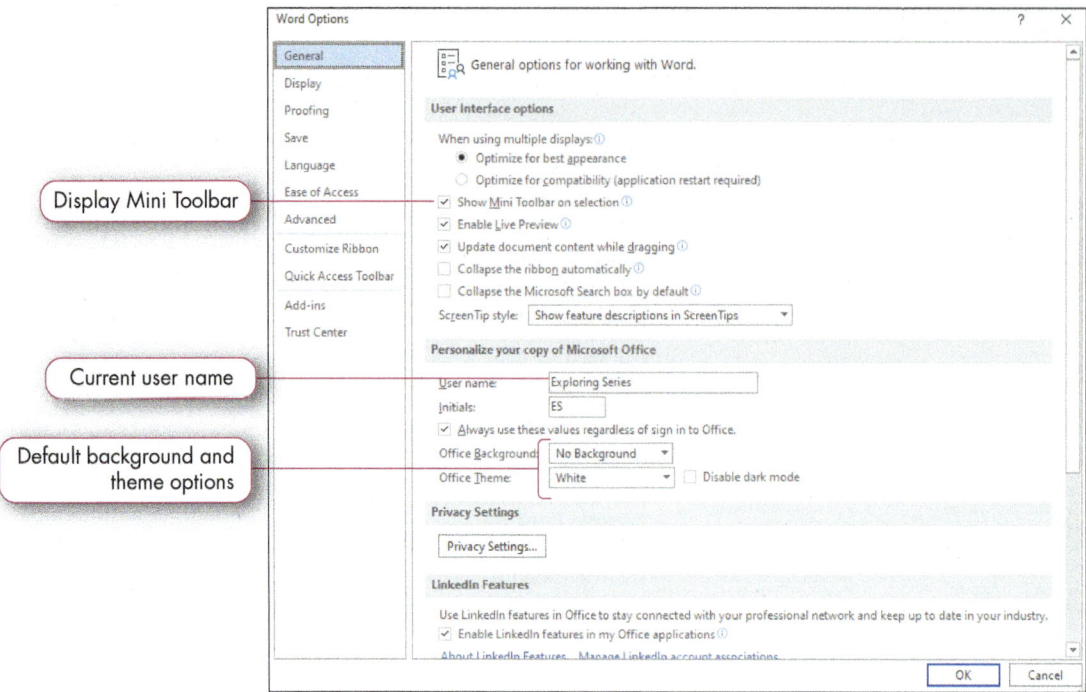

Display Mini Toolbar

Current user name

Default background and
theme options

FIGURE 1.12 Access Word Options

Although you can choose from many options as you customize your Word installation, you are likely to find a few that are more useful or more commonly accessed than others. The General category (refer to Figure 1.12) provides options to personalize Word by associating a particular name and initials. In the same area, you can select a background and theme for the Word interface. The Save category enables you to change the location where files are saved by default or to adjust the time between automatic saves. Other settings in other categories facilitate additional customization. (On a Mac, access Word Options when you click Word on the menu bar and click Preferences.)

TIP: SETTING WORD OPTIONS
Word options that you change will remain in effect until you change them again, even after Word is closed and reopened. Keep in mind that if you are working in a school computer lab, you might not have permission to change options permanently.

Use AutoCorrect

The **AutoCorrect** option in the Proofing category includes a standard list of typical misspellings and grammatical errors. As you type text in a Word document, you might notice that some items are automatically corrected, such as the automatic replacement of "teh" with "the." Because the mistake is so common, it is included in the standard set of AutoCorrect entries. AutoCorrect also corrects various capitalization errors and facilitates the inclusion of certain symbols. For example, typing (c) in a document automatically results in the copyright symbol of © because those keystrokes are included in AutoCorrect's standard set of replacements. You can check the list of automatic corrections or changes when you click AutoCorrect Options in the Proofing category in Word Options (see Figure 1.13).

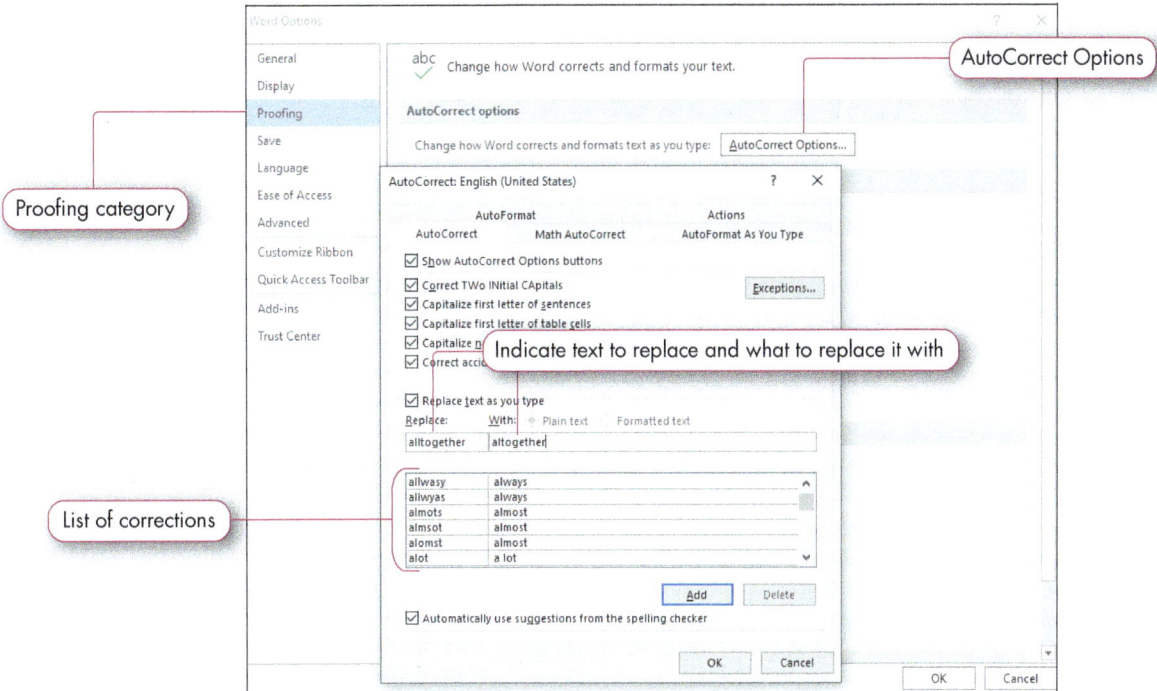

FIGURE 1.13 AutoCorrect Options

In the same dialog box (refer to Figure 1.13), you can customize AutoCorrect entries to include words or names that you often misspell or changes that you choose to make based on text typed. You might even consider using AutoCorrect to simplify the production of documents by replacing abbreviations with whole words. For example, you could include an entry that replaces an abbreviation for your company with the entire company name. That way, whenever you type the initials for a lengthy law firm name, for example, Word could automatically display the entire law firm name. To add AutoCorrect entries, indicate what to replace and what to replace it with in the AutoCorrect dialog box.

Critical Thinking

1. Provide a rationale for using a Word template instead of beginning with a blank document. *pp. 119–120*

2. Describe the process of reusing text from another document and compare the process to that of copying and pasting text. *p. 119*

3. Explain why Word's Editor might not catch all word usage errors in a document. *p. 123*

4. Describe how the use of AutoCorrect might make it easier to list long titles or names. *p. 127*

Hands-On Exercises

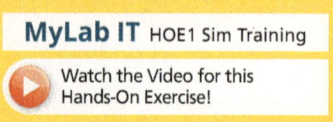
Skills covered: Create a Document • Reuse Text • Use a Template • Add Text and Navigate a Document • Find and Replace Document Content • Review Spelling and Grammar

1 Document Basics

As an employee of the Middleton Community Career Center (MCCC), you prepare a sample cover letter to support an upcoming job skills class. The document will serve as an example for students in the class, containing wording that can be modified to suit a particular job objective.

STEP 1 CREATE A DOCUMENT AND REUSE TEXT

As you create a cover letter for the job skills class, you will begin with a template. After inserting text from a previously created document, you will then add text to complete the letter. Refer to Figure 1.14 as you complete Step 1.

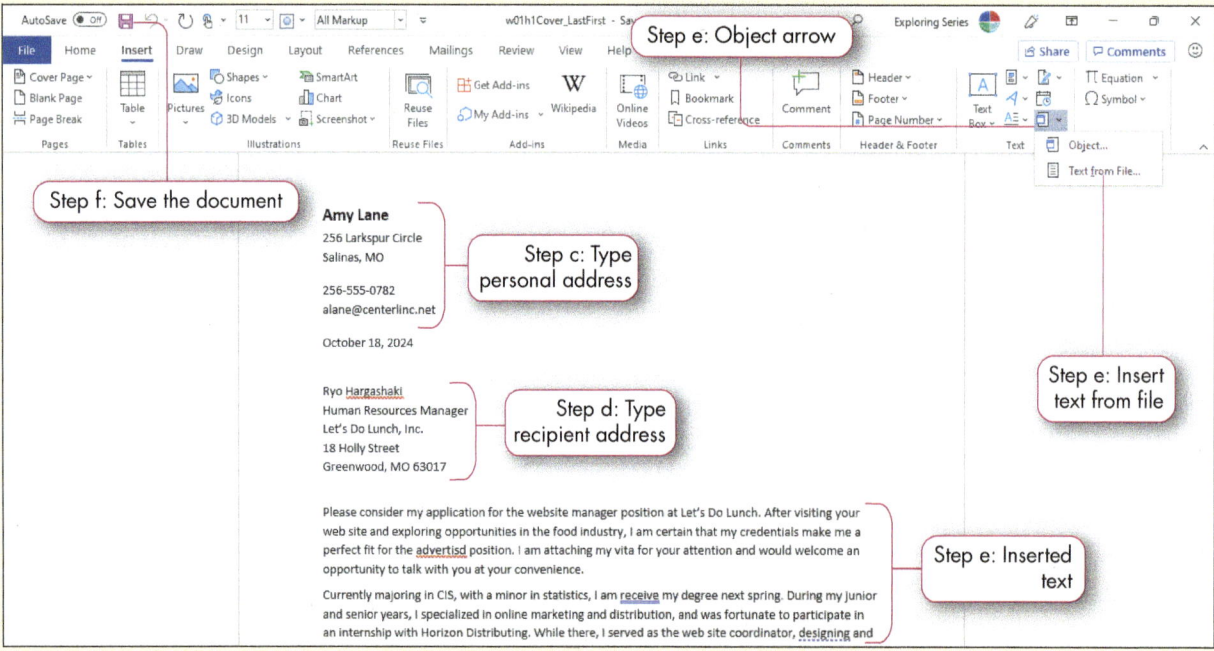

FIGURE 1.14 Begin a Document

a. Open Word. Click the **File tab** and click **New**. Click in the Search for online templates box and type **Job Cover Letter**. Press **Enter**. Scroll through the templates to locate **Cover letter in response to ad.** Click the selection. Click **Create**. Save the document as **w01h1Cover_LastFirst**, ensuring the file type is Word Document (not Word Template).

When you save files, use your last and first names. For example, as the Word author, I would name my document "w01h1Cover_HoganLynn."

> **TROUBLESHOOTING:** If you do not find the template, open *w01h1CoverTemplate.dotx* from your data files.

> **TROUBLESHOOTING:** If you make any major mistakes in this exercise, you can close the file without saving, open a blank document, and then start this exercise over.

b. Click **Get Started** in the Resume Assistant pane shown at the right of the document. Click **Add role** in the Resume Assistant pane and type **Website Manager**. Select a resulting match. Type **Food & Beverages** in the Industry box and press **Enter**. View a few wording examples shown in the pane. Close the Resume Assistant pane.

> **TROUBLESHOOTING:** If the Resume Assistant does not display, click the Review tab and select Resume Assistant from the Resume group.

c. Click **Show/Hide** in the Paragraph group on the Home tab to display nonprinting formatting marks (unless they are already displayed). Click **Your Name** and type **Amy Lane.** (Do not type a period following any address line.) Click **Street Address** and type **256 Larkspur Circle**. Complete remaining address lines as follows:

Salinas, MO 68112

256-555-0782

alane@centerlinc.net

d. Click **Date** and type **October 18, 2024**. (Do not type the period.) Click **Recipient Name** and press **Delete** three times. Press **Enter**. Click on the blank paragraph above *Title* and type **Ryo Hargashaki.** (Do not type the period.) Click **Title** and type **Human Resources Manager**. Click in each of the remaining address lines and type the following. Do not press Enter after any line.

Let's Do Lunch, Inc.

18 Holly Street

Greenwood, MO 63017

e. Select and delete the line containing the text *Dear Recipient Name:*. Press **Enter**. Select all body text in the letter, from *I am writing in response to your advertisement* through the end of the document. Click the **Insert tab** and click the **Object arrow** in the Text group. Click **Text from File**. Navigate to your student data files for this chapter and double-click *w01h1Letter.*

You borrow all wording for the cover letter from another letter that serves as a pattern, inserting all text from the other letter.

f. Click **Save** on the Quick Access Toolbar.

This saves the document without changing the name or the location where it is saved.

You decide to add a bit more detail to the cover letter. Refer to Figure 1.15 as you complete Step 2.

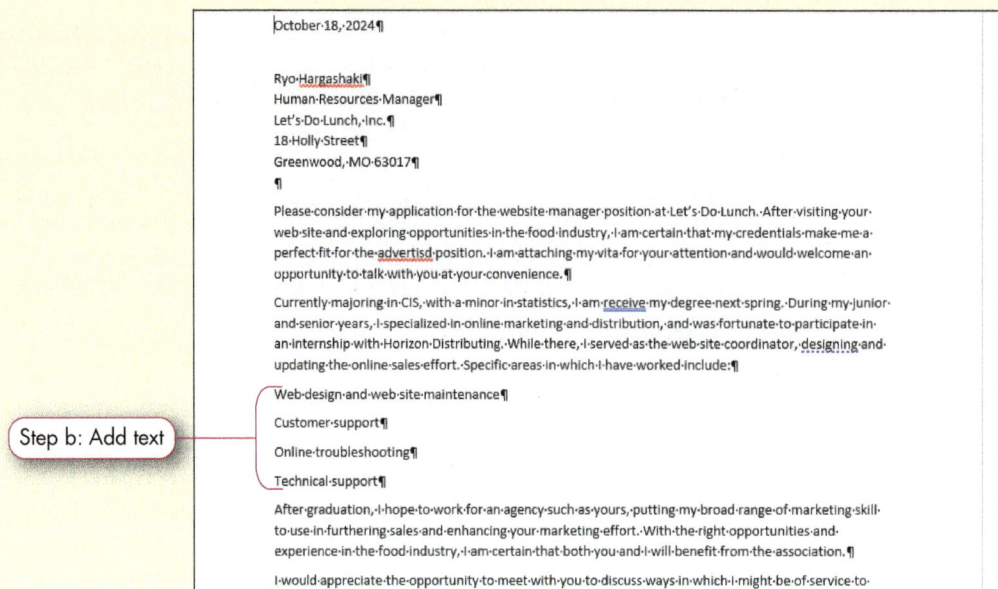

October·18,·2024¶

Ryo·Hargashaki¶
Human·Resources·Manager¶
Let's·Do·Lunch,·Inc.¶
18·Holly·Street¶
Greenwood,·MO·63017¶
¶
Please·consider·my·application·for·the·website·manager·position·at·Let's·Do·Lunch.·After·visiting·your·
web·site·and·exploring·opportunities·in·the·food·industry,·I·am·certain·that·my·credentials·make·me·a·
perfect·fit·for·the·advertisd·position.·I·am·attaching·my·vita·for·your·attention·and·would·welcome·an·
opportunity·to·talk·with·you·at·your·convenience.¶

Currently·majoring·in·CIS,·with·a·minor·in·statistics,·I·am·receive·my·degree·next·spring.·During·my·junior·
and·senior·years,·I·specialized·in·online·marketing·and·distribution,·and·was·fortunate·to·participate·in·
an·internship·with·Horizon·Distributing.·While·there,·I·served·as·the·web·site·coordinator,·designing·and·
updating·the·online·sales·effort.·Specific·areas·in·which·I·have·worked·include:¶

Step b: Add text

Web·design·and·web·site·maintenance¶

Customer·support¶

Online·troubleshooting¶

Technical·support¶

After·graduation,·I·hope·to·work·for·an·agency·such·as·yours,·putting·my·broad·range·of·marketing·skill·
to·use·in·furthering·sales·and·enhancing·your·marketing·effort.·With·the·right·opportunities·and·
experience·in·the·food·industry,·I·am·certain·that·both·you·and·I·will·benefit·from·the·association.¶

I·would·appreciate·the·opportunity·to·meet·with·you·to·discuss·ways·in·which·I·might·be·of·service·to·

FIGURE 1.15 Add Text

a. Click after the sentence ending in *sales effort* at the end of the second body paragraph. Be sure to click after the ending punctuation. Press **Spacebar** and type **Specific areas in which I worked include:** Press **Enter**.

b. Type the following text, pressing **Enter** at the end of every line except the last. Do not press Enter after the last line.

Web design and web site maintenance

Customer support

Online troubleshooting

Technical support

c. Click before the word *worked* in the last sentence of the second body paragraph. Type **have** and press **Spacebar** so that the sentence is *Specific areas in which I have worked include:* Ensure that only one space precedes and follows the newly inserted word.

d. Select and delete the first five lines of text in the document, beginning with *Amy Lane* and ending with *alane@centerlinc.net.* View the document in One Page view.

Given the length of the letter, you decide the inside address is not necessary.

> **TROUBLESHOOTING:** If a name placeholder displays after deleting the five lines of text, delete the placeholder and the following hard return.

e. Save the document.

As you consider the wording of the cover letter, you decide to replace one term with another. You are also concerned with the possible overuse of certain words. You will use Word's Replace feature to change text. Using the Navigation Pane, you will locate and consider replacement of another term, as well. Refer to Figure 1.16 as you complete Step 3.

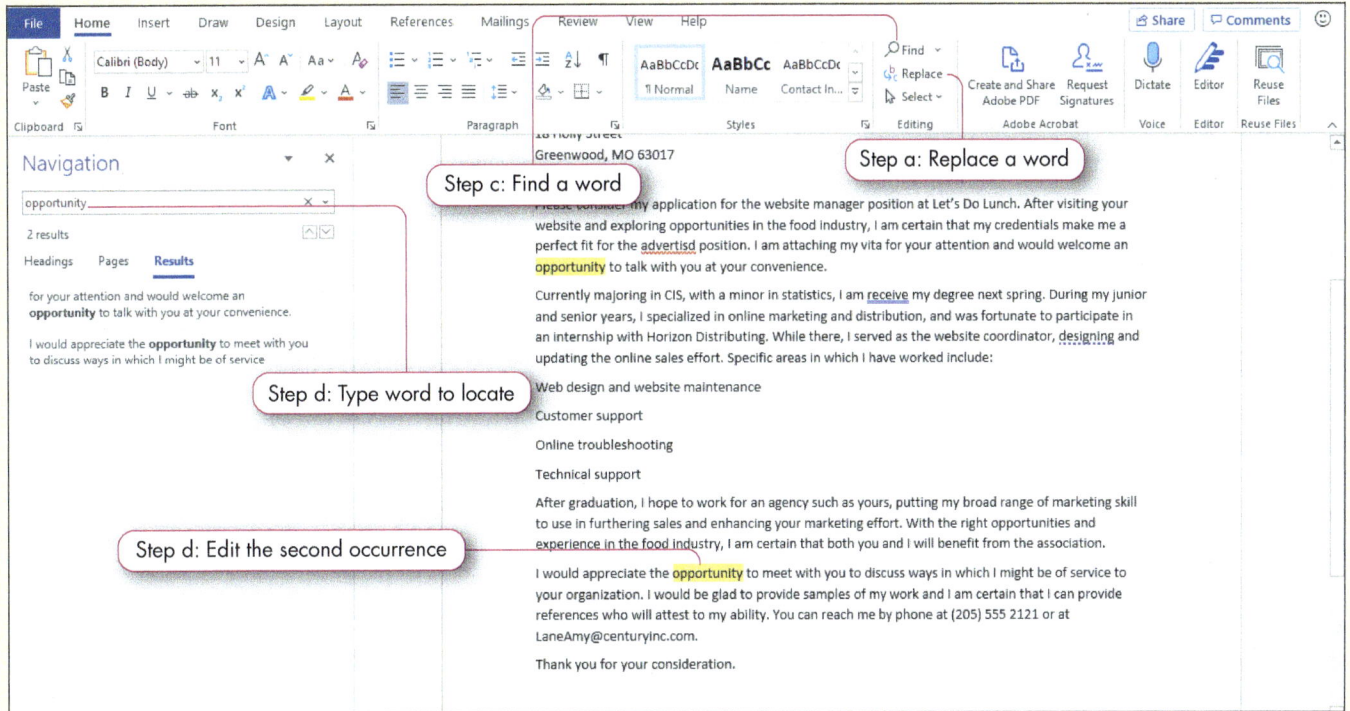

FIGURE 1.16 Find Text

a. Change the view to **100%**. Ensure that the insertion point is at the beginning of the document. Click the **Home tab**. Click **Replace** in the Editing group. (On a Mac, press control+H.) Click in the **Find what box** and type **web site**. Click in the **Replace with box** and type **website**. Click **Find Next**.

Although both *web site* and *website* are acceptable choices, the more common usage is *website*. You decide to replace every occurrence of *web site* in the cover letter with *website*. You evaluate each item found before replacing it.

b. Click **Replace** to change the first occurrence found. At the next stop, click **Replace**. Repeat the process once more. Click **OK**. Click **Close**.

Three items are replaced.

c. Click **Find** in the Editing group. (On a Mac, press shift+command+H.) In the Search box on the Navigation Pane, type **opportunity** (replacing *web site*). Locate the second highlighted incidence of the word (in the sentence beginning *I would appreciate*).

d. Change the second occurrence of the word *opportunity* to **pleasure**. So that the remainder of the sentence reads correctly, change the words *to meet* to **of meeting**. Close the Navigation Pane.

e. Save the document.

As you finalize the cover letter, you check for spelling, grammar, and word usage concerns. You also identify a synonym for a term. Refer to Figure 1.17 as you complete Step 4.

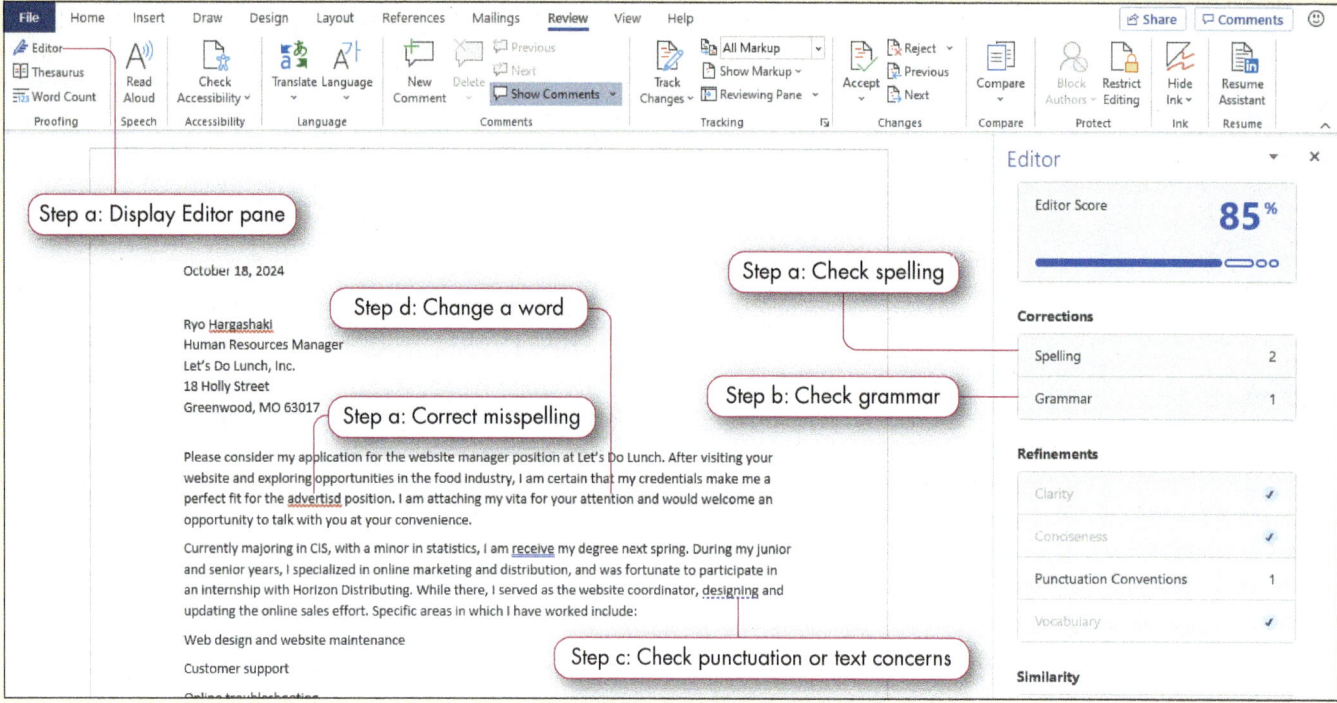

FIGURE 1.17 Proof a Document

a. Click the **Review tab** and click **Editor** (on a Mac, click Spelling & Grammar) in the Proofing group. Click **Spelling** in the Editor pane. The recipient's name is not misspelled, so ignore all occurrences of the error. The word *advertisd* is displayed as being misspelled. Select **advertised** from the list. Review any other errors that might be displayed for text that you typed, correcting any that should be addressed.

b. Click **Grammar** in the Editor pane. The word *receive* is identified as a grammar error. Select **receiving**. Close the Editor pane without considering other possible concerns.

c. Right-click the word **designing** in the second body paragraph if it is underlined in blue dashes to indicate a possible grammatical or word choice error. Because the suggestion is not actually suitable as a correction, click **Ignore Once**. Respond to any additional prompts and scroll through the letter to ensure that nothing else is flagged as a possible error.

Although it is not necessary to accept or ignore every flagged spelling or grammatical error, especially if they are not actually errors, you should check this document completely, given its potential importance to an applicant's job search.

d. Select the word **attention** in the last sentence of the first body paragraph. Click **Thesaurus** in the Proofing group on the Review tab. Click the arrow beside the word *consideration* in the Thesaurus pane and click **Insert**. Close the Thesaurus pane.

> **MAC TROUBLESHOOTING:** Delete the word *attention* and then drag the correct term from the Thesaurus pane into the document, positioning it where intended.

> **TROUBLESHOOTING:** If you click the word *consideration* instead of the arrow at the right, you will see related word choices, but the word will not be inserted. Click the back arrow at the top of the Thesaurus pane, and repeat Step d.

e. Save and close the document. Keep Word open if you plan to continue with the next Hands-On Exercise. If not, exit Word.

Format a Document

The overall appearance and organization of a document is the first opportunity to effectively convey your message to readers. You should ensure that a document is formatted attractively with coordinated and consistent style elements. Not only should a document be organized by topic, but also it should be organized by design, so that it is easy to read and so that topics of the same level of emphasis are similar in appearance. Major headings are typically formatted identically, with subheadings designed to indicate a subordinate relationship—in a smaller font, for example. Word includes tools on the Design tab that enable you to create a polished and professional-looking document. You will find options for creating a themed document, with color-coordinated design elements, as well as **style sets**, which are predefined combinations of font, style, color, and font size that can be applied to selected text. Organizing a document into sections enables you to combine diverse units into a whole, formatting sections independently of one another.

In this section, you will explore document formatting options, including themes and page background elements. You will work with sections and columns, learning to organize and format sections independently of one another to create an attractive document that serves your purpose.

Modify a Document

A document's layout, including font design, color scheme, columnar arrangement, and background elements, helps define the purpose of a document while also projecting a consistent and well-considered effort. Modifying the layout of a document and ensuring appropriate color and font design is a simple process, requiring just a bit of attention to the selection of a document theme and to the arrangement of text. Such a carefully designed document is attractive and easily readable, conveying a sense of attention to detail and professionalism.

In addition, the optional use of a watermark identifies a document's purpose or ownership. Applying a theme enables you to visually coordinate various page elements, while including a page border or page background contributes to an attractive and effective informal document. All those design options are available on the Design tab. When formatting a document, you should always keep in mind the document's purpose and its intended audience. Whereas a newsletter might use more color and playful text and design effects, a legal or business document should be more conservative. With the broad range of document formatting options available in Word, you can be as playful or formal as necessary.

TIP: APPLY DOCUMENT THEME

Themes are similar across the Office applications. If a Word document includes a table from Excel, both the Word and Excel files can be formatted with the same document theme, so the effects are consistent across the two applications.

STEP 1 **Select a Document Theme**

A *document theme* is a set of coordinating fonts, colors, and special effects that are combined into a package for use in document design. When you open a new blank Word document, it is based on the default Office theme. However, you can select and change the entire theme of the document or even customize theme fonts, colors, or effects. You will find a selection of options on the Design tab related to themes, colors, fonts, effects, watermarks, page background, and even page borders (see Figure 1.18). The Document Formatting group includes selections related to themes and theme effects, while the Page Background group enables you to change page color or page background, or to insert a watermark.

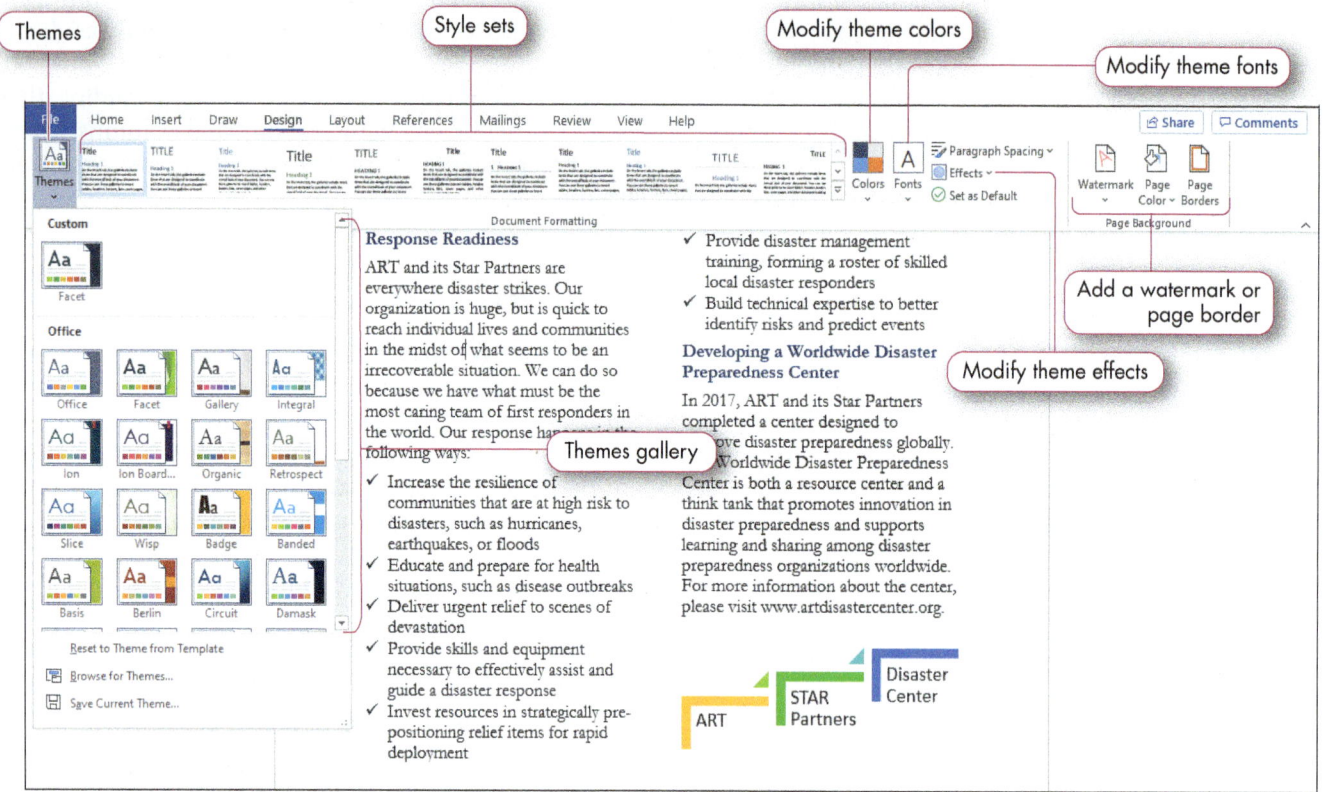

FIGURE 1.18 Design Tab

A document theme is applicable to text, objects, and other features of a document, contributing to a consistent color scheme that visually links various components of a document. Click Themes on the Design tab and point to any theme to see a preview of a theme's effect on existing text or objects before selecting the theme. Be aware that you may not see any noticeable difference as you peruse theme selections, depending upon the text or objects displayed in the document at the time. A theme typically applies color and font selections to objects, borders, and various heading levels, so if those items are not displayed as you preview a theme, you may not see much, if any, immediate effect as you preview its effect.

Having selected a theme, you can modify such theme options as color and font as shown in Figure 1.18. Doing so can yield more concise color and font coordination, resulting in a document that is consistent and professional in appearance.

It is not at all unusual for some areas of a document to be formatted differently from others. In fact, that is the norm. A heading might be bold and shown in larger font than text that follows. Other areas in the same document might be indented, bordered, or even shaded. Such formatting is not difficult to incorporate into a single document; however, when you find it necessary to significantly vary page layout within a single document—perhaps incorporating multiple columns of text in a document that also contains single columns in other areas—you will want to consider defining sections. In so doing, you can format sections independently of one another, while they collectively occupy the same document. For instance, a headline of an article can be aligned horizontally in the center, left, or right across the width of a page, while the remaining article text is divided into columns (see Figure 1.19). The key to such an arrangement is placing the headline in one section, while article text is set in another. Similarly, a report's cover page could be set apart in a section so that it is vertically centered, while subsequent report pages are in a section that is aligned at the top of each page.

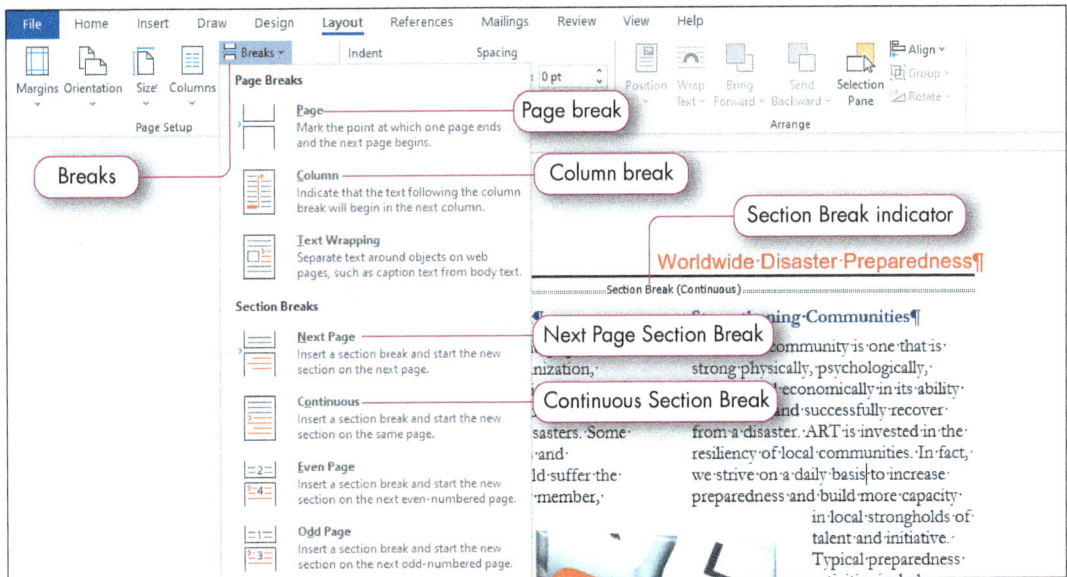

FIGURE 1.19 Select and Display a Section Break

A **section** is a part of a document that is independently defined with page layout settings, such as margins, columns, and orientation, and that varies from other document text. To define where one section ends and another begins, you place a section break. The Page Setup group on the Layout tab includes options for inserting section breaks within a document. Word stores the formatting characteristics of each section, such as columnar arrangement and page orientation, within the section break placed at the end of a section, making it possible to organize each section independently of others. If you delete a section break, you also delete the formatting for that section, causing the text above the break to assume the formatting characteristics of the following section. To delete a section break, click the section break indicator (refer to Figure 1.19) and press Delete.

Word provides four types of section breaks, as shown in Table 1.1. A commonly used break is Next Page, which forces text following the break to begin at the top of a new page. Such a break could divide a cover page from report text, for example. To format text on a single page in separate sections, perhaps placing a horizontally aligned headline by itself, while remaining text is displayed in two columns, you would insert a Continuous break. Even Page and Odd Page section breaks are often used in assembling printed material so that those page types are arranged independently.

TABLE 1.1	Section Breaks	
Type	**Text that follows...**	**Use to...**
Next Page	will begin at the top of the next page.	force a chapter to start at the top of a page.
Continuous	can continue on the same page.	format text in the middle of the page into columns.
Even Page	will begin at the top of the next even-numbered page.	force a chapter to begin at the top of an even-numbered page.
Odd Page	will begin at the top of the next odd-numbered page.	force a chapter to begin at the top of an odd-numbered page.

HOW TO

Place a section break in a document:

1. Click the location where the break should occur.
2. Click the Layout tab. Click Breaks in the Page Setup group.
3. Select a section break type (refer to Table 1.1). If nonprinting characters are displayed, a section break indicator will be shown (refer to Figure 1.19).

Format Text into Columns

Newsletters are often designed in *columns*, which are side-by-side vertical blocks of text flowing down one side and continuing at the top of the next. Such an arrangement is not a difficult process, requiring only that you identify where columns are to begin, and the number of columns to include.

To format text into columns, you must first place the insertion point where you want columns to begin. Click Columns in the Page Setup group on the Layout tab and specify the number of columns. You can, instead, click More Columns to display the dialog box shown in Figure 1.20, in which you can indicate the spacing between columns or whether the left or right column should be narrower than the other.

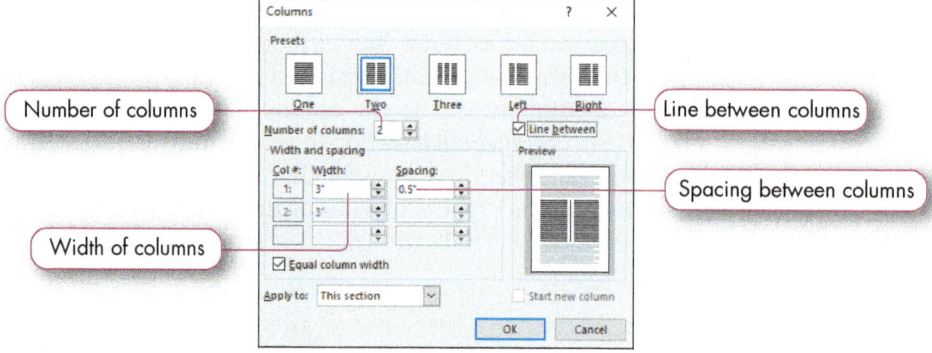

FIGURE 1.20 Columns Dialog Box

Text arranged in columns should be attractive. Most likely, you will want columns to be balanced on the page, so that one column is not far lengthier than the next. In addition, columns should not end awkwardly, as would be the case when a column heading is shown at the bottom of one column with remaining text picking up at the top of the next. One solution to such challenges is to place a column break where you intend to end a column. To insert a column break, place the insertion point where the break is to occur and then select Column from the list of breaks presented in the Page Setup group on the Layout tab (refer to Figure 1.19). With nonprinting characters displayed, a Column Break indicator will be shown where the break was placed.

STEP 3 Configure Page Background Elements

Using tools in the Page Background group, you can add a watermark, page color, or a page border. Such features can add interest or better identify a document's purpose or ownership.

A *watermark*, which is text or a graphic that displays behind text on a page, is often used to include a faded background image, such as a logo for a company, or to indicate the status of a document. For example, a watermark displaying Draft indicates that a document is not in final form. The document shown in Figure 1.21 contains a watermark. Watermarks do not display on a document that is saved as a webpage, nor will they display in Word's Web Layout view (discussed later in this chapter).

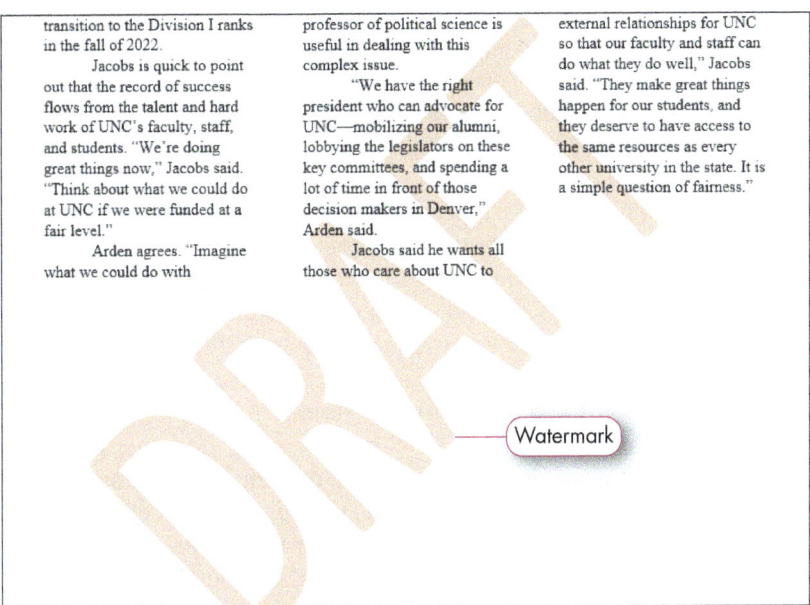

FIGURE 1.21 Use a Watermark

Insert a watermark by selecting Watermark in the Page Background group on the Design tab. Select from predesigned styles or click Custom Watermark to create your own, selecting text, color, and transparency settings. To remove a watermark, follow the same steps, choosing the option Remove Watermark.

Click Page Borders in the Page Background group on the Design tab to place a border around one or more selected pages. Options in the Borders and Shading dialog box, shown when you begin the process of adding a page border, enable you to select the type, color, and width of the border. You can also choose whether to apply the border to the entire document or only to a section. In addition, a page border can be shown on a particular side, or perhaps just at the top or bottom of each page. Note that it is appropriate to use page borders on documents such as flyers, newsletters, and invitations, but not on formal documents such as research papers and professional reports.

Depending upon a document's purpose and audience, you might find that a colored background is appropriate and may even enhance readability and interest, depending upon the hue chosen. Although most business documents are not well suited to brightly colored or graphic backgrounds, you might find that such interest livens up a newsletter, personal correspondence, or a more informal project. Although in general it is best to refrain from using color in formal documents, some might benefit from a light shade. For example, résumés delivered online often sport a bit of tint to set them apart from the crowd.

Not only should you consider a document's purpose, when considering a background choice, but you should also keep accessibility and readability in mind. Contrast is an important element in ensuring that those with visual impairment can read a document. A colored or graphic background could possibly detract and cause accessibility issues.

Using Word's Page Color selection in the Page Background group on the Design tab, you can add color, pattern, or even a picture to the background of pages in a document. Note that background color is visible only when a document is presented electronically. It does not show on a printed document.

Apply Styles

A characteristic of a professional document is uniform formatting. As you complete reports, assignments, and other projects, you are likely to apply the same text, paragraph, table, and list formatting to similar elements. For example, all major headings are likely to be designed with the same font, font size, and emphasis. Instead of formatting such document elements individually, you can select a predesigned style to apply the desired formatting quickly and consistently. A *style* is a named collection of formatting characteristics that can be applied to characters or entire paragraphs. An advantage of using styles, especially in the design of headings and subheadings, is that Word can then automatically generate reference pages such as a table of contents and indexes from headings that are formatted in various levels of heading styles. Selecting a document theme is a global approach to affecting the color and font format of an entire document. In contrast, applying a style to individual text or paragraphs changes the format of those specific items only, ensuring that similarly styled text is consistent and recognizable.

By default, Normal style is applied to new Word documents. Unless you specify otherwise when beginning a new document, Normal style features include 11 pt Calibri font, left alignment, and multiple line spacing. If that style is not appropriate for a document you are developing, you can select another style from Word's Style gallery shown on the Home tab (see Figure 1.22). For example, a business letter is typically single spaced. However, Normal style contains multiple line spacing, which would not be appropriate for the letter. In that case, you might choose the No Spacing style instead, before beginning the letter.

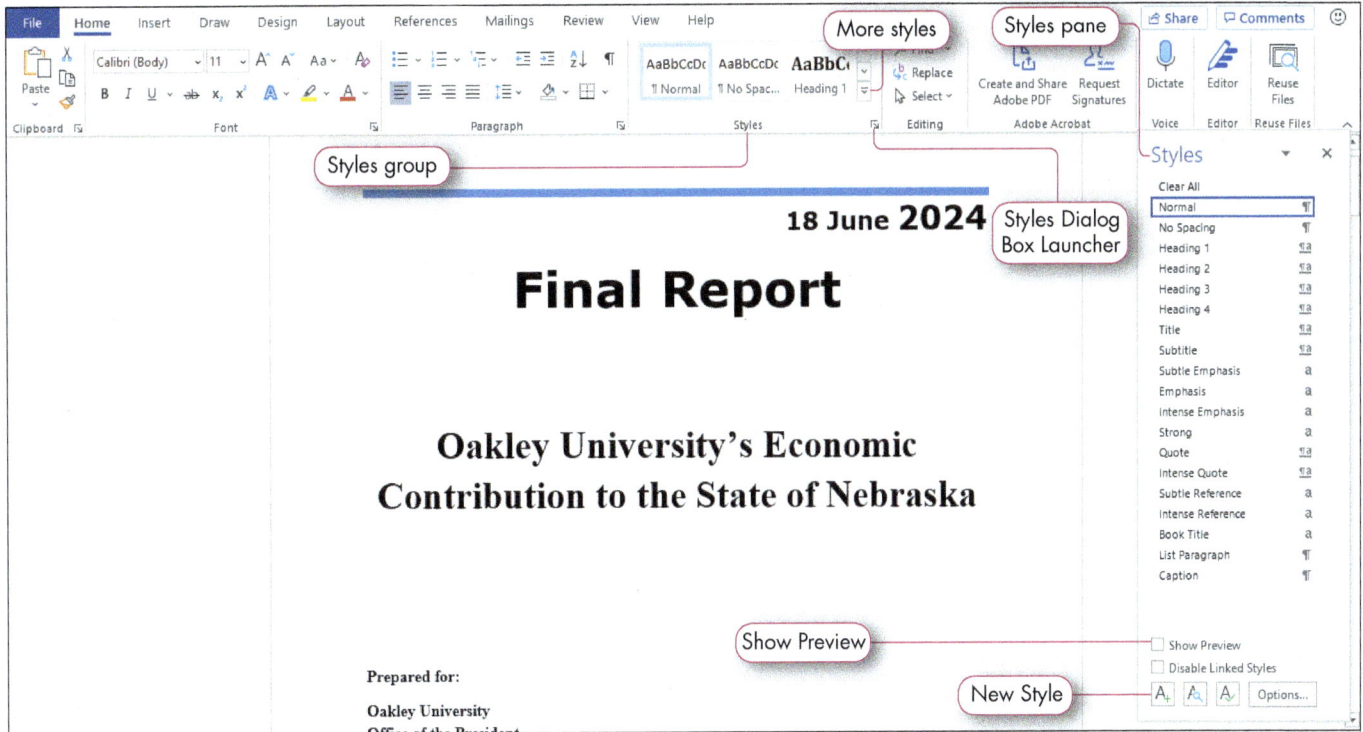

FIGURE 1.22 Styles

Select and Modify Styles

A style is typically identified as paragraph, character, or linked. Character styles are applied to selected text, while paragraph styles apply to all text within the current paragraph or within multiple selected paragraphs. A character style typically applies formatting located in the Font group on the Home tab, while paragraph styles are more concerned with formatting found in the Paragraph group. Linked styles are those in which both character and paragraph formatting settings are included. When the insertion point is located within a paragraph, but no text is selected, a linked style applies both font characteristics (such as bold or italic) and paragraph formats (such as paragraph and line spacing) to the entire paragraph. However, if text is selected within a paragraph when a linked style is applied, the style will apply font formatting only.

Applying a style is a simple process. When applying a character style, you should first select text to be modified. If applying a paragraph style, place the insertion point within a paragraph to be formatted or select multiple paragraphs. Then click a style in the Styles group on the Home tab (refer to Figure 1.22). For more style choices, click More or click the Dialog Box Launcher in the Styles group for additional options, such as modifying an existing style or even creating a new style.

Word provides a wide variety of style choices. Even so, you might find that modifying a style slightly would better suit your needs. For example, suppose that most of your work involves single-spaced documents. You find that the Normal style, which is applied to all new Word documents, is just what you need except that it does not include single spacing. In that case, you might consider modifying Normal style to include single spacing so that the current document, or even all new documents, are automatically designed in single spacing.

As you modify a style, you can indicate whether the style is to be changed only for the current document, or whether it is to be available in modified form for all documents created by your computer's Word installation. By default, modifying a style, or even creating a new style, affects only the current document. However, you can cause the style to be available to all documents that are based on the current template when you select *New documents based on this template* in the Modify Style dialog box (see Figure 1.23). To modify a style, click the Styles Dialog Box Launcher (refer to Figure 1.22), point to a style, click the arrow to the right, and select Modify. (On a Mac, click the Styles Pane on the Home tab.) The dialog box shown in Figure 1.23 displays the selected style's current format settings that you can change. During that process, you will either agree to apply those changes to the current document only or specify that all documents have access to the modified style settings.

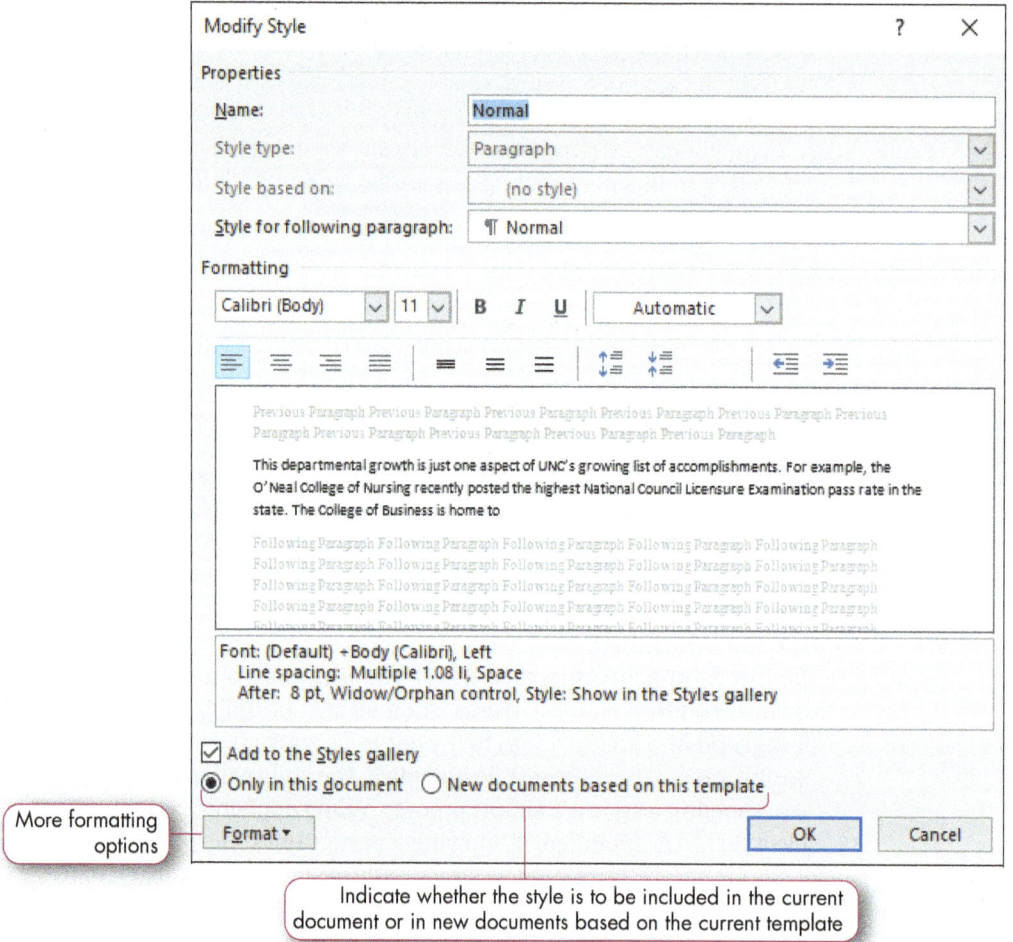

FIGURE 1.23 Modify a Style

When a style is modified, the changes are automatically applied to all text items formatted with that style. Suppose that you modify the Heading 1 style to include blue font. As soon as the style is modified, any headings already formatted in Heading 1 style within the current document will be shown in blue.

TIP: UPDATE A STYLE TO MATCH TEXT

A style can be quickly modified to match selected text. With text selected, or the insertion point within a paragraph, right-click the style to be modified in the Styles gallery on the Home tab or on the Styles pane. Select Update to Match Selection.

Create a New Style

Occasionally, modifying a current style is not the best way to ensure the formatting options you want. Suppose, for instance, that you are an English major who spends a great deal of time developing research papers. Your major requires that you follow a particular set of writing guidelines related to line and paragraph spacing, indentation, and font type. You find that the Normal style is not set up for those requirements, nor is any other style included in a typical Word installation. In that case, you can create a new style, titled whatever you like, with formatting that you need for research papers. The next time you begin a paper, select the newly created style and begin the paper.

To create a new style, open the Styles pane by clicking the Dialog Box Launcher in the Styles group (refer to Figure 1.22) and select New Style. Provide a name for the new style and indicate the formatting you want in the subsequent dialog box. A somewhat simpler approach is to base a new style on existing text. For example, with a research paper open, and the insertion point in a body paragraph that is formatted as you want, or with text selected, begin the process of creating a new style. Formatting selections included in the current paragraph or selected text will already be placed in the New Style dialog box, so you simply provide a style name and confirm the proposed settings. As a style is created, you can choose whether to make it available in the current document only (which is the default) or in all documents based on the same template.

Use a Style Set

Similar to a style, a style set is a combination of title, heading, and paragraph styles that are designed to work together and that are applied globally to an entire open document. Using a style set, you can format all elements in a document at one time. Style sets are located on the Design tab in the Document Formatting group (see Figure 1.24).

FIGURE 1.24 Style Sets

View a Document in Different Ways

Developing a document is a creative process. As you create, edit, or review a project, you will want to view the document in various ways. Word provides a view that enables you to see a document as it will print, as well as views that maximize typing space by removing page features. You might review a document in a magazine-type format for ease of reading, or perhaps a hierarchical view of headings and subheadings would help you better understand and proof the structure of a document. Zooming in on text and objects can make a document easier to proofread, while viewing a document page by page enables you to manage page flow—perhaps drawing attention to awkward page endings or beginnings. Taking advantage of the various views and view settings in Word, you will find it easy to create attractive, well-worded, and error-free documents.

Select a Document View

When you begin a new document, you see the top, bottom, left, and right margins. This default document view is called **Print Layout view**. You can choose to view a document differently, which is something you might do if you are at a different step in its production. For example, as you type or edit a document, you might prefer **Draft view**, which provides the most typing space possible without regard to margins and special page features. **Outline view** displays a document in hierarchical fashion, clearly delineating levels of heading detail. If a document is destined for the Web, you can view it in **Web Layout view**.

Designed to make a document easy to read and to facilitate access across multiple devices, **Read Mode** presents a document in a left-to-right flow, automatically splitting text into columns, for a magazine-like appearance. A document often displays in a two-page format. Text adjusts to fit any size screen, flowing easily from page to page with a simple swipe of a finger (if using a tablet or touch-sensitive device) or click of the mouse. Users of touch-based devices can rotate the device between landscape and portrait modes, with the screen always divided into equally sized columns. When in Read Mode (see Figure 1.25), the ribbon is removed from view. Instead, you have access to only three menu items: File, Tools, and View. One of the most useful features of Read Mode is object zooming. Simply double-click an object, such as a table, chart, picture, or video, to zoom in. Press Esc to leave Read Mode.

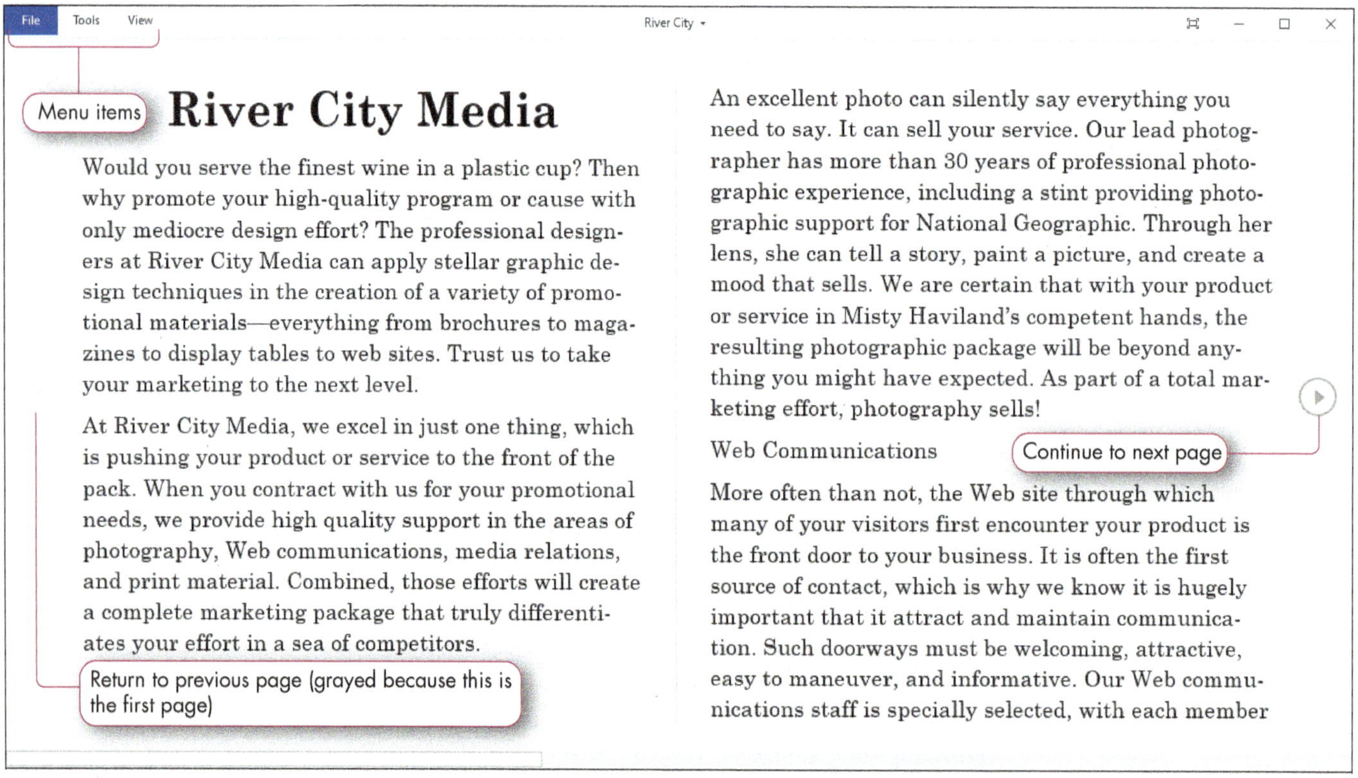

FIGURE 1.25 Read Mode

To change a document's view, click the View tab and select a view from the Views group (see Figure 1.26). Although slightly more limited in choice, the status bar also provides views to choose from (Read Mode, Print Layout, and Web Layout). Word views are summarized in Table 1.2.

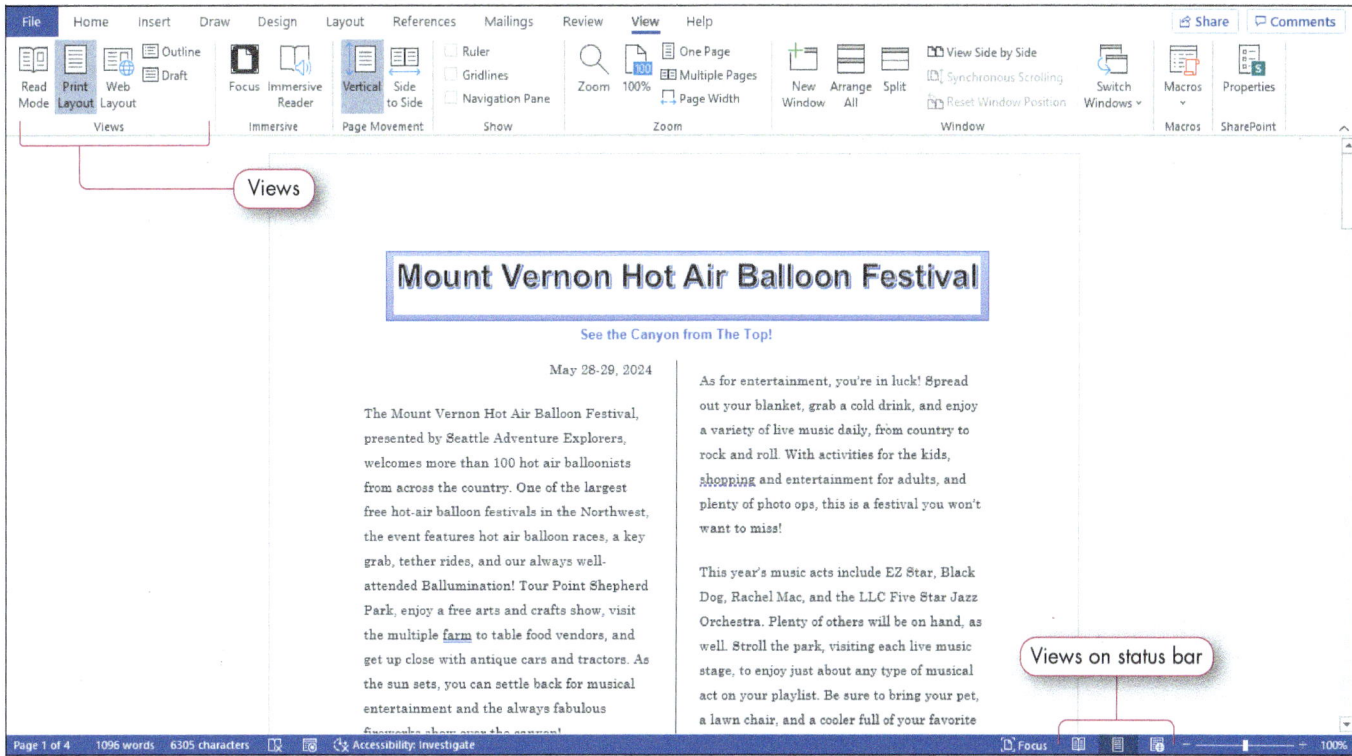

FIGURE 1.26 Word Views

TABLE 1.2	Word Views
View	**Appearance**
Read Mode	Primarily used for reading, with a document shown in pages, much like a magazine. The ribbon is hidden, with only a limited number of menu selections shown.
Print Layout	Shows margins, headers, footers, graphics, and other page features—much like a document will look when printed.
Web Layout	Shows a document as it would appear on a webpage.
Outline	Shows level of organization and detail. You can collapse or expand detail to show only what is necessary. Often used as a springboard for a table of contents or a PowerPoint summary.
Draft	Provides the most space possible for typing. It does not show margins, headers, or other features, but it does include the ribbon.

Change the Zoom Setting

Regardless of the view selected, you can use Word's Zoom feature to enlarge or reduce the view of text. Unlike zooming in on an object in Read Mode, the Zoom feature available on the View tab enables you to enlarge text, not objects or videos. Enlarging text might make a document easier to read and proofread. However, changing the size of text onscreen does not actually change the font size of a document. Zooming in or out is simply a temporary change to the way a document displays onscreen. The View tab includes options that change the onscreen size of a document (see Figure 1.27). You can also enlarge or reduce the view of text by dragging the Zoom slider on the status bar. Click Zoom In and Zoom Out on the status bar to change the view incrementally by 10% for each click.

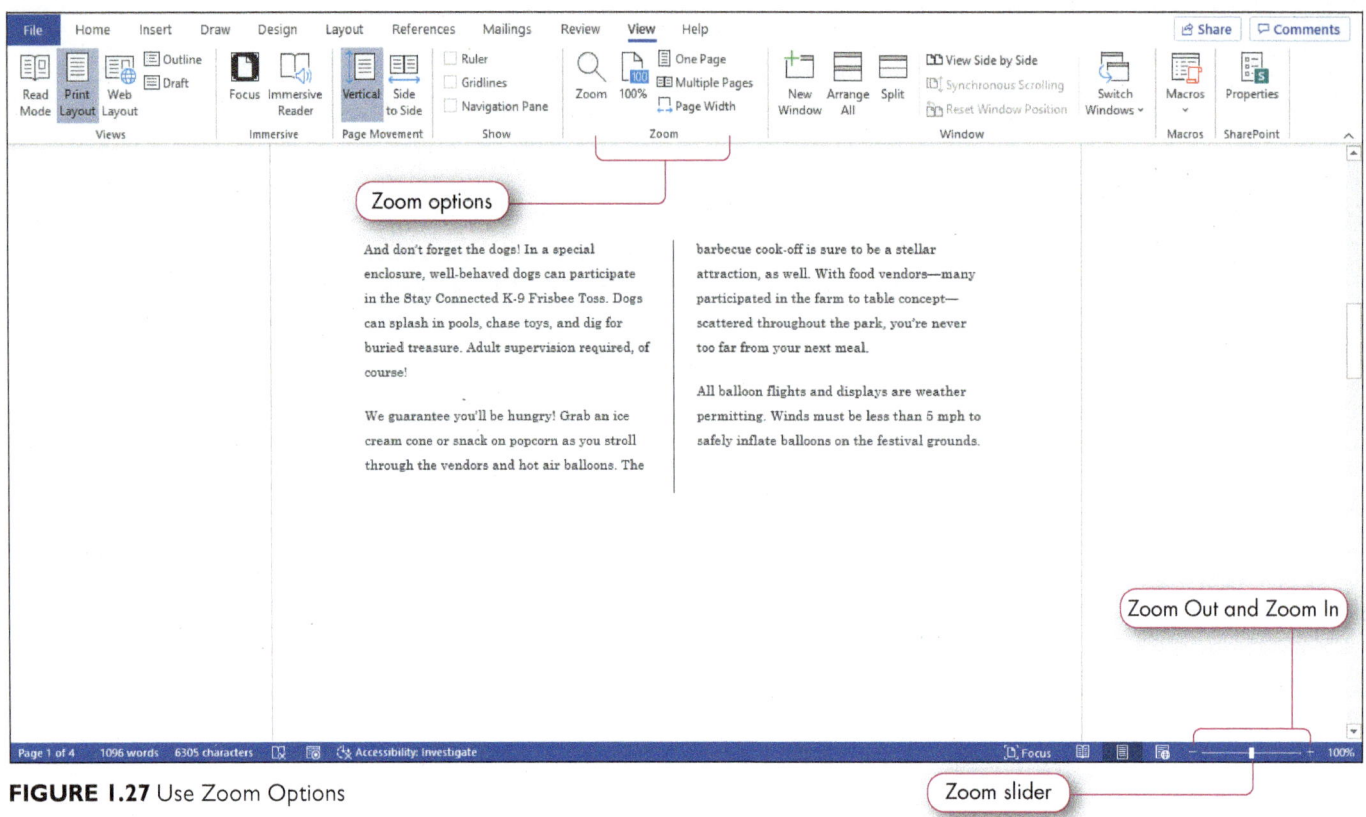

FIGURE 1.27 Use Zoom Options

Use the Zoom command on the View tab to select a percentage of zoom or to indicate a preset width (page width, text width, or whole page). Preset widths are also available as individual options in the Zoom group on the View tab (refer to Figure 1.27).

STEP 5 View a Document and Manage Page Flow

Document lengths can vary greatly. A research paper might span 20 pages, whereas a memo is seldom more than a few pages (most often, only one). Obviously, it is easier to view a memo onscreen than an entire research paper. Even so, Word enables you to get a good feel for the way a document will look when printed or distributed, regardless of document length.

Before printing, it is a good idea to view a document in its entirety. One way to do that is to click the File tab and click Print. A document is shown one page at a time in Print Preview (see Figure 1.28). You can use the Next Page or Previous Page navigation arrows to proceed forward or backward in pages. You can also view a document by using options on the View tab (refer to Figure 1.27). Clicking One Page provides a snapshot of the current page, while Multiple Pages shows pages of a multiple-page document side by side (and on separate rows, in the case of more than two pages).

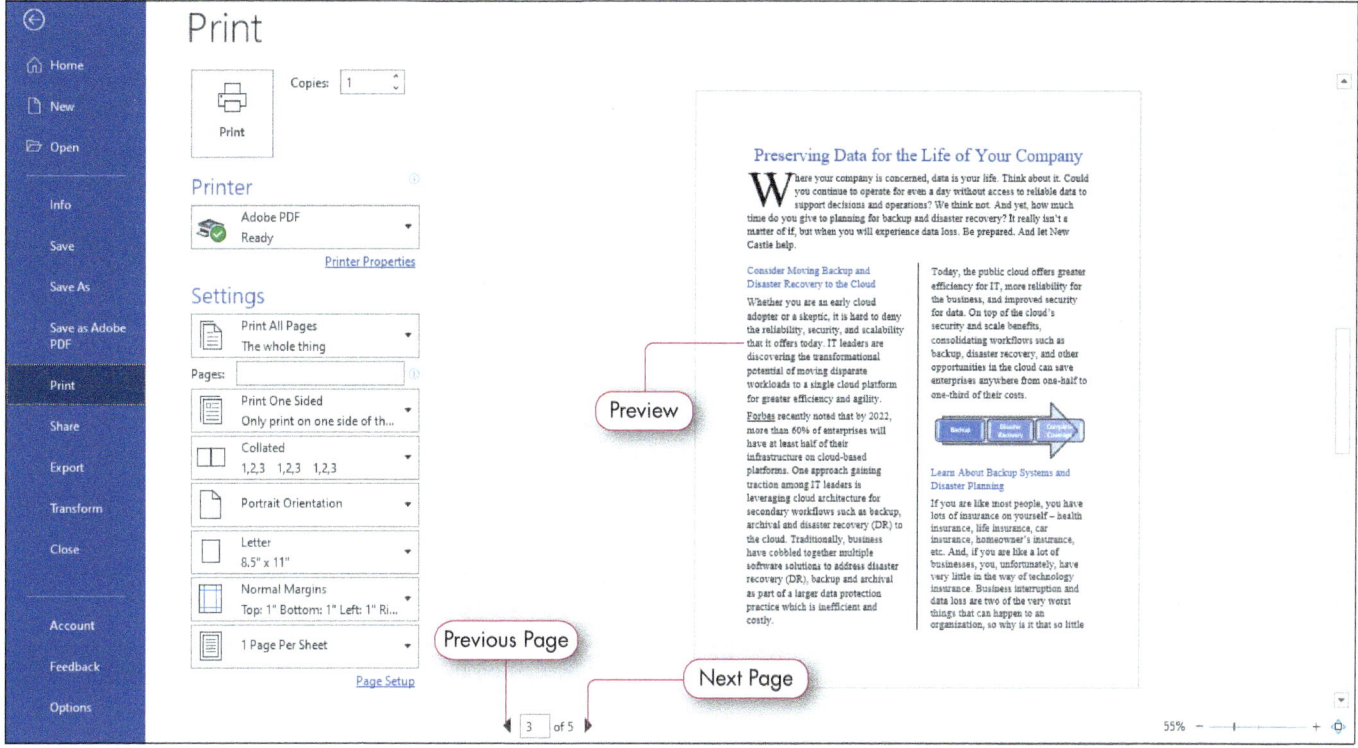

FIGURE 1.28 Preview a Document

Occasionally, a page will end poorly—perhaps with a heading shown alone at the bottom of a page or with a paragraph split awkwardly between pages. Or perhaps it is necessary to begin a new page after a table of contents, so that other pages follow in the order they should. To insert a page break, you can use the shortcut Ctrl+Enter (on a Mac, command+Enter) or click the Layout tab, click Breaks, and then select Page. Alternatively, click the Insert tab and click Page Break in the Pages group.

With nonprinting characters shown, you will see the Page Break indicator (see Figure 1.29). To remove a page break, click the Page Break indicator and press Delete.

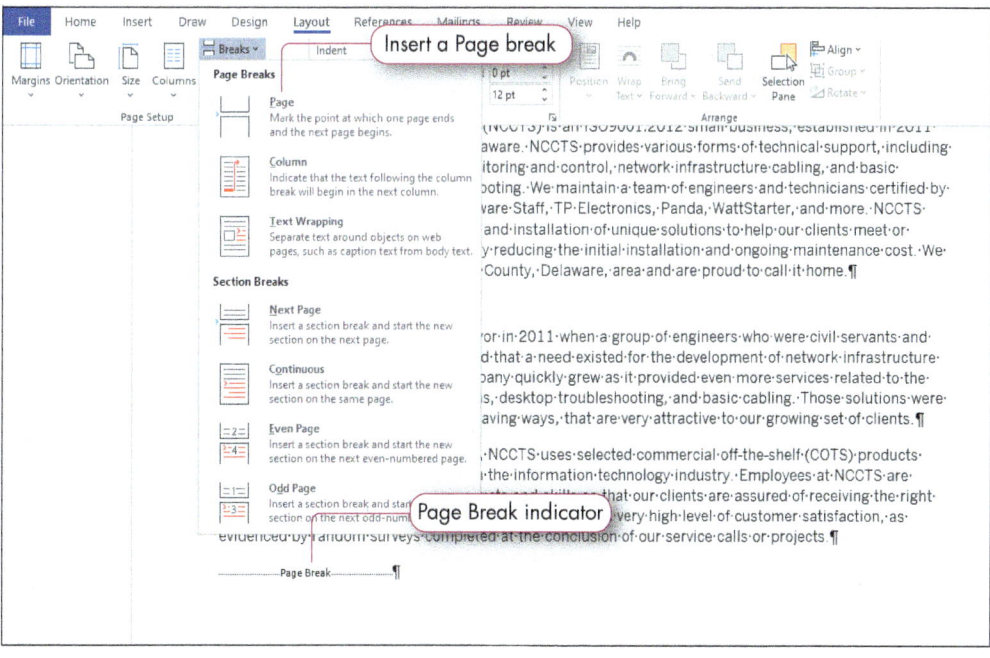

FIGURE 1.29 Insert a Page Break

Critical Thinking

5. Explain why might you choose to use a document theme instead of an individual style to modify formatting of a document. *p. 134*

6. Describe a document that would benefit from the use of a watermark. Explain why that is the case. *p. 137*

7. Describe a type of document that would benefit from page formatting, such as page color and border, as well as a document that would not. *pp. 137–138*

8. Describe a situation in which inserting a page break would be beneficial. *p. 145*

Hands-On Exercises

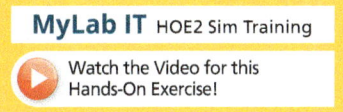

Skills covered: Select a Document Theme • Work with Sections • Format Text into Columns • Configure Page Background Elements • Select and Modify Styles • View a Document and Manage Page Flow

2 Format a Document

Students in the MCCC workplace readiness class should be introduced to various options in the design of job search documents, such as résumé. Although résumé templates are readily available, they are not always well suited to online application systems, and they may prove cumbersome to modify with personal information. In this exercise, you will format a sample résumé in a columnar arrangement, using section and column breaks to adjust layout and ensure an attractive arrangement. The choice of whether to use columns in a résumé depends upon personal preference, level of detail included, and whether a résumé is intended for online application, but such an arrangement is certainly an option that students should be aware of. Completing the design, you customize the document with a theme, border, and watermark.

STEP 1 SELECT A DOCUMENT THEME

You select a document theme, while also indicating a theme color selection as well as font options. Refer to Figure 1.30 as you complete Step 1.

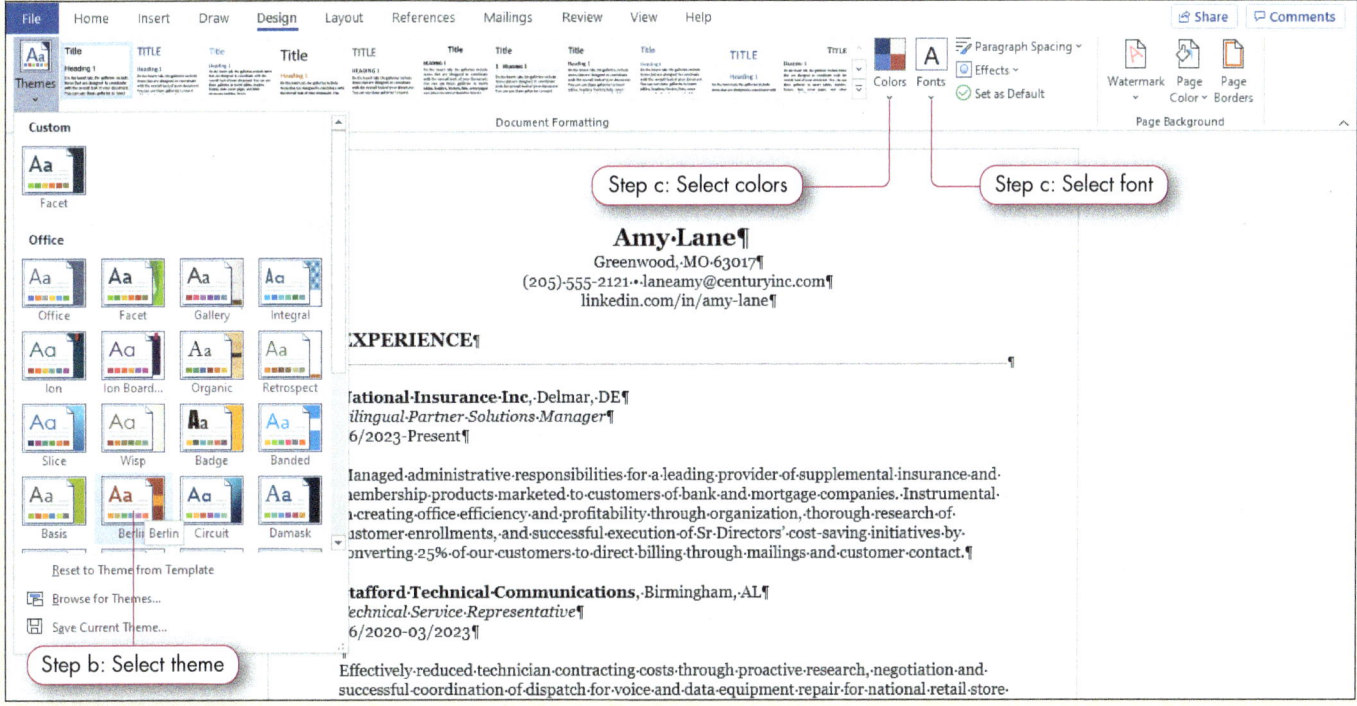

FIGURE 1.30 Select a Theme

a. Open *w01h2Vita* and save it as **w01h2Vita_LastFirst**. Click **Show/Hide** in the Paragraph group on the Home tab to display nonprinting formatting marks (unless they are already displayed).

b. Click the **Design tab**, click **Themes** in the Document Formatting group, and then select **Berlin**.

c. Click **Colors** in the Document Formatting group and select **Violet**. Click **Fonts** and select **Candara**.

The change in theme, color, and font selections will not immediately result in visible changes to the open document. A document theme becomes more evident when you work with page design features such as borders and color selections that are included in the theme settings. Such elements are not currently shown in the document.

d. Save the document.

WORK WITH SECTIONS AND FORMAT TEXT INTO COLUMNS

The résumé is to be arranged in a two-column display, with a column break ensuring balanced flow from one column to the next. Refer to Figure 1.31 as you complete Step 2.

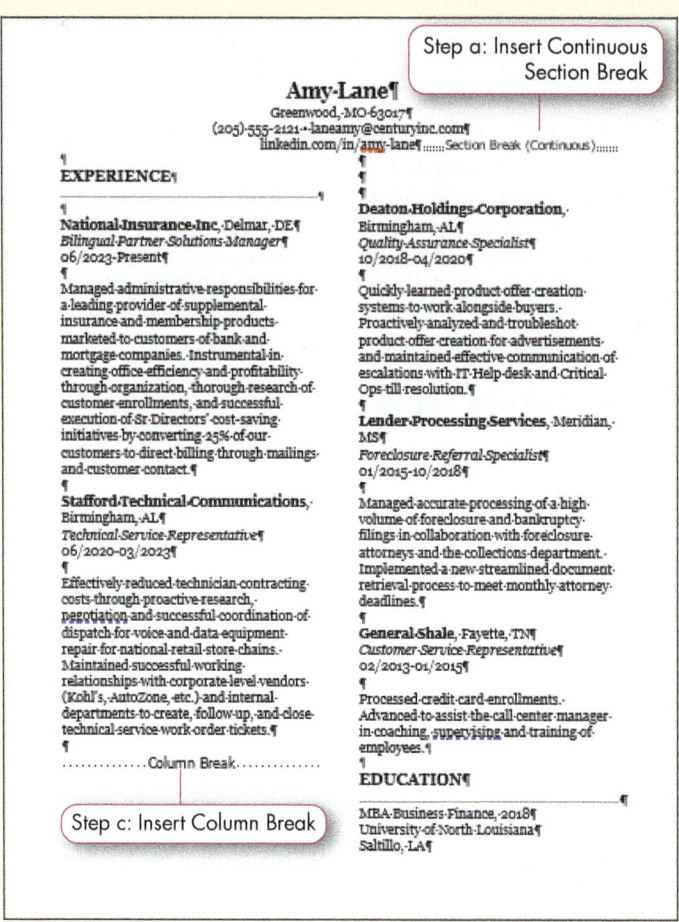

FIGURE 1.31 Insert Section and Column Breaks

a. Click to place the insertion point at the blank paragraph located just above the *EXPERIENCE* heading. Click the **Layout tab**, click **Breaks** in the Page Setup group, and then select **Continuous**.

Because you intend to format text following the address lines in two columns, you insert a section break. That way, the columnar layout from one section to the next can vary.

b. Ensure that the insertion point is still positioned at the blank paragraph. Click **Columns** in the Page Setup group and select **Two**. Scroll to the bottom of the page and note the company name and information that displays alone at the bottom of the left column.

c. Click before *Deaton Holdings Corporation*, ensuring that the insertion point is on the same line as the company name (not at the blank paragraph above). Click **Breaks** in the Page Setup group and select **Column**. Press **Enter** three times to reposition the company name slightly, resulting in a more attractive beginning to the second column.

d. Save the document.

You include an appropriate page border to add a bit of polish to the résumé while also using a watermark to identify the document as a sample. Refer to Figure 1.32 as you complete Step 3.

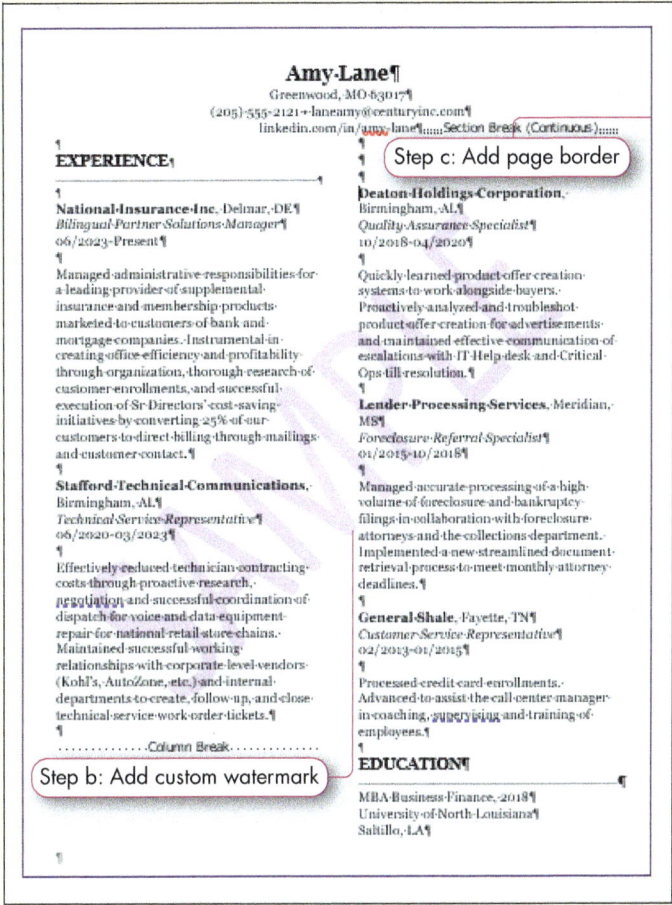

FIGURE 1.32 Configure Page Background

a. Click the **Design tab**. Click **Watermark** in the Page Background group. Scroll through watermarks and select **Sample 1**.

> **MAC TROUBLESHOOTING:** Select the Text option for a watermark and type SAMPLE in the text box. Change the orientation to Diagonal. Change the color as indicated in Step b.

b. Click **Watermark**. Click **Custom Watermark**. Click the **Color arrow** and select **Lavender, Accent 1, Darker 25%** (column 5, row 5). Click **OK**.

Because you limited theme colors to Violet, color choices are in a purple/gray/blue spectrum.

c. Click **Page Borders** in the Page Background group. Click **Box**. The line style should be the first one listed. Click the **Color arrow** and select **Lavender, Accent 1, Darker 50%** (column 5, row 6). Line weight is **½ pt**. Click **OK**.

d. Save the document.

By applying a style to headings in the résumé you ensure consistency. You then modify the heading style so that all text formatted in that style is adjusted at the same time. Refer to Figure 1.33 as you complete Step 4.

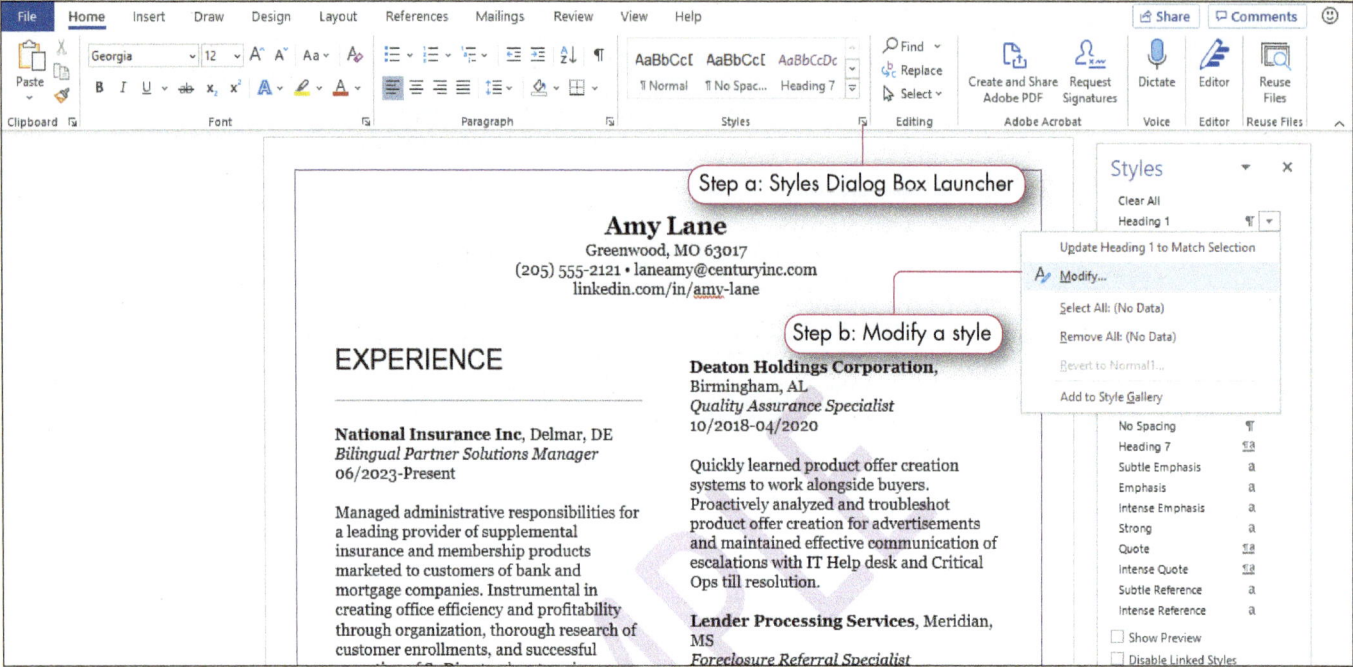

FIGURE 1.33 Modify a Style

a. Select **EXPERIENCE** near the top of page 1. Click the **Home tab**. Click the **Styles Dialog Box Launcher** to display the Styles pane. Click **Heading 1** in the Styles pane. Select the **EDUCATION** heading and click **Heading 1** in the Styles pane.

> **MAC TROUBLESHOOTING:** Click Styles Pane on the Home tab in the Styles group to display the Styles pane.

b. Right-click **Heading 1** in the Styles pane and click **Modify**. Click **Bold** and change the font in the Modify Style dialog box to **12**. Change the font to **Times New Roman**. Click **OK**. Close the Styles pane.

> **MAC TROUBLESHOOTING:** Click the arrow beside Heading 1 in the current style box and select Modify Style.

Both headings that are styled as Heading 1 are changed to reflect the new settings.

c. Save the document.

By changing the document view, you will see how text flows on and between pages. A manual page break ensures that no heading is left alone at the bottom of a page. Refer to Figure 1.34 as you complete Step 5.

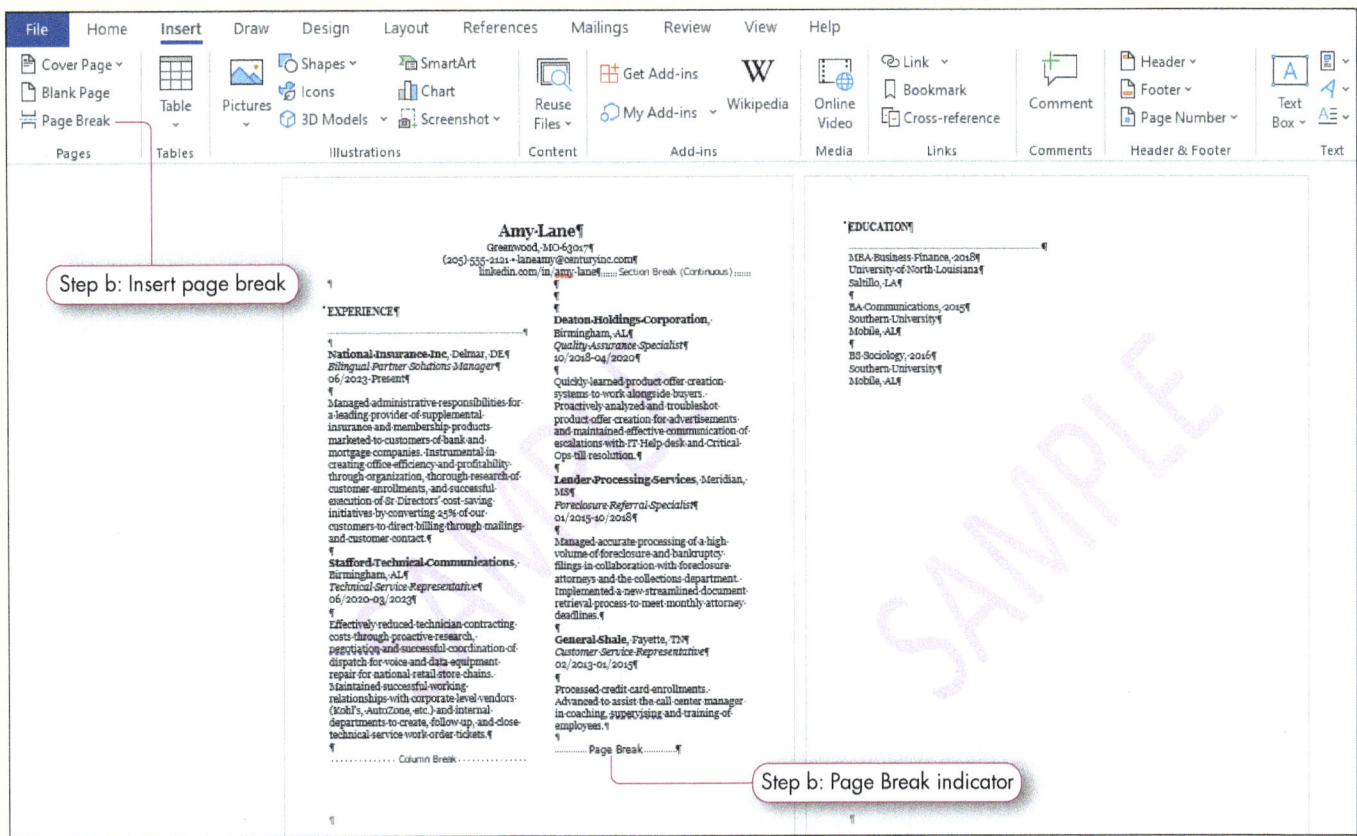

FIGURE 1.34 Manage Page Flow

a. Click the **View tab**. Click **Multiple Pages** in the Zoom group.

Note the poor placement of the Education heading at the bottom of the right column on page 1.

b. Click **100%** in the Zoom group. Click before the *Education* heading at the bottom of the right column on the first page. Ensure that the insertion point is on the same line as the *Education* heading, not on the blank paragraph above. Click the **Insert tab** and click **Page Break** in the Pages group.

You insert a page break so that the Education heading is more attractively placed on a new page.

c. Save and close the document. Keep Word open if you plan to continue with the next Hands-On Exercise. If not, exit Word.

Document Preparation and Distribution

After organizing and formatting a document, you often save it and prepare it for use by others. In so doing, you can take advantage of features in Word that enable you to manipulate the file in a variety of ways, including ensuring that people with different abilities are able to read and edit the document. You might also choose to include information about the file that does not display in the document, such as a title, author name, subject, and keywords. Such information further identifies the file and can be used as a basis on which to search for or categorize a document later. As you develop a document, you have the option to save the file so that you can access it later, and you should consider methods of document retrieval so that important documents are always available.

In this section, you will consider ways to save a document in alternative formats as well as to share a document electronically with others. In addition, you will explore ways to prepare a document for distribution, including ensuring that a document is as readable as possible, converting a file created in an earlier version to the most current, checking for sensitive information included in a file, and ensuring adequate document retrieval if a document is lost or corrupted. Finally, you will be introduced to Word's language and translation features.

Save and Share Documents

Documents are often developed by individuals who organize, format, and save them for later access. Those documents can be saved to cloud storage, such as OneDrive, for ease of access from any location, although they can also be saved locally on a USB drive or hard drive. In a global workplace, however, a document is often a shared project, necessitating simultaneous editing by people in different locations. Saving documents in formats and locations that facilitate easy retrieval while also sharing those documents so that global access is possible is a routine process within workplace communities and across the globe.

In addition, assigning document properties to a saved file both identifies the document and simplifies the search process, should it be necessary later. Using Word's language and translation features, you can ensure that a document is not only readily available from any location but also understandable by those who may not speak the same language.

STEP 1 › Save in Alternative File Formats

The typical workplace is no longer geographically confined to one location. Instead, documents are often saved in locations or formats that facilitate easy retrieval and editing by others. While saving a document to OneDrive and then sharing it electronically makes it possible for people in other locations to view and edit the document online, you should also consider how the file might be accessed and whether co-editors have appropriate software to open a shared file. In that case, it is important to ensure that the document is saved differently, perhaps in Rich Text Format (RTF) or Portable Document Format (PDF).

Saving a file as an RTF or a PDF makes it possible for the file to be opened in other software in addition to Word. When making a document available to others, you should consider the file format that would ensure simple access for them or that may be required. If you are uploading a file to a proprietary website, for example, a more globally accessible format such as PDF or RTF might be preferable. Or perhaps an employer's applicant website might require uploaded résumés to be saved in PDF format for ease of transfer and viewing. Finally, if you are not certain that those who will access a shared document have a current Word version, you might first save it in RTF format, which is easily opened and edited regardless of the Word version.

A Word document saved in PDF format is primarily intended for viewing, not editing, although you can use Word to open and minimally edit a PDF document. Some features of a PDF document, such as tables and graphics, are not always transferred seamlessly into a Word document if the intent is to edit the file. RTF file format also retains the original appearance of a document and is widely accessible across many platforms and programs. Regardless of Word version, an RTF file can be opened, making it a favorite format for sharing files with those who are using a much earlier Word version or who do not have access to Word at all. Like a PDF file, an RTF document is accessible on a Mac system as well as a Windows-based computer. Even so, you should remain aware that saving a Word document in PDF or RTF format is primarily used for viewing, as other software types might not be able to accommodate all the current Word features.

If you plan to save a document in a format other than Word (.docx), you should first save it in Word format. Then, browse to the location where you intend to save the document and change the file type (see Figure 1.35). Depending upon the Word update on your computer, you might first have to click More options, but before completing the save, you should consider the file type, selecting whatever is appropriate. Saving a document as a PDF is also an option when you click the File tab.

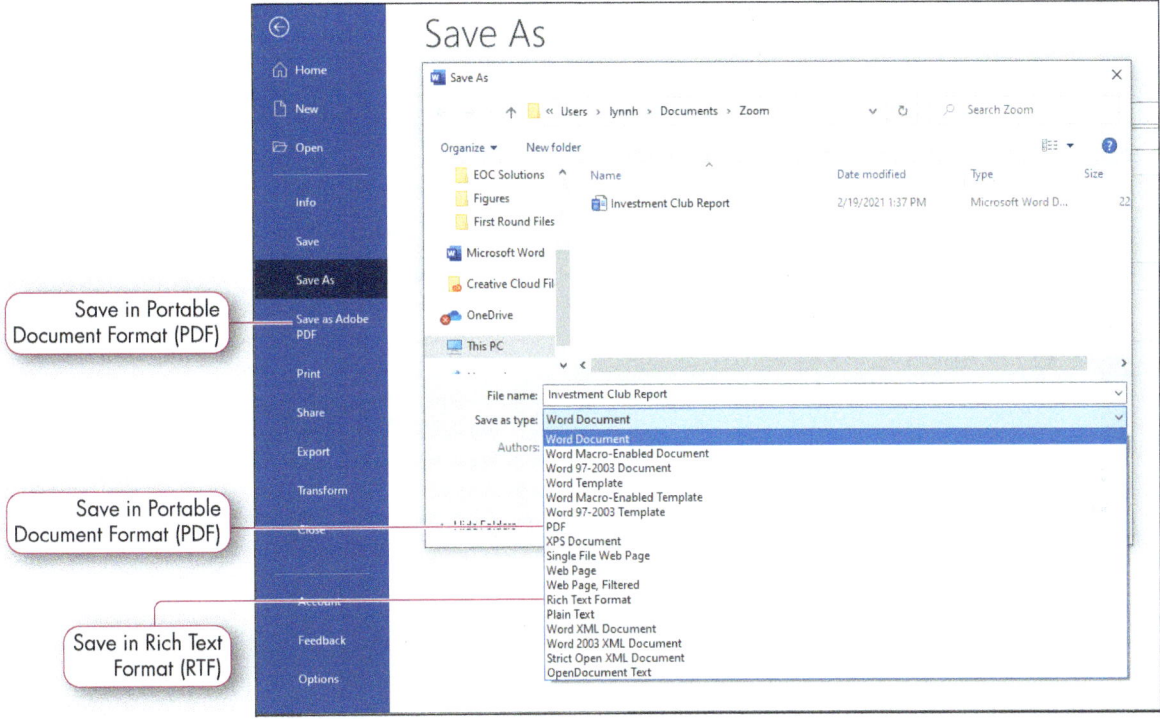

FIGURE 1.35 Select a File Type

STEP 2 ## Modify Document Properties

Occasionally, you might want to include information to identify a document, such as author, document title, or general comments. Those data elements, or **document properties**, are saved with the document, but do not appear in the document as it displays onscreen or is printed. Although you can instruct Word to print document properties, such print options are not the default. Standard document properties that you can assign include author, company, and subject, among others. Such document properties can be useful in categorizing documents and searching for them later. For example, suppose you apply a tag of Computer Applications 225 to all documents you create that are associated with that college class. Later, you can use that tag as a search term, locating all associated documents. Because tags are managed by the operating system instead of a single program such as Word, they are available across applications.

Tags can therefore be searched from different applications—perhaps identifying related PowerPoint presentations and Word documents.

Some properties are automatically updated, such as file size and file creation date, while others are optionally created or denoted by the document creator. If you change the author, or add a title or comments, that information is saved with the file. Comments are notes to yourself or other authors, documenting a process or intention, and they are especially helpful when several authors are collaborating.

To add tags and comments, as well as statistical information related to the current document, click the File tab and ensure that Info is selected. Data such as file size, number of pages, and total words are displayed in the right pane on the Info window (see Figure 1.36). You can modify some document information in this view, such as adding a title, tags, or comments. Additional document information can identify a document by author, subject, or title. For more possibilities, click Properties and then Advanced Properties (see Figure 1.36). You can then navigate through the file's dialog box, clicking the Summary tab to add or modify properties.

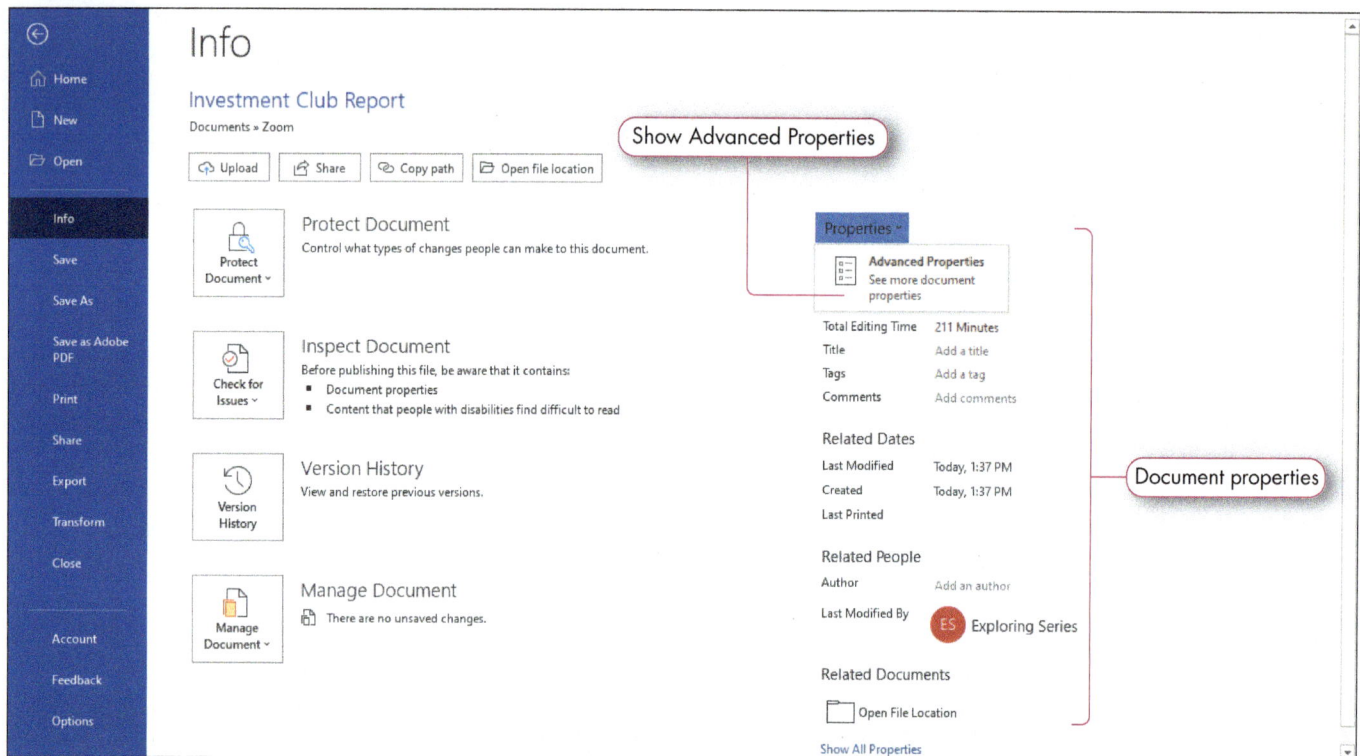

FIGURE 1.36 Work with Document Properties

Although standard document properties, such as title, author, and comments, are helpful in organizing documents by category, you can create your own custom document properties, as well. Suppose you want to identify a document by date assigned, or perhaps as a part of a particular project. Such properties are not considered standard property fields but can be created.

HOW TO

Create a custom property:

1. Click the File tab.
2. Ensure that Info is selected. Click Properties.
3. Click Advanced Properties.
4. Click the Custom tab. Scroll through existing fields or create a custom field, assigning a field type and value.

Share Documents Electronically

If a document requires collaboration and editing by several people, you can share it so that others can modify the document simultaneously. Other times, you might want to share the document so that others can view it but not change it. Using Microsoft 365, sharing a document is as simple as clicking an option on the ribbon.

If a document to be shared is open, click Share at the top right side of the ribbon (see Figure 1.37). If you have not yet saved the document to OneDrive or SharePoint Online, you will be prompted to do so. Once the file is saved, you will choose to email a link to collaborators or to copy a link to share in another way. At that point, you also have the option of attaching the document as a PDF or Word document through email as an alternative way to share the document.

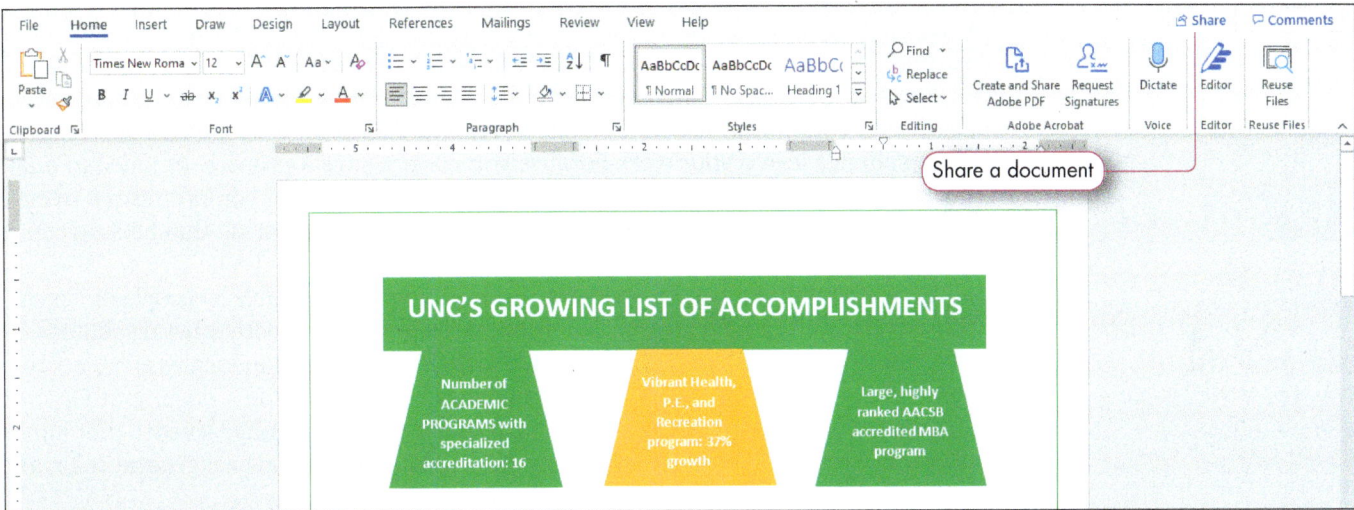

FIGURE 1.37 Share a Document

You can also begin the process of sharing an open document by clicking Share on the File tab. Yet another option to share a file is presented in the Save dialog box as you save a document for the first time.

If a document has already been saved to OneDrive, and you are signed onto your OneDrive account with OneDrive files shown onscreen, select the document to be shared and click Share (or right-click the document and select Share). At that point, you will indicate how you intend to share the document—through email or a copied link—and you can indicate whether it should be available for shared editing or merely viewing privileges.

A shared document does not need to be downloaded from its shared location. Instead, those who are editing the document work within the same online location, with changes being automatically saved to the original. There is no need to download the document unless it is necessary to use features that are available only in a full Word installation, instead of the more limited Word for the web version available in OneDrive.

STEP 3 ▶ Use Language and Translation Features

As a globally used application, Word enables you to work with different languages, setting a default language for editing, proofing, and display as well as translating between languages. In fact, Word gives you the option of working with more than 70 languages.

Entire documents can be translated into another language, creating a separate document as a result. Alternatively, you can select text to translate and then indicate the language to translate into, with the result displayed in a Translator pane. To translate an entire document into another language, click Translate on the Review tab and click Translate Document. Indicate the language you want to use in the Translator pane and within a short time a new document in that language is displayed. The original document is not affected by the translation. If, instead, only a single text selection is to be translated, select the text, click Translate and click Translate Selection. Indicate the language, with the result shown in the Translator pane.

Using the Language command on the Review tab, you can choose the default language to use for editing, proofing, or display. If you like, you can set the display and editing or authoring languages independently of each other. For example, the display language—what is shown on the ribbon and other displays—might be English, while the authoring language could be French, or another of the languages supported by Microsoft 365. Language options are also available when you click the File tab, Options, and Language.

Prepare a Document for Distribution

There will be occasions when you want to distribute a document to another individual or group. Whether it is a report to submit to your instructor or a memo on which you collaborated, most likely the document is something that will be shared with others. Regardless of how you plan to develop, save, and distribute a document, you will not want to chance losing your work because you did not save it properly or failed to make a backup copy. Inevitably, files are lost, systems crash, or a virus compromises a storage method. So, the importance of saving work frequently and ensuring that backup copies exist cannot be overemphasized.

A document developed for wide distribution should be readable by people of varying ability levels, even those who are visually impaired or who deal with other disabilities. To assist with that task, Word includes an ***Accessibility Checker*** that locates elements that might cause difficulty for people with disabilities. As you develop a document for such an audience, keep in mind the possible need to use simple language, ensure that font is sufficiently large, provide enough contrast between font color and background color, and provide other types of appropriate document organization.

STEP 4 ▶ Ensure Document Accessibility

In the United States alone, several million people rely on some sort of assistive technology to access electronic documents and webpages. If documents intended for wide distribution are not created with the need for that technology in mind, it is very likely that those documents will not be readable by many people. It may also be necessary to produce documents in compliance with federal legislation related to accessibility. Word assists with development of accessible documents through the Accessibility Checker, but you should keep the following points in mind as you develop a document so that a check will likely find few suggestions for improvement.

- Use appropriate font style and size. Sans serif fonts, such as Arial and Verdana, are good choices for readability, as they are clean and uncluttered. Make sure the font size is at least 12 pt.

- Use contrasting colors and do not rely solely on color to make a point. Readers with a level of color-blindness or those with glaucoma or macular degeneration typically have difficulty reading text that does not contrast strongly with the background. Do not assume that color choice necessarily conveys a message. For example, using a green X to indicate a positive result and a red X as a negative indicator might be less effective than a green Y and a red N, which represent the intended outcome both by color and by letter.

- Add alternative text and captions. Including alternative text and captions for images, pictures, tables, and various objects in a document makes them accessible by screen readers. In that way, the content of those items is understandable to those with certain disabilities.

- Construct simple tables with header rows. When developing a Word table, be sure to use only one row for a header, clearly formatted differently from remaining table text. Do not merge or split table cells and do not leave any rows or columns blank.

- Use meaningful hyperlink text. Do not create hyperlinks with such text as "Click here," as a person using assistive technology might navigate a document by skipping from hyperlink to hyperlink, without access to surrounding text that would provide meaning to such hyperlinks. Instead, make sure a hyperlink provides clear description of the link destination.

- Use built-in formatting styles, especially in the development of headings and lists. Headings that are defined using Word's built-in heading styles enable users to quickly skip through a document by navigating from one heading to another. Use bulleted or numbered lists where appropriate to clearly identify items as included in groups.

Before a document is distributed, run the Accessibility Checker so that questionable areas are first identified and corrected. Select Check Accessibility on the Review tab. As an alternative, you can also choose Check for Issues from the Info group on the File tab and indicate that you want to check accessibility. The Accessibility pane (see Figure 1.38) displays errors (content that is difficult or impossible for those with disabilities), warnings (content that is challenging for those with disabilities), and tips (suggestions for better organization or presentation).

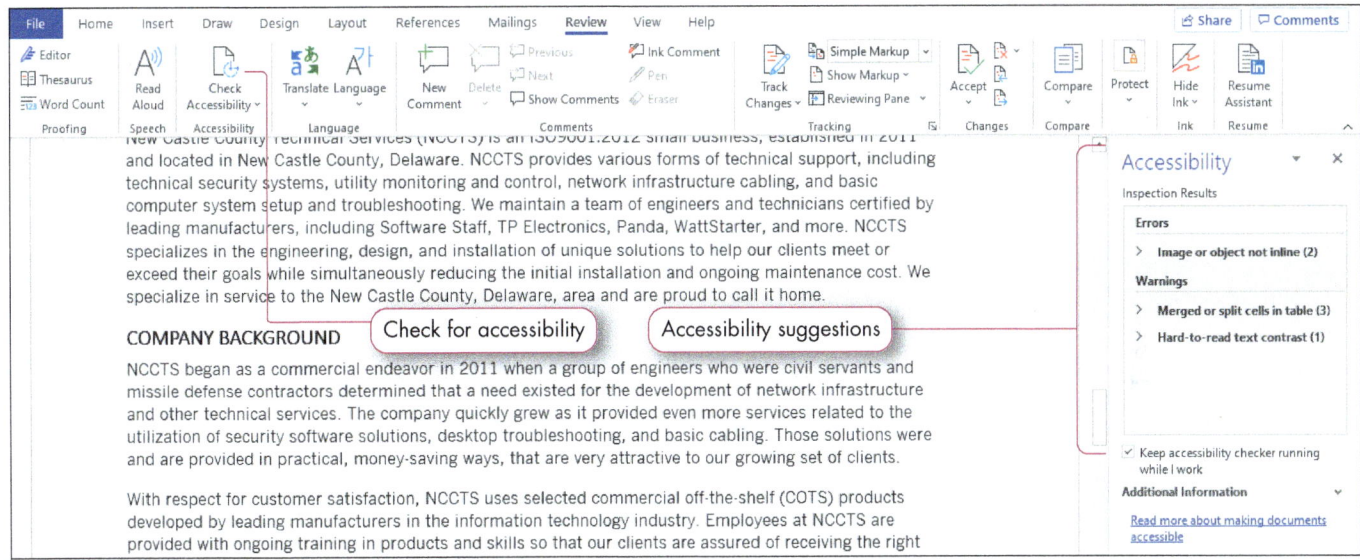

FIGURE 1.38 Use Accessibility Checker

Ensure Document Compatibility

Microsoft 365, a subscription plan that is preferred by most Word users, ensures that Word is continually updated with the most recent additions and software improvements. Whereas historically Microsoft relied solely on major updates—called versions—of its Microsoft Office software for purchase every few years, there is currently less reliance on that form of development and distribution. When that was the norm, however, each new software version was likely to incorporate a different type of file, so that users of early versions might not be able to open files created by newer software installations. While such a challenge is becoming much less likely, you should be aware of the possibility and should understand how to check a document for compatibility before distributing it to those with less up-to-date software installations. From the Info window on the File tab, select Check for Issues and then click Check Compatibility.

Occasionally, you might receive a Word document that was created in a much earlier Word version. In that case, the words *Compatibility Mode* are included in the title bar, advising you that some of Word's features may not be available or viewable in the document (see Figure 1.39). While in Compatibility Mode, you might not be able to use new and enhanced Word features; by keeping the file in Compatibility Mode, you ensure that people with earlier Word versions will still have full editing capability when they receive the document. Word simplifies the process of converting a Word document to the newest version. Click the File tab and click Convert (only shown if the file is not in the newest format). Click OK.

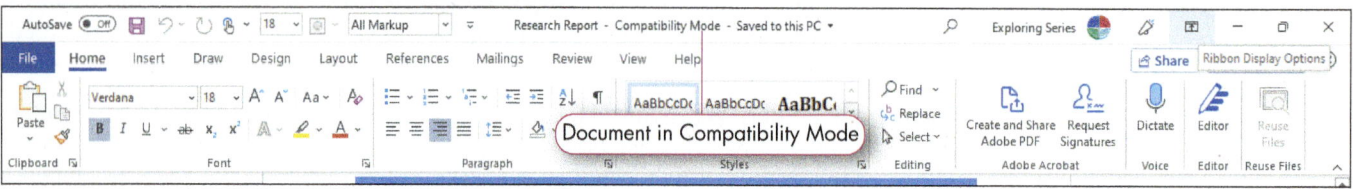

FIGURE 1.39 Compatibility Mode

Understand Document Retrieval

It is inevitable that you will, at some point, lose access to a document before you have saved it, or possibly after you have made a significant amount of progress since the last save. Perhaps the problem is a power disruption or an unexplainable failure that causes Word to become unresponsive. In these instances, the immediate need is to get your document back, without having lost too much content. In a proactive mode, you might have configured Word to create an automatic backup copy so that you can retrieve most, if not all, of what you have typed. If you are using OneDrive to save the document, you will find that the document was automatically saved and is readily available. Even if you have not yet saved a document at all, it is likely that Word can recover much of the document. Obviously, Word is well equipped to address many situations related to recovering documents. Even so, the best practice is to save a document often as you are creating it, perhaps even configuring Word to automatically create a backup copy, so that you are less likely to have to depend on Word's safety nets related to recovering files.

A possible scenario is one in which you close a document without saving it. You may fear that it is gone forever, but that may not be the case. A link to recover unsaved documents is shown at the bottom of the list of recent documents when you click the File tab and click Open, or when you manage documents from the Info window on the File tab.

HOW TO

Locate an unsaved document:

1. Click the File tab and ensure that Info is selected.
2. Click Manage Document.
3. Click Recover Unsaved Documents.
4. Open the file (with an ASD extension, indicating a recovered document) and then save it as a Word file, changing the type to Word Document during the save operation.

If you save a document to OneDrive, which is the default save location if you are logged in to a OneDrive account as you work with Word, you do not have to be quite as conscientious about saving often because an open document is automatically saved every few seconds. The **AutoSave** feature is applicable to files saved to OneDrive, OneDrive for Business, and SharePoint Online. If you prefer to save files on local storage, such as a flash drive or a folder on a hard drive, Word provides support through its **AutoRecover** feature, in which you can prescribe an interval of time at which a file should automatically be saved. Word can then recover a document, losing only those changes that might have occurred between saves. Word will be able to recover a previous version of your document when you restart the program, with any files that are recovered shown. By default, file information is saved every 5 minutes (see Figure 1.40), but you can adjust the setting so that the AutoRecover process occurs more or less frequently. You can access controls to adjust the time interval through selections in the Word Options dialog box.

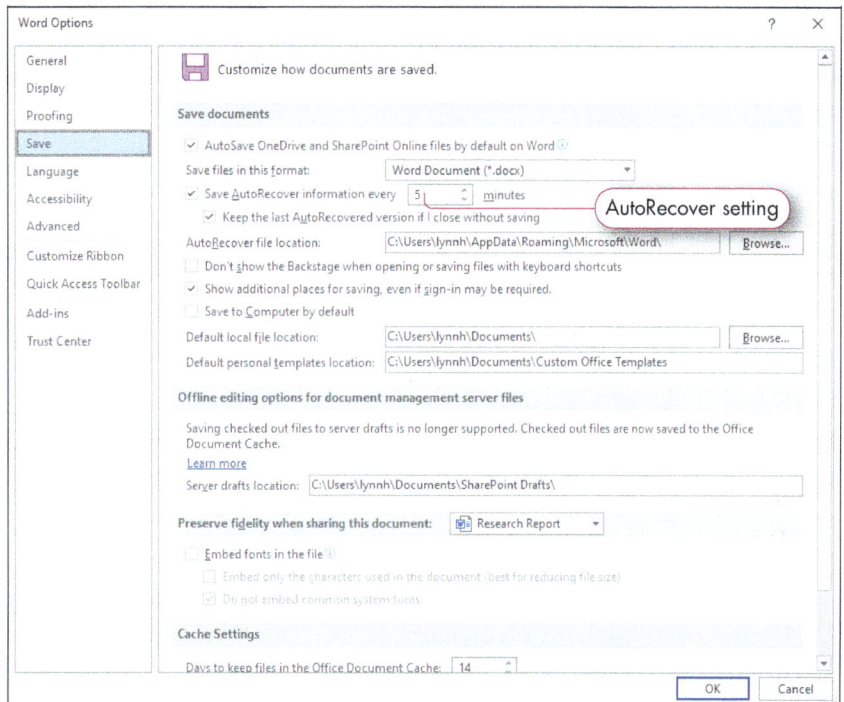

FIGURE 1.40 The AutoRecover Feature

You can also configure Word to create a backup copy each time a document is saved. Although the setting to always create a backup copy is not enabled by default, you can enable it from Word Options in the Advanced category. Even so, creating frequent backup copies can slow your system and may not be altogether necessary, given the excellent File History facility provided by Windows. Click the File tab and click Options. Click Advanced. Scroll to the Save group and select Always create backup copy. A backup copy is saved in the same folder as the original but includes a slightly different file name and the WBK extension, which represents a Word Backup file.

Run the Document Inspector

Before you send or give a document to another person, you should run the **Document Inspector** to reveal any hidden or personal data in the file. For privacy or security reasons, you might want to remove certain items contained in the document, such as author name, comments made by one or more people who have access to the document, or document server locations. Word's Document Inspector will check for and enable you to remove various types of identifying information, including:

- Comments, revisions, versions, and annotations
- Document properties and personal information
- Custom XML data
- Headers, footers, and watermarks
- Invisible content
- Hidden text

Because some information removed by the Document Inspector cannot be recovered with the Undo command, you should save a copy of your original document, using a different name, prior to inspecting the document.

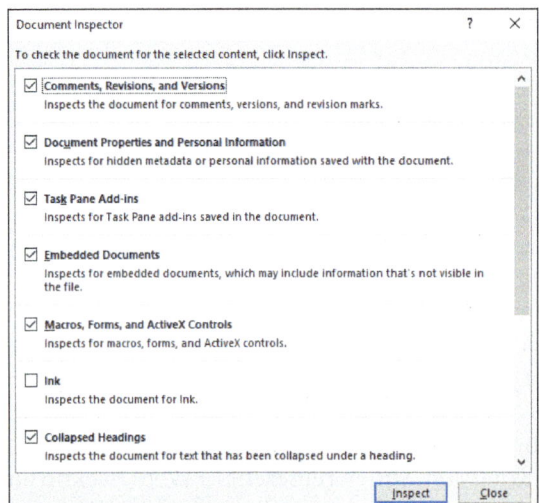

FIGURE 1.41 Inspect a Document

Critical Thinking

9. Explain why you might want to remove document properties from a file, especially because those document properties are not actually printed or shown when the document is onscreen. ***p. 159***

10. Explain the importance of using the Accessibility Checker for a document that you plan to distribute. Provide an example of what the Accessibility Checker might look for. ***pp. 156–157***

11. Provide a rationale for why OneDrive is the default location for saving documents (if a user is signed onto a Microsoft account). In other words, what advantages might there be to saving files to OneDrive instead of local storage such as a hard drive or flash drive? ***p. 158***

12. Provide an example of why you might want to share a document online instead of simply sending it as an attachment through email. ***p. 155***

Hands-On Exercises

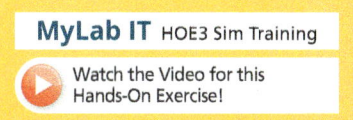
Skills covered: Save in Alternative File Formats • Modify Document Properties • Use Language and Translation Features • Ensure Document Accessibility • Run the Document Inspector

3 Document Preparation and Distribution

Employers often require that job search material be uploaded, occasionally in a readable format other than Word. You will combine the previously developed cover letter and résumé into one document and save it as a PDF file, illustrating the process for MCCC students. In a global economy, it is also possible that documents need to be translated into another language, which you will do in this exercise. Finally, using document properties and checking for accessibility, you ensure that job search material is properly categorized and without issues related to readability by those with vision challenges.

STEP 1   SAVE IN ALTERNATIVE FILE FORMATS

You combine the cover letter and résumé into one document and save it as a PDF file. Refer to Figure 1.42 as you complete Step 1.

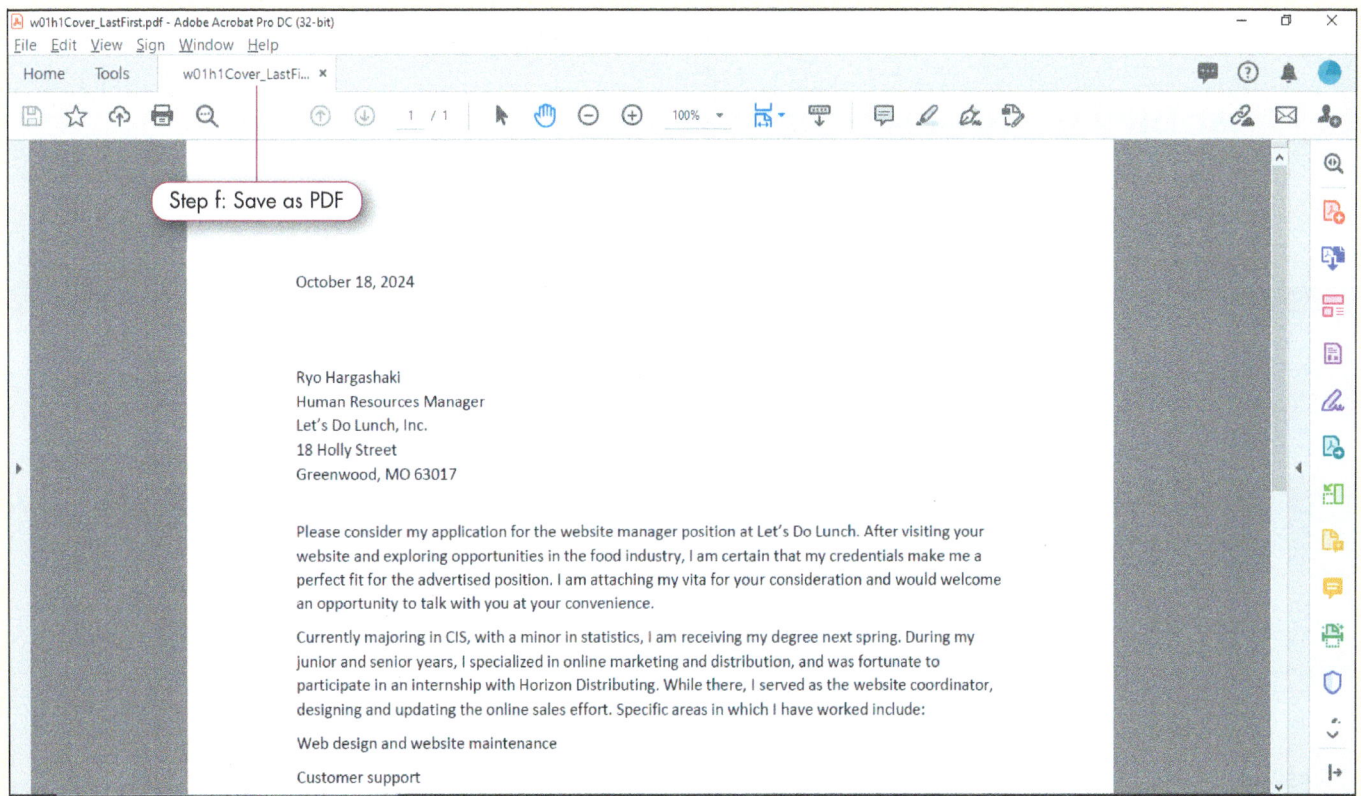

FIGURE 1.42 Save as a PDF

a. Open *w01h1Cover_LastFirst*. Click **Show/Hide** in the Paragraph group on the Home tab to display nonprinting formatting marks (unless they are already displayed).

b. Move the insertion point to the end of the document. Press **Enter**. Click the **Layout tab**, click **Breaks** in the Page Setup group, and then select **Continuous** to insert a section break.

Because you plan to insert a two-columned résumé after the cover letter, you create a section break. That way, the first page of the letter will remain formatted without columns, while the résumé that follows the letter in the same document can maintain its two-column format.

c. Click the **Insert tab**. Click the **Object arrow** and select **Text from File**. Navigate to the location where you saved *w01h2Vita_LastFirst* and double-click the file.

> **TROUBLESHOOTING:** If the résumé beginning with the Experience heading does not display in two columns, click before the Experience heading, click the Layout tab, click Columns, and select Two.

d. Scroll to the bottom of page 1 and ensure that the résumé begins on a new page, separately from the cover letter. If it does not, click before the first word of the résumé. Click the **Insert tab**, and click **Page Break** in the Pages group on the Insert tab.

Because the résumé should begin on a new page, you insert a page break.

e. Click at the top of page 3. Click the **Design tab**, click **Page Borders**, and select **None**.

You decide that a page border might detract from the résumé so you remove it.

f. Save the document with the filename **w01h3Job_LastFirst**. Click the **File tab** and click **Save As**. Change the document type to **PDF**, leaving the filename as is. Save the file. Close the PDF file, if it displays, leaving the Word document open.

STEP 2 ## MODIFY DOCUMENT PROPERTIES

By assigning document properties to the sample job search document, you identify it by author and by keywords. Refer to Figure 1.43 as you complete Step 2.

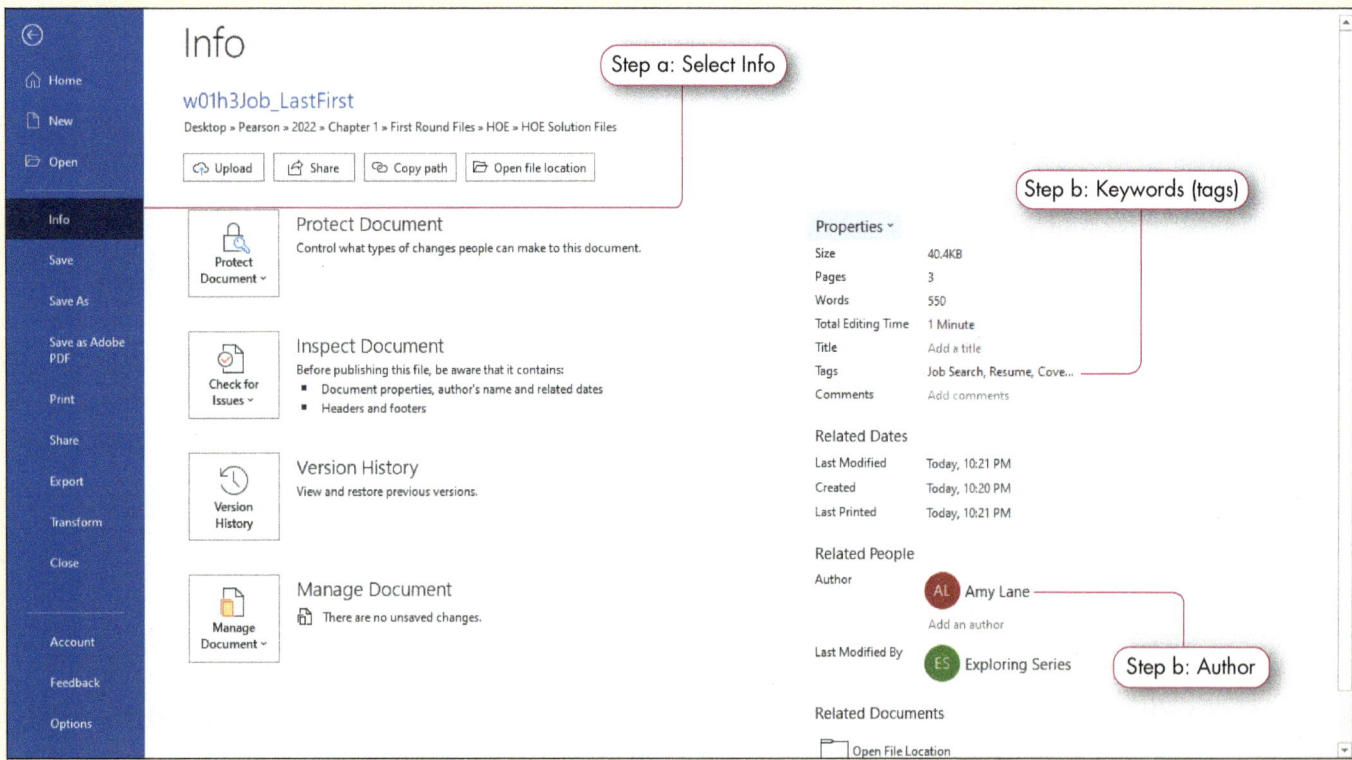

FIGURE 1.43 Modify Document Properties

a. Click the **File tab** and select **Info**. Click **Properties** on the right side of the Info window. Click **Advanced Properties**.

> **MAC TROUBLESHOOTING:** Select File on the menu bar and click Properties.

b. Click in the Author box in the Properties dialog box and remove the existing author. Type **Amy Lane**. Remove any other document properties. Click in the **Keywords box** and type **Job Search, Resume, Cover Letter**. Click **OK**.

Note the keywords that display as Tags in the Properties area of the Info window. As such, you can conduct a search for the document based on the tags included.

c. Press **Esc** to return to the document.

d. Save the document.

STEP 3 ⟩ **USE LANGUAGE AND TRANSLATION FEATURES**

You translate the document into Italian and save it as a separate document so that it can be shared in other areas of the world for a global job search. Refer to Figure 1.44 as you complete Step 3.

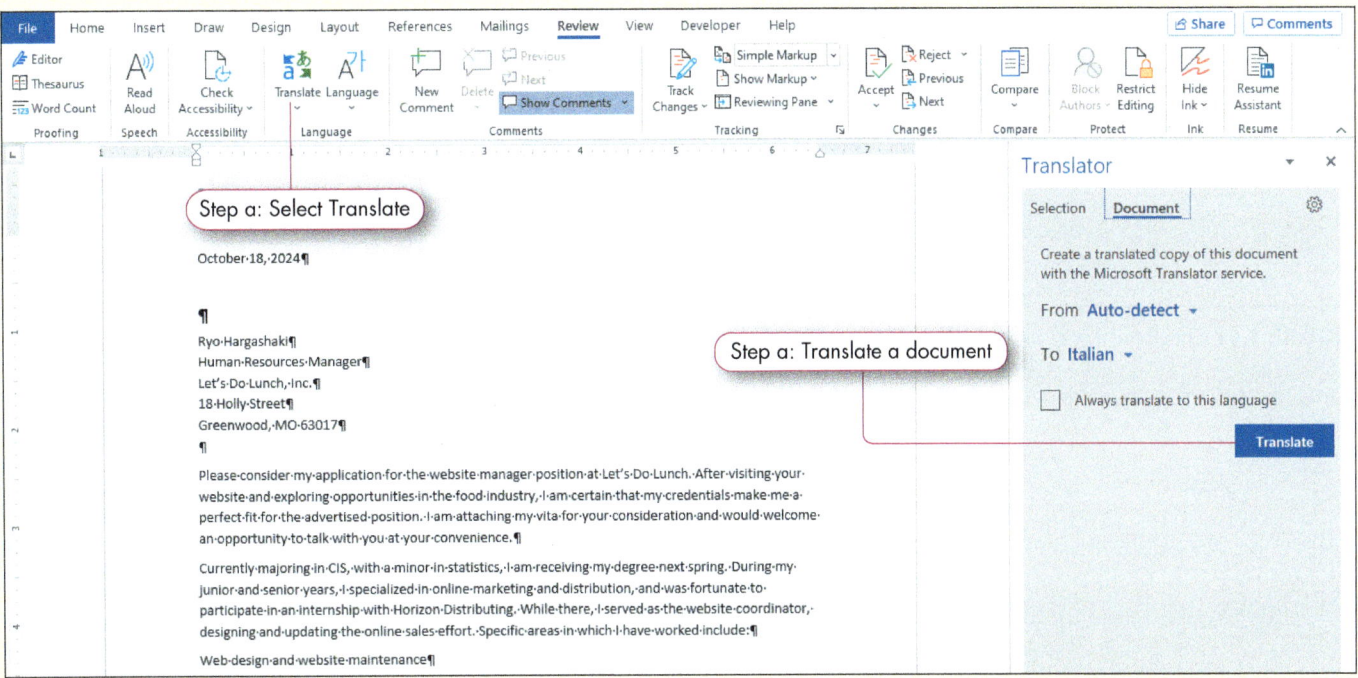

FIGURE 1.44 Translate a Document

a. Click the **Review tab** and click **Translate** in the Language group. Click **Translate Document**. Click the **To arrow** in the Translator pane and scroll to select **Italian**. Click **Translate**.

A new Word document opens with the translated text.

b. Scroll through the document, noting possible poorly placed page breaks. Note the scant amount of text on page 3.

Although the document is not as attractively arranged in its translated form, you will leave it as is, because the purpose was simply to translate its English equivalent.

c. Save the file as **w01h3ItalianVita_LastFirst**. Close the file but leave Word open.

The original document remains open.

d. Close the Translator pane. Save the document.

Because the job search material is likely to be read by others, you check it for accessibility by all. You also inspect the document for hidden or personal data. Refer to Figure 1.45 as you complete Step 4.

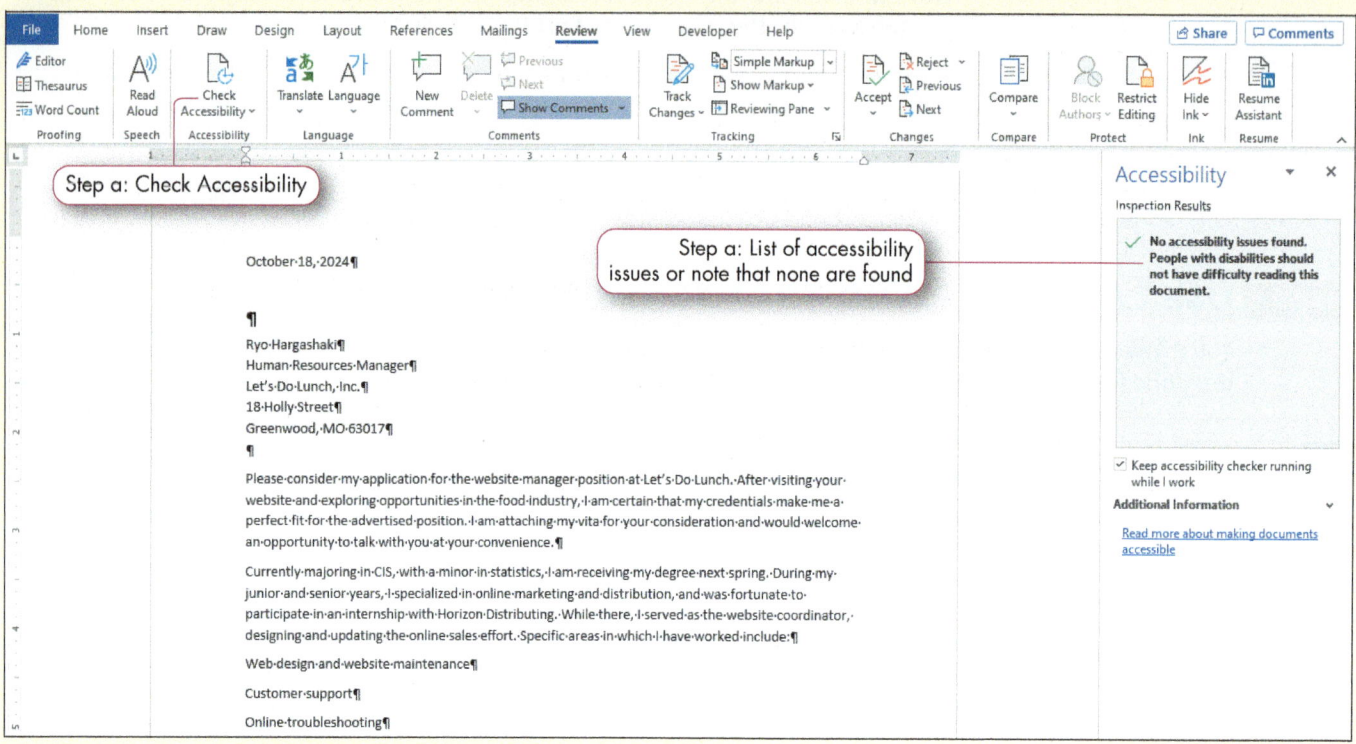

FIGURE 1.45 Check for Accessibility

a. Click **Check Accessibility** (not the arrow) in the Accessibility group. Inspection results display in the Accessibility pane. Although one or more issues may be identified, you will not make corrections now. Close the Accessibility pane.

> **MAC TROUBLESHOOTING:** Click Tools on the menu bar and click Check Accessibility.

b. Click **Save** in the Quick Access toolbar.

Before checking for and possibly removing personal and hidden information during a document inspection, you save the document.

c. Click the **File tab**. Click **Info**. Click **Check for Issues** and click **Inspect Document**. Click **Inspect**. Note that Document Properties and Personal Information as well as Headers, Footers, and Watermarks are areas flagged for possible removal. Because you do not need to remove that information, click **Close**.

> **MAC TROUBLESHOOTING:** Click Tools and click Protect Document. Because you do not intend to remove personal information, close the dialog box.

d. Save and close the file. Exit Word. Based on your instructor's directions, submit:
w01h3ItalianVita_LastFirst
w01h3Job_LastFirst
w01h3Job_LastFirst.pdf

Chapter Objectives Review

After reading this chapter, you have accomplished the following objectives:

1. **Begin and edit a document.**
   - **Create a document:** Begin a blank document when Word opens and type text.
   - **Reuse text:** Text from previously created documents can be inserted in another document.
   - **Use a template:** Predesigned documents save time by providing a starting point.
   - **Add text and navigate a document:** The insertion point indicates where the text you type will be placed. Use scroll bars or keyboard shortcuts to move around in a document.
   - **Find and replace document content:** Search a document to locate words or phrases, with the option of replacing them with others.
   - **Review spelling and grammar:** Use the Review tab to make sure all documents are free of spelling and grammatical errors.

2. **Customize Word.**
   - **Explore Word options:** Word options are global settings you can select, such as whether to check spelling automatically, or where to save a file by default.
   - **Use AutoCorrect:** The AutoCorrect feature automatically corrects many commonly misspelled words and enables you to create custom entries to simplify document development.

3. **Modify a document.**
   - **Select a document theme:** A document theme applies global settings related to color, font, and other formatting characteristics.
   - **Work with sections:** A document can be divided into sections so that layout can vary among them. For example, a cover page section can be vertically centered, while pages in another section of the same document are aligned from the top.
   - **Format text into columns:** A document or section divided into columns separates text attractively on a page. Such an arrangement is often used in newsletters.
   - **Configure page background elements:** Watermarks, page borders, and page color are page background features often used to add interest or identification to a document.

4. **Apply styles.**
   - **Select and modify styles:** A style applies preset formatting characteristics to paragraphs or selected text.

   - **Create a new style:** A new style can be created and applied to other selections. Often, a new style is based on existing text.
   - **Use a style set:** A style set combines title, heading, and paragraph styles so that all elements in a document can be formatted at once.

5. **View a document in different ways.**
   - **Select a document view:** Word includes various views that are useful in different stages of document production.
   - **Change the zoom setting:** Change zoom on a document to reduce or expand the view of various parts of a document.
   - **View a document and manage page flow:** A print preview shows a document in page-by-page view. Insert a page break to force a new page where it would not otherwise occur.

6. **Save and share documents.**
   - **Save in alternative file formats:** A document can be saved in a format that is accessible to others, regardless of specific software availability. PDF and RTF are common alternative file formats.
   - **Modify document properties:** Apply document properties such as author, comments, and keywords to better identify a document.
   - **Share documents electronically:** Sharing a document to facilitate global access and simultaneous editing is the norm in many workplaces, made possible by such online resources as OneDrive.
   - **Use language and translation features:** Word can translate a document or text selection into at least 70 languages.

7. **Prepare a document for distribution.**
   - **Ensure document accessibility:** The Accessibility Checker helps ensure that documents are readable by people with disabilities.
   - **Ensure document compatibility:** Word includes features that assist with converting documents from earlier file formats and saving files so they are easily accessible.
   - **Understand document retrieval:** Word's AutoSave, AutoRecover, and backup features address file recovery and help ensure that documents are not irretrievably lost.
   - **Run the Document Inspector:** Word's Document Inspector reveals any hidden or personal data in a file and enables you to remove sensitive information.

Key Terms Matching

Match the key terms with their definitions. Write the key term letter by the appropriate numbered definition.

a. Accessibility Checker

b. AutoCorrect

c. AutoRecover

d. AutoSave

e. Document Inspector

f. Document property

g. Document theme

h. Draft view

i. Insertion point

j. Microsoft Word

k. Outline view

l. Print Layout view

m. Read Mode

n. Style

o. Template

p. Thesaurus

q. Watermark

r. Web Layout view

s. Word processing software

t. Word wrap

1. _____ Text or graphic that displays behind text. **p. 137**

2. _____ A structural view of a document or presentation that can be collapsed or expanded as necessary. **p. 142**

3. _____ The feature that automatically moves words to the next line if they do not fit on the current line. **p. 117**

4. _____ The feature that enables Word to recover a previous version of a document. **p. 158**

5. _____ The tool that checks for document readability by people with disabilities. **p. 156**

6. _____ A computer application, such as Microsoft Word, used primarily with text to create, edit, and format documents. **p. 116**

7. _____ A view in which text reflows to screen-sized pages to make it easier to read. **p. 142**

8. _____ The feature that saves documents automatically so they can be retrieved later. **p. 158**

9. _____ The word processing application included in the Microsoft Office software suite. **p. 116**

10. _____ A predesigned document that may include formats that can be modified. **p. 119**

11. _____ A view that closely resembles the way a document will look when printed. **p. 142**

12. _____ A set of coordinating fonts, colors, and special effects that are combined into a package for use in document design. **p. 134**

13. _____ A feature that checks for and removes certain hidden and personal information from a document. **p. 159**

14. _____ A named collection of formatting characteristics that can be applied to characters or entire paragraphs. **p. 138**

15. _____ A view that shows a great deal of document space, but no margins, headers, footers, or other special features. **p. 142**

16. _____ A blinking bar that indicates where text that you next type will appear. **p. 120**

17. _____ A tool that enables you to find a synonym for a selected word. **p. 123**

18. _____ A feature that corrects standard misspellings and word errors as they are typed. **p. 126**

19. _____ A view that displays a document as it would appear on a webpage. **p. 142**

20. _____ A data element that is saved with a document but does not appear in the document as it is shown onscreen or is printed. **p. 153**

Multiple Choice

1. Which of the following activities enables various layout settings to be present within the same document?

   (a) Creating sections

   (b) Inserting a page break

   (c) Assigning document properties to various pages

   (d) Removing all soft returns between pages

2. What feature would you use to visually coordinate various elements of an entire document at one time, including color, font, and other format settings?

   (a) Template

   (b) Document theme

   (c) Watermark

   (d) Style

3. Which of the following is necessary before you rely on AutoSave to automatically save a document?

   (a) Check the AutoRecover setting in Word Options.

   (b) Ensure that Word is set to make an automatic backup every few minutes.

   (c) Save the document to local storage, such as a flash drive.

   (d) Save the document to OneDrive, OneDrive for Business, or SharePoint Online.

4. What happens when you modify an existing style?

   (a) The style is given a new name and location in the Styles pane.

   (b) The style replaces any previously defined style with the same name on the Design tab.

   (c) The new style settings are automatically applied to text formatted in that style.

   (d) The new style must be defined as a paragraph style and can be applied only to selected paragraphs.

5. Which of the following is a reason to use the Accessibility Checker?

   (a) To ensure compatibility with earlier Word versions

   (b) To comply with federal legislation related to disabilities

   (c) To provide access to appropriate document properties

   (d) To check for inaccessible styles

6. Suppose you find that a column heading within a newsletter is displayed at the end of a column, with remaining text continuing at the top of the next column. How would you keep the heading with the text so that it is not divided awkwardly?

   (a) Insert a Continuous section break before the heading.

   (b) Insert a soft return before the heading.

   (c) Insert a Column break before the heading.

   (d) Insert a hard return before the heading.

7. In which of the following situations would you consider inserting a soft return instead of a hard return?

   (a) At the end of a single line of an address, with more address lines to follow

   (b) At the end of a paragraph

   (c) At the end of a page

   (d) Before a section break

8. Why might you want to display nonprinting characters?

   (a) To simplify the process of converting a document to an earlier Word version

   (b) To facilitate the inspection of a document for hidden or personal information

   (c) To assist with troubleshooting a document and modifying its appearance

   (d) To enable spell checking on the document

9. Why might you consider saving a document in PDF format?

   (a) When uploading a document to a proprietary website for easy accessibility by others

   (b) To ensure that a file cannot be opened in any application other than Word

   (c) To make it possible to include document properties in the file

   (d) So that the document can be opened on a Mac

10. To identify a document as a draft, and not in final form, which of the following would you most likely add to the document?

    (a) Style

    (b) Watermark

    (c) Template

    (d) Document property

Practice Exercises

1 Therapy Dogs in Action

As the media relations specialist with the National Kennel Club (NKC), you are preparing an article with information on therapy dogs. Intended for novices who are considering selecting and training therapy dogs, the article provides helpful information. The document is to be distributed in the community, on social media, and in NKC printed material. You begin the article with a document prepared much earlier in another Word version and add to that some information provided by another NKC staff member. With attractive formatting and style application, you will prepare a two-columned article that is as attractive as it is informative. Refer to Figure 1.46 as you complete this exercise.

FIGURE 1.46 Therapy Dogs in Action

a. Open *w01p1Therapy*. The words *Compatibility Mode* in the title bar inform you the document was created in an earlier version of Word.

b. Click the **File tab** and select **Info**. (On a Mac, select Convert Document from the File menu.) Click **Convert**. Click **OK** in the dialog box, letting you know the document will be upgraded to the newest file format. Click the **File tab** and click **Save As**. Browse to the location to save and change the file name to **w01p1Therapy_LastFirst**. Click **Save**.

c. Ensure that nonprinting characters are displayed by clicking **Show/Hide** in the Paragraph group on the Home tab, if they are not already shown.

d. Click before the word *message* in the last sentence of the third body paragraph. Type **exact** and press **Spacebar**. Ensure that only one space precedes and follows the word *exact*.

e. Check the document for spelling and grammar concerns.
- Click the **Review tab** and click **Editor** in the Proofing group. (On a Mac, click the Review tab and click Spelling & Grammar. Proceed through any concerns presented, selecting correct spelling for *empathetic* and *attest*. Proceed to Step f.)
- Click **Spelling** in the Editor pane. Select a correct option for the two misspelled words presented.
- Click **Grammar** and check each grammatical error presented. In all cases, there is no need for concern, so click **Ignore Once** for each.
- Check and ignore all clarity and conciseness concerns, as the informality of the document is as intended and should not be changed.

f. Place the insertion point at the end of the document. Click the **Insert tab** and click the **Object arrow** in the Text group. Click **Text from File**. Navigate to the location of the data files and double-click *w01p1Text*.

g. Place the insertion point at the beginning of the document. Click the **Home tab**. Click **Replace** in the Editing group. (On a Mac, click Edit, point to Find, and then click Replace.) Type **Keehn** in the first or Find what box. Type **Keen** in the second or Replace with box. Click **Find Next**. Click **Replace** to replace the first occurrence. Similarly, click **Replace** twice more to replace the next two finds. Click **OK**. Click **Close**.

h. Click the **Design tab** and click **Themes** in the Document Formatting group. Select **Wisp**. Click **Colors** and select **Blue**.

i. Click after the word **Action** in the first heading of the document. Click the **Layout tab**. Click **Breaks** in the Page Setup group and select **Continuous**. Delete the hard return on the second line of the document.

j. Click **Columns** in the Page Setup group and click **More Columns**. Click **Two** and check **Line between** to select it. Click **OK**. Click the **Design tab** and click **Page Borders** in the Page Background group. Click **Box**. The style should be the first shown. Select a color of **Blue, Accent 1** (row 1, column 5) and a line width of **1½**. Ensure that the border applies to the whole document and click **OK**.

k. Select the first line in the document, *Therapy Dogs in Action*. It is OK if the section break indicator is also selected. Click the **Home tab**. Click **More** in the Styles group to display the Styles gallery. Click **Title**.

l. Scroll to page 2 and select the first subheading, **What is a Therapy Dog?** Click **More** in the Styles group and click **Heading 1** or select Heading 1 from the Styles pane. Apply Heading 1 style to all other subheadings: *Can Any Dog be a Therapy Dog?, Will Your Dog be a Good Therapy Dog?, Would You Make a Good Therapy Dog Handler?*, and *How Are Therapy Dogs Trained?*

m. Click the **Styles Dialog Box Launcher** to open the Styles pane unless it is already open. Right-click **Heading 1** and select **Modify**. Change the font color to **Black, Text 1** (row 1, column 2) and click **Bold**. Click **OK**. Scroll through the document to ensure that subheadings are now bold and in black font. If any headings were missed, select them and apply Heading 1 style. Close the Styles pane.

n. Click the **View tab** and select **Multiple Pages** in the Zoom group. Review the pages for overall layout and placement of subheadings but do not change anything. Note that the first body paragraph in the document is not indented, but all others are. Click **100%** in the Zoom group to return to the original view.

o. Click to place the insertion point at any location in the first body paragraph (beginning with *As a four-legged partner*). Click the **Home tab**. Click the **Styles Dialog Box Launcher** to open the Styles pane. Click **New Style** at the bottom (on a Mac, New Style will be at the top) of the Styles pane. Type **First Paragraph** in the Name box of the New Styles dialog box. Note that the style is a Paragraph type, that it applies only to the current document, and that it is to display in the Styles gallery. Click **OK**. Close the Styles pane.

p. Scroll to page 2 and click in the first body paragraph under the *What is a Therapy Dog?* heading. Click **First Paragraph** in the Styles Gallery. Apply the First Paragraph style to each first paragraph under the remaining four subheadings in the document.

q. Place the insertion point at the end of the document and type **Jassim Al Twedd**. Press **Shift+Enter** to insert a manual soft return. Type **National Kennel Club** and insert a manual soft return. Type **jatwedd@nkc.net**. (Do not type the period.) Do not press Enter.

r. Click the **Review tab** and click **Editor** (or Spelling & Grammar) to check spelling again. No names are misspelled, so ignore any noted misspelling of names. However, you should ensure that you have typed the name correctly as shown in the preceding step. Check and ignore any other concerns and close the Editor.

s. Click the **View tab** and click **Multiple Pages**. Scroll through the document one more time to check overall layout and placement of titles. You should not change anything. Save the document.

t. Click the **File tab** and select **Info**. Click **Properties**. Click **Advanced Properties**. (On a Mac, click the File tab and then Properties. Click the Summary tab.) Remove the current author and type **Jassim**. Click in the **Subject box** and type **Therapy Dogs**. Click **OK**. Click **Back** to return to the document.

u. Click the upper half of **Check Accessibility** in the Accessibility group on the Review tab. No issues should display in the Accessibility pane. Close the Accessibility pane. Save the document. (If using a Mac, skip to Step w.)

v. Click the **File tab**. Click **Info**. Click **Check for Issues**. Click **Inspect Document** and click **Inspect**. Note that the only issues found are related to document properties, which you do not want to remove. Click **Close**.

w. Save and close the document. Exit Word. Based on your instructor's directions, submit:

w01p1Therapy_LastFirst

You work with the Office of Media Relations at Tarrant State University. Several faculty researchers have been involved with a study on freshwater analysis, with their findings receiving national recognition. The university plans to post a news release describing the successful research. You will work with a draft of the press release, ensuring that it is properly formatted and readable by all. Refer to Figure 1.47 as you complete this exercise.

LAGIS
TARRANT STATE UNIVERSITY

FRESHWATER IN OUR FUTURE

To better understand the complex factors that threaten lake water quality, scientists need data on many lakes in various types of environmental settings. Unfortunately, much of the lake and geographic data needed for such studies is not easily accessible because the datasets exist in multiple formats scattered across government, university and private databases – sometimes only in file drawers. Until now.

A new "geography of lake water quality," known as LAGIS, allows scientists to understand entire populations of lakes to better inform water policy and management. LAGIS, which stands for Lake Area Geographic Information System is a database that includes information on 50,000 inland U.S. lakes in 17 northeastern and upper midwestern states.

A team of researchers in ecological, computer, geographic and information sciences built LAGIS, led by Susan Cassidy, ecology professor at Tarrant State University.

"We are at an exciting time in environmental science, when people are recognizing that the big problems we face require us to work together across disciplinary boundaries and to openly share data, methods and tools," said Kimberly Gray, TSU ecologist and co-author of the team's recent article published in the journal Lake.

With funding from the U.S. National Science Foundation's Freshwater Biology Program, the researchers collected water quality information from more than 70 individuals who took time to share data with the team, thousands of individuals who originally collected and processed the water quality data from 1995 to 2015, and more than 15 researchers at several institutions who worked together for six years to combine the information.

"Access to clean drinking water and the services lakes provide, such as fishing and recreation, are among the greatest environmental challenges we face today," said Kate Bloom, program director for NSF's Freshwater Biology program. "Now a comprehensive database has been created that will provide easy access to information on water quality and the physical and ecological factors that affect it across scales from individual lakes to entire regions." Included in that database are the following concerns:

Fresh water to a growing nearby population
Plenty of fishing and recreation
Scenic views and water frontage development

PAGE 1

FIGURE 1.47 Freshwater Research

a. Open Word. Click the **File tab** and select **New**. Click in the Search for online templates box and type **Student Report**. Press **Enter**. Click the template titled **Student report with photo**. Click **Create**. Close the Researcher pane that may open on the right. Click the **Home tab** and click **Show/Hide** in the Paragraph group to show nonprinting characters.

> **TROUBLESHOOTING:** If you cannot locate the template, open *w01p2Template.dotx* that is included in the data files.

b. Click **Report Title**. Type **LAGIS**. Click **REPORT SUBTITLE** and type **Tarrant State University**. As you type the university name, it will display in all caps. Select the last line on the first page of the document and press **Delete**. Do not delete the page break indicator at the bottom of the first page. Ensure that the insertion point is located before the Page Break indicator. Click the **Insert tab** and click the **Object arrow** in the Text group. Click **Text from File**. Navigate to the data files and double-click *w01p2Lake*.

c. Click the **File tab** and click **Save As**. Browse to the location to save and change the file name to **w01p2Lake_LastFirst.** Click **Save**.

d. Select the year **1990** in the fifth body paragraph. Change the year to **1995.** Click before *FRESHWATER IN OUR FUTURE* on page 1. Click the **Layout tab**, click **Breaks**, and click **Page**. Click the **View tab** and click **Multiple Pages**. Note the last page that should be deleted. Select all text on the last page and press **Delete**. Press **Backspace**, to ensure that only two pages remain. Click **100%** in the Zoom group.

e. Click the **Design tab**, click **Themes** in the Document Formatting group, and select **Berlin**. Click **Colors** and select **Red**. Click **Page Borders** in the Page Background group. Click **Box** and change the color to **Orange, Accent 2** (row 1, column 6). Change the line width to **1**. Click **OK**.

f. Place the insertion point after the word *population* on the second page near the end of the document. Press **Shift+Enter** to insert a soft return. Type **Plenty of fishing and recreation**. (Do not type the period.) Press **Shift+Enter**. Type **Scenic views and water frontage development**. (Do not type the period.)

g. Click before the first body paragraph on the second page, beginning with *To better understand*. Click the **Layout tab** and click **Breaks** in the Page Setup group. Click **Continuous**. Click **Columns** and select **Two**.

h. Click the **View tab** and select **One Page** in the Zoom group. Note the unbalanced column structure, especially related to the text box at the bottom of the page.

i. Click after the last sentence, ending in the word *Lake*, at the end of the fourth body paragraph on the second page. Be sure to click after the period ending the sentence. Click the **Layout tab**, click **Breaks** in the Page Setup group, and select **Column**. Delete the blank paragraph mark shown at the top of the right column.

j. Click the **View tab** and select **Multiple Pages** in the Zoom group. Check the overall layout of the document. Click **100%** in the Zoom group. Click the **Design tab**. Click **Watermark** in the Page Background group. Scroll through the Watermark gallery and select **Draft 2**. (On a Mac, select DRAFT from the Text menu.)

k. Click the **Review tab** and click **Editor** (or Spelling & Grammar) in the Proofing group. Click **Spelling** in the Editor pane and correct any spelling errors. No names are misspelled, so click **Ignore All** when a name is presented. Check any other concerns shown in the Editor pane, ignoring all, as they are not actually errors.

l. Click the **File tab** and click **Info**. Click **Properties** and select **Advanced Properties**. (On a Mac, click the Summary tab.) Remove the existing author. Click in the **Comments box** and type **Freshwater Flyer**. Click **OK**. Click **Back** to return to the document.

m. Click **Check Accessibility** in the Accessibility group. Click **Image or object not inline. (1)** in the Accessibility pane. Point to the Text Box problem shown in the Accessibility Checker pane and click the arrow. Note that a solution is presented. However, you determine instead to remove the text box, because it is not a critical element in the document. With the text box selected, press **Delete**. Close the Accessibility pane.

n. Click the **File tab** and click **Options**. (On a Mac, click Word on the menu bar and select Preferences.) Click **Proofing** (on a Mac, click Spelling & Grammar). Click **Show readability statistics** in the When correcting spelling and grammar in Word group. Click **OK**. Click the **Review tab** and click **Editor** in the Proofing group. (On a Mac, click Spelling & Grammar.) Note such items as the grade level and number of words per sentence that are shown in the Show Readability Statistics dialog box. Click **OK**. Click **OK** again to return to the document. If you are working in a school computer lab or prefer that Readability statistics not display each time you open the Editor, click the File tab, click Options, click Proofing, and deselect the same Readability statistics box.

o. Save the document. Click the **File tab** and click **Save As**. Ensure that the save location is correct and change the file type to **Rich Text Format**. Click **Save**. Save the document also as a Word (.docx) document.

p. Close the file. Exit Word. Based on your instructor's directions, submit:

w01p2Lake_LastFirst
w01p2Lake_LastFirst.rtf

Mid-Level Exercises

1   Basket Weaving

You are enrolled in a Western Civilization class that requires you to identify and research at least one ancient craft that is still practiced today in some form. You are to develop a document formatted as it would be for a newsletter, within guidelines provided by your instructor. Upon learning that traces of baskets have been found in ancient Egyptian pyramids, you decide to focus on the art of basket weaving. You have developed a draft document, although using a computer with a much earlier version of Word installed. You will convert the document to a newer version, include a cover page, and format it as required by your instructor.

a. Open *w01m1Baskets* and save it as **w01m1Baskets_LastFirst**. Show nonprinting characters.

b. Convert the document to a .docx file format. Change the words *devotion to* in the second sentence of the document to **focus on**. In the second paragraph of the document, change *us Tupperware* to **use Tupperware**.

c. Insert a blank page at the top of the document. Click before the page break indicator and insert text from *w01m1Cover*.

d. View the document in **Multiple Pages**. Return the view to **100%**. Insert a Continuous section break before the first body paragraph on page 2 (beginning with *The weaving of baskets is an art*).

e. Format text following the section break in two columns with a line between. Find the word *tolerate*. Select the word and use the thesaurus to identify a synonym that begins with the letter *b*. Replace the word *tolerate* with the synonym. Close the Thesaurus pane. Close the Navigation Pane.

f. Include a page border around only the cover page (ensure that the page border applies only to the current section). Choose a **single line Box** border that is colored **Orange, Accent 2, Darker 25%** (row 5, column 6) and with a width of **1½**.

g. Select the *Coiling* heading in the right column on page 2. Bold the text and change the font size to **16**. With the heading selected, create a new style with the title **Subheading**. The style should be placed in the current document only. Apply the new style to other subheadings of **Coiling with Sweetgrass, Splint Weaving, Round Fibered Weaving**, and **Today's Fibers**.

h. Modify the Subheading style to reduce the font to **14**. View the document in **Multiple Pages** to check for any unattractive or unbalanced columns. Insert a page break before the *Coiling with Sweetgrass* heading on page 2. Return the view to **100%**.

i. Modify document properties to replace the current author with **Jacob Enright**. Add a Subject of **Basket Weaving**. Change the word *BASKETWEAVING* on the cover page (page 1) to **BASKET WEAVING**.

j. Change the document theme to **Wisp**. Change the document colors to **Paper**.

k. Review the document for spelling and grammatical errors. The word *weavable* is not misspelled, so ignore the error. The words *stripped down* should be hyphenated. Check but ignore all clarity and conciseness concerns.

l. Run the Accessibility Checker. No concerns should be presented.

m. Check Word Options, selecting **Save**, and note the frequency with which an AutoRecover is conducted. Click **Cancel** so that any changes are not saved.

n. Save and close the file. Exit Word. Based on your instructor's directions, submit:
w01m1Baskets_LastFirst

With a degree in horticulture, you have recently been employed to work with Backyard Bonanza, a local outdoor living business specializing in garden gifts, statuary, outdoor fireplaces, landscaping materials, and pavers. The first Friday of each month, Backyard Bonanza participates in a downtown event in which vendors, artists, and musicians set up areas to perform or display products. To encourage those passing by to visit the store, you prepare a document describing a few do-it-yourself backyard projects—all of which can be completed with the help of products sold at Backyard Bonanza. The document is well under way, but you modify it slightly, making sure it is attractive and ready for distribution at the next event.

a. Open *w01m2Backyard*. The document was originally saved in an earlier version of Word, so you should save it as a Word Document with the file name of **w01m2Backyard_LastFirst**. Agree that the upgrade should proceed, if asked.

b. Display nonprinting characters. View the document in One Page to get a feel for the text flow. Return to 100%.

c. Insert text from *w01m2Fish* at the end of the document. View the document in Multiple Pages. Change the word *Create* at the bottom of page 1 to **Build**.

d. Select all text on page 2 (and page 3, if that page is shown). Format the selected text in two columns. Insert a page break before the heading shown alone at the bottom of page 1 (*Build a Backyard Fish Pond*).

e. Click anywhere on the first line of the document, containing the text *Build an Outdoor Fire Pit*. Create a new style based on the current text, calling it **Major Heading**. Ensure that the new style applies to the current document only. Apply the new style to the first line on the second page, *Build a Backyard Fish Pond*.

> **MAC TROUBLESHOOTING:** Press Enter after the heading, *Build a Backyard Fish Pond*, to force the section break to another line.

f. Create a custom watermark with the text **Backyard Bonanza**. The watermark should be horizontal.

g. Change the document theme colors to **Blue**. Select a **Box** page border, using the first style shown, with a color of **Blue, Accent 1, Darker 50%** (row 6, column 5) and a width of ½ **pt**. The page border should apply to the whole document.

h. Review the document for spelling and grammatical errors. The word *Delite* is not misspelled, so ignore the error. You must manually correct the word *layer*. *Fish Pond* should remain as two words.

i. Find the word *mature* on the first page of the document and replace the word *or* that precedes it with the word *of*. In the same sentence, replace the word *ad* with the word **and**. The entire sentence should read *Also, watch out for major root systems of mature trees, which can block too much of the sunlight that plants and fish need*.

j. Find the word *pone* and replace it with **pond**. Find the word *hold* and replace it with **hole**, but only where appropriate. Save the document before continuing to the next step.

k. Run the Document Inspector, removing all document properties and personal information.

l. Check the document for accessibility.

m. Save and close the file. Exit Word. Based on your instructor's directions, submit:
w01m2Backyard_LastFirst

Running Case

New Castle County Technical Services (NCCTS) provides technical services to clients in the greater New Castle County, Delaware, area. Founded in 2011, the company is rapidly expanding to include technical security systems, network infrastructure cabling, and basic troubleshooting services. With that growth comes the need to promote the company and to provide clear written communication to employees and clients. Microsoft Word is used exclusively in the development and distribution of documents, including an "About New Castle" summary that will be available both in print and online. You will begin development of the document in this case and continue working with it in subsequent Word chapters.

a. Open *w01r1NewCastle* and save it as **w01r1NewCastle_LastFirst**. Display nonprinting characters. Place the insertion point at the end of the document and insert a page break.

b. Ensure that the insertion point is at the top of the second page. Insert the text from *w01r1News*. View the document in Multiple Pages. Return to 100% view.

c. Change the document theme to **Berlin**. Change the document font to **Garamond**.

d. Select the words *set up* in the first paragraph on the third page. Change the selected words to **equipped**, ensuring that a space precedes and follows the newly inserted word.

e. Place the insertion point at the end of the first body paragraph on page 1, after the period following the word *offer*. Press **Spacebar** and type **We are proud to include the following new services, added to our inventory this past March.** (Include the period.) Press **Enter**. Type **Desktop troubleshooting**. (Do not type the period.) Insert a soft return. Type **Software training support**. (Do not type the period.)

f. Place the insertion point before the word *We* at the beginning of the first body paragraph on the fourth page (under the *A FEW OF OUR CUSTOMERS* heading). Type **At New Castle County Technical Services,** and press **Spacebar**. Ensure that a comma follows **New Castle County Technical Services**. Change the following word **We** to lowercase, as in *we*.

g. Apply a watermark using the **DRAFT 2** selection. Color the watermark **Blue** (eighth color from the left in Standard Colors). It does not matter whether the watermark is horizontal or diagonal. (On a Mac, insert a text watermark with the word *DRAFT*. Change the color in the Watermark dialog box.)

h. Check the document for spelling and grammatical errors. Ignore all possible misspellings of company names but correct any other spelling errors. If grammatical errors are shown, correct them as well. If Clarity and Conciseness concerns are shown, check but ignore any occurrence.

i. Insert a Continuous section break after the Page Break indicator on page 1. Ensure that the insertion point is on page 2. Add a **Box** page border using the third style shown (dashed). The color should not be changed, but the line width should be **1 pt**. The border should be applied to the current section only, resulting in all pages except the first being bordered.

j. Run the Accessibility Checker. Note the comments related to the picture in the first paragraph of the Company Background section. You may also see a warning flagging hard-to-read text contrast, although you will not address that issue at this time. Because the picture is not necessary, you will remove it. Click the picture of the keyboard on page 2 and press **Delete** to remove it. Close the Accessibility Checker pane.

k. Open Word Options and click **Save**. Note the number of minutes before saving AutoRecover information. Because you may be using a school computer, you will not adjust the setting. Click **Cancel** or otherwise close the dialog box.

l. Modify Heading 1 style to include a font size of **14**. All major headings in the document should immediately adjust, as they are based on Heading 1 style.

m. Open Document Properties, selecting **Advanced Properties** to display the dialog box. (On a Mac, click the Summary tab.) Add a Company name of **New Castle County Technical Services**. (Do not type the period.)

n. Save and close the file. Exit Word. Based on your instructor's directions, submit: w01r1NewCastle_LastFirst

Disaster Recovery

Small Business

Open *w01d1Business*. You are working with a local small business incubator, assigned the task of developing printed material for potential small business owners. You will finalize a document begun as a draft by an office assistant, making sure it is attractively formatted and error-free. First, ensure that the document is converted from an earlier Word version. Save the document as **w01d1Business_LastFirst**. Show nonprinting characters.

At the end of the document (the end of page 3), insert text from *w01d1Text*. In at least one location, the name of the U.S. entity related to small businesses is incorrectly titled *Startup Business Administration*. Find any occurrence of that text and replace it with **Small Business Administration**. Remove the page border from the document. Ensure that no heading or subheading is in colored text (the first major heading text should be Black, Text 1) and apply the Heading 1 style to all numbered subheadings so that they are consistent and can be categorized by level. Do not change any of the numbered items on page 3. Modify Heading 1 style to show a font color of Black, Text 1 (row 1, column 2).

You may further modify the report title (*How to Start a Small Business*) as you see fit to enhance it, perhaps applying another style, but ensuring that the text remains black. All text in the numbered section, beginning with *1. Refine your idea* and ending at the end of the document, should be formatted in two columns. Insert breaks (Column or Next Page) where necessary to ensure attractive text columns (making sure no column heading appears by itself or with very little text following). The document should include only 3 pages. Using a multiple page view, check the page layout of each page.

Replace the current author in document properties with your first and last names. Any other value in the dialog box should be removed. Using the Proofing category of Word Options, ensure that *Show readability statistics* is selected. Check for spelling and grammatical errors. Any error suggested in a formula is not an error, so ignore it. Check but ignore all other concerns shown in the Editor pane, including any related to a comma punctuation. Several sentences do require a space following a period, however, so accept those changes. Note the grade level shown in the Readability Statistics dialog box and record it on the last line of text in the document (beside *Reading Grade Level*). Ensure there are no blank pages in the document. Check the document for accessibility.

Save and close the document. For later display online, you will also save the document as a PDF file with the same name as the Word document. Exit Word. Based on your instructor's directions, submit:

w01d1Business_LastFirst

w01d1Business_LastFirst.pdf

Cumulative Exercise

You have always been fascinated with the science behind flying kites—the aerodynamics and maneuverability of keeping them aloft and controlled. As an engineering student, you and a few friends are considering forming a club to compete in various kite-flying competitions. A potential faculty sponsor has asked that you research the sport and prepare a summary for him to consider before moving forward. You are using Word to prepare a short summary in the form of an informative flyer for distribution campus-wide, encouraging student interest. In the process, you will apply various formatting and readability features, and will ensure an error-free and informative document.

Inserting Text, Editing a Document, and Working with Styles

Inserting text from another document can save time in creating a document, so you insert text to provide additional information in the flyer. You also edit the document, making a few changes and applying styles, to ensure attractive text appearance. Viewing the document in different ways gives an overall understanding of page layout.

1. Open *w01c1Kite* and save it as **w01c1Kite_LastFirst**.
2. Display nonprinting characters. Insert text from *w01c1Info* in the blank paragraph at the top of the last column on the page.
3. Remove the two blank paragraphs after the inserted text in the last column on page 1.
4. View the document in **Multiple Pages**. Change the view back to **100%**. Apply **Title** style to the heading *Kite High Fliers*.
5. Modify the Title style to center alignment and bold.
6. Insert a manual soft return after the title, *Kite High Fliers*, and type **Join Us!** (include the exclamation point). Select **Join Us!** and change the font size of the subtitle to **20**.
7. Create a new style using text in the first body paragraph (beginning with *Go fly a kite!*), calling the new style **Body Paragraph**. The style should be available in the current document only. Apply the Body Paragraph style to all other body paragraphs in the document, including the contact information. Do not apply the style to the heading lines.
8. Insert a blank paragraph before the second to last line in the document, containing the word *Contact*.

Working with Columns, Changing the Document Theme, and Replacing Text

You decide that two columns are more appropriate for the flyer, so you make that change. You also select a different document theme and narrow the colors to a selected group. A page border adds interest and a bit of informality to the flyer. Finally, you settle on a modified club name that replaces the existing name in the document.

9. Select all body paragraphs that follow the two heading lines and change the number of columns to **2**. Ensure that a line displays between the columns.
10. View the document in **Multiple Pages** to make sure that all columns are attractively arranged. Change the document theme to **Slice** and change the theme colors to **Red**.
11. Add a **Box** page border, selecting the third line style (dashed). The color is **Orange, Accent 2** (row 1, column 6), and the line width is **1 pt**. Apply the page border to the whole document, not just a single section.
12. Replace all occurrences of *Kite High Fliers* with **High Fliers**. The word *Kite* should not be part of the club name anywhere in the document. Three replacements should be made. Return the view to **100%**.

Working with the Editor and Thesaurus, Checking Document Statistics, and Changing Word Options

As you review the document, you determine alternative wording and check for spelling or grammatical errors. Because the university limits student flyers to 700 words or less, you also ensure that the flyer stays within that count. Using Word Options, you get a better understanding of the document's readability.

13. Identify a synonym for the word *controller* in the first body paragraph. Ensure that you are replacing *controller*, not *controllers*. The synonym you select should begin with the letter *m*. Replace the word in that paragraph.
14. Check the word count. If the number of words is greater than 700, remove the entire third body paragraph (beginning with *The High Fliers*). However, make that change only if the word count exceeds 700.
15. Select the Proofing group in Word Options and select *Show readability statistics*. Check the document for spelling and grammatical errors. *Hadzicki* is not misspelled, so ignore that error. Ignore all grammatical and conciseness errors, with the exception of replacing the word *that* where it may be flagged. All hyphenated words are correct, so ignore any related errors. Note the number of sentences (not the average) for use in the next section.

Modifying Document Properties, Inspecting a Document, and Checking Accessibility

Document properties identify the author of the flyer. Before it is distributed, the document is checked for accessibility and inspected for any personal or hidden information.

16. Modify document properties to include **Mason Gibbons** as the author, replacing any existing author. Click in the Comments box and type the number of sentences you noted in Step 15. You should type only the number, no words.

17. Check for accessibility, addressing any concerns that may be shown. If none are identified, simply close the Accessibility pane.

18. Save the document and inspect the document for any personal or hidden properties. If anything other than Document Properties and Personal Information are identified, remove the item. (On a Mac, click Tools and then select Protect Document.)

19. Save and close the document. Exit Word. Based on your instructor's directions, submit: w01c1Kite_LastFirst

Document Presentation

LEARNING OUTCOME

You will modify a Word document with formatting and objects.

OBJECTIVES & SKILLS: After you read this chapter, you will be able to:

CASE STUDY | Phillips Studio L Photography

Having recently opened your own photography studio, you are engaged in marketing the business. Not only do you hope to attract customers from the local community who want photos of special events, but you will also offer classes in basic photography for interested amateur photographers. In addition, you have designed a website to promote the business and to provide details on upcoming events and classes. The business is not large enough yet to employ an office staff, so much of the work of developing promotional material falls on you.

Among other projects, you are currently developing material to include in a quarterly mailing to people who have expressed an interest in upcoming studio events. You have prepared a rough draft of a newsletter describing photography basics—a document that must be formatted and properly organized before it is distributed to people on your mailing list. You will modify the document to ensure attractive line and paragraph spacing, and you will format text to draw attention to pertinent points. Formatted in columns, the document will be easy to read. The newsletter is somewhat informal, and you will make appropriate use of colors, borders, pictures, and graphics so that it is well received by your audience.

Document Appearance and Graphics

FIGURE 2.1 Phillips Studio L Photography Document

CASE STUDY | Phillips Studio L Photography

Starting Files	File to Be Submitted	MyLab IT HOE Grader
w02h1Studio w02h2Winter.jpg	w02h2Studio_LastFirst	

MyLab IT Grader: This project is available as a Hands-On Exercise project in MyLab IT.

Format Text and Paragraphs

When you format text, you change the way it looks. Your goal in designing a document is to ensure that it is well received and understood by an audience of readers. Seldom will your first attempt at designing a document be the only time you work with it. Inevitably, you will identify text that should be reworded or emphasized differently, paragraphs that might be more attractive in another alignment, or words that might need to be bold, underlined, or italicized to call attention to selected text. As you develop a document or after reopening a previously completed document, you can make all these modifications and more. That process is called ***formatting***.

In this section, you will learn to change font and font size and format text with character attributes, such as bold, underline, and italics. In addition, you will learn to use symbols and special characters in a document. At the paragraph level, you will adjust paragraph and line spacing, set tab stops, change alignment, and apply bullets and numbering.

Apply Font Attributes

A ***font*** is a combination of typeface and type style. The font you select should reinforce the message of the text without calling attention to itself, and it should be consistent with the information you want to convey. For example, a paper prepared for a professional purpose, such as a résumé, should have a standard font, such as Times New Roman, instead of one that looks casual or frilly. Additionally, more than one font might need to be used to distinguish the purpose of the text, such as paragraph headings, body text, captions, and so on, but you will want to minimize the variety of fonts in a document to maintain a professional look. Typically, you should use no more than three fonts within a document. Not only can you identify font selections for various purposes, but you can also change font size and apply text attributes, such as bold, italic, or underline. Several of the most commonly used text formatting commands are located in the Font group on the Home tab.

STEP 1 ▶ Select Font Options

A definitive characteristic of any font is the presence or absence of serifs, thin lines that begin and end the main strokes of each letter. A ***serif font*** contains a thin line or extension at the top and bottom of the primary strokes on characters. Times New Roman is defined as a serif font. A ***sans serif font*** (*sans* from the French word meaning "without") does not contain the thin lines on characters. Calibri, for example, is a sans serif font.

Serifs provide a visual connection from one letter to the next, as the thin lines bridge the gap between characters. A serif font is especially useful with large amounts of text, as in a lengthy report or printed manual. The paragraphs in this book, for example, are shown in a serif font. A sans serif font, such as Calibri, Arial, or Verdana, is more effective with smaller amounts of text such as titles, headlines, corporate logos, and webpages. For example, the heading "Select Font Options" at the beginning of this section is set in a sans serif font. Web developers often prefer a sans serif font because the extra strokes that begin and end letters in a serif font can blur or fade into a webpage, making it difficult to read. Examples of serif and sans serif fonts are shown in Figure 2.2.

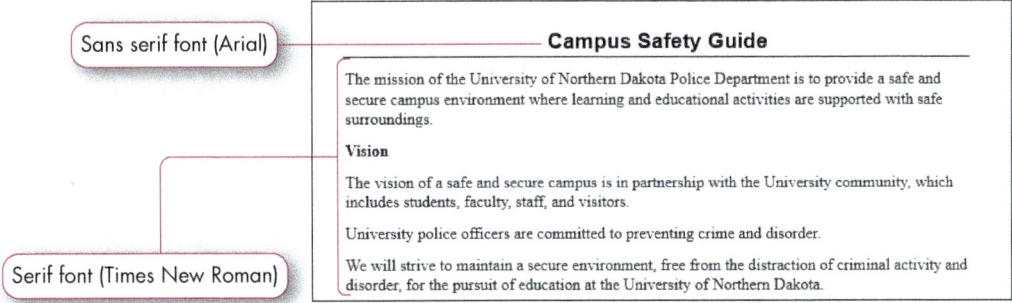

FIGURE 2.2 Serif and Sans Serif Fonts

New blank documents are based on Normal style, which includes a font selection that may or may not be appropriate for a document being developed. You can always choose a different font and font size from options in the Font group on the Home tab. Changes apply to text that is to be typed or to a text selection you want to modify. To change font settings, click the Font arrow and select a font from those displayed (see Figure 2.3). Each font shown in the list is a sample of the actual font, so you have an idea of how the font will look before you choose it. If text is already selected as you point to a font in the list, you will also see a preview of the effect on the selected text—called **Live Preview**—before finalizing the choice.

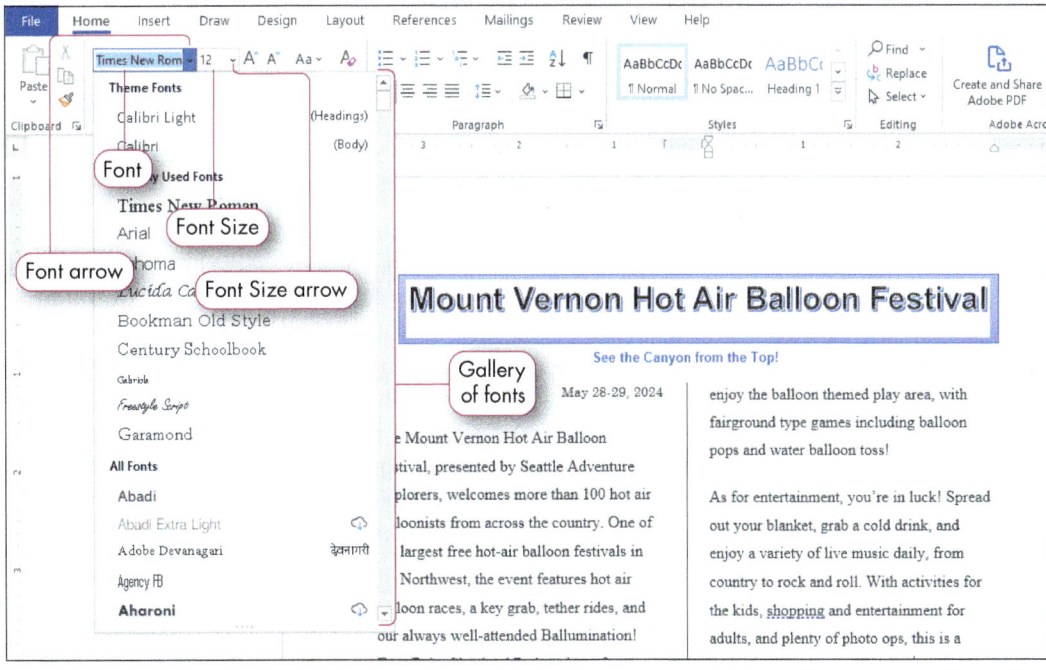

FIGURE 2.3 Select a Font and Font Size

Not only can you select a different font from the Font group, but you can also identify a font size (refer to Figure 2.3), measured in points. Each point is equivalent to 1/72 of an inch; the larger the point size, the larger the font. A document often contains several sizes of the same font. For example, various levels of headings are often differentiated by different font sizes. A major heading, for example, might be 16 pt size, setting it apart from a subheading, which could be a bit smaller at 13 pt.

Fonts are typically categorized as either TrueType or OpenType. Unless you are involved with designing documents that require elaborate script or stylistic character combinations, the distinction between OpenType and TrueType font is not of great importance. TrueType fonts were first developed as a joint effort between Apple and Microsoft, ensuring a selection of fonts that both platforms could read and that most printers could reproduce. OpenType fonts are also cross-platform, but there the differences begin. OpenType fonts are much more robust, with advanced typesetting features such as ligatures, that give text designers many more options. A ligature is a decorative joining of two different letters, commonly found in script font. For example, the letters *f* and *i* are often bound together in a ligature, as are the letters *t* and *h*. Using OpenType fonts, with associated style settings, you can design beautiful specialty documents, such as wedding invitations.

Change Text Appearance

In addition to font type and size, various other attributes are often applied to document text. Such settings as boldface, italics, underline, and font color are found in the Font group on the Home tab, often used to emphasize or draw attention to wording (see Figure 2.4). Text effects including shadow, glow, and outline add style, and you can highlight text for added emphasis. For even more choice, click the Font Dialog Box Launcher in the Font group and select from additional formatting commands that are not as commonly used (see Figure 2.5). Using the Font dialog box, you can select from various underline styles or format text as a subscript or superscript, among other options. Or, with text selected, you can instead choose from font options on the Mini Toolbar, negating the need to use the ribbon for equivalent options.

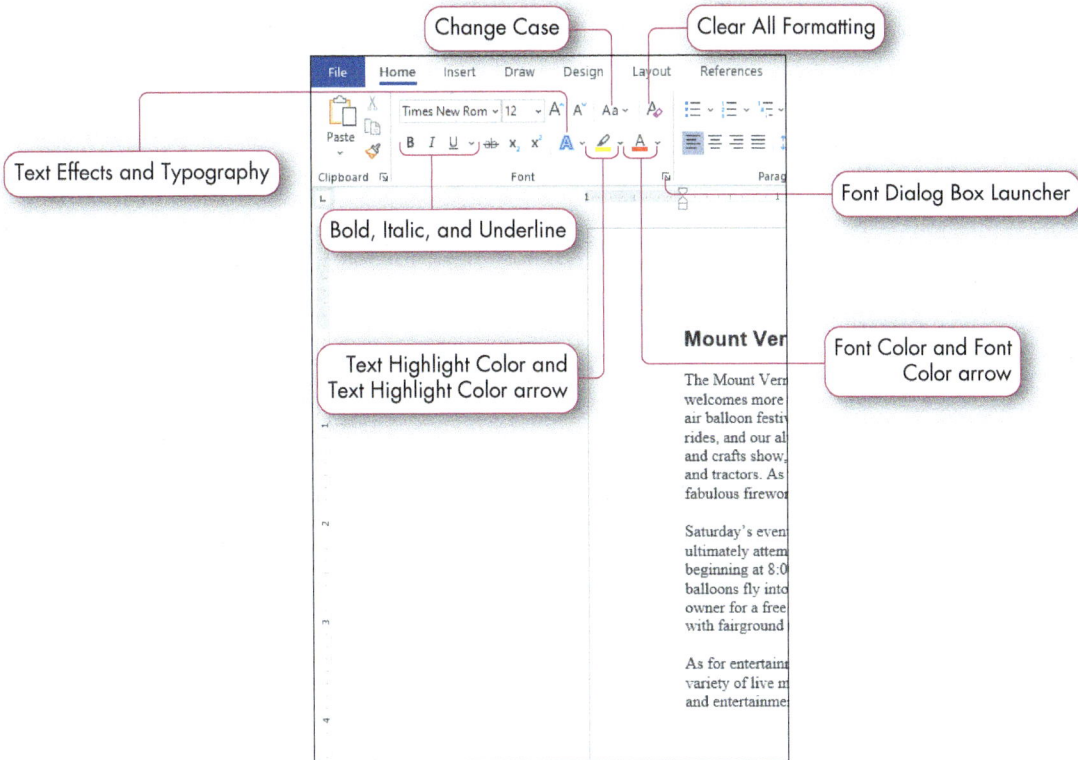

FIGURE 2.4 Font Options

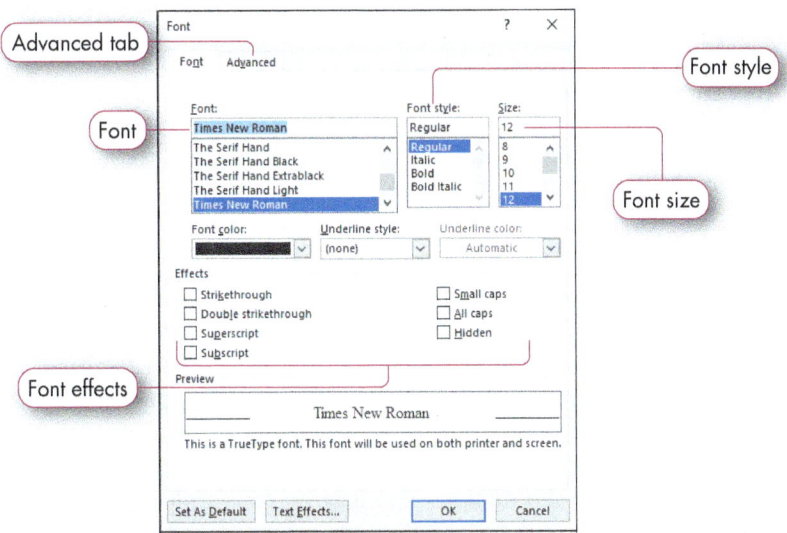

FIGURE 2.5 Font Dialog Box

Using Word's Text Effects and Typography option on the Home tab, you can apply special formats such as shadow, outline, reflection, or glow to text. The Text Effects and Typography gallery (see Figure 2.6) provides access to those effects as well as to WordArt styles, number styles, ligatures, and stylistic sets, collectively known as *typography*.

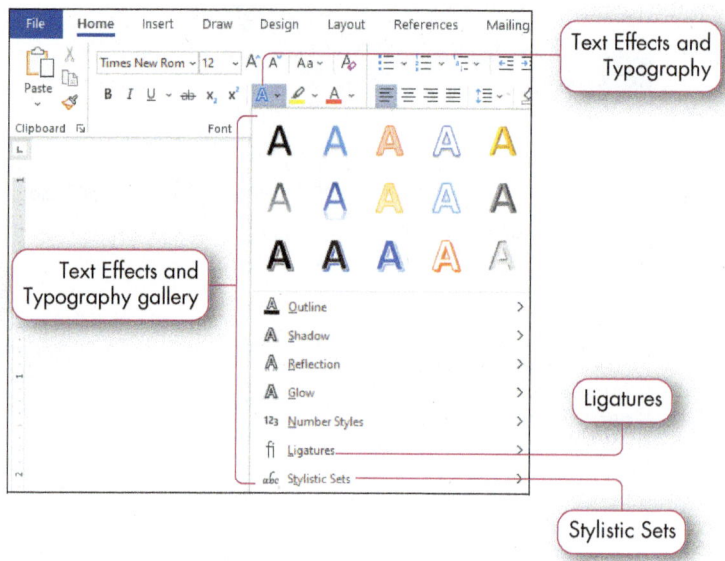

FIGURE 2.6 Text Effects and Typography Gallery

Certain OpenType fonts contain embedded appearance options, called **stylistic sets**, which enable subtle appearance changes based on stylistic set selection, character spacing, and other settings. Some fonts include more stylistic sets than others. For example, with a text selection formatted in Gabriola font (an OpenType font that enables various stylistic sets), click Text Effects and Typography, point to Stylistic Sets, and choose from any one of several options.

> **TIP: ADVANCED FONT SETTINGS**
> If you intend to use a ligature and/or stylistic set, you may select it via the Advanced tab in the Font dialog box (refer to Figure 2.5). Ligatures and stylistic sets are also readily available in the Text Effects and Typography gallery as shown in Figure 2.6.

At some point in your academic career, you might have used a highlighting marker to draw attention to text in a printed book or class paper. Word provides an equivalent tool with which you can shade text in a document—the Text Highlight Color command— located in the Font group on the Home tab (refer to Figure 2.4). Click the tool and then drag over one or more text selections to apply color. Or select text first and then click Text Highlight Color from the Font group or the Mini Toolbar to immediately shade the selection. Although the default highlight color is yellow, you can choose from other options when you click the Text Highlight Color arrow. To remove highlight color from a selection, select No Color.

Among other options in the Font group on the Home tab is Change Case, a command that enables you to quickly change the capitalization of selected document text (refer to Figure 2.4). Suppose you determine that a heading currently shown in upper and lowercase should be all caps. Select the heading, click Change Case in the Font group, and select UPPERCASE. No typing is involved. Similarly, change selected case to sentence case, or perhaps you want to capitalize each word. The less you type, the less likely you are to make mistakes, so using Change Case to adjust capitalization likely results in less typos and saves time.

By default, text color is black. For a bit of interest, or to draw attention to text within a document, you can change the font color of previously typed text or of text that you are about to type. Click the Font Color arrow (refer to Figure 2.4) and select from a gallery of colors. For even more choice, click More Colors and select from a variety of hues or shades. As shown in Figure 2.7, you can click the Custom tab in the Colors dialog box and select a color hue by dragging along a hue continuum.

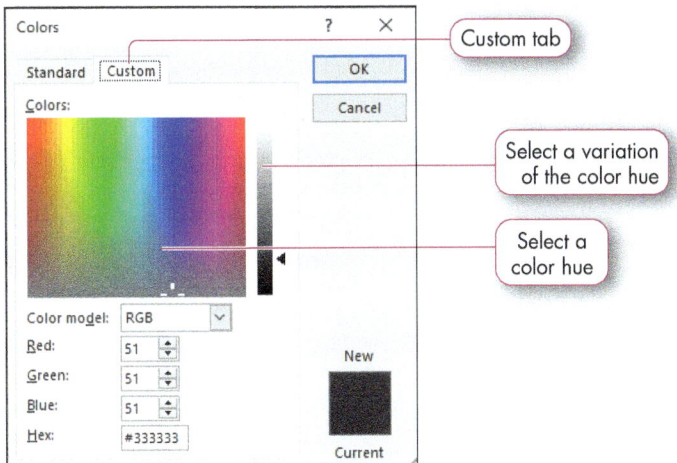

FIGURE 2.7 Apply a Custom Color

Insert Symbols and Special Characters

A *symbol* is text, a graphic, or a foreign language character that can be inserted into a document. Some symbols, such as $ and #, are located on the keyboard; however, others are only available from Word's collection of symbols. Symbols such as © and ™ can be an integral part of a document; in fact, those particular symbols are necessary to properly acknowledge a source or product. Because they are typically not located on the keyboard, you can access them in Word's library of symbols or use a shortcut key combination, if available.

Some symbols serve a very practical purpose. For example, it is unlikely you will want a hyphenated word to be divided between lines in a document. In that case, instead of typing a simple hyphen between words, you can insert a nonbreaking hyphen, which is available as a symbol. Such a symbol is included in a document for instruction purposes but does not show in the document. That special-purpose symbol, along with others, is located in the Special Characters section of the Symbol dialog box. Similarly, you can insert a nonbreaking space when you do not want words divided between lines. For example, a person's first name on one line followed by the last name on the next line is not a preferred placement. Instead, make the space between the words a nonbreaking space by inserting the symbol, so the names are never divided. Mathematical symbols, foreign currency marks, and popular emoticons are also available in Word's symbol library.

A typical Microsoft Office installation includes a wide variety of fonts categorized for selection in the Symbols gallery. Depending upon the font selected (Symbol text is shown in Figure 2.8), your symbol choices will vary. Fonts such as Wingdings, Webdings, and Symbol contain a wealth of special symbols, many of which are actually pictures. Each symbol is assigned a character code. If you know the character code, you can type the code instead of searching for the symbol itself.

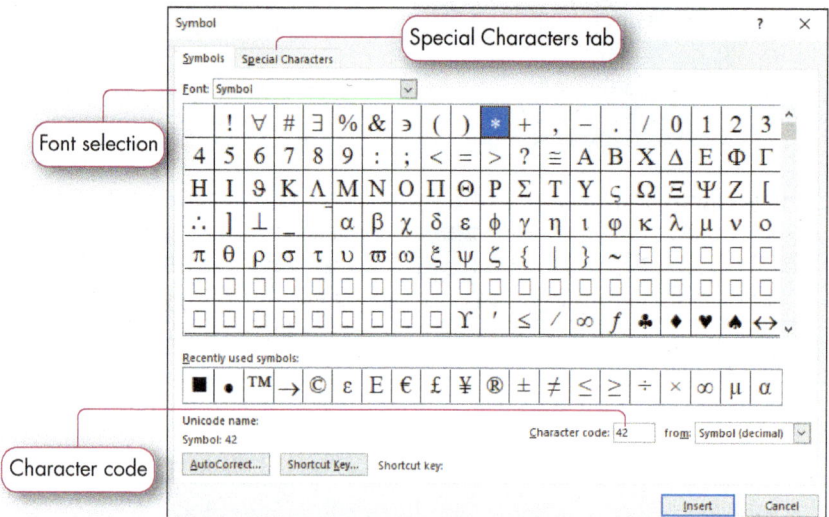

FIGURE 2.8 Insert a Symbol

MAC TIP: SYMBOL CHARACTER CODES
Mac does not include the option to type a character code, so it can be difficult to locate a particular symbol. Using various key combinations, you can insert certain symbols, but the list is not as comprehensive or as easily accessible as what you find on a Windows computer. Check online for a list of options available for a Mac keyboard.

TIP: USING SYMBOL SHORTCUTS
Some symbols, such as © and ™, are included in Word's list of AutoCorrect entries. When you type (c), Word will automatically "correct" it to display ©. Type (tm), and Word shows ™. If you do not want an entry to be changed by AutoCorrect, point to the resulting symbol and click AutoCorrect Options. Select from a list of preferred actions, one of which is to change back to the original text.

Format a Paragraph

Formatting selected text is only one way to alter the appearance of a document. You can also change the alignment, indentation, tab stops, or line spacing for any paragraph within the document. Recall that Word defines a paragraph as text followed by a hard return, or even a hard return on a line by itself (indicating a blank paragraph). You can include borders or shading for added emphasis around selected paragraphs, and you can number paragraphs or enhance them with bullets. The Paragraph group on the Home tab contains several paragraph formatting commands (see Figure 2.9). If you are formatting only one paragraph, you do not have to select the entire paragraph. Simply click to place the insertion point within the paragraph and apply a paragraph format. However, if you are formatting several paragraphs, you must select them before formatting.

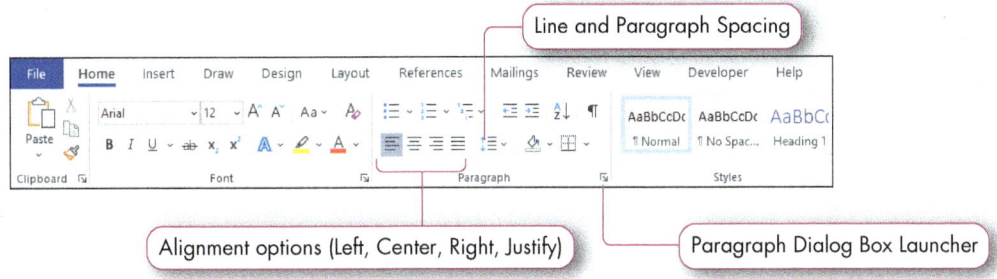

FIGURE 2.9 Paragraph Options

STEP 2 ## Select Paragraph Alignment

Alignment refers to how text is positioned relative to document margins. *Left alignment* is the most common alignment, often seen in letters, reports, and memos. When you begin a new blank Word document, paragraphs are left aligned by default. Text begins evenly at the left margin and ends in an uneven ("ragged") right edge. The opposite of left alignment is *right alignment*, a setting in which text is aligned at the right margin with a ragged left edge. Short lines including dates, figure captions, and headers are often right aligned. A *center alignment* positions text horizontally in the center of a line, at an equal distance from both the left and right margins. Report titles and major headings are typically centered. Finally, *justified alignment* positions text evenly between left and right margins so that text begins at the left margin and ends uniformly at the right margin. Newspaper and magazine articles are often justified. Such text alignment often causes awkward spacing as text is stretched to fit evenly between margins. Figure 2.10 shows examples of paragraph alignments.

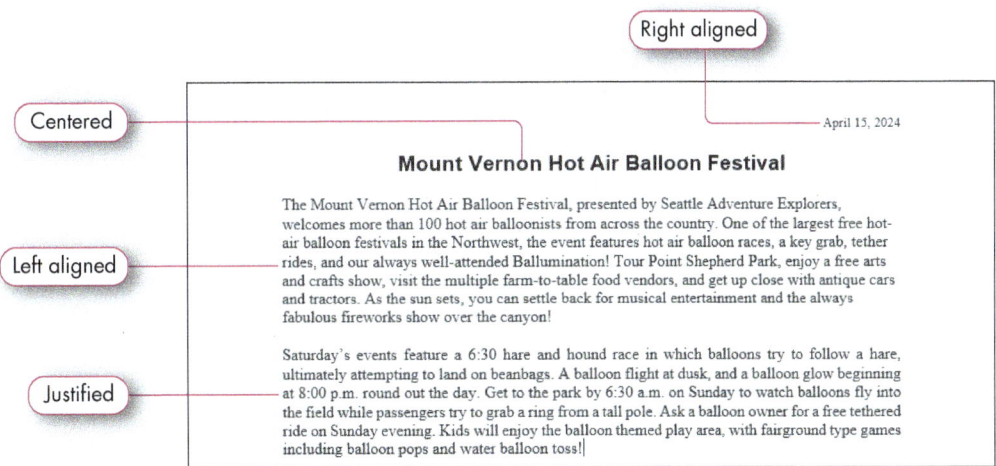

FIGURE 2.10 Paragraph Alignment

To change paragraph alignment, select text (or position the insertion point in a paragraph, if only one paragraph is to be affected) and select an alignment from the Paragraph group on the Home tab. You can also change alignment by selecting from the Paragraph dialog box (see Figure 2.11), which opens when you click the Paragraph Dialog Box Launcher (refer to Figure 2.9).

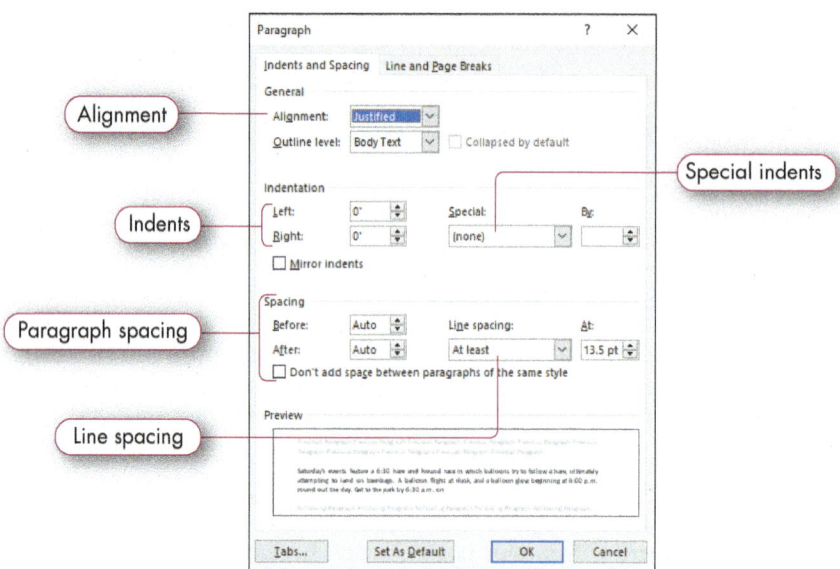

FIGURE 2.11 Paragraph Dialog Box

Select Line and Paragraph Spacing

Paragraph spacing is the amount of space between paragraphs, measured in points. (Recall that one point is 1/72 of an inch.) Paragraph spacing is a good way to differentiate between paragraphs, especially if the beginning of each paragraph is not clearly identified by an indented line. In such a case, paragraph spacing identifies where one paragraph ends and another begins. Spacing used to separate paragraphs usually comes after each affected paragraph, although you can specify that it is placed before the affected paragraph. Use the Paragraph dialog box to select paragraph spacing (refer to Figure 2.11). Use any of the following methods to change paragraph spacing.

- Click Line and Paragraph Spacing in the Paragraph group on the Home tab (see Figure 2.12). Click to Add Space Before Paragraph (or to Add Space After Paragraph).

- Click the Paragraph Dialog Box Launcher in the Paragraph group on the Home tab. Type a number to indicate the amount of Spacing Before or After in the respective areas (refer to Figure 2.11) or click the spin arrows to adjust spacing. Click OK.

- Change the Before or After spacing in the Paragraph group on the Layout tab (see Figure 2.13).

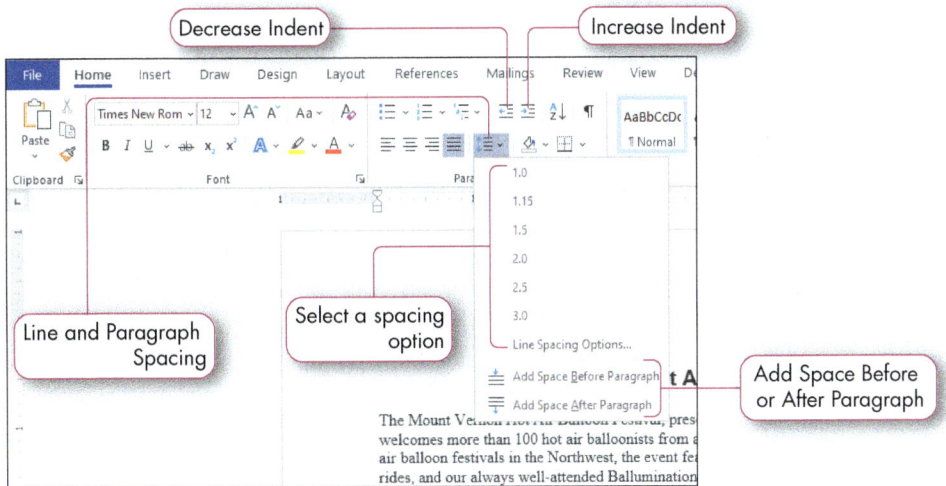

FIGURE 2.12 Paragraph Spacing Options

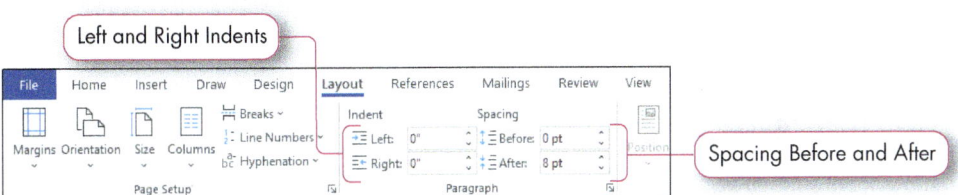

FIGURE 2.13 Paragraph Spacing and Indents

Just as paragraph spacing is the amount of space between paragraphs, **_line spacing_** is the amount of space between lines in a paragraph. Typically, line spacing is determined before beginning a document, such as when you know that a research paper should be double-spaced, so you identify that setting before typing. Of course, you can change line spacing of a current paragraph or selected text at any point as well.

You can change line spacing using either the Paragraph dialog box or the Line and Paragraph Spacing option in the Paragraph group on the Home tab. The most common line spacing options are single, double, 1.15, or 1.5 lines. Word provides those options and more. From the Paragraph dialog box (refer to Figure 2.11), you can select Exactly, At Least, or Multiple, along with the more standard line spacing selections. To specify an exact point size for spacing, select Exactly. If you select At Least, you will indicate a minimum line spacing size while enabling Word to adjust the height, if necessary, to accommodate such features as drop caps (oversized letters that sometimes begin paragraphs). The Multiple setting enables you to select a line spacing interval other than single, double, 1.15, or 1.5 lines.

Select Indents

An **indent** is a setting associated with how part of a paragraph is distanced from the margin. One of the most common indents is a ***first line indent***, in which the first line of each paragraph is set off from the left margin. For instance, your English instructor might require that the first line of each paragraph in a writing assignment is indented 0.5″ from the left margin, which is a typical first line indent. If you have ever prepared a bibliography for a research paper, you have most likely specified a ***hanging indent***, where the first line of a source begins at the left margin, but all other lines in the source are indented. Indenting an entire paragraph from the left margin is a ***left indent***, while indenting an entire paragraph from the right margin is a ***right indent***. A lengthy quote is often set apart by indenting from both the left and right margins.

Using the Paragraph dialog box, you can select an indent setting for one or more paragraphs. First line and hanging indents are considered special indents. You can select left and right indents from either the Paragraph dialog box or from the Paragraph group on the Layout tab.

You can use the Word ruler to set indents. If the ruler does not display above the document space, you can control the ruler display by toggling it on or off on the View tab (see Figure 2.14). The ***three-part indent marker*** located at the left side of the ruler enables you to set a left indent, a hanging indent, or a first line indent (see Figure 2.15). The marker is comprised of two triangles and a rectangle; the upper triangle is the first line indent marker; the lower triangle is the hanging indent marker. The rectangle below the lower triangle indicates the location of the current left margin. You can exert more complete control of these indents through the Paragraph dialog box. Another way is to drag the indent along the ruler to apply the indent to the current paragraph (or selected paragraphs). The first body paragraph shown in Figure 2.14 includes a first line indent at 0.5″.

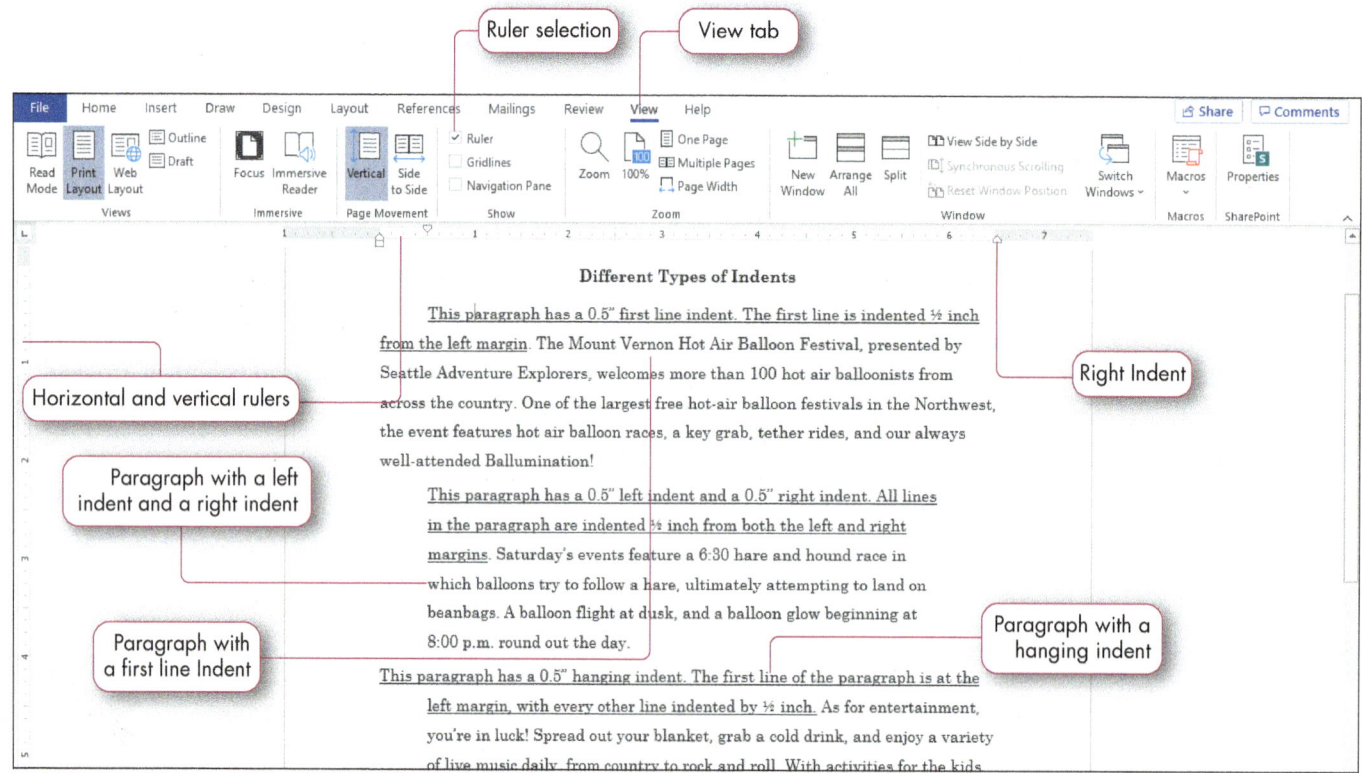

FIGURE 2.14 Work with Indents

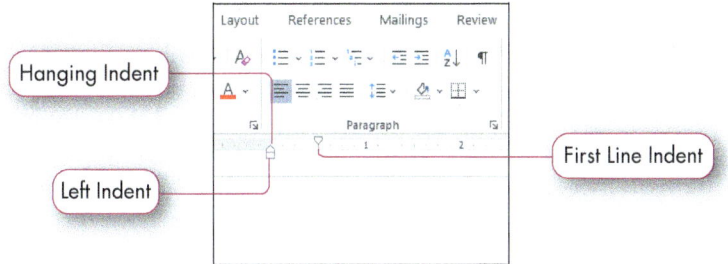

FIGURE 2.15 Three-Part Indent Marker on the Ruler

STEP 3 Set Tab Stops

Each time you press Tab, the insertion point moves to the right by 0.5″. Typically, you would set a first line indent or press Tab to indent the first line of each new paragraph within a document. When creating a professional document, you can draw attention to certain information by setting the content apart from the body text. There are times when moving the insertion point by different intervals or positions and alignments helps to increase the readability of the document. Tabs enable you to add organization to a document, arranging text in easy-to-read columns. A table of contents and indexes are examples of tabbed text, as is a restaurant menu. In those instances, setting tab stops that overwrite the default tabs is useful. A ***tab stop*** is a marker on the horizontal ruler specifying the location where the insertion point stops after Tab is pressed to align text in a document. By using tab stops, you can easily arrange text in columns or position text a certain distance from the left or right margins. The most common tab stops are left, right, center, and decimal. By default, a left tab is set every 0.5″ when you start a new document.

Table 2.1 describes the types of tabs that are available in the ***tab selector***, which is the small box at the leftmost edge of the horizontal ruler. The tab selector (see Figure 2.16) enables you to repeatedly cycle through tabs, including left, center, right, decimal, bar, first line indent, and hanging indent. Using the tab selector, you can select and apply any of these indents to your document.

TABLE 2.1 Tab Markers		
Tab Icon on Ruler	**Type of Tab**	**Function**
⌊	Left	Sets the start position on the left, so as you type, text moves to the right of the tab setting.
�

Center	Sets the middle point of the text you type. Whatever you type will be centered on that tab setting.
⌋	Right	Sets the start position on the right, so as you type, text moves to the left of that tab setting and aligns on the right.
⊥	Decimal	Aligns numbers on a decimal point. Regardless of how long the number, each number lines up with the decimal point in the same position.
▮	Bar	This tab does not position text or decimals but inserts a vertical bar at the tab setting. This bar is useful as a separator for text printed on the same line.
▽	Hanging	Sets the first line of a paragraph to begin at the left margin, but all other lines in the paragraph are indented.
△	First Line	Sets the start position on the left for the first line of each paragraph, so as you type, text moves to the right of the tab setting

Tab stops that you set override default tabs. For example, if a 1″ left tab is set, when Tab is pressed the insertion point moves directly to a position that is 1″ from the left margin without stopping at the 0.5″ mark. Tab stops can be inserted and applied in two ways. Tab stops are applied to text you have selected. If you do not select text, the tab stops will apply to the current paragraph and any new paragraphs you type.

To set a tab, click the tab selector on the left of the horizontal ruler until the tab stop option that you want displays. Then click the location of the tab stop on the horizontal ruler. To reposition a tab stop, drag it along the horizontal ruler, or you can drag a tab stop off the ruler to remove it. An alternative is to click the Paragraph Dialog Box Launcher, click Tabs, select the tab (in the Tab stop position box), and then click Clear. Click OK.

A more precise way to set tab stops or to include tab leaders is to use the Tabs dialog box. To open the dialog box you can either double-click an existing tab stop on the ruler or click the Paragraph Dialog Box Launcher (in the Paragraph group on the Home tab) and then click the Tabs option.

A *leader* is a series of dots or hyphens that leads the reader's eye across the page to connect two columns of information, as shown in Figure 2.16. A leader can include dots, dashes, or underlines. For example, the row of dots that typically connects a food item with its price on a restaurant menu is an example of a dot leader. A leader is a tab setting that is associated with the tab that follows the dot leader you select. In the restaurant example, a leader would be associated with the food price that it leads to. The leader shown in Figure 2.16 is a dot leader.

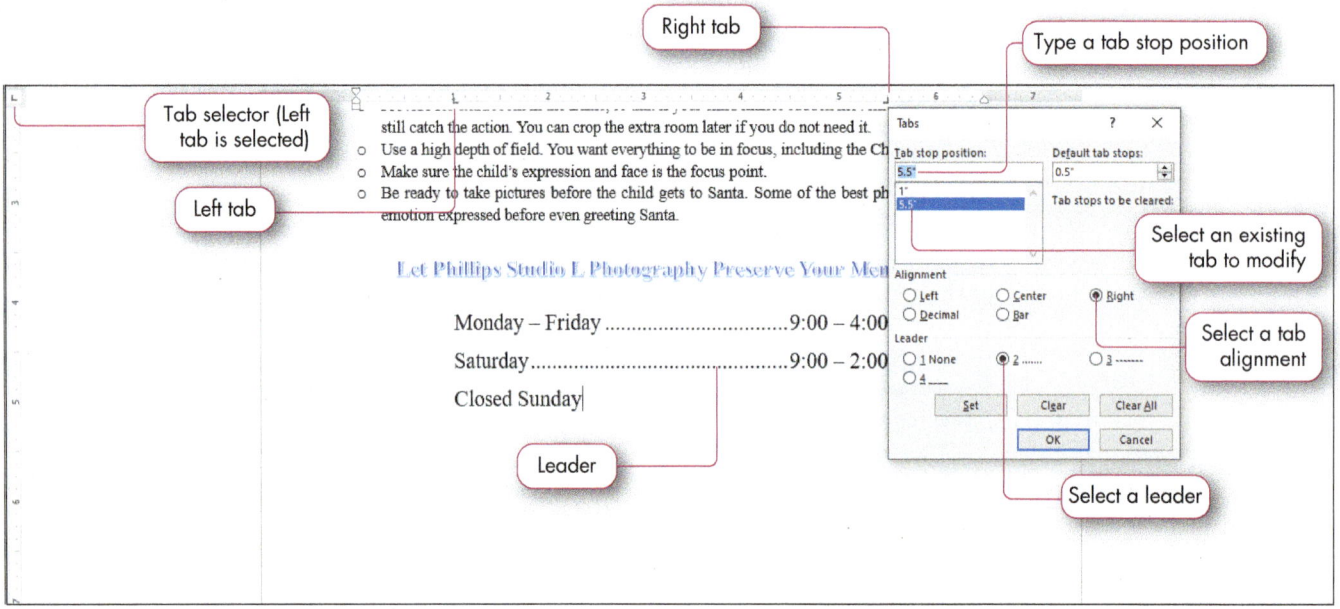

FIGURE 2.16 Set Tab Stops and Leaders

Apply Borders and Shading

You can draw attention to a document or an area of a document by using the Borders and Shading command. A *border* consists of lines that display at the top, bottom, left, or right of a paragraph, a page, a table, or an image, similar to how a picture frame surrounds a photograph or piece of art. *Shading* is a background color behind text in a paragraph, a page, or a table. Shading has more color selections than the Text Highlight Color command; it can add a graphical perspective and draw attention to the selected text. Figure 2.17 illustrates the use of borders and shading.

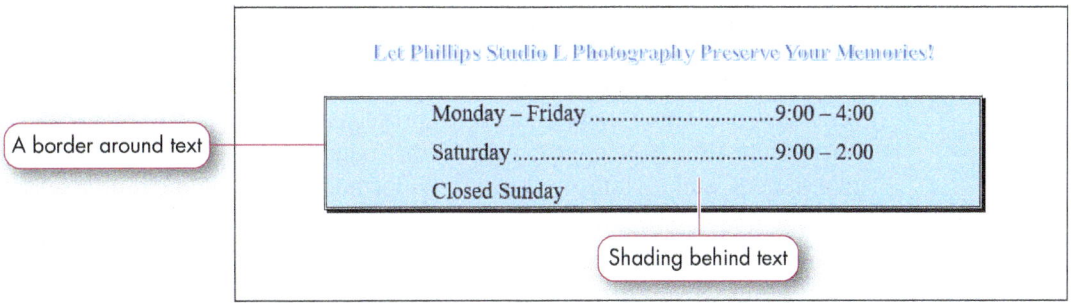

FIGURE 2.17 Borders and Shading

Borders are used throughout this text to surround Tip and Troubleshooting boxes. You might surround a particular paragraph with a border, possibly even shading the paragraph, to set it apart from other text on the page, drawing the reader's attention to its contents. You must first select all paragraphs to which you will apply a border or shading format. If you have not selected text, any border or shading you identify will be applied to the paragraph in which the insertion point is located.

When you click the Borders arrow in the Paragraph group on the Home tab and select Borders and Shading, the Borders and Shading dialog box displays (see Figure 2.18), containing three tabs—Borders, Page Border, and Shading. If your intention is to place a border around one or more paragraphs, you would use options on the Borders tab, first selecting a Box, Shadow, 3D, or Custom design. A Box border places a uniform border around a paragraph. A Shadow border places thicker lines at the right and bottom of the bordered area. A 3D border adds more dimension to the border, while a Custom border enables the user to select a specific style, color, width, and side. If you are removing existing borders from a paragraph or selection, you would choose the None setting. The Preview area of the dialog box displays results of any selected border options before you finalize the design.

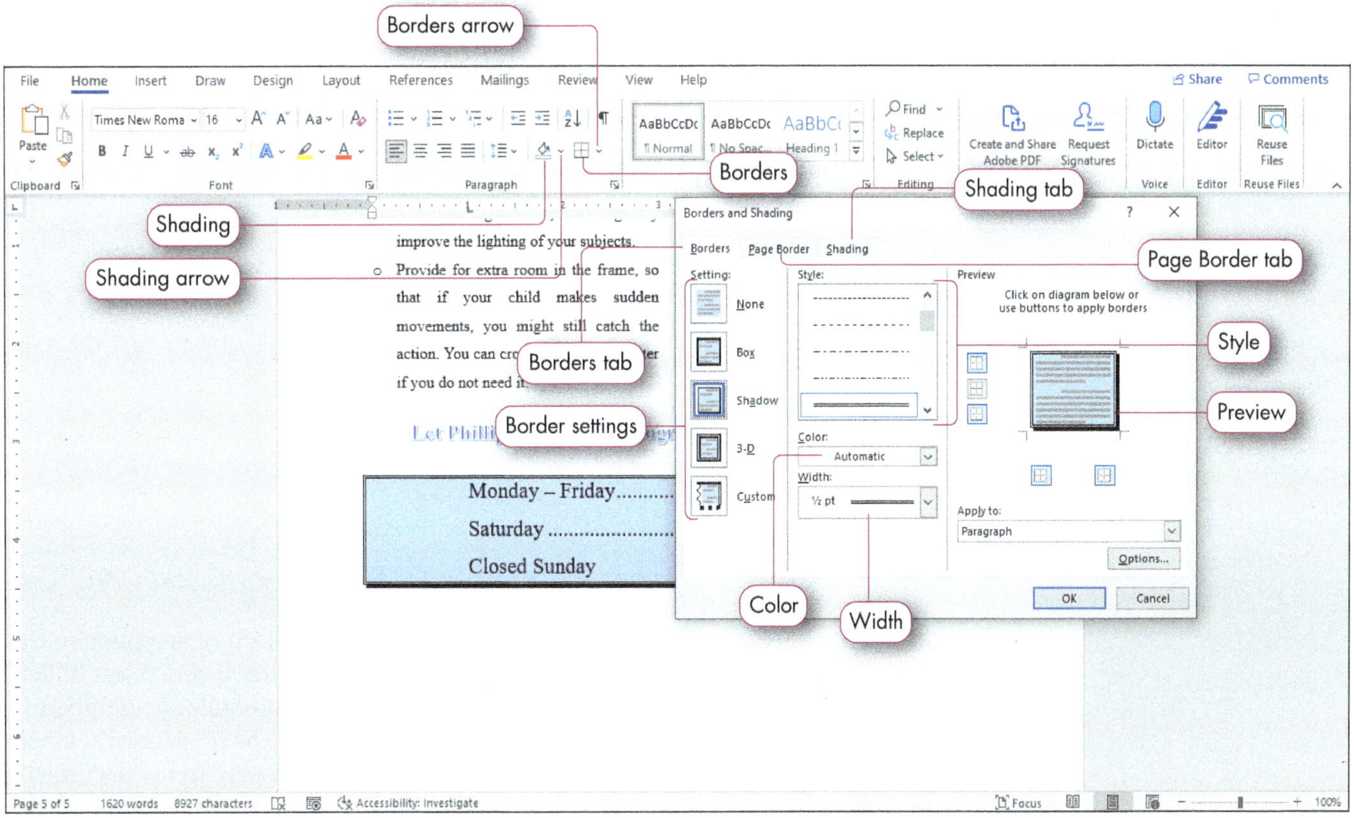

FIGURE 2.18 Select a Border and Shading

The Page Border tab in the Borders and Shading dialog box is used to place a border around one or more selected pages. As with a paragraph border, you can place the border around the entire page, or you can select one or more sides. The Page Border tab also provides an additional option to use a preselected image as a border instead of ordinary lines. Note that it is appropriate to use page borders on documents such as flyers, newsletters, and invitations, but not on formal documents such as research papers and professional reports.

You can apply shading to one or more selected paragraphs using the Shading arrow in the Paragraph group on the Home tab. Select a solid color, a lighter or darker variation of a color, or More Colors for even more variety. You can also select shading options from the Shading tab of the Borders and Shading dialog box.

STEP 4 · Create Bulleted and Numbered Lists

A list organizes information by topic or in a sequence. Word enables you to format a **numbered list** for a sequence of steps. In that case, if you add or remove items, the list items are automatically renumbered. If the list is a simple itemization of points, use a **bulleted list** (see Figure 2.19). A multilevel list extends a numbered or bulleted list to several levels, and it, too, is updated automatically when topics are added or deleted. A multilevel list is helpful for listing major categories as well as subordinate items below each category. Both numbering and bullets are options in the Paragraph group on the Home tab.

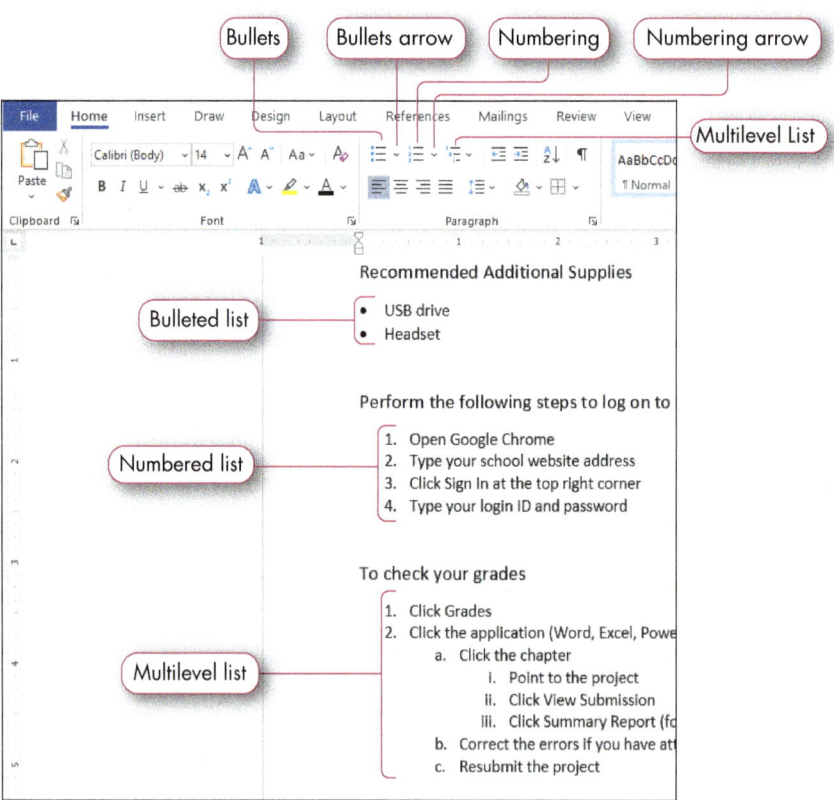

FIGURE 2.19 Bullets and Numbering

With text selected, you can apply bullets or numbering by selecting an option in the Paragraph group. If, instead, you want to format text that is yet to be typed, select Bullets (or Numbering) before typing. For options other than the default bullet or numbering style, click the Bullets (or Numbering) arrow and point to one of the predefined symbols or numbering styles in the library. A preview of the style will display in the document. Click the style you want to use. To apply multiple levels to a list, as shown in Figure 2.19, click Multilevel List.

Word provides a gallery of bulleting and numbering styles. Instead of a solid round bullet, you might prefer a checkmark or arrow. Instead of plain numbering, you might want Roman numerals, or perhaps letters of the alphabet would better suit the project. Those options and more are available when you click the Bullets arrow (or Numbering arrow) and choose from a list (or click Define New Bullet or Define New Number Format).

Critical Thinking

1. Explain why you might select a serif font instead of sans serif for a printed document. *p. 180*

2. Explain why you would choose to use paragraph spacing in a document, such as a report, in which paragraphs are not indented. *p. 188*

3. Describe the type of tabs you would use in developing a table of contents listing chapters of a book and corresponding pages. Provide rationale for the choices you are describing. *pp. 191–192*

4. Explain whether you would choose bullets or numbering to list items required for an upcoming camping trip, providing rationale. *pp. 194–195*

Hands-On Exercises

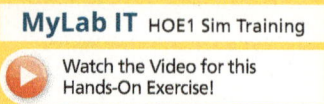
Skills covered: Select
Font Options • Change Text
Appearance • Select Paragraph
Alignment • Select Line and
Paragraph Spacing • Select Indents
• Set Tab Stops • Apply Borders
and Shading • Create Bulleted and
Numbered Lists

1 Format Text and Paragraphs

The newsletter you are developing needs a lot of work. You want to format it so it is much easier to read. After selecting an appropriate font and font size, you will emphasize selected text with bold and italic text formatting. Paragraphs must be spaced so they are easy to read. You know that, to be effective, a document must capture the reader's attention while conveying a message. You will begin the process of formatting and preparing the newsletter in this exercise.

STEP 1 SELECT FONT OPTIONS AND CHANGE TEXT APPEARANCE

The newsletter will be printed and distributed by mail. As a printed document, you know that certain font options are better suited for reading. Specifically, you want to use a serif font in an easy-to-read size. Refer to Figure 2.20 as you complete Step 1.

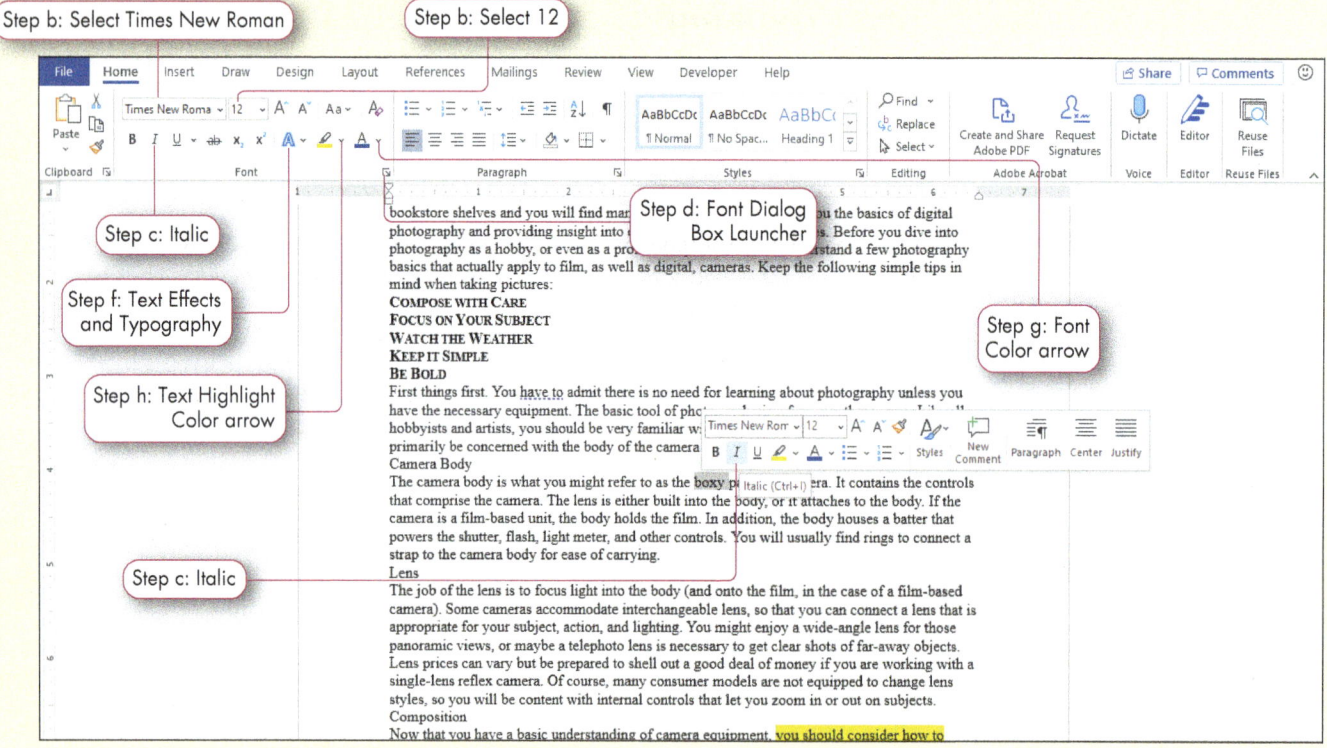

FIGURE 2.20 Format Text

a. Open *w02h1Studio* and save it as **w02h1Studio_LastFirst**.

> **TROUBLESHOOTING:** If you make any major mistakes in this exercise, you can close the file, open *w02h1Studio* again, and then start this exercise over.

b. Press **Ctrl+A** to select all the text in the document (on a Mac, command+A). Click the **Font arrow** in the Font group on the Home tab and scroll to select **Times New Roman**. Click the **Font Size arrow** in the Font group and select **12**.

You use a 12-pt serif font on the whole document because it is easier to read in print.

c. Select the second paragraph in the document, *Courtesy of Phillips Studio L Photography*. Click **Italic** on the Mini Toolbar. Locate and double-click **boxy** in the paragraph below *Camera Body*. Click **Italic** in the Font group or on the Mini Toolbar.

d. Select the five paragraphs beginning with *Compose with Care* and ending with *Be Bold*. Click the **Font Dialog Box Launcher** in the Font group.

MAC TROUBLESHOOTING: Click the Format menu and click Font.

The Font dialog box displays with font options.

e. Ensure that the Font tab is displayed in the Font dialog box and click **Bold** in the Font style box. Click to select the **Small caps check box** under Effects. Click **OK**.

Formatting a list differently helps set it apart from surrounding text, drawing attention to its content.

f. Scroll to the end of the document. Select the last paragraph in the document, *Let Phillips Studio L Photography Preserve Your Memories!* Click **Text Effects and Typography** in the Font group. Select **Fill: Blue, Accent color 5; Outline: White, Background color 1; Hard Shadow: Blue, Accent color 5** (row 3, column 3). Change the font size of the selected text to **16**. Click anywhere to deselect the text.

g. Press **Ctrl+Home** to position the insertion point at the beginning of the document (on a Mac, command+fn+up arrow). Select the second paragraph in the document, *Courtesy of Phillips Studio L Photography*. Click the **Font Color arrow** and select **Blue, Accent 5, Darker 25%** (row 5, column 9).

h. Select the words **you should consider how to become a better photographer** in the paragraph under the *Composition* heading. Click the **Text Highlight Color arrow** and select **Yellow**.

i. Click the **Review tab** and click **Editor** in the Proofing group to check spelling and grammar. Correct all suggested spelling and grammatical errors, but ignore any concisement or refinement flags.

j. Save the document.

INSERT SYMBOLS AND SPECIAL CHARACTERS, AND SELECT PARAGRAPH ALIGNMENT, SPACING, AND INDENTS

The lines of the newsletter are too close together. It is difficult to tell where one paragraph ends and the next begins, and the layout of the text is not very pleasing. Overall, you will adjust line and paragraph spacing, and apply indents where necessary. Refer to Figure 2.21 as you complete Step 2.

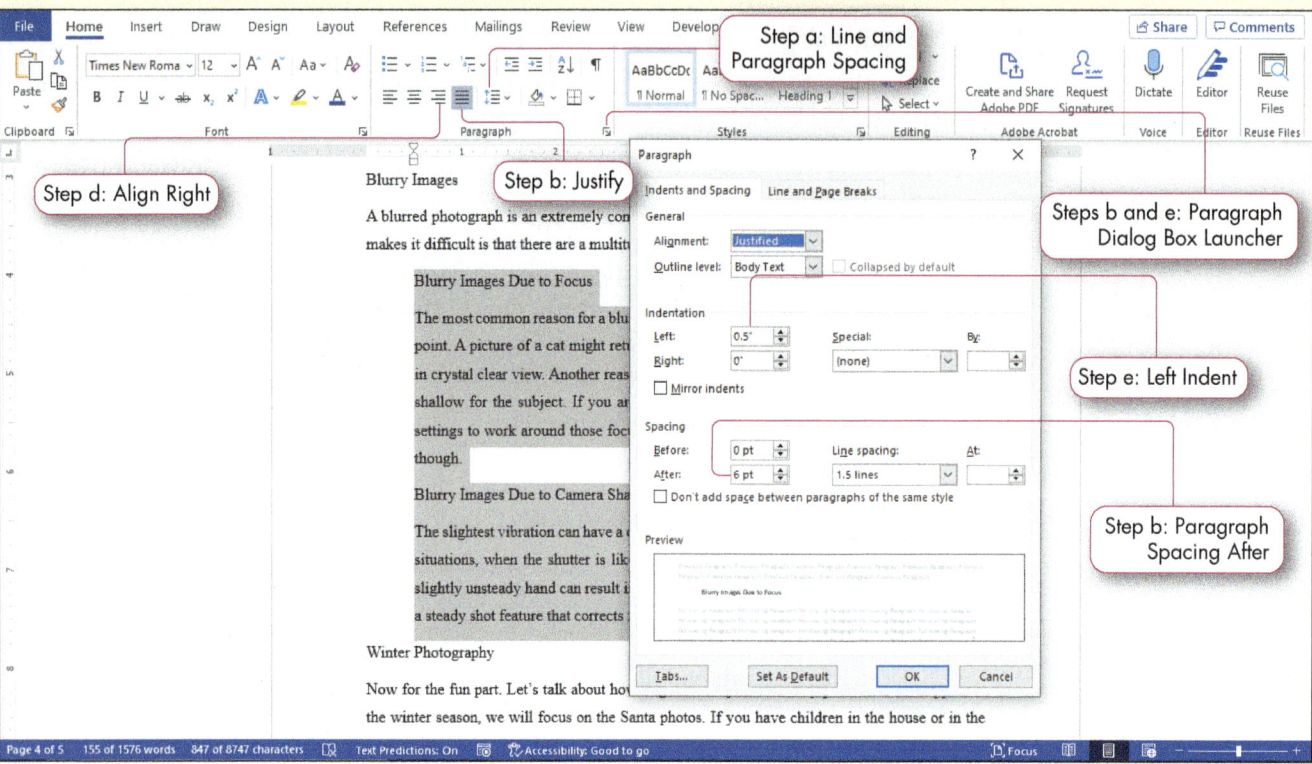

FIGURE 2.21 Adjust Spacing and Indents

a. Select most of the document beginning with the sentence *If you enjoy taking digital pictures* and ending with *emotion expressed before even greeting Santa.* Click the **Home tab**. Click **Line and Paragraph Spacing** in the Paragraph group. Select **1.5**. Do not deselect the text.

All lines within the selected text are spaced at 1.5, resulting in a more attractive, easy-to-read display.

b. Click **Justify** in the Paragraph group. Click the **Paragraph Dialog Box Launcher** (on a Mac, click Format and select Paragraph). With the Indents and Spacing tab selected, click the **After up arrow** in the Spacing section to increase spacing after to **6 pt**. Click **OK**. Click anywhere to deselect the text.

Additional paragraph spacing clearly delineates where one paragraph ends and another begins, improving readability of the document.

c. Click to place the insertion point after *Courtesy of Phillips Studio L Photography* on the second paragraph of page 1. Ensure that the insertion point is placed on the same line as the text, not on the blank paragraph following. Click the **Insert tab**, click **Symbol**, and select **More Symbols**. Click the **Special Characters tab** and click **Registered**. Click **Insert**. Click **Close**.

Adhering to any legal requirements, such as identifying a registered name or a copy-righted item, is an important part of a well-designed document.

d. Ensure that the insertion point is on the second paragraph of text in the document, *Courtesy of Phillips Studio L Photography*. Click the **Home tab**. Click **Align Right** in the Paragraph group. Click anywhere on the last paragraph in the document, *Let Phillips Studio L Photography Preserve Your Memories!* Click **Center** in the Paragraph group.

e. Select four paragraphs of text on page 4, beginning with *Blurry Images Due to Focus* and ending with *feature that corrects for a bit of shake*. Click the **Paragraph Dialog Box Launcher.** (On a Mac, click Format and select Paragraph.) Click the **Left up arrow** in the Indentation group five times to increase the Left indent to **0.5″**. Click **OK.**

The paragraphs that are sublevels of the Blurry Images section are indented uniformly from the left, identifying their status as sublevels of the Blurry Images discussion.

f. Save the document.

STEP 3 ▸ SET TAB STOPS AND APPLY BORDERS AND SHADING

You realize that you left off the studio hours and want to include them at the end of the document, and you also want to draw attention to the business hours using borders and shading. Refer to Figures 2.22 and 2.23 as you complete Step 3.

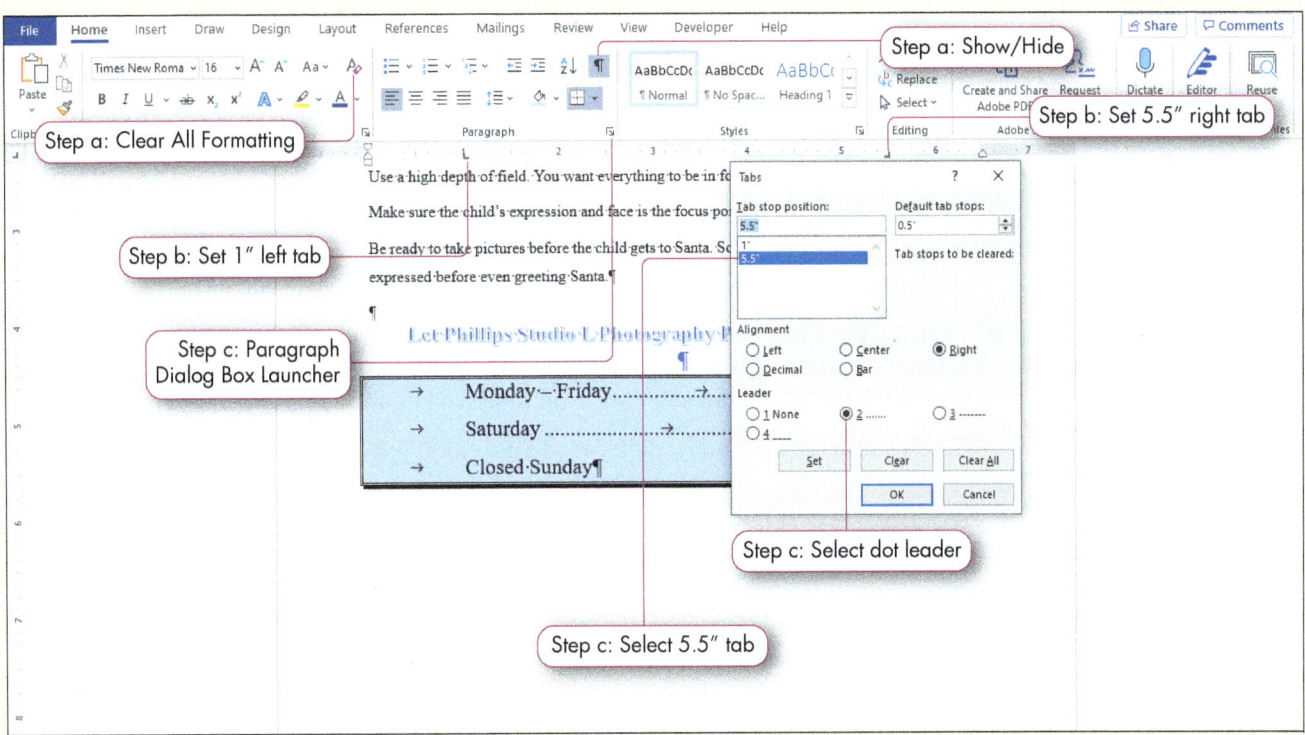

FIGURE 2.22 Set Tab Stops

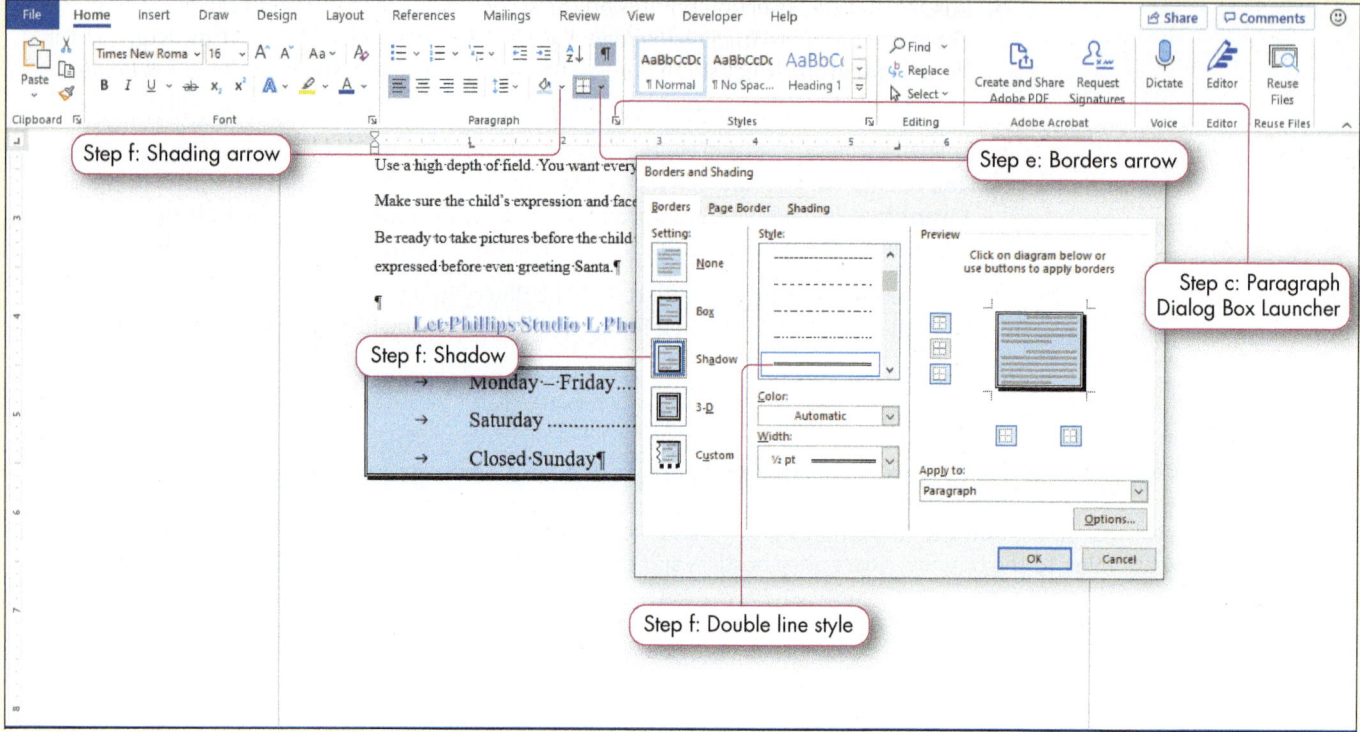

FIGURE 2.23 Apply Borders and Shade Text

a. Place the insertion point at the end of the document. Click **Show/Hide** in the Paragraph group to display nonprinting characters. Press **Enter** twice. Click **Clear All Formatting** in the Font group on the Home tab. Select **Times New Roman font** and **16 pt size**.

You clicked Clear All Formatting so that the text effect formatting from the paragraph above the insertion point is not carried forward to text that you will type next.

b. Click the **View tab** and ensure that Ruler in the Show group is selected. Ensure the tab selector (shown at the top of the vertical ruler) specifies a left tab and click at **1** on the horizontal ruler. Click the **tab selector** twice to select a right tab and click at **5.5″** on the ruler.

You set a left tab at 1″ and a right tab at 5.5″.

> **TROUBLESHOOTING:** If the tabs you set are incorrectly placed on the ruler, click Undo in the Quick Access Toolbar and repeat Step b. You can also drag a tab off the ruler to remove it or drag it along the ruler to reposition it.

c. Click the **Home tab.** Click the **Paragraph Dialog Box Launcher** and click **Tabs** at the bottom-left corner. Click **5.5″** in the Tab stop position box. Click **2** in the Leader section and click **OK**.

You modified the right tab to include dot leaders, which means dots will display before text at the right tab.

d. Press **Tab**. Type **Monday – Friday** and press **Tab**. Type **9:00 – 4:00**. Be sure to leave a space before and after the dash. Press **Enter**. Press **Tab**. Type **Saturday** and press **Tab**. Type **9:00 – 2:00**. Press **Enter**. Press **Tab**. Type **Closed Sunday**.

e. Select the three paragraphs at the end of the document, beginning with *Monday – Friday* and ending with *Closed Sunday*. Click the **Borders arrow** in the Paragraph group on the Home tab and select **Borders and Shading**.

> **TROUBLESHOOTING:** If you click Borders instead of the Borders arrow, you will not see the Borders and Shading dialog box and the most recent border will be applied to selected text. Click Undo on the Quick Access Toolbar, click the Borders arrow, and then select Borders and Shading.

f. Click **Shadow** in the Setting section. Scroll through the Style box and select the seventh style—**double line**. Click **OK**. Do not deselect the text. Click the **Shading arrow** and select **Blue, Accent 1, Lighter 60%** (row 3, column 5). Click anywhere to deselect the text.

Studio hours are bordered and shaded to draw attention.

g. Save the document.

CREATE BULLETED AND NUMBERED LISTS

At several points in the newsletter, you include either a list of items or a sequence of steps. You will add bullets to the lists and number the steps. Refer to Figure 2.24 as you complete Step 4.

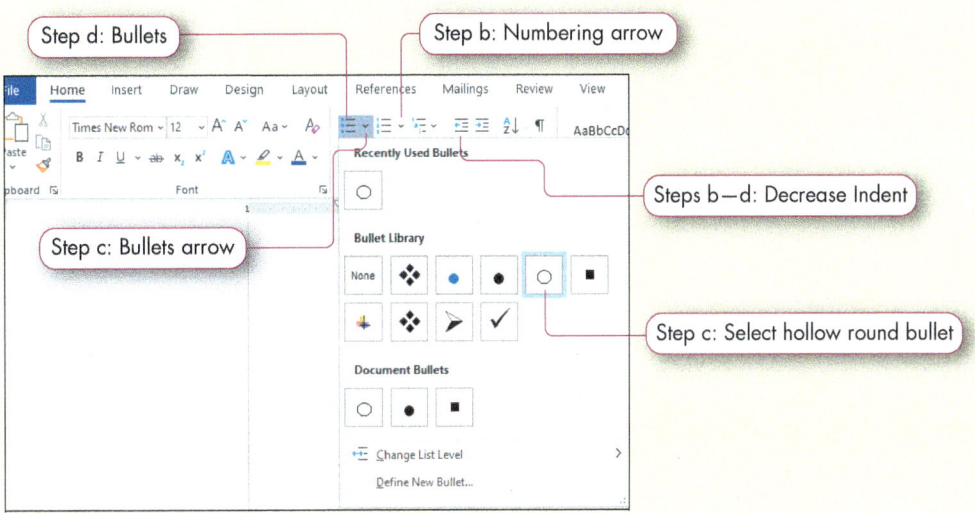

FIGURE 2.24 Add Bullets and Numbers

a. Scroll to the top of the document. Select the five boldfaced paragraphs, beginning with *Compose with Care* and ending with *Be Bold*.

b. Click the **Numbering arrow** in the Paragraph group and select **Number Alignment: Left** showing each number followed by a right parenthesis (row 1, column 3 under Numbering Library). Click **Decrease Indent** in the Paragraph group to move the numbered items to the left margin. Click anywhere to deselect the text.

c. Scroll to the second page and select the four paragraphs following the sentence *Depth of field is determined by several factors*, beginning with *Aperture/F-Stop* and ending with *Point of View* on the third page. Click the **Bullets arrow** and select the **hollow round bullet**. Decrease the indent to move the selected text to the left margin. Deselect the text.

Lists are often delineated by bullets to clearly identify them.

d. Scroll to the last page and select the six paragraphs above the last paragraph of text, beginning with *Where kids are involved*, and ending with *even greeting Santa*. Click **Bullets** to apply a hollow round bullet to the selected paragraphs. Decrease the indent so the bullets begin at the left margin.

Clicking Bullets applies the most recently selected bullet style to selected text. You did not have to click the Bullets arrow and select from the Bullet Library.

e. Save the document. Keep the document open if you plan to continue with the next Hands-On Exercise. If not, close the document, and exit Word.

Graphic Objects

An ***object*** is an item that can be individually selected and manipulated within a document. Objects, such as pictures, tables, text boxes, and other graphic types are often included in documents to add interest or convey a point (see Figure 2.25). Newsletters typically include pictures and other decorative elements to liven up what might otherwise be a somewhat mundane document. Reports might include descriptive drawings or tables to help clarify data. As you work with a document, you can search for appropriate pictures and graphics online, or you can create objects using Word's selection of illustrations and art—all without ever leaving your document workspace.

FIGURE 2.25 Word Objects

One thing all objects have in common is that they can be selected and worked with independently of surrounding text. You can resize them, add special effects, and move them to other locations within the document. Word includes convenient text wrapping controls so that you can adjust the way text wraps around an object. With Live Layout and alignment guides, you can line up pictures and other diagrams with existing text.

In this section, you will explore the use of objects in a Word document. Specifically, you will learn to include pictures, searching for them online as well as obtaining them from your own storage device. You will create text boxes and learn to create impressive text displays with WordArt and SmartArt. Using 3D models, you will diagram multidimensional objects, and you will learn to create objects using various combined shapes.

Work with Graphic Objects

Objects such as pictures, icons, and illustrations can be selected from online locations or a local storage device. When using images that you do not own, you should ensure that all copyright concerns are addressed and you have the permission of the images' owners. You can also use Word to create other objects, such as WordArt, SmartArt, text boxes, screenshots, and 3D models. An object is selected independently of surrounding text so that it can be modified, moved, or deleted. With an object selected, an additional tab displays on the ribbon with options related to the object, making it convenient to quickly modify and enhance an object. For example, with a picture selected, a Picture Format tab is included on the ribbon, containing options for modifying and working with the picture. When the picture is deselected, the tab is no longer visible.

Graphic objects—such as stylized text, shapes, diagrams, and text boxes—add visual interest to documents and often illustrate processes in a more understandable way than text alone. Word provides a variety of objects that you can use individually or in combination to illustrate a point or emphasize text. For example, you can insert a process diagram to describe a set of steps. Or perhaps your intent is to provide a callout to better describe an area of text. You can even combine objects for an intended effect, positioning and overlapping shapes.

STEP 1 Insert a Picture

A ***picture*** is a graphic image, such as a drawing or photograph. You can insert pictures in a document from your own library of digital images or you can access abundant picture resources online. Once placed in a document, a picture can be resized and modified with styles, special borders, and artistic effects. Other options enable you to easily align a picture with surrounding text, rotate or crop it if necessary, and even recolor it so it coordinates with an existing color scheme.

To insert a picture in a document, click the Insert tab and select Pictures in the Illustrations group, as shown in Figure 2.26. Choose a picture type—This Device, Stock Images, or Online Pictures. Microsoft provides access to thousands of royalty-free images, icons, stickers, and other graphics, including backgrounds and clip art in its searchable stock images. Online Pictures include a wide range of Creative Commons images, which are free of copyright restrictions as long as they are not sold or used for profit.

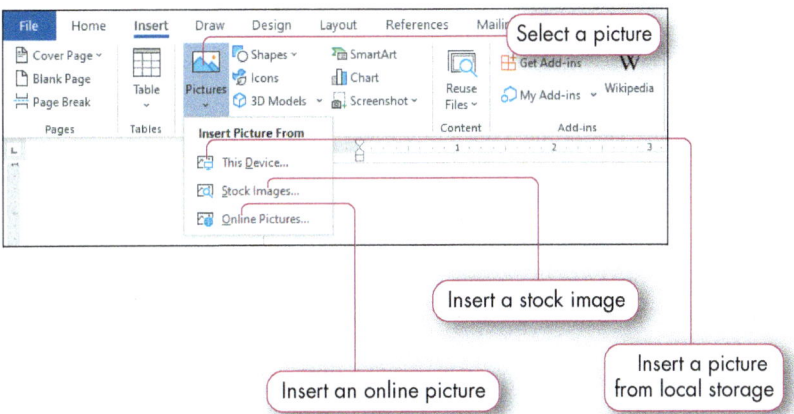

FIGURE 2.26 Insert a Picture

Insert a Screenshot

To capture information that displays onscreen, whether from a website, another program, or another document that you have open on your computer, you can take a ***screenshot*** without leaving Word. A screenshot is a picture of a device display. You can either capture the whole screen or a screen clipping of an open—not minimized—window. For example, with a Word document open, and the insertion point positioned where the screenshot is to be placed, click the Insert tab and select Screenshot in the Illustrations group. If one or more windows are open, perhaps a Web browser and also another document, those windows will be shown as thumbnails in the Available Windows gallery. Click one of the windows to insert the full screenshot of that item. The Available Windows gallery will display any open window, but not those that are minimized. The window is automatically inserted into the document as an object.

If the intent is to capture only part of an open window, open the item to be captured, ensuring that it is the only open window other than the Word document. Begin the process of capturing a screenshot, but select Screen Clipping after clicking Screenshot, as shown in Figure 2.27. Drag to select any part of the subsequent screen display, which is then placed in the document as an object.

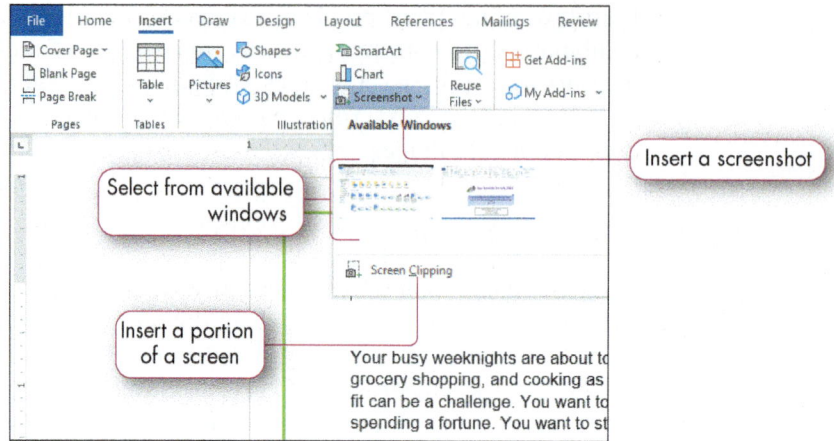

FIGURE 2.27 Insert a Screenshot

> **TIP: SNIP & SKETCH**
> Snip & Sketch is an app that facilitates the capture of screenshots. It is pre-installed on Windows computers, but you can also download it from the Microsoft Store. It is an alternative to the Snipping tool with slightly more drawing features. On a Mac, to get a full screenshot, use the Grab tool or press shift+command+3.

Insert SmartArt

Although Word provides ample shapes and drawing tools to enable you to create diagrams, it can be extremely time consuming and difficult to create complex, designer-quality illustrations using those tools alone. To simplify that task, Word includes *SmartArt*, which is a group of visual representations of information that can be created to effectively communicate a message or idea in one of many visually appealing layouts. For example, you might insert a SmartArt diagram of an organization chart, a list, or a process to illustrate an important concept that is difficult to explain with simple text but easier to understand when viewed as an illustration. SmartArt is an option in the Illustrations group on the Insert tab. From the Choose a SmartArt Graphic dialog box, you can select a category in the left pane and any of a number of diagrams to the right. Click a selection in the middle pane to see a short description, as shown in Figure 2.28.

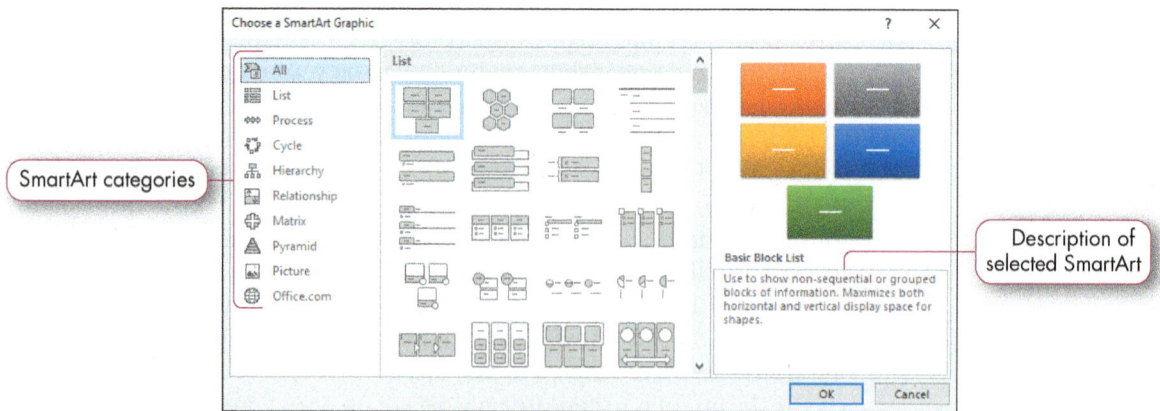

FIGURE 2.28 Choose a SmartArt Graphic

When a SmartArt diagram is inserted into a document, text placeholders display, as shown in Figure 2.29. You can click a placeholder and type text directly into the diagram. Alternatively, you can click the Text pane arrow in the middle left side of the diagram frame to view the Text pane if it is not already visible. The **SmartArt Text pane**, shown in Figure 2.29, displays an outline view for typing text items that are then placed in the SmartArt diagram. With a SmartArt object selected, SmartArt Design and Format tabs display on the ribbon. The Design tab provides a toggle button for the SmartArt Text pane, along with other tools to change the appearance of the diagram, such as changing shapes and style. The Format tab provides options to modify the appearance of diagram text.

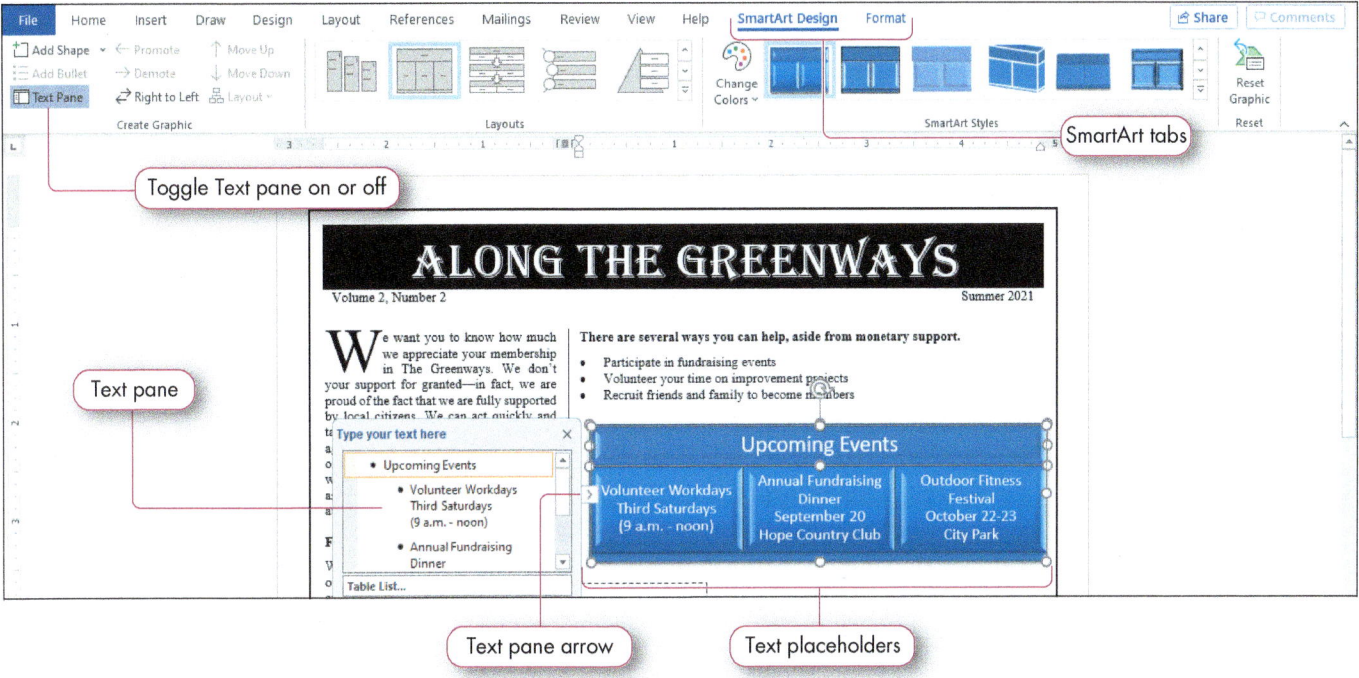

FIGURE 2.29 Design a SmartArt Graphic

Insert WordArt

WordArt is a decorative text feature that is especially useful for designing banners or headings. Incorporating special effects that include colors, shadows, gradients, and 3D effects, a WordArt object presents text in a vibrant and eye-catching way. WordArt text can be rotated in any direction, even upside down, and text can be oriented in a slanted, arched, or wavy pattern. WordArt design is not appropriate for all documents, especially more conservative business correspondence, but it can give life to newsletters, flyers, and other more informal projects, especially when applied to headings and titles.

WordArt is well suited for single lines, such as document headings, where the larger print and text design draws attention and adds style to a document title. However, it is not appropriate for body text because a WordArt object is managed independently of surrounding text and cannot be formatted along with other document text. In addition, if WordArt were incorporated into body text, the more ornate text design would most likely adversely affect the readability of the document. You can format existing text as WordArt, or you can insert new WordArt text into a document by selecting WordArt in the Text group on the Insert tab. A heading that is formatted as WordArt is shown in Figure 2.30.

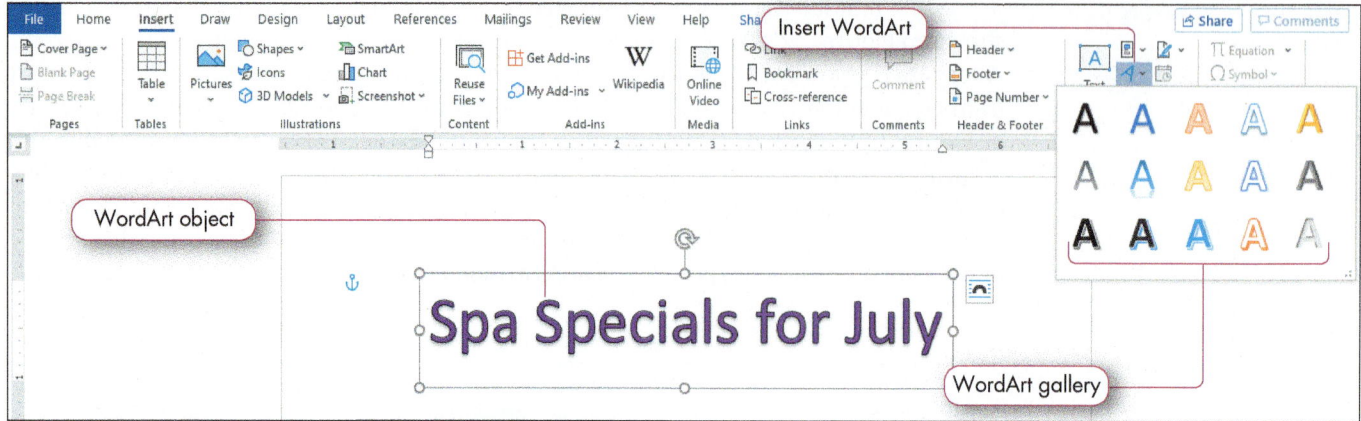

FIGURE 2.30 WordArt

STEP 2 **Insert a Text Box**

As the name suggests, a ***text box*** is a rectangular object that contains text. Magazine and newspaper articles often use text boxes to help control the placement of text as well as provide a visual tool to draw a reader's attention. A text box can be bordered and shaded, serving the purpose of setting text apart from other text in the document. Conversely, a text box can also be designed to contain no shape color and no visible outline so that text is more fully incorporated or at least more seamlessly linked to surrounding text, giving little indication of its origin as a text box. For example, some Word templates use text boxes to format newsletter text into columns. With no borders or shading, such an arrangement makes quick work of organizing text into columns. Similarly, a text box with no shading or border often houses a ***pull quote***, which is a short excerpt from document text, often formatted in larger font and creatively placed within existing document text, used to draw attention to a fact or point. A text box might even be used as a banner for a newsletter, attractively shaded and bordered.

A text box can be used to house a ***sidebar***, which is a long vertical block of text displayed along the side of a document. Sidebars might display supplementary information, or they can simply display information of interest to the reader. Several designs in the text box gallery are suitable for a sidebar or pull quote in a document, as shown in Figure 2.31, but you can also create your own, starting with a simple text box.

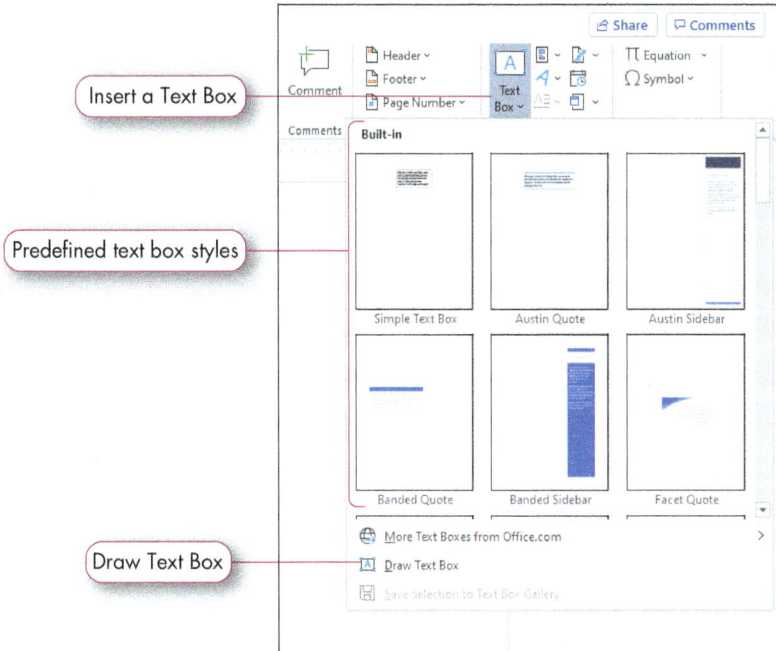

FIGURE 2.31 Insert a Text Box

Use the Text Box selection in the Text group on the Insert tab to begin the process of inserting a text box. Alternatively, you can select Text Box in the Basic Shapes gallery when you click the Insert tab and select Shapes. As shown in Figure 2.31, you will find a variety of text box selections, including some that are preformatted, when you choose Text Box from the Insert tab. Regardless of how you begin the process of inserting a text box, you can click in a document to place the text box or drag to draw the box. The text box size can be modified later through settings on the Shape Format tab that displays when a text box is selected.

> **TIP: LINK TEXT BOXES**
>
> Newsletters are sometimes designed with columnar text organized in text boxes instead of being formatted in columns. In that case, text flows from one text box in one column or page to another text box. You can link text boxes so that when text runs out of space in one box it automatically flows into another. Although text can be present in a text box to link to another, you can only link to an empty text box. As the first text box becomes populated with text, it will automatically continue in the linked text box. To link text boxes, place the insertion point in the first text box and type text. Click Create Link in the Text group on the Shape Format tab. Click in the empty text box to link to it.

Insert a Shape

Occasionally, a predefined object, such as a text box or SmartArt, is not sufficient for your purpose. Perhaps you are designing an award document in which you will include a banner shape with text. Or maybe a thought bubble would be helpful to illustrate a point. In both cases, you can use the Shapes gallery to access and modify shapes. A *shape* is an object, such as a circle or an arrow, that can be used as visual enhancement in a document. Use one shape or combine multiple shapes to create a more complex image. When you click the Insert tab and click Shapes in the Illustrations group, the Shapes gallery displays, as shown in Figure 2.32. Select a shape from the gallery. The pointer becomes a crosshair. At that point, click in the document to insert the shape or drag to draw the shape in any size.

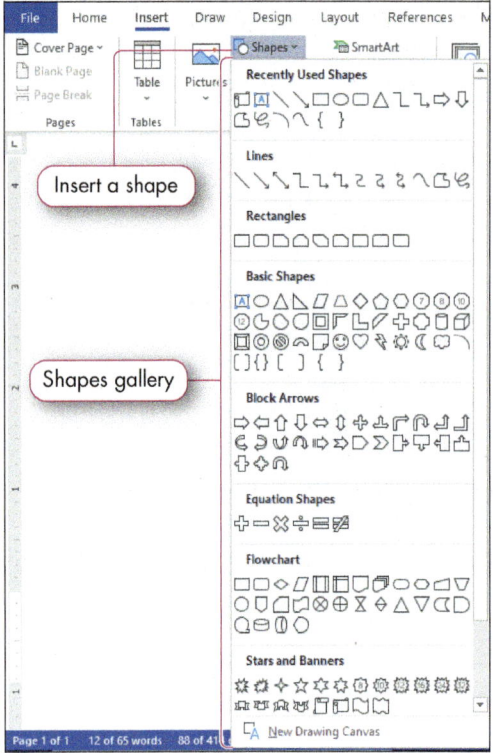

FIGURE 2.32 Use the Shapes Gallery

TIP: TEXT BOXES AND RECTANGLE SHAPES

Unlike a rectangle shape that can be selected from the Illustrations group on the Insert tab, a text box modifies its size to accommodate the amount of text included. In contrast, a rectangle shape can also include text, but its size does not automatically adjust for text included.

Although predesigned shapes are readily available when you access the Shapes gallery from the Insert tab, you can also create your own drawings and shapes using the Draw tab. If it is not shown on the ribbon, you can right-click the ribbon and choose to customize the ribbon to include the Draw tab. Using a set of pens, available when you click the Draw tab, you can write, draw, or highlight text. Click a pen once to select it and then click it again to further define color and thickness settings. Drawing tools include pens, a pencil, and a highlighter. An eraser is also available to toggle on and use to remove drawn elements. Choosing Ink to Shape in the Convert group, you can draw a shape freehand, and Word will convert the shape into a well-designed and recognizable replica. Having used a drawing tool to illustrate, you can take advantage of Word's Ink Replay command to repeat ink strokes.

TIP: DUPLICATING SHAPES

An object, such as a shape, is treated as a separate entity that can be moved, resized, formatted, or even duplicated. A duplicated object is the same size and appearance as the original. To duplicate an object, including a WordArt selection, text box, shape, image, or SmartArt, select the object, and press Ctrl+D. Once the object is duplicated, you can drag to reposition it or use tools on the ribbon to adjust the appearance.

After you have drawn one shape, you might want to continue drawing the same shape. For example, if you are creating a flowchart or organization chart, you might want to use a shape several times, although not necessarily in the exact same size as the first shape that was drawn. Use the Lock Drawing Mode command to quickly draw additional shapes while retaining the latitude to adjust size or dimensions as the shape is redrawn. Unlike the process of copying and pasting, or duplicating, in which an exact duplicate of an original is created, the process of drawing additional shapes does not necessarily result in shapes that are identical.

Insert a 3D Model

A 3D object can be manipulated in three dimensions, rotated in any direction at any angle. You might find 3D objects useful in online or electronic sales brochures where potential customers can explore facets of an item, such as a house they are considering purchasing. 3D objects can accurately represent items that must be assembled or they can provide detail in technical manuals. Although 3D objects can also be inserted in documents designed for printing, they are especially beneficial in online documents where they can be rotated, resized, panned, and zoomed. When placed in a Word document and deselected, a 3D model becomes a 2D image that cannot be further manipulated unless selected in an onscreen view.

Insert a 3D image by selecting 3D Models from the Insert tab. If you click the 3D Models arrow, you can choose to obtain a stock image online or from files on your computer. If you click the 3D Models command, you will be directed to Microsoft's collection of stock images. Select an image from various categories or navigate to the file and insert the graphic.

> **TIP: CREATE YOUR OWN 3D IMAGES**
> You can create your own 3D images or obtain them from various online content sharing locations. Paint 3D, a desktop app included with Windows or available from the Microsoft Store, enables you to create your own 3D images, saving them for inclusion in a Word document.

After you have inserted a 3D object, you can choose from various formatting options on the 3D Model tab, shown in Figure 2.33. The 3D Model Views group includes various three-dimensional views of the selected object. You can change the object's orientation, tilting or rotating it, when you drag the 3D rotation handle that displays in the center of the object. A rotation handle at the top of the object enables you to rotate it clockwise or counter-clockwise, and sizing handles are available if you want to drag to resize. Click Pan & Zoom and then drag the magnifying glass that displays beside the object up or down to increase or reduce the view. When you pan and zoom, however, the object's dimensions do not change; you merely use more or less of the allocated space for the object's display. As with more traditional images, you can wrap text around a 3D model, position and align it on the page, and adjust the height and width. All of those options are available on the 3D Model tab when the object is selected.

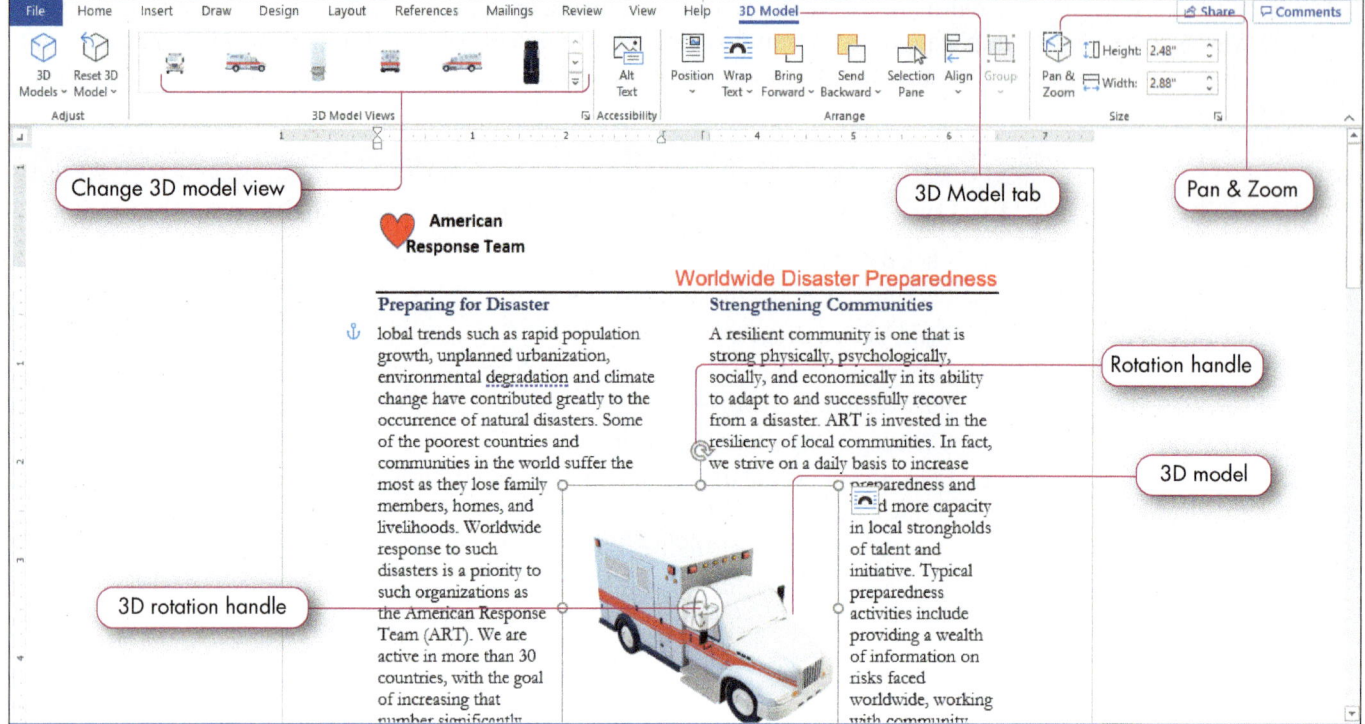

FIGURE 2.33 Insert a 3D Model

Depending on the purpose of a document and its intended audience, objects such as pictures, text boxes, SmartArt, and WordArt can help convey a message and add interest. As you learn to incorporate objects visually within a document so that they appear to flow seamlessly within existing text, you will find it easy to create attractive, informative documents that contain an element of design apart from simple text.

Modify Graphic Objects

Generally speaking, objects are selected and managed similarly, but each type of object is unique not only in purpose but also in choices that are shown on associated ribbon tabs. For example, with a picture chosen, you can select from various photo editing and correction options that are unique to the Picture Format tab (see Figure 2.34). Selecting a SmartArt object results in not only a Format tab but also a Design tab with even more possibilities related to shapes and color. You can also easily resize objects, either by dragging a sizing handle or by more precisely adjusting settings on an associated Format tab. Using text wrapping, alignment guides and positioning options, you can ensure that an object is placed exactly where it should be, attractively situated within surrounding text.

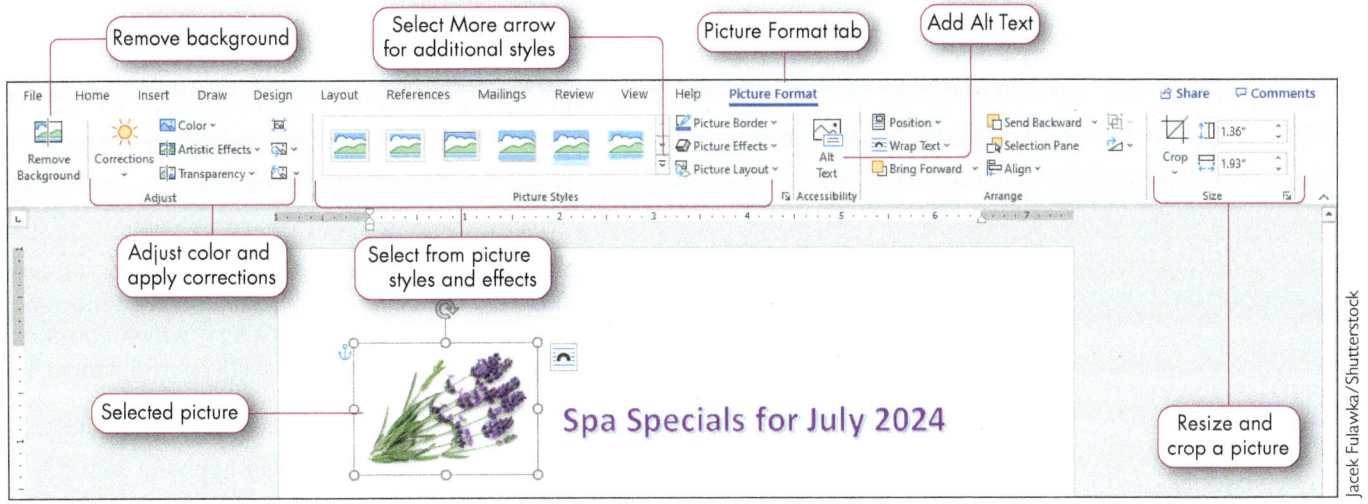

FIGURE 2.34 Picture Format Tab

STEP 3 ▶ Format an Object

Although graphic objects vary in purpose and appearance, they can all be modified through options on an associated Format tab. After selecting a picture or screenshot, you can choose from a wide variety of styles, effects, and photo editing options aimed at customizing a picture's appearance. With WordArt or SmartArt selected, choices center around color, style, shape and text formatting. A 3D model comes with its own set of adjustments related to views and positioning. Text boxes and shapes share format options for shape fill and outline color, among other settings. The Format tab is definitely the place to start when you want to modify the appearance of a selected object.

The Picture Format tab is available when a picture or screenshot is selected, including a variety of options related to styles, effects, corrections, and text wrapping. In addition, resizing, cropping, and repositioning options ensure a precisely placed and sized picture. You can apply a picture style or effect, as well as add a picture border, from selections in the Picture Styles group. The More arrow (refer to Figure 2.34) provides a gallery of picture styles. As you point to a style, the effect of the style is shown in Live Preview, but the style is not applied until you select it. Options in the Adjust group simplify changing a color scheme, applying creative artistic effects, and even adjusting the brightness, contrast, and sharpness of an image.

Adjusting contrast increases or decreases the difference in dark and light areas of the image. Adjusting brightness lightens or darkens the overall image. These adjustments often are made to a picture taken with a digital camera in poor lighting or if a picture is too bright or dull to match other objects in your document. The Brightness/Contrast adjustment is available when you click Corrections in the Adjust group on the Picture Format tab (refer to Figure 2.34).

You can remove the background or portions of a picture you do not want to keep. When you select a picture and click the Remove Background tool in the Adjust group on the Picture Format tab, Word creates a marquee selection area in the picture that determines the background, or area to be removed, and the foreground, or area to be kept. Word identifies the background selection with magenta coloring. Using tools on the Background Removal tab, you can mark areas to keep or mark additional areas to remove. Click Keep Changes to remove the background.

Shapes, text boxes, and WordArt contain two main components to which color can be applied—the line or border of the object and the fill or interior space of the object. So that you can customize shapes, Word provides a Shape Styles gallery, which contains predefined styles with a combination of colors, lines, and other effects. As shown in Figure 2.35, the Shape Format tab includes not only a Shape Styles gallery but also options for modifying the shape outline or fill color of a selected object. Some shapes, such as a straight line, obviously do not contain an interior area for applying a fill color, but you can change the color, width, and style of the line itself. You can also enhance the shape by adding visual effects such as shadow, reflection, glow, soft edges, bevel, and 3D rotation.

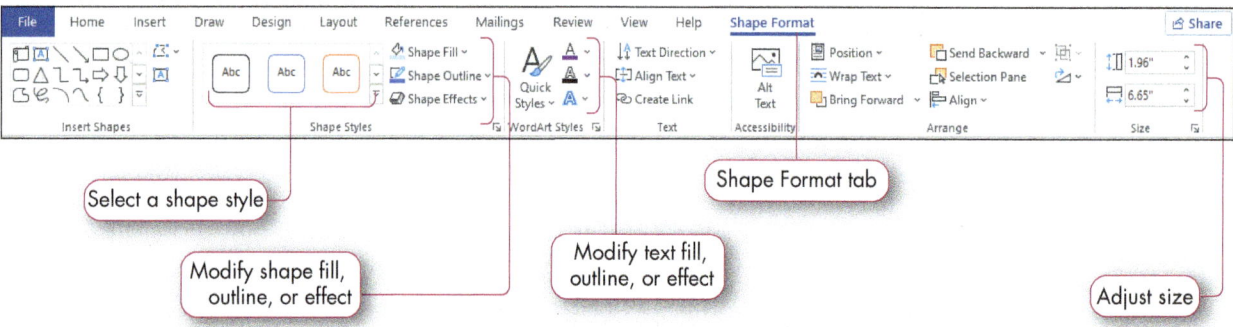

FIGURE 2.35 Shape Format Tab

Remember that both a text box and WordArt are text-oriented objects, sharing many of the same characteristics as typical shapes, but with an additional text component. In fact, the Shape Format tab displays when either a text box or WordArt is selected and is the same as that displayed when a shape is in use, albeit with a few more text formatting possibilities. Not only the shape, but also the text inside those objects can be formatted. Simply drag to select the text to be formatted or click the shape border to select all text (even though text will not be shaded). At that point, you can select an alignment option on the Home tab to left align, right align, center, or justify text. Other text formatting options, like bold, underline, and font color, can also be applied.

A 3D model is unique in its design, sharing few of the same formatting options as other objects. As shown in Figure 2.36, the 3D Model tab focuses on managing views and positioning the object, without the availability of style and color options prevalent with other graphic objects. Similarly, a SmartArt object comprised of multiple shapes and text not only sports a Format tab but also a Design tab that contains varying layout and text options.

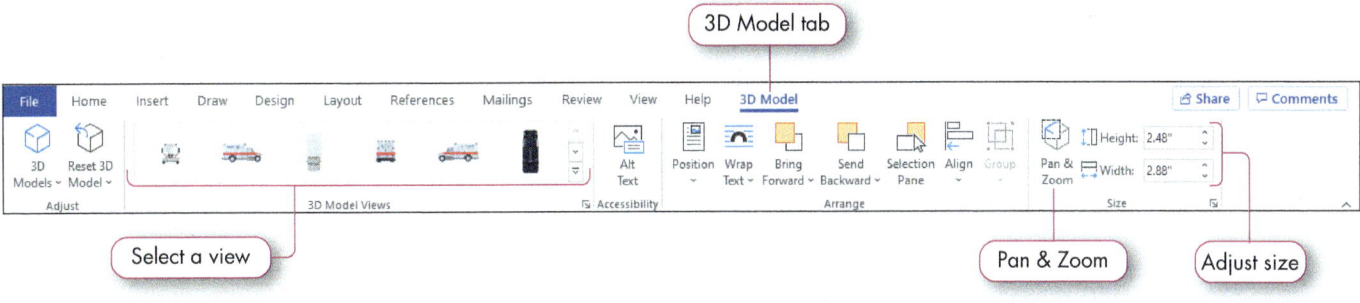

FIGURE 2.36 3D Model Tab

Resize and Position an Object

Often, an object placed in a document is in a size that is too large or too small for your purposes. You can resize an object either by dragging a sizing handle or by adjusting settings in the Size group of the Format tab.

A *sizing handle* is a circle on each corner and in the center of each side of a selected object. When you drag a corner sizing handle, an image will be resized proportionally, which is what you want to ensure when resizing a picture. If you drag a center sizing handle instead, a picture is skewed. Other shapes can typically be resized within reason by dragging either a corner or center sizing handle, as they are not as susceptible to skewing, but a good rule of thumb is to stick with a corner handle if at all possible. A text box is a notable exception, where contents will not be skewed regardless of how you resize. A second approach to resizing an object is much more precise, that of adjusting height and width of many objects in the Size group on the Shape Format tab (refer to Figure 2.35).

> **TIP: LOCK ASPECT RATIO**
> By default, the Lock aspect ratio setting is on, which means that when you change a dimension—either width or height—of a picture, the other dimension is automatically adjusted as well. To confirm or deselect the Lock aspect ratio, click the Size Dialog Box Launcher and adjust the setting in the Layout dialog box. Unless you deselect the setting, you cannot change both width and height distinctly from each other, as that would distort the picture. On a Mac, Lock Aspect Ratio is not on by default. Instead, a selection at the right side of the size options on the Shape Format tab enables you to indicate whether changing one dimension should automatically resize the other.

If a picture contains more detail than is necessary, you can *crop* it, which is the process of trimming edges that you do not want to display. The Crop tool is in the Size group on the Picture Format tab (refer to Figure 2.34). When the Crop tool is used, it will surround the selected object with eight *cropping handles*, evident by dark, thick lines—around the four corners and on the left, right, top, and bottom sides of the selected image. Click on any of these eight handles and drag to remove a portion of the selected object. Even though cropping enables you to adjust the amount of a picture that displays, it does not actually delete the portions that are cropped out. Therefore, you can later restore parts of the picture, if necessary.

> **TIP: CROPPING AND FILE SIZE**
> Cropping a picture does not reduce the file size of the picture or of the Word document in which it displays. However, if you are adamant on removing the cropped portion, you may permanently remove it by using the Delete cropped areas of pictures option, Compress Pictures command, in the Adjust group on the Format tab. You may also use the same command to shrink down the file size of high-resolution photos.

When an object is inserted in a document, it becomes part of the overall flow of text. As such, you should ensure that text flows around, above, or below the object in a way that serves your purposes. You can even insert and configure an object so that text flows behind, in front of, or through the object. All of those options are possible when you manage *text wrapping*. The Format tab of a selected object includes a Wrap Text option in the Arrange group, containing options described in Table 2.2. The same options are available when you click Layout Options, located just outside the upper right corner of a selected object, shown in Figure 2.37.

TABLE 2.2 Text Wrap Options

Type	Effect
In Line with Text	The image is part of the line of text in which it is inserted. Typically, text wraps above and below the object.
Square	Text wraps on all sides of an object, following an invisible square.
Tight	Text follows the shape of the object, but it does not overlap the object.
Through	Text follows the shape of the object, filling any open spaces in the shape.
Top and Bottom	Text flows above and below the borders of the object.
Behind Text	The object is positioned behind text. Both the object and text are visible (unless the fill color exactly matches the text color).
In Front of Text	The object is positioned in front of text, often obscuring the text.

FIGURE 2.37 Text Wrap Options

Once text wrapping has been identified, you can drag an object to move it within existing document text. As you do so, you will work with Live Layout and alignment guides. *Live Layout* enables you to watch text flow around an object as you move it, so you can position the object exactly as you want it. *Alignment guides* are horizontal or vertical green bars that display as you drag an object, so you can align an object with text or with another object. To ensure that alignment guides display, click the Layout tab, click Align, and select Use Alignment Guides. The green alignment guide shown in Figure 2.38 helps align the picture object with paragraph text.

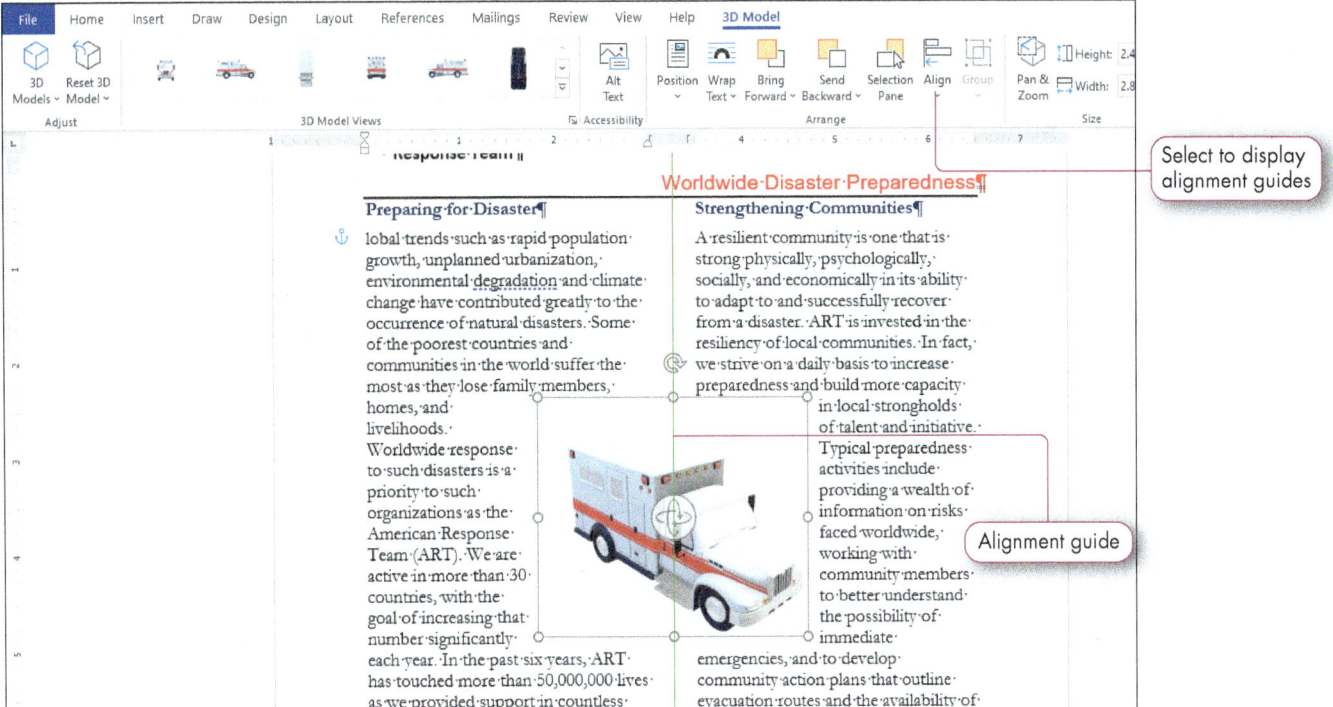

FIGURE 2.38 Use Alignment Guides

To move an object, position the pointer on a border so it displays as a small, four-headed arrow. Drag to reposition it. The Format tab also includes a Position command in the Arrange group that enables you to align the object in various ways within existing text.

STEP 4 — Group, Layer, and Rotate Objects

Occasionally, you may want to insert several shapes and combine them into one object. Such could be the case if you create a logo containing several shapes that should be grouped as one. *Grouping* shapes or objects combines them into one entity. A single border surrounds all grouped objects when you select the item, so you can move, copy, delete, resize, or adjust the collection as one object. Even though several objects are grouped, you can still modify a single item within the group when you double-click the individual item. To group objects, hold Shift as you click each object to be grouped or use the Select option on the Home tab. The objects shown in Figure 2.39 have not yet been grouped into one object, although they have all been selected. Choose to group the objects using the Group Objects command in the Arrange group on the Format tab.

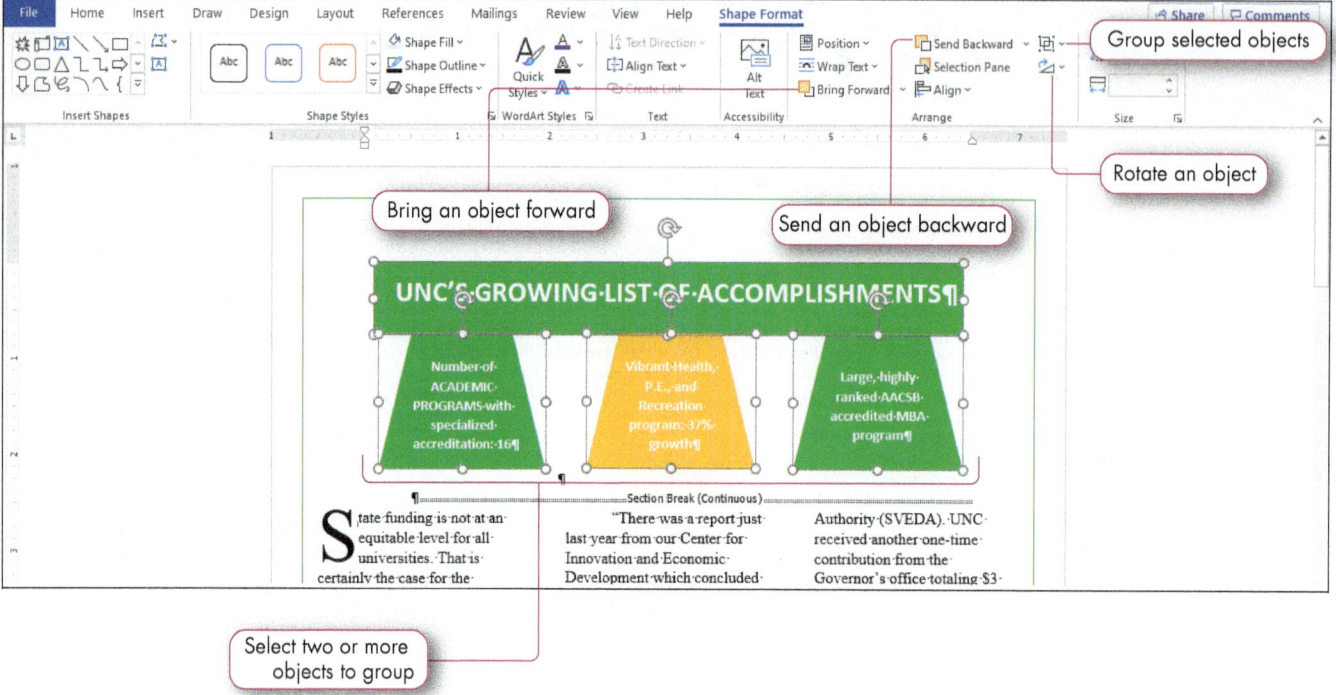

FIGURE 2.39 Group Objects

You can separate grouped objects by ungrouping them. ***Ungrouping*** breaks a grouped object into separate individual objects. You might ungroup objects because you want to make modifications to one individual part of the group rather than to the entire group, such as sizing or repositioning an individual object in the group. Ungrouping also makes it possible to delete an object or add another object to the group. To ungroup objects, select the grouped object and follow the steps to group several objects, selecting Ungroup instead of Group.

When you want to place all or part of an object on top of another, as when an arrow shape is intended to overlap a text box, the objects become layered. ***Layering*** combines objects into a hierarchy with the most recently added object placed on a higher layer than a previously created object.

When working with layered shapes in Word, you can bring a shape to the front by one layer, push a shape back by one layer, move a shape to the front of all layers, or push a shape to the back of all layers. You can even position an object behind or in front of text. With multiple objects selected, you can change layering order with commands on the Format tab that are related to the selected object. To layer objects, select an object to be rearranged and select from the options described in Table 2.3. After objects are arranged in the order of layers, it is useful to group them so they can be moved, resized, and adjusted together as one object.

TABLE 2.3	Layering Options on the Shape Format Tab
Command	**Outcome**
Bring Forward	Moves an object on top of another object directly in front of it
Bring to Front	Moves an object to the top of all other objects
Bring in Front of Text	Moves an object to display in front of text
Send Backward	Moves an object below the object directly behind it
Send to Back	Moves an object to the back of all other objects
Send Behind Text	Moves an object to display behind text

An object's angle can be adjusted in several different directions by flipping or rotating it. The Rotate Objects command is in the Arrange group on the Shape Format tab, as shown in Figure 2.39. Select from several commands to rotate the object in a particular direction or to flip horizontally or vertically.

Critical Thinking

5. Describe the type of text wrapping that might be best for a WordArt banner that serves as a newsletter heading, providing rationale for your choice. *p. 214*

6. Explain how a text box differs from simple shaded text. *p. 206*

7. Explain why WordArt is most often used to format headings or titles and not text in the body of a document. *p. 205*

Hands-On Exercises

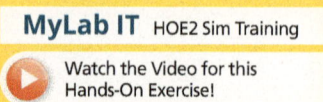
MyLab IT HOE2 Sim Training

▶ Watch the Video for this Hands-On Exercise!

Skills covered: Insert a Picture • Insert SmartArt • Insert WordArt • Insert a Text Box • Insert a Shape • Format an Object • Resize and Position an Object • Group, Layer, and Rotate Objects

2 Graphic Objects

After you format the document for easier reading, you want to insert objects into the document to better describe its contents and give it a bit more visual appeal. A picture brightens up a newsletter section, while a SmartArt object describes a list of common photography mistakes. Finally, you will format the newsletter heading in an attractive WordArt choice.

STEP 1 INSERT A PICTURE, SMARTART, AND WORDART

You place a picture in the winter break section, adding visual interest. A plain list is livened up and formatted in a SmartArt object, while WordArt facilitates design of the newsletter heading. Refer to Figure 2.40 as you complete Step 1.

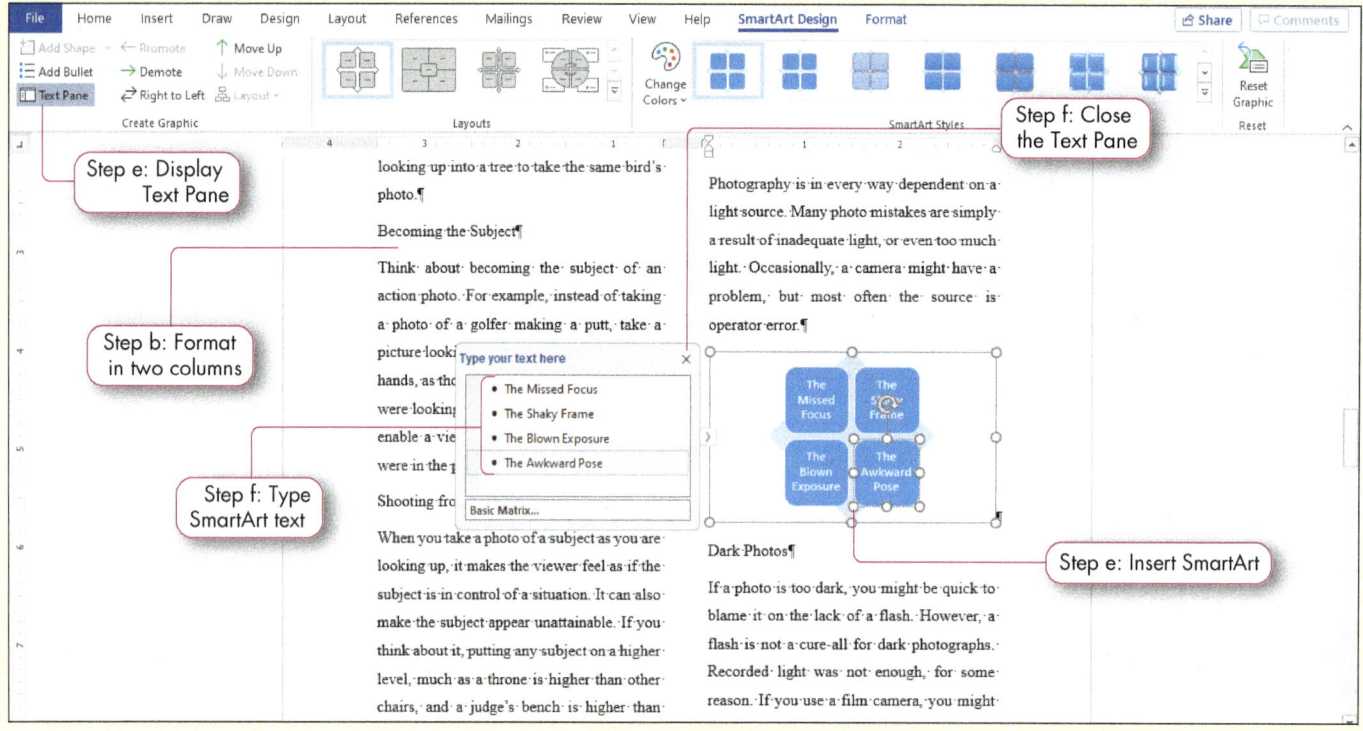

FIGURE 2.40 Insert SmartArt

a. Open *w02h1Studio_LastFirst* if you closed it at the end of Hands-On Exercise 1, and save it as **w02h2Studio_LastFirst**, changing h1 to h2. Click **Show/Hide** in the Paragraph group on the Home tab to display nonprinting characters, unless they are already shown.

b. Select all text from *Courtesy of Phillips Studio Photography* on page 1 through *before even greeting Santa* on page 5. Click the **Layout tab**, click **Columns**, and select **Two**.

> **TROUBLESHOOTING:** If the first line, *Basics of Photography*, is included in the two-column layout, you included it in the selection by mistake. Click Undo on the Quick Access Toolbar and repeat Step b, ensuring that the first line of the document is not included.

c. Click before the paragraph on page 4, beginning with *Now for the fun part*. Ensure that the insertion point is on the same line as the paragraph beginning. Click the **Insert tab**, click **Pictures** in the Illustrations group, select **This Device**, and then double-click *w02h2Winter.jpg* from the data files.

The picture will most likely display at the bottom of the left column on page 4, but it is OK if it shows at the top of the right column.

d. Ensure that the picture is selected. Click **Layout Options** beside the picture and select **Tight** (row 1, column 2 under With Text Wrapping). (On a Mac, click Wrap Text in the Arrange group on the Picture Format tab and select Tight.) Close Layout Options.

e. Click before the *Dark Photos* heading in the right column on page 3, on the same line as the text. Press **Enter**. Click beside the newly inserted blank paragraph above *Dark Photos*. Click the **Insert tab** and click **SmartArt** in the Illustrations group. Click **Matrix** in the left pane of the Choose a SmartArt Graphic dialog box. Select **Basic Matrix** (column 1). Click **OK**. Ensure that the Text pane displays beside the SmartArt diagram. If it does not, click Text Pane in the Create Graphic group on the SmartArt Design tab.

f. Type **The Missed Focus** beside the first bullet in the Text pane. Click beside the next bullet and type **The Shaky Frame**. Click beside the third bullet and type **The Blown Exposure**. Click beside the fourth bullet and type **The Awkward Pose**. Close the Text pane.

You create a SmartArt object that lists several common photography mistakes made by beginners.

g. Select the first paragraph in the document on page 1, *Basics of Photography*. Click the **Insert tab** and select **WordArt** in the Text group. Click **Fill: Blue, Accent color 1; Shadow** (row 1, column 2). Click **Layout Options** at the top right side of the WordArt object. (On a Mac, click Wrap Text in the Arrange group on the Shape Format tab.) Select **Top and Bottom** (row 2, column 1 under With Text Wrapping). Close Layout Options. Click anywhere outside the WordArt object.

Using WordArt, you format the major heading in an attractive manner.

h. Save the document.

INSERT A TEXT BOX AND INSERT A SHAPE

You add a pull quote to a text box, drawing attention to a fact related to beginning photography. The text box is formatted differently from surrounding text. The newsletter title is enhanced with the addition of a shape. Refer to Figure 2.41 as you complete Step 2.

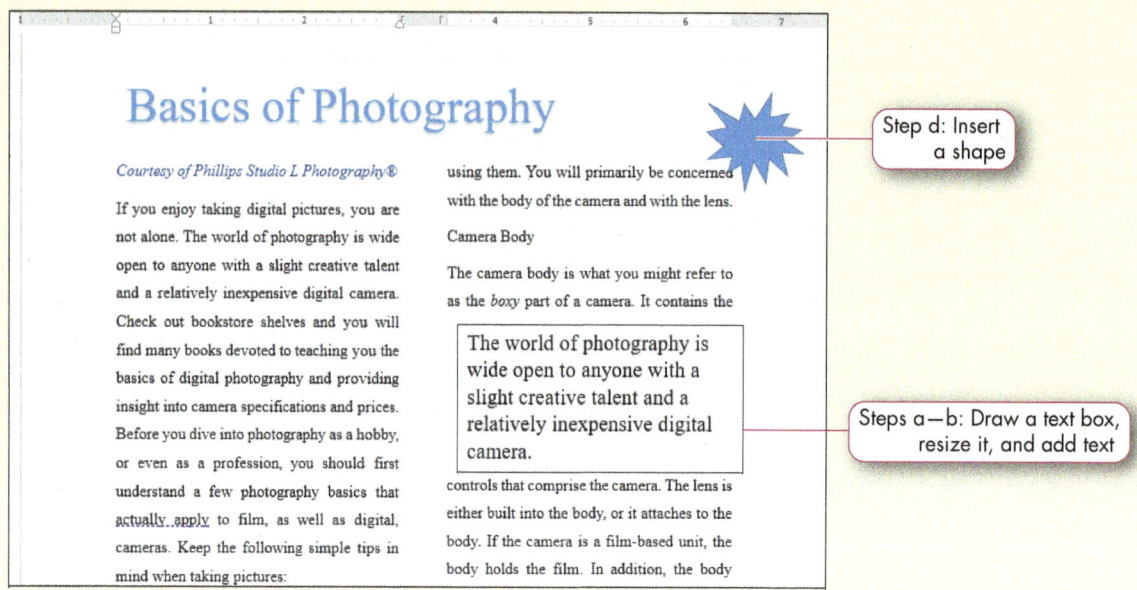

FIGURE 2.41 Insert a Text Box and Shape

a. Click the **Insert tab** and click **Text Box** in the Text group. Click **Draw Text Box**. Click anywhere in the right column on page 1 to insert a text box. Change the height in the Size group on the Shape Format tab to **1.5"**. Change the width to **3"**. Point to a border of the text box and drag to position it approximately as shown in Figure 2.41.

A text box is placed in the right column, obscuring existing text. It will be better positioned in Step 3.

b. Select the second sentence in the first body paragraph, *The world of photography is open to anyone with a slight creative talent and a relatively inexpensive digital camera.* Click the **Home tab** and click **Copy** in the Clipboard group. Click in the text box and click **Paste** (not the arrow) in the Clipboard group. Drag to select the sentence in the text box, or click a text box border to select all text (although it will not be shaded), and change the font size to **16**.

c. Click **Layout Options** beside the text box and choose **Square** text wrapping. Close Layout Options.

d. Click the **Insert tab** and click **Shapes** in the Illustrations group. Select **Explosion: 8 Points** in the Stars and Banners section. (On a Mac, select Explosion 2.) Click at the right of the *Basics of Photography* heading, near the right margin, as shown in Figure 2.41.

Precise positioning is not necessary. It is OK if the shape overlaps text.

FORMAT AN OBJECT, RESIZE AND POSITION AN OBJECT

You format the inserted objects so that they fit well amid surrounding text, adding visual appeal to newsletter text. Objects are resized and positioned to flow seamlessly. Refer to Figures 2.42 and 2.43 as you complete Step 3.

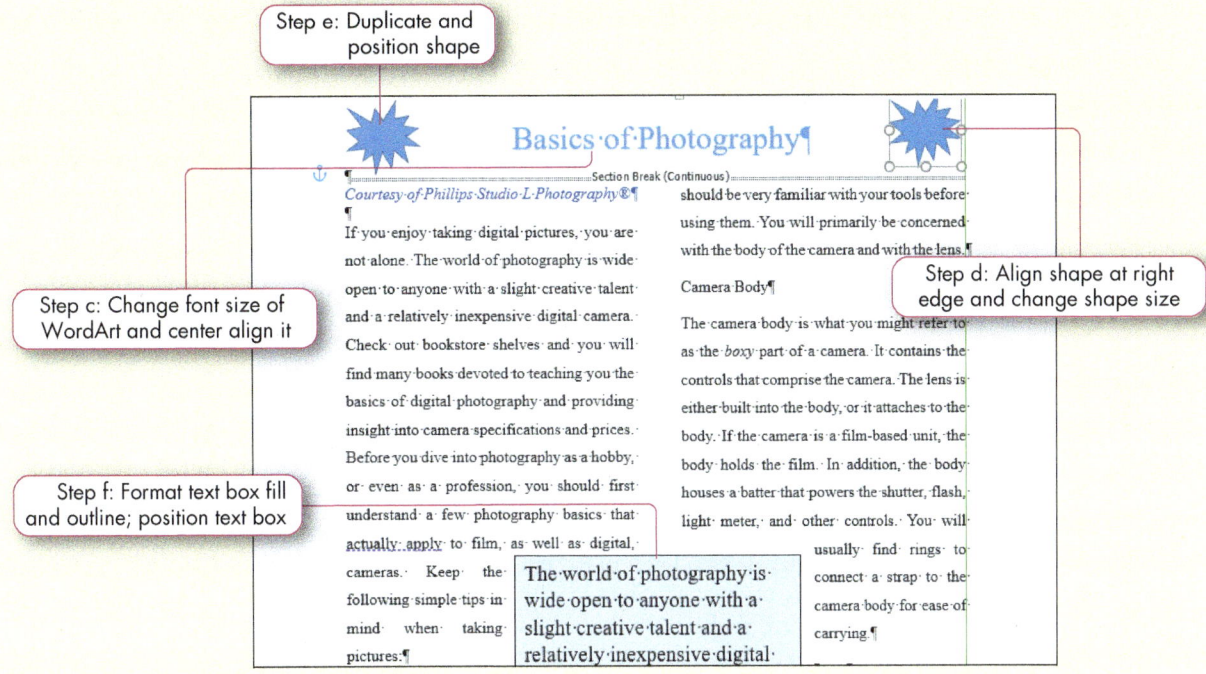

FIGURE 2.42 Format WordArt, Shape, and Text Box

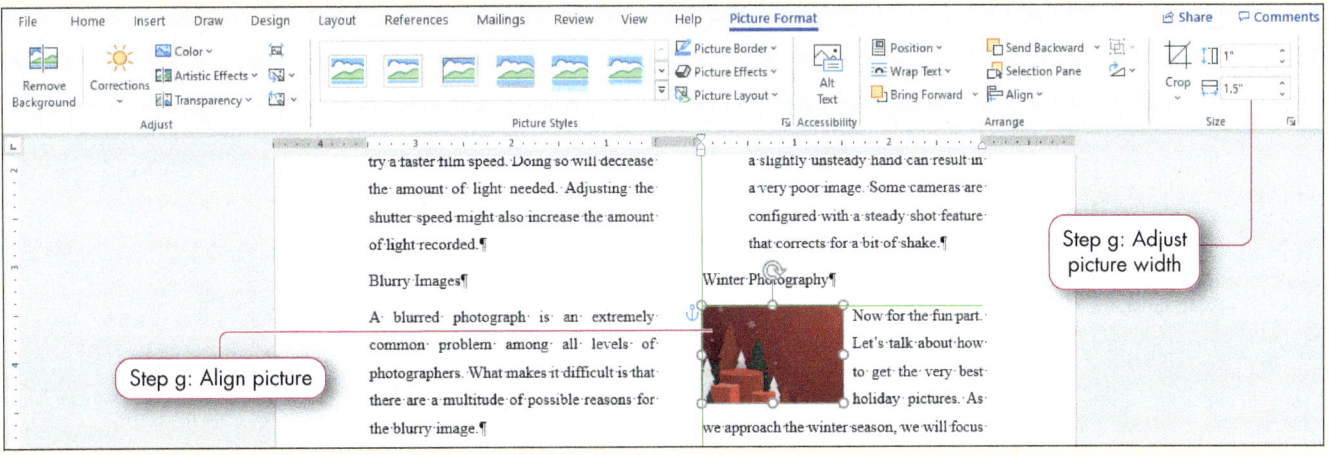

FIGURE 2.43 Modify Picture

a. Select the SmartArt object. Click near an outside border of the diagram to ensure that the entire object is selected and not a single shape. Click the **SmartArt Design Tab** and select **Polished** in the SmartArt styles group (sixth selection in the SmartArt styles group). Click the **Format tab**. Click **Size** and change the height to **2** and the width to **2.5**.

b. Click **Layout Options** beside the SmartArt object. Click **Square** (row 1, column 1 under With Text Wrapping). Close Layout Options. Drag the SmartArt object up to position it directly under the *Common Photography Mistakes* heading near the end of the right column on page 3. Use an alignment guide to ensure that the object is aligned at the left edge of the right column.

TROUBLESHOOTING: If you do not see alignment guides, click the Layout tab, click Align, and select Use Alignment Guides.

c. Scroll to the top of page 1 and click the WordArt object, *Basics of Photography*. Drag to select the text in the object, or click an outside border of the WordArt. Change the font size of the selection to **24**. Drag the WordArt object to the right, using green alignment guides to position it in the center of the top row. A green alignment guide should show at the top and middle of the WordArt object, indicating that it is centered and aligned.

d. Click the explosion shape near the right side of the WordArt object. Click the **Shape Format tab** and change the height and width to **0.75**. Position the shape as shown in Figure 2.42, aligning it along the right margin with the assistance of an alignment guide.

e. Ensure that the shape is selected. Press **Ctrl+D** to duplicate the shape (on a Mac, command+d). Drag the copied shape to the left, positioning it as shown in Figure 2.42. An alignment guide should assist with placing it at the left side of the page.

f. Click to select the text box near the top of page 1. Click the **Shape Format tab**, click **Shape Fill**, and choose **Blue, Accent 1, Lighter 80%** (row 2, column 5). Click **Shape Outline** and choose **Black, Text 1**. Ensure that the text box is positioned approximately as that shown in Figure 2.42, using an alignment guide to center the object.

The text box is shaded and outlined to differentiate it from surrounding text.

g. Click to select the winter picture on page 3 or 4. Click the **Picture Format tab** and change the width in the Size group to **1.5**. The height automatically adjusts. Drag the picture to position it directly below the *Winter Photography* heading in the right column of page 4. Position it at the left edge of the column, below the heading, and at the left side of the paragraph, aligned with a green alignment guide at the top and left side of the picture, as shown in Figure 2.43.

h. Save the document.

GROUP, LAYER, AND ROTATE OBJECTS

The shapes and WordArt object at the top of page 1 are individual entities that should be grouped so they can be managed as one item. Refer to Figure 2.44 as you complete Step 4.

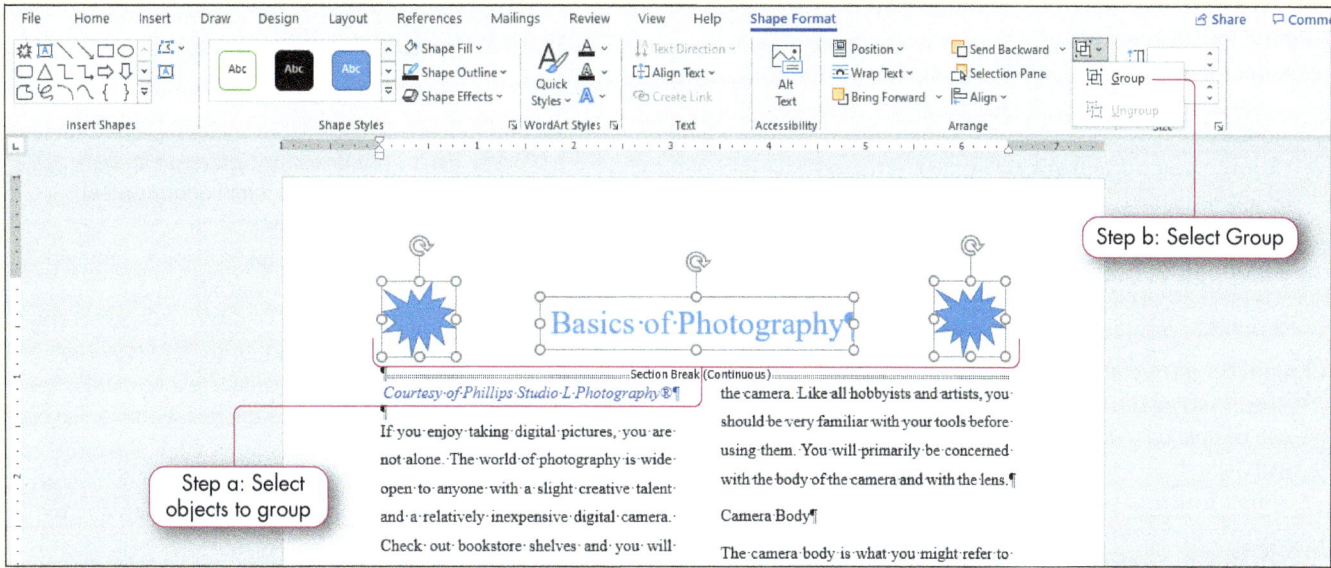

FIGURE 2.44 Group Objects

a. Scroll to the top of page 1. Select the explosion shape on the left side of the page. Press and hold Shift as you click the WordArt banner and the explosion at the right side.

All three objects are selected.

b. Click the **Shape Format tab**. Click **Group Objects** in the Arrange group and select **Group**. Click **Layout Options** beside the grouped object and select **Top and Bottom** (row 2, column 1 under With Text Wrapping). Close Layout Options.

All three shapes are grouped together so they can be managed as a unit.

c. Save and close the file. Exit Word. Based on your instructor's directions, submit: w02h2Studio_LastFirst

Chapter Objectives Review

After reading this chapter, you have accomplished the following objectives:

1. Apply font attributes.

- **Select font options:** The Font group on the Home tab includes options for changing font appearance, size, and emphasis.
- **Change text appearance:** Format characters by applying bold, italics, underline, font color, text highlighting, and text effects.
- **Insert symbols and special characters:** A symbol is typically a graphic or text that is not found on the keyboard.

2. Format a paragraph.

- **Select paragraph alignment:** Paragraph alignment can be applied as left or right aligned, centered, or justified.
- **Select line and paragraph spacing:** Line spacing refers to the amount of space between lines within a paragraph, whereas paragraph spacing is the amount of space between paragraphs.
- **Select indents:** Options for indenting paragraphs include left indent, right indent, hanging indent, and first line indent.
- **Set tab stops:** Use tabs to indent the first line of the paragraph, or to arrange text in columns, including leaders as needed.
- **Apply borders and shading:** Borders and shading draw attention to selected paragraphs.
- **Create bulleted and numbered lists:** Itemized lists can be set apart from other text with bullets, while sequential lists are formatted with numbers.

3. Work with graphic objects.

- **Insert a picture:** Insert pictures from online sources or from a storage device connected to your computer.

- **Insert a screenshot:** Capture the whole or a portion of a computer screen and insert it into a document as an object.
- **Insert SmartArt:** SmartArt is a visual representation of a process, list, or relationship. SmartArt is often more effective than simple text when communicating interconnected ideas or processes.
- **Insert WordArt:** A WordArt object displays text with special effects, such as color, size, gradient, and 3D appearance.
- **Insert a text box:** Include text in a bordered area by inserting a text box. You can format a text box with shape styles and effects, and you can align text within a text box.
- **Insert a shape:** A shape is an object, such as a circle or an arrow, which you can use as a visual enhancement. You can use one shape or combine multiple shapes to create a more complex image.
- **Insert a 3D model:** A 3D model is an object that can be rotated 360 degrees and tilted up or down to illustrate a point or show specific features in three-dimensional view.

4. Modify graphic objects.

- **Format an object:** Use a ribbon tab related to the specific object to apply styles, effects, corrections, and other settings to modify an object's appearance.
- **Resize and position an object:** Reposition objects easily using Live Layout and alignment guides. You can also resize objects and wrap text around objects.
- **Group, layer, and rotate objects:** Two or more objects are grouped so that they can be managed as one entity. Layering is the process of placing one shape on top of another or rearranging the order of stacked objects. Rotating an object means changing the angle of the object.

Key Terms Matching

Match the key terms with their definitions. Write the key term letter by the appropriate numbered definition.

a. Alignment

b. Border

c. Bulleted list

d. Crop

e. First line indent

f. Font

g. Group

h. Hanging indent

i. Line spacing

j. Live Preview

k. Object

l. Paragraph spacing

m. Sans serif font

n. Sizing handle

o. SmartArt

p. Symbol

q. Tab stop

r. Text box

s. Three-part indent marker

t. WordArt

1. _____ How text is positioned relative to document margins. **p. 187**

2. _____ Represented by a dot on each corner and in the center of each side of a selected object. **p. 213**

3. _____ A list of points that is not sequential. **p. 194**

4. _____ An item, such as a picture or text box, that can be individually selected and manipulated. **p. 202**

5. _____ A marker on the horizontal ruler specifying the location where the insertion point stops after Tab is pressed to align text in a document. **p. 191**

6. _____ A typeface or complete set of characters. **p. 180**

7. _____ A visual representation of information that can be created to effectively communicate a message or idea in one of many visually appealing layouts. **p. 204**

8. _____ A mark that indicates the location to indent only the first line in a paragraph. **p. 190**

9. _____ The amount of space before or after a paragraph. **p. 188**

10. _____ An Office feature that provides a preview of the results of a selection when you point to it. **p. 181**

11. _____ The vertical space between the lines in a paragraph. **p. 189**

12. _____ A boxed object that can be bordered and shaded, providing space for text. **p. 206**

13. _____ An icon located at the left side of the ruler that enables you to set a left indent, a hanging indent, or a first line indent. **p. 190**

14. _____ Two or more objects that are collected into a unit that can be managed as an entity. **p. 215**

15. _____ The first line of a paragraph begins at the left margin, but all other lines in the paragraph are indented. **p. 190**

16. _____ Typeface that does not contain the thin lines on characters that several other selections include. **p. 180**

17. _____ The process of trimming edges of a picture. **p. 213**

18. _____ Text, a graphic, or a foreign language character, not typically located on a keyboard, that can be inserted into a document. **p. 185**

19. _____ Decorative text feature that is especially useful for designing banners or headings. **p. 205**

20. _____ A top, bottom, side, or all-around outline that enhances a selected paragraph. **p. 192**

Multiple Choice

1. Why is paragraph spacing necessary for some documents?
   (a) To specify spacing between lines within a paragraph, selecting single, double or another appropriate setting
   (b) So that paragraphs can be indented as required, perhaps with a first line or left indent
   (c) To ensure that paragraphs can be differentiated from one another, particularly if the first line of each paragraph is not indented
   (d) So that paragraph settings, such as alignment, bullets, and numbering can be applied

2. How would you identify a series of sequential steps to several levels?
   (a) Design multilevel tabs.
   (b) Create a bulleted list.
   (c) Create a multilevel list.
   (d) Create a numbered list.

3. When might it be necessary to use a dot leader when setting a tab?
   (a) When you want to draw a reader's eye across the page from one area to another
   (b) When you want to add style and interest to a mundane document
   (c) To ensure adherence to accessibility recommendations
   (d) When the tab in question is a bar tab

4. What kind of indent is often used in preparing a bibliography for a research paper?
   (a) First line indent
   (b) Hanging indent
   (c) Right indent
   (d) Left indent

5. What object is most useful for drawing attention to such items as contact information or store hours?
   (a) Text box
   (b) SmartArt object
   (c) Model
   (d) Online picture

6. Which type object would you include in a document describing a house that should be visible from all angles within the document?
   (a) 4D SmartArt
   (b) Stock photo
   (c) Screenshot of online newspaper clipping
   (d) 3D model

7. Why might you choose to use tabs when arranging text?
   (a) To clear all existing indents
   (b) To align text in columns
   (c) To restrict text alignment to the left margin only
   (d) So that text can be bordered

8. Which of the following objects is best suited to diagramming an organization chart?
   (a) WordArt
   (b) Online picture
   (c) 3D model
   (d) SmartArt

9. What feature enables you to apply special formats such as shadow, outline, reflection, or glow to text?
   (a) Ligatures
   (b) Formatting sets
   (c) Text Effects
   (d) Style options

10. What would you consider adjusting to correct for text that flows to the side of a newsletter heading (WordArt object) that you intended to occupy a line by itself?
    (a) Tab settings
    (b) Text wrapping
    (c) Paragraph alignment
    (d) Text effects

Practice Exercises

MyLab IT Grader
Office for the web: Word project available in **MyLab IT**.

1 Campus Safety

You are the office assistant for the police department at a local university. As a service to students, staff, and the community, the police department publishes a campus safety guide, available both in print and online. With national emphasis on homeland security and local incidents of theft and robbery, it is obvious that the safety guide should be updated and distributed. You will work with a draft document, formatting it to make it more attractive and ready for print. Refer to Figures 2.45 and 2.46 as you complete this exercise.

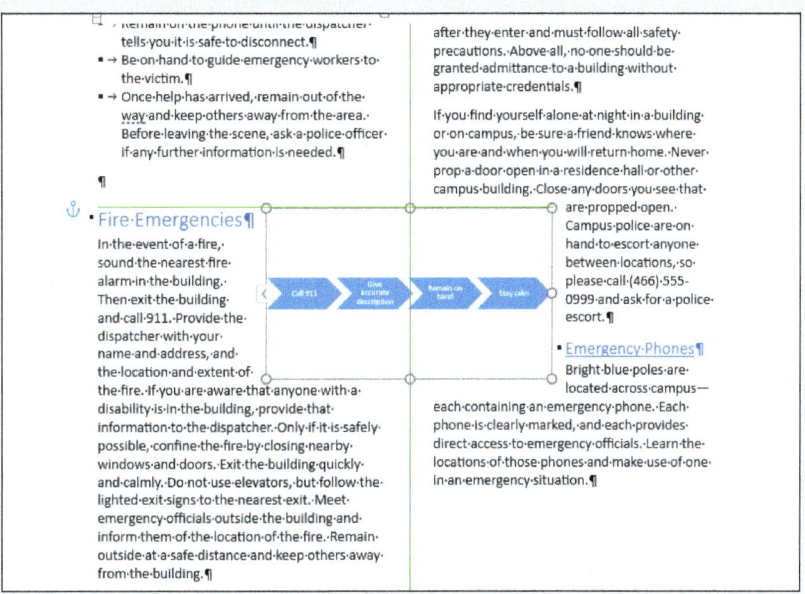

FIGURE 2.45 Position SmartArt

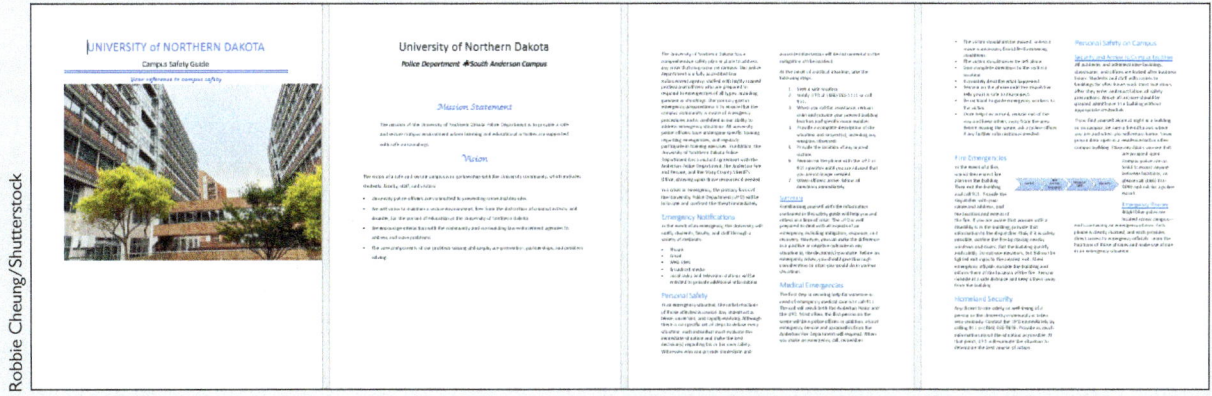

FIGURE 2.46 Campus Safety

Robbie Cheung/Shutterstock

a. Open *w02p1Campus* and save the document as **w02p1Campus_LastFirst**. Ensure that non-printing characters are displayed.

b. Format the first and second paragraphs in the document as follows:
   - Select the first paragraph in the document and click **Center** in the Paragraph group on the Home tab. Click the **Font Color arrow** in the Font group and select **Blue, Accent 5**.
   - Click the **Font Size arrow** and select **26**. Click **Change Case** in the Font group and select **UPPERCASE**. Double-click **OF** in the first paragraph in the document, click **Change Case**, and then select **lowercase**.

- Select the second paragraph in the document. Center the paragraph, change the font color to **Blue, Accent 5**, change the font size to **16**, and then change the case to **Capitalize Each Word**. Do not deselect the text.

c. Shade the second paragraph in the document as follows:
  - Click the **Borders arrow** in the Paragraph group and click **Borders and Shading**. Click **Custom** in the Setting section of the Borders and Shading dialog box.
  - Click the **Color arrow** and select **Blue, Accent 5**. Scroll through the styles in the Style box and select the seventh style (double line).
  - Click the **Width arrow** and select **1 1/2 pt**. Click **Bottom** in the Preview group and click **OK**.

d. Select the paragraph containing the text *Your reference to campus safety*. Click **Font Color** on the Mini Toolbar or the ribbon to apply the most recent font color selection. Use either the Mini Toolbar or selections on the Home tab to change the font to **Lucida Calligraphy** and center the selection.

e. Click at the end of the currently selected paragraph to position the insertion point immediately after *Your reference to campus safety*. Click the **Insert tab** and click **Pictures** in the Illustrations group. Click **This Device** (on a Mac, click Picture from File). Navigate to the location of your student data files and double-click *w02p1Campus.jpg*.

f. Change the height in the Size group on the Picture Format tab to **5**. Click **Corrections** in the Adjust group and select **Brightness: 0% (Normal), Contrast: +20%** under Brightness/Contrast (row 4, column 3 under Brightness/Contrast).

g. Click before the words *University of Northern Dakota* immediately below the picture and press **Ctrl+Enter** to insert a manual page break (or click the Insert tab and click Page Break). (On a Mac, press fn+command+enter.) Scroll up and select the first paragraph on page 1 of the document, *University of Northern Dakota*. Click the **Home tab** and click **Format Painter** in the Clipboard group. Scroll to the second page and select the first paragraph (*University of Northern Dakota*) to copy the formatting. (Note that the Format Painter does not copy the Uppercase format.) Change the font color of the selected line to **Black, Text 1**.

h. Complete the following steps on page 2 to format the text:
  - Select the second paragraph containing the text *Police Department*. Apply **Center, Bold**, and **Italic** to the selection. Change the font size to **16 pt**. Click to position the insertion point after the words *Police Department* and press **Enter** twice.
  - Select text in the document beginning with *Mission Statement* and ending with *prevention, partnerships, and problem solving* (on the same page). Click **Line and Paragraph Spacing** in the Paragraph group and select **1.5**. Click the **Paragraph Dialog Box Launcher** and change Spacing After to **6 pt**. Click **OK**. (On a Mac, click Format and click Paragraph to display the dialog box.)

i. Select the *Mission Statement* heading near the top of page 2 and change the font color to **Blue, Accent 5**. Center the selection and change the font size to **16** and the font to **Lucida Calligraphy**. Copy the format of the selection to the *Vision* heading on the same page. Insert a page break after the sentence ending with the words *problem solving* on page 2.

j. Select the body paragraph under the *Mission Statement* heading, and click the **Paragraph Dialog Box Launcher**. (On a Mac, click Format and click Paragraph.) Change the Left and Right indents to **0.5″** and click **OK**. Click **Justify** in the Paragraph group.

k. Select the paragraphs on page 2 in the *Vision* section, beginning with *University police officers are committed to* and ending with *prevention, partnerships, and problem solving*. Click the **Bullets arrow** in the Paragraph group and select the **square filled bullet**. Click **Decrease Indent** in the Paragraph group to move the bullets to the left margin.

l. Scroll to page 3 and select the five paragraphs in the *Emergency Notifications* section, beginning with *Phone* and ending with *provide additional information*. Apply **square filled bullets** to the selection. Click **Decrease Indent**.

m. Select the seven paragraphs in the *Personal Safety* section, beginning with *Seek a safe location* and ending with *follow all directions immediately*. Click the **Numbering arrow** and click the **Number alignment: Left** (the option showing 1., 2., 3.) to apply it to the selection.

n. Place the insertion point at the beginning of the document. Spell check the document. The word *of* in the university name is correct in lowercase, so do not correct it. Ignore any errors related to punctuation.

o. Scroll to page 3 and select all text beginning with *The University of Northern Dakota* and ending at the end of the document. Click the **Layout tab**, click **Columns**, and then select **Two**. Click the **View tab** and click **Multiple Pages** in the Zoom group to view pages of the document, getting a feel for document layout. Click **100%** in the Zoom group.

p. Insert a symbol by completing the following steps:
- Click after *Police Department* on the second line on page 1. Ensure that the insertion point is on the same line as the heading, not the line above it.
- Press **spacebar**. Click the **Insert tab**, click **Symbol** in the Symbols group and click **More Symbols**. (On a Mac, click Advanced Symbols.)
- Click the **Font arrow** in the Symbols dialog box and scroll to select **Wingdings**. Click in the **Character code box** and type **172**. (On a Mac, locate a round filled circle symbol and click to select it.) Click **Insert**. Click **Close**.
- Press **spacebar**. Type **South Anderson Campus**. (Do not type the period.)

q. Insert SmartArt by completing the following steps:
- Click the **Home tab**. Click after the last bulleted item at the top of page 4 (ending in *if any further information is needed*). Press **Enter**. Click **Bullets** in the Paragraph group to turn off the display of bullets.
- Click the **Insert tab** and click **SmartArt** in the Illustrations group. Click **Process** and select **Basic Chevron Process** (row 5, column 2 on a Windows computer). Click **OK**.
- Click **Text Pane** in the Create Graphic group on the SmartArt Design tab, unless the Text pane is already displayed.

r. Enter SmartArt data by completing the following steps:
- Type **Call 911** beside the first bullet.
- Click beside the second bullet and type **Give accurate description**. (Do not type the period.)
- Click beside the last bullet and type **Remain on hand**. (Do not type the period.) Press **Enter** to begin a new bullet, which also results in a new shape.
- Type **Stay calm**. (Do not type the period.) Click **Text Pane** in the Create Graphic group to close the text pane.

s. Click a border of the SmartArt graphic to select it. Click **Layout Options** at the top right corner of the selected object, or click Wrap Text on the Format tab. Click **Square** (row 1, column 1 under With Text Wrapping on a Windows computer). Drag to position SmartArt graphic as shown in Figure 2.46, using alignment guides.

t. Ensure the SmartArt graphic is selected. Click **Subtle Effect** in the SmartArt Styles group on the SmartArt Design tab (third selection from left).

u. Save and close the file. Exit Word. Based on your instructor's directions, submit: w02p1Campus_LastFirst

2 DIY Arbor

You work with a local garden center, promoting the business with various publications and online material. Your latest project is the development of documents describing selected do-it-yourself projects related to the enjoyment of home landscaping and gardens. A local builder is helping with a step-by-step outline for putting together an arbor to enhance a garden. The plans for the arbor need to be as descriptive and complete as possible, which means you will need to include numbered steps, an itemized materials list, and diagrams or models detailing the process. In addition, the document must be attractive and error-free. You will apply various font and paragraph formatting features as well as graphic objects to enhance the document and describe the building process. Refer to Figures 2.47 and 2.48 as you complete this exercise.

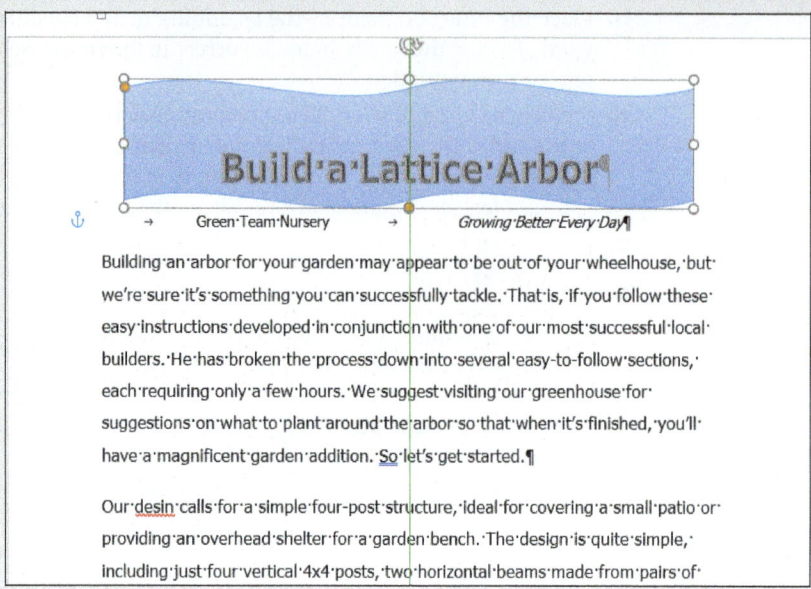

FIGURE 2.47 Position an Object

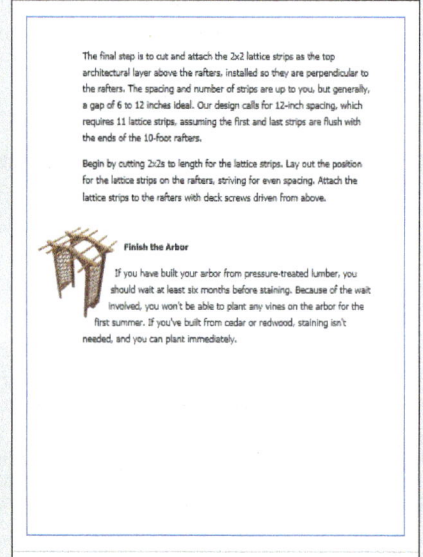

FIGURE 2.48 Insert a 3D Model

a. Open *w02p2Arbor* and save it as **w02p2Arbor_LastFirst**.

b. Click **Show/Hide** if nonprinting characters are not displayed. Press **Ctrl+A** (on a Mac, command+A) to select all document text. Click the **Font arrow** and select **Tahoma**.

c. Click in the blank paragraph after *Build a Lattice Arbor*. Click the **View tab** and select **Ruler** in the Show group unless it is already selected. Click at **1″** on the ruler to set a left tab. Click the tab selector twice to change to a Right Tab. Click at **5.5″** on the ruler to set a right tab. Press **Tab**. Type **Green Team Nursery**. Press **Tab**. Click the **Home tab** and click **Italic** in the Font group. Type **Growing Better Every Day**. (Do not type the period.)

d. Select the first line on page 1, *Build a Lattice Arbor*. Click the **Insert tab**. Click **WordArt** in the Text group. Click **Fill Gray, Accent Color 3: Sharp Bevel** (row 2, column 5). Click the **Home tab** and change the font size to **28**. Click **Text Effects and Typography** in the Font group, point to **Glow**, and select **Glow: 5 point; Gray, Accent color 3** (row 1, column 3 under Glow Variations).

e. Click **Layout Options** at the top right side of the WordArt object, or click Wrap Text in the Arrange group on the Shape Format tab. Click **Top and Bottom** (row 2, column 1 under With Text Wrapping). Close Layout Options. Drag the WordArt object to visually center it, using the center alignment guide, if shown, to position it at the top of the document on a line by itself.

f. Select all text in the body of the document from *Building an arbor for your garden* to the end of the document. Click the **Paragraph Dialog Box Launcher**. (On a Mac, click Format and click Paragraph.) Click the **Spacing After arrow** to a setting to **6 pt**. Change Line spacing to **1.5**. Click **OK**.

g. Select the five bulleted paragraphs at the top of page 2. Click the **Numbering arrow** and select **Number alignment: Left** (row 1, column 3 under Numbering Library). Select the nine items listed under *Equipment/Tools*. Click the **Bullets arrow** and select a **square filled bullet**. Click **Line and Paragraph Spacing** in the Paragraph group and select **1.0**.

h. Select all items listed under *Materials* and change the bullet to a **square filled bullet**. Change line spacing of the bulleted list to **1.0**. Click the **Paragraph Dialog Box Launcher** (on a Mac, click Format and click Paragraph) and change Spacing After to **0 pt**. Select *Instructions* on the same page. Click **Center** in the Paragraph group.

i. Select *Dig Post Holes* and click **Bold** in the Font group. Bold *Position the Posts, Anchor the Posts, Cut and Attach the Beams, Attach Rafters, Attach Lattice Strips,* and *Finish the Arbor*. Select the heading *Finish the Arbor* and the two paragraphs below the heading. Drag the Left Indent marker on the ruler to the right to **0.5″**.

j. Click after the third body paragraph on page 1, ending in *actual labor are involved*. Press **Enter**. Click the **Insert tab**. Click **SmartArt** in the Illustrations group. Click **List** and select **Vertical Box List** (row 2, column 2 on a Windows computer). Click **OK**. Click in the top box of the SmartArt diagram and type **Working Time: 8 hours**. (Do not type the period.). Click in the second box and type **Total Time: 2 days.** (Do not type the period.) Click in the third box and type **Material Cost: $350 - $550**. Leave a space before and after the hyphen and do not type the period.

k. Click **Change Colors** in the SmartArt Styles group on the SmartArt Design tab and select **Gradient Range – Accent 1** (column 3 under Accent 1). Click **More** in the SmartArt Styles group and select **Inset** (column 2 under 3D). Click a border of the SmartArt graphic to select the object. Click the **Format tab** and change the height in the Size group to **2″** and the width to **4.5″**.

l. Triple-click the last paragraph in the document, beginning with *In some communities* to select it. Click **Cut** in the Clipboard group on the Home tab. Click after the second to last body paragraph on page 5, ending in *moved as the concrete dries*. Click the **Insert tab** and click **Text Box** in the Text group. Click **Draw Text Box**. Click anywhere below the current paragraph to place a text box. Precise placement is not important at this point. Press **Ctrl+V** to paste the copied text in the text box.

m. Change the width in the Size group on the Shape Format tab to **5″**. Change the height to **2.5″**. Click the **Home tab**. Ensure that all text in the text box is in Tahoma font. Change the font size to **14 pt**. Change line spacing of all text in the text box to **1.15**. Click the **Shape Format tab** and click **Shape Fill** in the Shape Styles group. Click **Blue-Gray, Text 2, Lighter 80%** (row 2, column 4).

n. Click **Layout Options** at the top right side of the text box, or click Wrap Text in the Arrange group on the Shape Format tab. Click **Top and Bottom** (row 2, column 1 under Text Wrapping). Close Layout Options. With the text box selected, click **Align** in the Arrange group on the Shape Format tab and select **Align Center**.

o. Click before the first body paragraph on page 1, beginning with *Building an arbor*. Click the **Insert tab**, click **Shapes**, and select **Double Wave** in the Stars and Banners group. Starting at the top left, drag to place the shape directly over the WordArt title at the top of the document. The shape should completely cover the title. If you make a mistake, click Undo on the Quick Access toolbar and try it again. With the shape selected, click the **Send Backward arrow** in the Arrange group on the Shape Format tab and click **Send to Back**.

p. Change the height of the shape to **1.3″** and change the width to **6″**. Click **More** in the Shape Styles group and select **Subtle Effect – Blue, Accent 5** (row 4, column 6 on a Windows computer). Drag to position the shape in the center of the line, using an alignment guide as shown in Figure 2.47.

q. Press and hold **Shift** while you click **Build a Lattice Arbor** to select both items. Click **Group Objects** in the Arrange group on the Shape Format tab and select **Group**. Click **Layout Options** beside the grouped object, or click Wrap Text in the Arrange group on the Shape Format tab, and select **Top and Bottom** (row 2, column 1 under With Text Wrapping). Close Layout Options.

r. Click before the third sentence in the paragraph following *Anchor the Posts* on page 5, beginning in *Not too wet and not*. Backspace to delete the space and the period preceding the current position. Click the **Insert tab** and click **Symbol** in the Symbols group. (On a Mac, click Advanced Symbols.) Click **More Symbols**. Click the **Special Characters tab**. Ensure that *Em Dash* is selected. Click **Insert**. Click **Close**. Change the uppercase N in *Not* to a lowercase *n*.

s. Click the **Design tab**. Click **Page Borders** in the Page Background group. Click **Box** and change the color to **Blue, Accent 1**. Click **OK**.

t. Click the blank paragraph above *Finish the Arbor* on page 8. Click the **Insert tab** and click **3D Models**. Type **garden** in the Search box and press **Enter**. Click the arbor picture shown in Figure 2.48 and click **Insert**. Drag the 3D Rotate handle to adjust the picture approximately as that shown in Figure 2.48. Change the height to **2″**.

u. Click **Layout Options** beside the 3D model, or click Wrap Text on the 3D Model tab, and select **Through** (row 1, column 3 under With Text Wrapping). Position the model as shown in Figure 2.48.

v. View the document in Multiple Pages. Note the poorly placed heading at the bottom of page 3. Click before *Materials* on that page and insert a page break. Check for any spelling and grammatical mistakes. Correct spelling but ignore all grammatical concerns.

w. Save and close the file. Exit Word. Based on your instructor's directions, submit: w02p2Arbor_LastFirst

Mid-Level Exercises

As chair of the Mount Vernon Hot Air Balloon Festival, you are responsible for promoting the upcoming event. You started a document providing details on the festival. You plan to distribute the document both in print and online. First, you must format the document to make it more attractive and well designed. You will use styles, bullets, and line and paragraph spacing to coordinate various parts of the document. In addition, you will add interest by including objects, such as pictures and WordArt.

a. Open *w02m1Festival* and save it as **w02m1Festival_LastFirst**.

b. Select the first paragraph in the document, *Mount Vernon Hot Air Balloon Festival*. Insert WordArt, selecting **Fill: Black, Text color 1; Outline: White, Background color 1; Hard Shadow: Blue, Accent color 5** (row 3, column 2). Change the font size of the WordArt object to **24**.

c. Wrap text around the WordArt object as **Top and Bottom**. Format the WordArt object with Shape Style **Subtle Effect – Blue, Accent 5** (row 4, column 6). Visually center the WordArt object on the first line of the document.

d. Select the second paragraph in the document, *See the Canyon From The Top!* Center and bold the text and apply a font color of **Blue, Accent 5**.

e. Select the remaining text on page 1, beginning with *May 28-29, 2022* and ending with *on the festival grounds*. Change the font of the columned text on page 1 to **Century Schoolbook**. Change line spacing to **1.5**. Insert a page break on page 2 before the *Frequently Asked Questions* heading.

f. Check spelling and grammar—the word *Ballumination* is not misspelled (for the purposes of this document). Accept the grammatical correction related to the word *from* in the second line of the document. Ignore all other grammatical concerns.

g. Click in the third paragraph on page 1—*May 28-29, 2022*—and right align it. Select all columned text, including the line containing festival dates, and apply paragraph spacing after of **6 pt**.

h. Click to place the insertion point before the paragraph beginning *As for the kids*. Insert *w02m1Balloon.jpg*. Size the picture with a width of **1″**. Click **Remove Background** in the Adjust group on the Picture Format tab to remove the picture background and click **Keep Changes**. Select **Square text wrapping** and a picture style of **Reflected Bevel, White** (row 5, column 2).

i. Position the picture so that it is on the left side of the paragraph beginning with *As for the kids*, and aligned with the top of the paragraph. Select the picture and choose the **Paint Brush Artistic effect** (row 2, column 3).

j. Scroll to page 3 and bold all headings on that page that are in the form of a question, beginning with *When is the best time to see balloons?*

k. Scroll to page 4 and apply **solid round bullets** to the first nine paragraphs on the page. Decrease the indent so the bullets begin at the left margin. With the bulleted items selected, click the **Bullets arrow** and click **Define New Bullet**. Click **Font** and change the font color to **Blue, Accent 5**. Click **OK**. Click **OK** again.

l. Insert a page break before the heading *How can I plan for the best experience?* on page 3. Click the **View tab** and ensure that the ruler shows. Select the schedule of items under the heading *Saturday (5/28/2022)*, beginning with *6:00 AM* and ending with *Balloon Glow*. Set a left tab at **1″** and another left tab at **3″**. Double-click either tab on the ruler to display the Tabs dialog box. Click **3″** in the Tab stop position box, select option **2** in the Leader section, and click **OK**.

m. Click before the first line in the selected text (beginning with 6:00 AM) and press **Tab**. Click before each remaining Saturday time and press **Tab**. Click before *Pilots Briefing* and press **Tab** to move to the second tab (with the dot leader). Similarly, move all remaining Saturday activities to the 3″ tab. Select the schedule of items under *Sunday (5/29/2022)* and repeat the process of setting a left tab at 1″ and 3″ (with dot leader). Move all times and activities as you did for Saturday.

n. Click before *Frequently Asked Questions* at the top of page 3. Click the **Insert tab** and select **Icons** in the Illustrations group. Type **question mark** in the Search box. Select the first question mark shown in the list and click **Insert**. Change text wrapping to **Square**.

o. Scroll to the bottom of page 4 and draw a text box below the list of Sunday's activities. Any size will do. Type **Where Your Dreams Take Flight** in the text box and press **Enter**. Type **Mount Vernon Hot Air Balloon Festival**. (Do not type the period.) Select the first line of text in the text box, *Where Your Dreams Take Flight* and apply a text effect of **Gradient Fill: Blue, Accent color 5; Reflection** (row 2, column 2). Change the font size of the first line to **18**.

p. Adjust the text box size to a height of **0.8″** and a width of **3.5″**. Select the second line of text in the text box, *Mount Vernon Hot Air Balloon Festival*. Bold the text and change the font color to **Blue, Accent 5**. Center both lines horizontally in the text box.

q. Click **Position** in the Arrange group on the Shape Format tab. Click **More Layout Options**. Select Horizontal alignment of **Centered** relative to **Margin**. Select Vertical Absolute position of **0.5″** below **Paragraph**. Click **Shape Outline** and choose **No Outline**. Click outside the text box.

r. Save and close the file. Exit Word. Based on your instructor's directions, submit: w02m1Festival_LastFirst

2 Franelli Pediatric Dentistry

MyLab IT Grader

You are the office manager for Dr. Franelli, a general dentist for children, who periodically conducts informational sessions for young patients. You have written a letter to children in the neighborhood reminding them about the upcoming monthly session, but you want to make the letter more professional looking. You decide to use paragraph formatting such as alignment, paragraph spacing, borders and shading, and bullets that describe some of the fun activities of the day. You also want to include fun and informative graphics.

a. Open the document *w02m2Dentist* and save it as **w02m2Dentist_LastFirst**.

b. Show nonprinting characters, if they are not already displayed. Apply **Justify alignment** to body paragraphs beginning with *On behalf* and ending with *September 12*.

c. Select the paragraph mark under the first body paragraph and create a bulleted list, selecting a filled square bullet. Type the following items in the bulleted list. Do not press Enter after the last item in the list.

Finding hidden toothbrushes in the dental office
Participating in the dental crossword puzzle challenge
Writing a convincing letter to the tooth fairy
Digging through the dental treasure chest

d. Select text from the salutation *Dear Wooseok:* through the last paragraph that ends with *seeing you on September 12*. Select paragraph spacing after of **12 pt.** Remove the paragraph mark after the *Dear Wooseok* paragraph.

e. Select the italicized lines of text that give date, time, and location of the meeting. Remove the italics, do not deselect the text, and then complete the following:

- Increase left and right indents to **1.25** and select paragraph spacing after of **0 pt.**
- Apply a **double-line box border** with the color **Purple, Accent 4**, and a line width of **3/4 pt**. Shade selected text with the **Purple, Accent 4, Lighter 40%** shading color.
- Delete the extra tab formatting marks to the left of the lines containing *September 4, 2024; 4:00 p.m.;* and *Dr. Franelli Pediatric Dentistry Office* to align them with other text in the bordered area.

f. Click in the paragraph following the bordered text, beginning with *Dr. Franelli is pleased to let you know*. Adjust paragraph spacing before to **6 pt**. Select the entire document and change the font to **12 pt. Bookman Old Style**.

g. Click before the first line in the document, *August 2, 2024*. Insert *w02m2Tooth.jpg*. Apply a **Square text wrap** and resize the picture to a height of **1.1″**. Position the picture in the top right corner of the document, using alignment guides to place it just inside the right margin and aligned with the date line. Apply an artistic effect of **Photocopy** (row 5, column 2).

h. Move to the end of the document and insert a page break. Change paragraph spacing after to **6 pt**. Change the font size to **14**.

i. Type **Wellington Water Park and Slide Fun Day!** Press **Enter** and type **September 12, 2024**. Press **Enter**. Change the font size to **12**. Center the first two lines on the page. Click at the blank paragraph following the two heading lines on page 2.

j. Ensure that the ruler shows. Set a left tab at **2″** and a right tab at **5.5″**. Drag the 2″ tab on the ruler back to **0.5″** to reposition it. Type the following text, with the first column at the 0.5″ tab and the next column at the 5.5″ tab. Do not press Enter after typing the last line.

Check-in	**9:00**
Wave pool	**9:30–11:00**
Lunch at the pavilion	**11:00–12:00**
Bungee	**12:00–2:00**
Water slide	**2:00–3:00**
Parent pickup at the gate	**3:00–3:30**

k. Select *Wellington Water Park and Slide Fun Day!* on page 2 and insert WordArt with the style **Gradient Fill: Purple, Accent color 4; Outline: Purple, Accent 4** (row 2, column 3). Wrap text around the WordArt object at **Top and Bottom**, change the font size of the WordArt object to **24**, and ensure that the WordArt object is visually centered horizontally on the first line of the page.

l. Select the tabbed text, beginning with *Check-in* and ending with *3:00-3:30*. Open the Tabs dialog box and modify the 5.5″ right tab to include a dot leader.

m. Click at the end of the document, following *3:00-3:30*. Press **Enter** twice. Insert a **Star: 5 Points shape**, drawing it to approximately 1″ in height at the left margin near the final paragraph mark. Adjust the height and width to **1″**. Change the shape fill to **Purple, Accent 4 Lighter 60%** and remove the shape outline.

n. Ensure that the star shape is selected. Press **Ctrl+D** to duplicate the shape. Move the copy to the right side of the original star, positioning it so that the longest horizontal star tips touch, as if the stars were holding hands. Repeat the process of duplicating and positioning so that four stars occupy the space, with star tips touching. They do not need to be centered or horizontally aligned.

o. Click the first star on the left, hold **Shift**, and click each remaining star so they are all selected. Click the **Shape Format tab** and group the selected objects. Click **Align** and click **Align Center**.

p. Check spelling and grammar, correcting any errors and ignoring those that are not errors. No names are misspelled.

q. Save and close the file. Exit Word. Based on your instructor's directions, submit: w02m2Dentist_LastFirst

New Castle County Technical Services

New Castle County Technical Services (NCCTS) provides technical services to clients in the greater New Castle County, Delaware, area. Founded in 2011, the company is rapidly expanding to include technical security systems, network infrastructure cabling, and basic troubleshooting services. With that growth comes the need to promote the company and to provide clear written communication to employees and clients. Microsoft Word is used exclusively in the development and distribution of documents, including an "About New Castle" summary that will be available both in print and online. You make a few changes to the document, ensuring a well-formatted and descriptive summary of the company.

a. Open *w02r1NewCastle* and save it as **w02r1NewCastle_LastFirst**. Show nonprinting characters.

b. Select the first paragraph on page 3 of the document, *About New Castle, Inc.* Insert WordArt, selecting **Fill: Olive Green, Accent color 3; Sharp Bevel** (row 2, column 5). Ensure that the font size of the WordArt object is **36**.

c. Select **Top and Bottom** text wrapping. Visually center the WordArt object on the first paragraph of the document, using alignment guides to ensure placement.

d. Place the insertion point before the *ON STAFF PERSONNEL EXPERIENCE AND CERTIFICATIONS* heading on page 4 (on the same line as the heading) and insert a page break. Select all the bullets in the section, beginning with *Electrical, Mechanical* and ending with *CompTIA Security+, A+, Server+, Network+*. Change the bullets to **hollow round bullets**. Do not deselect the text.

e. Click the **Layout tab**, click **Columns**, click **More Columns**, click **Two**, and select **Line between**. Click **OK**. Change the font of all bulleted items to **Century Schoolbook**.

f. Click to place the insertion point before the *EXPERIENCE AND CERTIFICATIONS* heading on page 4 (on the same line as the heading). Insert *w02r1Digital.jpg*. Change the picture height to **2″**. Select **Top and Bottom text wrapping** and a picture style of **Reflected Rounded Rectangle**. Position the picture so that it is immediately below the *EXPERIENCE AND CERTIFICATIONS* heading, aligned at the left margin.

g. Delete the page break following page 4 along with any remaining blank paragraph between pages 3 and 4. Select the last three bulleted items in the list on page 4. The items begin with *Cisco* and end with *Network+*. Change the bullets for those items to a **filled square bullet**. Increase the indent of the three items by one level.

h. Scroll to the end of the document, and remove the bullets from the list of 6 companies in the *A FEW OF OUR CUSTOMERS* section. Delete all the tab stops between company information and time frame information. Select all six lines containing company information. Set a left tab at **1″** and a right tab with a dot leader at **5″**. Tab each company in the list to the first tab stop. Tab all time frame information to the next tab stop.

i. Click anywhere in the first body paragraph under the *About New Castle, Inc.* heading, beginning with *New Castle County Technical Services (NCCTS)*, and change the alignment to **Left Align**. Insert a page break before *A FEW OF OUR CUSTOMERS* on page 5.

j. Click at the end of the document. Insert a SmartArt object, selecting **Continuous Arrow Process**. Change text wrapping to **Top and Bottom**. Change the first text block on the left to **Prompt**. (Do not type the period.) Change the next text block to **Experienced** and the next to **Dependable**. (Do not type the period.)

k. Change the SmartArt height to **1.5″** and change the width to **5″**. Ensure that the SmartArt object is shown under the list of customers, dragging to reposition it if necessary. Change the SmartArt style to **Subtle Effect** and change the color to **Colored Fill – Accent 3**. Use the SmartArt Align command to center the SmartArt horizontally.

l. Check the document for spelling errors, No company names are misspelled. Save and close the file. Exit Word. Based on your instructor's directions, submit:
w02r1NewCastle_LastFirst

Fairhope

You are working with the South Alabama Tourism Group to promote various events, munici-palities, and landmarks of the region. One of your assignments is the preparation of a monthly spotlight on an item of interest—this month is the burgeoning real estate potential of Fairhope, Alabama, a small town situated on the eastern side of Mobile Bay, favored by artists, authors, and those who want to invest in a second home for enjoyment or rental. Several of your coworkers have contributed to a document that you will now format and modify so that it conveys in words and graphics all that Fairhope has to offer in the way of prime real estate. Open *w02d1Fairhope* and notice how unprofessional and unorganized the document looks so far. You will improve the ap-pearance in whatever ways you think appropriate. Specifically, consider the following suggestions:

- Group the scroll shape and the two star shapes so they can be managed as a single entity. Adjust text wrapping so the grouped scroll is shown at the top of the document. Consider changing shape fill of the star shapes to differentiate them from the scroll fill.
- Adjust paragraph spacing, font selection, and font size for consistency. You might also work with line spacing and indents. Change font color where necessary and remove any unattractive shading. Consider formatting document headings to better identify them.
- Locate a Zillow.com listing of a home on the bay currently for sale in Fairhope and insert a screenshot, taking a screen clipping of the house picture and price to include in the document where it is indicated. Adjust the screenshot and text wrapping to ensure attractive placement.
- Format the "DID YOU KNOW" heading and text as a text box, formatted as you like and placed within the document wherever you think it might be most effective.
- Adjust tabs to better organize the tabbed information shown at the end of the document, in-cluding appropriate text formatting in the tabbed area, as well.
- Check for spelling and grammatical errors and ensure that there are no awkward page end-ings, perhaps with a heading shown alone.

Save your work as **w02d1Fairhope_LastFirst** and close the file. Exit Word. Based on your instructor's directions, submit:

w02d1Fairhope_LastFirst

Cumulative Exercise

You and a friend from college are starting a new business, Pool Pros, a pool maintenance and supplies operation. You plan to carry inventory in a retail storefront and also contract out pool maintenance and installation services. You know that if new pool owners are educated on how to maintain a pool, they are more apt to enjoy their purchase and frequent your store for supplies. Therefore, you plan to have on hand various documents and brochures related to pool ownership, one of which you are working with now. The document on pool maintenance will be a quick summary, with supporting graphics and attractive formatting. You will use skills presented in this chapter to format text, adjust alignment and indents, bullet and number lists, and incorporate various types of graphic objects that help describe the process of caring for a pool.

Apply Font Attributes and Format a Paragraph

By formatting text and adjusting paragraph and line spacing, you greatly improve the cohesiveness and readability of the document.

1. Open *w02c1Pool* and save it as **w02c1Pool_LastFirst**. Show nonprinting characters. Display the ruler.

2. Select *crystal-clear perfection* at the end of the first body paragraph and bold it. Select all text and change the font to **Arial** with a font size of **12**. Change the alignment of selected text to **Justify**.

3. Select the first two body paragraphs on page 1 and adjust the line spacing to **1.5**. Ensure that paragraph spacing before and after is **0 pt** for the selected paragraphs. Apply a First line indent for the two paragraphs of **0.5″**.

4. Select all subheadings that are formatted in bold and change the font size to **14**.

5. Select the four paragraphs that precede the *Get Rid of Debris* heading, beginning with *Check the pool's water balance* and ending with *Add an algaecide*. Add a **Box, double-line** border with **¾ line width** and a color of **Blue-Gray, Text 2**. Shade the bordered area with **Blue-Gray, Text 2 Lighter 60%**.

6. Click at the top of the document and press **Enter**. Click the newly inserted blank paragraph. Drag the First line indent marker back to the left margin to remove the First line indent from the blank paragraph.

7. Set a left tab at **1″** and a right tab at **5″**. Ensure that the right tab includes a dash leader. Press **Tab** and type **Your Pool**. (Do not type the period.) Press **Tab** and type **Your Way**. (Do not type the period.) Change the font for *Your Pool* and *Your Way* to **Lucida Calligraphy**. Bold the selection and change the font size to **10**.

8. Click before the second sentence in the first body paragraph at the top of page 3. The sentence begins with *Add more in hot weather*. Delete the preceding space and period that ends the first sentence. Insert an **Em dash** symbol and change the case of *Add* to *add*.

9. Select the four paragraphs in the shaded area near the top of page 1. Apply numbering, choosing **Number alignment: Left** (1., 2., 3.) with each number ending in a period.

Insert and Modify WordArt and SmartArt

An informal document can benefit from graphics that add interest and explanation. You format a heading as WordArt and include SmartArt to outline the process of maintaining a pool.

10. Click at the top of the document and insert WordArt, selecting **Fill: Blue, Accent color 1; Shadow** (row 1, column 2). Type **Pool Maintenance**. (Do not type the period.) Change the font size to **24** and change the Text Fill to **Black, Text 1**. Change WordArt font to **Arial**. Wrap text at **Top and Bottom** and visually center the WordArt horizontally on the first line.

11. Click at the end of the document and press **Enter**. Insert SmartArt, selecting **Basic Cycle**. Display the Text pane. Type **Get rid of debris** beside the first bullet. Type **Vacuum pool** beside the second bullet. Type **Adjust chemicals** beside the next bullet. Type **Backwash filter** and **Add chlorine** beside the next two bullets. Close the Text pane.

12. Adjust the SmartArt height to **3″** and the width to **5″**. Choose **Polished** SmartArt style and change colors to **Gradient Range – Accent 3**. Choose text wrapping of **Square**. Align the SmartArt object in the center.

Insert and Group Shapes, Insert a Text Box

Combining shapes, you develop a fun graphic for the document's heading line. A text box contains a summarizing pull quote.

13. Click at the top of the document. Insert a **Sun** shape from the Basic Shapes category. Draw the shape approximately 1″ wide and 1″ high, near the left margin on the top line of the document. Using the Shape Format tab, adjust the height and width to exactly **1″**.

14. Change the shape fill of the sun to **Yellow**. Insert a **Cloud** shape from the Basic Shapes category, sizing it to be approximately ¾″ high and ¾″ wide. Position the shape so that it overlaps the top right corner of the Sun shape. Change the shape fill of the cloud to **Light Gray, Background 2**. Send the cloud to the back so that it appears to be peeking out from behind the sun.

15. Group the cloud and sun shapes into one object. Duplicate the shape and drag the copy to the right, aligning it at the right margin on the same line as the WordArt heading. Align the first shape at the left margin, approximating a mirrored placement of the copied shape.

16. Copy the first sentence in the document, *On a searing summer day, a swimming pool is a welcome respite from the heat.* Deselect the sentence after copying it. Draw a text box of any size near the middle of page 2 and paste the copied sentence in the text box. Adjust text box height to **1″** and width to **3″**. Apply **Square** text wrapping.

17. Change the font size of text in the text box to **14** and change the font to **Tahoma**. Center the text. Click **Align** in the Arrange group on the Shape Format tab and align the text box in the middle and also in the center of the page. If the text box awkwardly divides a heading, drag it down slightly to better position it visually. Remove the outline from the text box and apply a shape fill of **Blue-Gray, Text 2**, **Lighter 80%**.

18. View the document in Multiple Pages and check for any poorly placed headings. Insert a page break before *Vacuum the Pool* at the bottom of page 1. Insert a page break before *Add Chlorine to the System* at the bottom of page 2. Drag to reposition the text box if it interrupts a heading.

19. Save and close the file. Exit Word. Based on your instructor's directions, submit: w02c1Pool_LastFirst

Document Productivity

CASE STUDY | Oakley University Economic Impact Study

As director of marketing and research for Oakley University, a midsize university in northwest Nebraska, you have been involved with an economic impact study during the past year. The study is designed to measure as closely as possible the contribution of the university to the local and state economy. An evaluation of data led university researchers to conclude that Oakley University serves as a critical economic driver in the local community and, to a lesser extent, the state of Nebraska. It is your job to summarize those findings and see that they are accurately reflected in the final report.

Your assistant has prepared a draft of an executive summary that you will present to the board of trustees, outlining the major findings and conclusions. The best way to present some of the data analysis will be through tables, which your assistant is not very familiar with, so you will take responsibility for that phase of the summary preparation. You will send an executive summary, along with a cover letter, to community and university leaders. You will use Word's mail merge feature to prepare personalized letters.

Work with Tables and Mail Merge

NDAB Creativity/Shutterstock

CHAPTER 3

Table 2 presents impact sources, with a description of each.

Table 2 – Impact Sources	
Source	**Description**
Capital Investment	New construction expenditures, creating additional "indirect" and "induced" jobs
Employee Compensation	Salary and wages to faculty and staff circulate in the local and regional economy
	es for goods and services needed to tions

omic Impact

Key Findings

Primary data utilized in this analysis was obtained from Traylor University's Office of Research and Development. Data included capital expenditures, operational expenditures, jobs data, payroll and benefits information, and taxes. We took a decidedly conservative approach in the analysis and determination of key findings. Not unexpectedly, study findings compare favorably to other top universities in the country.

Overall, this study suggests that the University stabilizes and strengthens the local and statewide tax base through its local spending as well as direct and indirect support of jobs. As an integral part of the state's economy, Traylor University generates revenue, jobs, and spending. In fact, state and local government revenues attributable to the presence of Traylor University totaled over $422.4 million in the previous fiscal year. State and local governments throughout Nebraska all received tax revenues that were University-related.

y University.

	Total Employment
	902 jobs
	420 jobs
	319 jobs
	311 jobs
	281 jobs
	178 jobs

y Employment

October 15, 2024

Ms. Rebecca Hardin
Belk, Inc.
3008 Beltline Hwy.
Suite 10
Dinsford, NE 68445

Dear Ms. Hardin,

Oakley University is making a difference in the local community and in the state of Nebraska, as confirmed by the results of the recently completed biannual economic impact study. As a member of the Oakley University Board of Trustees, you can be assured that you are leading a stellar university—one that contributes millions of dollars to the economy of the state each year, and one that is improving the lives of the state's populace.

The attached executive summary provides a snapshot of the university's monetary effect on its service area and the state. The expanded report will be printed and available at the November board meeting. As you review the executive summary, please let me know of any questions or suggestions.

Sincerely,

Melinda Roberts, Executive Director
Office of Marketing and Research
Oakley University

ectors in which Oakley University makes a difference in terms of

Sectors			
Description	**Economic Impact**	**Percentage of Total**	
es and universities	1,770,281,355	41.83%	
interests	1,256,390,688	29.69%	
e hospitals	544,871,166	12.88%	
estate companies	338,999,342	8.01%	
services and drinking lishments	321,381,992	7.59%	
Total	4,231,924,543		

Table 1: Economic Impact by Industry

FIGURE 3.1 Oakley University Documents

CASE STUDY | Oakley University Economic Impact Study

Starting Files	Files to Be Submitted	MyLab IT HOE Grader
w03h1Oakley	**w03h2Oakley_LastFirst**	
w03h3Letter	**w03h3Merged_LastFirst**	
w03h3Trustees.xlsx		

MyLab IT Grader: This project is available as a Hands-On Exercise project in MyLab IT.

Tables

A ***table*** is a grid of columns and rows that organizes data. As shown in Figure 3.2, a table is typically configured with headings in the first row and related data in the following rows. The intersection of each column and row is a ***cell***, in which you can type data. A table is an excellent format in which to summarize numeric data because you can easily align numbers and even include formulas to sum or average numbers in a column or row. Text can be included in a table as well. Although you can use tabs to align text in columns in a Word document, you might find it quicker to create a table than to set tabs, and you have more control over format and design when using a table. Even so, using tabs is necessary in some situations, such as when using dot leaders to lead the eye from one tabbed area to another.

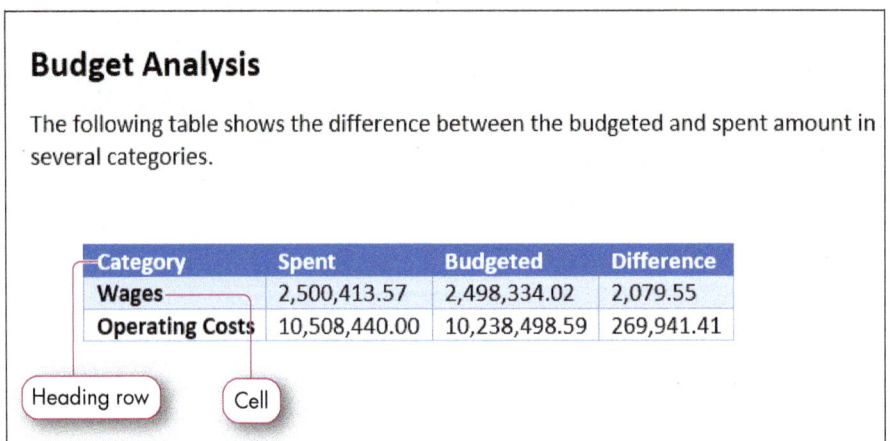

FIGURE 3.2 A Word Table

Word's Table feature is a comprehensive but easy-to-use tool, enabling you to insert a table, add and remove rows and columns, format table elements, include formulas to summarize numbers in a table, and customize borders and shading. You can always change a table or format it differently, even after it is developed.

In this section, you will learn to insert a table. After positioning the table within a document, you will explore inserting and deleting columns and rows, merging and splitting cells, and adjusting row height and column width. Using table styles, you will modify the appearance of a table, and you will adjust table position and alignment.

Insert a Table

You can either create a table with uniformly spaced rows and columns or draw a table with the pointer, creating rows and columns of varying heights and widths. Regardless of how a table is created, you can always change table settings so that rows and columns better fit the data included in the table.

When you create a table, you specify the number of columns and rows that should be included. For example, the table shown in Figure 3.2 is a 4×3 table, which means it contains four columns and three rows.

> **TIP: INSERT AN EXCEL SPREADSHEET**
> If you are familiar with Microsoft Excel, you can insert an Excel spreadsheet into a document and format it as a Word table. The option to insert an Excel table is not available on a Mac, however. The advantage is that when you double-click a cell in the table, it reverts to an Excel spreadsheet, so you can use Excel commands and functionality to modify the table and create formulas. Although a Word table attractively aligns numbers and text in columns, it is not as adept as a comparable Excel spreadsheet in updating formulas when values change. To insert an Excel spreadsheet, click the Insert tab, click Table, and then select Excel Spreadsheet. Enter data in the Excel spreadsheet and click outside the spreadsheet to view it as a Word table. Double-click any cell to return to Excel.

STEP 1 ## Create or Draw a Table

A table is an object; as such, it can be selected and manipulated independently of surrounding text. You can insert a table in a few ways, beginning by clicking the Insert tab and clicking Table. At that point, you can select from three different methods of creating tables, as shown in Figure 3.3:

- Drag to select the number of columns or rows to include in the table, as shown in Figure 3.3. Click in the bottom-right cell of the selection.
- Click Insert Table to display the Insert Table dialog box, where you can indicate the number of rows and columns you want to include. Click OK.
- Click Quick Tables (not available on a Mac) to insert a predesigned table, including such items as calendars, tabular lists, and matrices.

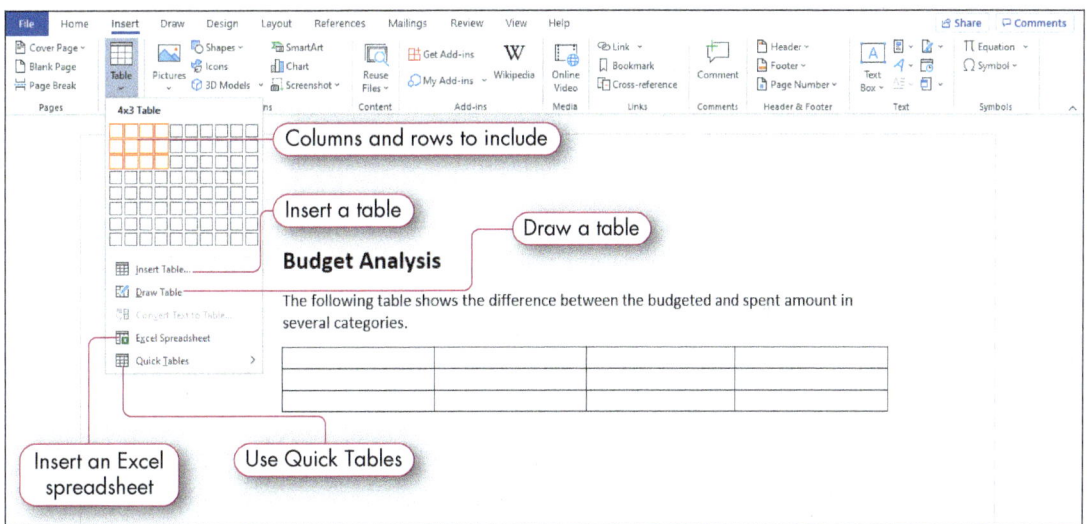

FIGURE 3.3 Insert a Table

Instead of inserting a table by indicating the number of columns or rows to include, as described in the previous set of steps, you can draw a table. You might choose to draw a table if you know that rows and/or columns should have varying heights or widths. It is sometimes easier to draw rows and columns of varying dimensions when a table is created rather than to modify the dimensions later, as would be necessary if you use the Insert Table feature to create evenly distributed columns and rows.

Draw a table:

1. Click the Insert tab and click Table in the Tables group.
2. Click Draw Table (refer to Figure 3.3). As you move the pointer over the document, it resembles a pencil.
3. Drag a rectangle and then draw horizontal and vertical lines to create rows and columns within the rectangular table space.
4. Press Esc when the table is complete.

After the table structure is created, you can enter characters, numbers, or graphics in cells, moving from one cell to another when you press Tab or a directional arrow key. You can also click a cell to move to it. As you type text in a cell, it is automatically left-aligned, although you can adjust alignment with options on the Table Layout tab or on the Home tab. Although the Layout tab associated with a table does not include the word Table, it is referred to in that way throughout this chapter to differentiate it from the other Layout tab on the ribbon. If typed text requires more space than is available, the text will wrap and the row height will adjust when it reaches the right edge of the cell. To force text to a new line in a cell (before reaching the right cell border), press Enter. You can instead insert a soft return by pressing Shift+Enter, which forces text to a new line in a cell, but without any additional paragraph spacing.

Insert and Delete Rows and Columns

If a table structure needs to be modified, you can insert or delete columns and rows. For example, suppose you have inserted a table and typed text in cells. As you enter data into a table and complete the last row, you find that an additional row is required. Press Tab to begin a new row. Continue entering data and pressing Tab to create new rows until the table is complete.

Occasionally, you will want to insert a row above or below an existing row when the row is not the last row in the table. You might even want to insert a column to the left or right of a column in a table. You can insert rows or columns by clicking an **Insert Control** that displays when you point to the edge of a row or column gridline, as shown in Figure 3.4. To insert several rows or columns, drag to select the number of rows or columns to insert, and click the Insert Control.

Although it is convenient to use the Insert Control to insert rows and columns, the Table Layout tab includes more comprehensive options that enable you to insert both columns and rows. Select from options in the Rows & Columns group to insert rows or columns. You can also delete rows or columns.

When you delete a table, you remove the entire table, including all table contents. When you select and delete table contents, the table structure remains as an empty set of rows and columns. To delete a table you must first select the entire table by clicking the Table move handle in the top left corner of the table (see Figure 3.4). At that point, you can complete any of the following options:

- Right-click the selected table and select Delete Table from the shortcut menu.
- Click Delete in the Rows & Columns group on the Table Layout tab and select Delete Table.
- Press Backspace.

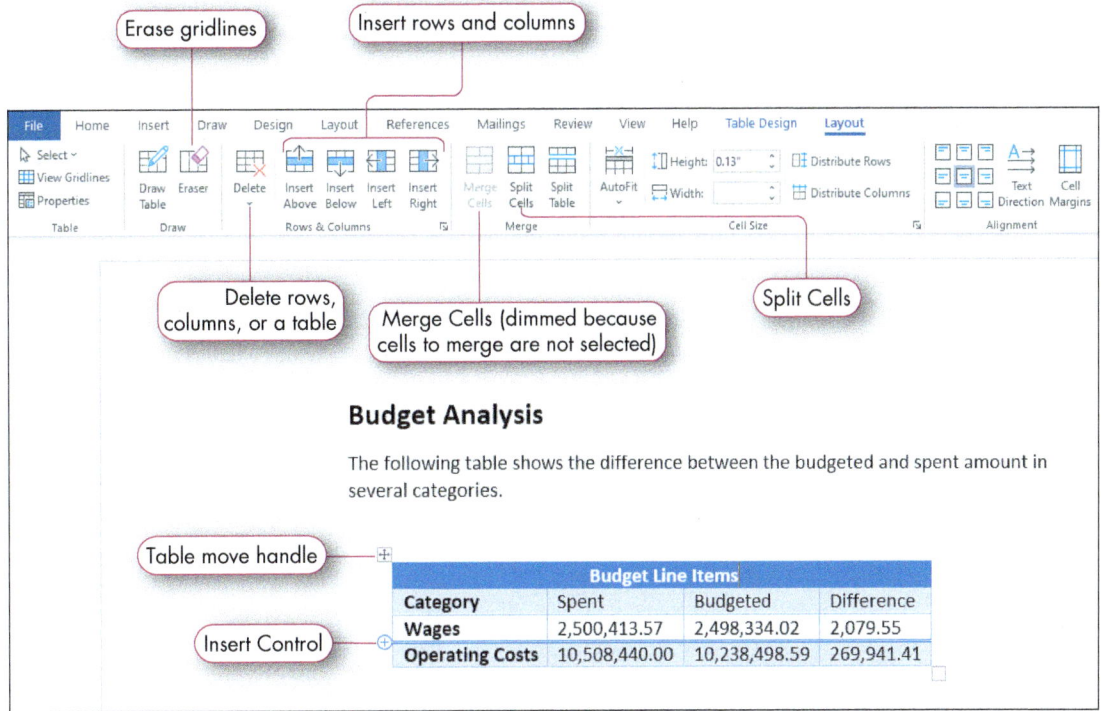

FIGURE 3.4 Work with Rows and Columns

STEP 2 ## Merge and Split Cells

The first row of the table shown in Figure 3.4 is a merged cell. When several cells are combined into one, the new cell is considered a merged cell. If you want to place a title across the top of a table or center a label over columns or rows of data, you can merge cells. After selecting cells to merge, use Merge Cells on the Table Layout tab to complete the merge. Once cells are merged, you can align data in the merged cell and change the font size to create a table title. You can also erase one or more gridlines within the table. Eraser on the Table Layout tab enables you to remove gridlines (refer to Figure 3.4). Click Eraser and click any table gridline to erase it. Press Esc or click Eraser again to toggle off the eraser.

Conversely, you might want to split a single cell into multiple cells. You can split a selected row or column to provide additional detail in separate cells. Split Cells is an option on the Table Layout tab.

Change Row Height and Column Width

An inserted table is a grid of evenly spaced columns and rows. As mentioned earlier, text automatically wraps within a cell and the row height adjusts to accommodate the entry. Row height is the vertical distance from the top to the bottom of a row, whereas column width is the horizontal space from the left to the right edge of a column. You can manually adjust row height or column width to modify the appearance of a table, perhaps making it more readable or more attractive. Increasing row height can better fit a header that has been enlarged for emphasis. You can increase column width to display a wide area of text, such as a first and last name, to prevent wrapping of text in a cell.

A simple but not very precise way to change row height or column width is to position the pointer on a border so that it displays as a double-pointed arrow ◄║► and drag to increase or reduce height or width. For more precision, you can use ribbon commands to adjust row height or column width. After selecting a row or column to be adjusted, change the height or width in the Cell Size group on the Table Layout tab. Alternatively, you can right-click the selected row or column and select Table Properties on the shortcut menu. You can then work with selections from the Column tab or Row tab in the dialog box, as shown in Figure 3.5.

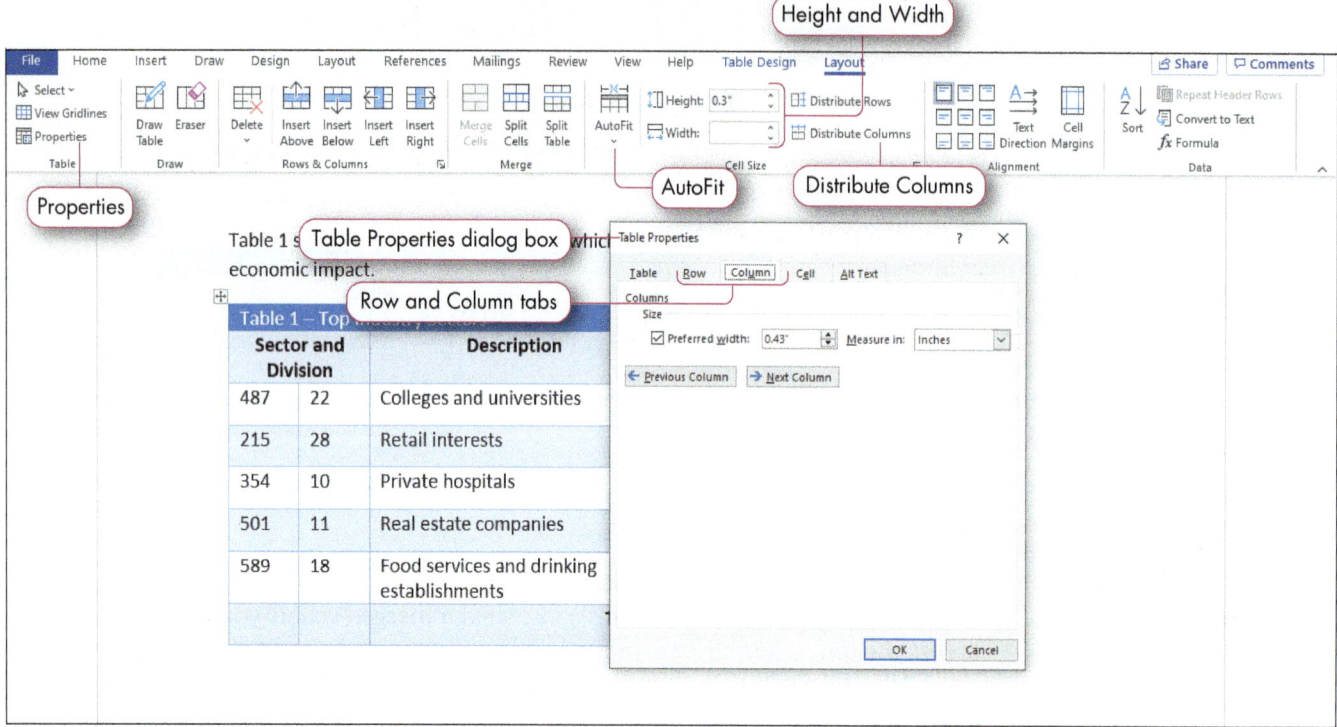

FIGURE 3.5 Change Row Height and Column Width

You can evenly distribute selected columns and rows to ensure that they are the same height and/or width. Select the columns and rows and click Distribute Rows (or Distribute Columns) in the Cell Size group on the Table Layout tab. Distributing rows and columns ensures uniformity within a table.

Instead of adjusting individual columns and rows, you can format a table with column and row dimensions that accommodate all cell entries. The feature, called AutoFit, automatically adjusts rows and columns. After clicking in any cell, select AutoFit in the Cell Size group on the Table Layout tab and choose AutoFit Contents.

Format a Table

After a table is inserted in a document, you can enhance its appearance by applying coordinated colors, borders, shading, and other design elements. Just as you format other document text by boldfacing, italicizing, or otherwise modifying it, you can format text within a table. You can also align text within cells by selecting an alignment from the Alignment group on the Table Layout tab. Lists or series within cells can be bulleted or numbered, and you can indent table text. A table can be positioned and moved to any location on a page.

Apply and Modify Table Styles

Word provides several predesigned *table styles* that contain borders, shading, font sizes, and other attributes that enhance the readability of a document. Use a table style when you want to create a color-coordinated, professional document or when you do not want to design your own custom borders and shading.

> **TIP: USE TABLE STYLES WITH THEMES**
>
> When you apply a table style or manually modify table shading and color selections, the color choices are associated with the theme in use. Therefore, if you change the document theme, the color selections applied through a table style or manual selections are likely to also change.

As shown in Figure 3.6, the Table Styles gallery provides styles for Plain, Grid, and List tables, although the size of each gallery prohibits all three groups from displaying at once. A table style format is also affected by the Table Style Options that are selected, such as Header Row, Banded Rows, and so on. Select a style from the Table Styles group on the Table Design tab. In Live Preview, the result of a style selection will display as you point to a style in the gallery.

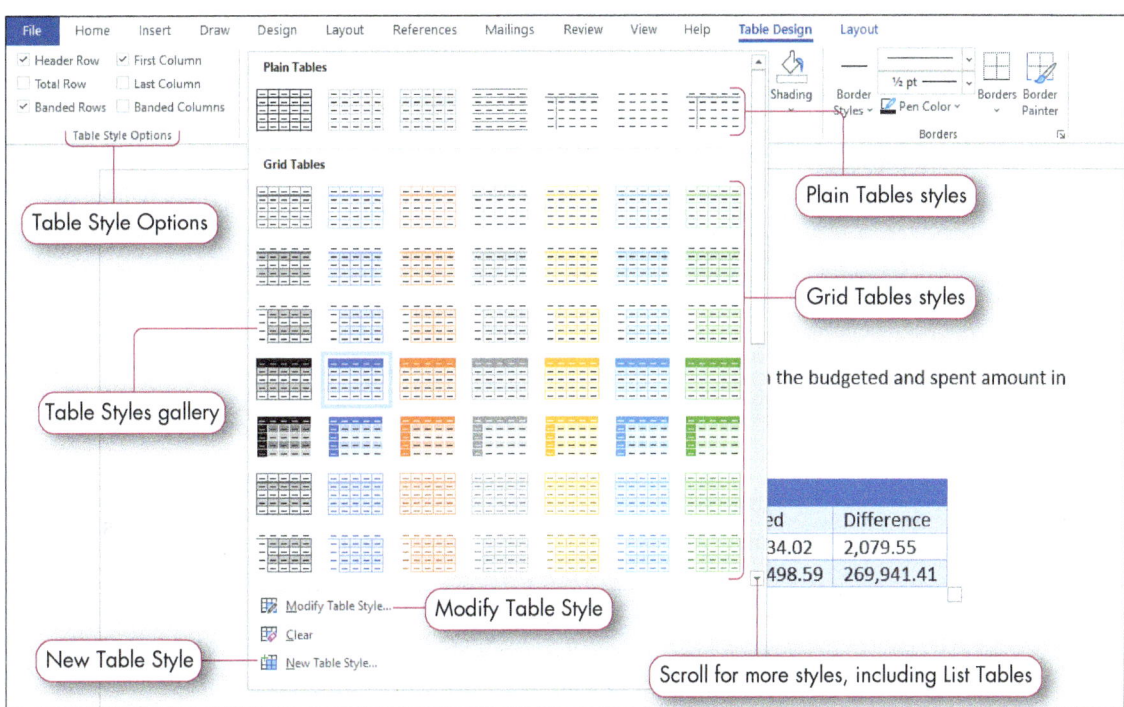

FIGURE 3.6 Work with Table Styles

After choosing a table style, you can modify it, as shown in Figure 3.6. As you modify a table style, you can apply changes to the entire table or to elements such as the header row. In that way, you can adjust a style so that it better suits your purposes. If you have modified a table style and want to make the style available for use in other documents, select New Table Style at the bottom of the Table Styles gallery. Otherwise, choose to save the changes for use only in the current document.

Adjust Table Position and Alignment

Table alignment refers to the horizontal position of a table between the left and right document margins. When you insert a table, it aligns at the left margin, although you can change the alignment, choosing to center the table or align it at the right margin. Right-click any cell and choose Table Properties (or select Properties from the Table Layout tab in the Table group) to display the Table Properties dialog box shown in Figure 3.7. You can also select alignment options in the Alignment group on the Table Layout tab.

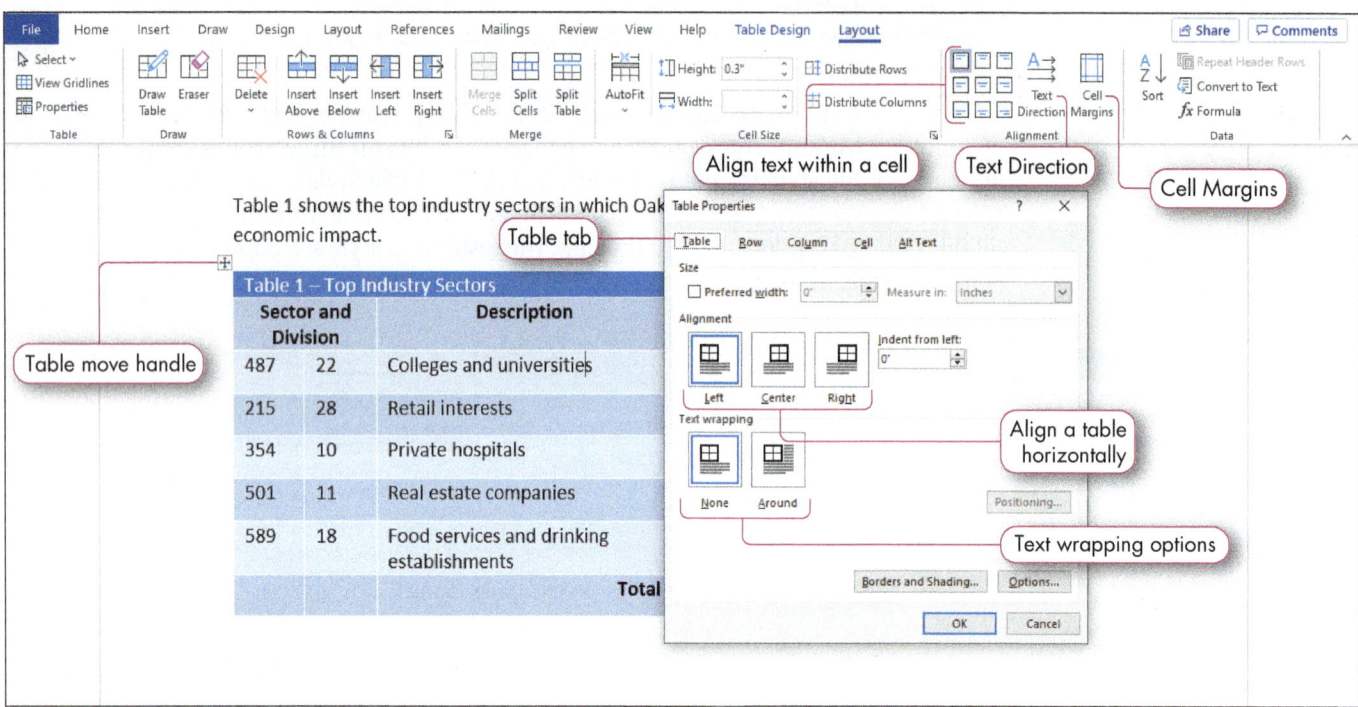

FIGURE 3.7 Adjust Table and Text Alignment

Move a table to any location within the document when you drag the Table move handle. As you move the table, a dashed border displays, indicating the position of the table. Release the mouse button to position the table.

Text within cells can be aligned using alignment options on the Table Layout tab. You can align cell contents both vertically and horizontally within the current cell, as indicated in Figure 3.7. Especially when working with a small table that does not require much document space, you might find it useful to wrap text around the table so that the table is better incorporated visually into the document, much as you would do when wrapping text around a picture or object in a document. Figure 3.7 illustrates the use of text wrapping with a table. Text will wrap on the right side of a left-aligned table, on both sides of a centered table, and on the left side of a right-aligned table. If you select None in the Text Wrapping section, text is prevented from wrapping, ensuring that text displays only above and below a table.

Format Table Text

Text within a cell can be formatted just as any other text in a document. Select text to format and apply one or more font attributes such as font type, font size, underline, boldface, or italics.

> **TIP: SELECT TEXT IN A TABLE**
> To select a cell's contents, you can drag over the text or click just inside the left edge of a cell.

By default, text within a cell is oriented horizontally so that it reads from left to right. On occasion, you might want to change that direction. Lengthy column headings can be oriented vertically so that they require less space. Or perhaps a table includes a row of cells repeating a telephone number, with each cell designed to be ripped from the bottom of a printed document. Such cells are often in a vertical format for ease of removal. Cycle through Text Direction options in the Alignment group on the Table Layout tab (refer to Figure 3.7) to rotate text in the current cell.

The Cell Margins command in the Alignment group enables you to adjust the amount of white space inside a cell as well as spacing between cells. With additional empty space shown between typed entries, a table can appear more open and readable. Other times, you will want to remove extra space created by cell margins such as when preparing a photo layout in a Word table in which you do not want to display any space at all between photos.

Critical Thinking

1. Explain whether you would format a table of contents for a book by using tabs or a table, providing rationale for your choice. *p. 242*

2. Describe a table that would be best designed by drawing instead of inserting. *p. 243*

3. Explain why it would or would not be good practice to distribute rows and columns for every table that you create. *p. 246*

Skills covered: Create or Draw a Table • Insert and Delete Rows and Columns • Merge and Split Cells • Change Row Height and Column Width • Apply and Modify Table Styles • Adjust Table Position and Alignment • Format Table Text

1 Tables

The executive summary is the first section of the economic impact report for Oakley University. Although the summary is already well organized, the data analysis part of the summary needs some attention. Specifically, you develop tables to organize major findings.

STEP 1 ▶ **CREATE A TABLE AND INSERT AND DELETE ROWS AND COLUMNS**

You modify a couple of tables to summarize study findings, including those tables in the executive summary. As you develop or edit the tables, you find it necessary to insert rows to accommodate additional data and to delete columns that are not actually required. Refer to Figure 3.8 as you complete Step 1.

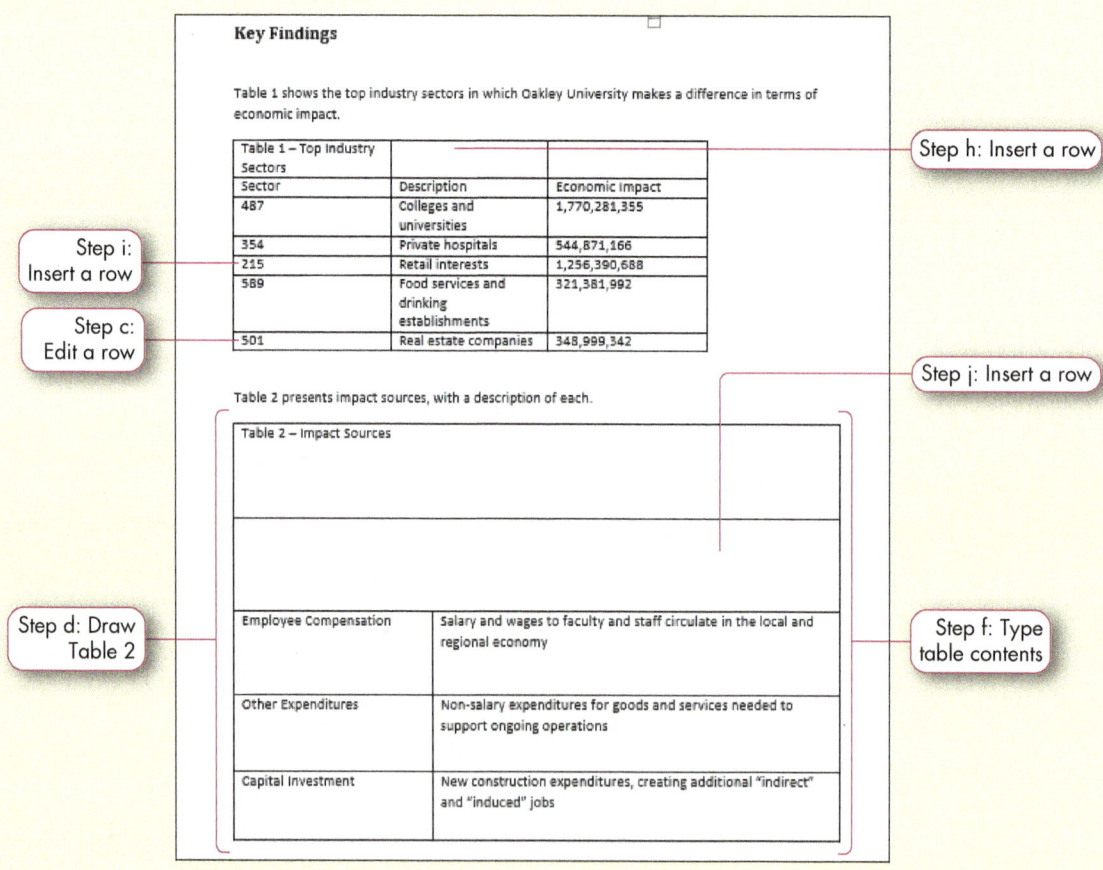

FIGURE 3.8 Report Tables

a. Open *w03h1Oakley* and save it as **w03h1Oakley_LastFirst**.

TROUBLESHOOTING: If you make any major mistakes in this exercise, you can close the file, open *w03h1Oakley* again and then start this exercise over.

---

b. Click the **View tab** and ensure that Ruler is selected in the Show group. Ensure that nonprinting characters are shown. Scroll to the last page of the document and click in the first cell on the last row of the table.

c. Type the following text on the last row, tabbing between cells. Do not press Tab after the last entry.

501	Real estate companies	Land	348,999,342

You completed the entry of data in a table to indicate community and state interests that are positively impacted by the presence of Oakley University.

> **TROUBLESHOOTING:** If you press Tab after the last entry, a new row is created. Click Undo. If the insertion point moves to a new line within a cell instead of advancing to another cell or row, you pressed Enter instead of Tab between entries. Press Backspace and press Tab. Do not press Tab if you are in the last cell on the last row.

d. Place the insertion point at the end of the document and complete the following steps:

- Click the **Insert tab**, click **Table** in the Tables group, and then click **Draw Table**.
- Drag a box approximately six inches wide and four inches tall, using the vertical and horizontal rulers as guides. Draw one vertical gridline at two inches from the left to create two columns—the first column approximately two inches wide and the second about four inches wide.
- Draw three horizontal gridlines to divide the table into four approximately evenly spaced rows of about one inch each. Press **Esc** or click **Draw Table** in the Draw group on the Table Layout tab to toggle the tool off. Although the ribbon tab does not include the word *Table*, it is used in this context to differentiate it from the other Layout tab.

> **TROUBLESHOOTING:** It is possible that the lines you draw to form the table are in a color or style other than black. That occurs if someone using the same computer previously selected a different pen color. For this exercise, it will not matter what color the table borders are.

It is OK if the row height is not identical for each row. Simply approximate the required height for each.

e. Click **Eraser** in the Draw group and click to erase the vertical gridline in the first row so that the row includes only one column. Click **Eraser** again to toggle off the setting.

> **TROUBLESHOOTING:** If you make any mistakes while erasing gridlines, press Esc. Click Undo to undo your actions.

f. Ensure the insertion point is in the first row and type **Table 2 - Impact Sources**. (Do not type the period.) Press **Tab** and complete the table as follows (do not press Tab at the end of the last entry):

Employee Compensation	Salary and wages to faculty and staff circulate in the local and regional economy
Other Expenditures	Non-salary expenditures for goods and services needed to support ongoing operations
Capital Investment	New construction expenditures, creating additional "indirect" and "induced" jobs

Text you type will wrap within some cells. You will resize the columns later, so leave the text as it appears.

g. Position the pointer just above the *Category* column in Table 1 so that the pointer resembles a downward-pointing arrow ⬇. Click to select the column. Click **Delete** in the Rows & Columns group and select **Delete Columns**.

h. Click anywhere in **row 1** of Table 1. Click **Insert Above** in the Rows & Columns group. Click in the **first cell** in the new row and type **Table 1 - Top Industry Sectors**. (Do not type the period and leave a space before and after the hyphen.)

Text will wrap within the first cell.

i. Point to the left edge of the horizontal gridline dividing Sector 354 from 589 to display an Insert Control. Click the **+ indicator** on the end of the Insert Control to insert a new row. Ensure that the insertion point is in the **first cell** of the new row and type the following. Press **Tab** between cells.

215	Retail interests	1,256,390,688

> **MAC TROUBLESHOOTING:** Use ribbon selections on the Table Layout tab to insert a row instead of the Insert Control.

j. Click anywhere in **Table 2** to select the table. Point to the left edge of the gridline dividing rows 1 and 2, and click the **Insert Control** to insert a row above row 2 (*Employee Compensation*). Leave the row blank, for now.

Depending on the size of the rows you drew for Table 2, it is possible that Table 2 spans over two pages with the last row shown on a separate page. You will correct that in the following step.

> **TROUBLESHOOTING:** If you do not see an Insert Control between rows 1 and 2, click in row 1 and click Insert Below in the Rows & Columns group on the Table Layout tab.

k. Check spelling and correct any errors. The *Salida* campus is spelled correctly, so ignore the error if presented. Ignore any grammatical or refinement concerns. Save the document.

STEP 2 MERGE AND SPLIT CELLS AND CHANGE ROW HEIGHT AND COLUMN WIDTH

As you work with the tables in the executive summary, you notice that the first row of Table 1 is not very attractive. The title in that row should not be limited to one small cell. More uniformity of row height and column width would also improve the appearance of Table 2, and you want to add data to the second row. You explore ways to modify both tables by merging and splitting cells and changing row height and column width. Refer to Figure 3.9 as you complete Step 2.

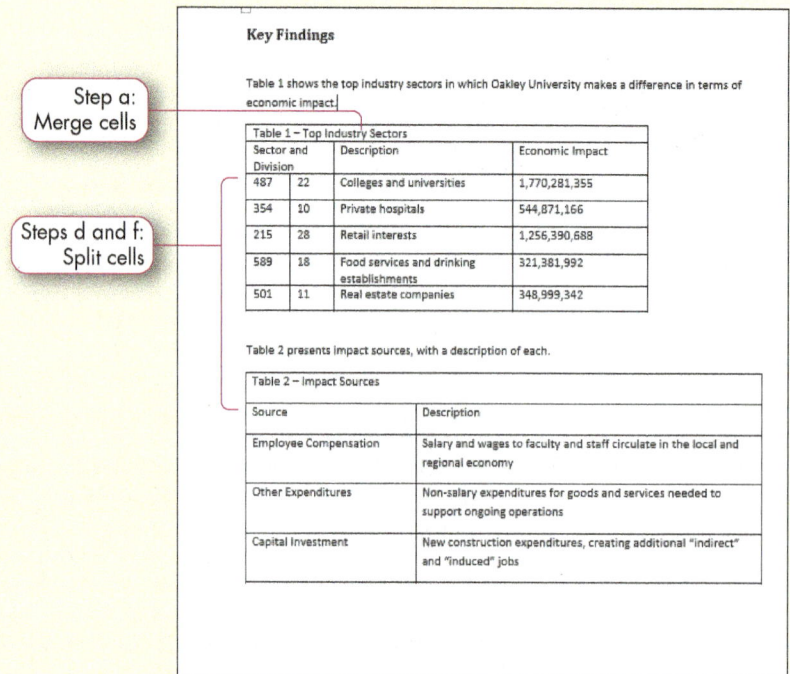

FIGURE 3.9 Merged and Split Cells

a. Position the pointer just outside the left edge of the first row of Table 1 so that it resembles an angled pointing arrow ⟨⟩. Click to select **row 1**. Click the **Table Layout tab** and click **Merge Cells** in the Merge group.

You merge the cells in row 1 to create one cell in which text can be better positioned across the table.

b. Position the pointer in row 2 on the border between the first and second column of Table 1. The pointer displays as a double-pointed icon ⟨↔⟩. Drag to the left to reduce the column width to approximately 1 inch.

The column is resized to better accommodate the contents of the column.

c. Position the pointer just outside the left edge of row 2 in Table 1 and drag down to select row 2 as well as all remaining rows. Use the Height up arrow in the Cell Size group to change the height to **0.3"**.

Row height of rows 2, 3, 4, 5, and 7 is adjusted to 0.3". However, because text wraps in row 6, the height of that row is not adjusted to 0.3". Click anywhere in the table to deselect text.

> **TROUBLESHOOTING:** If items in the first column are selected instead of every cell in every row, you have selected cells instead of rows. Repeat Step c, making sure to position the pointer outside the table and very near the left edge.

The first column of Table 1 lists a sector in which an area of economic impact is identified. Each sector should be further identified by a division, which you now add.

d. Position the pointer just inside the left edge of the third row of Table 1 (containing *487*). The pointer should resemble a right-angled black arrow. Drag down to select the contents of the first column in row 3 as well as all remaining rows in that column. Click **Split Cells** in the Merge group on the Table Layout tab. Check to ensure that *2* displays as the number of columns and *5* displays as the number of rows. Make necessary adjustments. Uncheck **Merge cells before split**. Click **OK**.

Column 1 is split into two columns so that the first column includes the sector and the second will contain the associated division.

> **TROUBLESHOOTING:** If all sector numbers display in the first cell instead of remaining in separate cells, you did not deselect *Merge cells before split*. Click Undo and repeat Step d.

e. Click in the **first cell** on the second row in Table 1 (containing *Sector*). Type **and Division** after *Sector*. Ensure that a space is included after *Sector*. Type the data underneath the heading as follows, using Figure 3.9 as a guide:

487	22
354	10
215	28
589	18
501	11

f. Click in the **second row** of Table 2. Click **Split Cells** in the Merge group. Ensure that *2* displays as the number of columns and *1* displays as the number of rows. Click **OK**. Place the pointer on the vertical gridline dividing the two columns in row 2. The pointer displays as a double-pointing arrow ⟨↔⟩. Drag to the left to align the gridline with the vertical gridline in row 3.

g. Type **Source** in the first cell of row 2. Press **Tab**. Type **Description**. (Do not type the period.)

h. Click the **Table move handle** (at the top-left corner of Table 2) to select the entire table. Use the Height down arrow in the Cell Size group on the Table Layout tab to reduce the height to **0.01"**.

Row height of all rows in Table 2 is reduced, resulting in a more attractive table.

i. Save the document.

APPLY AND MODIFY TABLE STYLES, ADJUST TABLE POSITION AND ALIGNMENT, AND FORMAT TABLE TEXT

The tables included in the Key Findings section are complete with respect to content, but you realize that they could be far more attractive with a bit of color and appropriate shading. You explore Word's gallery of table styles. You also bold and center column headings and explore aligning the tables horizontally on the page. Refer to Figure 3.10 as you complete Step 3.

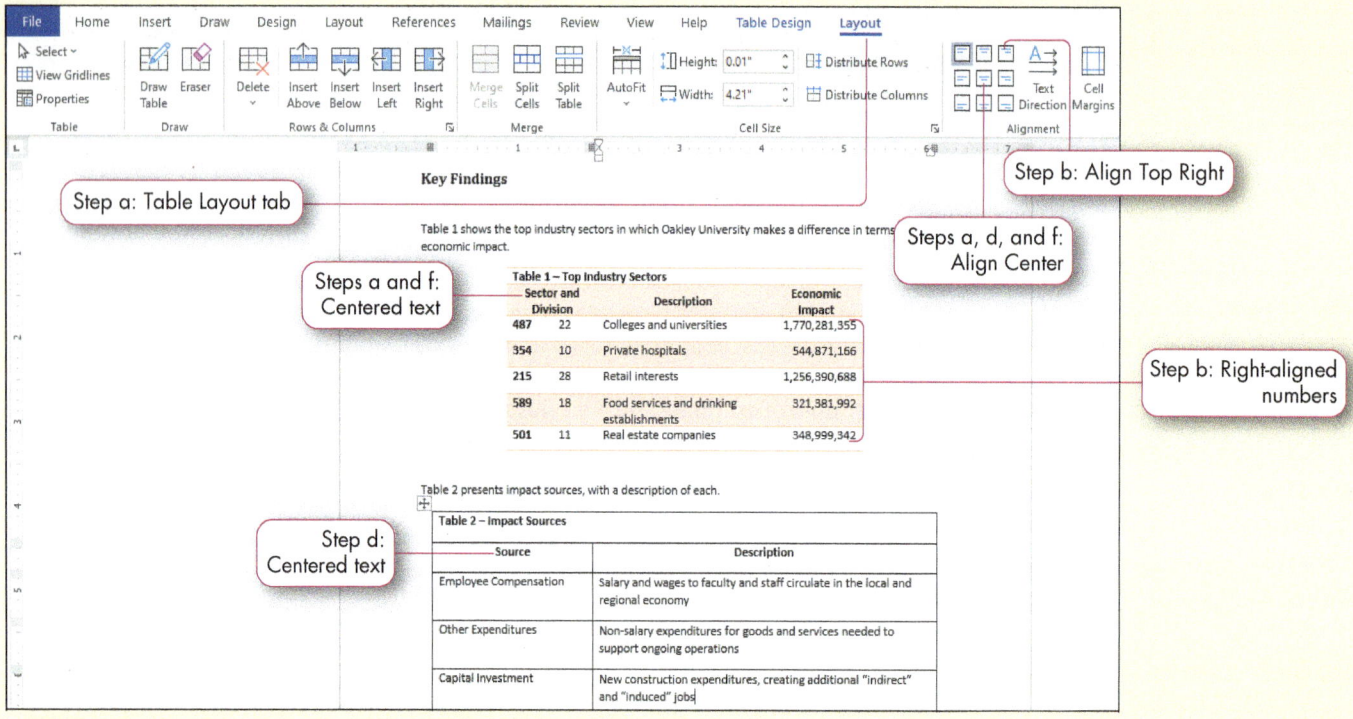

FIGURE 3.10 Format and Align a Table

a. Select the **second row** in Table 1. Click **Align Center** in the Alignment group on the Table Layout tab.

Text in row 2 is centered both vertically and horizontally within each cell.

b. Select the cells containing numbers in the Economic Impact column of Table 1 (beginning with 1,770,281,355 and ending with 348,999,342). Click **Align Top Right** in the Alignment group. Click anywhere to deselect the cells.

c. Position the pointer on the right border of the Economic Impact column of Table 1 so that it resembles a double-pointed arrow . Drag to the left to reduce the column so that the width is approximately **1"**, better accommodating the contents of the column.

The heading in the Economic Impact column will most likely wrap as you reduce the column width.

d. Select the **second row** in Table 2, containing column headings. Click **Align Center** in the Alignment group. With the column headings selected, click the **Home tab** and click **Bold** in the Font group. Bold the contents of row 1 in Table 2.

e. Click anywhere in Table 1, click the **Table Design tab**, and then click **More** in the Table Styles group. Scroll through the gallery and select **List Table 2 - Accent 6** (row 2, column 7 under List Tables). You may need to scroll through the list of styles to locate the List Tables area. Bold the contents of the first two rows in Table 1.

The table style removed some of the formatting from Table 1, applying color-coordinated font color and shading. The style also removed the inside vertical borders.

f. Click the **Table Layout tab**. Select the **second row** in Table 1 (containing column headings) and click **Align Center** in the Alignment group.

g. Click the **View tab** and click **One Page** in the Zoom group to view the current page. Note that the tables are not centered on the page horizontally. Click **100%** in the Zoom group.

h. Right-click anywhere in **Table 1** and select **Table Properties**. Click **Center** in the Alignment group on the Table tab in the Table Properties dialog box to center the table horizontally. Click **OK**. Repeat this technique to center Table 2 horizontally. Click **One Page** in the Zoom group to view the effects of the realignment. Click **100%**.

i. Save the document. Keep the document open if you plan to continue with the next Hands-On Exercise. If not, close the document, and exit Word.

Advanced Table Features

Having developed a basic table, you can enhance it by using features that improve its readability. Many of the tasks typically associated with an Excel spreadsheet can be accomplished in a Word table, such as summing or averaging a numeric column or row. By using advanced table features in Word, you can create tables that not only organize data but also present table contents in an attractive, easy-to-read format.

In this section, you will enhance tables with borders and shading. In addition, you will sort table data and learn to include formulas and functions in a table. You will learn to include captions with tables so that tables are correctly identified. Finally, you will simplify the task of creating a table by converting plain text into a table, and you will learn to convert a table to plain text.

Manage Table Data

A table is often used to summarize numeric data. For example, the table shown in Figure 3.11 organizes a list of students receiving college scholarships. The last row of the table shows column totals, calculated using functions, which are discussed in a later section. The table is sorted by student last name. Because the college awards many individual scholarships, there is a likelihood that the table could extend beyond one page. In that case, the first row (containing table headings) should be set to recur across all pages so that table data are identified by column headings, regardless of the page on which the table is continued. You can manage table data to include calculations, sort table contents, and cause header rows to recur across pages. Planning a table ahead of time is always preferable to recognizing the need for a table after text has already been typed. However, in some cases, you can convert plain text into a table. Conversely, after a table has been created, you can convert table text back to plain text.

Recipient Name	Major	Date Awarded	Amount Awarded	Amount Spent
Alim, Nisheeth	Accounting	5/15/2024	1,850	1,200
Dininsha, Ahmed	Finance	4/23/2023	1,200	1,200
Don, Clarke	Management	2/1/2024	1,350	728
Edge, Latisha	Finance	6/4/2021	2,550	1,014
Gonzalez, Patricia	Accounting	3/16/2024	1.500	0
Green, Amber	Entrepreneurship	5/10/2022	1,225	1,225
James, Greg	CIS	4/23/2022	2,850	350
McDonald, June	Accounting	5/15/2024	2,335	2,001
Marish, Tia	CIS	2/10/2021	1,895	1,400
Pintlala, Sarah	Management	8/1/2023	3,950	2,100
Tellez, Anthony	Finance	6/2/2023	2,350	2,300
Wallace, April	Marketing	2/28/2024	1,100	250
		TOTAL	22,657	13,768

FIGURE 3.11 Manage Table Data

STEP 1 ▶ Use a Formula

Organizing numbers in columns and rows within a Word table not only creates an attractive and easy-to-read display but also simplifies the task of totaling, averaging, or otherwise summarizing those numbers. Although Word is not designed to perform heavy-duty statistical calculations, it is possible to determine basic solutions, such as a sum, an average, or a count of items, in cells using built-in functions.

A **formula** is a calculation that can add, subtract, divide, or multiply cell contents. To use formulas, you must understand the concept of cell addresses. A Word table is very similar to an Excel worksheet, so if you are familiar with Excel, you will understand how Word addresses cells and develops formulas. Each cell in a Word table has a unique address. Columns are designated with letters (although such labeling is understood—letters do not actually display above each column) and rows with numbers. For example, Nisheeth Alim's award amount, shown in Figure 3.12, is in cell D2 (fourth column, second row). The amount he has spent is in cell E2, and the amount remaining is to be calculated in cell F2. The formula to calculate the amount remaining is =D2-E2, which subtracts the amount spent from the award amount. When indicating a cell reference, you do not have to capitalize the address. For example, =A10+A11 is evaluated identically to =a10+a11.

Unlike the way you would manage formulas in an Excel worksheet, you do not actually type a formula or function in a cell. Instead, you use the Formula dialog box to build a formula or use a function (see Figure 3.12).

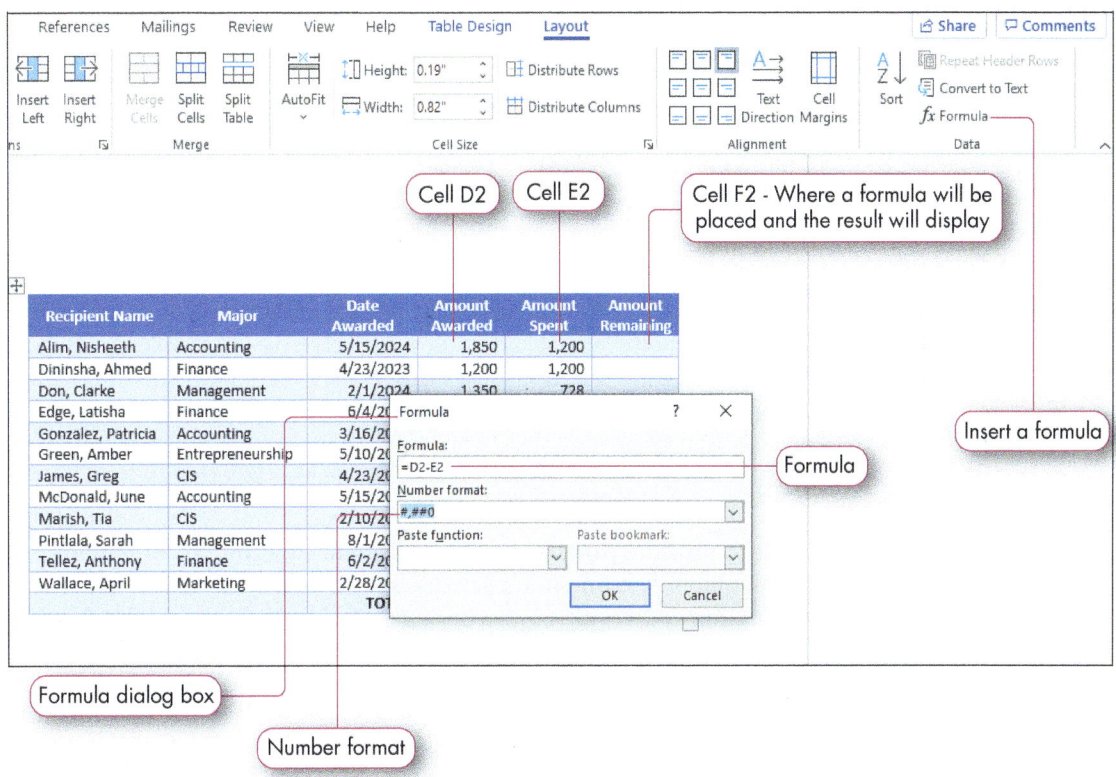

FIGURE 3.12 Use the Formula Dialog Box

> **TIP: NUMBER FORMAT**
> When identifying a number format, you have several options to select from when you click Number format in the Formula dialog box. A # in a format indicates that leading zeroes will be suppressed. A 0 in a format indicates that leading zeroes will be displayed. Other format options enable you to display dollar signs or percent signs in the formula result.

A formula can contain more than one mathematical operator. The minus sign in the formula described in the preceding steps is considered an operator. Mathematical operators that you can use in creating formulas include exponentiation (^), multiplication (*), division (/), addition (+), and subtraction (-).

When more than one operator is included in a formula, evaluation of the formula follows a set procedure, called the ***order of operations***. The order of operations requires that the following operations be evaluated in the this order:

1. Parenthetical information (any calculation in parentheses)
2. Exponentiation

3. Multiplication and Division—evaluated from left to right if both operators are present in a formula

4. Addition and Subtraction—evaluated from left to right if both operators are present in a formula

As an example, the expression =C12+C15*1.8 is evaluated as follows: Multiply cell C15 by 1.8 and add the result to cell C12. If, however, you wanted the addition to be performed first, you would enclose that calculation in parentheses. Because the use of parentheses has a higher order of operation than multiplication, that addition would be done first, and the result would be multiplied by 1.8.

> **TIP: UPDATING A FORMULA**
> Unlike Microsoft Excel, a formula in a table is not automatically updated when the contents of cells referenced by the formula change. However, you can manually update a formula. Right-click the cell containing the formula and select Update Field. (On a Mac, you must first select the value and then update the field.)

Common equations, such as the area of a circle, and more complex equations, such as the quadratic formula, are available to be incorporated into a document or table. The Equation command in the Symbols group on the Insert tab provides a list of equations and enables you to create your own. The formula is created in a placeholder, so you can manage it independently of surrounding text. Most math symbols and operators are not located on the keyboard; however, you can create a formula so that it seamlessly integrates with surrounding text by making selections from the Symbols group on the Insert tab or the Equation tab, shown when you click the Insert tab and select Equation from the Symbols group.

Use a Function

Word provides *functions*, which are built-in formulas, to simplify the task of performing calculations. A function uses values in a table to produce a result. For example, the SUM function totals values in a series of cells, whereas the COUNT function identifies the number of entries in a series of cells. The total scholarship amount, which is included in the Total row shown in Figure 3.11, is calculated with a SUM function, which adds the values in the column above. In most cases, a function provides an alternative to what would otherwise be a much lengthier calculation.

To determine a final scholarship amount in the Total row of the table shown in Figure 3.11, you could click in the cell underneath the last scholarship award amount and add all cells individually in the fourth column, as in =D2+D3+D4+D5+D6, continuing to list cells in the range through D13. A *range* is a series of adjacent cells. Although the formula would produce a final total, the formula would be extremely lengthy. Imagine the formula length in a more realistic situation in which hundreds of students received a scholarship! A much more efficient approach would be to use the SUM function, in which you indicate, by position, the series of cells to total. For example, the function to produce a total scholarship amount is =SUM(ABOVE). Similarly, a function to produce an average scholarship amount is =AVERAGE(ABOVE). In fact, you can select from various table functions, as shown in Table 3.1. The positional information within parentheses is referred to as an *argument*. Positional information indicates the position of the data being calculated. You can use positional notation of ABOVE, BELOW, LEFT, or RIGHT as arguments. An argument of ABOVE indicates that data to be summarized is located above the cell containing the function. Although not a comprehensive list, Table 3.1 shows the functions that are commonly used. Note that an argument will be included within parentheses in each function.

TABLE 3.1	Table Functions
Function	**Action**
=SUM(argument)	Totals a series of cells
=AVERAGE(argument)	Averages a series of cells
=COUNT(argument)	Counts the number of entries in a series of cells
=MAX(argument)	Displays the largest number in a series of cells
=MIN(argument)	Displays the smallest number in a series of cells

To include a formula in a cell, you must click the cell that is to contain the calculation result. For example, click in cell D14 of the table shown in Figure 3.11 to include a function totaling all scholarship amounts. Click Formula in the Data group on the Table Layout tab. Type a formula in the Formula dialog box or edit the suggested function. Alternatively, you can click the Paste function and type an argument. Click OK.

TIP: COMBINING ARGUMENTS

Combine arguments in a function to indicate cells to include. For example,
=SUM(ABOVE,BELOW) totals numeric cells above and below the current cell.
=SUM(LEFT,ABOVE) totals numeric cells to the left and above the current cell, whereas
=SUM(RIGHT,BELOW) totals numeric cells to the right and below the current cell. Combine any two arguments, separated by a comma, to indicate cells to include.

STEP 2 ▶ **Sort Data in a Table**

Columns of text, dates, or numbers in a Word table can be sorted alphabetically, chronologically, or numerically. The table shown in Figure 3.11 is sorted alphabetically in ascending order by last name. It might be beneficial to sort the data in Figure 3.11 by date so that scholarship awards are shown in chronological order. Or you could sort table rows numerically by award amount, with highest awards shown first, followed in descending order by lesser award amounts. You might even want to sort awards alphabetically by major, with scholarship award amounts within programs of study shown in order from low to high. Such a sort uses a primary category (major, in this case) and a secondary category (award amount). You can sort a Word table by up to three categories.

A table is often designed so that the first row contains column headings. Those column headings, also called a header row, serve as categories that you can sort by. As you conduct a sort, described in the following steps, you should first indicate whether the table has a header row. In doing so, you can then select one or more sort categories. Even if a table has no header row, you can select rows to sort and indicate which column to sort by.

HOW TO

Sort table rows:

1. Click anywhere in the table (or click in the column to sort by).
2. Click Sort in the Data group on the Table Layout tab.
3. Specify whether the table includes a header row.
4. Indicate or confirm the primary category, or column, to sort by (along with the sort order, either ascending or descending), as shown in Figure 3.13.
5. Select any other sort columns and indicate or confirm the sort order. Click OK.

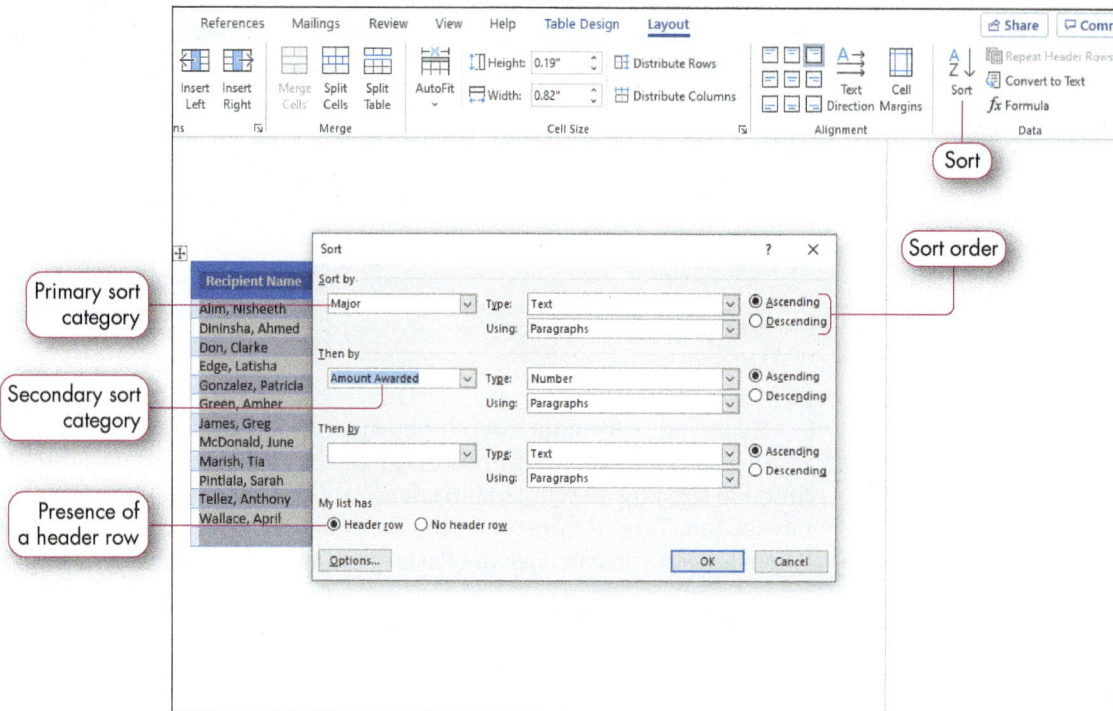

FIGURE 3.13 Sort a Table

> **TIP: INCLUDE A RECURRING TABLE HEADER**
> A table is typically composed of a header row followed by several rows of data. If a table extends beyond one page, the header row will not show on the second page. To remedy that situation, you can cause one or more rows of headings to repeat at the top of every page on which a table extends. Select the header row(s) and click Repeat Header Rows in the Data group on the Table Layout tab.

Enhance Table Data

You include data in a table to organize it in a way that makes it easy for a reader to comprehend. Using table styles and table formulas, you have learned to configure a table so it is attractive and so that it provides any necessary summary information. To further enhance table data, you can select custom shading and borders. Certain writing styles require the use of captions to identify tables included in reports; you will also learn to work with captions in this section.

STEP 3 ## Include Borders and Shading

Enhancing a table with custom borders and shading is possible when you use Word's Border tools. A border is a line style you can apply to individual cells, to an entire table, or to individual areas within a table. You can design your own border, selecting a pen color, line style, and line weight, or you can select from a gallery of predesigned borders that coordinate with existing table styles. When a table is inserted, it is automatically formatted in Table Grid style, with all cells bordered with a ½ pt single line border.

Word makes use of ***Border Painter***, a tool that enables you to apply border settings you have identified (or a border style selected from the Borders gallery) to one or more table borders. Using Border Painter, you can apply preselected borders by "brushing" them on a table border with the pointer. Figure 3.14 shows various border selections that are available on the Table Design tab when a table is selected.

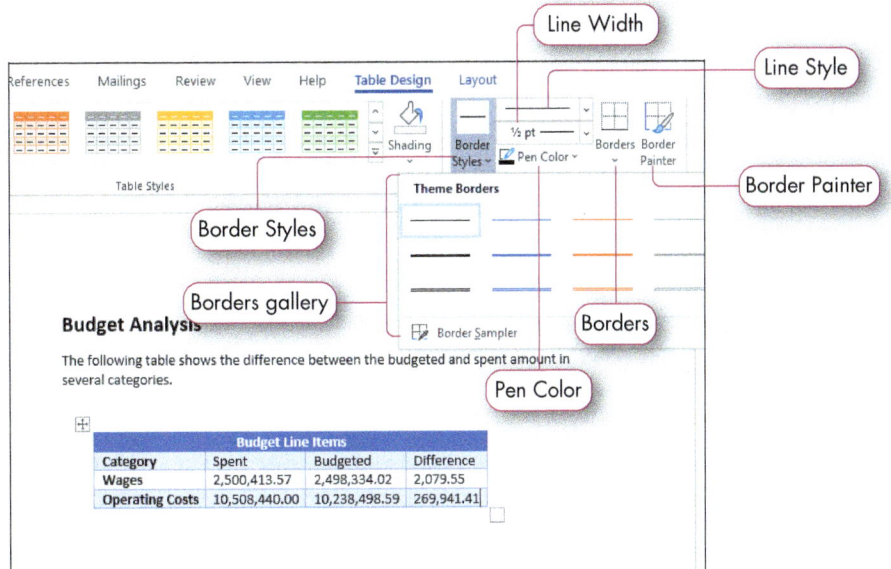

FIGURE 3.14 Work with Borders

In most cases, using the Borders and Shading dialog box is the simplest approach to changing borders and shading within a table. Options include border style, color, line width, and shading (background) color. Select cells to modify, or click the Table move handle to select an entire table. Click the Borders arrow in the Borders group on the Table Design tab and select Borders and Shading to display the dialog box shown in Figure 3.15. Choose from options to add, remove, or modify table and cell borders. In addition, you can select shading when you click the Shading tab in the dialog box.

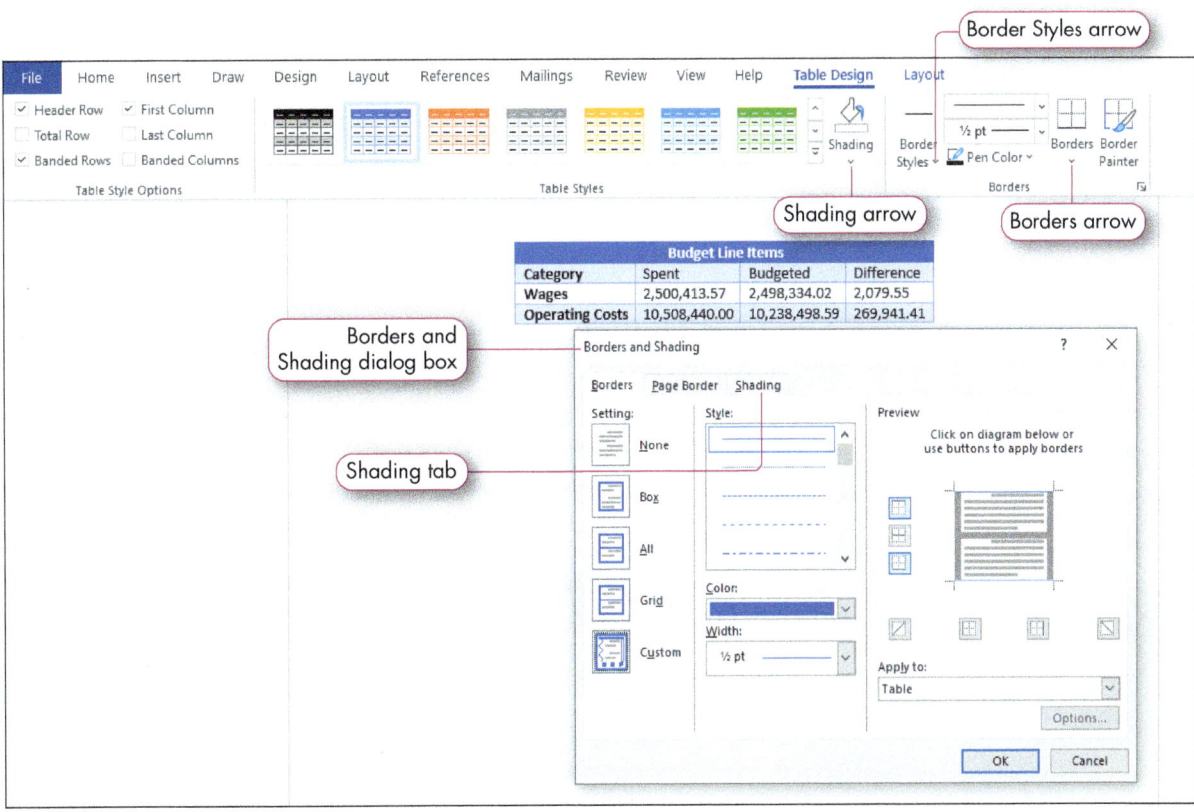

FIGURE 3.15 Use Borders and Shading

For more specificity than what might be found in the Borders and Shading dialog box, you can design a custom border. You can create a custom border by selecting a pen color, line style, and line width, and then apply it to table borders, or you can select from a gallery of predesigned border styles. You should be aware that if you change the document theme later, the border style and color choice will change to match the theme. Regardless of whether you are applying a custom border or a predesigned style, you can select the borders to apply the selection to when you click the Borders arrow (refer to Figure 3.15) and select a type (Outside Borders, Right Border, Left Border, etc.).

HOW TO

Design and apply custom borders:

1. Choose a pen color, line style, and line width (refer to Figure 3.14). The pointer displays as a pen. Alternatively, click Border Styles and select a border style. Each border style combines border width, color, and size.
2. Click the Borders arrow (refer to Figure 3.15) and select a border to apply the border selections to. Alternatively, drag the insertion pointer across a border to apply the selected border design.
3. Click Border Painter to toggle off the border application or press Esc.

As shown in Figure 3.15, the Table Design tab also includes options for selecting shading. Shading applies color or a pattern to the background of a cell or group of cells. You can apply shading to a header row to emphasize it, setting it apart from the rows beneath. Apply shading to selected areas by choosing from options on the Table Design tab. The Shading option provides various color selections, whereas the Borders option enables you to open the Borders and Shading dialog box, from which you click the Shading tab for shading choices.

> **TIP: USE BORDER SAMPLER**
> After applying a custom border or border style to one or more borders in a table, you can copy the selection to other table borders. You can accomplish this task using Border Sampler. Click the Border Styles arrow and select Border Sampler. The pointer becomes an eyedropper tool; click a table border that you want to copy. The pointer automatically switches to the Border Painter tool, as indicated by the ink pen designation or a paintbrush. (On a Mac, you can brush another border to apply the border selection.)

Convert Text to a Table and Convert a Table to Text

Suppose you are working with a list of items organized into two areas, with each item separated from the next by a comma, tab, or a paragraph marker. For example, you develop a list of items in a sale along with each respective price, with the items and prices separated by a tab. You know that if the areas, or columns, were organized as a table, you could apply a table style, sort rows, and even use formulas to summarize numeric information. In that case, you can convert text to a table. Having selected text to be converted, click table in the Tables group on the Insert tab. Click Convert Text to Table and select options from the Convert Text to Table dialog box shown in Figure 3.16. Click OK.

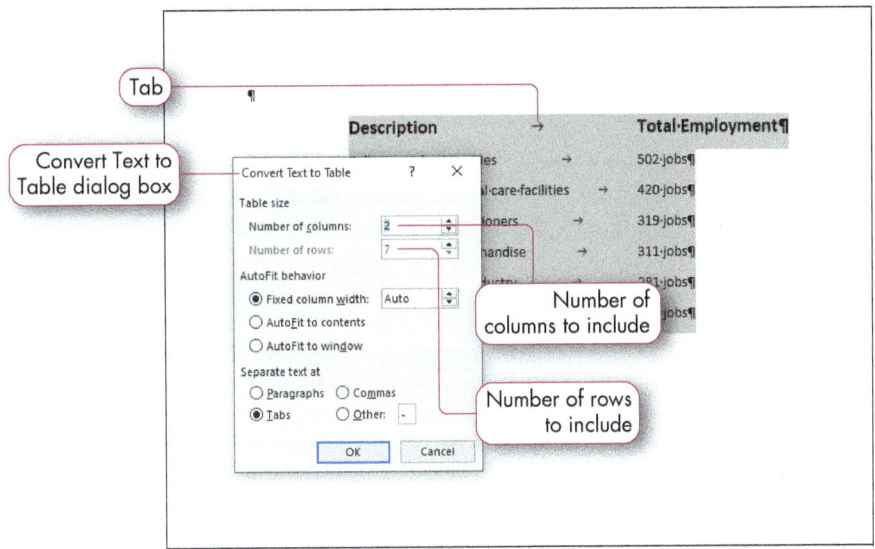

FIGURE 3.16 Convert Text to a Table

Conversely, you might decide to convert table text to plain text, removing special table features, and then organizing columns into simple tabbed columns. Click anywhere in the table and click Convert to Text in the Data group on the Table Layout tab. Indicate how table text is to be divided in the Convert Table to Text dialog box shown in Figure 3.17. Click OK.

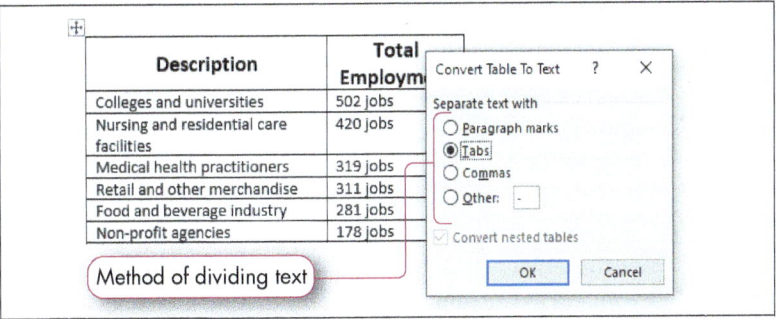

FIGURE 3.17 Convert a Table to Text

Include a Table Caption

A *caption*, such as *Table 1*, is a numbered item of text that identifies a table, figure, or other object in a Word document. A particular writing style may be required for class papers or published works. This style will prescribe a standard set of guidelines, including the usage of captions. A caption is often used to cite a table that came from a research source. A caption typically includes a label, such as the word *Figure* or *Table*, followed by a sequential number that can be automatically updated with the addition of new tables or captioned objects.

HOW TO

Include a caption:

1. Click a cell in a table. Click the References tab and select Insert Caption in the Captions group. The Caption dialog box displays, as shown in Figure 3.18.
2. Confirm that the caption label should be Table, or click the Label arrow and change the label to Figure or Equation. Depending on the wording of the caption, you might find that a label is unnecessary or even redundant. In that case, select the check box to exclude the label from the caption.
3. Type the caption in the Caption box. Indicate whether the caption should be above or below the table by clicking the Position arrow and making a selection.
4. Click Numbering to select a numbering style and click OK.

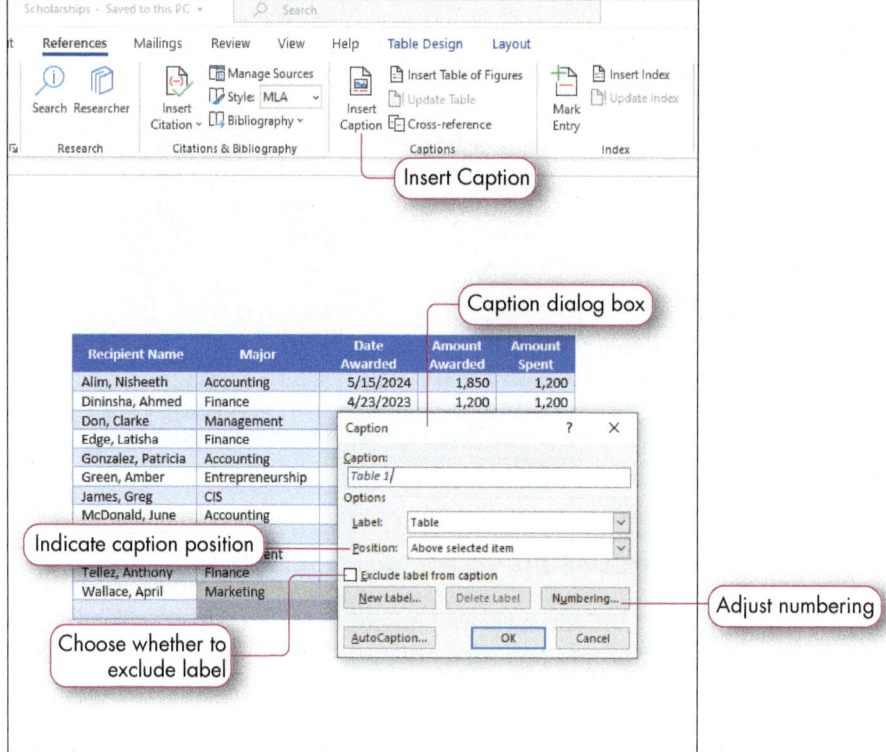

FIGURE 3.18 Insert a Caption

When a caption is created, it is formatted in Caption style. You can use the Styles pane to modify the Caption style applied to all captions in the document. Using the Styles gallery on the Home tab, you can identify and modify the caption style.

As you continue to add captions to tables in a document, each caption is shown in sequence. For example, if the first caption is Table 1, then the second caption you add will automatically be labeled Table 2. If you insert a table between existing tables, the caption you add to the table will automatically be shown in sequence, with captions on following tables updated accordingly. However, if you delete a table from a document, remaining captions are not automatically renumbered. In that case, you must manually update the captions. To update all captions in a document, select all document text, right-click anywhere in the selection, and then select Update Field. Or to update only one caption, right-click the caption number, and then click Update Field.

Critical Thinking

4. Differentiate between the use of a function and a formula in a table. When would one be preferable to another? *pp. 256–258*

5. Provide an explanation of why a table formula that sums row data does not include data from a newly added row. Explain what can be done to cause the sum to be correct. *p. 258*

6. In a report, you provide a tabbed list of club expenses so that club members can see the total spent each month. However, you are considering converting that list to a table. Provide at least one major advantage to summarizing those expenses in a table rather than a tabbed list. *p. 256*

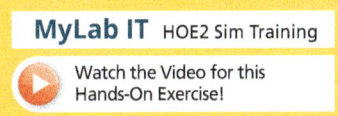

Hands-On Exercises

Skills covered: Use a
Formula • Use a Function • Sort
Data in a Table • Include Borders
and Shading • Include a Table
Caption

2 Advanced Table Features

As you continue to work with the Key Findings section of the executive summary, you modify the two
tables you previously created. The first table, showing major areas in which the university contributed to
the economy, is modified to include a total row and to indicate the percentage represented by each sector.
You also explore Word's Borders gallery and design options as you customize the tables to reflect the
color scheme of the university. Adding a caption to each table serves to identify the table and will be useful
for your assistant when he prepares a Table of Figures later. You also apply a sort order to each table to
organize each in a more understandable manner.

STEP 1 ### USE A FORMULA AND USE A FUNCTION

Table 1 includes a numeric column showing Oakley University's economic impact in several sectors. You add a row
showing the total for all of the sectors. You also insert a column showing the percentage of the total represented by
each sector's value. Refer to Figure 3.19 as you complete Step 1.

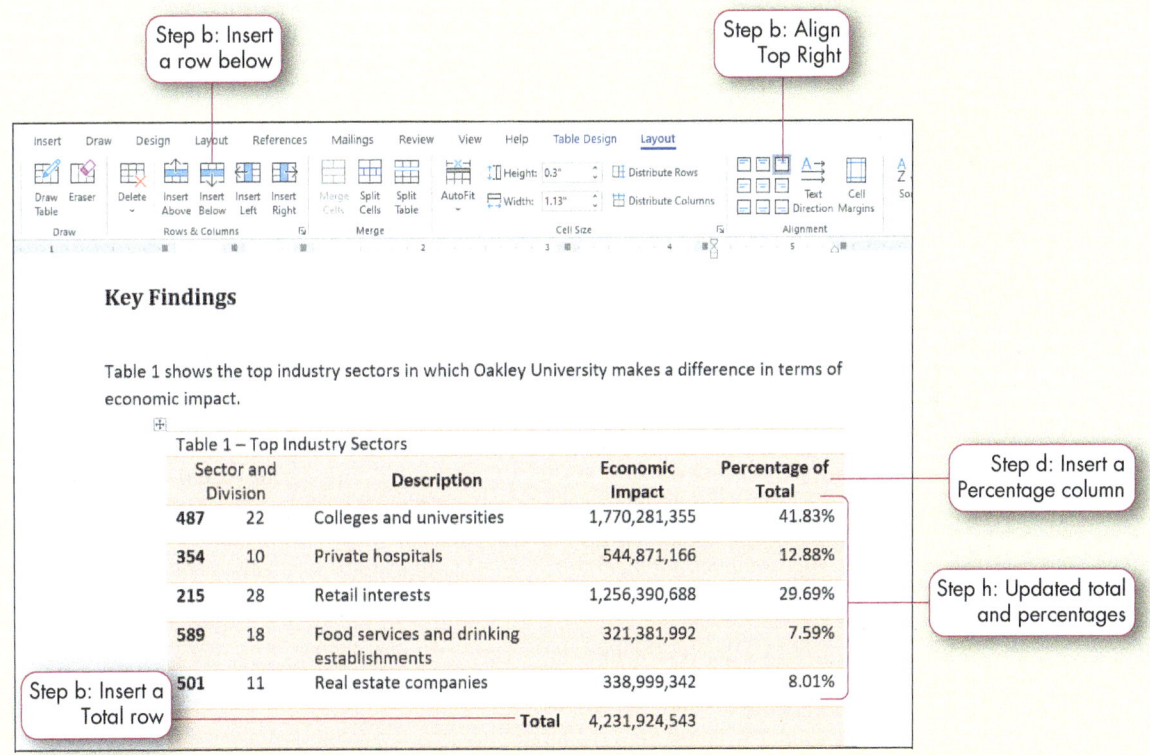

FIGURE 3.19 Work with Table Formulas

a. Open *w03h1Oakley_LastFirst* if you closed it after Hands-On Exercise 1 and save it as
w03h2Oakley_LastFirst, changing h1 to h2.

b. Scroll to the last page. Click in the **last row** of Table 1. Click **Insert Below** in the Rows
& Columns group on the Table Layout tab. Click in the **third cell** of the new row (the
Description column), type **Total**, and then apply **bold** formatting to the word *Total*.
With the word still selected, click **Align Top Right** in the Alignment group on the Table
Layout tab.

You add a row in which to place a total economic impact figure.

c. Click in the **cell** immediately below the last economic impact number. Click **Formula** in the Data group. The suggested function, =SUM(ABOVE) is correct. Click the **Number format arrow** and select **#,##0**. Click **OK**.

The total economic impact is 4,241,924,543.

> **TROUBLESHOOTING:** If the total is incorrect, you most likely typed a number incorrectly in the column above. Refer to Figure 3.9 in the previous Hands-On Exercise for the correct numbers. Make any necessary corrections in Table 1. The total will not show the correct number until you complete Step h to update the field.

d. Click **Insert Right** in the Rows & Columns group. Click the **last cell** in the second row and type **Percentage of Total**.

Text will wrap in the cell. You added a new column that will show the percentage each sector's value represents of the total economic impact.

e. Click in the **last cell** of the third row (in the *Colleges and universities* row). Click **Formula** in the Data group. Remove any formula or function that may be presented and type **=D3/D8*100**. (Do not type a period.) Click the **Number format arrow**, scroll through the options, and then select **0.00%**. Click **OK**.

You create a formula to obtain the result. The formula divides the value in the cell to the left (cell D3) by the total value of economic impact in the last row of the table (cell D8). The result is multiplied by 100 to convert it to a percentage. The format you chose displays the result with a percent sign and two places to the right of the decimal.

The percentage represented by Colleges and universities is 41.73%.

> **TROUBLESHOOTING:** If an error message displays in the cell instead of a percentage, or if the percentage is incorrect, click Undo and repeat Step e.

f. Click in the **last cell** of the *Private hospitals* row. Click **Formula** in the Data group. Remove any formula or function that may be presented and type **=D4/D8*100**. (Do not type a period.) Click **OK**.

The number format remains at 0.00%, so there is no need to change it. The resulting value is 12.84%.

g. Click in the **last cell** of the *Retail interests* row and repeat Step f, changing *D4* in the formula to **D5** (because you are working with a value on the fifth row). Create a formula for *Food services and drinking establishments* and *Real estate companies,* adjusting the row reference in each formula. Do not enter a formula in the last cell on the last row.

> **TROUBLESHOOTING:** If text indicating a syntax error displays in the cell instead of a percentage, you made a typo in the formula. Click Formula in the Data group on the Table Layout tab and check the formula, correcting it as necessary.

h. Change the number in *Economic Impact* for *Real estate companies* in the second to last row in the table from *348,999,342* to **338,999,342**. Update formulas that are affected by the change as follows:

- Right-click (on a Mac, control+click) the total in the next row, *4,241,924,543,* and click **Update Field** to update the total.
- Right-click the percentage of total for Real estate companies in the last column of the second to last row. Click **Update Field**.
- Right-click each remaining percentage figure in the last column, updating each field. Refer to Figure 3.19 to check numbers in the table.

i. Save the document.

SORT DATA IN A TABLE

You will sort Table 1 so that the dollar amounts are arranged in descending order. That way, it is very clear in which sectors the university had the most impact. You will also sort Table 2 in alphabetical order by Source. The resulting table is well organized. Refer to Figure 3.20 as you complete Step 2.

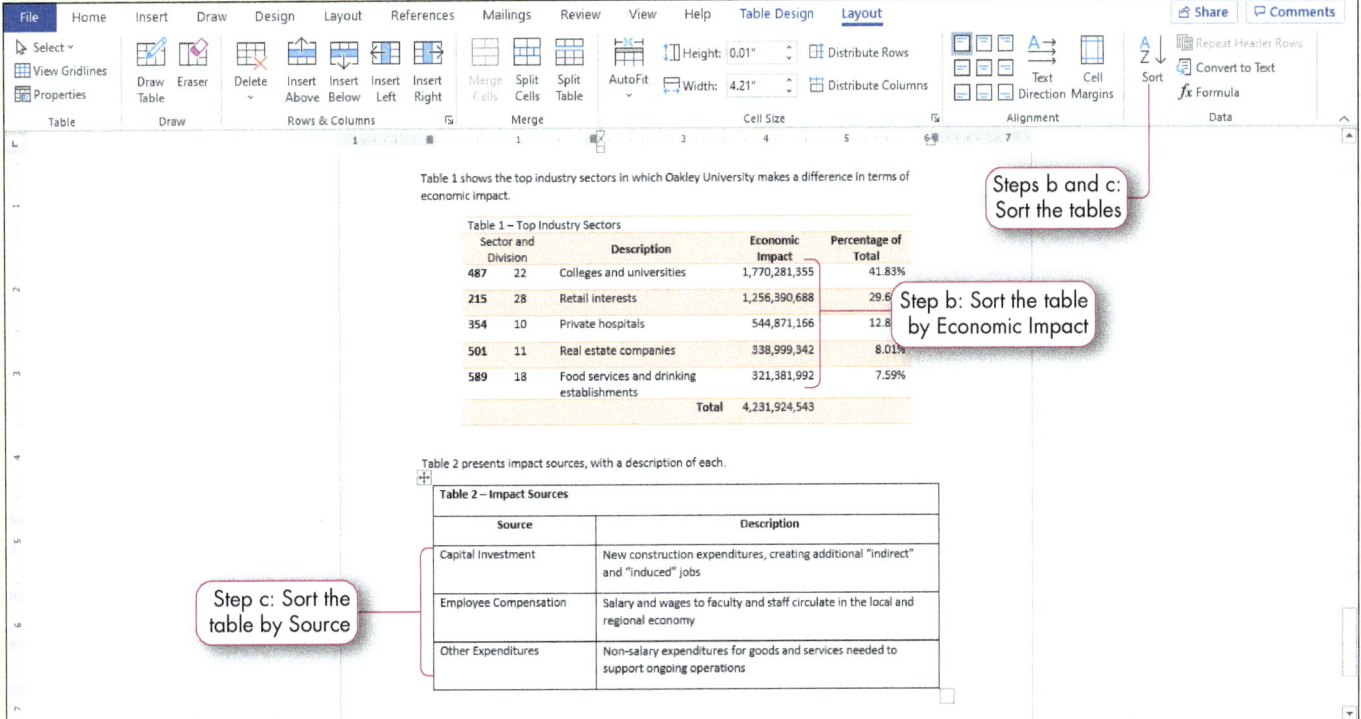

FIGURE 3.20 Sorted Tables

a. Show nonprinting characters if they are not already displayed. Position the pointer just outside the left edge of the third row of Table 1 (beginning with 487). The pointer should be a right-directed white arrow ⬀. Select the third through the seventh row. Do not include the final total row.

> **TROUBLESHOOTING:** If only data in the first column is selected instead of entire rows, you dragged inside the table instead of outside the left edge of a row. Deselect the data and repeat Step a.

The table rows that are to be sorted are selected. You do not want to include the first two rows or the final total row in the sort because they do not contain individual values to sort.

b. Click **Sort** in the Data group on the Table Layout tab. Click the **Sort by arrow** and select **Column 4**. Click **Descending**. Click **OK**.

The five rows containing a sector name (Colleges and universities, Retail interests, etc.) are sorted in descending order by the value in the fourth column (Economic Impact). It is clear that the sector most affected is Colleges and universities.

c. Position the pointer just outside the left edge of the third row of Table 2. Drag to select the remaining rows. Click **Sort** in the Data group. Click the **Sort by arrow** and select **Column 1**. Click **Ascending** and click **OK**.

The three rows containing a source (Capital Investment, etc.) are sorted in ascending order alphabetically.

d. Save the document.

You expect to add more tables later but decide to format Tables 1 and 2 so they are more attractive and color-coordinated. You explore border and shading options, learning to paint borders and considering border selections from the Borders gallery. Because you expect to include numerous figures throughout the report, you insert captions to identify those tables. Refer to Figures 3.21 and 3.22 as you complete Step 3.

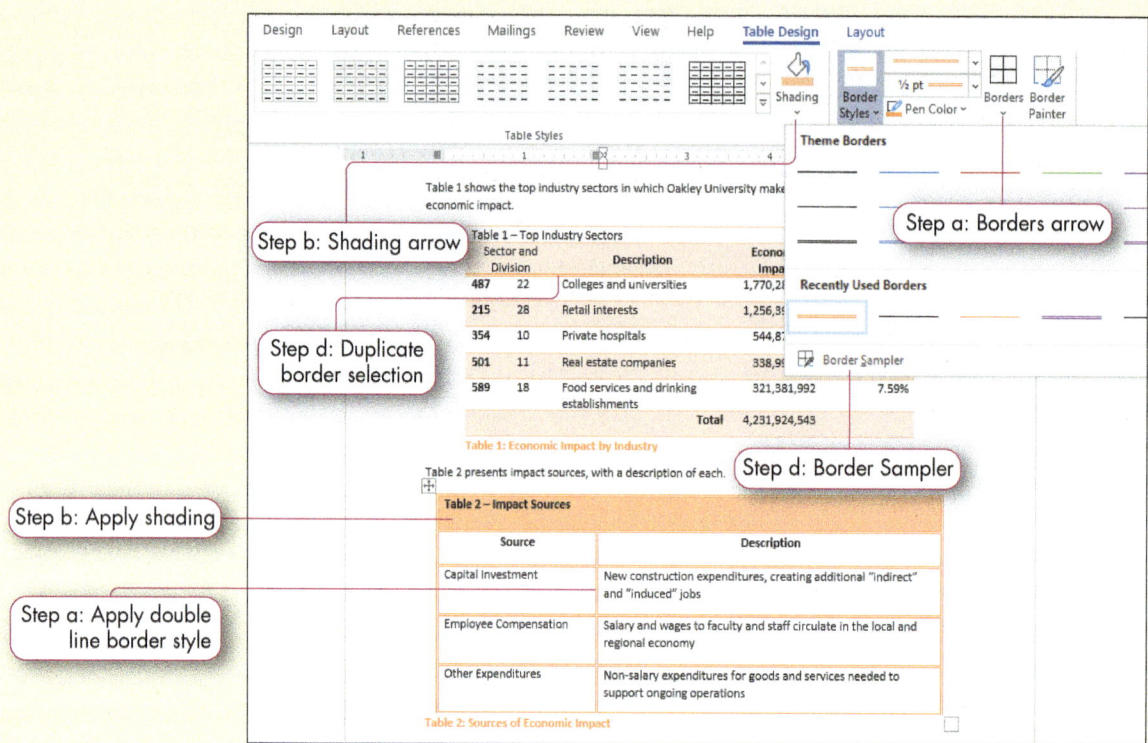

FIGURE 3.21 Include Borders and Shading

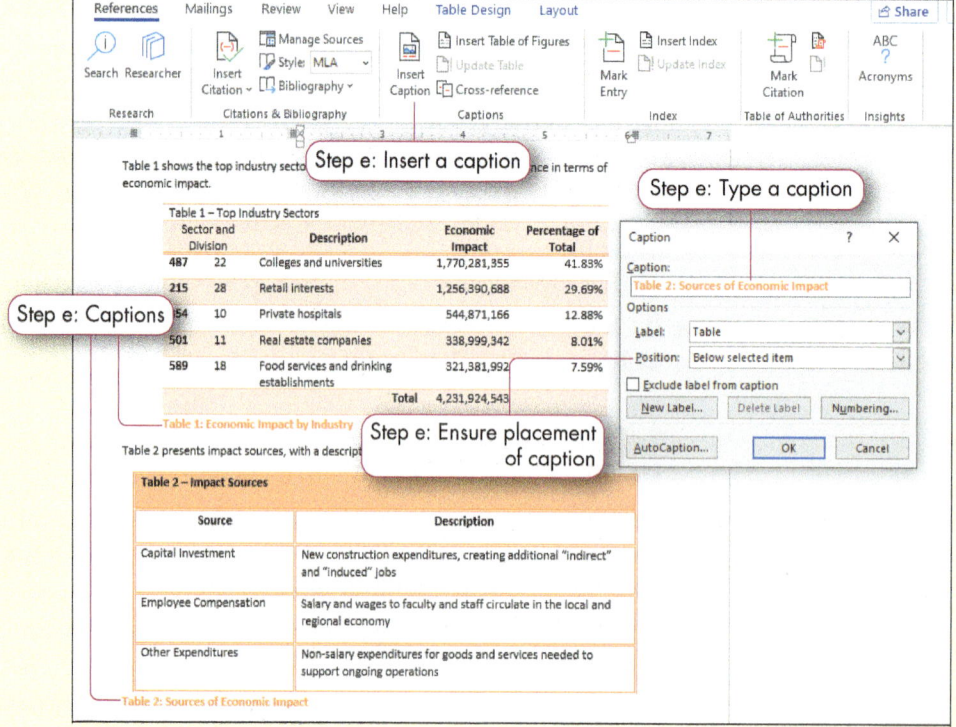

FIGURE 3.22 Include Captions

a. Click the **Table move handle** to select Table 2. Click the **Table Design tab** and click **Border Styles** in the Borders group. Select **Double solid lines, ½ pt, Accent 6** (row 3, column 7 under Theme Borders). Click the **Borders arrow** in the Borders group and select **All Borders**.

> **TROUBLESHOOTING:** If you do not see the Table move handle, point to or click any cell in the table and move to the top-left corner of the table to click the Table move handle (or click the Table Layout tab, click Select in the Table group, and then click Select Table).

b. Select **row 1** in Table 2. Click the **Shading arrow** in the Table Styles group on the Table Design tab and select **Orange, Accent 6, Lighter 40%** (row 4, column 10).

> **MAC TROUBLESHOOTING:** This particular orange shade may not be available, so select another that is similar.

c. Select the **first two rows** in Table 2. Click the **Table Layout tab** and increase the row height in the Cell Size group to **0.4"**.

The first two rows in Table 2 are resized slightly.

d. Use Border Sampler to duplicate a border selection as follows:

- Click the **Table Design tab**. Click the **Border Styles arrow** in the Borders group and select **Border Sampler**.
- Click the horizontal border dividing row 1 from row 2 in Table 2 to sample the border.
- Drag the horizontal border in Table 1 that separates row 2 (containing column headings) from the first record (487) to paint the double-line border.
- Press **Esc** to toggle off the tool.

Border Sampler was used to duplicate a border from one location to another.

e. Add a caption to each table as follows:

- Click anywhere in **Table 1**. Click the **References tab**.
- Click **Insert Caption** in the Captions group. With the insertion point immediately after the phrase *Table 1* in the Caption box, type **:** and press **Spacebar**. Type **Economic Impact by Industry**. (Do not type the period.)
- Ensure that *Below selected item* is shown as the caption position. Click **OK**.
- Click the **Home tab** and click **Increase Indent** in the Paragraph group.
- Click anywhere in **Table 2** and insert a caption below the selected item that reads **Table 2: Sources of Economic Impact**. (Do not type the period.)

f. Click the **Home tab**. Click the **Dialog Box Launcher** in the Styles group. Scroll down and point to **Caption** in the Styles pane. Click the **Caption arrow** and select **Modify**. Change the font size to **11 pt** and the font color to **Orange, Accent 6**. Click **OK**. Close the Styles pane.

The Caption style was modified to include orange font so the caption text coordinates with the table color scheme.

g. Check the document for spelling errors, addressing any that might be identified. Ignore any refinement concerns.

h. Save and close the document. You will submit this file to your instructor at the end of the last Hands-On Exercise.

Mail Merge

At some point in your personal or professional life, you may want to send the same document to a number of different people. The document might be an invitation, a letter, or a memo. For the most part, document text will be the same regardless of how many people receive it. However, certain parts of the document may contain personalized information, such as the inside address included in a letter. Consider the task of conducting a job search. You have created a cover letter and want to personalize the letter with the recipient's name and address, include the recipient's name in the salutation, and perhaps reference the company name in the body of the cover letter for all companies to which you are sending your résumé and cover letter. In addition, you want to generate envelopes with each recipient's address. Word's Mail Merge feature enables you to easily generate those types of personalization within one common document. *Mail merge* is a process that combines content from a main document and a data source with the option of creating a new document. A data source is a list of variable data to include in the document, effectively personalizing it, such as recipient name and address.

You can use mail merge to create a set of form letters, personalizing or modifying each one for the recipient. A *form letter* is a document that is often mass produced and sent to multiple recipients. The small amount of personal information included in the form letter—perhaps the salutation or the recipient's address—can be inserted during the mail merge procedure.

Mail merge may also be used to send personalized email messages to multiple recipients. Unlike sending email to a group of recipients or listing recipients as blind carbon copies, creating a mail-merged email makes it appear as if each recipient is the sole addressee. You can also use mail merge to send an email in which the message is personalized for each recipient, referring to the recipient by name within the body of the message.

In this section, you will learn to use Mail Merge to create a main document and select a recipient list. You will then combine, or merge, the main document and data source to produce a document that is personalized for each recipient.

Create a Mail Merge Document

The mail merge process begins with a *main document* that contains wording that remains the same for all recipients. In the case of the cover letter used in your job search, the main document would include paragraphs that are intended for all recipients to read— perhaps those that describe your qualifications and professional goals. Placeholders are also included in the main document. They are intended to contain variable data, which might include a recipient's address or a salutation directed to a particular person. During the mail merge process, a *data source* that contains variable data is combined with the main document to produce personalized documents. You can merge a data source of employer names and mailing addresses with a main document to produce a personalized letter for each potential employer. Mail merge also enables you to print labels or envelopes, obtaining addresses from a data source.

If creating a form letter in which certain variable data will be inserted, you can begin with the main document, or letter, open. If you have not yet created the form letter, you will begin with a blank document. Similarly, you would begin with a blank document when creating envelopes or labels.

The main document used in a mail merge process can be a new or existing document. In creating a document to be merged with a data source, you can select from ribbon options, or you can work with the Mail Merge Wizard, which is a guided step-by-step approach. In either case, begin with a main document (or a blank document) and select from options on the Mailings tab.

Select or Create a Recipient List

The data source that is merged with the main document is often referred to as a recipient list. It provides variable data to include in the document, such as recipient name, address, phone number, and company information. Each item of information is referred to as a *field*. For example, the data source might include a last name field, a first name field, a street address field, and so on. A group of fields for a person or thing, presented as a row in the data source, is called a *record*. Figure 3.23 illustrates a sample data source. Note that each record in the data source represents a person, with each record subdivided into fields. The data source shown in Figure 3.23 is an Access database table.

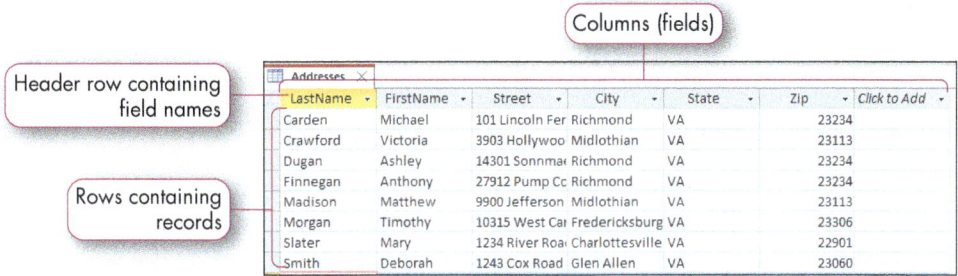

FIGURE 3.23 Mail Merge Data Source

A data source can be obtained from:

- A Word document that contains records stored in a table, where each row after the first is a record and the top row contains headings (field names)
- An Access database table or query
- An Excel worksheet, where each row after the first contains records and the top row shows headings (field names)
- A group of Outlook contacts
- A list that you create during the mail merge process
- Any database to which you can connect

The first row in the data source is called the *header row* and identifies the fields in the remaining rows. Each row beneath the header row contains a record, and every record contains the same fields in the same order—for example, Title, FirstName, LastName, and so on.

Typical data sources are those you might have saved in a Word table, Excel worksheet, or Access database table. The existing list can also be any database that you can connect to. If you do not have a preexisting list to use as a data source, you can create one during the Word mail merge process that is saved as a Microsoft Office Address List with a file extension of .mdb (mailing list database).

HOW TO

Create a new data source (not an existing list):

1. Click Select Recipients in the Start Mail Merge group on the Mailings tab.
2. Select Type a New List. The New Address List dialog box displays with the most commonly used fields for a mail merge.
3. Type data or click Customize Columns to add, delete, or rename the fields to meet your needs.

STEP 1 ## Use a Data Source

An Excel worksheet organizes data in columns and rows, so it is a natural choice as a data source listing variable data, such as addresses. Similar to entering data in a Word table, you can learn to enter data in an Excel worksheet, designing columns and rows of data so that a lengthy address list can be maintained. With many columns and rows available in a single worksheet, Excel can store a huge number of records, making them available as you create a mail merge document. Figure 3.24 shows an Excel worksheet that can be used as a data source. Note the header row, with records beneath.

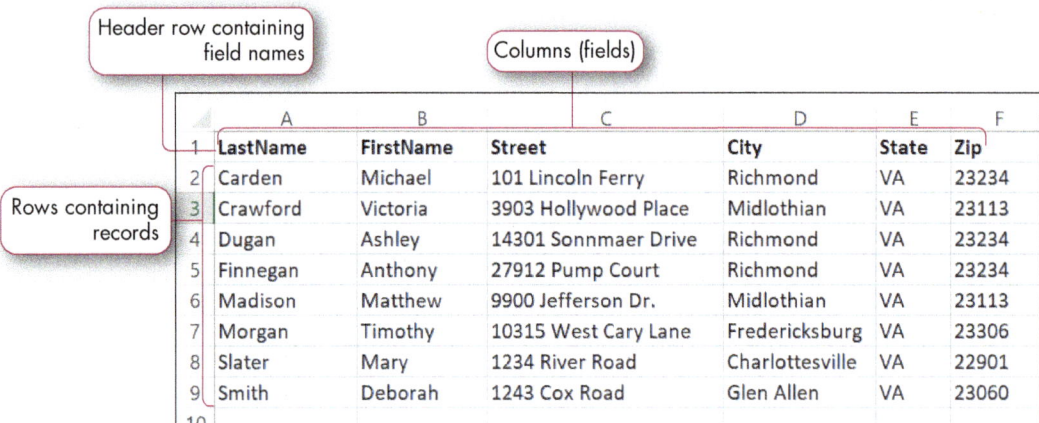

FIGURE 3.24 Excel Worksheet

As a database program, Microsoft Access is designed to manage large amounts of data. An Access database typically contains one or more tables; each table is a collection of related records that contains fields of information. Access enables you to query a table, which is the process of filtering records to show only those that meet certain search criteria. For example, you might want to send a personalized letter or email to employees who work in the Accounting department. Using Access, you can create a query showing only those records of employees in the Accounting department, and then use that query as a data source for a mail merge. An Access database table is well suited for use as a mail merge data source, due to its datasheet design (approximating an Excel worksheet). Figure 3.23 shows a sample Access database table that could be used as a data source.

Because a Word table is organized in rows and columns, it is also ideal for use as a data source in a mail merge. The first row in the Word table should include descriptive headers, with each subsequent row including a record from which data can be extracted during a mail merge process. The document used in a mail merge must contain a single table.

> **TIP: USING A DATABASE OTHER THAN ACCESS AS A DATA SOURCE**
> To access a data source other than a Word table, an Access database table, an Excel worksheet, or a file that you create during a mail merge process, click Mailings, Select Recipients, Use an Existing List, and then select New Source to open the Data Connection Wizard. Choose the type of data source you want to use and then follow through remaining steps of the wizard.

To merge a main document with an existing data source, click Select Recipients in the Start Mail Merge group on the Mailings tab. Click Use an Existing List (see Figure 3.25). Navigate to the Excel, Access, or Word data source and double-click the file.

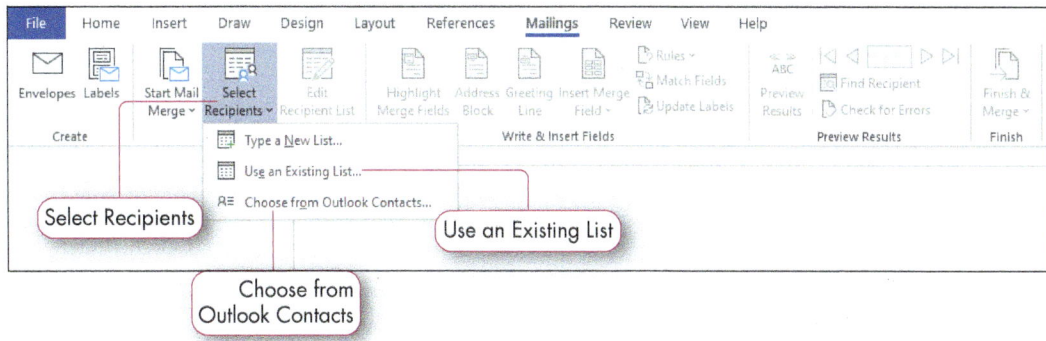

FIGURE 3.25 Select an Existing List

You can also use a list of Outlook contacts as a data source, which is especially helpful when you have a bulk mailing to send to your contacts. If you have an Outlook account, you can access basic information included with your contacts, including name, email address, mailing address, and phone number. Select Choose from Outlook Contacts in the Start Mail Merge group on the Mailings tab when you begin the process of selecting recipients (refer to Figure 3.25).

STEP 2 ❯ **Edit a Data Source**

Before merging a data source with the main document, you can rearrange records in the data source so that output from a mail merge is arranged accordingly. For example, you can sort the data source in alphabetical order by last name so that letters are arranged alphabetically or so that mailing labels print in order by last name. Or perhaps data in the data source should be updated, as might be the case if a recipient's address has changed. In addition, you could consider filtering a data source to limit the mail merge output based on criteria. You might want to print letters to send to clients in a specific region or state. Select Edit Recipient List on the Mailings tab and work with the dialog box shown in Figure 3.26 to edit, sort, filter, or otherwise modify the data source before including its contents in the main document during the mail merge process.

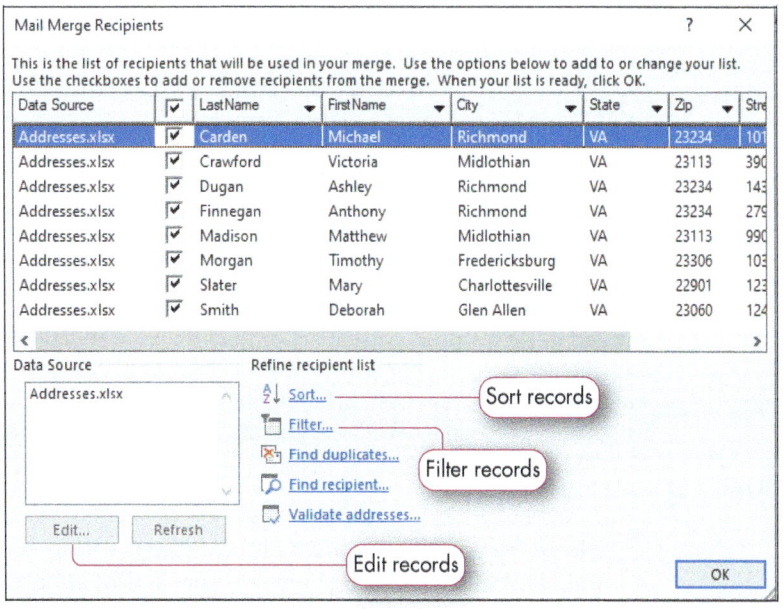

FIGURE 3.26 Edit, Sort, and Filter a Data Source

The same data source can be used to create multiple sets of form documents. You could, for instance, create a marketing campaign in which you send an initial letter to the entire list, and then send follow-up letters at periodic intervals to the same mailing list. Alternatively, you could filter the original mailing list to include only a subset of names, such as individuals who responded to the initial letter.

Complete a Mail Merge

After a data source has been identified and prepared for merging with a main document, the mail merge process is near completion. Items of text in the main document that are considered variable, such as an address block or a greeting, must be copied from the data source and inserted so that the resulting document is personalized to the recipient or purpose. Upon completion of the mail merge process, a merged document contains several copies, each uniquely prepared with areas of variable data. For example, the result of a mail merge used in preparation of job search material could be a personalized letter to each potential employer.

STEP 3 ▶ Insert Merge Fields

The goal of a mail merge is often to produce a document or email that is personalized and sent to multiple recipients. As the document is prepared, you will indicate locations of variable data, such as a mailing address or a personalized greeting. Such areas of information are called *merge fields*. When you write a letter or create an email in preparation for a mail merge, you will insert one or more merge fields in the main document in the location(s) of variable data. As shown in Figure 3.27, the Write & Insert Fields group on the Mailings tab enables you to select Address Block, Greeting Line, or other items that can be included as a placeholder in the main document. The data source must contain fields that are recognizably named. For example, a field containing last names is given a field name that is likely to be recognized as containing a person's last name, such as LastName. Because a merge field corresponds with a field in the data source, matching the two fields guarantees that the right data will be inserted into the main document when you complete the merge.

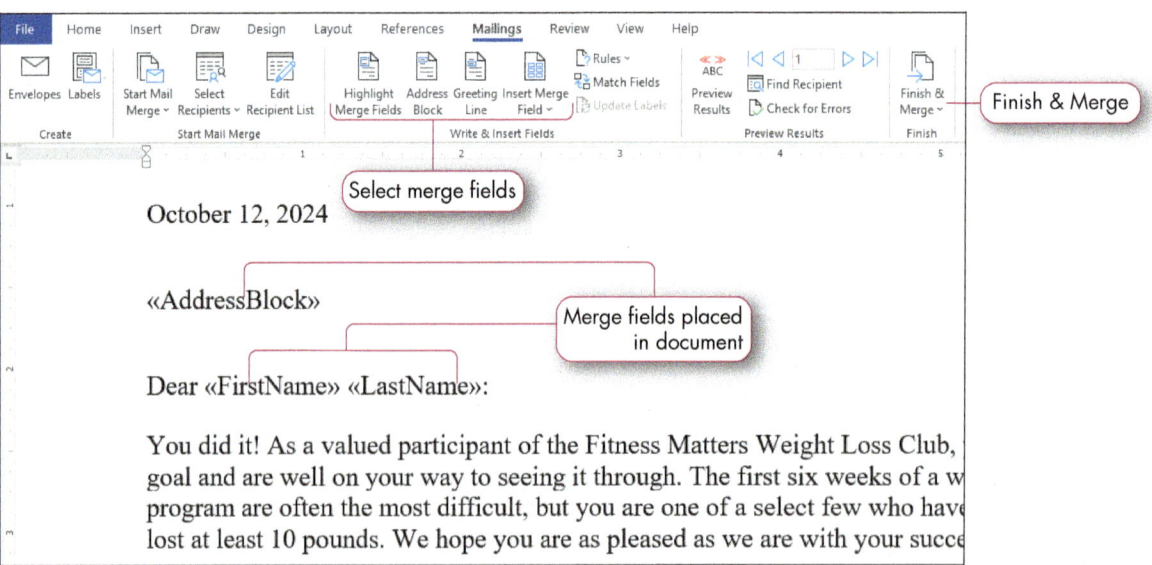

FIGURE 3.27 Insert Merge Fields

Merge fields display in the main document within double angle brackets, for example <<AddressBlock>>, <<FirstName>>, or <<Donation>>. Those entries are not typed explicitly but are entered automatically when you select Insert Merge Field in the Write & Insert Fields group on the Mailings tab and then identify a field to include (refer to

Figure 3.27) or when you choose from selected merge fields in the Write & Insert Fields group. As the document is merged with a data source, data from the data source will be placed in the position of the merge fields. Therefore, <<AddressBlock>> will not display in the merged document; instead a recipient's multi-line mailing address will be shown, followed by the same letter addressed to another recipient in the data source. Having inserted merge fields, you will preview the document to ensure correct placement and content.

TIP: CREATE MAILING LABELS AND ENVELOPES

Word's Mail Merge Wizard simplifies the process of creating mailing labels or adding addresses to envelopes. With a data source of addresses handy, click Start Mail Merge from the Mailings tab and select Labels or Envelopes. You can instead choose Step-by-Step Mail Merge Wizard from Start Mail Merge in the Start Mail Merge group for a guided step-by-step approach. Proceed through dialog boxes or wizard steps presented, depending upon how you began the process. You will browse for an existing list of recipient addresses or create a new list and also select label or envelope options, resulting in a list of formatted addresses to be printed on mailing labels or envelopes.

STEP 4 ▸ **Complete a Merge**

After you create the main document and identify the source data, you are ready to begin the merge process. The merge process examines each record in the data source, and when a match is found, it replaces the merge field in the main document with the information from the data source. A copy of the main document is created for each record in the data source, creating individualized documents.

Finish the merge by selecting that action from the Mailings tab (refer to Figure 3.27). You can then choose to edit individual documents, providing a preview of each page of the merged document, or you can choose to immediately print the merged items.

HOW TO

Use mail merge to send personalized email:

1. Ensure that you have an email program like Outlook or Gmail installed. Create a data source, possibly an Excel worksheet with a column that includes email addresses. You can also create a data source as you work through the mail merge steps.

2. Open a blank document in Word and type the body of the email message—the wording that should go to all recipients.

3. Click Start Mail Merge in the Start Mail Merge group on the Mailings tab and select E-mail Messages. Click Select Recipients and choose a data list or choose to create a new data source.

4. Click in the message area where a greeting should go and click Greeting Line in the Write & Insert Fields group. Adjust settings as needed in the dialog box and click OK.

5. Click Preview Results, Finish & Merge, and Send E-mail Messages. Ensure that the Email address column from the data source shows in the To box and type a Subject.

6. Choose All to send to all recipients in the data source and click OK.

Critical Thinking

7. Explain the importance of giving fields in a data source recognizable headings, such as LastName or Title. *p. 274*

8. Suppose you are running for political office and plan to send a mailing to potential voters asking for support. How could Word's Mail Merge feature help in that situation? *p. 270*

Hands-On Exercises

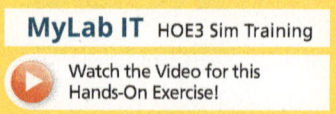
Skills covered: Select or Create a Recipient List • Edit a Data Source • Insert Merge Fields • Complete a Merge

3 Mail Merge

The executive summary is ready for you to send to members of the board of trustees. You merge a form letter with a data source of addresses, merging fields in the process to personalize each letter.

STEP 1 ▷ SELECT A RECIPIENT LIST

You select a recipient list, including the names and addresses of members of the board of trustees. Refer to Figure 3.28 as you complete Step 1.

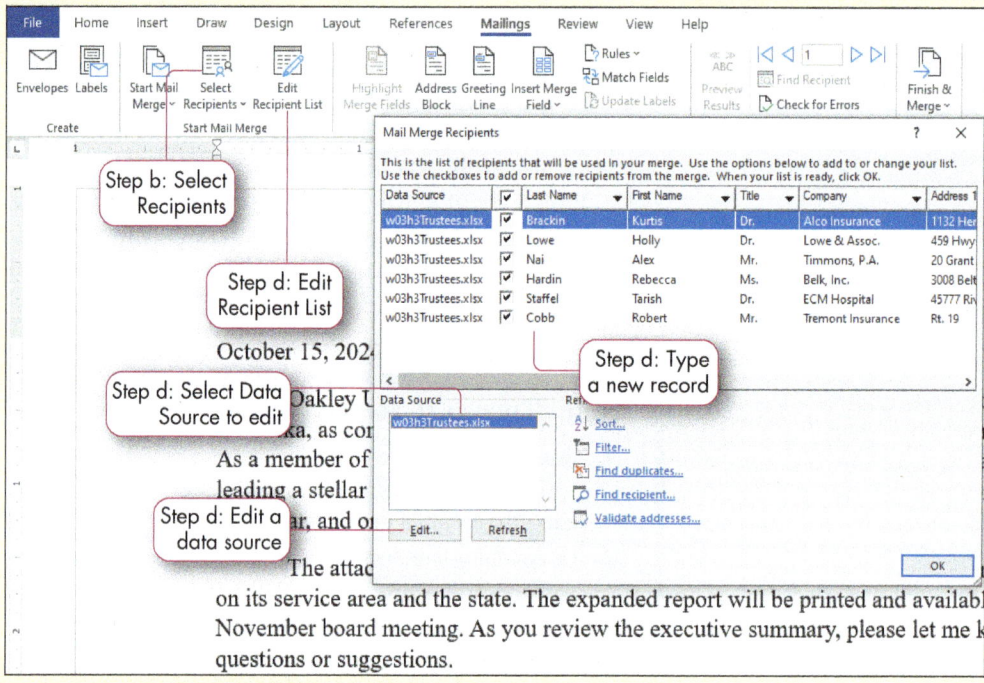

FIGURE 3.28 Select and Edit a Recipient List

---

a. Open *w03h3Letter* and save it as **w03h3Letter_LastFirst**.

b. Click the **Mailings tab** and click **Select Recipients** in the Start Mail Merge group.

c. Select **Use an Existing List**. Navigate to the location of your data files and double-click *w03h3Trustees.xlsx*. With **Sheet1$** selected, click **OK**.

d. Click **Edit Recipient List** in the Start Mail Merge group. Click **w03h3Trustees.xlsx** in the Data Source box and click **Edit**. Click **New Entry** and add the following record, leaving the Address 2 area blank.

Mr.	Robert	Cobb	Tremont Insurance	Rt. 19	Navarre	NE	68811

e. Click **OK**. Click **Yes**. Click **OK**.

You inadvertently left off one of the trustees, so you add him to the data source.

You sort the records alphabetically by city and then by recipient last name. Refer to Figure 3.29 as you complete Step 2.

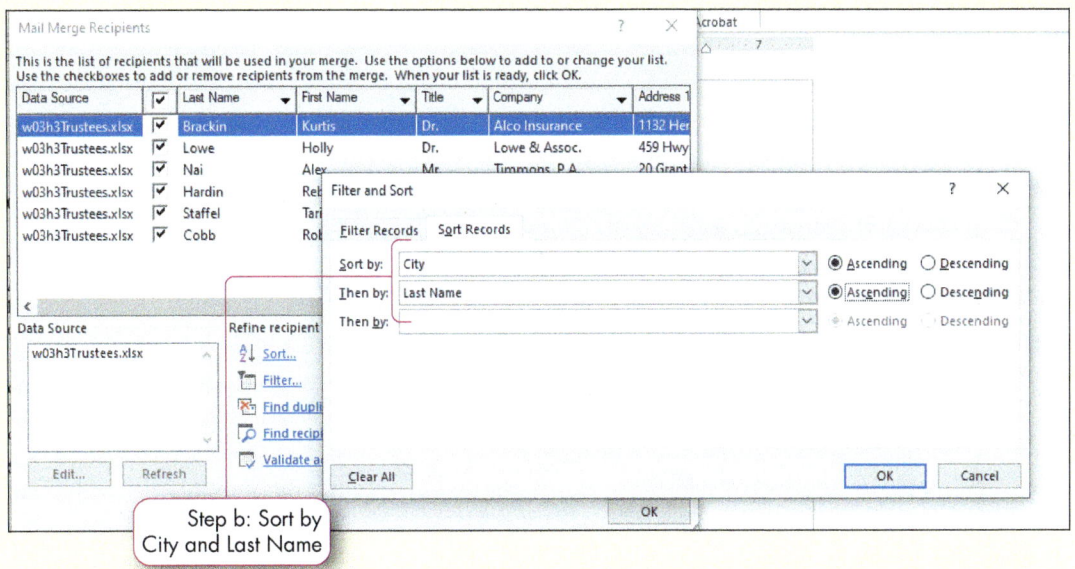

FIGURE 3.29 Sort a Recipient List

a. Click **Edit Recipient List** in the Start Mail Merge group. Click **Sort** in the *Refine recipient list* area of the Mail Merge Recipients dialog box.

You open the data source in order to sort it.

b. Click the **Sort by arrow**, scroll down, and then click **City**. Ensure that sort order is Ascending. Click the **Then by arrow** and click **Last Name**. Ensure that sort order is Ascending. Click **OK**.

c. Scroll to the right to confirm that records are sorted by City. Scroll back to the left and confirm that the two records with a city of Navarre (records 3 and 4) are also sorted by Last Name. Click **OK**.

Although the body of the letter will be the same for all recipients, you create merge fields to accommodate variable data, including each recipient's name and address. Refer to Figure 3.30 as you complete Step 3.

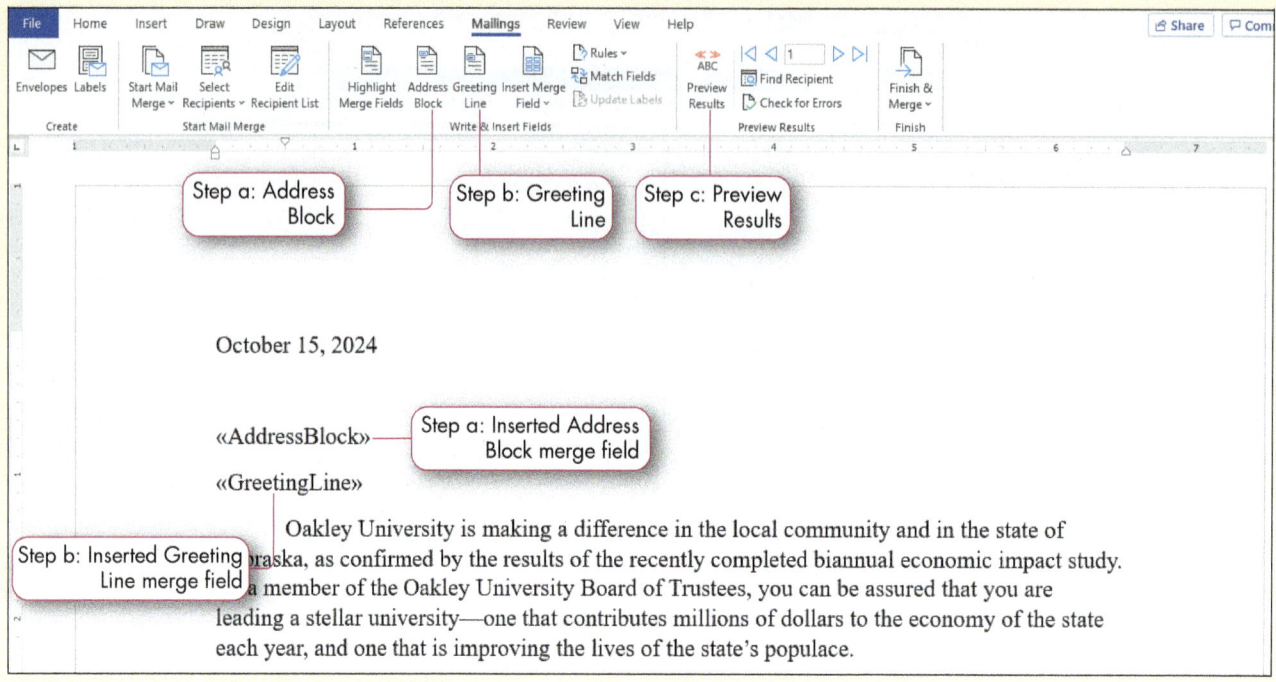

FIGURE 3.30 Insert Merge Fields

a. Click after *2024* in the first line of the document. Press **Enter** twice. Click **Address Block** in the Write & Insert Fields group. Note the address in the Preview area. Ensure that *Insert recipient's name in this format, Insert company name,* and *Insert postal address* are selected. Click **OK**.

The AddressBlock merge field is inserted, with double angle brackets on each side, indicating its status.

> **MAC TROUBLESHOOTING:** Because the Address Block and Greeting Line selections may not be available, click Insert Merge Field and choose fields that comprise the address block and greeting line—Title, FirstName, LastName, and so on—ensuring that a space is shown between fields where necessary.

b. Press **Enter**. Click **Greeting Line**. Click **OK**.

A salutation is added, using the Greeting Line placeholder.

> **TROUBLESHOOTING:** If you make a mistake when entering merge fields, you can backspace or otherwise delete a field.

c. Click **Preview Results** in the Preview Results group.

d. Select the first four lines of the address block, from *Ms. Rebecca Hardin* through *Suite 10*. Click the **Layout tab** and remove any paragraph spacing shown in the Paragraph group.

Now that you have inserted merge fields into the form letter, the letter is complete. You will merge the main document with the data source so that each letter is personally addressed and ready to be printed. Refer to Figure 3.31 as you complete Step 4.

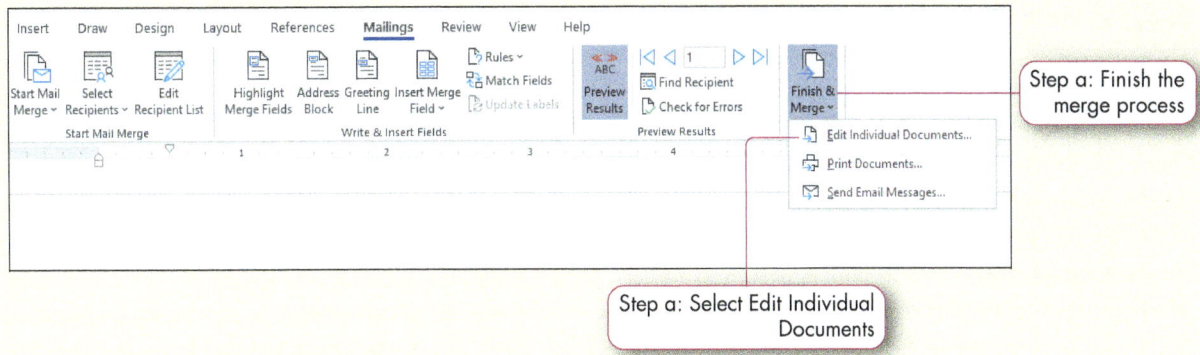

FIGURE 3.31 Complete a Mail Merge

a. Click the **Mailings tab**. Click **Finish & Merge** in the Finish group. Click **Edit Individual Documents**. Ensure that *All* is selected in the Merge to New Document dialog box and click **OK**.

b. Scroll through the letters, noting that each address and salutation is unique to the recipient. The main document and data source were merged to create a new document titled *Letters1* containing six letters. You will save the document.

c. Save the document as **w03h3Merged_LastFirst** and close the document.

d. Save and close w03h3Letter_LastFirst. Exit Word. Based on your instructor's directions, submit:
   w03h2Oakley_LastFirst
   w03h3Merged_LastFirst

Chapter Objectives Review

After reading this chapter, you have accomplished the following objectives:

1. Insert a table.

- **Create or draw a table:** You can include a table in a document by indicating the number of rows and columns, enabling Word to create the table, or you can draw the table, designing rows and columns of varying height and width.
- **Insert and delete rows and columns:** You can insert or delete rows and columns in a table to accommodate additional data or to otherwise update a table.
- **Merge and split cells:** As you update a table, you can merge cells in a row or column, accommodating text that is to be aligned within the row or column, and you can split cells within an existing row or column as well.
- **Change row height and column width:** You can increase or decrease row height and column width in several ways—using selections on the Table Layout tab as well as manually dragging column or row borders.

2. Format a table.

- **Apply and modify table styles:** Apply predesigned color, borders, and shading to a table by selecting a table style. Modify an existing style to adjust settings that better suit your purposes.
- **Adjust table position and alignment:** A table can be aligned horizontally on a page; in addition, you can align cell contents within each cell horizontally and vertically.
- **Format table text:** Format text included in a cell just as you would format text outside a table, with bold, italics, underlining, and so on. You can also apply paragraph formatting, such as alignment, bullets, and numbering.

3. Manage table data.

- **Use a formula:** A formula includes table cells and mathematical operators to calculate data in a table.
- **Use a function:** A function is a simplified formula, such as SUM or AVERAGE, that can be included in a table cell.
- **Sort data in a table:** You can sort table columns in ascending or descending order, including up to three sort categories. For example, you can sort a table by department name, and then by employee name within department.

4. Enhance table data.

- **Include borders and shading:** Use borders and shading to customize a table's design. You can use Word's Borders gallery, Border Painter, or the Borders and Shading dialog box to enhance a table with borders and shading.
- **Convert text to a table and convert a table to text:** You can convert text that is arranged in columns, with tabs separating columns, to a table. Conversely, you can convert text arranged in a table into text that is tabbed or otherwise divided into columns.
- **Include a table caption:** A table caption identifies a table, numbering each table in a document sequentially. You can modify the caption style and update caption numbering when tables are deleted.

5. Create a mail merge document.

- **Select or create a recipient list:** To prepare a form letter or other document type so that it is personalized with variable data, such as recipient name and address, you select or create a recipient list that will be merged with the main document.
- **Use a data source:** A data source contains variable data to be combined with a main document in a mail merge procedure. Typical data sources include an Excel worksheet, an Access database table, a Word table, an Outlook contacts list, or a data source you created during a mail merge.
- **Edit a data source:** Records in a data source can be sorted or filtered before they are merged with the main document. In addition, you can update records and add or delete them.

6. Complete a mail merge.

- **Insert merge fields:** Merge fields are placeholders in a main document to accommodate variable data obtained from a data source.
- **Complete a merge:** As you complete a mail merge procedure, you update a main document with variable data from a data source, resulting in a new document that is a combination of the two.

Match the key terms with their definitions. Write the key term letter by the appropriate numbered definition.

a. Argument
b. Border Painter
c. Caption
d. Cell
e. Data source
f. Field
g. Form letter
h. Formula
i. Function
j. Header row

k. Insert Control
l. Mail merge
m. Main document
n. Merge field
o. Order of operations
p. Range
q. Record
r. Table
s. Table alignment
t. Table style

1. _____ The horizontal position of a table between the left and right document margins. **p. 248**

2. _____ A descriptive title for a table. **p. 263**

3. _____ A document used in a mail merge process with standard information that you personalize with recipient information. **p. 270**

4. _____ The first row in a data source. **p. 271**

5. _____ A named collection of color, font, and border design that can be applied to a table. **p. 247**

6. _____ Area of information including variable data that is included in a data source. **p. 271**

7. _____ A combination of cell references, operators, and values used to perform a calculation. **p. 256**

8. _____ The intersection of a column and row in a table. **p. 242**

9. _____ A process that combines content from a main document and a data source. **p. 270**

10. _____ Contains the information that stays the same for all recipients in a mail merge. **p. 270**

11. _____ An indicator that displays between rows or columns in a table, enabling you to insert one or more rows or columns. **p. 244**

12. _____ Organizes information in a series of rows and columns. **p. 242**

13. _____ A list of information that is merged with a main document during a mail merge procedure. **p. 270**

14. _____ Determines the sequence by which operations are calculated in an expression. **p. 257**

15. _____ Serves as a placeholder for the variable data that will be inserted into the main document during a mail merge procedure. **p. 274**

16. _____ A pre-built formula that simplifies creating a complex calculation. **p. 258**

17. _____ Feature that enables you to choose border formatting and click on any table border to apply the formatting. **p. 260**

18. _____ A positional reference contained in parentheses within a function. **p. 258**

19. _____ A group of related fields representing one entity, such as a person, place, or event. **p. 271**

20. _____ A series of adjacent cells. **p. 258**

Multiple Choice

1. In which of the following scenarios would you filter a data source in preparation for a mail merge?

   (a) When an Outlook contact list is not readily available

   (b) When mailing a promotional document to recipients in a particular zip code, excluding others

   (c) When records in a data source have not yet been sorted

   (d) When a data source is in a format other than a Word table and must be filtered prior to importing the data source

2. Which of the following features formats a table with column and row dimensions that accommodate all cell entries, even if resulting widths and heights are not uniform?

   (a) AutoFit

   (b) Distribute Rows and Columns

   (c) BestFit

   (d) Table Properties

3. A mail merge process requires which of the following?

   (a) A main document and a merged list

   (b) A data source and an email list

   (c) A main document and a data source

   (d) A form letter and a main document

4. Why might you choose to apply a table style to an existing table?

   (a) To match the table theme to the document theme

   (b) To ensure that the table can include formulas

   (c) To enhance the readability of the table

   (d) To automatically remove any blank columns or rows

5. You plan to place a function or formula in cell B4 of a Word table to total the cells in the column above. How would that function or formula display?

   (a) =SUM(ABOVE)

   (b) =B1+B2+B3+B4

   (c) =TOTAL(ABOVE)

   (d) =SUM(B1-B3)

6. Which of the following is a purpose of a caption?

   (a) To add a comment to a particular table element

   (b) To provide documentation of the style used to design the table

   (c) To provide appropriate citation of a source from which the table was drawn

   (d) To provide a title in the first row of the table

7. Why is it recommended that a table include column headings if data in the table is to be sorted later?

   (a) Because without column headings, it is impossible to sort a table

   (b) Because column headings can be used as categories to sort by

   (c) Because the Sort function requires column headings

   (d) Because the Sort style cannot be applied without column headings in place

8. Which of the following best describes the purpose of a mail merge process?

   (a) To produce a document or email message in which variable data is drawn from a data source and combined with a main document

   (b) To produce a document or email message with fields containing data that should not vary from one document to the next

   (c) To produce only printed material, primarily mailing labels and envelopes

   (d) To produce only electronic material that is mass distributed, such as newsletters, for delivery through email

9. How could you modify the appearance of a caption so that any changes affect all captions in a document?

   (a) Select a caption in a document and format it differently.

   (b) Make changes in the Caption dialog box that displays when you first insert a caption.

   (c) Right-click an existing caption and select Format.

   (d) Modify the Caption style.

10. Having applied custom borders to a table, what feature do you use to copy the border style to another table?

    (a) Borders gallery

    (b) Format Painter

    (c) Border Painter

    (d) Border style

1 Academics

As an executive assistant working in the Admissions Office at Carnes State University, you are involved with a research project that is exploring the relationship between student GPA and involvement in academic clubs and scholarly activities. Academic and extracurricular data from a random sample of students in the College of Business has been summarized in a Word table that will be included in a brief memo to others on campus. You edit and format the report, preparing it for final submission. Refer to Figure 3.32 as you complete this exercise.

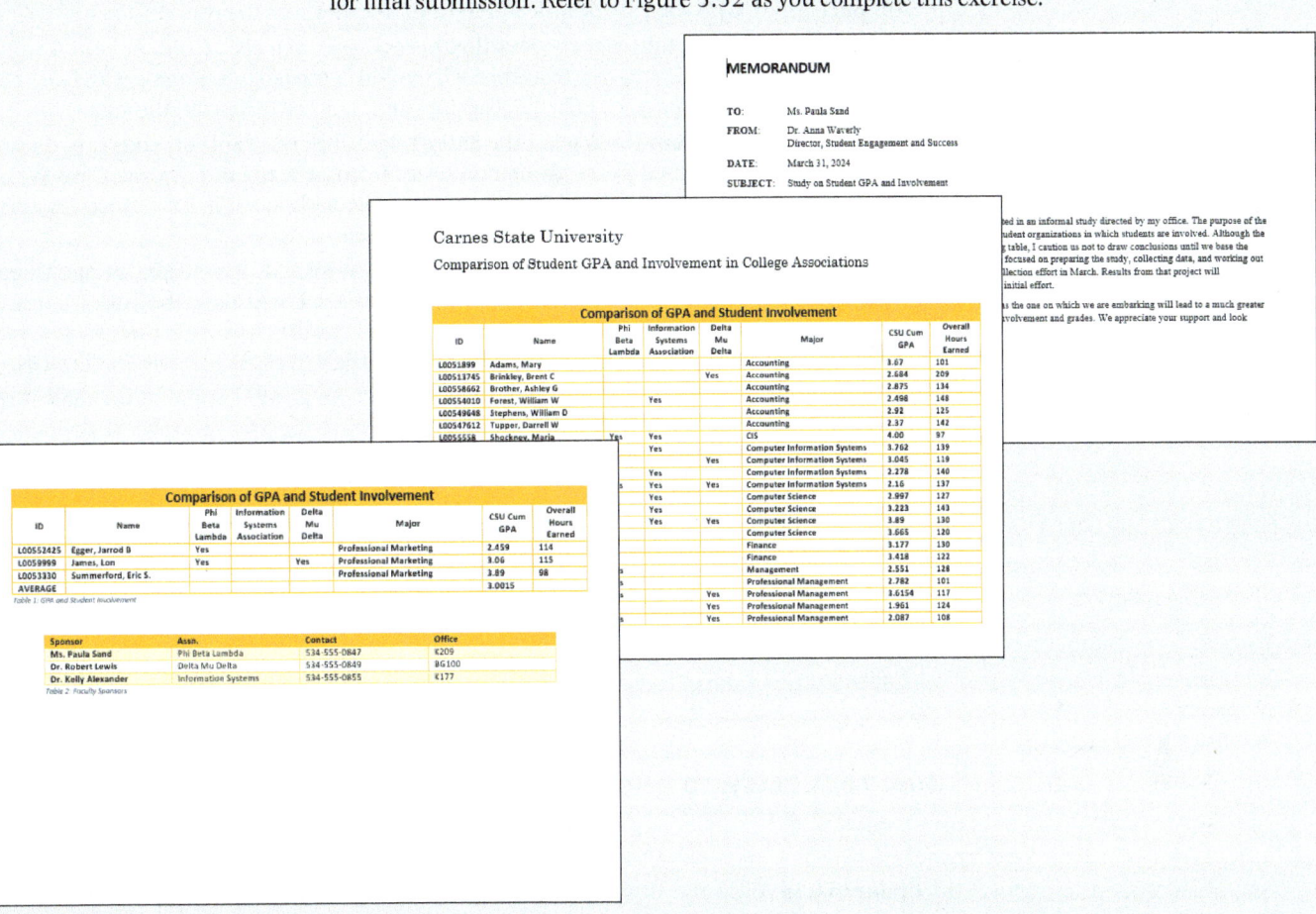

FIGURE 3.32 Academic Documents

a. Open *w03p1Academics* and save the document as **w03p1Academics_LastFirst**. Ensure that nonprinting characters are displayed.

b. Click before the blank paragraph mark at the top of page 2. Using Century Schoolbook font at 20 pt size, type **Carnes State University** and press **Enter**. Change the font size to **16 pt**. Type **Comparison of Student GPA and Involvement in College Associations**. Press **Enter**. Check the document for spelling and grammatical errors. All names in the table are correct.

c. Select the first row in the table. Click the **Table Layout tab** and click **Align Center** in the Alignment group so that entries are centered both vertically and horizontally.

d. Click after the last entry in the last row, ending in *115*. Press **Tab**. Type the following data, tabbing between all entries except the last. Do not press Tab after the last item. Do not type the word (blank) but leave the cell empty.

L0051899	Adams, Mary	(blank)	(blank)	(blank)	Accounting	3.67	101
L0055558	Shockney, Maria	Yes	Yes	(blank)	CIS	4.00	97

e. Right-click any name identified as misspelled and click **Ignore All**. Click **Sort** in the Data group. In the Sort dialog box, click the **Sort by arrow** and select **Major**. The sort should occur in ascending order. Click the **Then by arrow** and sort by **Name** in ascending order. Click **OK**.

f. Indicate that Michael Simpson and Andrew Sams are both active in Delta Mu Delta by typing **Yes** in the *Delta Mu Delta* column for each of those students.

g. Click anywhere in the first row. Click **Insert Above** in the Rows & Columns group on the Table Layout tab. Click **Merge Cells** in the Merge group. Change the font size to **16 pt**. Type **Comparison of GPA and Student Involvement**. (Do not type the period.)

h. Click the **Table Design tab,** click the **Shading arrow**, and then click **Gold, Accent 4** (row 1, column 8). Select all text in the third row through the end of the table, beginning with *L0051899* and ending with *98* (on page 3). Bold the selection. Click any cell to deselect the area.

i. Click the **Table move handle** to select the entire table. Click the **Table Design tab**. Click the **Pen Color arrow** in the Borders group and select **Gold, Accent 4**. Click the **Line Weight arrow** and click **1½ pt**. Ensure that a single line border is shown. Click the **Borders arrow** and select **All Borders**. Click any cell to deselect the area.

j. Click after **98** at the end of the last row. Press **Tab**. Type **AVERAGE**. Press **Tab** six times to reach the *CSU Cum GPA* column. Click the **Table Layout tab**. Click **Formula** in the Data group. Click between *SUM* and *(ABOVE)* in the Formula dialog box. Press **Backspace** repeatedly to remove the word *SUM*, and type **AVERAGE**. The formula should be *=AVERAGE(ABOVE)*. Click **OK**.

k. Click the **View tab** and click **Multiple Pages** in the Zoom group. Note that the table is split between two pages. Click **100%** in the Zoom group. Select the first two rows of the table on page 2. Click the **Table Layout tab** and click **Repeat Header Rows** in the Data group. View the document in multiple pages once more to see the change. Change the view back to **100%**.

l. Click anywhere in the table. Point to the outside left edge of the table between *Frederick Davidson* and *David Stumpe*. Click the **Insert indicator**. Click in the first cell of the new row and type the following record, tabbing between cells. Do not type (blank) in the cell containing that text, but leave the cell empty.

L00500932	Johns, Lacey	(blank)	Yes	Yes	Computer Science	3.89	130

> **MAC TROUBLESHOOTING:** Insert a new row using ribbon selections.

m. Move to page 3 and right-click the **average** (in the second to last column) in the last row. Click **Update Field**. Click the **References tab** and click **Insert Caption** in the Captions group. Ensure that the caption begins with *Table 1*. Type a colon (:) and press **Spacebar**. Type **GPA and Student Involvement**. (Do not type the period.) Ensure that the caption will display below the table and click **OK**.

> **MAC TROUBLESHOOTING:** Before updating the field, you must first select the value in the cell.

n. Press **Enter** twice. Click the **Insert tab** and click the **Object arrow** in the Text group. Select **Text from File**. Navigate to the location of the student data files and double-click *wO3p1Sponsors*.

o. Select the newly inserted text, from *Sponsor* through *K177*. It does not matter whether you select the paragraph mark following K177, but do not select the blank paragraph on the next line. Click **Table** in the Tables group and select **Convert Text to Table**. Confirm that the new table will include four columns and four rows. Click **OK**.

p. Ensure that the entire table is selected. Right-click anywhere in the selected table and click **Table Properties**. Click the **Column tab**. Select the Preferred width check box so that a checkmark shows. Change the width to **2** and ensure that the measurement is in Inches. Click **OK**. Do not deselect the table. Click **More** in the Table Styles group and select **Grid Table 4 - Accent 4** (row 4, column 5 under Grid Tables). Select the first row of the table and change the font color to **Black, Text 1**.

q. Right-click anywhere in the selected table and click **Table Properties**. Click the **Table tab**. Click **Center**. Click **OK**. Insert a caption below the table that reads **Table 2: Faculty Sponsors**. (Do not type the period.) Click **OK**. Click the **Home tab** and click **Increase Indent** in the Paragraph group to indent the caption.

r. Save the document. Place the insertion point at the beginning of the document.

s. Click the **Mailings tab** and click **Start Mail Merge** in the Start Mail Merge group. Select **Letters**. Click **Select Recipients**. Select **Use an Existing List**. Navigate to your data files and double-click *w03p1Faculty.xlsx*. Click **OK** to select the *Sheet1$* worksheet.

t. Click before the paragraph mark following *TO:*. Click the **Insert Merge Field arrow** in the Write & Insert Fields group. Click **Title**. Press **Spacebar**. Click the **Insert Merge Field arrow** and select **First_Name**. Press **Spacebar.** Click the **Insert Merge Field arrow** and select **Last_Name.** Click before the paragraph mark following *DATE:* and type **March 31, 2024**.

u. Click **Preview Results**. Click **Finish & Merge**. Select **Edit Individual Documents**. Ensure that *All* is selected and click **OK**. Scroll through the merged document to see that three recipients will receive the memo and tables. The document should include nine pages.

v. Save the document as **w03p1AcademicsMerged_LastFirst** and close the document. Save w03p1Academics_LastFirst. Exit Word. Based on your instructor's directions, submit: w03p1AcademicsMerged_LastFirst

2 | Berkeley Bill's Coffee Creations

You recently bought a local coffee shop, Berkeley Bill's. As a fixture in the community, Berkeley Bill's caters to a varied crowd of coffee drinkers including college students, business professionals, and local retirees. You have a few changes in mind for the business, starting with an expanded and well-trained barista crew. Each Saturday for a month, your new employees will be attending a half-day workshop on various topics related to running the coffee shop business and providing a quality product. You have begun a document that will be used in this Saturday's workshop, but it is in draft form. You will format the included table so that it is attractive and complete. You will also prepare a personalized handout for each barista in training so they can prepare for the workshop beforehand. Refer to Figure 3.33 as you complete this exercise.

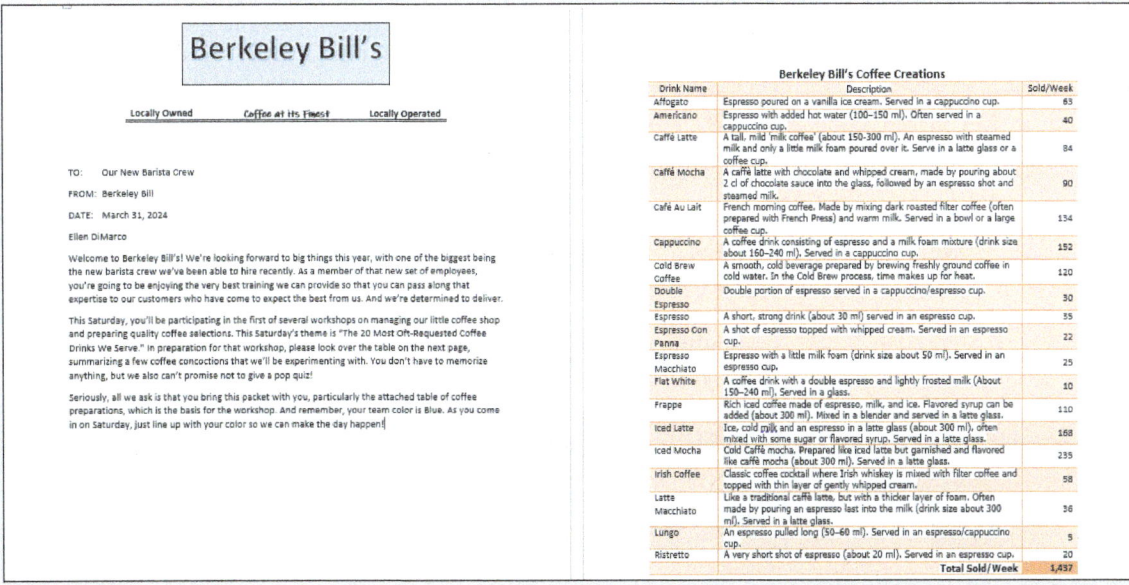

FIGURE 3.33 Coffee Letter

a. Open *w03p2Coffee* and save the document as **w03p2Coffee_LastFirst**. Show nonprinting characters if they are not already displayed.

b. Click before the second blank paragraph mark after the letterhead on page 1. Click the **Insert tab**. Click **Table**. Drag to select 3 columns and 1 row. Click to insert the table. Type **Locally Owned** and press **Tab**. Type **Coffee at its Finest** and press **Tab**. Type **Locally Operated**. (Do not type the period and do not press Tab.)

c. Select *Coffee at its Finest* in the middle cell. Click the **Table Layout tab** and select **Align Center** in the Alignment group. Change the font to **Ink Free**. Select the contents of the last cell, *Locally Operated*, click the **Table Layout tab**, and change the alignment to **Align Center Right**.

d. Click the **Table move handle**. Change the width in the Cell Size group on the Table Layout tab to **1.6**. Click the **Home tab** and bold the table contents. Right-click the table, click **Table Properties**, and select **Center** on the Table tab. Click **OK**.

e. Ensure that the table is selected. Click the **Table Design tab**, click the **Borders arrow**, and select **No Border**. Click the **Borders arrow** and select **Borders and Shading**. Scroll through selections in the Style box in the Borders and Shading dialog box and select the seventh style (double underline). Select a line width of **¾ pt**.

f. Click the **left border option**, the **right border option**, and the **top border option** in the Preview box so that the bottom border option is the only one still shaded. The preview window should show a double bottom border only. Click **OK**.

g. Scroll to page 2. Point to the top of the middle table column so that the pointer looks like a downward-pointing arrow ⬇. Click to select the middle column. Change the font to **Tahoma** and change the font size to **10**.

h. Click anywhere in the first row. Click the **Table Layout tab** and select **Insert Above** in the Rows & Columns group. Type **Drink Name** in the first cell on the top row and press **Tab**. Type **Description** and press **Tab**. Type **Sold/Week**. (Do not type the period.).

> **MAC TROUBLESHOOTING:** Insert a new row using ribbon selections.

i. Click the **Table Design tab**, click **More** in the Table Styles group, and select **Grid, Table 2 – Accent 2** (row 2, column 3 under Grid Tables). Deselect **First Column** in the Table Style Options group.

j. Click the **Table Layout tab**, click **Select** in the Table group, and then click **Select Table**. Click **AutoFit** in the Cell Size group, and select **AutoFit Contents**. Select the first row and apply **Align Center** alignment.

k. Click in the last row of the table and insert a new row below. Click in the middle cell on the last row and type **Total Sold/Week**. (Do not type the period.) Bold the entry in the current cell and apply **Align Center Right** alignment.

l. Click in the last cell on the last row. Click **Formula** in the Data group. Ensure that the formula is *=SUM(ABOVE)* and select a Number Format of **#,##0**. Click **OK**. Select all numbers in the last column and click **Align Center Right** in the Alignment group.

m. Select **1,417** in the last cell on the last row in the table. Click the **Table Design tab**, click the **Shading arrow**, and select **Orange, Accent 2, Lighter 40%**. Bold the selection.

n. Scroll to locate the *Iced Mocha* row. Change the number of Iced Mocha sold/week to **235**. Right-click the last number in the last row, representing the total sold/week, and click **Update Field** to update the total.

> **MAC TROUBLESHOOTING:** Before updating the field, you must first select the value in the cell.

o. Insert a new row above the top row of the table. Click **Merge Cells** in the Merge group on the Layout tab. Type **Berkeley Bill's Coffee Creations**. Change the font size to **14 pt**.

p. Check spelling. No coffee names are misspelled so ignore any errors of that type. Save the document.

q. Scroll to page 1. Click the **Mailings tab**. Click **Start Mail Merge** in the Start Mail Merge group, and select **Letters**. Click **Select Recipients**, click **Use an Existing List**, navigate to the location of your data files, and double-click *w03p2Coffee.accdb*.

r. Click **Edit Recipient List** in the Start Mail Merge group. Click **Sort** in the Refine recipient list area. Click the **Sort by arrow** and select **Team** (in ascending order). Click the **Then by arrow** and select **Last Name** (in ascending order). Click **OK**.

s. Filter records in the data source as follows:
- Click **Filter** in the Refine recipient list area.
- Click the **Field arrow** and select **Hire Date**.
- Click the **Comparison arrow** and select **Greater than or equal**.
- Type **1/1/2024** in the Compare to box. Click **OK** and then click **OK** again.

t. Insert merge fields as follows:
- Click the blank paragraph below the Date line on page 1.
- Click the **Insert Merge Field arrow** in the Write & Insert Fields group on the Mailings tab. Click **First_Name**. Press **spacebar**.
- Click the **Insert Merge Field arrow** and select **Last_Name**.
- Click at the end of the second to last sentence on page 1, after the space following *color is*. Click the **Insert Merge Field arrow** and select **Team**.

u. Click **Preview Results.** Note the crew member's name near the top of the letter and the team color near the end of page 1. Click **Finish & Merge**. Click **Edit Individual Documents**, ensure that **All** is selected, and click **OK**.

v. Save the resulting merged document, containing 10 pages, as **w03p2CoffeeMerged_LastFirst** and close the file. Save and close w03p2Coffee_LastFirst. Exit Word. Based on your instructor's directions, submit:

w03p2CoffeeMerged_LastFirst

Mid-Level Exercises

1 Football Statistics

As a communication specialist for the Midwest Athletic Conference, you are preparing a summary of football statistics for inclusion in material published by the conference. Specifically, you highlight stats from the offensive units of leading teams in the conference. A Word table is an ideal way to summarize those statistics, so you prepare and populate several tables. Where appropriate, you include formulas to summarize table data. The tables must be attractively formatted, so you use Word's design and bordering tools as well.

a. Open *w03m1Football* and save it as **w03m1Football_LastFirst**.

b. Select text in the document from # (in the top-left corner) to *13.4* (in the bottom-right corner) and convert the text to a table. Whether you include the paragraph mark following 13.4 is irrelevant, but do not include the paragraph mark on the following line. Change page orientation to **Landscape**. Change the font of the second and third lines (*Midwest Athletic Conference* and *Season Statistics*) to **Cambria 16 pt**.

c. Delete column 1. Change the font of all table data to **Cambria 10 pt**. AutoFit the contents of the table.

d. Ensure that no team names in column 1 are bold or underlined. However, entries in row 1 should remain bold and underlined.

e. Insert a row above row 1 in the table. Complete the following steps to populate and format the new row:

- Type **Offensive Statistics** in the first cell on the new row.
- Type **Rushing Statistics** in the next cell on the first row.
- Select the second, third, fourth, fifth, and sixth cells on the first row. Merge the selected cells.
- Align *Rushing Statistics* in the center of the merged cell.
- Type **Passing Statistics** in the next cell on the first row.
- Select the cell containing *Passing Statistics* and the next three cells on the first row. Merge the cells.
- Align *Passing Statistics* in the center of the merged cell.
- Merge the remaining cells on row 1, type **Total** in the merged cell, and then center the word *Total*.

f. Insert a row between *HARKINSVILLE* and *DAKOTA STATE* and type the following data in the new row:

JAMES COLLEGE	38.2	41.0	220.5	4.2	19.7	32.7	0.601	199.2	7.6	57.9	449.3	5.9	12.7

g. Select a table style of **Grid Table 5 Dark - Accent 2** (row 5, column 3 under Grid Tables). Select all table text. Apply a Pen Color of **Orange, Accent 2, Darker 50%** (row 6, column 6 under Theme Colors) with a line width of **½ pt** and a line style of a **single line** to outside borders.

h. Ensure that the pen color is Orange, Accent 2, Darker 50% and the line weight is ½ pt. Select a **double-line style** and apply the selection to the border along the horizontal line separating row 1 from row 2, and also along the vertical line separating the first column from the second. The vertical line border should begin in row 2 and continue down the table.

i. Move to the end of the document, press **Enter** twice, and then insert a 3×5 table. Enter the following data in the table.

Calvin Spraggins	SPR	1428
Demaryius Schuster	DEN	1197
Taylor Marchant	CHI	1182
Wayne McAnalley	IND	1156
Sparky Hall	HOU	1114

j. Change the column width of all columns in the table to **1.5"**. Center all entries in the last two columns.

k. Insert a new blank row at the top of the second table and complete the following steps:
- Type **Receiving Yards** in the first cell on row 1.
- Change the font size of the entry on row 1 to **14 pt**.
- Merge all cells on row 1.
- Center *Receiving Yards*.

l. Shade the first row with **Orange, Accent 2, Lighter 60%** (row 3, column 6 under Theme Colors).

m. Add a new blank row at the end of the second table and type **Average** in the first cell of the new row. Enter a formula in the last cell of the new row to average all entries in the column above. You do not need to select a number format.

n. Align both tables horizontally in the center of the page. Check for spelling and grammatical errors. All names in both tables are correct.

o. Change the receiving yards for *Calvin Spraggins* to **1451**. Update the average to reflect the change.

p. Click any cell in the first table. Click the **Table Design tab** and click **Border Painter** in the Borders group. With the pointer resembling a pen, click the double-line border that divides the first and second rows of the first table to "sample" it. Drag to apply the sampled border to the border dividing the first and second rows in the second table. Press **Esc** or click Border Painter to toggle off the tool.

> **MAC TROUBLESHOOTING:** When working with Border Painter, the pointer resembles a paintbrush instead of a pen.

q. Add a caption below the first table with the following text: **Figure 1: Midwest Athletic Conference Offensive Statistics**. (Do not include the period.) Add a caption below the bottom of the second table that reads **Figure 2: Average Receiving Yards**. (Do not include the period.) Modify the Caption style to include a font color of **Orange, Accent 2, Darker 50%**. Caption style font should be bold (not italicized) and centered. Save the document.

r. Begin a mail merge procedure, selecting as a recipient list *Sheet1$* of *w03m1Universities.xlsx*.

s. Sort the data source by **University** in ascending order. Merge the University field with the source document so that the university name displays after the text *Draft Prepared for:* on page 1. Ensure that a space is shown before the University placeholder. Preview the results and finish the merge, merging all records.

t. Save the merged document as **w03m1FootballMerged_LastFirst** and close the file. Save and close w03m1Football_LastFirst. Exit Word. Based on your instructor's directions, submit: w03m1FootballMerged_LastFirst

2 BMI

As a nursing student, you are completing a Capstone course that requires focused study and class reports on various health topics. This week, you and a team are developing a presentation on body mass index and its use in helping determine overall health of individuals. Your task is putting together an overall summary of the topic with information on how BMI is actually determined. You will use Word—specifically Word tables—to organize that information. In so doing, you will ensure that the summary and tables are attractive and well-constructed, with appropriate formatting and formulas where necessary.

a. Open *w03m2BMI* and save the document as **w03m2BMI_LastFirst**. Ensure that nonprinting characters are displayed.

b. Select all text on page 2 and insert a table by converting the text to a table. The new table should include 18 columns and 19 rows. Insert two rows at the top of the table. Add text to the top row as follows.

BMI	19	20	21	22	23	24	25	26	27	28	29	30	31	32	33	34	35

c. Adjust the width of Column 1 in the table to **0.8**. Modify the second row, merging columns 2 through 18, and adding text as follows. Press **Shift+Enter** after typing *Height* in the first cell on the second row to insert a soft return within the cell. Apply **Align Center** alignment to text in the merged cell so that it is centered both horizontally and vertically.

Height (Inches)	Body Weight (Pounds)

d. Bold all text in the first two rows. Remove bold from all numbers in the first column (rows 3 through the end of the column). Center the contents of the first column.

e. Select the table and format it as follows:
- Choose a pen color of **Blue-Gray, Text 2, Lighter 40%**, and apply the selection to all borders.
- Select the first two rows and apply a shading of **Blue-Gray, Text 2, Lighter 60%**. Change the font color in the first two rows to **Blue-Gray, Text 2**.
- Shade the remaining rows with **Blue-Gray, Text 2, Lighter 80%**.

f. Select the first two rows and apply a single line, **1 pt** border with a pen color of **Black, Text 1** to the **Outside Borders**.

g. Insert a row between 63 and 65 in the Height column. Type the following in the new row.

64	110	116	122	128	134	140	145	151	157	163	169	174	180	186	192	197	204

h. Place the insertion point at the end of the document. Insert a table with 3 columns and 2 rows. Type the following in the first row.

Weight	Height (Inches)	BMI

i. Type **140** in the first cell on the second row and **66** in the second cell. Click in the third cell on the second row. Insert a formula that multiplies weight by 703 and divides the result by the height squared. The formula would be **=A2*703/(B2*B2)**.

j. Insert a row at the end of the table, type **160** in the first cell on the new row, **66** in the second cell, and type the same formula as the row above, but adjust for the new row position.

k. Select the new table and AutoFit the contents. Apply a table design of **Grid Table 4 – Accent 3** (row 4, column 4 under Grid Tables). Deselect **First Column** in the Table Style Options group. Center the table horizontally on the page. Adjust the width of the middle column to **1** inch.

l. Insert a caption below the first table with the text **Table 1: BMI Table**. (Do not include the period.) Insert a caption below the second table with the text **Table 2: Sample BMI Measures and Results**. (Do not include the period.)

m. Modify the Caption style to increase the font size to **11 pt** and change the alignment to **Centered**.

n. Insert a column at the right of the last column in Table 2. Include text as follows.

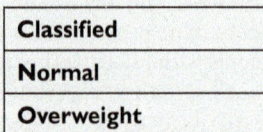

Classified
Normal
Overweight

o. Save and close the file. Exit Word. Based on your instructor's directions, submit: w03m2BMI_LastFirst

Running Case

New Castle County Technical Services

You continue to work with promotional material for New Castle County Technical Services (NCCTS). In so doing, you create and modify a couple of tables, further outlining company services for potential clients. In addition, you prepare a cover letter to merge with a data source as you prepare to mail the promotional document.

a. Open *w03r1NewCastle.docx* and save it as **w03r1NewCastle_LastFirst**.

b. Show nonprinting characters. Scroll to page 5. Select the six clients listed in the tabbed area at the bottom of page 5 and near the top of page 6, making sure to include everything from the first nonprinting tab character through the paragraph mark after the words *Since 1999*. Convert the selected text to a table, accepting all dialog box settings.

c. Delete the first column in the table, which is empty. Change the column width of the new second column to **1.5"**.

d. Insert a row above the first row of the table. Type **Our Valued Connections** in the first cell of the newly inserted row. Merge both cells on the first row and apply center alignment to the text in the first row. Change the font size of text in the first row to **16 pt**.

e. Apply **Grid Table 4 – Accent 5** table style to the table (row 4, column 6 under Grid Tables). Deselect **First Column** in the Table Style Options group. Place the insertion point after the last body paragraph on page 5 (ending in *a few of our current clients*). Press **Enter**. The table should display completely on page 6.

f. Select the table. Select a border style of **Single solid line, 1½ pt**. Apply the border style to all borders in the table. Center the table horizontally on the page.

g. Insert a row after the last row in the table and type **Call Us Today at 256-555-7100.** (Include the period.) Merge all cells on the last row and center the text. Apply shading to the last row, selecting a shading color of **Dark Gray, Accent 6, Darker 25%**. Change the font size of text in the last row to **16 pt** and bold the text.

h. Place the insertion point on the blank paragraph that precedes the last paragraph on page 1. Insert a 4×6 table. The table will span two pages. Beginning in the first cell on the first row of the table, type the following data:

Active accounts			
	2022	2023	Increase
Network Security	48	81	
IT Consulting	124	145	
Cloud Integration	38	40	
Disaster Recovery	109	132	

i. Adjust the column widths of columns 2, 3, and 4 to **1"**. Merge all cells in the first row and center the text. Adjust the font size of text in the first row to **16 pt** and bold the text.

j. Apply a table style of **Grid Table 4** (row 4, column 1 under Grid Tables). Bold all table entries in row 2. Center the table horizontally on the page.

k. Click in the last cell on the third row of the table. Insert a formula to determine the percentage increase from 2022 to 2023. The formula is **=(C3-B3)/B3*100**. Change the Number format to **0.00%**. Continue down the column, placing an appropriate formula in each cell to indicate the percentage increase. The Number format for all formulas in the last column is **0.00%**.

l. Change the number in the *2023* column for *Cloud Integration* to **59**. Update the formula field on the same row to adjust for the new entry.

m. Add a row at the end of the table. Type **Total** in the first cell on the last row. Include a formula in each of the next two cells to total the active accounts in 2022 and 2023. The formula should be **=SUM(ABOVE)-B2**, which sums the column above but removes the year from the calculation. Include a similar formula in the next cell, adjusting for the year reference. Do not include a formula in the last cell on the last row.

n. Place the insertion point before the page break designation at the end of page 2. Click the **Layout tab**, click **Breaks**, and then insert a **Continuous** section break. Click anywhere in the body of the letter on page 1 or 2 and change the orientation of the letter to **Portrait**. All pages following the letter remain in Landscape orientation.

o. Delete the page break on page 3. Delete the first three lines of text (address lines) on page 1 and delete a space that may display before the Date placeholder. Select and replace *[Date]* on the first line of the letter with the current date by clicking the Insert tab and selecting **Insert Date and Time** in the Text group. Select the **month, day, year** format and do not choose to have the date update automatically. Ensure that the date displays on a line by itself. Press **Enter** after the date, ensuring that the date is followed by a blank paragraph. Save the document.

p. Begin a mail merge procedure to combine the data source, *w03r1Clients.xlsx*, with the open document. Use the *Company Addresses$* worksheet. Edit the recipient list to filter records for an Account Manager of **Andrea Macon** and a State of **MS**. Sort the filtered records by **Name** in ascending order.

q. Replace [Recipient Name] on the first line of the address block on page 1 with the merge field of **Name**. Ensure that the square brackets are also removed and that <> displays on a line by itself. Replace text on the next three lines with merge fields of the same name, ensuring that square brackets are removed. Replace [City, ST Zip] with the merge field of **City**. Type a comma and press **Spacebar**. Insert the merge field of **State**. Press **Spacebar** and insert the merge field of **Zip**.

r. Replace [Business Type] in the first body paragraph (including the square brackets) with the merge field **Business_Type**. Ensure that a space precedes and follows the new insertion. Similarly, replace [Account Manager] and [Account No] with merge fields of the same name.

s. Replace [Your Name] at the end of the letter with your first and last names. Check spelling, correcting any misspellings and ignoring any names or company names that may be identified as errors.

t. Click the **Mailings tab** and click **Preview Results** to view a merged document. Merge all of the records into individual documents. The newly merged document should contain 12 pages.

u. Save the newly merged document as **w03r1NewCastleMerged_LastFirst**. Close the document. Save w03r1NewCastle_LastFirst. Exit Word. Based on your instructor's directions, submit:
w03r1NewCastleMerged_LastFirst

Disaster Recovery

Boston Travels

Your family runs a travel agency in the Boston area. Between college semesters, you are helping in the home office and have been charged with developing a document to promote various tour packages for the city of Boston. Another employee began the document but was not able to finish it and so has left it for you. The body of the flyer is complete, but it is in need of a table to summarize tour packages. At this point, the tour information is shown in a tabbed list at the end of *w03d1Boston*. You should convert the tabbed list to a Word table and then format it to include the data shown in the following table. As closely as possible, replicate what is shown. Make sure to include all information shown, including the discounted admission values. The final column, shown in red, is a 40% discount that is now available. For example, the Back Bay/Fenway tour that is normally $20 is now $12. Assuming Back Bay/Fenway is on row 2 of the table you create, the formula to determine that discount would be =C2-(.40*C2). Each subsequent row's formula would be adjusted by row. The Beacon Hill/Science Park tour, for example, would be =C3-(.40*C3). Continue the pattern down the column. Open *w03d1Boston* and save it as **w03d1Boston_LastFirst**. Convert the tabbed text at the end of the document to a table. Exit Word. Based on your instructor's directions, submit:

w03d1Boston_LastFirst

Tour Package	Attraction	Discounted Admission	
Family Fun Tour	Back Bay/Fenway	20.00	12.00
	Beacon Hill/Science Park	25.00	15.00
	Quincy Market/Waterfront	27.95	16.77
Patriot Tours	Freedom Trail/Statehouse	15.00	9.00
	Boston Sunset Cruise	18.95	11.37
	USS Constitution	24.50	14.70
JFK/Harvard Tours	Harvard and Cambridge Guided	15.95	9.57
	JFK Presidential Library	25.00	15.00
	Edward M. Kennedy Institute for the United States Senate	16.00	9.60

Cumulative Exercise

With a passion for the outdoors, you are interested in a wide range of outdoor activities. You are also a firm believer in preserving the ecosystem for future generations. As a member of a local chapter of the Audubon Society, you are involved with an outreach to promote ecotourism, which encourages travel to natural habitats while conserving the environment in the process. You will finalize a short flyer that identifies eight unique destinations for ecotourism, describing them in a Word table. Business sponsors have agreed to support the effort and will be distributing flyers, so you plan to include each business name and contact in the flyer.

Insert and Format a Table

You will create a table at the end of the flyer where Sponsor information can be placed during a later mail merge process. The one-row table will be formatted before data is included.

1. Open *w03c1Tourism* and save it as **w03c1Tourism_LastFirst**. Display nonprinting characters.

2. Place the insertion point at the end of the document. Insert a 2x1 table. Adjust the width of the first column to **2** inches. Apply a table style of **List Table 2 – Accent 6** (row 2, column 7 under List Tables).

3. Center the newly created table horizontally. Select the table and apply shading of **Gray, Accent 3, Lighter 80%** (row 2, column 7).

Enhance Table Data

The first table in the document, listing top ecotourism destinations, requires a bit of work. You will finish entering data in the table, inserting columns in the process, and you will ensure that the table is attractive.

4. Insert a row between the first and second rows of the first table shown (under the *Eco_Friendly World Destinations* row). Type **Destination** in the first cell on the new row. Type **Description** in the next cell. Type **C2 Rating** in the last cell on the row.

5. Insert a column at the right of the last column in the table. Type **Approximate Visitors/Year** in the last cell on the current row. Type data in the final two columns of the table as shown below:

C2 Rating	Approximate Visitors/Year
8	250,300
7	524,000
9	2,000,700
6	34,900
9	190,000
10	3,500
7	145,000
8	348,000

6. Select the first table. Select a border style of **Double solid lines, ½ pt, Accent 3** (row 3, column 4). Apply the selection to outside borders. AutoFit contents of the table.

7. Select the first row of the first table and merge cells. Center text in the first row. Apply shading of **Light Gray, Background 2, Darker 50%** (row 4, column 3). Change font color of text in the first row to **White, Background 1.** Bold text in the selected row and change the font size to **14 pt.**

8. Select rows 2 through the end of the table and apply shading of **Light Gray, Background 2** (row 1, column 3). Use Border Painter to copy the double-line format from an outside border and apply it to each vertical gridline within the table.

9. Apply **Align Center** alignment to all text in the second row so that contents are both horizontally and vertically centered. Apply **Align Center** alignment to all text in the first and third columns in rows 3 through the end of the table. Select all numbers in the last column and apply **Align Center Right** alignment.

10. Include a caption that reads *Table 1: Data provided by the National Conservation Fund* below the first table.

Manage Table Data

Before the table is considered complete, you will summarize numeric data. By sorting rows, you ensure a well-organized presentation listing destinations in alphabetical order.

11. Select rows 3 through the end of the first table. Sort the rows in ascending order by Column 1. All destinations should be shown in alphabetical order.

12. Insert a row at the bottom of the first table. Type **Average** in the second cell on the last row. Choose **Align Center Right** alignment and bold the entry.

13. Include a function in the third cell on the last row (below the *C2 Rating* column) that determines the average of the values in the column above. You do not need to select a number format.

14. Include a function in the last cell on the last row (below the *Approximate Visitors/Year* column) that determines the average of the values in the column above. You do not need to select a number format.

Create and Complete a Mail Merge Document

Several sponsors generously support the cause of ecotourism you are promoting. You want to mention them in the flyer so they will be recognized. You will prepare a mail merge document, including personalized information at the bottom of the flyer, identifying the business to which you will be sending packets of flyers.

15. Begin a mail merge process, selecting a recipient list from *w03c1Members.xlsx*. Data is located in *Sheet1$* of the workbook. Edit the recipient list to include a business you left off, as follows:

Sloan Outfitters	171 Wood Avenue	Anderson	SC	34408	Serena Blake	sloan@ingroup.net

16. Sort the recipient list in ascending order by Business, and filter results to show only those from SC.

17. Click in the first cell of the last table on the page (following *Thanks for Supporting Us!*). Insert the **Business** merge field. In the second cell of the table, insert the **Contact** merge field. Preview results and finish the merge, editing individual documents and merging all. The merged document should contain six pages.

18. Save the merged document as **w03c1Tourism Merged_LastFirst**. Save w03c1Tourism_LastFirst. Exit Word. Based on your instructor's directions, submit:
w03c1TourismMerged_LastFirst

LEARNING OUTCOME You will model professional use of research and collaboration tools.

OBJECTIVES & SKILLS: After you read this chapter, you will be able to:

CASE STUDY | Literature Analysis

You are a college student enrolled in a literature class in which you are required to write papers. As a requirement for the class, you will prepare an analysis of "A White Heron," a short story by Sarah Orne Jewett. The analysis is a group effort, completed by four students, including you. You are required to develop the paper based on a particular writing style, and you will include citations and a bibliography. Your instructor, Mr. Carpenter, will provide feedback in the form of comments that the group will then incorporate into the paper. Because you are a commuting student with a part-time job, you are not always on campus, and your time is very limited. As is typical of many college students, even those in your literature group, time and availability are in short supply. The group is quick to realize that much of the coordination on the project must be done from a distance. You will share the project in such a way that each student can contribute, although not in a group setting. Instead, the document will be available online, with each student reviewing, contributing, and reposting the project.

Nd3000/Shutterstock

Produce Professional Papers

CHAPTER 4

An Analysis of "A White Heron"

Sarah Orne Jewett's short story, "A White Heron" centers on a few days in the life of Sylvia, a nine-year-old girl spending the summer in Maine with her grandmother. Having left the bustle of the city, Sylvia enjoys spending a great deal of time in the woodland, as "there never was such a child for straying about out-of-doors" (Jewett 532). One summer... walking the family cow home, she is approached by a handsome young stra... to hunt, kill, and stuff birds, specifically a white heron. Sylvia is attracted to... help in his quest. Although the first day's search proves fruitless. Sylvia cli... tree on the next day and locates a beautiful white heron, its mate, and nest. ... realizes that she cannot give the bird's location away. She is too tenderhear... heron family to the hunter. Although wracked with guilt to the point of "a s... conviction holds firm (Jewett 537). Her attachment to nature and the beauty... proves stronger than her desire to please the hunter.

Theodore R. Hovet, university researcher and scholar, analyzed Jew... the short story to a fairy tale, in "'Once Upon a Time': Sarah Orne Jewett's ... A Fairy Tale." Identifying various components of a typical fairy tale, Hovet... "A White Heron" includes many facets of a typical fairy tale. In fact, his an... Jewett's tale, elaborating on twenty functions that are often found to be pre... functions that are also present in "A White Heron" (63). Hovet borrows the ... function from Vladimir Propp, author of "Morphology of the Folk Tale", w... function as "an act of a character, defined from the point of view of its signi... course of action" (Propp). For example, a villain appearing, and the use of a ...

both examples of functions in a fairy tale. Hovet's analysis is an eye-opening approach to interpreting "A White Heron" as a fairy tale.

A typical fairy tale includes a hero and a disguised villain. The villain plunders or causes harm to others. ... Conflict often ... returns to a hap... whose underly... suggests that J... villain and her... Combat betwe... the hunter atte... "despite great i... with a resoluti... takes the form ... advantage" and ... easily scale the...

masculine will". As he continues his analysis of Jewett's tale, Hovet explores the story's connection to "the imperialistic bent of industrial America". The hunter's money and gun represent the power and i... attempts to illustrate that... the hunter in destroying t... influences and is not swa...

On an e... disguised in th... feminist who p... stronger sex. S... prey and those... evident throug... refusal to give ...

The analysis prov... underlying influences tha... White Heron," I was ent... to save a heron from des... someone to whom she wa... interest. However, the rev... think about the story on a... depiction of Jewett's inte... connections to a feminist... conclusions. It is always... however, each reader mu... underlying meaning or sy... intended.

Works Cited

Hovet, Theodore R. "Once Upon a Time: Sarah Orne Jewett's 'A White Heron' as a Fairy Tale." *Studies in Short Fiction* 25 Sept. 2011: 63-68.

Jewett, Sarah Orne. "A White Heron." *The American Tradition in Literature*. Ed. George Perkins and Barbara Perkins. Vol. 2. New York: McGraw-Hill, 2009. 531-537.

Propp, Vladimir. "Morphology of a Folk Tale." New York: Anniston, 2004.

FIGURE 4.1 Literature Analysis Document

CASE STUDY | Literature Analysis

Starting Files	Files to Be Submitted	MyLab IT HOE Grader
w04h1Analysis w04h2WhiteHeron w04h2Entry.pdf	w04h2WhiteHeron_LastFirst w04h2Entry_LastFirst.pdf w04h3Analysis_GroupName	

MyLab IT Grader: This project is available as a Hands-On Exercise project in MyLab IT.

Research Paper Basics

Researching a topic and preparing a research paper are common components of most college degrees. Although Word cannot replace the researcher, it can provide a great deal of support for properly citing sources and adhering to specific style manuals. In addition, Word assists with designing footnotes and endnotes and preparing a bibliography.

In this section, you will explore the use of Word features that support the preparation of a research paper. Specifically, you will learn how to use style manuals, create source references and insert citations, develop a bibliography, and work with footnotes and endnotes.

Use a Writing Style and Acknowledge Sources

As you write a research paper, you will develop content that supports your topic. You will also be expected to adhere to a prescribed set of rules regarding page design and the citing of sources. Those rules are spelled out in a **style manual** that you can refer to as you develop a research paper. A style guide prescribes such settings as margins, line and paragraph spacing, the use of footnotes and endnotes, the way sources are cited, and the preparation of a bibliography.

It is common practice to use a variety of **sources** to supplement your own thoughts when writing a paper, report, legal brief, or other type of research-based document. A source is original material from which you pull some fact or statistic or quote used in a research paper. In fact, the word *research* implies that you are seeking information from other sources to support or explore your topic when writing a research paper. Properly citing, or giving credit to, your sources of information ensures that you avoid plagiarizing. Merriam-Webster's Collegiate Dictionary's definition of **plagiarizing** is "to steal and pass off (the ideas or words of another) as one's own."[1] Not limited to failure to cite sources, plagiarism includes buying a paper that is already written or asking (or paying) someone else to write a paper for you. In addition to written words, plagiarism applies to spoken words, multimedia works, or graphics. Plagiarism has serious moral and ethical implications and is typically considered as academic dishonesty in a college or university.

STEP 1 Select a Writing Style

When assigning a research paper, your instructor will identify the preferred **writing style**. The choice of writing style is often a matter of the academic discipline in which the research is conducted. A writing style provides a set of rules that results in standardized documents that present citations in the same manner and that include the same general page characteristics. In that way, research documents contain similar page features and settings so a reader can focus on the content of a paper without the distraction of varying page setups.

The humanities disciplines, including English, foreign languages, philosophy, religion, art, architecture, and literature, favor the **Modern Language Association (MLA)** style, which has been in existence for more than 50 years. Brief parenthetical (synonymous with

---

[1] By permission. From Merriam-Webster's Collegiate Dictionary, 11th edition © 2019 by Merriam-Webster, Inc. (www.Merriam-Webster.com).

in-text) citations throughout a paper identify sources of information. MLA style is used in many countries around the world, including the United States, Brazil, China, India, and Japan. Current MLA guidelines are published in the *MLA Handbook for Writers of Research Papers* and the *MLA Style Manual and Guide to Scholarly Publishing*.

Such disciplines as business, economics, communication, and social sciences promote the use of ***American Psychological Association (APA)*** writing style. Developed in 1929, APA attempts to simplify the expression of scientific ideas and experiment reports in a consistent manner. Its focus is on the communication of experiments, literature reviews, and statistics. The *Publication Manual of the American Psychological Association* provides current rules and guidelines associated with the writing style.

The ***Chicago writing style*** is an excellent choice for those who are preparing papers and books for publication. In fact, it is one of the most trusted resources within the book publishing industry. True to its name, the Chicago writing style was developed at the University of Chicago in 1906. It is currently in its 17th edition. The style is often referred to as CMS or CMOS. Often associated with the Chicago writing style, the ***Turabian writing style*** originated as a subset of Chicago. The dissertation secretary at the University of Chicago, Kate Turabian, narrowed the Chicago writing style to focus on writing papers. To do so, she omitted much of the information that is relevant for publishing. Currently, Turabian style is used mainly for the development of papers in the field of history. As you start working on your research paper, you may ensure the correct writing style is applied to your Word document from the Citations & Bibliography group on the References tab (see Figure 4.2).

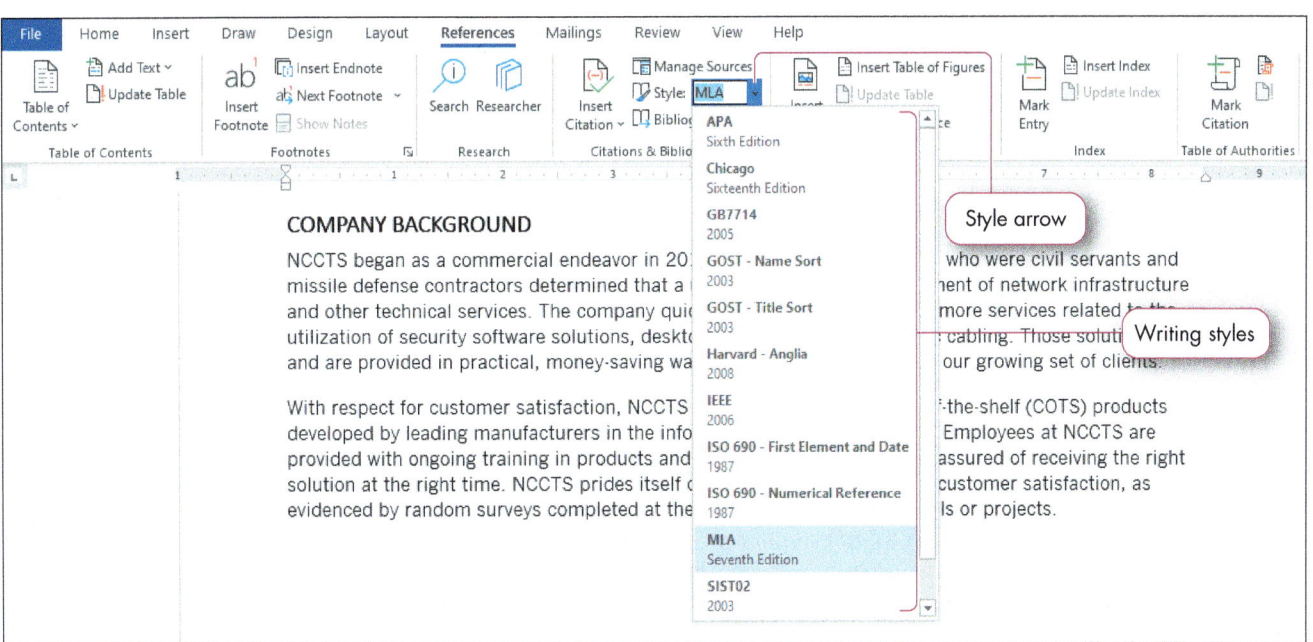

FIGURE 4.2 Select a Writing Style

Format a Research Paper

Regardless of the writing style used, most research papers in academic writing share several common formatting features to maintain some uniformity and consistencies across disciplines and to help produce a professional-looking document. With the exception of the title or cover page, some commonly established guidelines for a research paper include:

- Align text at the left
- Set double-space between lines
- Include no paragraph spacing before or after
- Set all margins (top, bottom, left, and right) to 1″
- Indent the first line of all body paragraphs by 1/2″
- Indent quotations 1″ from the left margin
- Separate sentences by only one space
- Use a serif font, such as Times New Roman, at 12 pt size
- Create a right-aligned header, including the page number in Arabic numerals, positioned 1/2″ from the top of the page

Create a Source and Include a Citation

By its very nature, a research paper is a collection of ideas and statements related to a topic. Many of those ideas are your own, summarizing your knowledge and conclusions. However, you will often include facts and results obtained from other sources. When you quote another person, glean ideas from others, or include information from another publication, you must give credit to the source by citing it in the body of your paper and/or including it in a bibliography. A *citation* is a brief, parenthetical reference that directs a reader to a source of information you used. Typically, a citation includes an author or publication name with an optional page number. For more information, the reader can check the source on your bibliography or works cited page. As you create a citation, you also add a reference source or refer to a preexisting source. A cited reference includes the type of source (book, journal article, report, website, etc.), title, publisher, page number(s), and other items specific to the type of source. At the conclusion of a report, you can use Word to create a bibliography, listing all of the sources you have cited.

Proper placement of a citation within a research paper is critical. A citation should be placed at the end of a sentence or paragraph. Use your judgment in placing a citation. For example, a long section of text that comes from one source should be cited at the end of the section—not after every sentence within the section. In other cases, a sentence that includes a quote or a direct reference to a particular source should be cited at the end of the sentence. Check the manual for the writing style you are working with for assistance with determining where to place a citation. Citations are typically placed before a punctuation mark that ends a sentence.

HOW TO

Insert a citation and source:

1. Place the insertion point at the end of the sentence that you want to cite, typically before the ending punctuation mark.
2. Click the References tab.
3. Click Insert Citation in the Citations & Bibliography group.
4. Click the source if inserting a previously defined source. Click Add New Source and type the new source information if creating a new source (see Figure 4.3).

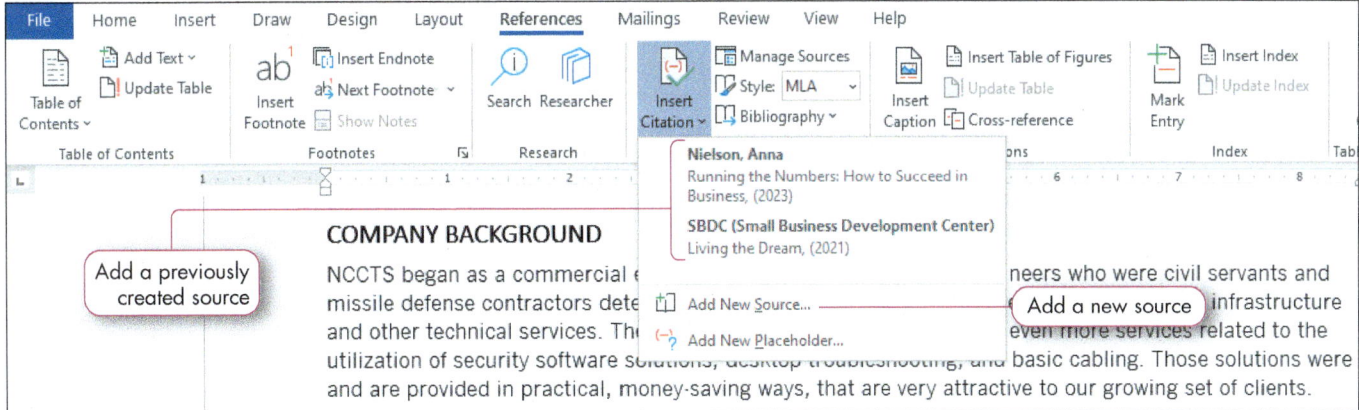

FIGURE 4.3 Add a Source

Depending on the writing style in use, the way a citation is worded may vary. Although Word automatically formats parenthetical citations (citations in parentheses in the body of the text) with the author's last name and other information, you might want to modify the wording or placement of items to accommodate the writing style. For example, if a sentence you are citing includes the author's name, most writing styles require only the page number in the citation, not the author's name. However, Word will place the author's name in the citation, so you must edit the citation to remove the name. A citation can be edited after selecting it, with options that include adding a page reference and/or suppressing the author, year, or title. When you click a parenthetical citation and click the Citation Options arrow, you can do more than simply edit the citation. You can also choose Edit Source (updating the source citation wherever it appears in the document) or Convert citation to static text (removing the field designation from the citation so that you can treat it like normal text) as shown in Figure 4.4. After you convert the citation to text, it will still be included in a bibliography generated by Word.

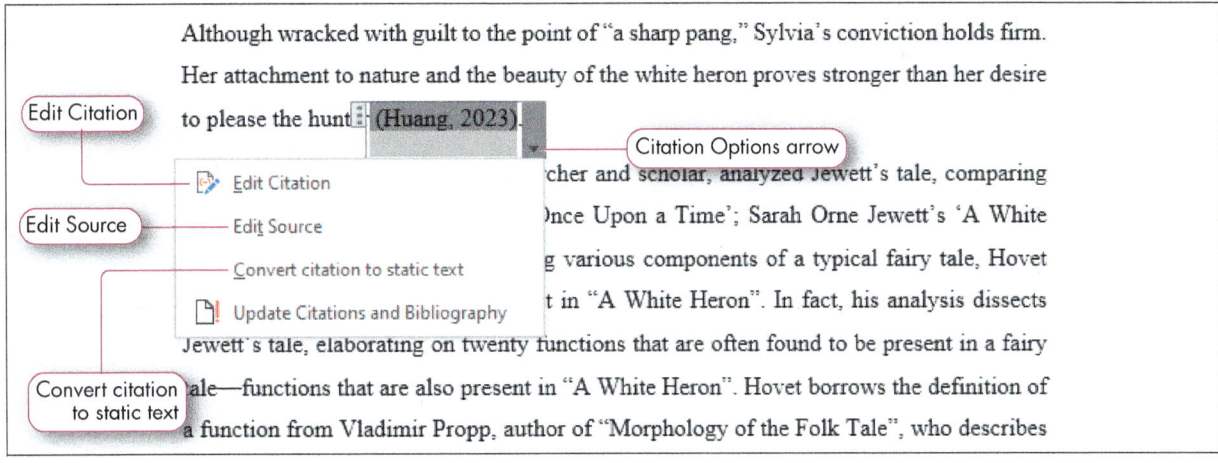

FIGURE 4.4 Citation Options

STEP 2 Manage Sources

When you create a source, it is available for use in the current document, saved in the document's *Current List*. It is also placed in a *Master List*, which is a database of all sources created in Word on a computer. Sources saved in the Master List can be shared in any Word document. This feature is helpful to those who use the same sources on multiple occasions. Suppose you are working on a research paper that addresses a topic similar to that of another paper you created on the same computer; you can access the same source from the Master List.

Access a source from the Master List for inclusion in the current document:

1. Click the References tab.

2. Click Manage Sources in the Citations & Bibliography group. (On a Mac, click Citations and click Settings in the bottom right corner of the Citations pane. Select Citation Source Manager.)

3. Select a source in the Master List that you intend to use in the current document (see Figure 4.5).

4. Click Copy to move it to the Current List.

5. Click Close.

6. Click in the location of the citation in the current document and click Insert Citation. (On a Mac, double-click the source shown in the Citations pane.)

7. Select the source reference.

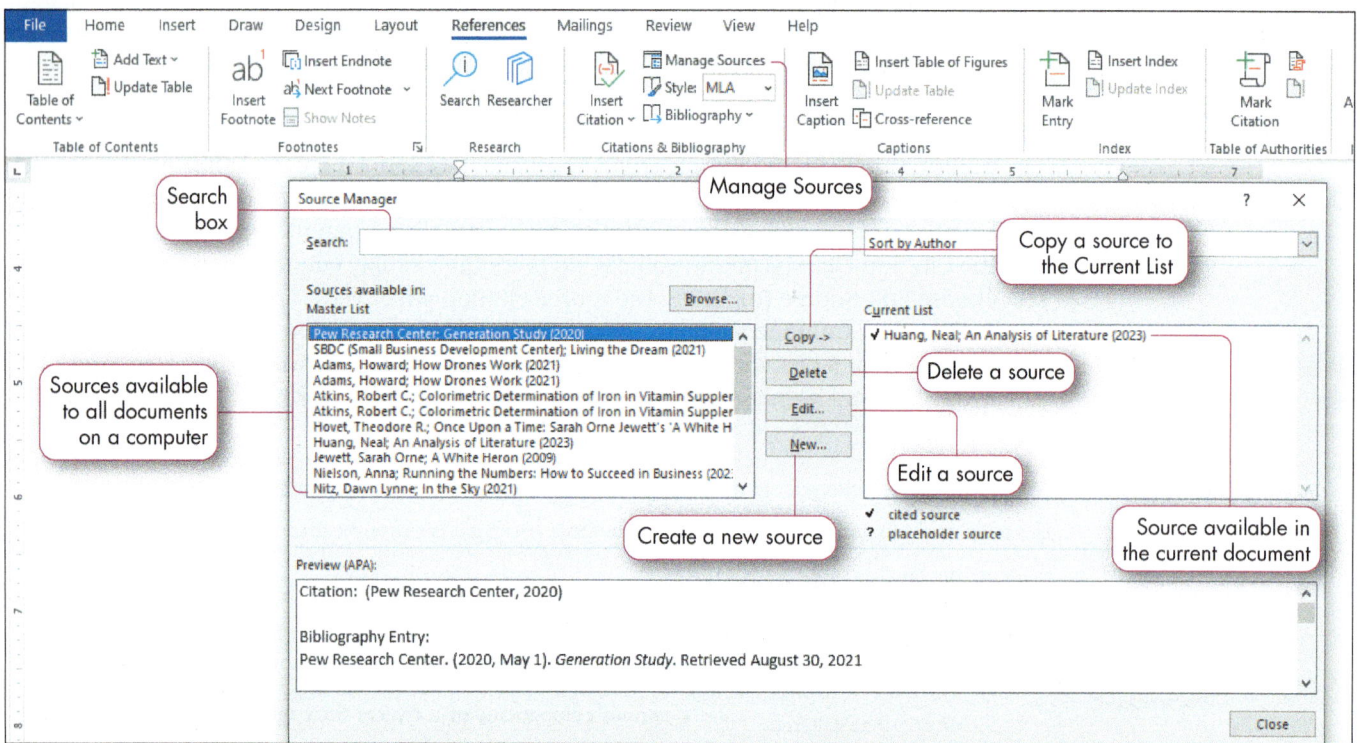

FIGURE 4.5 Manage Sources

The Source Manager not only enables you to share sources among several documents, it also makes it easy to delete and edit sources. In the Source Manager dialog box, select a source from either the Master or Current List, and then click Delete or Edit (refer to Figure 4.5). If sources are numerous, you might appreciate a quick way to search for a particular source. Search by author, title, or year by typing a search term in the Search box of the Source Manager dialog box. As you type, Word narrows the results so you can more easily determine if a source exists that meets your search criteria.

Create a Bibliography

A **bibliography** is a list of documents or sources that are consulted by an author during research for a paper. It guides a reader to sources of your research for additional study, and it also provides a reader with an opportunity to validate your references for accuracy. In theory, a bibliography lists not only those references that were cited in parenthetical terms throughout the paper but also those that were not cited but were helpful as you prepared the paper. A **Works Cited** page, on the other hand, is designed to contain only those sources that were cited in the paper, which is the way most research documents are expected to be prepared. However, a bibliography and a Works Cited page are considered synonymous terms when working with Word, and they both include consulted and cited sources. After a bibliography is prepared, you can always edit it to add additional references if required. Figure 4.6 shows a bibliography developed in Word and formatted according to the APA writing style, which requires the use of *References* as a title. Note that all sources include a hanging indent, which is typical of all writing style requirements. Further, entries are listed in alphabetical order by the last names of authors or editors or by the first words of the titles.

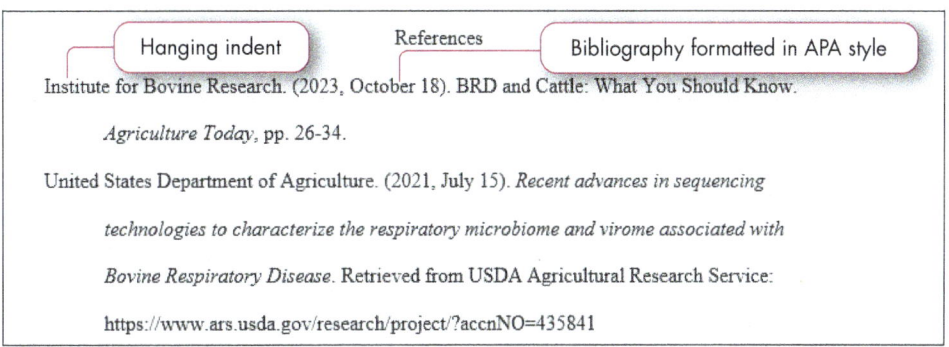

FIGURE 4.6 Bibliography

Depending on the writing style you are following, the term used for the list of references varies. MLA uses the term *Works Cited*, whereas APA requires *References*. Still others prefer *Bibliography*. You should be familiar with the preferred term and organization before using Word to develop a list of references.

The bibliography should be placed on a separate page by selecting Bibliography, References, or Works Cited (depending on the particular writing style requirement) in the Citations & Bibliography group on the References tab. If you want no heading but simply the formatted references, select Insert Bibliography. You can then add a heading, formatted as required by the writing style.

Regardless of which approach you take, you should always confirm that the resulting page meets all requirements of the style to which you are writing. Just as you would proofread a document instead of relying solely on Word's spelling checker, you should also consult a writing style manual to make sure your bibliography is correct.

When Word creates a bibliography page, it formats all citations as a single field. As shown in Figure 4.7, when you insert a bibliography list that Word has prepared, the entire list is shown as a unit, called a Bibliography field. The bibliography page does not update automatically should your sources change. However, if sources are added or edited later, you can update the bibliography by selecting the bibliography and clicking Update Citations and Bibliography. You can also choose to format the existing bibliography with a different title (perhaps changing from *Works Cited* to *References*), and you can convert the bibliography to static text.

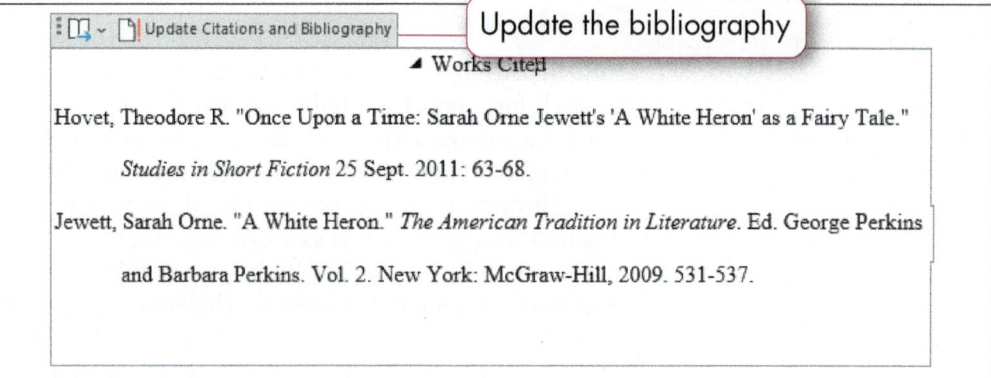

FIGURE 4.7 Update a Bibliography

Create and Modify Footnotes and Endnotes

A ***footnote*** is a citation or note that displays at the bottom of a page, while an ***endnote*** serves the same purpose but is at the end of a document. Like parenthetical citations, the purpose of a footnote and endnote is to draw a reader's attention to a specific source of information. In addition, footnotes and endnotes are often used to further describe a statistic or statement used in the report without including additional detail in the text. For example, a statistic on the number of victims in a natural disaster or the amount of money given through a government program could be further detailed in a footnote. You might also define or illustrate a concept included in the report, providing a personal comment. Much of business writing is persuasive text, in which you explain a situation or encourage others to take some action. Using a footnote is a great way to further describe a statistic used in your text without having to incorporate it into the written paragraph. That way, you do not risk cluttering the document with overly explanatory text, perhaps losing or diverting the attention of the reader. A footnote, providing clarification of a statistic, is shown in Figure 4.8. Note that the footnote is linked by a superscript (elevated number) to the corresponding reference in the paper.

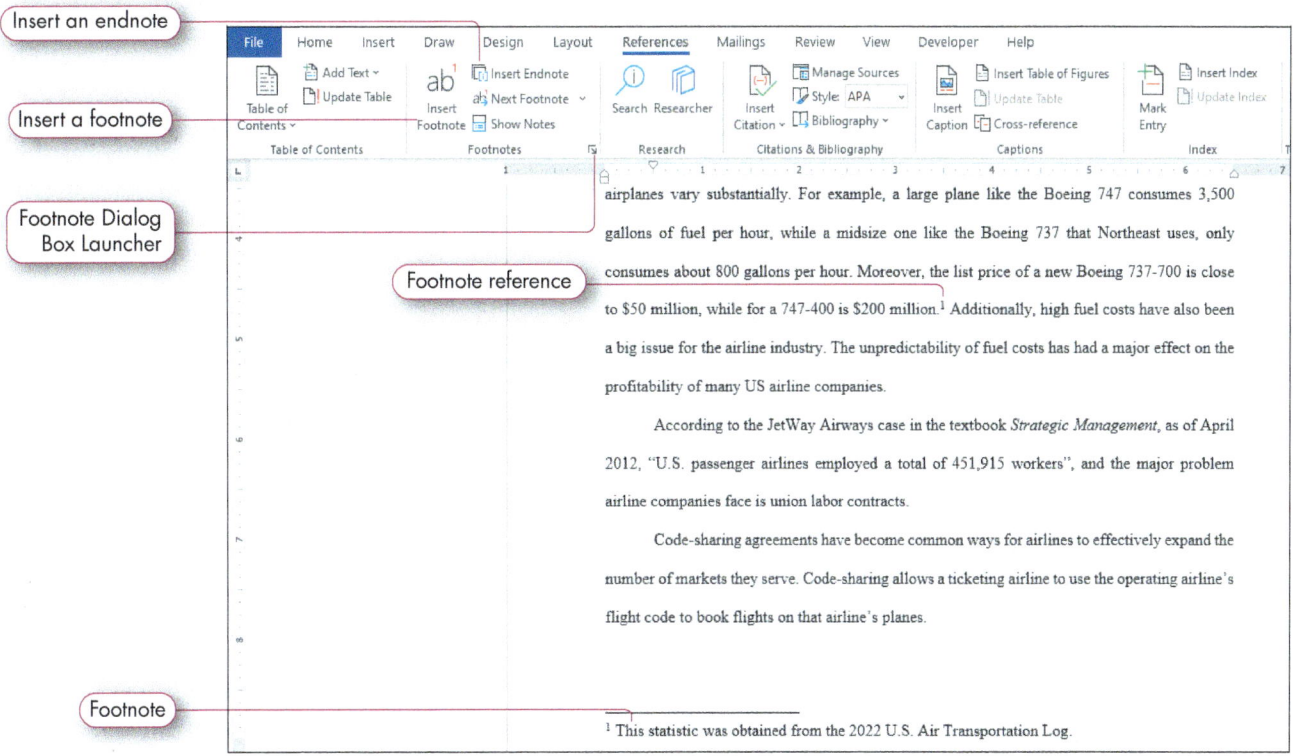

Insert an endnote

Insert a footnote

Footnote Dialog Box Launcher

Footnote reference

Footnote

airplanes vary substantially. For example, a large plane like the Boeing 747 consumes 3,500 gallons of fuel per hour, while a midsize one like the Boeing 737 that Northeast uses, only consumes about 800 gallons per hour. Moreover, the list price of a new Boeing 737-700 is close to $50 million, while for a 747-400 is $200 million.[1] Additionally, high fuel costs have also been a big issue for the airline industry. The unpredictability of fuel costs has had a major effect on the profitability of many US airline companies.

According to the JetWay Airways case in the textbook *Strategic Management*, as of April 2012, "U.S. passenger airlines employed a total of 451,915 workers", and the major problem airline companies face is union labor contracts.

Code-sharing agreements have become common ways for airlines to effectively expand the number of markets they serve. Code-sharing allows a ticketing airline to use the operating airline's flight code to book flights on that airline's planes.

[1] This statistic was obtained from the 2022 U.S. Air Transportation Log.

FIGURE 4.8 Include a Footnote

You should never use both footnotes and endnotes in the same paper. Choosing whether to use footnotes or endnotes, if at all, depends in part on the number of citations included and the way you want your reader to process the report's information. Because endnotes are included as a list at the end of the document, they do not add clutter to the bottom of pages. In addition, they might make the report easier to read because a reader's gaze is not constantly shifting back and forth from the bottom of a page to the text. Conversely, a footnote provides immediate clarification of a source and enables the writer to make additional comments related to a statement on the same page as the footnote.

The choice of whether to use a footnote or a parenthetical citation to reference a source depends somewhat on the writing style you are following. Always refer to the writing style guide when considering which to use, as each style tends to prefer one or the other. The choice is also related to the type of document. For example, legal documents almost always rely heavily on footnotes instead of parenthetical citations or even endnotes.

Although you might choose to include footnotes to provide additional information related to a statement on the same page, you will most likely use a bibliography or Works Cited page to provide a complete list of referenced sources in a paper. An advantage to using a bibliography for that task is that each source is listed only once. In contrast, a footnote or endnote displays each time a source is referenced, regardless of how many times the same source is cited in a paper.

Including a bibliography does not mean that you cannot use footnotes to provide more detailed descriptions of statements or facts in the paper. You should be aware, however, that most writing styles limit a footnote to only one sentence. Therefore, any planned explanation of a report statement should be condensed to just one sentence.

STEP 3 ▶ **Create Footnotes and Endnotes**

Source information in a document that you reference with a footnote or endnote includes a number or symbol in superscript. The reference is then keyed to the same number or symbol at the end of the page (footnote) or at the end of the document (endnote). The References tab includes the Insert Footnote and Insert Endnote commands as shown in Figure 4.8. By default, Word sequentially numbers footnotes with Arabic numerals (1, 2, and 3) and endnotes with lowercase Roman numerals (i, ii, and iii). If you add or delete footnotes or endnotes, Word renumbers the remaining notes automatically.

Modify Footnotes and Endnotes

Occasionally, you will determine that different wording better suits a particular footnote or endnote. Or perhaps you want to remove a footnote or endnote completely. You can even change the format of a footnote or endnote, changing the font, font size, or character formatting. To modify a footnote or endnote, double-click the numeric reference in the body of the document. The insertion point will be placed to the left of the footnote or endnote number.

To insert a footnote or endnote while specifying settings other than those selected by default, use the Dialog Box Launcher in the Footnotes group on the References tab to open the Footnote and Endnote dialog box (refer to Figure 4.8). As shown in Figure 4.9, you can modify the placement, number format, symbol, and initial number before you insert a new footnote or endnote. You can delete any unwanted footnote or endnote by selecting the numeric footnote or endnote indicator in the document and pressing Delete.

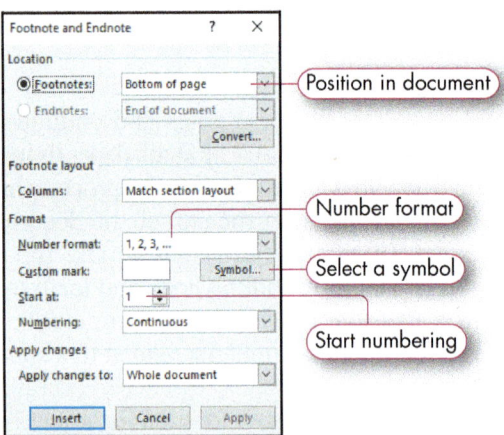

FIGURE 4.9 Footnote and Endnote Dialog Box

You can remove note text and replace it with alternate wording, just as you would adjust wording in a document. If you plan to change the format of a single note instead of affecting all footnotes or endnotes in a document, you can select the note text and apply different formatting—perhaps italicizing or bolding words. More often, you might want to adjust the format of every footnote or endnote in a document. Footnotes are formatted in Footnote Text style and endnotes are formatted in Endnote Text style. Those styles include a specific font type, font size, and paragraph spacing, and can also be accessed from the Styles pane.

HOW TO

Modify the style of either a footnote or endnote, affecting all footnotes or endnotes in a document:

1. Right-click a footnote or endnote and select Style.
2. Click Modify in the Style dialog box.
3. Adjust the font and alignment settings or click Format for more selections.
4. Click OK. Click Apply.

Explore Special Features

Although writing a research paper is a typical requirement of a college class, it is not the only type of paper you are likely to write. In the workplace, you might be asked to contribute to technical reports, grant proposals, and other types of business documents. Those reports are not likely to be as strictly bound to writing style rules as are reports written for academic purposes. In fact, you might find it necessary to include special features such as a table of contents, an index, and even a cover page to properly document a paper and make it easier to navigate. Such features are not usually included in a college research report or required by academic writing style guides, but they are common components of papers, chapters, and articles to be published or distributed.

Create a Table of Contents

For a long, written report or research paper, a *table of contents* lists headings and subheadings in the order they appear in the document, along with the page numbers on which the entries begin. The key to enabling Word to create a table of contents is to apply heading styles to headings in the document at appropriate levels. You can apply built-in styles, Heading 1 through Heading 9, or identify your own custom styles to use when generating the table of contents. For example, if you apply Heading 1 style to major headings, Heading 2 style to subordinate headings, and lower-level heading styles to remaining headings as appropriate, Word can create an accurate table of contents. The table of contents is displayed in a separate section of the document.

HOW TO

Insert a predefined table of contents:

1. Ensure that headings in the document are formatted with heading styles according to level.
2. Click the References tab.
3. Click Table of Contents in the Table of Contents group.
4. Select an Automatic table style to create a formatted table of contents that can be updated when heading text or positioning changes (or select Manual Table to create a table of contents that is not updated when changes occur).

For more flexibility as you design a table of contents, you can choose Table of Contents (on the References tab) and select Custom Table of Contents. From the Table of Contents dialog box, select options related to page numbering and alignment, general format, level of headings to show, and leader style (the characters that lead the reader's eye from a heading to its page number).

A table of contents is inserted as a field. When you click a table of contents, the entire table is shown as an entity that you can update or remove. As shown in Figure 4.10, controls at the top of the selection enable you to update, modify, or remove a table of contents. As you make changes to a document, especially if those changes affect the number, positioning, or sequencing of headings, you will want to update any associated table of contents. You will indicate whether you want to update page numbers only or the entire table.

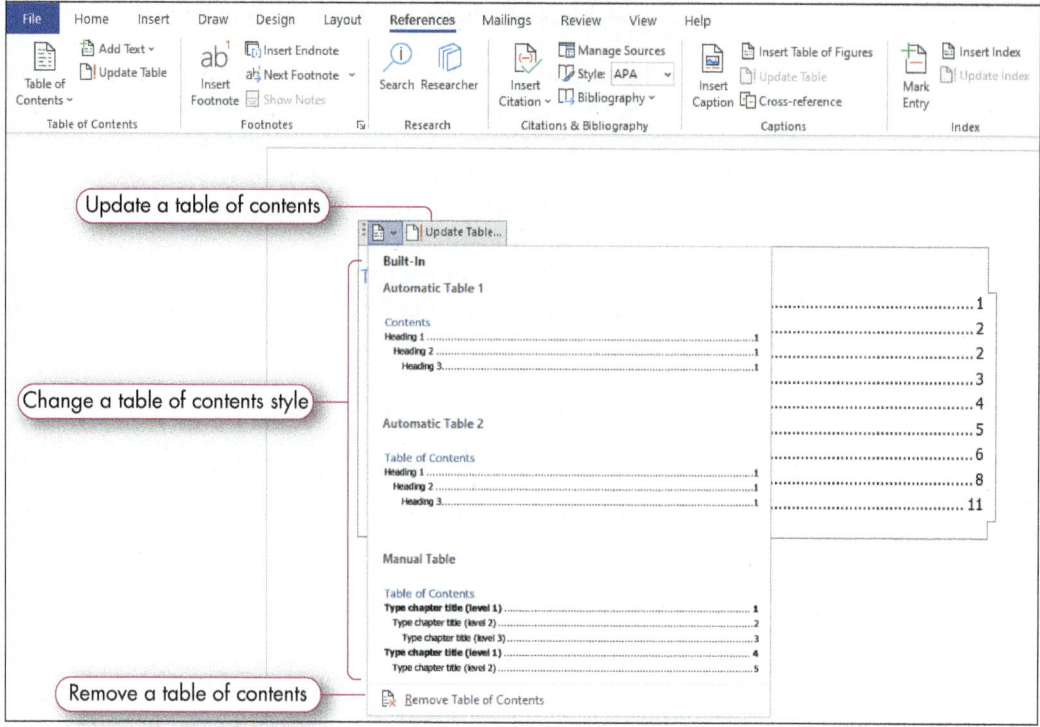

FIGURE 4.10 Update a Table of Contents

Create an Index

No doubt you have used an *index* to locate a topic of interest in a book. In doing so, you were able to move quickly to the topic. Most books and many lengthy papers include an index. Typically located at the end of a book or document, an index provides an alphabetical listing of topics included in a document, along with related page numbers. In a document, you can mark items to include and have them automatically formatted as an index. In situations where there is more than one name or term to describe the same content, you can mark the item for cross reference.

To mark terms for inclusion in an index, select any word or phrase and click Mark Entry in the Index group on the References tab. Select or confirm settings in the Mark Index Entry dialog box, identifying any cross references and indicating whether all occurrences of the selected text should be marked for inclusion in the index.

As you mark entries for inclusion in the index, they will be coded in the document with a tag. After marking entries to include, you are ready to create the index. There are several layouts available for the Index page, with Word arranging index entries in alphabetical order and supplying page references.

HOW TO

Create an index:

1. Insert a blank page at the end of the document or at a location where the index is to display.
2. Click Insert Index in the Index group on the References tab.
3. Adjust or confirm settings in the Index dialog box, including the format style, number of columns, language, and alignment. Click OK.

Creating an index is usually among the last tasks related to preparing a paper, chapter, or book. However, even if an index has been created, you can still update the index with new entries. New entries are alphabetized along with the original entries in the index. An index can be updated to include newly marked entries with the correct page numbers by using Update Index in the Index group on the References tab.

STEP 4 ▸ Create a Cover Page

A ***cover page***, sometimes called a *title page*, is placed at the beginning of a report. Some writing styles do not require a cover page for a research report, whereas others do. For example, APA writing style requires a cover page for a research report, while MLA style does not. When writing a research paper, consult the writing guide of the style you are following for information related to the format of a cover page (if a cover page is required). You can create a cover page in any of a variety of styles available in the Pages group on the Insert tab. After selecting a design, you can personalize the cover page with your name, report title, and any other required information.

Manage a Table of Figures

It is not unusual for a report, especially one that is scientific in nature, to include a large number of media items, such as tables, figures, and images. Those items are often captioned for identification. Even so, it is also helpful to provide a table of figures so that a reader can quickly navigate to specific figures of interest. In a lengthy document, such as a dissertation, a table of figures is an invaluable navigational aid, much as a table of contents might be. A table of figures is a list, sorted by page number, of figure captions throughout a document.

You should consult the writing style manual that you are following for information on where to locate a table of figures and for any required formatting. Click where the table is to be placed and select Insert Table of Figures in the Captions group on the References tab. The Table of Figures dialog box will open, showing both a print and Web preview of the table. After adjusting any settings included in the dialog box, click OK. The table of figures is placed in the document. With continued editing of the document, it is possible that additional figures are added, or perhaps captioned items are rearranged. In that case, a table of figures should be updated. Click the table of figures to select it, and then select Update Table in the Captions group on the References tab. At that point, you will choose whether to update the entire table or only the page numbers. Click OK to complete the update process.

Critical Thinking

1. Explain how the purpose of a footnote differs from that of a citation to a source in a paper. ***p. 305***

2. Explain how the length of a report or paper might contribute to the necessity, or lack thereof, of an index. ***p. 308***

3. Provide rationale for the requirement that both footnotes and endnotes should never be used in the same paper. ***p. 304***

Hands-On Exercises

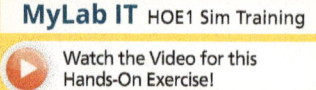

Skills covered: Select a
Writing Style • Format a Research
Paper • Create a Source and
Include a Citation • Manage
Sources • Create a Bibliography •
Create Footnotes and Endnotes •
Modify Footnotes and Endnotes •
Create a Cover Page

1 Research Paper Basics

You have completed a draft of an analysis of the short story "A White Heron." As a requirement for the literature class in which you are enrolled, you must format the paper according to MLA style, including citations and a bibliography. In addition, you will include a cover page. Although a cover page is not included in MLA style, your instructor has asked that you prepare one for this class.

STEP 1 **SELECT A WRITING STYLE, FORMAT A RESEARCH PAPER, CREATE A SOURCE, AND INCLUDE A CITATION**

You will format the analysis of "A White Heron" in MLA style and include citations where appropriate. Refer to Figure 4.11 as you complete Step 1.

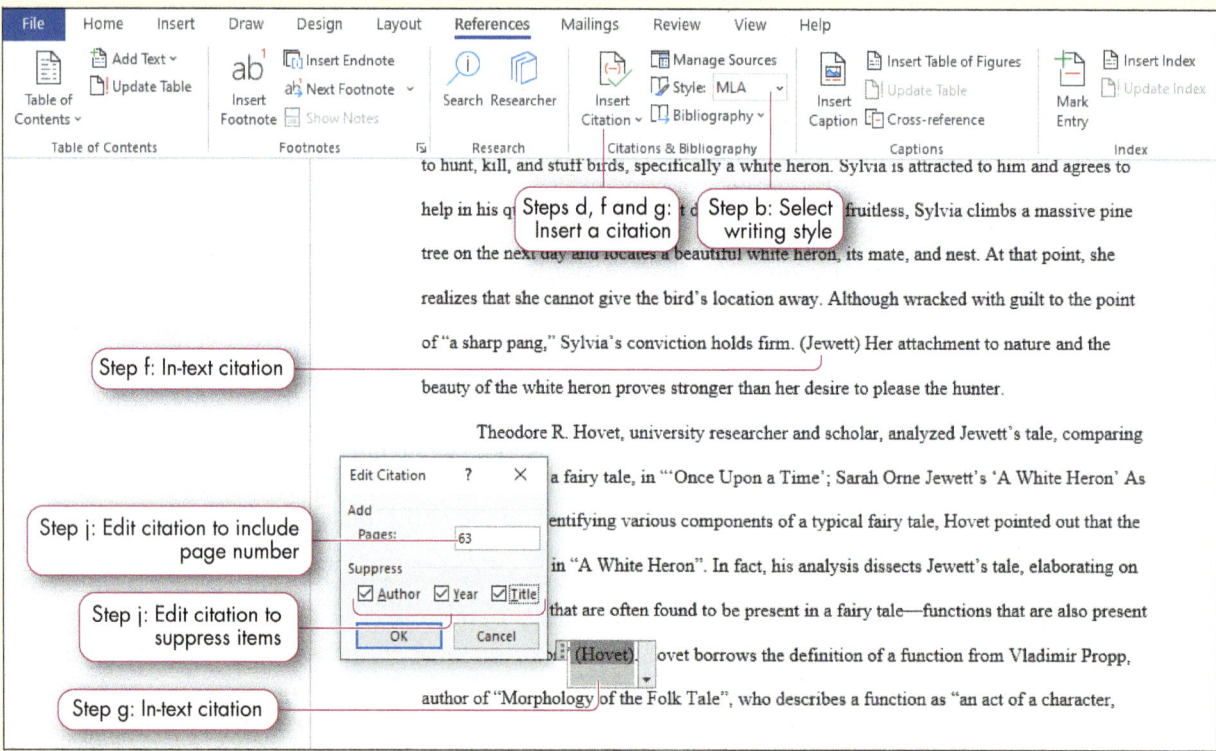

FIGURE 4.11 Add Sources and Insert Citations

a. Open *w04h1Analysis* and save it as **w04h1Analysis_LastFirst**.

> **TROUBLESHOOTING:** If you make any major mistakes in this exercise, you can close the file, open *w04h1Analysis* again, and then start this exercise over.

b. Click the **References tab** and click the **Style arrow** in the Citations & Bibliography group. Select **MLA Seventh Edition**. Select all of the document and apply the following MLA style settings:

- Text is **left** aligned.
- Line spacing is **2.0** (or double).
- Paragraph spacing Before and After is **0**.

- Font is **12 pt Times New Roman**.
- Margins are **1″** at the top, bottom, left, and right.
- First line of all body paragraphs are indented **0.5″**. (Select all paragraphs except the report title, click the **Dialog Box Launcher** in the Paragraph group on the Home tab, click the **Special arrow** and select **First line**.)
- Report title (*An Analysis of "A White Heron"*) is centered.

c. Insert a right-aligned header that includes your last name, followed by a space and a plain page number. Make sure the page number is inserted as a field, not simply typed. Format the header as **Times New Roman 12 pt**. Select **Different First Page** in the Options group on the Header & Footer tab. Close the header or double-click in the body of the report.

d. Place the insertion point after the ending quotation mark and before the ending period in Jewett's notation in the first body paragraph (ending in *straying about out-of-doors*). Click the **References tab** and click **Insert Citation** in the Citations & Bibliography group. Select **Add New Source**. Click the **Type of Source arrow** and select **Book Section**. Complete the citation as follows, but do not click OK after completing the source.

Author: **Jewett, Sarah Orne**

Title: **A White Heron**

Book Title: **The American Tradition in Literature**

Year: **2009**

Pages: **531–537**

City: **New York**

Publisher: **McGraw-Hill**

e. Click to select **Show All Bibliography Fields**. Scroll down and click in the **Editor box** and type **Perkins, George**. Click **Edit** beside Editor. Type **Perkins** in the Last box. Click in the **First box** and type **Barbara**. Click **OK**. Click in the **Volume box** and type **2**. Click **OK**.

You have added a source related to a section of a book in which the short story is printed. Because more than one editor was involved, you added two editor names.

f. Click after the word *firm* and before the ending period in the sentence that ends in *Sylvia's conviction holds firm* in the first paragraph. Click **Insert Citation** in the Citations & Bibliography group and select **Jewett, Sarah Orne** to insert a citation to the same source as that created earlier.

> **MAC TROUBLESHOOTING:** Click Citations on the References tab, double-click the citation in the Citations pane, and then close the pane.

g. Place the insertion point after the ending quotation mark and before the ending period in Hovet's notation in the second body paragraph (ending in *functions that are also present in "A White Heron"*). Add a new source, selecting **Article in a Periodical** as the source and type:

Author: **Hovet, Theodore R.**

Title: **Once Upon a Time: Sarah Orne Jewett's 'A White Heron' as a Fairy Tale**

Periodical Title: **Studies in Short Fiction**

Year: **2011**

Month: **Sept.**

Day: **25**

Pages: **63–68**

You have to use single quotes for the title of the source because double quotes will be added around the full title in the Bibliography.

h. Click to select **Show All Bibliography Fields**, set the Volume to **15** and the Issue to **1**, and then click **OK**.

i. Click Jewett's parenthetical citation in the first body paragraph beside the words *straying about out-of-doors*. Click the **Citation Options arrow** and select **Edit Citation**. Type **532** in the Pages box. Click **OK**.

You have added a page number to identify the source as required by MLA writing style.

j. Edit the next citation in the first body paragraph (following the sentence that ends in *Sylvia's conviction holds firm*) to include page number **537**. Click the only Hovet citation in the second body paragraph. Click the **Citation Options arrow** and select **Edit Citation**. Suppress the display of Author, Year, and Title, but include a Page Number of **63**. Click **OK**.

k. Save the document.

MANAGE SOURCES AND CREATE A BIBLIOGRAPHY

Now that sources are cited and stored in the document, you will insert the bibliography at the end. You will also explore the sharing of sources. Refer to Figure 4.12 as you complete Step 2.

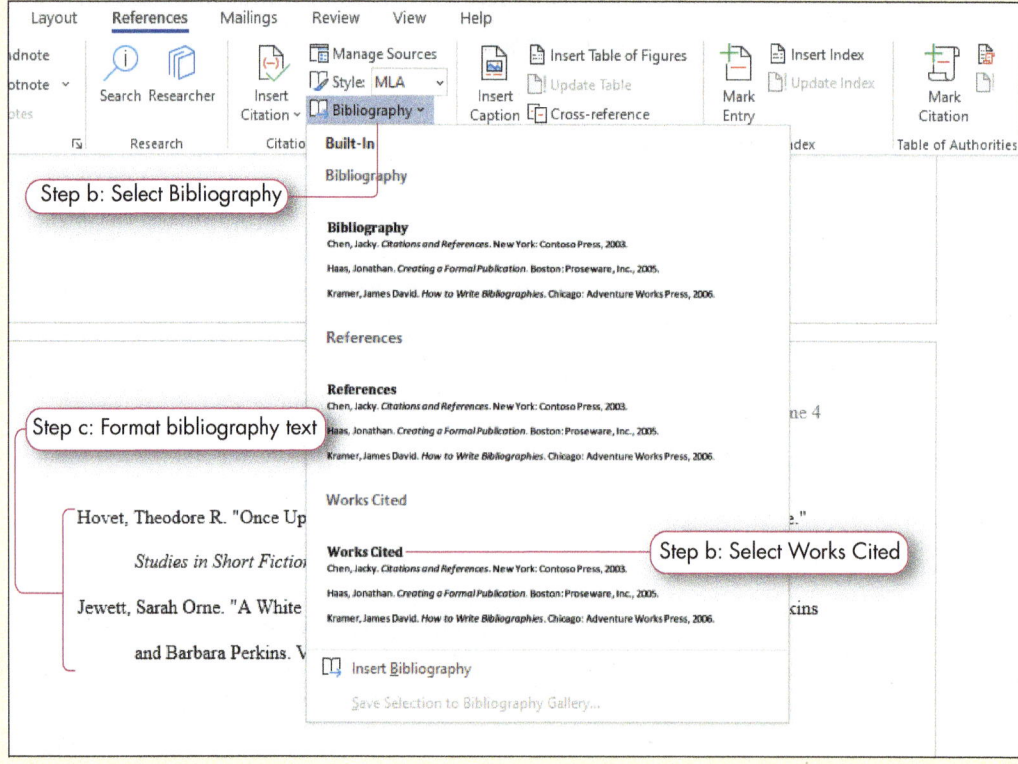

FIGURE 4.12 Create a Bibliography

a. Click **Manage Sources** in the Citations & Bibliography group on the References tab.

Note that the sources you created in the previous step are shown in the Master List and the Current List. They are available for use in other documents as well as in the current document.

> **MAC TROUBLESHOOTING:** Click Citations on the References tab, click Settings in the Citations pane, and then click Citation Source Manager.

> **TROUBLESHOOTING:** It is possible that sources other than those you just added are also shown in the Master List. The list includes all sources you have included in other documents as well as those in the current document.

b. Click **Close**. Place the insertion point at the end of the document. Press **Ctrl+Enter** to insert a page break. Click **Bibliography** in the Citations & Bibliography group and select **Works Cited**.

A bibliography is always included as a separate page at the end of the document. Therefore, you inserted a page break before adding the bibliography. The bibliography includes the heading Works Cited. The two sources you used in your analysis are listed, although you may have to scroll up to see them.

c. Drag to select all text on the Works Cited page, including the heading *Works Cited* and all sources. Change the line spacing to **2.0** (or double), the paragraph spacing Before and After to **0**, and the font to **Times New Roman 12 pt**. Select the *Works Cited* heading, remove the bold format, and then center the line.

The Works Cited page adheres to MLA writing style guidelines.

d. Save the document.

STEP 3 **CREATE AND MODIFY FOOTNOTES**

Footnotes are used to clarify statements or provide additional information. You identify a couple of places in the paper where a footnote would be helpful. Because footnotes and endnotes are mutually exclusive—you only use one or the other in a single paper—you will not use endnotes. However, you know that the way in which endnotes and footnotes are added is very similar. Having added footnotes, you will modify the style so that they match the format of other text in the research paper. Refer to Figure 4.13 as you complete Step 3.

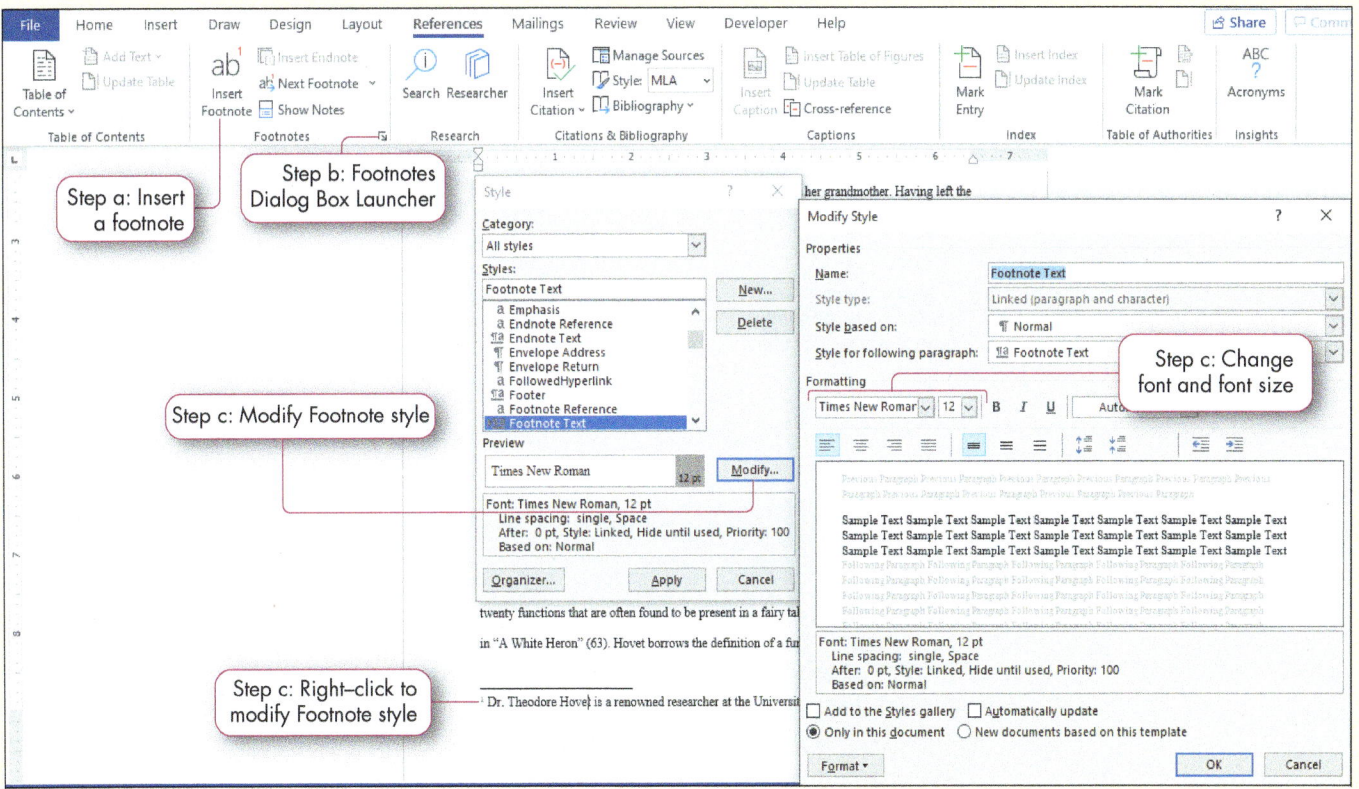

FIGURE 4.13 Modify Footnote Style

a. Click after the quotation mark ending the first sentence in the last paragraph on page 1, ending in *as a Fairy Tale*. Click the **References tab** and click **Insert Footnote** in the Footnotes group. Type **Dr. Theodore Hovet is a renowned researcher at the University of Southern Colorado.** (Include the period.)

You inserted a footnote, numbered with a superscript, providing additional information.

b. Scroll to page 2 and place the insertion point after the period ending the first sentence in the first full paragraph on the page (ending in *and a disguised villain*). Click the **Dialog Box Launcher** in the Footnotes group and click **Insert**. Type **Grimm's Fairy Tales is a classic collection of such stories.** (Include the period.)

You inserted another footnote, numbered sequentially after the first footnote. Using the Footnote and Endnote dialog box, you have options to specify various choices, including numbering.

c. Right-click the footnote at the bottom of page 2 and click **Style**. Click **Modify**. Change the font type to **Times New Roman** and the font size to **12**. Click **OK** and click **Apply**.

You changed the footnote style for this document to include a font type and size that is similar to the body text. The new format applies to all footnotes in the document.

d. Save the document.

STEP 4 ## CREATE A COVER PAGE

As a final touch, you create a cover page with information related to the report title, your name, the course number, and the current date. Although MLA writing style does not require a cover page, your instructor has asked for a cover page so he can quickly identify each student submission. Refer to Figure 4.14 as you complete Step 4.

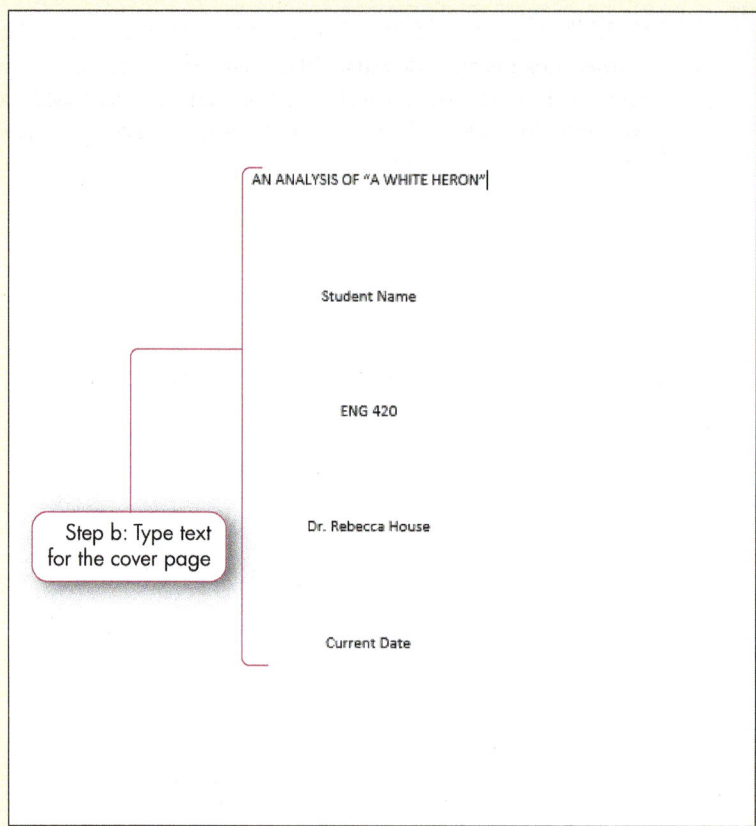

FIGURE 4.14 Create a Cover Page

a. Insert a page break at the beginning of the document and place the insertion point at the top of the new blank page. Click the **Home tab** and click **Center alignment** in the Paragraph group. Change the font size to **16 pt** and font color to **Black, Text 1**.

The change in font and font color will apply to text that is to be typed in the cover page.

b. Press **Enter** five times. Type **An Analysis of A "White Heron"**. Press **Enter** three times and type your first and last names. Press **Enter** three times again and type **ENG 420**. Press **Enter** three times and type **Dr. Rebecca House**. Press **Enter** three times and type the current date, as month day, year (e.g. *March 10, 2024*). Ensure that text on the cover page is neither bold nor italicized. Select the text *An Analysis of The White Heron*, click **Change Case** in the Font group on the Home tab, and select **UPPERCASE**.

Although Word provides predesigned colorful cover page choices, you design a more conservative cover page to accompany the research report.

c. Save and close the document. You will submit this file to your instructor at the end of the last Hands-On Exercise.

Document Tracking

Whether in a college class or in the workplace, it is likely that you will seek feedback from others or collaborate with them on the completion of a project. Knowing how to use *Track Changes* to keep track of all additions, deletions, and document formatting can enhance collaborative efforts. Further, you can use *markup* to help customize the way tracked changes are displayed in a document. As a document is reviewed by several people, you can track changes and view any comments that have been made.

Although group editing is often a reason to share a document, you might also want to share a completed document with others with the assurance that they can open it regardless of specific software availability. Documents are often saved as *Portable Document Format (PDF)* files for ease of access, as they can be opened by several programs, including Word and Adobe Acrobat Reader (a free download). Especially useful for documents like magazine articles, brochures, and flyers, PDF format accurately represents all page elements, including graphics and text effects. Although a PDF file is not necessarily intended for sharing and group editing, you can convert a PDF document into a Word document and edit content.

In this section, as you track changes in a document, you will learn to control the level of detail shown and you will work with accepting or rejecting changes made by others. As you explore the review of documents, you will learn to add and reply to comments. Finally, you will learn to edit and share a PDF document.

Track Changes

Whether you work individually or with a group, you can monitor any revisions made to a document. Track Changes in the Tracking group on the Review tab enables you to track all changes (for example, content and formatting) made to a document. Track Changes is particularly useful in situations in which a document must be reviewed by several people—each of whom can offer suggestions or change parts of the document—with those changes and comments reviewed before being accepted. In effect, changes made to a document when Track Changes is activated are much like suggestions that a reviewer can accept or reject later. When you no longer want changes to be tracked, you can toggle off the Track Changes feature. You can also lock tracking with or without a password to prevent other authors from turning off Track Changes (see Figure 4.15). However, if you forget the password, tracking changes will always be on, so carefully consider whether a password is necessary.

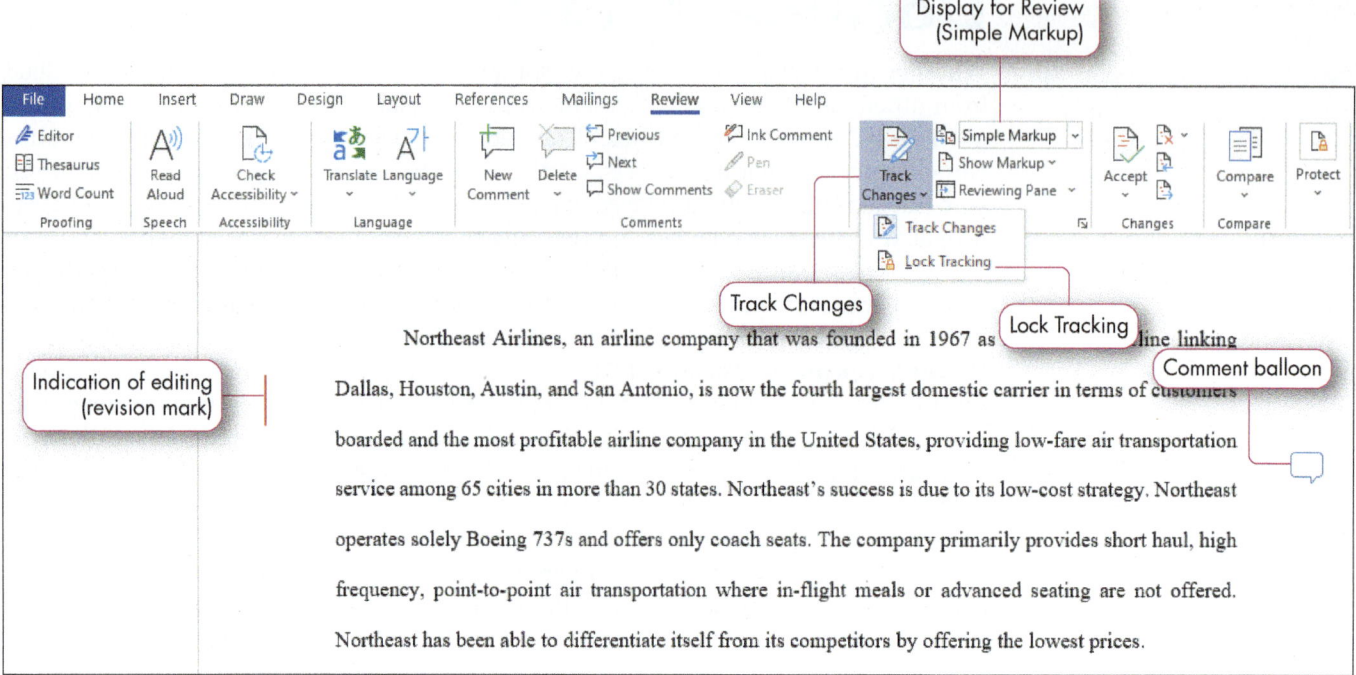

FIGURE 4.15 Track Changes

STEP 1 **Use Track Changes**

When Track Changes is not active, any change you make to a document is untraceable, with no indication that editing has occurred. However, when you select Track Changes on the Review tab and begin to monitor editing, *revision marks* are shown, color-coded depending on who made the changes if more than one person is involved. Added text is underlined, while deletions are shown with a strikethrough if a document is shown with full markup. As described later in this chapter, you can control the level of markup shown, from full markup through a simpler view in which a vertical bar in the margin indicates the general location of changes made in a document (refer to Figure 4.15). For various purposes, you can display markups in full detail or choose a simpler view to minimize clutter and distraction.

For even more control over how changes are tracked and displayed, you can access one or more dialog boxes related to tracking. Click the Dialog Box Launcher in the Tracking group on the Review tab to show the Track Changes Options dialog box. There you can select which changes are shown, although you can do much the same when you click Show Markup in the Tracking group on the Review tab. The Advanced Track Changes Options dialog box, shown when you click Advanced Options (see Figure 4.16), enables you to customize a wide array of tracking settings—everything from the width of comment balloons to the colors assigned various edits and whether a vertical revision mark should show in the left or right margin.

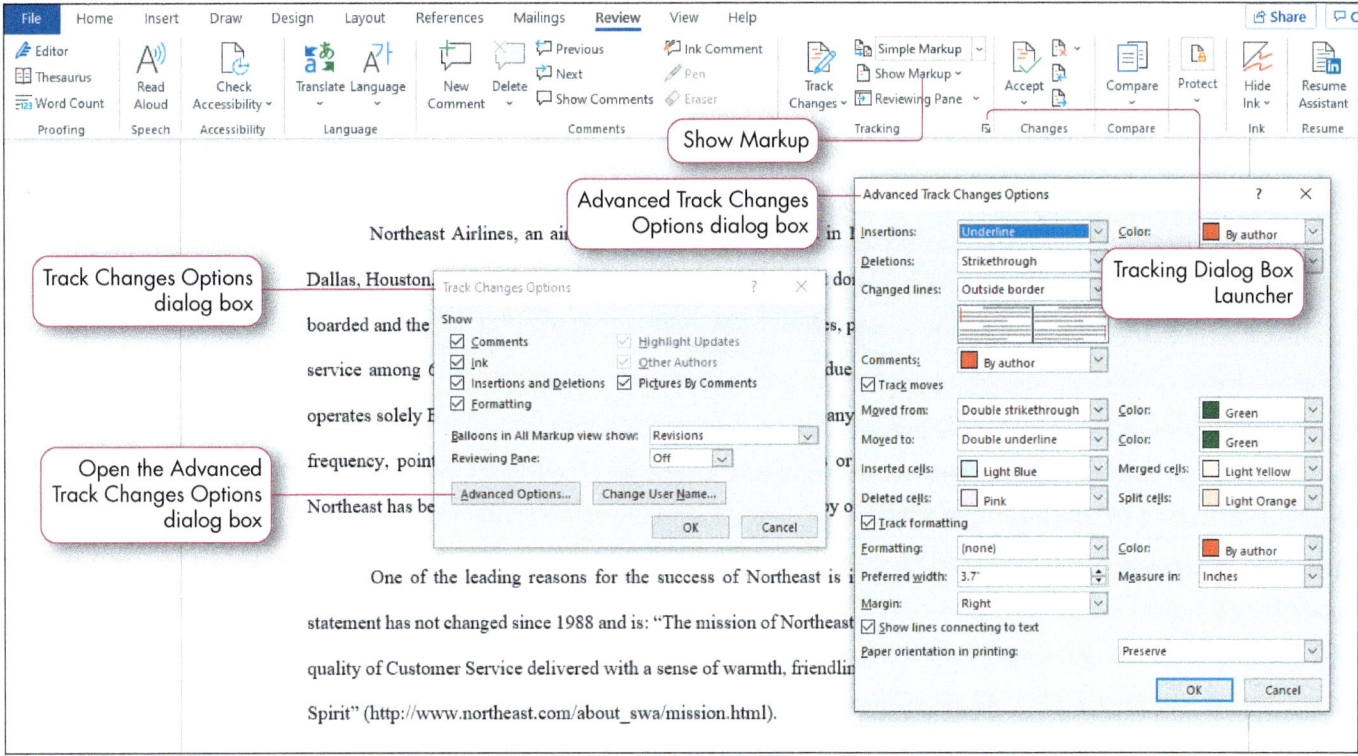

FIGURE 4.16 Format Track Changes

Accept Changes

During the review and revision process, you will most likely check all comments and act on them or otherwise reply to the reviewer. You might also view all edits, including changes in wording and formatting, accepting or rejecting such changes during the review process. As shown in Figure 4.17, you can step through each change by clicking Next in the Changes group, or you can revisit others by clicking Previous. At any point, you can accept or reject a change, or you can accept or reject all changes at one time while also ending tracking. When a review is complete, you will want to ensure that all changes have been accepted and tracking has ended so that a clean copy is available. Until that is done, edits remain in the document as revision marks even if the markup view is such that they are not currently visible in text.

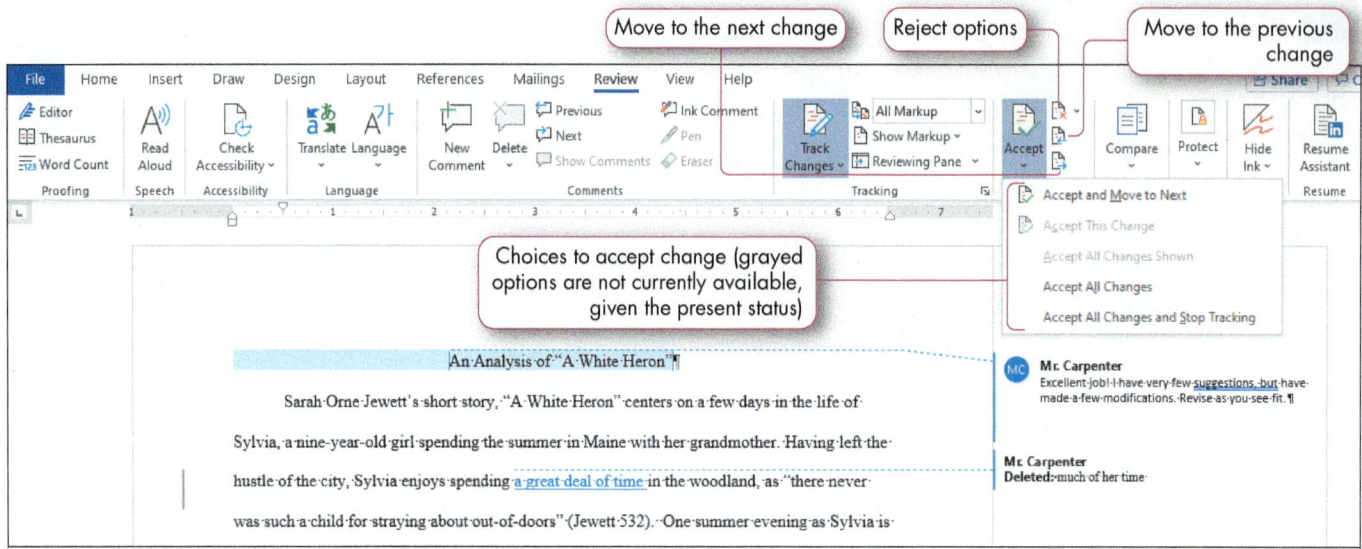

FIGURE 4.17 Accept or Reject Changes

Review a Document

In today's organizational environment, it is common for teams of people with diverse backgrounds, skills, and knowledge to prepare documents as a group. A large part of that process is reviewing or editing work begun by others. As several people contribute to a document, it may be helpful to view the document with all changes, or markups, shown; conversely, such markup could result in a cluttered view that is difficult to work with. In reviewing a document, you are likely to identify alternate wording or you may have suggestions on items to include or ways to approach content differently. You might want to communicate such suggestions with others through **comments** that are included in the document but that do not actually change any content. Comments are typically directed to the attention of another author or editor, suggesting actions or otherwise critiquing a selection, available for others to reply to or resolve in some way. You can also use a comment much as you might a sticky note, as a notation to yourself or others related to a particular text selection.

Use Markup

Markup is a way of viewing tracked changes, enabling you to customize the way edits are displayed. If editing has occurred, with deletions, additions, and changes, the resulting display can become distracting and cluttered. In fact, a heavily edited document can become a jumbled mass of underlined and colored text, so that continued review and editing is difficult. One way to control the level of detail shown in a marked-up document is to select options from Show Markup in the Tracking group on the Review tab (see Figure 4.18). There, you can choose to view document revisions by category, showing or hiding comments, formatting, and other changes. If multiple people are involved in a document's development, you can filter the changes shown by those belonging to particular people.

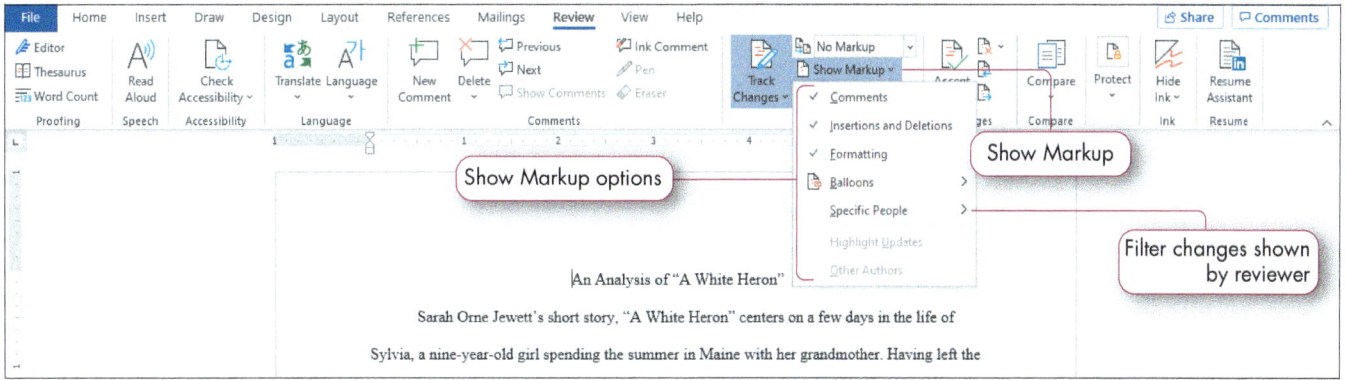

FIGURE 4.18 Show Markup

Another way to control the display of edits is by choosing a Markup view. The Display for Review arrow (see Figure 4.19) provides access to four markup views, each of which shows document changes in different ways. ***Simple Markup*** is a clutter-free display of tracked changes, subtly indicating revisions by vertical bars in the margin and comments by balloons that you can click to view content. ***All Markup*** shows revisions, markups, and comments using default revision formats or those predefined in Track Changes Options. For example, deletions will typically be shown with strikethrough lines while additions are underlined. Such a comprehensive view can become difficult to interpret as changes mount up; even so, it is a complete visual record of all that has changed. ***No Markup*** provides a completely clean view of a document, temporarily hiding all comments and revisions, and displays the document as it would be if all changes were applied. In that view, you can see how the document would look if all changes are accepted. Be reminded, though, that edits and revisions are only hidden from view in No Markup; before a document is final, those changes should either be accepted or rejected. The last option, Original, displays the document in its initial form, as it was before any changes were applied. Even then, edits remain but are hidden from view.

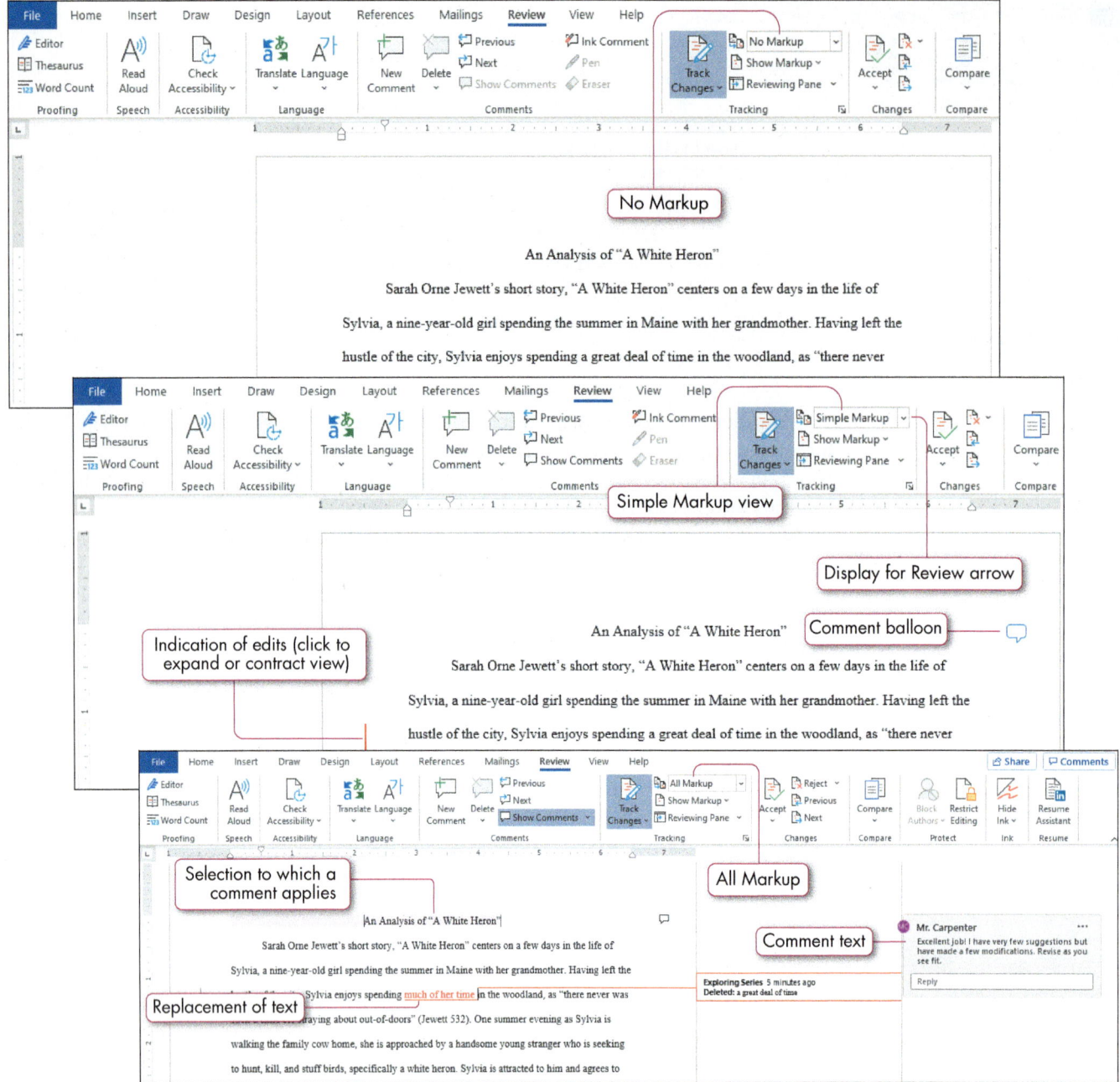

FIGURE 4.19 Markup Views

Add a Comment

In addition to tracking changes and controlling the level of editing detail shown, the Review tab includes a Comments group that enables you to create new comments, delete existing comments, or navigate through the document and review each individual comment (see Figure 4.20). Comments can also be added using the Comments option just above the right side of the ribbon. That option remains available, regardless of the currently selected ribbon tab, simplifying the addition of comments at any time.

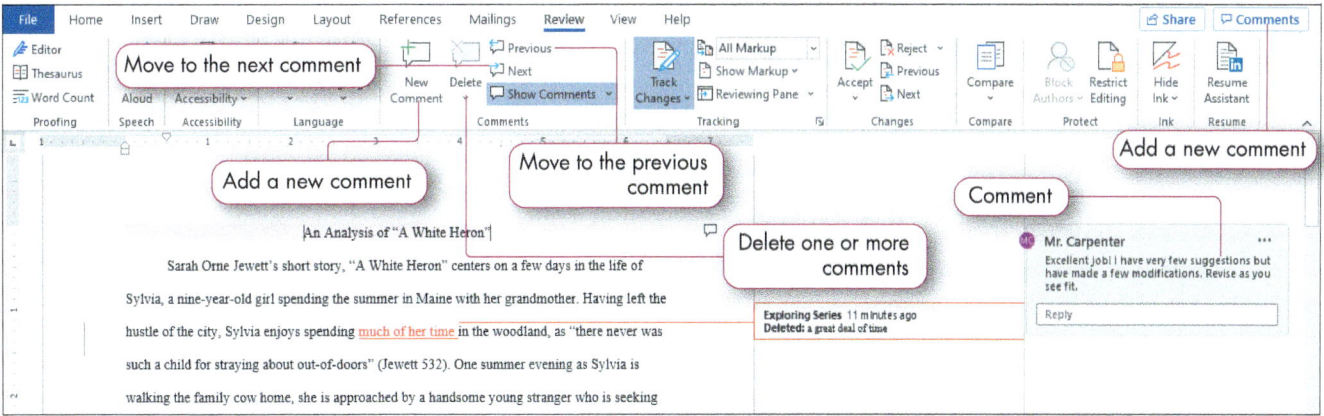

FIGURE 4.20 Work with Comments

To add a comment, click in the document or select a word or phrase that you want to comment on. Click New Comment in the Comments group on the Review tab. Alternatively, you can click Comments above the right side of the ribbon and click New. As a third option, right-click selected text and select New Comment. In addition, the Mini toolbar, shown when text is selected, includes a New Comment option. After typing a comment, you will be identified as the author. If you do not select anything prior to adding a comment, the comment is assigned to the word or object closest to the insertion point. Click Post in the Comment box to complete the process.

> **TIP: CONFIRMING THE USER NAME**
> Before you use the Comments feature, make sure your name displays as you want it to in any comments. To do so, click the Dialog Box Launcher in the Tracking group, and then select Change User Name. Confirm that your name and initials display as the user. Word uses that information to identify the person who uses collaboration tools, such as Comments. If you are in a lab environment, you might not have permission to modify settings or change the user name; however, you should be able to change those settings on a home computer.

STEP 2 ▶ **View Comments**

All comments are displayed in the right margin, near the text to which they refer. In Simple Markup view, comments are shown as ***comment balloons*** that you can click to view the content, with the commented-upon text highlighted in the document itself. Comments in All Markup view display as shown in Figure 4.20, with commented-upon text highlighted and full comment text shown.

> **TIP: WORD VIEWS AND COMMENTS**
> Regardless of the Word view chosen—Print Layout, Draft, Read Mode, Web Layout, or Outline—working with comments is possible when you choose either Simple Markup or All Markup in the Tracking group on the Review tab and point to an area of text that has been commented on. Text selection will highlight with comment text displaying in a boxed area nearby. Comments will not display if the Markup chosen on the Review tab is either No Markup or Original.

Reply to Comments

Replying to a comment creates a conversation around it. Point to a comment, click Reply, and type a response (see Figure 4.21). If the markup view is Simple Markup, you will need to click the comment balloon before adding a reply, unless Show Comments in the Comments group is selected, in which case the full comment shows. The response will be placed within the original comment space, below the initial comment, identifying the responder by name. Such identification documents the progression of a comment through its replies. If a comment has been addressed, you can acknowledge that by pointing to the comment, clicking Resolve thread, and then selecting Resolve thread although that action is certainly not required. A resolved comment is removed from view.

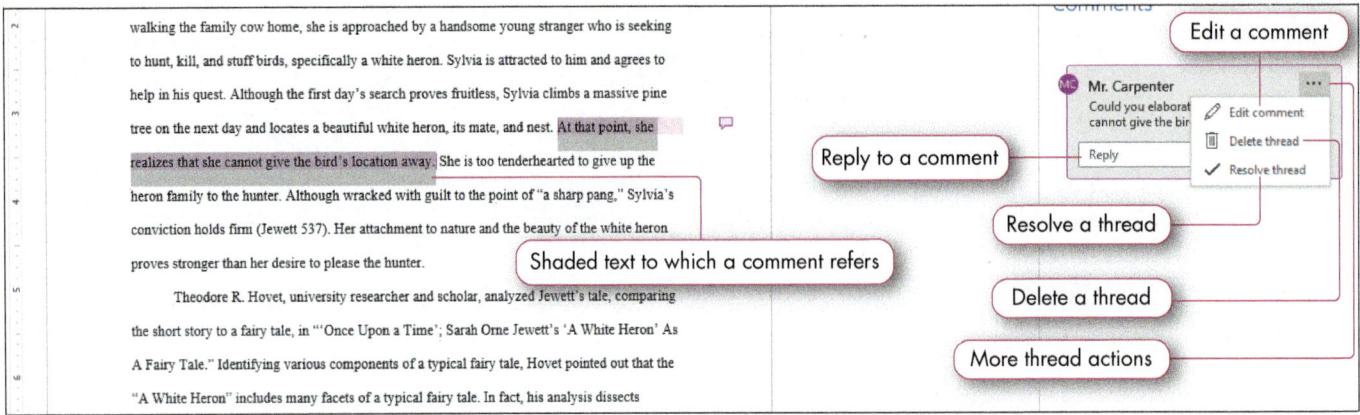

FIGURE 4.21 Reply to a Comment

Especially in a heavily edited and commented-upon document, keeping track of all changes can be a challenge. To simplify that task, Word provides a Reviewing pane, which is a collection of all edits and comments in one easily accessible area. In any view, you can select Reviewing Pane in the Tracking group on the Review tab, indicating whether to show the pane in a vertical or horizontal fashion. Figure 4.22 shows a vertical Reviewing Pane. You can toggle the Reviewing Pane on and off by clicking Reviewing Pane in the Tracking group.

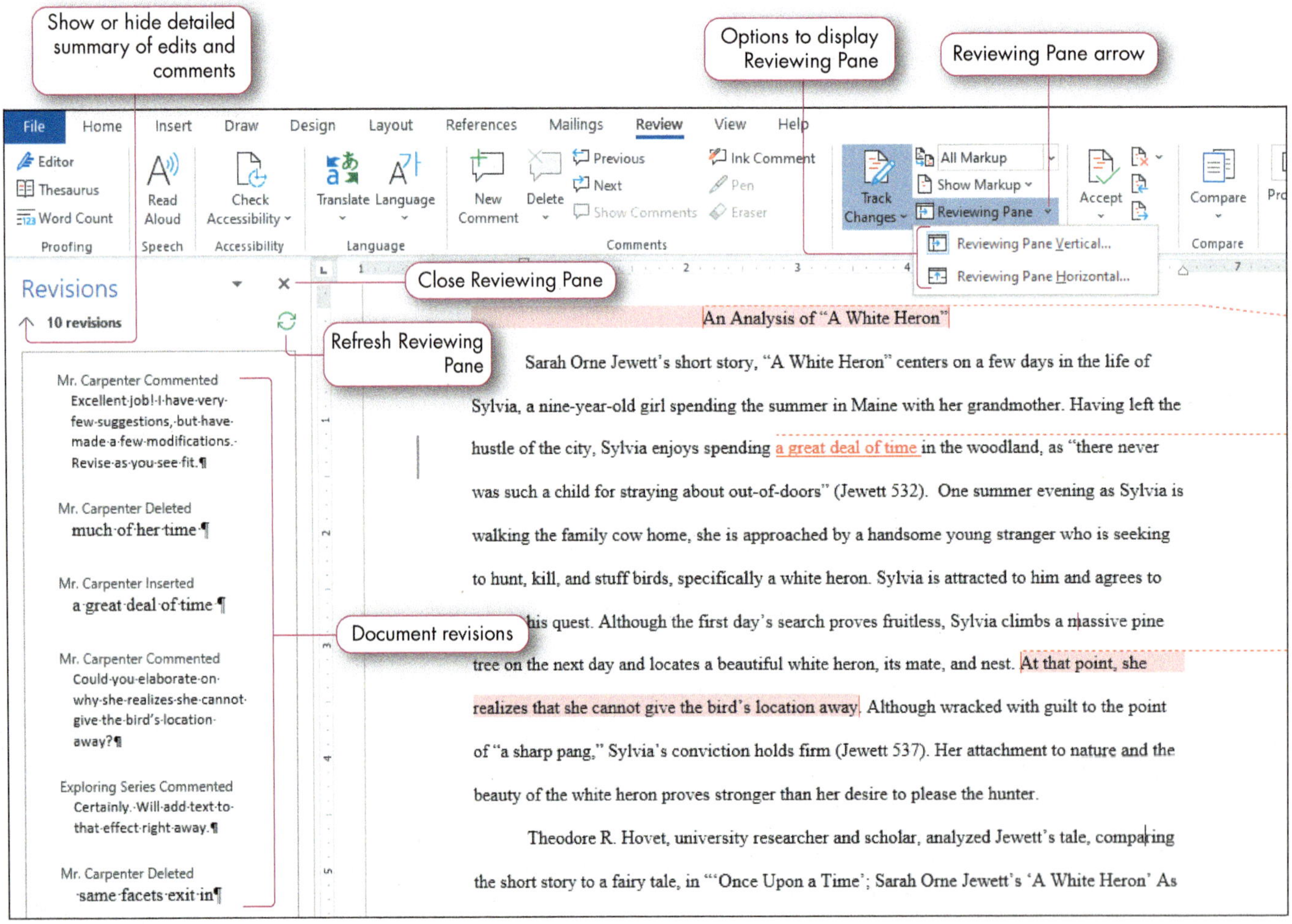

FIGURE 4.22 Reviewing Pane

STEP 3 ## Work with a PDF Document

Documents are often saved in PDF format to preserve the layout, font formats, and images of the original Word document. This format is especially useful for documents such as magazine articles, brochures, and flyers, as it accurately represents all page elements, including graphics and text effects. Software that will read a PDF file, such as Adobe Acrobat Reader, is free to download, making PDF files accessible to everyone. In addition, Microsoft Edge and other browsers, including macOS versions, can also display PDF files. Not only can Microsoft Word open a PDF file, but it enables you to edit the document, including the use of Review features found on the Review tab.

PDF Reflow is a process that converts PDF content into a Word document, retaining the original layout so that it flows correctly across pages in the resulting Word document. PDF Reflow seeks to convert recognizable features of a PDF document into items that are native to Word. For example, a table in a PDF document is converted into a table in a Word document so you can use Word's table feature to modify and update the item. Similarly, bulleted lines in a PDF file become bulleted paragraphs in a Word document. Although using PDF Reflow does not always convert every feature flawlessly, the result is usually a close imitation of the original.

HOW TO

Convert a PDF document to Word:

1. Click Open on the File tab.
2. Browse to the folder of the PDF document you want to open and double-click the selected file.
3. Click OK if warned that the conversion might take a while and that the PDF document contains interactive features that are not supported by PDF Reflow. Within a few seconds, the PDF file opens as a Word document which you can edit as you would any Word document.

Critical Thinking _____

4. Discuss why it might be helpful to mark a comment as resolved. *pp. 321–322*

5. Explain why a reviewer might choose to change from All Markup to Simple Markup when reviewing the content of a document that has been thoroughly edited. *p. 319*

6. Provide rationale for saving a Word document as a PDF file. Conversely, explain why PDF files are often converted into Word files. *p. 323*

Hands-On Exercises

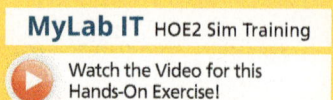

MyLab IT HOE2 Sim Training

Watch the Video for this Hands-On Exercise!

Skills covered: Use Track Changes • Accept Changes • Use Markup • Add a Comment • View Comments • Reply to Comments • Work with a PDF Document

2 Document Tracking

Your literature group submitted a draft copy of the analysis of "A White Heron." Your literature instructor, Mr. Carpenter, made comments and suggested some additional editing before the paper is considered complete. Even at this early stage, however, he is very pleased with your group's initial analysis. In fact, he suggested that you prepare to submit the paper to the campus Phi Kappa Phi Honor Society for judging in a writing contest. He will provide a copy of the entry form in PDF format so you can have it on hand when you submit the paper. Now, you will review his comments and changes and act on his suggestions.

STEP 1 USE TRACK CHANGES, USE MARKUP, AND ACCEPT CHANGES

Your instructor returned to you an electronic copy of the analysis with a few edits and comments. You are ready to review the paper using track changes and markup and to accept changes. Refer to Figure 4.23 as you complete Step 1.

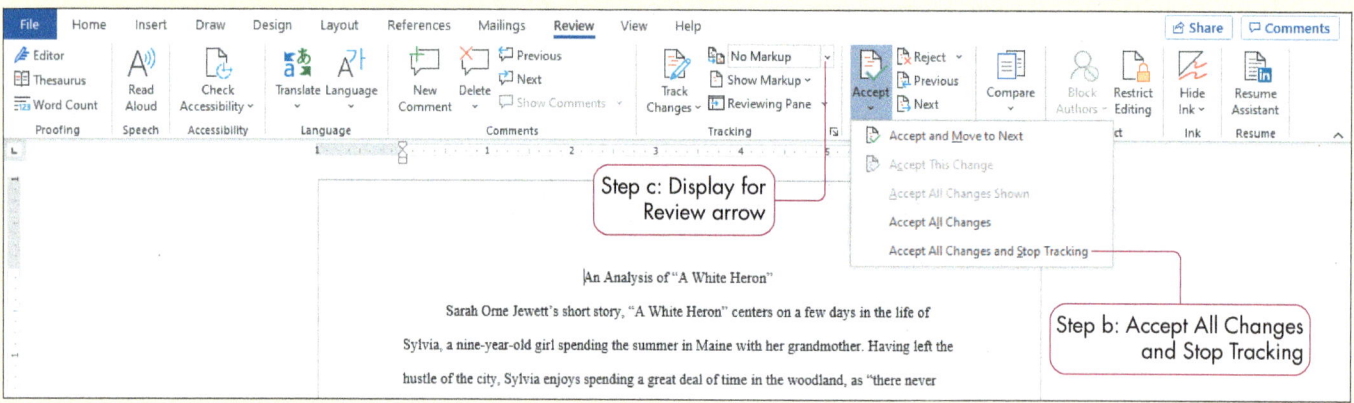

FIGURE 4.23 Track Changes

a. Open *w04h2WhiteHeron* and save it as **w04h2WhiteHeron_LastFirst**.

b. Click the **Review tab** and change the markup to **All Markup**. Point to a section of text that has been changed and note the author of the change. Click the **Accept arrow** in the Changes group, and then select **Accept All Changes and Stop Tracking**.

   You have accepted all remaining changes and turned off Track Changes. Comments are still displayed.

c. Click the **Display for Review arrow** and click **No Markup**.

The document looks completely clean, without any markups or comments. Be reminded, though, that even though you accepted all changes, any comments remain even though they are not visible.

d. Save the document.

ADD A COMMENT, VIEW COMMENTS, AND REPLY TO COMMENTS

You will review and reply to your instructor's comments, make a few changes, and save the document for final review and group collaboration later. Refer to Figure 4.24 as you complete Step 2.

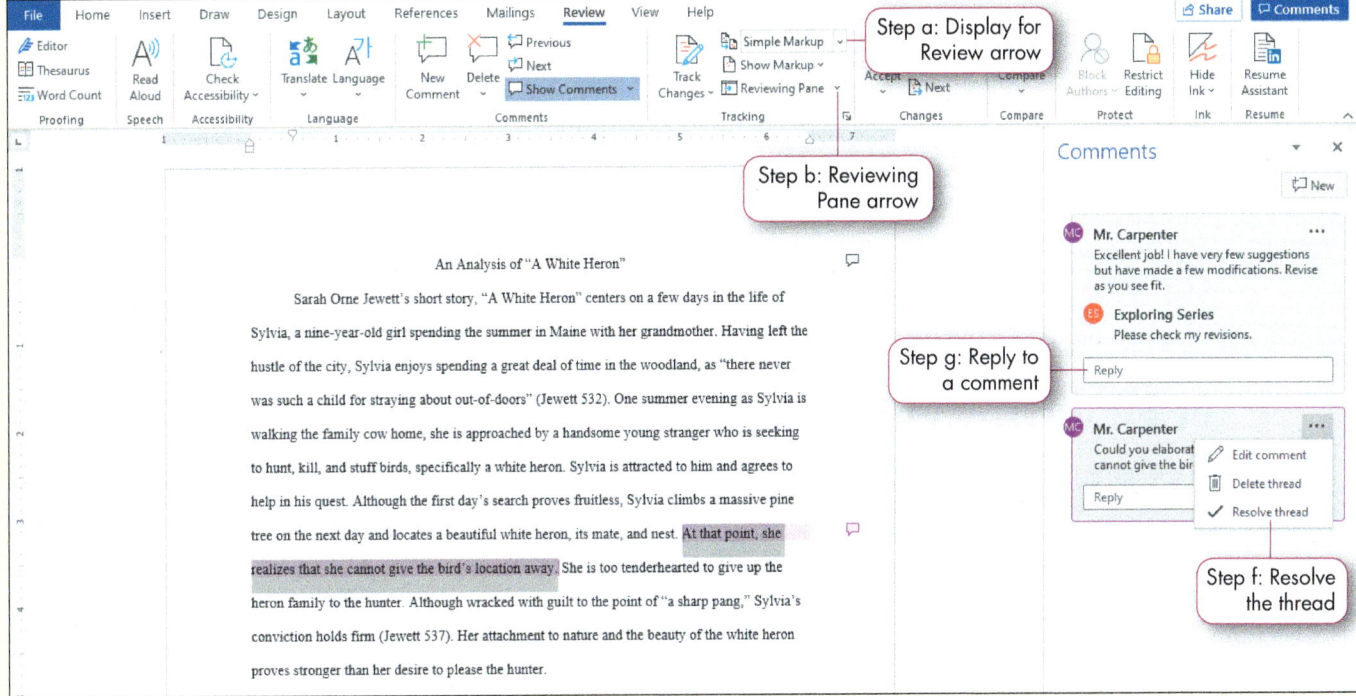

FIGURE 4.24 Work with Comments

a. Click the **Display for Review arrow** in the Tracking group on the Review tab, and then select **Simple Markup**. Ensure that **Show Comments** is selected in the Comments group. Review the comments made by your instructor.

In the Simple Markup view, you can also display comments by clicking Show Comments in the Comments group.

b. Click the **Reviewing Pane arrow** in the Tracking group and select **Reviewing Pane Vertical**. Review the comments shown in the Reviewing Pane. Close the Reviewing Pane (titled *Revisions*).

> **MAC TROUBLESHOOTING:** There is no arrow for the Reviewing Pane and it can only display vertically. Click Reviewing to toggle the pane on and off.

c. View the **third comment balloon** on the first page and note that you need to add a citation. Click after the quotation mark and before the period in the sentence in the last paragraph on the first page (ending with *for the course of action*). Add a new source for the following book:

Type of Source: **Book Section**

Author: **Propp, Vladimir**

Title: **Morphology of a Folk Tale**

Year: **2004**

City: **New York**

Publisher: **Anniston**

    d. Scroll to the end of the document and click anywhere in the bibliography text. Click **Update Citations and Bibliography**.

        You added a new source and updated the Works Cited page to include the newly added source.

    e. Point to the third comment on page 1 and click **Resolve**.

        You have addressed the comment, so you marked it as resolved.

    f. Scroll up and view the **second comment balloon** on page 1. Click before the word *Although* in the sentence in the first body paragraph (that begins with *Although wracked with guilt*). Type **She is too tenderhearted to give up the heron family to the hunter.** (Include the period.) Press **Spacebar**. Point to the second comment on page 1 and click **Resolve**.

    g. Point to the first comment on page and click **Reply**. Type **Please check my revisions**.

    h. Save and close the document. Keep Word open for the next step. You will submit this file to your instructor at the end of the last Hands-On Exercise.

STEP 3 WORK WITH A PDF DOCUMENT

You are ready to finalize the paper, and your instructor has let you know that you must include an entry form with the submission. You are not on campus, so Mr. Carpenter emailed the entry form as a PDF document. You will convert the form to Word and complete it with your name and report information. You will then save it as a PDF document for later submission. Refer to Figure 4.25 as you complete Step 3.

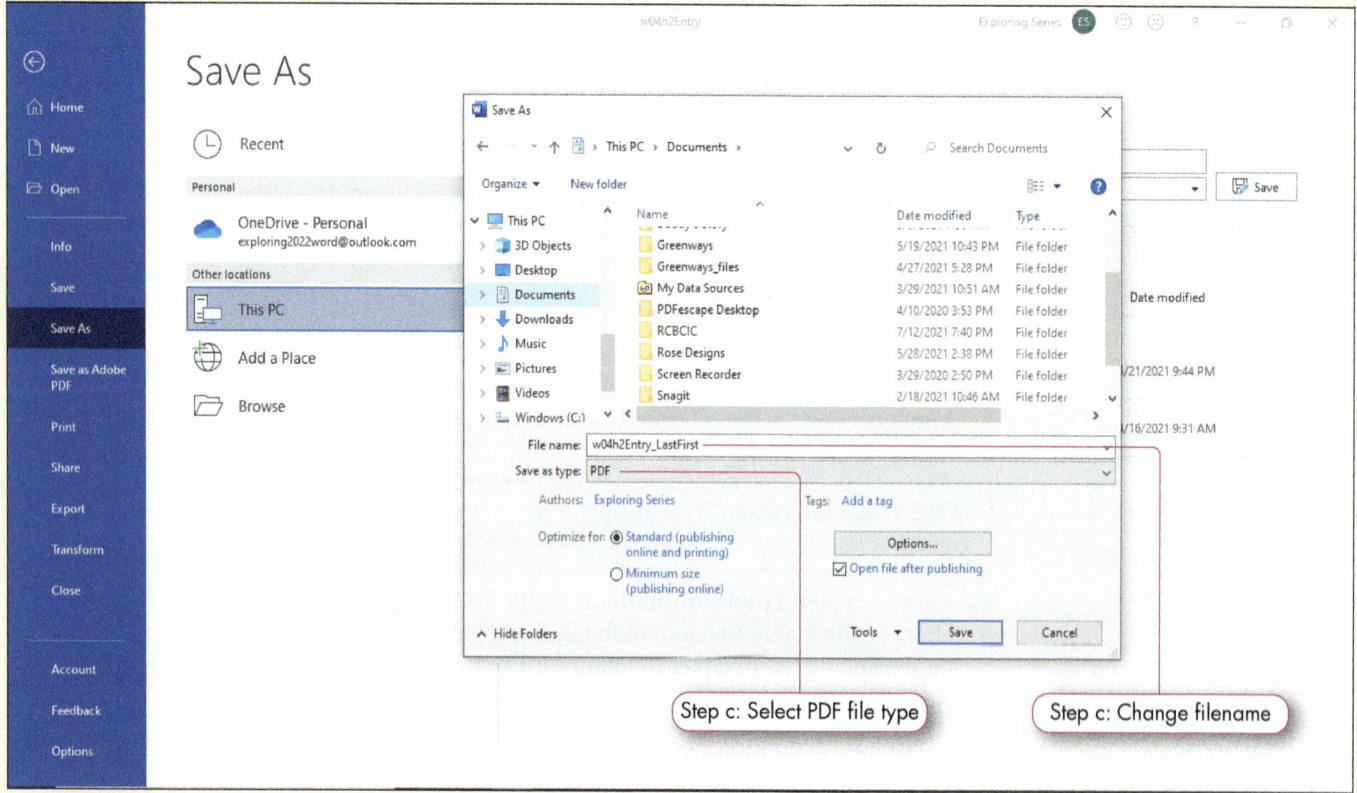

FIGURE 4.25 Work with a PDF Document

a. Click the **File tab**, click **Open**, click **Browse**, and then navigate to the student data files folder. Change the type of files in the Open dialog box to **PDF Files**. Double-click *w04h2Entry.pdf* to open the file. Click **OK** if warned that the conversion might take a while.

> **TROUBLESHOOTING:** If the document opened as an Adobe PDF file instead of as a Word document, you opened the file from File Explorer. Instead, you should open the document from within Word. Click the File tab and click Open.

Word has converted the original PDF version of the entry form and opened it in Word so you can modify it.

b. Click after *Date* and type today's date in the month day, year format (as *March 10, 2024*). Complete the remaining information, including your name, instructor's name (**Mr. Avery Carpenter**), college class (**Sophomore**), email (**CollegeStudent@act.edu**), and **An Analysis of "A White Heron"** as the report title.

c. Click the **File tab** and click **Save As**. Click **Browse**. Change the file type to **PDF (*.pdf)**. Change the filename to **w04h2Entry_LastFirst.pdf**. Browse to the location where you save your assignments, ensure that *Open file after publishing* is selected, and click **Save**.

You saved the entry form you completed in Word as a PDF file for later submission with the entry.

d. Close the PDF version of the completed entry form. Close the Word version of the entry form without saving it. You will submit the PDF file to your instructor at the end of the last Hands-On Exercise.

Online Document Collaboration

With its continuing commitment to incorporate collaboration features, Microsoft is simplifying how people in any location can work together in groups to complete projects. Marketing proposals, company reports, and all sorts of other documents are often prepared by several people working with shared documents to which all can contribute at the same time. Similarly, group projects in classes can be completed by sharing documents online for review and completion. The key to much of that global access is Microsoft 365, which is now considered an industry standard for enabling collaboration anywhere, anytime, on any device. Its total online access is facilitated by the use of such file storage and sharing resources as OneDrive.

In this section, you will learn to use OneDrive, not only for file storage but also as a resource for sharing documents with others so that group editing can occur. You will also explore the use of Word for the web in sharing and saving documents intended for access by more than one person.

Use OneDrive

Word facilitates document saving and sharing through *OneDrive*, which is a Web-based storage site and sharing utility. Saving a document to OneDrive is sometimes referred to as "saving to the cloud," because the file is saved and stored online. After downloading the OneDrive mobile app, you can access, edit, and share OneDrive files on any of your devices. Not limited to Microsoft 365 files, OneDrive provides ample free storage for the backup of photos and other files, with additional storage available for purchase or as part of a Microsoft 365 subscription.

Using OneDrive as a storage location, you can upload and retrieve files from any Internet-connected device and share documents with others. OneDrive not only serves as a location for file storage, but it facilitates sharing those files with others for group editing. In addition, a OneDrive account provides access to Office for the web, which is a free, although limited, set of online apps (Word, PowerPoint, Excel, and OneNote). You may even choose to use OneDrive as a primary location for saving all of your Word documents, regardless of whether they are intended for sharing, for no other reason than to be assured that the AutoSave feature is activated. AutoSave, which saves an open file every few seconds, is automatically enabled for all files saved to OneDrive and SharePoint Online.

> **TIP: USE AUTOSAVE**
> The AutoSave status is shown just above the ribbon on the left side of the Quick Access Toolbar. If an open document is saved in OneDrive, AutoSave is shown as On. You can also toggle the setting off, although doing so affects the current document only. You might want to toggle the setting off if you are working with a shared document and are not ready to show others the changes you are making. To globally disable AutoSave so that you can choose whether to toggle it on, click Options on the File tab and select Save. Deselect *AutoSave OneDrive and SharePoint Online files by default on Word*.

STEP 1 ▸ Use OneDrive with File Explorer

Windows incorporates OneDrive into File Explorer, listing it along with other storage devices and locations. In that way, you can treat it much as you would local storage such as a hard drive or flash drive, creating folders and saving and retrieving files. Although OneDrive is considered cloud storage because it is not physically housed on your computer, you can mirror any or all of the files you save to OneDrive, also called syncing, so that they are available both locally and backed up on OneDrive. Once configured, that process is transparent, occurring behind the scenes as you work with your computer.

With a typical laptop or desktop computer, such duplication of files and folders may not pose a problem; however, such is not the case with tablets and mobile devices with more limited local storage, or possibly none at all. To identify which files and folders, if any, should be synced, right-click OneDrive in File Explorer and select Settings. The Settings option is also available from the OneDrive icon on the Windows taskbar. Click Account and select Choose Folders. Finally, select folder and file settings that are appropriate for the device with which you are working, selecting those that should be saved both locally and on OneDrive. If storage space on a device is limited, you may want to leave most files on OneDrive without syncing them to the device. That way, you can access them only when needed.

Use OneDrive in a Browser

With a Microsoft account, you have access to OneDrive, with a certain amount of free online storage. The amount of storage varies, depending upon whether you also have a Microsoft 365 subscription or whether you have purchased a higher-level plan. Just as other cloud-based services provide online storage for backup purposes, OneDrive fills that need as well. In addition, it is a favorite for Microsoft 365 users as it is seamlessly incorporated into the Office interface.

Although you can save files directly to OneDrive from within Word, you can also manage file storage from within a browser interface. Visit onedrive.com and sign in to your Microsoft account to view the hierarchy of folders and files you might have organized there. Using the OneDrive toolbar, shown in Figure 4.26, you can upload files from local storage or create new folders. As discussed later in this chapter, you can also use *Office for the web*—previously titled Office Online—from within the OneDrive interface to create Word documents regardless of whether you have purchased access to the Microsoft 365 suite. The online version of Office also includes access to other online apps such as Excel and PowerPoint.

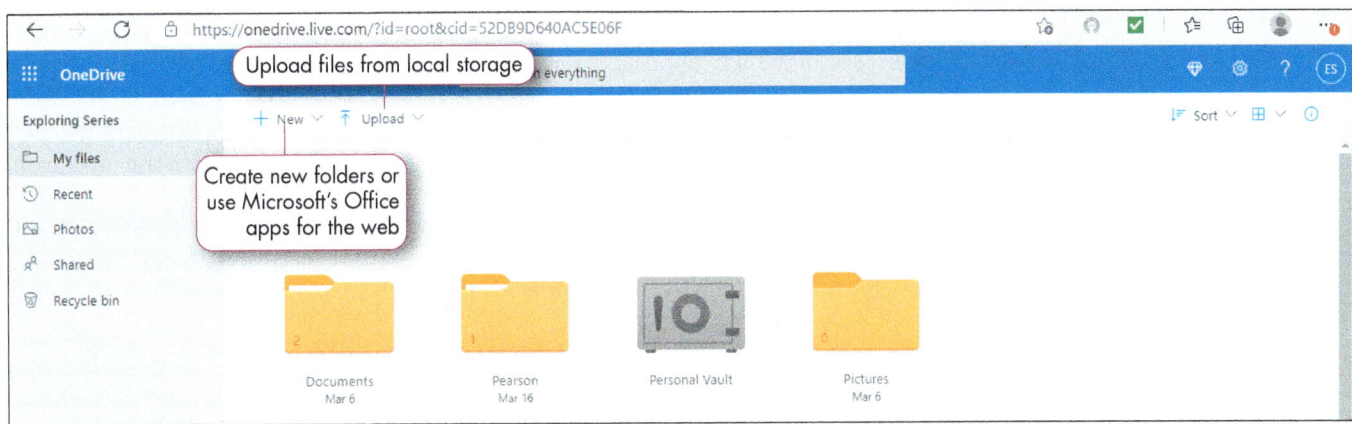

FIGURE 4.26 Use OneDrive Online

Share Documents

OneDrive not only provides cloud storage, but it facilitates online collaboration. Saving a document to OneDrive, OneDrive for Business, or SharePoint Online and then sharing it with others, you make a document available for simultaneous editing. As members of your group work with the file saved in OneDrive, their edits and comments are automatically saved to the document. Because only one copy is being edited by all group members, there is no need to collect multiple marked-up copies and merge all edits into one, as would be the case with a file shared through email attachment or otherwise distributed. The key to such group editing is the use of OneDrive to share a document.

> **TIP: CONSIDER DROPBOX FOR FILE SHARING**
>
> An alternative to OneDrive, Dropbox has partnered with Microsoft to provide shared space for Office documents as well as to facilitate real-time co-authoring. Users can create new documents from Dropbox, using Microsoft's Word for the web app, and edit those documents as a team. As a cloud-based storage and sharing resource, Dropbox offers seamless mobile and Web integration with the online Office suite, making it an attractive alternative to OneDrive for those who may be more familiar with its interface.

Invite Others to Share

Coordinating with Word and OneDrive, you can share a document in several ways:

- Open File Explorer to display files saved on OneDrive. Then right-click a file to be shared.

- Open a Word document to be shared. Click Share above the right side of the ribbon.

- Open a Word document to be shared. Click the File tab and select Share.

- Sign in to your OneDrive account at onedrive.com. Select a file and click Share on the OneDrive toolbar (or right-click the file and click Share).

Regardless of which approach you take to sharing a file, you will next select a method of sharing—through a link that you can distribute, through email to addresses you provide, or through a social media site such as Facebook or LinkedIn. You will also indicate whether a co-author can only view the shared document or whether you want to convey editing privileges.

If you are working in a Word document, you might find it simpler to share the file from within Word. Be reminded that shared files must reside in the cloud; you cannot share them from local storage on your computer if real-time collaboration is the goal. Regardless of whether a file has been saved yet, you can begin the sharing process by clicking Share above the top right side of the ribbon (see Figure 4.27). You will be asked to upload a copy of the document to OneDrive if the file has not yet been saved. As shown in Figure 4.27, you will then choose from various options related to how the link is to be shared and whether to assign a password or expiration date for the link.

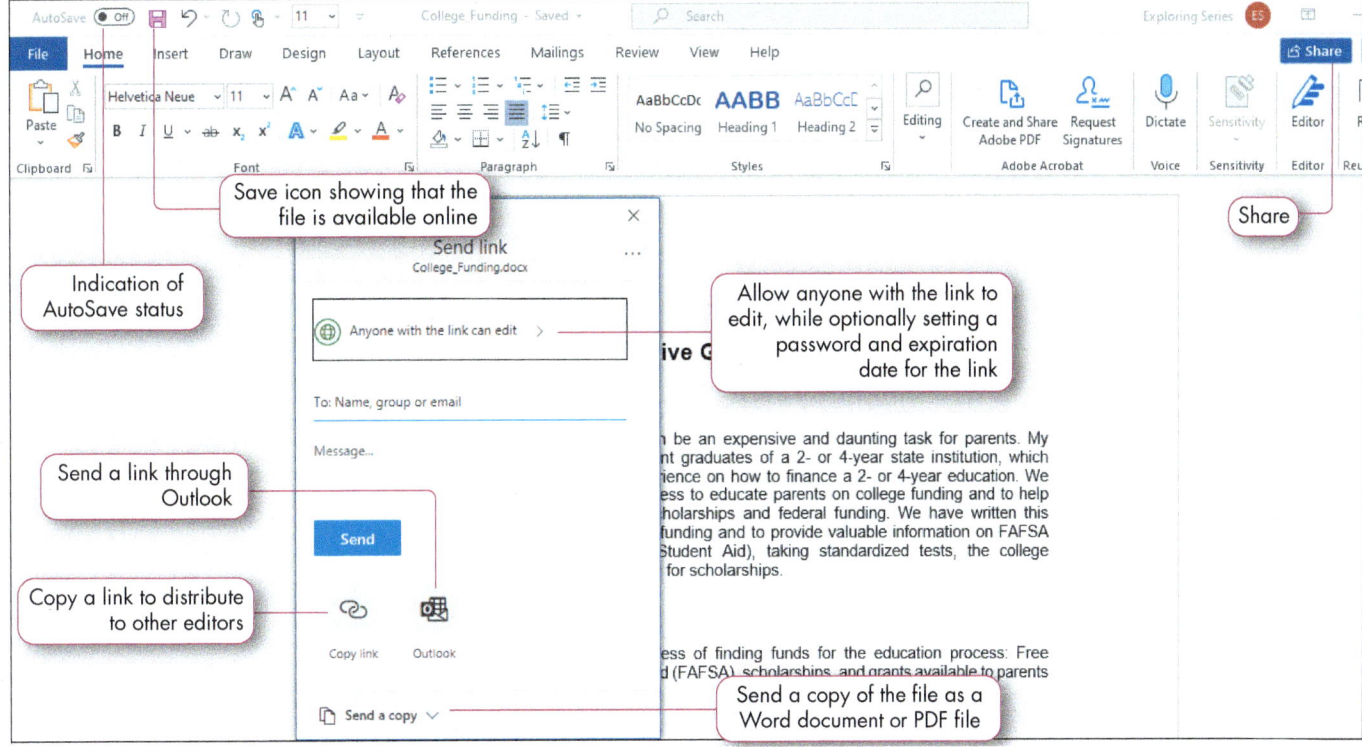

FIGURE 4.27 Share a Document (from the Share option above ribbon)

As shown in Figure 4.28, you can also share a document by selecting Share from the File tab (first saving the document to OneDrive) and selecting options related to how the link is to be shared and with whom. If you are working with a browser and have signed in to your OneDrive account, right-click a file to be shared and select Share, as shown in Figure 4.29, or select a file in OneDrive (in a browser) and click Share on the OneDrive toolbar.

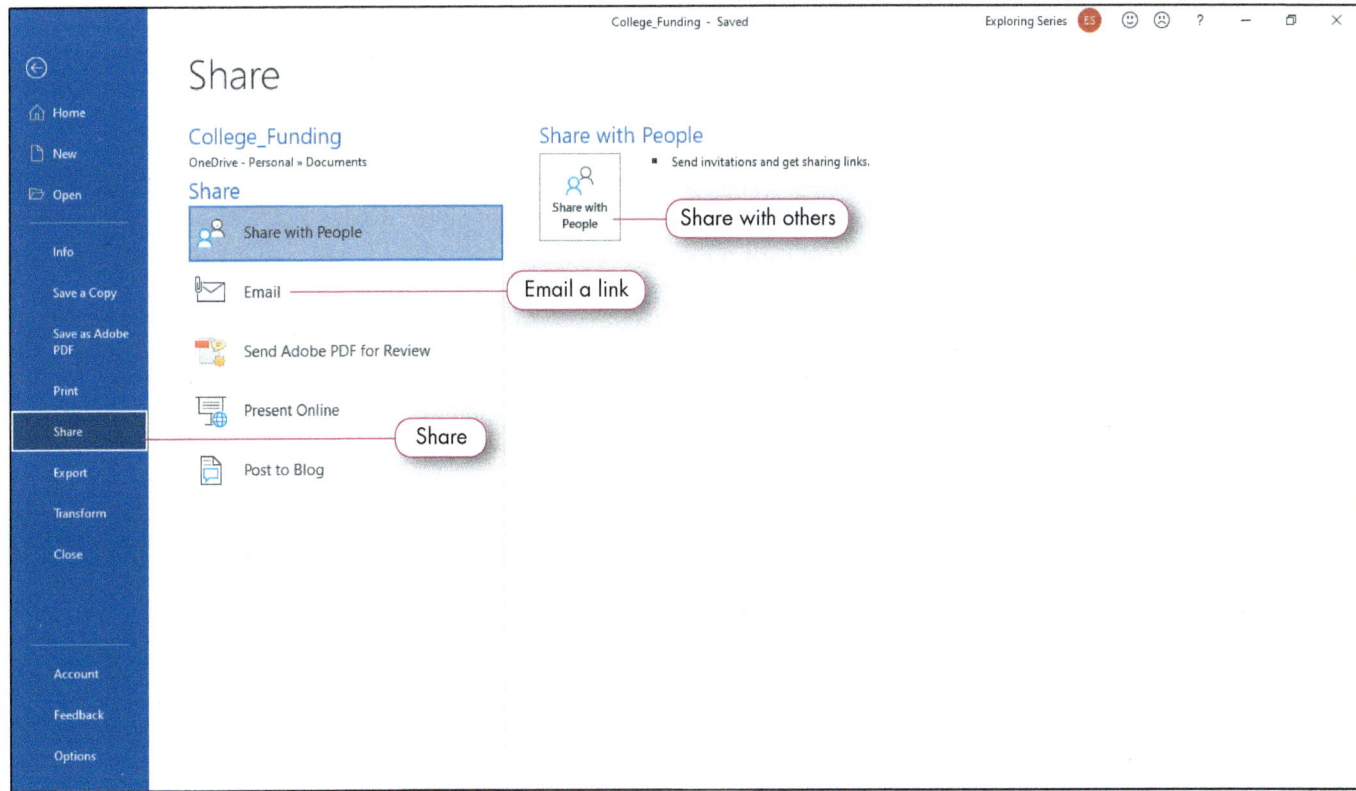

FIGURE 4.28 Share a Document (from the File tab)

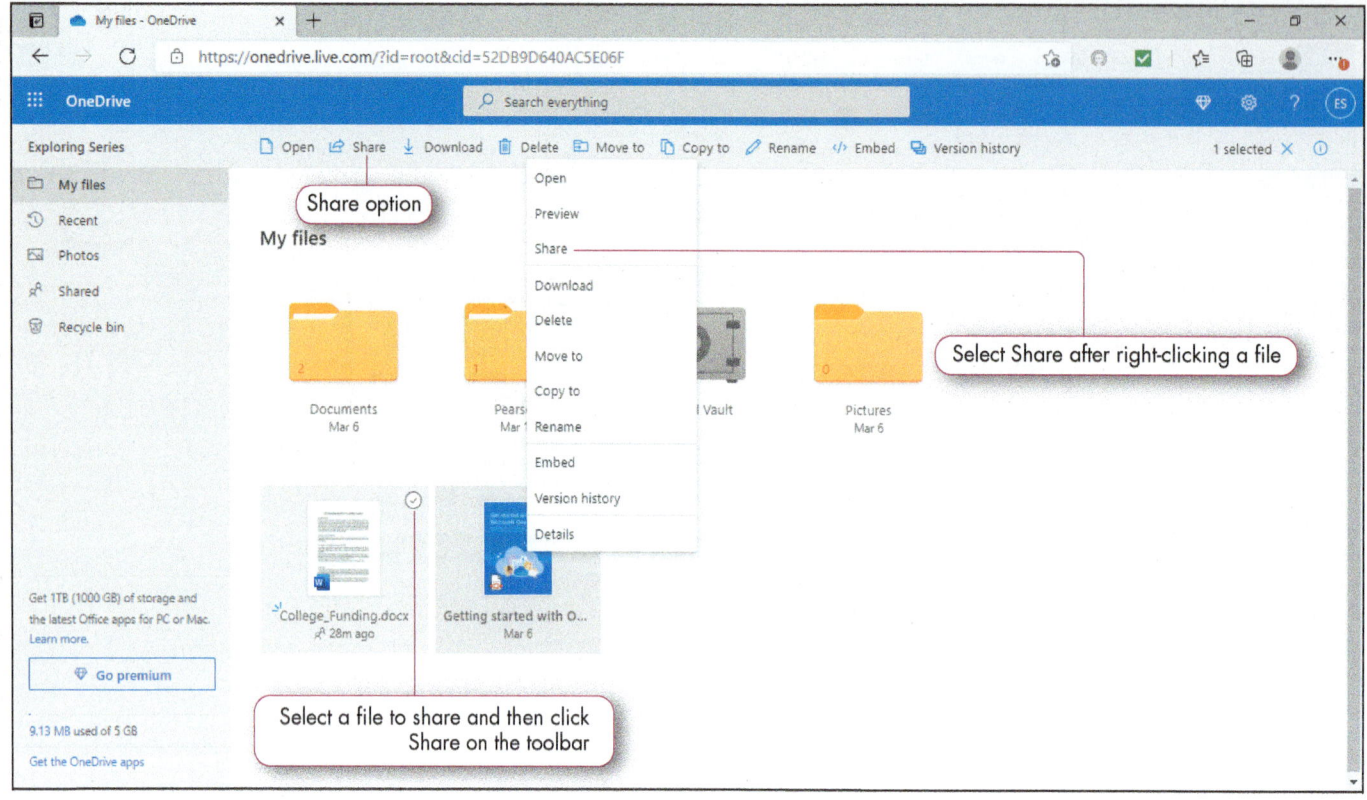

FIGURE 4.29 Share a Document (from OneDrive in a browser)

Send as an Attachment

If group editing of a single document is not the goal, but you want to share a document with someone else, you can send the file as an attachment. You can begin that process in several ways, with a common approach being to open the document and click Share above the right side of the ribbon. Regardless of whether the file has been saved to OneDrive, which is not a requirement when sending an attachment, you can indicate whether the attached file should be sent as a Word document or as a PDF file. As described in a previous section of this chapter, a PDF file preserves all formatting but is typically not intended for a great deal of additional editing. Depending upon the purpose of the file share, you will determine the most appropriate format. The recipient of the attachment can edit the document and return it to you, but simultaneous editing by multiple people is not possible in that situation.

The same outcome can be achieved when you click the File tab and select Share. As shown in Figure 4.30, you can then select from various options related to sharing a file, including sending as an attachment (Word document) or as a PDF file. The Send a Link option is grayed out and unavailable if the document has not been saved to cloud storage. Although you can also send a file as an XPS document (Windows format that is similar to PDF), that option is not as popular or as universally accepted as the PDF format.

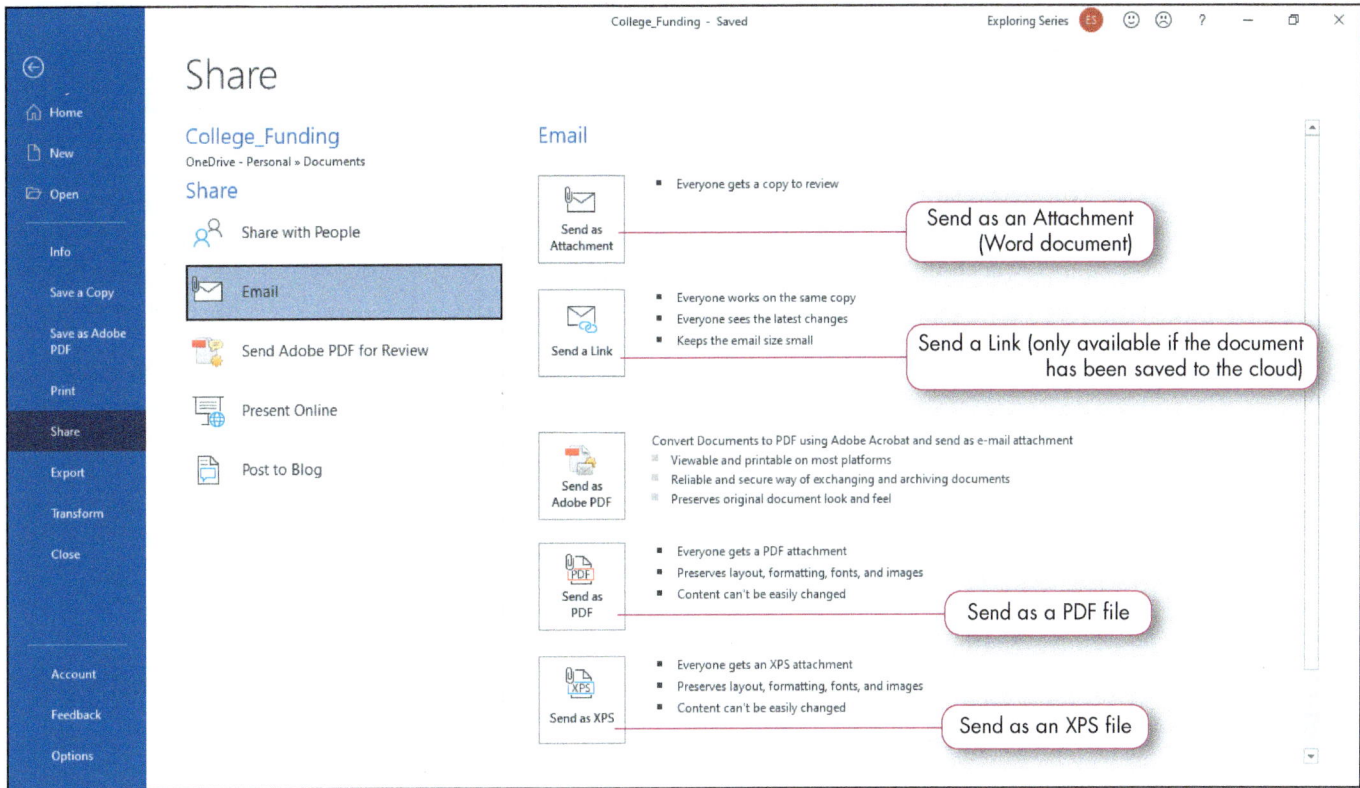

FIGURE 4.30 Send as an Attachment

Collaborate with Word and Word for the Web

Imagine gathering around a conference table to work on a document with others. The group shares ideas and comments on content, working to produce a collaborative document that is representative of the group's best effort. Now expand that view to include co-authors who are widespread geographically instead of gathered in a conference room. Because the far-flung group members have access to shared online material, they can view a document and collaborate on its content, each editing the document at any time. Whether your goal is to present a document for discussion (but no editing) or to seek input from a group, you will appreciate the ease with which documents saved to OneDrive and opened in Word or **Word for the web** facilitate that task. Word for the web is the online equivalent of the desktop version of Word; however, it is missing some of the functionality of the full version. Even so, it is free and accessible to anyone with a OneDrive account.

After you have saved a document to OneDrive and shared it with others, you are ready to collaborate in real time. As mentioned previously, a recipient of a link that grants editing privileges to a shared document can access the document at any time from any Internet-connected device. The document will initially be opened in Word for the web, but at any time, the editor can switch to a local Word installation to continue editing. As Word for the web is a limited version of Word, it may not include some features that a reviewer finds necessary, such as adding a bibliography or checking a document in Outline view. Any document saved to OneDrive and shared with editing privileges has real-time, group-editing functionality.

Use Word for the Web

Microsoft Office has evolved significantly since its inception, from a product developed for primary use on a standalone system, such as a desktop or laptop, to a globally accessible suite of software that is available any time on any device, with emphasis on cloud storage so that files are always available and easily shared with others. Most users of Microsoft Office now prefer the subscription method of delivery, purchasing annual access through Microsoft 365. Although a subscription to the Office suite is not required for a OneDrive account, Microsoft Office users appreciate the close integration with the cloud-based system, as they become familiar with its facility for storing and sharing files.

A key to the use of OneDrive for document sharing and group editing is the availability of online Office apps, collectively referred to as Office for the web. Although those apps are free to any OneDrive user, those who are most apt to use the online versions are those who are familiar with Microsoft Office, most likely using the full installation of that Office suite on a work or home computer. When a Word document is uploaded or saved to OneDrive and then shared with others, those with a link can open the document in Word for the web, formerly called Word Online, a component of Office. Using Word for the web, you can create and edit Word documents from any Internet-connected computer, and across any platform. In addition, you can open documents in that app if they have been uploaded to OneDrive or a comparable cloud-based service, regardless of whether they have been shared with others. The more limited version of Word is usually sufficient for most routine word processing tasks, but a shared or uploaded document can also be edited in a full installation if more functionality is required or if a user prefers that interface.

A shared link for a Word document will open the file in Word for the web so that you can immediately begin to work with it. You can also open a file saved to OneDrive, even if it has not been shared, by double-clicking it in the online OneDrive interface. The document will open in Word for the web. In either case, you can click Editing in the OneDrive toolbar and select from various options, one of which opens the document in the full-featured desktop Word app (see Figure 4.31).

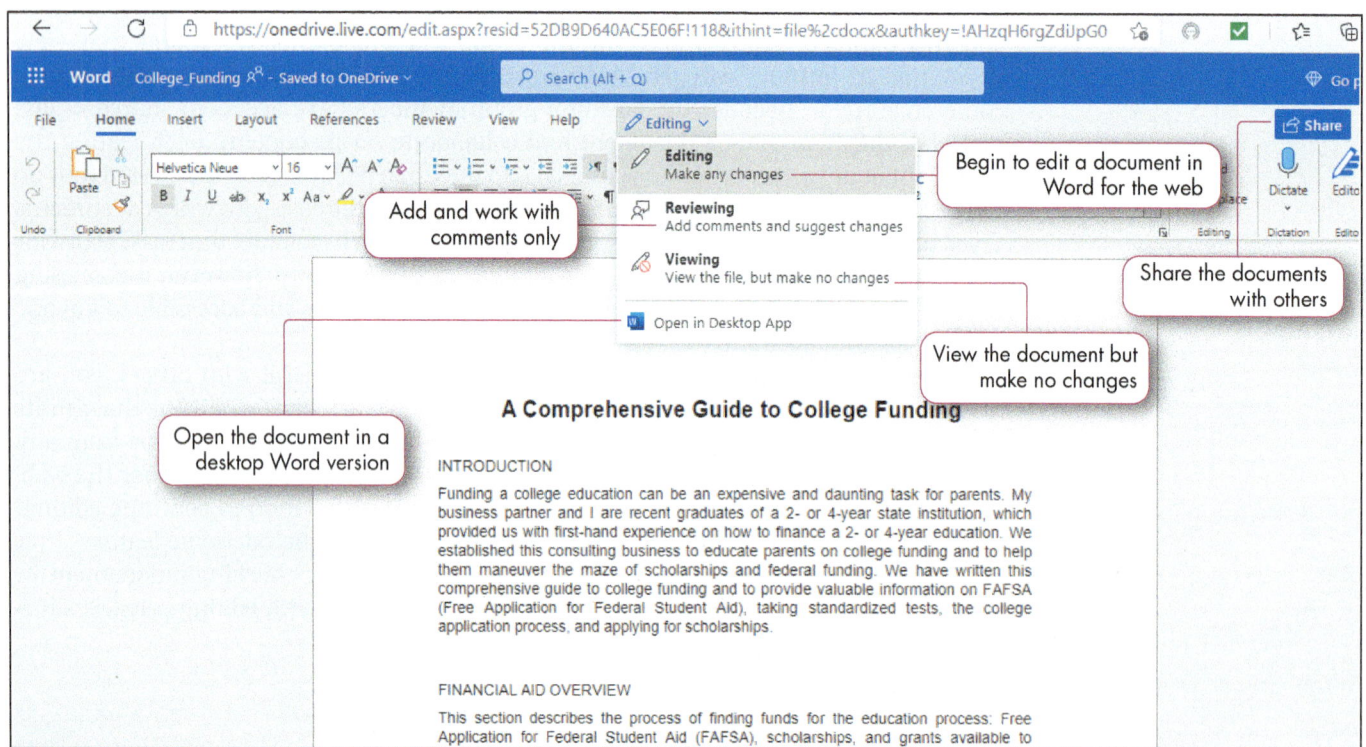

FIGURE 4.31 Work with Word for the Web

Word for the web has the familiar look and feel of Microsoft Word; however, you will note that the ribbon in the online version has fewer tabs than the ribbon in a desktop Word version (refer to Figure 4.31). Other limitations, such as fewer Dialog Box Launchers and lack of access to many reference features, such as a cover page and bibliography, can present a challenge to those who may be reliant on the online Word version. And yet the availability of editable documents in an online format, even for those who have no access to a desktop Word version, more than makes up for the somewhat limited features in most cases.

Co-authoring a document is straightforward, with no specific commands required to begin editing. Simply open a shared document, possibly using a link you received from the document owner, and use either Word or Word for the web to modify the document. Several people can access and edit the same document at the same time, with the only requirement being that two people cannot edit the same paragraph at the same time. While one is working in that space, it is temporarily locked to others. Simultaneous editing is called *real-time co-authoring*. As you edit a shared document, you will see an indication onscreen of others who are also working with the document.

As editing continues on a shared document, changes are automatically saved, so that a document is always up to date. With only one iteration of a document being worked with, the outcome is sure to be reflective of an entire group effort, all made possible by the collaborative nature of Word and the availability of cloud-based resources.

Critical Thinking

7. Explain why you might choose not to sync all files from OneDrive to your computer, preferring to leave some stored only on OneDrive. *p. 329*

8. Explain why, after opening a document in Word for the web on OneDrive, you might choose to continue editing the document in the desktop version of Word. *p. 335*

9. Explain why you might choose to share a file with others through a link instead of sending the file as a copy through email. *p. 330*

Hands-On Exercises

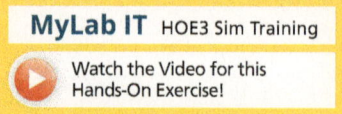

Skills covered: Use OneDrive with File Explorer • Invite Others to Share • Use Word for the web

3 Online Document Collaboration

Your literature group will finalize the analysis of "A White Heron" by collaborating on a few last-minute edits online. Your instructor will assign you to work in a group of four students to complete this Hands-On Exercise. A member of your group should be selected as the group leader who will assume the task of posting and sharing the document. You will work with a draft of the analysis of the short story, co-authoring the document online and then addressing final comments with classmates in your group.

STEP 1 **USE ONEDRIVE WITH FILE EXPLORER AND INVITE OTHERS TO SHARE**

You know that OneDrive provides storage space that can be accessed by others and can be used as a backup. Therefore, you plan to use OneDrive to share the analysis of "A White Heron" so that classmates can collaborate on the project. Your group leader will save a copy of the analysis paper to their OneDrive folder on File Explorer. From that point, changes made to the document can be synchronized with the online version stored in OneDrive. Because coordinating schedules is difficult for group members, your group decides to edit the document online. That way, each group member can work with the document at any time from any location, while all group members can see edits that have been made. **Only the group leader should complete Step 1, sharing the document with others in the group.** Your instructor should assign your group a name, which will be included in the name of the file that you submit. Refer to Figure 4.32 as you complete Step 1.

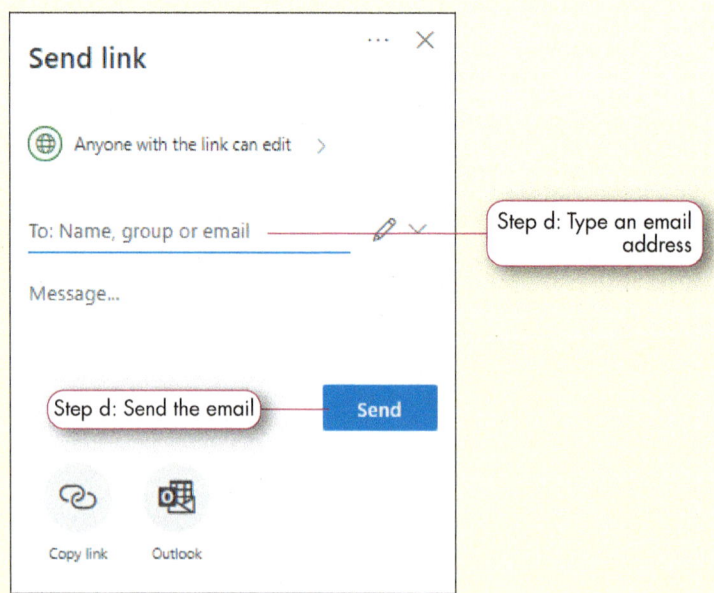

FIGURE 4.32 Share a Document

a. Ensure that you have a Microsoft account and that the OneDrive folder displays in File Explorer. Alternatively, you will be able to upload the file directly to your OneDrive space.

> **TROUBLESHOOTING:** Before beginning this exercise, you must have a Microsoft account. If you do not have a Microsoft account, create one at signup.live.com. It is possible that you might have more than one Microsoft account—a personal account as well as one assigned to you by your college. This project might be more easily conducted if all group members use a OneDrive account associated with your college or university.

b. Open *w04h1Analysis_LastFirst* and save it as **w04h3Analysis_GroupName** to OneDrive, first selecting or creating a folder in which to store it. Also save the file locally, perhaps in the Documents folder. Close **w04h1Analysis_LastFirst.**

> **TROUBLESHOOTING:** If you are not able to select OneDrive, or otherwise have difficulty during the save process, go to onedrive.com, sign in to your account, and navigate to a folder or space where you want to upload the file, creating a new folder in OneDrive. (To do so, click New on the OneDrive toolbar and then select Folder. Type a folder name and press Enter.) Click Upload in the toolbar and click Files. Navigate to *w04h3Analysis_GroupName* (in the Documents folder or wherever it was saved locally) and double-click the file to begin the upload.

c. Double-click **w04h3Analysis_GroupName** from its OneDrive location in File Explorer to open it. Click **Share** at the top right corner. (If using OneDrive in a browser, right-click w04h3Analysis_GroupName and select Share.)

d. Type an email address of a group member, clicking a resulting address suggestion if presented. Continue typing email addresses of group members. Type an optional message and click **Send**.

> **TROUBLESHOOTING:** The group leader should also copy the link, recording it as a backup to give a group member if email is unavailable to them or if they have difficulty retrieving the email. To do so, begin the share process again, this time copying and recording the link.

> **TROUBLESHOOTING:** If no group members have been assigned, consider sharing documents with a friend, family member, or with yourself, using an email address that is different from the email address associated with the current Windows account.

e. Close w04h3Analysis_GroupName.

STEP 2 ▶ USE WORD FOR THE WEB

Each team member should have received an email with a link to the shared document—w04h3Analysis_GroupName. If an email is unavailable, they would have received a link from the group leader that can be typed into a browser. Each person will access w04h3Analysis_GroupName, reviewing and editing the report individually on his or her computer at any time. You do not have to access the report simultaneously, although that is an option. Refer to Figure 4.33 as you complete Step 2.

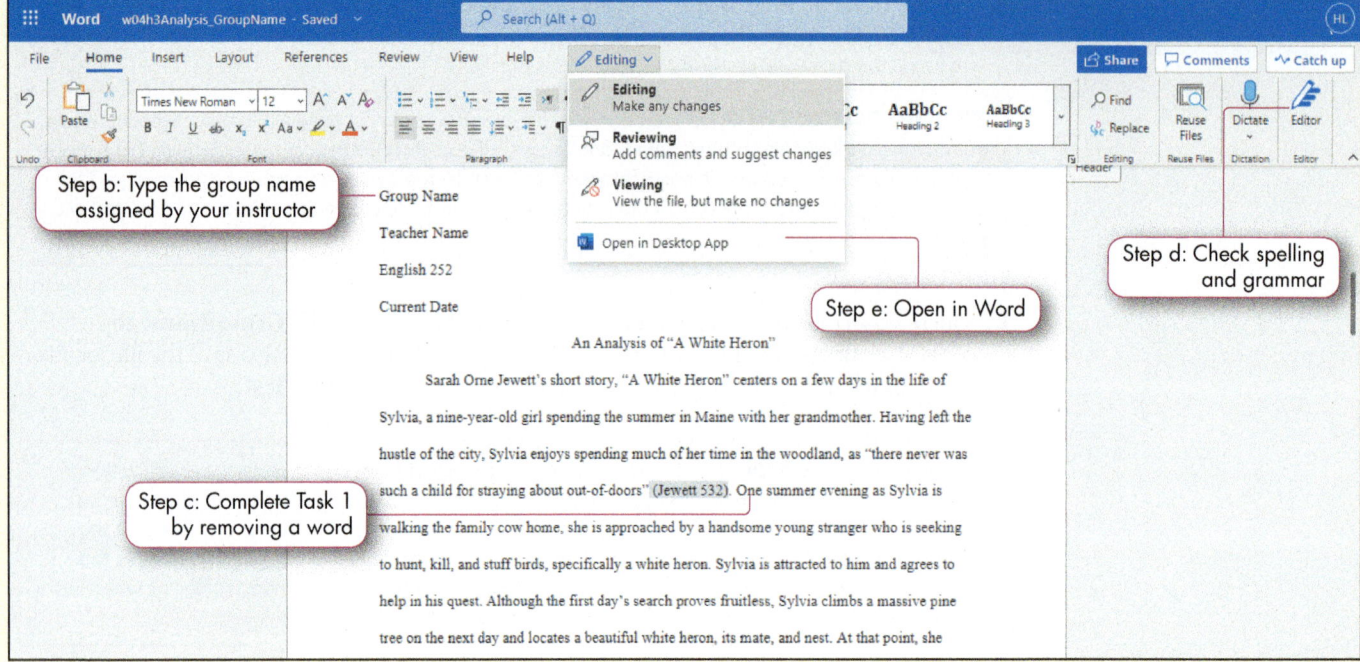

FIGURE 4.33 Work in Word for the Web

> **TROUBLESHOOTING:** To complete all steps of this exercise, every group member must have a Microsoft account. If you do not have a Microsoft account, create one at signup.live.com.

a. Open a browser window and open your email account. Open the email with the shared link and click **Open**.

   The document opens in Word for the web on your computer.

> **TROUBLESHOOTING:** It is possible that the email containing the shared link is sent to a spam folder. You may have to mark the email as not spam before the shared file can be opened. Otherwise, the group leader can provide a direct link to the shared document.

b. Type the Group Name assigned by the instructor to replace the first and last name on the first line of page 2, unless another group member has already changed the name.

c. Divide the following tasks among group members, with each task completed by only one team member (unless there are fewer team members than tasks; in that case, assign the tasks as appropriate). As each group member completes a task, it is automatically saved. These tasks can be done simultaneously and you will see indicators showing that someone is currently editing the document as well.

   - Task 1: Remove the word *On* from the third sentence of the first paragraph on page 1, and capitalize the word *One*, so that the sentence begins, *One summer evening as Sylvia is walking*.
   - Task 2: Change the word *components* in the second sentence of the second paragraph to **facets**.
   - Task 3: Change the word *bribe* in the last full paragraph of page 3 to **convince**.
   - Task 4: Change the word *helpful* to **interesting** in the last paragraph of the document.

d. Check the document for spelling errors. All authors' names are correctly spelled, so ignore flagged errors of names. Ignore any grammatical errors centered on punctuation or capitalization. Correct any misspelled words.

e. Click **Editing** and **Open in Desktop App** to open the document in Word on your computer. Click the **File tab** and select **Save a copy**. Navigate to the location on your computer where you save your student files and click **Save**.

f. Exit Word. Based on your instructor's directions, submit:
w04h2Entry_LastFirst.pdf
w04h2WhiteHeron_LastFirst
w04h3Analysis_GroupName

Chapter Objectives Review

After reading this chapter, you have accomplished the following objectives:

1. Use a writing style and acknowledge sources.
- **Select a writing style:** A research paper is typically written to adhere to a particular writing style, often dictated by the academic discipline.
- **Format a research paper:** Research papers share a set of common formatting features to maintain consistency and help to make the document look more professional.
- **Create a source and include a citation:** Each source consulted for a paper must be cited, according to the rules of a writing style.
- **Manage sources:** Sources are included in a Master List, available to all documents created on the same computer, and a Current List, available to the current document. You can edit, delete, and add new sources to either list and share sources between them.
- **Create a bibliography:** A bibliography, also known as works cited or references, lists all sources used in the preparation of a paper.

2. Create and modify footnotes and endnotes.
- **Create footnotes and endnotes:** Footnotes (located at the bottom of a page) and endnotes (located at the end of a paper) enable you to expand on a statement or provide a citation.
- **Modify footnotes and endnotes:** You can change the format or style of footnotes and endnotes, or delete them.

3. Explore special features.
- **Create a table of contents:** If headings are formatted in a heading or hierarchical style, Word can prepare a table of contents, listing headings and associated page numbers.
- **Create an index:** Mark entries for inclusion in an index, which is an alphabetical listing of marked topics and associated page numbers. Items can also be cross referenced.
- **Create a cover page:** Some writing styles require a cover page, which you can create as the first page, listing a report title and other identifying information.
- **Manage a table of figures:** A table of figures is a list, sorted by page number, of figure captions throughout a document.

4. Track changes.
- **Use Track Changes:** With Track Changes active, all edits in a document are traceable so you can see what has been changed.
- **Accept changes:** With Track Changes active, you can evaluate each edit made, accepting or rejecting it.

5. Review a document.
- **Use markup:** Markup views enable you to customize how tracked changes are displayed in a document. There are four markup views: Simple Markup, All Markup, No Markup, and Original.
- **Add a comment:** A comment is located in a comment balloon in the margin of a report, providing a note to the author.
- **View comments:** Comments are viewed in comment balloons in the document.
- **Reply to comments:** Replying to comments creates a conversation around the comment with the reply placed within the original comment balloon.
- **Work with a PDF document:** Documents can be saved in PDF format to preserve the layout and images of the original Word document.

6. Use OneDrive.
- **Use OneDrive with File Explorer:** Windows incorporates OneDrive into File Explorer to simplify the process of organizing and managing OneDrive folders (and contents) as well as ensuring that files are synchronized.
- **Use OneDrive in a browser:** Although you can save files directly to OneDrive from within Word, you can also manage file storage from within a browser interface.

7. Share documents.
- **Invite others to share:** Use Word and Word for the web to share documents through email or links with varying levels of permission.
- **Send as an attachment:** Send an email to recipients with an attached document, either in PDF or the original format.

8. Collaborate with Word and Word for the Web.
- **Use Word for the web:** Word for the web is a Web-based version of Word that enables you to create, edit, and format a document online without having to install Word on your computer.

Key Terms Matching

Match the key terms with their definitions. Write the key term letter by the appropriate numbered definition.

a. American Psychological Association (APA)
b. Bibliography
c. Citation
d. Comment
e. Comment balloon
f. Cover page
g. Footnote
h. Index
i. Markup
j. Modern Language Association (MLA)
k. OneDrive
l. PDF Reflow
m. Real-time co-authoring
n. Revision mark
o. Simple Markup
p. Source
q. Table of contents
r. Track Changes
s. Word for the web
t. Writing style

1. _____ An online app that enables you to create and edit Word documents from any Internet-connected computer and across any platform of all sources created in Word on a computer. **p. 333**

2. _____ An alphabetical listing of topics covered in a document along with the page numbers where the topic is discussed. **p. 308**

3. _____ A list of sources cited by an author in his or her work, shown at the end of a research report. **p. 303**

4. _____ A parenthetical note recognizing a source of information or a quoted passage. **p. 300**

5. _____ A Web-based storage site and sharing resource. **p. 328**

6. _____ A page that lists headings in the order they appear in a document and the page numbers where the entries begin. **p. 307**

7. _____ A Word feature that monitors all additions, deletions, and formatting changes you make in a document. **p. 315**

8. _____ A writing style used primarily in the fields of business, economics, and social science. **p. 299**

9. _____ A view that simplifies the display of comments and revision marks, resulting in a clean, uncluttered look. **p. 319**

10. _____ A note, an annotation, or additional information to the author or another reader about the content of a document, shown in the right margin. **p. 318**

11. _____ A shape that displays on the right side of a paragraph in which a comment has been made. **p. 321**

12. _____ A Word feature that shows several authors simultaneously editing the document in Word or Word for the web. **p. 335**

13. _____ A writing style used primarily in humanities disciplines. **p. 298**

14. _____ Text that displays at the bottom of a page, providing additional detail to text in the document. **p. 304**

15. _____ A way of viewing tracked changes, enabling you to customize the way edits are displayed. **p. 315**

16. _____ Indicates where text is added, deleted, or formatted. **p. 316**

17. _____ The first page of a report, including the report title, author or student name, and other identifying information. **p. 309**

18. _____ A publication, person, or media item that is consulted in the preparation of a paper and given credit. **p. 298**

19. _____ A set of guidelines that results in standardized documents that present citations in the same manner and that include the same general page characteristics. **p. 298**

20. _____ A process that converts PDF content into a Word document, retaining the original layout. **p. 323**

Multiple Choice

1. How would you choose whether to use a footnote or an endnote?

   (a) If the number of footnotes is excessive, the overflow would be directed to an endnote list, so you might actually use both.

   (b) It would depend upon the document type, with legal and medical documents requiring footnotes, while research reports always use endnotes.

   (c) You would consult the writing style you are following.

   (d) It is a matter of preference; either is always acceptable.

2. Office for the web is a collection of Microsoft Office apps with what primary purpose?

   (a) Group editing of an online document

   (b) Tracking document changes

   (c) Serving as a subscription version of Microsoft Office

   (d) Limiting the amount of local computer storage required for Office installation

3. How is Word for the web limited?

   (a) A document opened in Word for the web cannot be simultaneously edited by more than one person.

   (b) A document opened in Word for the web is formatted as a PDF file, with limited Word editing possible.

   (c) Word for the web is not as full featured as its desktop equivalent, with fewer ribbon tabs and less functionality.

   (d) Word for the web can only open Word documents that are less than 15 KB in size.

4. Which of the following is not considered an accepted writing style?

   (a) Purdue Owl

   (b) MLA

   (c) Chicago

   (d) APA

5. Why might it be beneficial to show the Reviewing Pane?

   (a) So that you can see a complete list of all reviewers of a group-edited document

   (b) So that you can filter edits by reviewer

   (c) So that you can add all comments in one location

   (d) So that you can more easily keep track of all changes and comments in a heavily edited document

6. In which of the following situations would you need to edit a citation?

   (a) If you misspelled an author's name when creating a source

   (b) If you need to include a page number in the citation

   (c) If the citation is not included in the Master List of sources

   (d) If you initially selected the wrong writing style

7. Which of the following is an advantage of saving Word documents to OneDrive?

   (a) AutoSave is on, which means a document is automatically saved every few seconds as it is being edited.

   (b) The AutoRecover setting for documents saved to OneDrive is adjusted to occur every 3 minutes.

   (c) A folder structure is not necessary in OneDrive as files are categorized and stored by revision date.

   (d) A Microsoft account is not necessary to access OneDrive.

8. What is required before a table of figures can be created?

   (a) Captions in a document identifying tables and figures

   (b) A citation for every table that is included

   (c) Permission from any copyright holders being cited in a table of figures

   (d) That the table is formatted with PDF Reflow

9. Which feature provides the most uncluttered view of comments and tracked changes made to a document?

   (a) Normal Style

   (b) All Markup

   (c) Simple Markup

   (d) Original

10. How does a table of contents differ from an index?

   (a) A table of contents is arranged alphabetically by topic, while an index lists items in page number order.

   (b) A table of contents can be created from a References tab selection, while an index must be manually created.

   (c) A table of contents is based on a hierarchy of headings in a document, shown in page number order, while an index is an alphabetical listing of selected terms and related page numbers.

   (d) A table of contents is only used in books, while an index can appear in shorter reports.

Practice Exercises

1 Live. Work. Dine. Shop.

You are the assistant publicity manager of a construction company that is building a community where residents can live, work, dine, and shop within the community without having to get into a car. You and a team of colleagues are designing promotional materials for this project. You conducted your research online for such communities in other states and wrote a promotional article. You will share your research with your team members online so that they can contribute, comment, and collaborate with you before finalizing the document. Refer to Figure 4.34 as you complete this exercise.

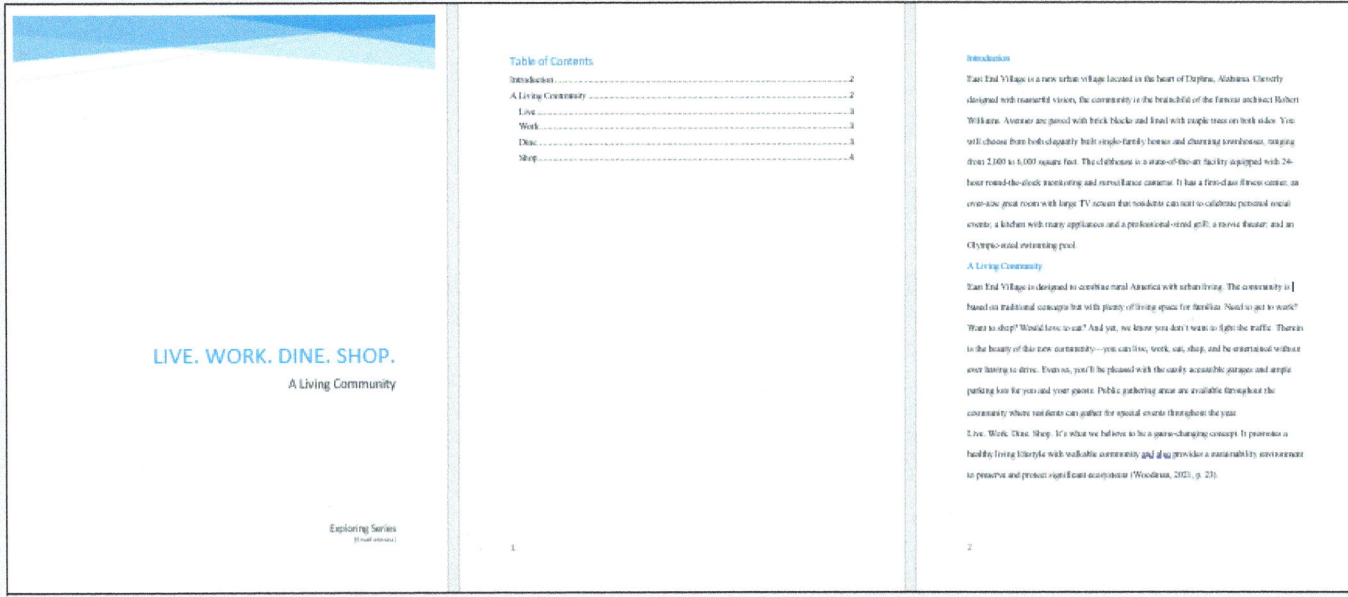

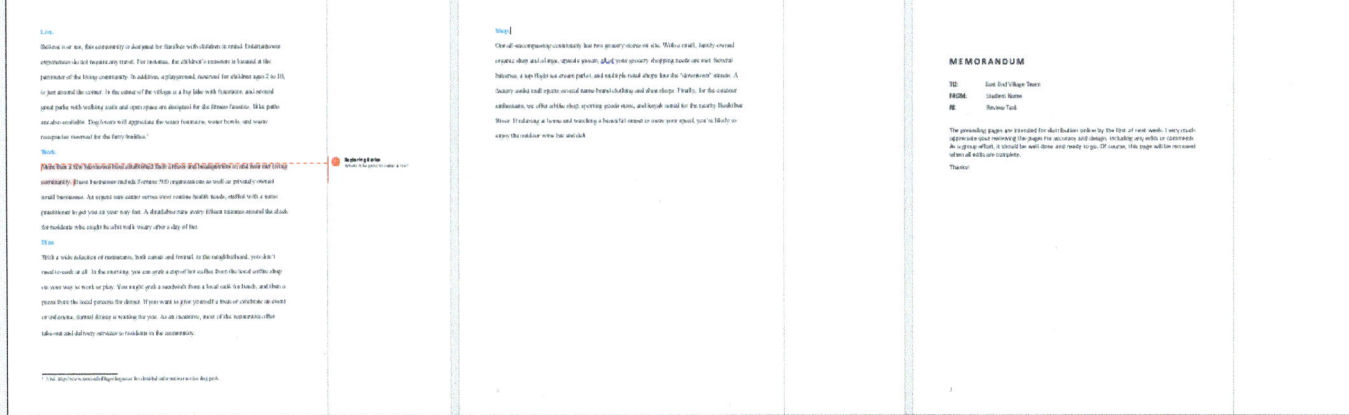

FIGURE 4.34 Design a Promotional Document

a. Open Word. Click **Open** and navigate to your student data files. Double-click *w04p1Memo.pdf*, agreeing to convert the PDF file to an editable Word document. Enable content if asked.

b. Show nonprinting characters. Insert a hard return before the first body paragraph, beginning with *The preceding pages*. Change the last sentence of the first body paragraph to *Of course, this page will be removed when all edits are complete.*

c. Save the memo as a Word document with the filename **w04p1Memo_LastFirst**. Close the document.

d. Open *w04p1Live* and save it as **w04p1Live_LastFirst**. Show nonprinting characters.

e. Format the document as follows:
   - All text is double-spaced.
   - Font is Times New Roman 12 pt size.
   - No paragraph spacing before or after any paragraph.
   - Margins are 1″ at the top, bottom, left, and right.
   - Alignment is left.

f. Place the insertion point at the beginning of the document. Click the **Insert tab**, click **Cover Page**, and then select **Facet**. Complete the cover page as follows:
   - Click **Document title** and type **Live. Work. Dine. Shop.** (Include the periods.) Text will be shown in all caps.
   - Click **Document subtitle** and type **A Living Community**. (Do not type the period.)
   - Ensure that your name shows as the author at the bottom right corner of the page. You will not type an email address.
   - Right-click the **Abstract paragraph** (not the word *Abstract*) and click **Remove Content Control**.
   - Delete the text box in which the word *Abstract* is shown.

g. Click the **Review tab**. Click the **Track Changes arrow** in the Tracking group and select **For Everyone**. All of your edits will be marked as you work. Ensure that the markup view is **All Markup**. Make the following changes to the document:
   - Change the heading *A New Community* on page 2 to **A Living Community**. (Do not type the period.)
   - Select the first sentence under the *Work* heading on page 3. Click **New Comment** in the Comments group on the Review tab. Type **Would it be good to name a few?** Click the **Post comment arrow.**

h. Insert a page break at the end of the document. Click the **Insert tab** and click the **Object arrow** in the Text group. Select **Text from File**. Navigate to and double-click **w04p1Memo_LastFirst**. It is the document you saved in Step c. Replace *Student Name* on the last page with your first and last names.

i. Scroll through the document, noting the edits that were tracked as well as the comment. Click the **Review tab** and change the markup view to **No Markup**. Scroll through the document to note that revision marks (indicating edits) do not display. Change the markup view to **Simple Markup**. Scroll to page 2 and click the vertical red bar in the left margin to display edits in that area. Click the bar again to remove the edit from view.

j. Check the document for spelling and grammatical errors. The river name is not misspelled. The words *life style* should be one word. Scroll to page 3 (it is the third page, but the page number is 2 because the cover page is not numbered) and view the comment referring to the last sentence in the Live section. Point to the comment and click **Reply**. Type **I am including a footnote.** (Include the period.) Post the reply.

k. Click after the period at the end of the last sentence in the *Live* section. Click the **References tab** and click **Insert Footnote** in the Footnotes group. Type **See http://www.eastendvillage.com/dognews for detailed information on the dog park.** (Include the period.) Right-click the **hyperlink** in the footnote and click **Remove Hyperlink**.

l. Click the **Review tab** and change the view to **No Markup**. Right-click the footnote at the bottom of page 3 and click **Style**. Click **Modify**. Change the font to **Times New Roman** and ensure that the font size is **10 pt**. Click **OK** and click **Apply**.

m. Place the insertion point at the top of page 2 (beginning with the *Introduction* heading). Insert a page break. Click before the Page Break indicator on the new blank page. Click the **References tab**, click **Table of Contents** in the Table of Contents group, and then select **Automatic Table 2**.

n. Select the *Conclusion* heading and the following paragraph on the fifth page (numbered page 4), taking care not to remove the Page break indicator that follows the selected paragraph. Press **Delete**. Scroll to page 2 and click **Table of Contents**. Click **Update Table** in the content control and select **Update entire table**. Click **OK**. Note that the Conclusion section is no longer included in the table of contents.

o. Click the **Review tab** and change the view to **Simple Markup**. Click the **Accept arrow** and select **Accept All Changes and Stop Tracking**. Scroll through the document and note that edits are no longer marked. However, comments remain.

p. Click before the period in the last sentence in the second paragraph in the *A Living Community* section that ends *protect significant ecosystems*. Click the **References tab** and click the **Style arrow** in the Citations & Bibliography group. Select **APA Sixth Edition**. Click **Insert Citation** in the Citations & Bibliography group and click **Add New Source**. Add the following source from a **Journal Article** and click **OK**:

Author: **Woodman, Jennifer Lynn**

Title: **Protecting Ecosystems**

Journal Name: **Journal of Ecosystems Studies**

Year: **2021**

Pages: **23–30**

Volume: **6**

Issue: **4**

(Hint: Click **Show All Bibliography Fields** to enter the volume and issue.)

q. Click the **citation** you just created, click the **Citation Options arrow**, and then select **Edit Citation**. Type **23** in the Pages box. Click **OK**.

r. Save the document. Save the document again, selecting **OneDrive** as the save location. If prompted, sign in to your Microsoft account. Click **Share** at the top right corner, enter your own email address, and click **Send**. Close **w04p1Live_LastFirst**, first making sure you have saved it to your student files (you will select Save a Copy and select a save location).

s. Check the email account to which you sent the link in Step r. Open the email message and click **Open**. Scroll to the last page in the shared document and change the first line of the memorandum from *M E M O* to **M E M O R A N D U M**. (Do not type the period, but do include a space between letters.)

TROUBLESHOOTING: If you do not find the email in your inbox, check your Spam or Junk folder. If it is not there, open a browser and go to onedrive.com. Sign into the account from which you sent the link, and click w04p1Live_LastFirst. Change M E M O to M E M O R A N D U M and proceed to Step t.

---

t. Click **Editing** in the OneDrive toolbar and select **Open in Desktop App**. Click the **File tab**, click **Save a Copy**, browse to your student files, and save the document as **w04p1Live_LastFirst**, replacing the existing file.

u. Save and close the file. Exit Word. Based on your instructor's directions, submit: w04p1Live_LastFirst

2 College Funding

You and a partner are beginning a consulting business related to helping students secure college funding. The funding landscape is vast and challenging for many students who might become overwhelmed with the process; you hope to help with that so that students who want to go to college are able to do so. You are beginning an informational document as an overview of the consulting company's mission and activities. You plan to share it with your partner before it is finalized and distributed. Your current task is formatting the document and ensuring appropriate section headings. You will include a table of contents that will be updated as edits continue. In addition, you will cite funding agencies and scholarship opportunities correctly. By tracking all changes, you will ensure that only those that are appropriate are ultimately included. Refer to Figure 4.35 as you complete this exercise.

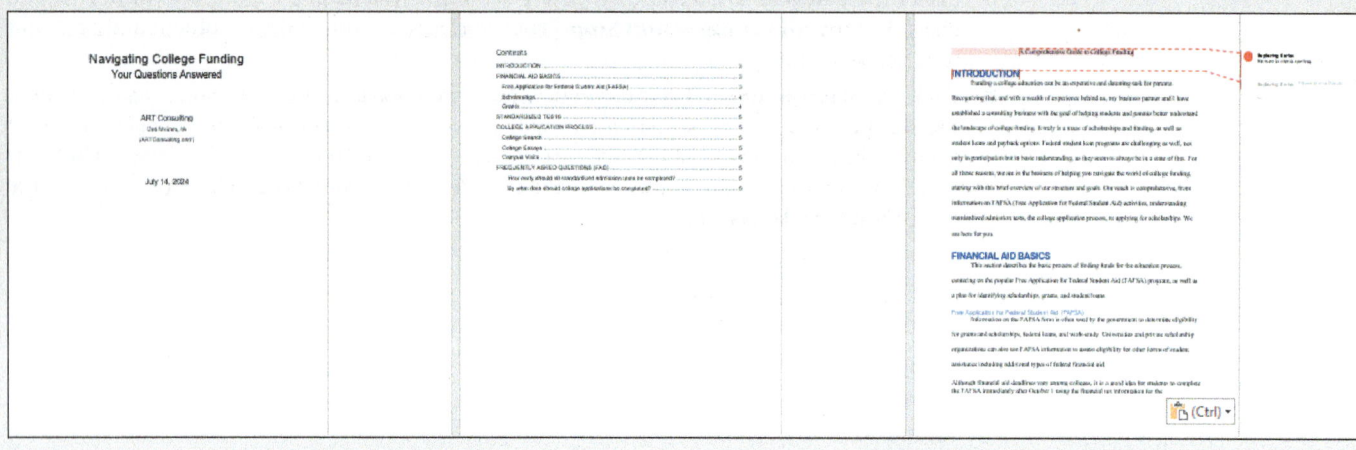

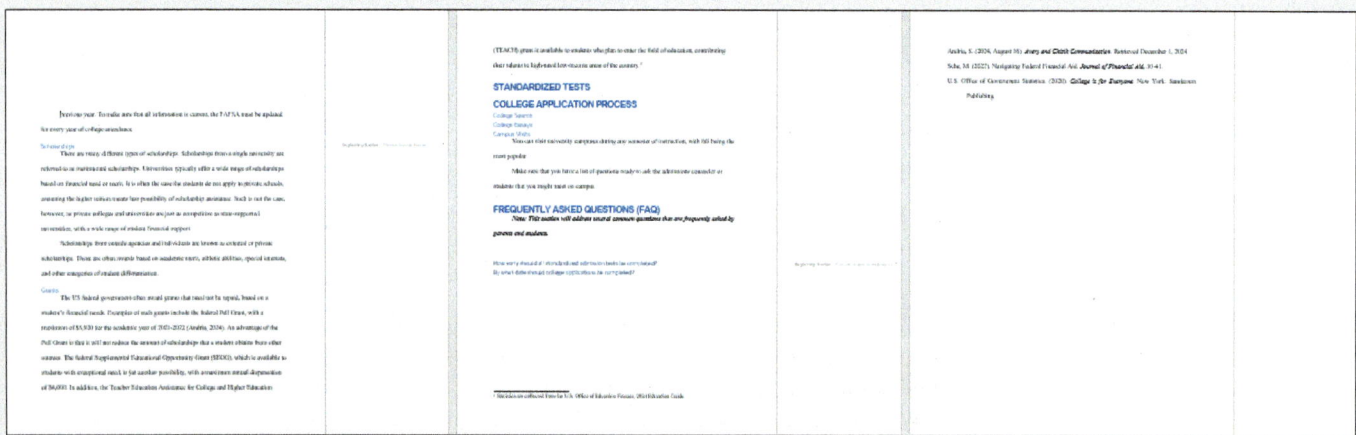

FIGURE 4.35 Design an Informational Document

a. Open *w04p2College* and save as **w04p2College_LastFirst**. Show nonprinting characters.

b. Format the document as follows:
- All text is double-spaced.
- Font is Times New Roman 12 pt size.
- No paragraph spacing before or after any paragraph.
- Margins are 1″ at the top, bottom, left, and right.
- Add a First line indent of 0.5″ to each paragraph.

c. Place the insertion point at the beginning of the document and insert a blank page. Click before the Page Break indicator on page 1. Click the **Insert tab**. Click the **Object arrow** in the Text group and select **Text from File**. Navigate to your student files and double-click *w04p2Cover*.

d. Click the **Review tab**. Click the **Track Changes arrow** in the Tracking group and select **For Everyone**. All of your edits will be marked as you work. Ensure that the markup view is **Simple Markup**. Make the following changes to the document:
- Change the heading *FINANCIAL AID OVERVIEW* on page 2 to **FINANCIAL AID BASICS**. (Do not type the period.)
- Click before the period that ends the last sentence on page 2, ending in *for other forms of student assistance*. Press **spacebar** and type **including additional types of federal financial aid**. (Do not type the period.)
- Select the report title on page 2, *A Comprehensive Guide to College Funding*. Click **New Comment** in the Comments group on the Review tab. Type **Be sure to check spelling.** (Include the period.) Click **Post comment**.

e. Work with comments in the document as follows:
- Review the second comment on page 2, indicating that headings in all caps should be format-ted differently. Follow the suggestion and make the changes. Click **More thread actions** and select **Resolve thread**. when the task is complete.
- Review the comment on page 3 and follow the formatting directions. Mark the comment as resolved when the task is complete.
- Review the comment on page 4 and follow the formatting directions. Mark the comment as resolved when the task is complete.

f. Scroll to page 2 and click any of the vertical bars in the left margin indicating that edits have occurred. Click a bar again to close the view. Click the **Review tab** and change the markup view to **All Markup**. Scroll through the document, noting the changes and formatting that have occurred.

g. Click before the report heading on page 2, *A Comprehensive Guide to College Funding*. Click the **View tab** and show the ruler. Drag the **First Line Indent indicator** on the ruler back to the left margin so that the report heading is not indented. Center the report heading. Delete the blank paragraph that follows the report heading.

h. Click the **Review tab** and change the markup view to **Simple Markup**. Check the document for spelling and grammatical errors. Ignore any grammatical errors. Mark the remaining comment on page 2 as resolved.

i. Click **Reviewing Pane** (not the Reviewing Pane arrow) in the Tracking group on the Review tab to display the Revisions Pane. Click the arrow beside the number of revisions at the top left of the Revisions pane to view editing statistics. Close the Revisions Pane.

j. Click the **Accept arrow** in the Changes group on the Review tab and select **Accept All Changes and Stop Tracking**.

k. Click after the period that ends the last sentence on page 3 ending in *low-income areas of the country*. Click the **References tab** and click **Insert Footnote** in the Footnotes group. Type **Statistics are collected from the U.S. Office of Education Finance, 2024 Education Guide.** (Include the period.)

l. Right-click the footnote at the bottom of page 3 and click **Style**. Click **Modify**. Change the font to **Times New Roman** and ensure that the font size is **10 pt**. Click **OK** and click **Apply**.

m. Place the insertion point before the report heading at the top of page 2. Insert a page break. Click before the Page Break indicator on the new blank page. Click **Table of Contents** in the Table of Contents group on the References tab, and then select **Automatic Table 1**. Select the word *Contents* at the top of the table of contents and change the font color to **Black, Text 1**.

n. Scroll to page 5 and delete the last question, *What are the qualifications for a federal Pell Grant?* Scroll to page 2 and click in the table of contents. Click **Update Table** in the content control and select **Update entire table**. Click **OK**. Note that the question is removed from the table of contents.

o. Insert a citation by completing the following steps:
- Click the References tab. Click the **Style arrow** in the Citations & Bibliography group and select **APA Sixth Edition**
- Scroll to page 4 and click before the period at the end of the second sentence under the *Grants* heading (ending in *2021-2022*).
- Click **Insert Citation** in the Citations & Bibliography group. Select the **Andria** source.
- Click the **Andria citation** and click the **Citation Options arrow**. Select **Edit Source**. Correct the spelling of the author's first name to **Solomon**. Click **OK**. Agree to change both the master and current list.

p. Place the insertion point at the end of the document and insert a page break. Click **Bibliography** in the Citations & Bibliography group and select **Insert Bibliography** (the last selection in the list). Select all text on the Bibliography page and format it as double-spaced, no paragraph spacing before or after paragraphs, and with **Times New Roman** font at **12 pt** size.

q. Save and close the file. Exit Word. Based on your instructor's directions, submit: w04p2College_LastFirst

Mid-Level Exercises

1 Maroney Design Agency

You are employed as a Web designer at Maroney Design Agency and have been charged with developing a document for use in a workshop for beginners to the field of Web design. You want to provide the basic elements of good design and format the document professionally. You will use the information you have already prepared in a Word document and revise it to include elements appropriate for a research-oriented paper.

a. Open *w04m1Maroney* and save as **w04m1Maroney_LastFirst**. Replace the current author with your name in the text box on the cover page.

b. Apply the following formatting to all text in the document, with the exception of the cover page.
   - Alignment is left.
   - Document is double-spaced.
   - The font is Times New Roman 12 pt.
   - Paragraph spacing before or after any paragraph is 0.
   - Margins are 1″ at the top, bottom, left, and right.
   - A First line indent of .05″ is applied to all paragraphs, with the exception of the shaded text on page 3 and the table text on page 5.

c. Change writing style to **APA Sixth Edition**. Place the insertion point at the end of the last sentence in the *Proximity* paragraph (after the period) on the second page of the document (ending in *more white space indicates less proximity*). Insert the following footnote: **Max Rebaza, Effective Websites, Chicago: Windy City Publishing (2023)**. (Do not type the period.)

d. Change the footnote number format to lowercase letters. (Use the Footnote and Endnote dialog box.)

e. Insert a table of contents on a new page after the cover page. Use **Automatic Table 2** style.

f. Display the ruler. Remove the First line indent from the following single-line headings: *Proximity and Balance, Contrast and Focus, Consistency, Additional Design Guidelines, Appropriate Background, Effective Color Choices, Effective Typography*, and *Graphical and Multimedia Effects*.

g. Add a bibliography to the document by inserting citation sources from the footnotes already in place. Because you will not use in-text citations, you will use the Source Manager to create the sources. If asked at any point, you will update both the Current List and the Master List. To add new sources, complete the following steps:
   - Scroll to page 3, where the first footnote is shown. Click **Manage Sources** in the Citations & Bibliography group on the References tab.
   - Click **New** in the Source Manager dialog box. The source is a **Book** written in **2023** and titled **Effective Websites**, written by **Max Rebaza**. The publisher is **Windy City Publishing** based in **Chicago**.
   - Create entries for the two additional sources identified in the document footnotes. They are as follows:
     - The footnote on the fourth page, numbered page 3 is from an **Article in a Periodical**. The author is **Kaylene Durocher** and the title is **ABC's of Web Site Consistency**. The Periodical title is **Web Site Magazine**. The volume is **7**, pages are **33–34**, and the year is **2020**. (Hint: To add the volume, select Show All Bibliography Fields.)
     - The footnote on the fifth page, numbered page 4 is from a **Journal Article**. The author is **Cheyenne Kinyon** and the title is **Color Background and Themes: Making Wise Decisions**. The Journal is **Web Guidelines and Conventions**. Pages are **166–167** and the year is **2021**.

h. Insert a bibliography at the end of the document on a separate page, selecting **Bibliography**. Center the bibliography heading. Double-space the bibliography and ensure that there is no paragraph spacing before or after. Update the table of contents to include this new addition and ensure that the font for *Bibliography* in the table of contents is **Times New Roman**.

i. Mark all occurrences of *web, content*, and *site* as index entries. Create an index on a separate page after the bibliography, accepting all defaults.

j. Check the document for spelling errors. All names are spelled correctly, including *TypoUpright*. Ignore all grammatical errors and disregard any other refinement concerns.

k. Begin to track changes. Ensure that the markup view is **All Markup**. Select the heading **Proximity and Balance** on the third page, numbered page 2. Add a new comment, typing **This section seems incomplete. Please expand.** (Include the period.)

l. Complete the following edits:
- Select and delete the word *that* in the third sentence of the first paragraph on the third page, numbered page 2.
- Add the following sentence as the second sentence in the first body paragraph of the *Contrast and Focus* section: **You are most likely familiar with the concept of contrast when working with pictures in an image editor.** Ensure that a space follows the sentence.
- Select the first paragraph on the fifth page, numbered page 4, beginning with *Consultants recommend white or black backgrounds.* Click the **Shading arrow** in the Paragraph group on the Home tab and select **No Color**.

m. Accept all changes and stop tracking.

n. Save and close the file. Exit Word. Based on your instructor's directions, submit: w04m1Maroney_LastFirst

2 Study Abroad   MyLab IT Grader

You plan to participate in a study abroad program in France. For the application process, you are required to write a proposal describing the program that you are interested in. You have begun that process, with a draft document underway. You conducted online research, found a foreign university that appeals to you, and developed a list of activities that you would like to participate in while away. In continuing to work with the document, you will apply a few formatting changes and add a cover page, table of contents, and index. As it is a work in progress, you will track all changes before deciding which to keep, and you will make note of things to remember by adding comments.

a. Open *w04m2Study* and save it as **w04m2Study_LastFirst**.

b. Turn on **Track Changes** so any further changes will be flagged.

c. Apply **Heading 1 style** to section headings that display in all capital letters. Apply **Heading 2 style** (scroll to locate the style) to section headings that display alone on a line in title case (the first letter of each word is capitalized). Format the items in the *Included in the Tuition* section as a bulleted list.

d. Place the insertion point at the beginning of the document. Ensure that the markup view is **All Markup**. Change the word *INTRODUCTION* on the first line of the report to **STUDY ABROAD IN FRANCE**. (Do not type the period.) Center the first line and change the font size to **20 pt**.

e. Accept all changes and stop tracking. Modify comments as follows:
- Right-click the first comment on page 2, related to formatting an item as Heading 1, and click **Delete Comment** to remove the comment.
- Delete the next comment related to formatting the list with bullets.
- Reply to the next comment, related to formatting an item as Heading 2. Type **I assume you meant to include Day 3 as well?**

f. Ensure that the writing style is **APA Sixth Edition**. Insert a footnote on page 1 at the end of the first sentence in the first paragraph, ending with *Strasbourg, France*. Be sure to click after the period. Type **EU Studies Program in Strasbourg, France is open by application only.** (Include the period.) Modify the footnote style to **Times New Roman** font at **12** pt size.

g. Click the **Insert tab** and click **Header**. Click **Edit Header** and type **Study Abroad**, followed by a space and a **Plain Number** page number. The header should be right-aligned. Click **Different First Page** in the Options group on the Header & Footer tab to refrain from showing the header on the first page.

h. Create a cover page choosing **Banded** style. Ensure that your name shows as author at the bottom of the cover page. Right-click any other content controls and click **Remove Content Control** to remove them. Click the *Document Title* placeholder and type **Study Abroad**.

i. Insert a blank page after the cover page for the table of contents. On the new blank page, generate a table of contents, choosing **Automatic Table 1** style.

j. Mark all occurrences of the following text for inclusion in the index: *Alsace, Black Forest, European Union, and France.* On a separate page at the end of the document, create the index, choosing a **Classic** format.

k. Check spelling and grammar. Although many place names are flagged, no name is misspelled, so ignore all errors attributed to such. The words *fresh water* should be one word, *freshwater*. Ignore any other grammatical flags.

l. Click after the second to last sentence in the paragraph above the *About the University* section on the third page, numbered page 2. Ensure that the insertion point is before the ending period in the sentence that ends with *the Klinglin.* Insert a citation to a new source which is a **Book Section**. The author is **Kaytrina Lawler**. The title is **The Culture of Strasbourg**. The book title is **European Study and Travel**, authored by **Anders Fuqua**. The year is **2018** and the pages are **252-259**. The publisher is **Goforth Publishing**, based in **Dallas**.

m. Edit the Lawler citation to include a page number of **254**.

n. Save and close the file. Exit Word. Based on your instructor's directions, submit: w04m2Study_LastFirst

Running Case

New Castle County Technical Services

New Castle County Technical Services (NCCTS) provides technical services to clients in the greater New Castle County, Delaware, area. Founded in 2011, the company is rapidly expanding to include technical security systems, network infrastructure cabling, and basic troubleshooting services. With that growth comes the need to promote the company and to provide clear written communication to employees and clients. Microsoft Word is used exclusively in the development and distribution of documents, including an "About New Castle" summary that will be available both in print and online. You made a few changes to the document and you are now ready to make this into a professional-looking business document in this exercise.

a. Open *w04r1NewCastle* and save it as **w04r1NewCastle_LastFirst** to your OneDrive folder on File Explorer, signing in to your Windows account if prompted.

b. Click the **Review tab.** Click the first formatting indication of a change of font to Times New Roman, shown in the right margin on page 1. Click the **Accept arrow** in the Changes group and select **Accept This Change**. Scroll through all pages of the document, accepting all changes to Times New Roman.

c. Click **Share** at the top right corner, enter your own email address, and then click **Send**.

d. Check the email address to which you sent the link, opening the email containing the link. Click **Open**. Confirm that Track Changes are active, if prompted. Scroll through the document. Click the **Review tab** and click **Show Comments** in the Comments group. Select **Student Name** at the end of the first page. Click **New Comment** in the Comment pane and type **Be sure to change this to your name.** (Include the period.) Click **Post comment**.

> **TROUBLESHOOTING:** If you do not find the email in your inbox, check your Spam or Junk folder. If it is not there, open a browser and go to onedrive.com. Sign into the account from which you sent the link, and click w04r1NewCastle_LastFirst. Revisit Step d, beginning with the directions related to adding a comment.

e. Ensure that nonprinting characters are shown. Click the second comment shown in the Comments pane related to providing more detail. Click after the space following the period ending the last sentence in the *Active Accounts* section to which the comment refers. Type **It is not surprising to see that network security and cloud integration have a larger increase than IT consulting and disaster recovery.** (Include the period.) Reply to the comment by typing **Done**. Click **Post reply**. Close the Comments pane.

f. Click **Reviewing** in the toolbar and click **Open in Desktop App**. Insert and modify a footnote by completing the following steps:

- Scroll to page 6 and click after the period that ends the second sentence in the first body paragraph (ending in *of the past two years*).
- Insert a footnote with the text **Information for the past five years is available upon request.** (Include the period.)
- Click the **Dialog Box Launcher in the Footnotes group**. Click the **Number format arrow** and select the lowercase alphabet format (a, b, c,...). Click **Insert**.

g. Accept all changes and stop tracking. Create an **Integral** cover page before the first page of the document. Change the document title to **About New Castle** and ensure that your name is shown as the author. Delete any placeholders that you are not using, including the abstract and document subtitle. Be sure to delete the entire placeholder, not just the text within. (Right-click the placeholder and click **Remove Content Control.)** Delete the word *ABSTRACT*.

h. Scroll to page 2 and follow the directions given in the comment addressing the Student Name paragraph. It is OK if the comment is deleted as you change the name.

i. Create a blank page for the table of contents after the cover page and generate a table of contents using the **Automatic Table 2** style.

j. Create an index for the report by completing the following steps:

- Find an occurrence of the word *computer* and select the word.
- Click the **References tab** and click **Mark Entry** in the Index group. Click **Mark All**. Click **Close**.
- Repeat the process, marking all entries for **network, NCCTS, training support**, and **troubleshooting**.
- Create a blank page at the end of the document. Click the **References tab** and click **Insert Index** in the Index group. Click **OK**.

(Hint: Click Find in the Editing group on the Home tab to open the Navigation Pane. Type the word or phrases you are seeking in the Search box to locate them quickly.)

k. Click the **File tab** and click **Save a Copy**. Browse to the location of your student files, change the filename to **w04r1NewCastleRevised_LastFirst**, and click **Save**.

l. Save and close the file. Exit Word. Based on your instructor's directions, submit: w04r1NewCastleRevised_LastFirst

Disaster Recovery

Computer History

You are preparing a brief history of computers for inclusion in a group project. Another student began the project but ran out of time and needs your help. You need to turn the draft into a professional-looking document by including proper citations of the sources used in your research. Adding a cover page and a table of contents to the research paper will also help to enhance the document. Open *w04d1Computers* and save it as **w04d1Computers_LastFirst**. Act on all comments left for you by the previous student, marking each as resolved when complete. Insert a citation to an existing source (Natasha Brevard), positioning it after the sentence in the IBM PC section ending in *$50,000*. Insert a citation to an existing source (Nichola Tsaviv), positioning it after the last sentence in the Apple Macintosh section, ending in *trade secrets*. Edit the citation to include a page number of 68. Include a bibliography on its own page at the end of the document, titled **References** and formatted as the rest of the paper. The bibliography heading should not be bold but should be centered. Save and close the file. Exit Word. Based on your instructor's directions, submit: w04d1Computers_LastFirst

Cumulative Exercise

Bovine Research

As a pre-veterinary major, you are steeped in classes related to scientific research and analysis of veterinary practices. Most recently, you were assigned the task of creating a brief overview of livestock genomics, especially as the topic relates to cattle. You have completed a draft of the paper and submitted it for review by your instructor. Having made several comments, primarily regarding formatting, your instructor has returned it to you for completion. You will modify the format, add a cover page and a table of figures, and ensure that sources are properly acknowledged both in text and in a bibliography. Because the paper might be selected for inclusion in the department's online database of relevant research, you will save the file in PDF format (which is required by the university for online publications) as well as in Word.

Use Track Changes, Accept Changes, Use Markup, Select a Writing Style, and Format a Research Paper

The content of your paper seems to be in order, but its formatting must be adjusted to adhere to the writing style required, which is APA (widely used in undergraduate science disciplines).

1. Open *w04c1Cattle* and save as **w04c1Cattle_LastFirst**. Display nonprinting characters.
2. Click the **Review tab** and ensure that the view is **All Markup**. Click the first edit in the right margin, indicating that the words *can foster* were deleted. Click **Reject and Move to Next** in the Changes group. Delete the words *often fosters* in the same paragraph.
3. Change the view to **No Markup** and ensure that the modified sentence reads correctly, with the words *can foster* instead of *often fosters*.
4. Change the view to **Simple Markup**. Accept all changes and stop tracking.
5. Ensure that the writing style is **APA**. Format the body of the research paper, including the two tables, as follows:
   - Document is double-spaced.
   - No paragraph spacing before or after any paragraph.
   - Margins are 1" at the top, bottom, left, and right.
   - Alignment is left.

Create a Source and Include a Citation, Create a Footnote, Modify a Footnote, and Create a Bibliography

The brief paper includes several sources which should be cited in-text and documented in a bibliography. A footnote provides additional explanation of a statement as well.

6. Click before the period that ends the second sentence in the second paragraph, ending *in beef cattle*. Insert a citation to a new source (**Article in a Periodical**) as follows:

   Corporate Author: **Institute for Bovine Research**
   Title: **BRD and Cattle: What You Should Know**
   Periodical Title: **Agriculture Today**
   Year: **2023**
   Month: **October**
   Day: **18**
   Pages: **26–34**

7. Click before the period that ends the first sentence on page 2, ending in *is survived*. Insert a citation to the United States Department of Agriculture source.
8. Click the parenthetical citation for the Institute of Bovine Research shown in the second paragraph on page 1. Edit the citation to include page **31**.
9. Click after the period that ends the fourth sentence in the last paragraph on page 2, ending in *and exhibit symptoms*. Ensure that the insertion point is after the period. Insert a footnote that reads **A diagnosis of BRD will be confirmed by attending veterinarians.** (Include the period.)
10. Modify the footnote style to include **12 pt Times New Roman** font.
11. Insert a blank page at the end of the report and insert a bibliography without a heading, selecting **Insert Bibliography**.
12. Add a centered heading to the bibliography at the top of the page on a line by itself. The heading is **References**. Ensure that the heading is not bold.
13. Select all text in the bibliography, including the heading, and change the font to **12 pt Times New Roman**. Line spacing should be **double**, and there should be no paragraph spacing.
14. Double-click in the header area and change *Name* to **Agrawal**. Close the header.

Manage a Table of Figures, Create a Cover Page, and Create an Index

Because there are several figures included, you will include a table of figures. In addition, a cover page will identify the paper and its author.

15. Insert a blank page at the beginning of the document. Click at the top of the new page. Click the **References tab**. Click **Insert Table of Figures** in the Captions group. Change the Caption label to **Table** and change the format to **Distinctive**. Click **OK**.

16. Insert a blank page before the Table of Figures. Click at the top of the blank page and insert text from *w04c1CoverPage*. Change *Student Name* to **Sherry Agrawal**.

17. Mark all occurrences of *Bovine Respiratory Disease, genomic,* and *pathogen* as index entries. Cross-reference *BRD* with *Bovine Respiratory Disease*. Create an index on a separate page after the bibliography using the **Formal format**. Use all other default settings.

Add Comments, View Comments, Reply to Comments, Work with a PDF Document, and Invite Others to Share

18. Scroll to page 3 and mark the comment related to formatting the report as a research paper resolved. Reply to the comment on page 4 with the text **Does a table of figures include a title?**

19. Check spelling and grammar. *Virome* is not misspelled and *qRT* is correct. Ignore all grammatical errors.

20. Save the document. Click **Share** at the top right side of the ribbon and sign in to your Microsoft account if prompted. Send an email to yourself with the shared link.

21. Open the email that shares the file and click **Open** in the email message. When the document opens in Word for the web, scroll to the second table and change the column heading from *BRD Tested* to **BRD (2023)**.

> **TROUBLESHOOTING:** If you do not find the email in your inbox, check your Spam or Junk folder. If it is not there, open a browser and go to onedrive.com. Sign into the account from which you sent the link, and click w04cCattle_LastFirst. Scroll to the second table and change the column heading from BRD Tested to BRD (2023). Proceed to Step 22.

22. Click **Editing** at the top of the Word for the web window and select **Open in Desktop App**. When the document opens, click the **File tab** and click **Save a Copy**. Navigate to the location of your student files, change the filename to **w04c1CattleRevised_LastFirst** and click **Save**.

23. Click the **Review tab**, click **Delete** in the Comments group, and click **Delete All Comments in Document**. Save the document as a PDF file with the same filename. Close the PDF file. Close w04c1CattleRevised_LastFirst without saving.

24. Close the Word file. Exit Word. Based on your instructor's directions, submit:
    w04c1CattleRevised_LastFirst
    w04c1CattleRevised_LastFirst.pdf

Document Publications

CASE STUDY | Along the Greenways

Scelena Allen is director of The Greenways, a nonprofit organization. The organization was formed to generate interest in outdoor activities as well as to provide support and funding for additional walking and biking trails in the city and surrounding counties. Maintaining positive public relations is key to generating support for the organization, and providing a quarterly newsletter, along with a supporting webpage, is one way to do this.

Ms. Allen has asked you to create a newsletter in a format that is easy to read but also informative. In addition, you will consider including professional design elements and graphics to add visual interest. Ms. Allen wants to limit the newsletter to one page. You will also use Word to develop a webpage summarizing the nonprofit and encouraging support.

Document Publications and Forms

NDAB Creativity/Shutterstock

FIGURE 5.1 Greenways Documents

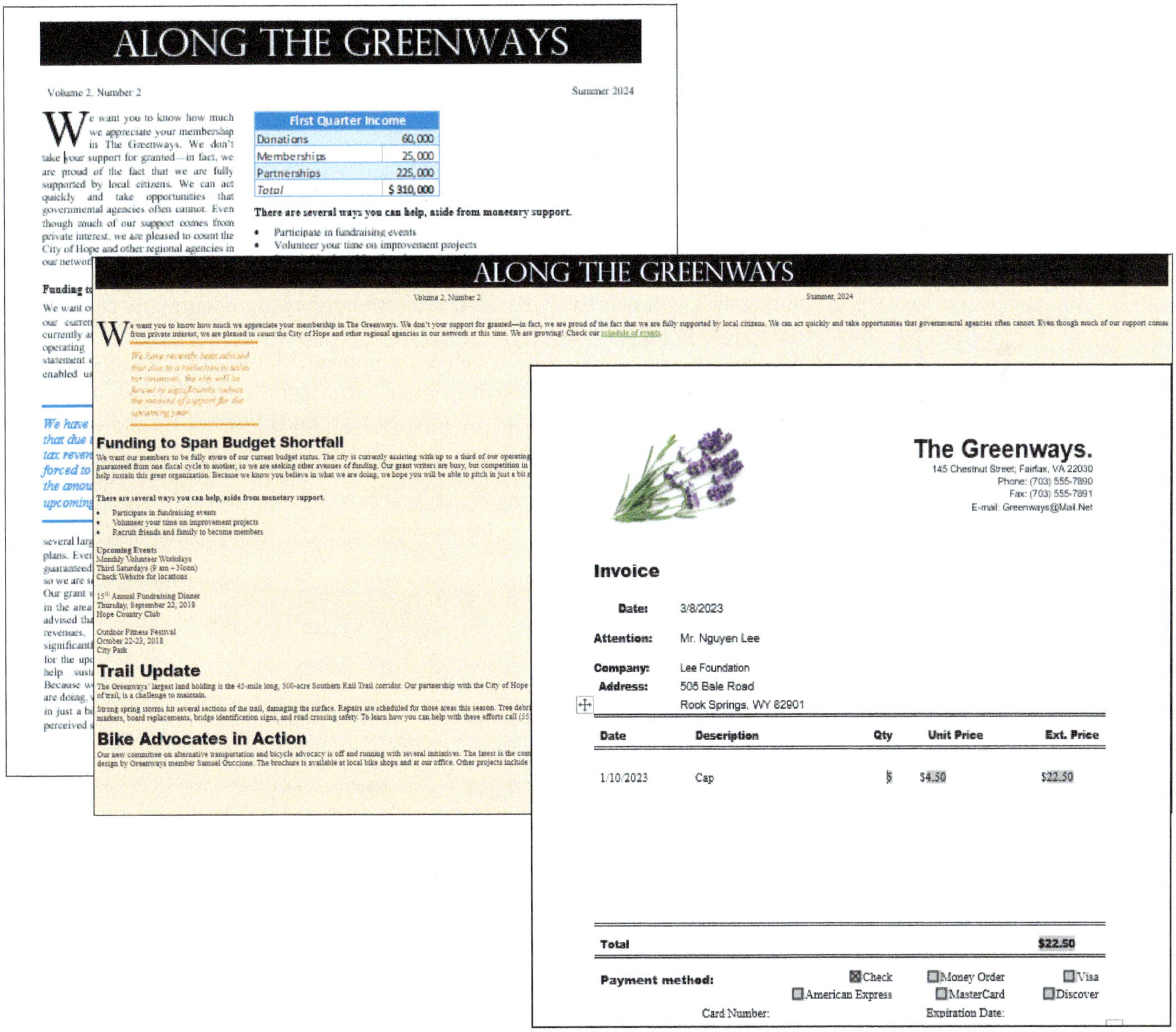

Jacek Fulawka/Shutterstock

CASE STUDY | Along the Greenways

Starting Files	File to Be Submitted	MyLab IT HOE Grader
w05h1Greenways w05h1Budget.xlsx w05h3GreenwaysInvoice	W05h1Greenways_LastFirst W05h2Greenways_LastFirst.html w05h3GreenwaysInvoice_LastFirst	

MyLab IT Grader: This project is available as a Hands-On Exercise project in MyLab IT

Desktop Publishing

Desktop publishing is a process that uses software, such as Microsoft Word, to design commercial-quality printed material. Through a combination of technologies and page composition software, desktop publishing enables users to manipulate text and graphics to produce attractive documents. Some desktop publishing tasks, such as a college catalog, require a high level of precision and typesetting capability; in those cases, you might opt for dedicated desktop publishing software that includes sophisticated typesetting and graphic tools. However, Word's comprehensive set of desktop publishing tools is often sufficient for such applications as newsletters, brochures, and other documents requiring unique type and artwork. In fact, Word's enhanced graphic design features have narrowed the gap between typical word processing tasks and desktop publishing flair, such that many companies find that Word is the only tool necessary for the production of high-quality, graphic-rich printed material.

Designing an attractive document that includes eye-catching features and graphics is often time-consuming, requiring software proficiency and attention to detail. Although the development of high-quality marketing and informational material often requires the attention of skilled professionals and graphic designers, you can use Word to produce attractive newsletters, brochures, and flyers without needing a great deal of desktop publishing skill on your part. With a bit of practice using Word and basic proficiency in graphic design, you can easily develop professional-looking documents such as the newsletter shown in Figure 5.2.

In this section, you will learn to develop a simple newsletter that includes multiple columns situated in an attractive arrangement. The inclusion of images and other objects, positioned within the flow of newsletter text, adds interest to and enlivens a newsletter as well.

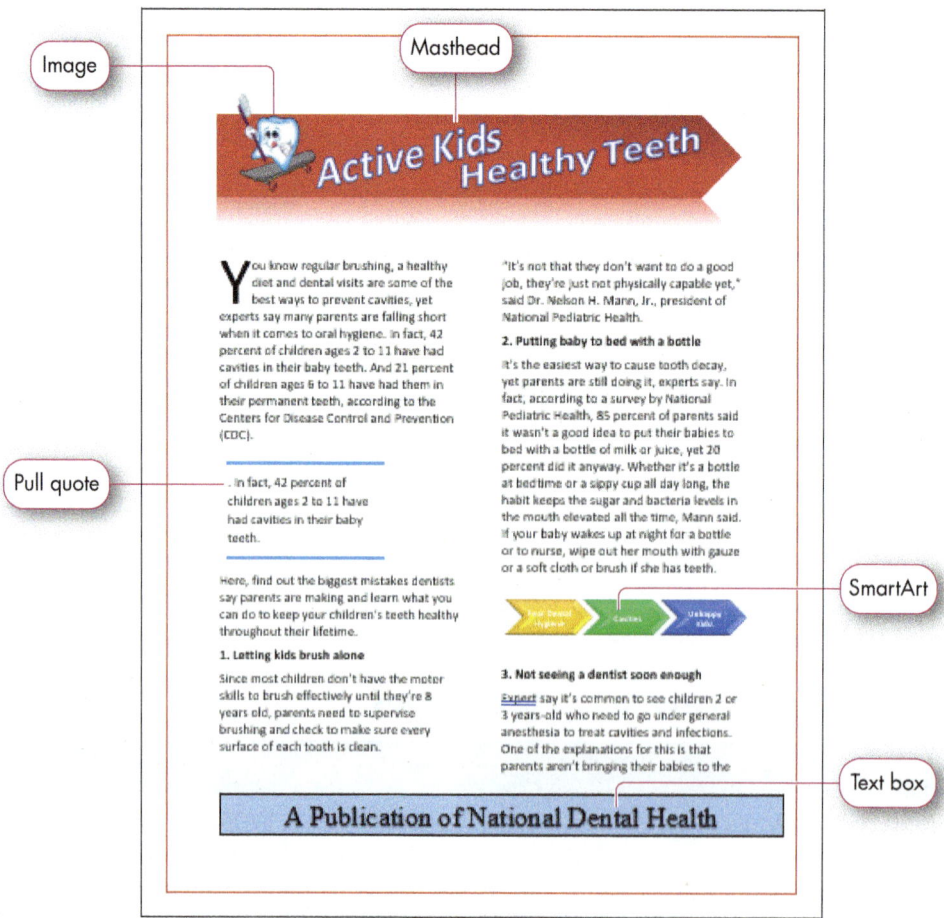

FIGURE 5.2 Sample Newsletter

Design a Newsletter

Perhaps the most difficult aspect of creating a document is to develop an overall design. Designing a document is a creative process in which you consider your audience and purpose, combining overall appearance, wording, and specific formatting features to create a document that accomplishes the goal of effectively conveying your message. Let your eye be the judge and follow your instincts. It also helps to seek inspiration from others by collecting samples of documents that succeed in capturing attention and using those document principles as the starting point for an effective design. In addition, newsletter templates available in Word might be helpful for layout and formatting suggestions. Newsletters and other informal documents benefit from a creative design approach, such as the use of columns and other formatting features, while more conservative business documents and reports are best formatted in a one-column arrangement with minimal clutter.

TIP: LIMIT USE OF TYPOGRAPHY

Less is more—a rule that especially applies to typefaces and styles. Too many of either will produce cluttered documents. Try to limit the design to a maximum of two fonts per document but choose multiple sizes or a variety of formatting treatments. Use boldface or italics for emphasis—not underlining—but do so in moderation. Too much emphasis on too many elements is distracting. A simple design is often the best design.

Develop Overall Document Layout

The design of a newsletter is developed on a grid, an underlying set of horizontal and vertical lines that determine the placement of major elements. A grid may be simple or complex, but it is always distinguished by the number of columns it contains. The three-column grid of Figure 5.3 is one of the most common and utilitarian designs. Other grid designs include multiple columns of various widths and heights. You would typically use a one-column grid for term papers and letters. A two-column, wide-and-narrow format is appropriate for some newsletters, textbooks, and manuals.

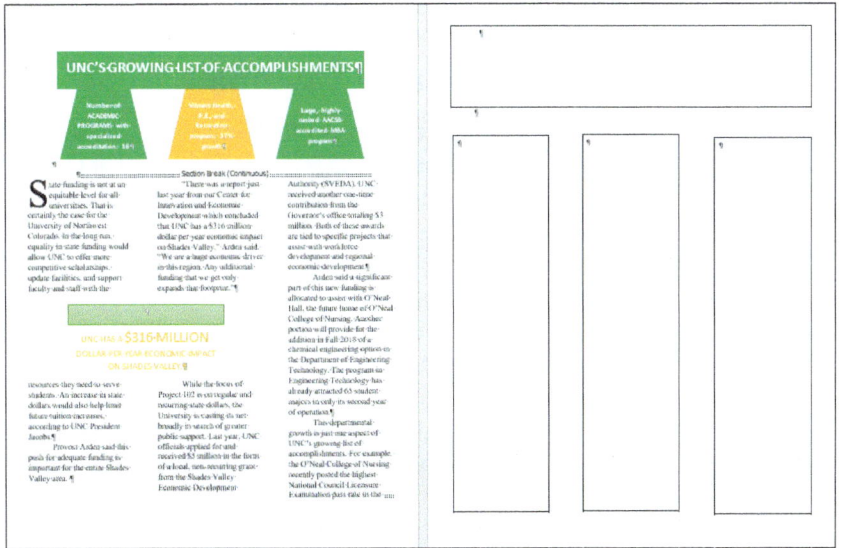

FIGURE 5.3 Design on a Grid

The grid concept simplifies a document design task, as it affords a strong foundation upon which you can manage various formatting options. It enables you to develop a plan for positioning newsletter elements appropriately with relation to one another.

Moreover, the conscious use of a grid encourages consistency from page to page within a document (or from issue to issue of a newsletter), resulting in a polished publication.

> **TIP: SIDE TO SIDE VIEW**
>
> As you develop a multi-page publication, a global view of the document in a side-to-side arrangement provides an overview of page layout that enhances your understanding of the document flow. You can page through a document much like reading a book instead of scrolling through pages vertically. Select the Print Layout view and the Side to Side option in the Page Movement group on the View tab to flip through pages by swiping a touchscreen or using a mouse. For quick navigation or general overview, use the Thumbnails command in the Zoom group (having selected Side to Side movement) and click any page or pinch on a touchscreen to zoom in or out. Click Vertical in the Page Movement group or select another view to return to a single-page view.

Once you have determined an overall document layout, you will next focus on specific formatting features, such as font style, boldface, and italics. Such formatting not only yields an attractive document but also assists in emphasizing essential points. Consider the following suggestions when formatting text:

- Vary font size and/or font style to delineate various sections, such as major headings and subheadings. Format headings in a font size at least two points larger than that of the body text.

- Use bold and italic formatting sparingly. Both are effective at drawing attention, but excessive variation in font results in a document that looks choppy and disjointed.

- Limit the use of all uppercase letters and underlining. Uppercase letters are often associated with screaming, while underlining typically indicates a hyperlink.

- Avoid overusing such techniques as drop caps, color, and objects. While appropriate use of such items can generate interest and entertainment, overuse can result in a document that is cluttered and difficult to follow.

> **TIP: CUSTOMIZING THE STATUS BAR**
>
> Designing a document that is intended for publication often requires that you work within certain constraints related to overall document design and placement of page elements. You might even be required to remain within a range of words or characters. Customizing the status bar to provide document information can help. Right-click the status bar and select from various options, including a character and word count that updates immediately as you type. Accessibility status is also noted on the status bar.

STEP 1 **Apply and Modify Column Layout**

Newsletters often include multiple columns, as illustrated by the document shown in Figure 5.2. A newsletter title is typically located at the top of the first page of a newsletter, followed by text that is formatted in multiple columns. Columns can be equally sized, or you can arrange them in varying widths, even including a line between them for additional interest or definition. You can format text into columns by using Columns in the Page Setup group on the Layout tab and selecting the number of columns you want. If you do not first select text to format, column selections are applied to all text in the document or in the current section.

For more specificity, click More Columns from the Columns option in the Page Setup group on the Layout tab to open a dialog box, shown in Figure 5.4, from which you can choose additional settings, such as the inclusion of a line between columns or the selection of a preset column design (One, Two, Three, Left, or Right). Word calculates the width of each column based on the number of columns, the left and right margins, and the space between columns. The One, Two, and Three column selections result in columns of equal width, while the Left and Right options apply two columns of unequal width, with the narrower column on the left or right, respectively. Varying column width can add interest to a newsletter, modifying the predictability of more uniform text design. Regardless of column design, text that has been formatted in columns flows continuously from the bottom of one column to the top of the next.

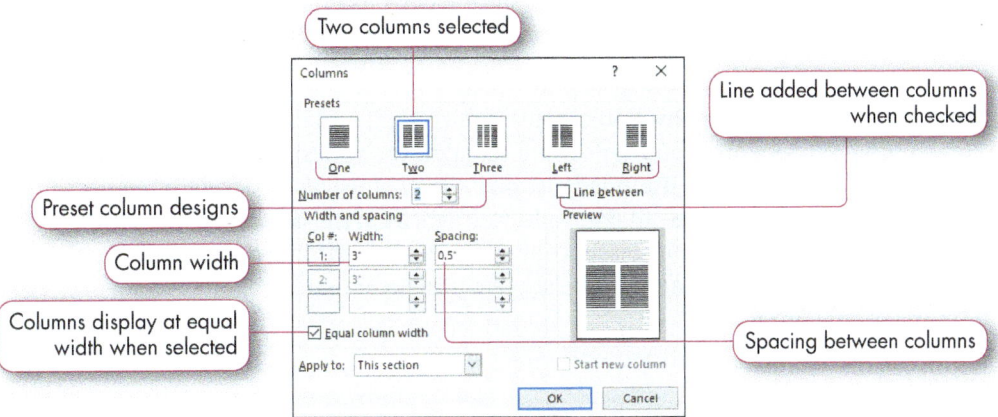

FIGURE 5.4 Columns Dialog Box

As you design a newsletter, you can also use the Columns dialog box to specify custom column widths. In the dialog box shown in Figure 5.4, ensure that *Equal column width* is deselected and indicate a measurement for the width of each column and column spacing.

Apply Design Features

Companies, civic clubs, schools, and even families use Word to design newsletters. You can create a newsletter using a newsletter document template or design a newsletter from a blank document. Using Word, you can design and format newsletters, arranging text in columns and incorporating such objects as pictures, SmartArt, and text boxes, as shown in Figure 5.2. Objects and formatting features that are often found in newsletters include:

- **Images.** Pictures and graphics visually break a long line of text, adding interest and drawing attention to a topic. Images direct the eye to relevant textual information, providing a bit of color and making the document more entertaining to read.

- **WordArt.** WordArt enables you to apply predefined styles to major headings, banners, or other text elements. A WordArt object is often large and colorful, drawing attention to a specific area of a newsletter.

- **SmartArt.** A SmartArt graphic, showing relationships or processes, can enhance understanding. Diagrams tend to convey ideas much more effectively than words do alone.

- **Shapes.** Word's drawing tools simplify the addition of shapes and objects to a document. Such shapes as arrows and callouts enable you to create descriptive drawings or to clarify elements within a document.

- **Tables.** A table provides a grid of columns and rows in which you can summarize data in an understandable way. With Word's comprehensive table design and layout tools, you can add style, color, and structure to a simple table.

- **Charts.** Presentation of data in a chart, such as a pie or column design, often enhances understanding and adds interest to a document. Charts created and formatted using Microsoft Excel can bc easily inserted into a Word document.

- **Screenshots.** A screenshot is a graphic image of a screen display. You can use Word to capture a screenshot and include it in a document.

- **Borders.** Documents such as newsletters often include bordered text or even a page border surrounding one or more pages. Not limited to simple lines, borders can be designed with various line thicknesses and colors as well as small graphics.

- **Shading.** When used as the background color of an item, such as a text box or paragraph, shading is an effective way to set an element apart.
- **Lists.** Whether bulleted or numbered, lists organize and emphasize information.
- **Typography.** You can use stylized text and enhanced text effects to design document contents that best achieve the desired visual effect and to effectively convey the intended message. Good typography design often goes unnoticed, whereas poor typography detracts from the message. The selection of fonts, font styles, and font sizes that enhance text within a document is a critical, often subtle, element in the success of a document.
- **Styles.** You can use predefined styles in desktop publishing to add personality to your newsletter. Remember that a style is a set of formatting options you apply to characters or paragraphs. A style includes such settings as alignment, line spacing, indents, tabs, borders, and shading. You can use the same styles from one edition of a newsletter to the next to ensure consistency. Additionally, the use of styles in any document promotes uniformity and increases flexibility.

No hard and fast rules exist to dictate how many or which features you should include when designing a newsletter. Your objective should be to create a document that is easy to read and visually appealing—one that conveys your message as intended. You may find that a design that works well in one document is not at all appropriate for a different document. For example, a technical newsletter on best practices for critical care nurses would not be formatted in the same way as a more informal newsletter developed by a local swim team. Therefore, you should experiment with various design techniques as you develop documents for different purposes.

STEP 2 ▸ Create a Masthead

Most often located at the top of a newsletter, a *masthead* typically includes a title, perhaps incorporating graphics or a logo, as well as other identifying information such as company address and contact information, a volume and issue number, and the date of publication. The purpose of the masthead is to communicate the identity of the publication in an easily recognizable fashion, as shown in Figure 5.5. You can employ various Word techniques and formatting features to create a masthead, including designing a WordArt object, text box, or shaded text.

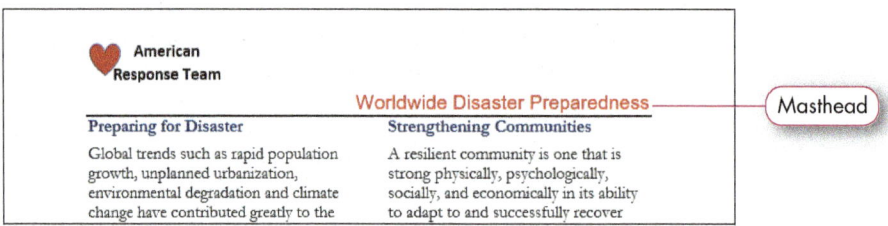

FIGURE 5.5 Newsletter Masthead

> **TIP: CREATE A REVERSE MASTHEAD**
> Borders and shading are often applied to a masthead. A border around the masthead can be used to distinguish the content from the rest of the document. To add additional emphasis, a masthead is sometimes designed in reverse effect, which uses light-colored text on a dark background. Often used in newsletter mastheads, a reverse masthead provides a distinctive look to a publication, clearly identifying the document and enabling the newsletter title to stand out from remaining text. The masthead shown in Figure 5.6 is an example of a reverse effect.

STEP 3 Create a Drop Cap

Paragraphs in a newsletter can begin with a *drop cap*, which is a capital letter formatted in a font size larger than the body text. A drop cap adds interest and a bit of style to text within a document. Drop caps can align with text or display in the margin, and they can be designed in various sizes. The choice depends on the style and design of the newsletter. To insert a drop cap, place the insertion point before the letter that is to be converted to a drop cap and click Drop Cap in the Text group on the Insert tab. You can point to either the Dropped option or In margin to see a preview of the effect before selecting one, or you can select Drop Cap Options to display the dialog box shown in Figure 5.6.

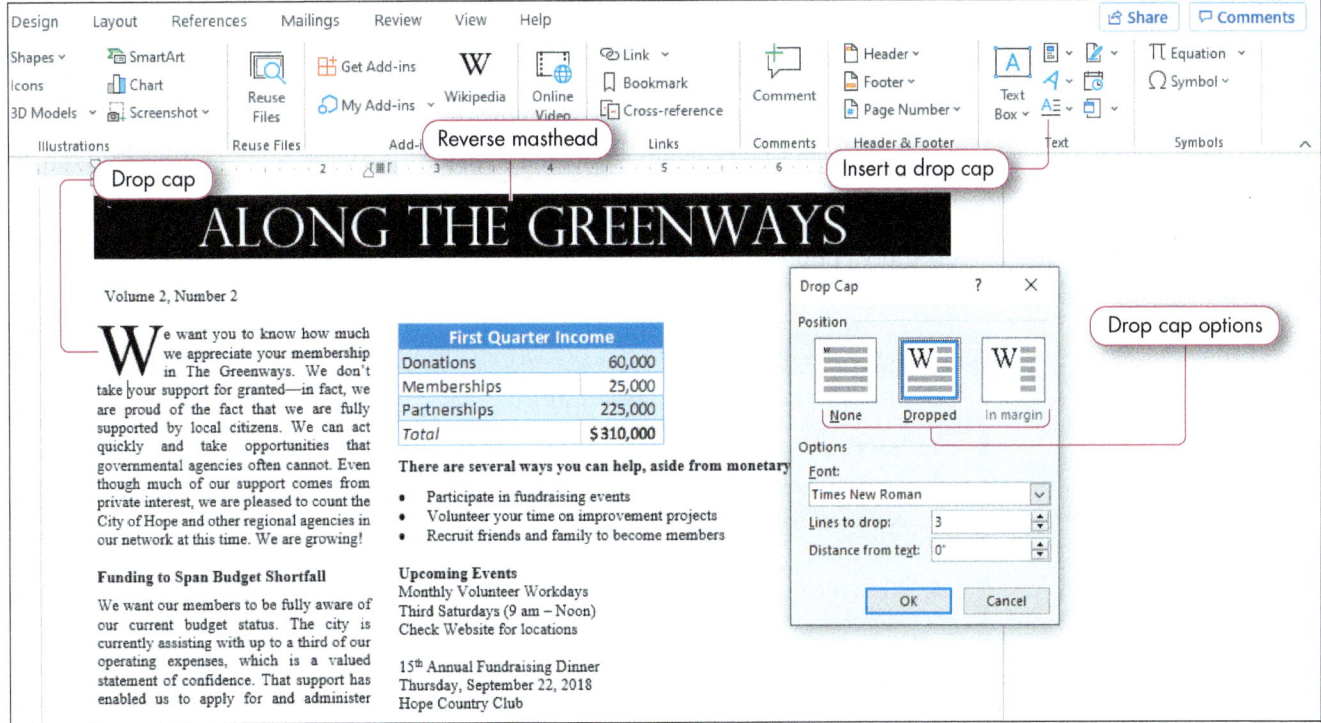

FIGURE 5.6 Drop Cap Dialog Box and Reverse Masthead

STEP 4 Copy and Link Objects from Other Files

Using Microsoft 365, you can share objects across applications. For example, suppose you are composing a report in Word that explains survey results. You used Excel to summarize those results in the form of a worksheet and accompanying chart. The worksheet arrangement of columns and rows enables you to organize data and then prepare a chart to graphically illustrate the data. You plan to use a portion of an Excel worksheet and chart in a Word document. The process of placing the data and chart in the Word document is not complicated; however, you must first determine whether you want the objects to be automatically updated when the original data changes (the Excel data, in this example) or whether you prefer to modify them in Word independently of the Excel source. The feature that enables you to insert and link objects into different applications is called *Object Linking and Embedding (OLE)*.

When you copy an object from one application to another, you can either embed the object or link it. *Embedding* an object into a Word document imports the object into the document and enables editing directly in the document without changing the source data. For example, if you embed a portion of an Excel worksheet, it becomes part of the Word document. You can modify the inserted data at any time without affecting the original worksheet. Likewise, any changes to the original Excel worksheet do not display in the Word document. An embedded object is a snapshot of information at the time the data was embedded into the file.

Embed an object in a Word document:

1. Select an object or section in a source file (Excel, for example).
2. Click Copy from the Clipboard group on the Home tab.
3. Navigate to the location in the Word document where the object or data is to be placed.
4. Click the Paste arrow in the Clipboard group and then select a Paste option (related to formatting).

Linking is the process of importing an object from another application so that the object retains a connection to the file that contains the original data. If you change the data in the original source file, the data in the destination file reflects the changes, and vice versa. A data file used as a linked object may be linked to multiple documents. The same Excel chart, for example, can be linked to a Word document and a PowerPoint presentation. Any changes to the Excel chart are reflected and updated in the document and the presentation to which the chart is linked when you update the link in the document or presentation.

Link an object in a Word document:

1. Select an object or section in a source file (Excel, for example).
2. Click Copy from the Clipboard group on the Home tab.
3. Navigate to the location in the Word document where the object or data is to be placed.
4. Click the Paste arrow in the Clipboard group on the Home tab and select Paste Special. Select the appropriate object from the right pane of the Paste Special dialog box and click OK.

The choice of whether to embed or link an inserted object depends upon your purpose. A linked object will reflect the most current information. This might be important, for example, when you insert stock prices for a particular company into a newsletter—you might want the most current prices to display. If the current prices that you insert into the document are copied from an Excel worksheet, you would want the prices in the Word document to change when the Excel worksheet prices change. If the prices are linked to the original Excel worksheet data, changes to the original price data would reflect in the Word document. On the other hand, if you want to retain the data shown in a Word document, without the possibility of change occurring when the source data is modified, then embedding would be the best choice.

In addition to using copy and paste, Word provides another option for linking objects or data from other applications whereby you can choose to insert an object from a file. As you do so, you will choose whether to include contents of the inserted object or to cause an icon to display that provides access to data only when you double-click the icon. For example, you might want to provide access to an Excel workbook from within a Word document. However, if the Excel workbook contains a large amount of data that would clutter the Word document or significantly increase the file size of the document, you can insert the Excel workbook as an icon so the data is available and can even be linked to the Word document but without occupying a great deal of document space. On the other hand, if the object you are linking to is relatively small and would not clutter the document or be distracting, you can choose to include the contents of the object within the document.

Link an object or data, including either a selection or an icon:

1. Click the Insert tab and click Object in the Text group (in a Word document).

2. Click the Create from File tab, browse to the location of the source file (the file you are copying from), and then double-click the file.

3. Click *Link to file* and click OK (to show the full file). Optionally, you can also click *Display as icon* (to show an icon that can be clicked to show the linked file). To embed the file, click OK (to show the full file). Optionally, you can click *Display as icon* (to show an icon that can be clicked to show the file).

If you choose to link an object in a document, you can modify the source data, ensuring that any edits are also reflected in the Word document. However, you must manually update the object to ensure that changes are carried over. To begin, open the source file in its native application—Excel, for example—and make modifications. You can also open the application from within the Word document containing the linked object. Double-click the linked object or click the application icon if you chose to display one. After making changes in the source file, you must update the linked data in the Word document to reflect the changes there. To update the linked data, right-click the inserted object text in the Word document or the icon representing inserted text, and select Update Link.

STEP 5 ## Create a Pull Quote or Sidebar

A pull quote is a phrase or sentence taken from an article to emphasize a key point. A pull quote is typically set in larger type, often in a different font or in italics, and may be offset with borders at the top, at the bottom, or on the sides. Pull quotes are frequently displayed in professional publications, such as newsletters and annual reports, to draw attention to important topics or facts, as shown in Figure 5.7. A sidebar displays along the side of a document to call attention to certain information. You can select from several specialized designs in the Text Box gallery or you can create your own design.

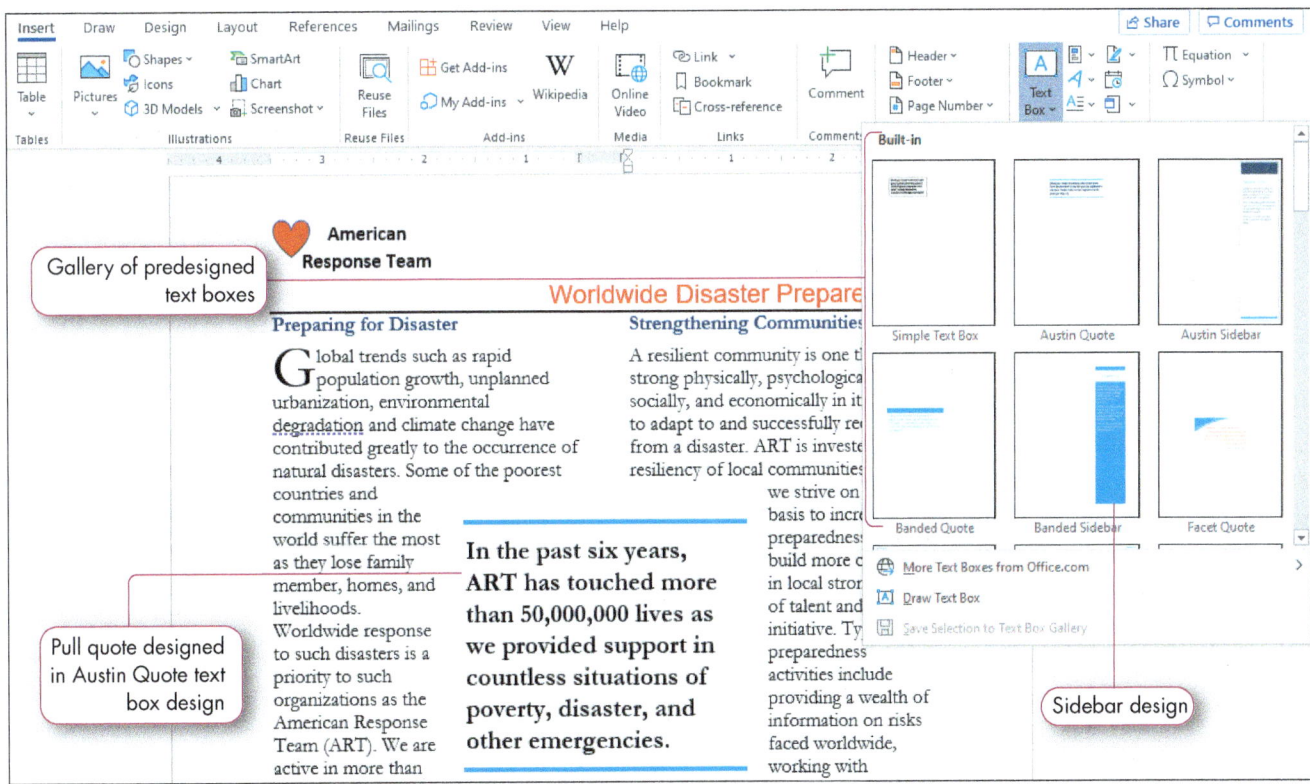

FIGURE 5.7 Insert a Text Box for Use as a Pull Quote or Sidebar

Both a pull quote and sidebar are designed as text boxes. To begin the process of creating a pull quote or sidebar, select from preformatted text boxes in the Text Box gallery (shown when you click the Insert tab and then click Text Box in the Text group). Then add text in the pull quote or sidebar. You can also draw a text box and add design features as you see fit.

Because a pull quote and sidebar are designed in a text box, they are considered graphic objects. As such, you can apply shape formatting options such as text wrapping, horizontal alignment, outside borders, shape fill, and font treatments.

TIP: ANCHOR AN OBJECT

To position an object so that it does not move, even if text around it changes, you can lock its anchor to an adjacent paragraph. Much like a boat anchor, text will flow around the anchored object (like water), but the object remains fixed in position (as an anchored boat remains fixed relative to the shoreline). You can lock an anchor so that an object remains in place from the object's Position settings (in the Arrange group on the object's Format tab). If you want to see anchors in a document, ensure that Object anchors in the Display category of Word Options is selected.

Critical Thinking

1. Provide examples of documents that should include columns as well as those that should not. *p. 359*

2. Explain how you might decide whether to embed or link a file within a Word document. *p. 363*

3. Explain how envisioning a grid structure as you design a newsletter is beneficial. *p. 359*

Hands-On Exercises

Skills covered: Apply and Modify Column Layout • Create a Masthead • Create a Drop Cap • Copy and Link Objects from Other Files • Create a Pull Quote or Sidebar

1 Desktop Publishing

Selena Allen, director of The Greenways, forwarded a document with short articles that she wants to include in the newsletter you are preparing. You design a layout that will display the information in an easy-to-read and visually appealing manner. You also consider how to display the masthead and other visual elements.

STEP 1 APPLY AND MODIFY COLUMN LAYOUT

Upon reviewing the file, you consider the structure necessary to design an attractive newsletter. You decide to modify the margins and to arrange the newsletter in two columns. In considering the best way to arrange the newsletter, you decide it would be more attractive with columns of unequal width. You experiment with column layouts and adjust column width. You also add a line to separate columns. Refer to Figure 5.8 as you complete Step 1.

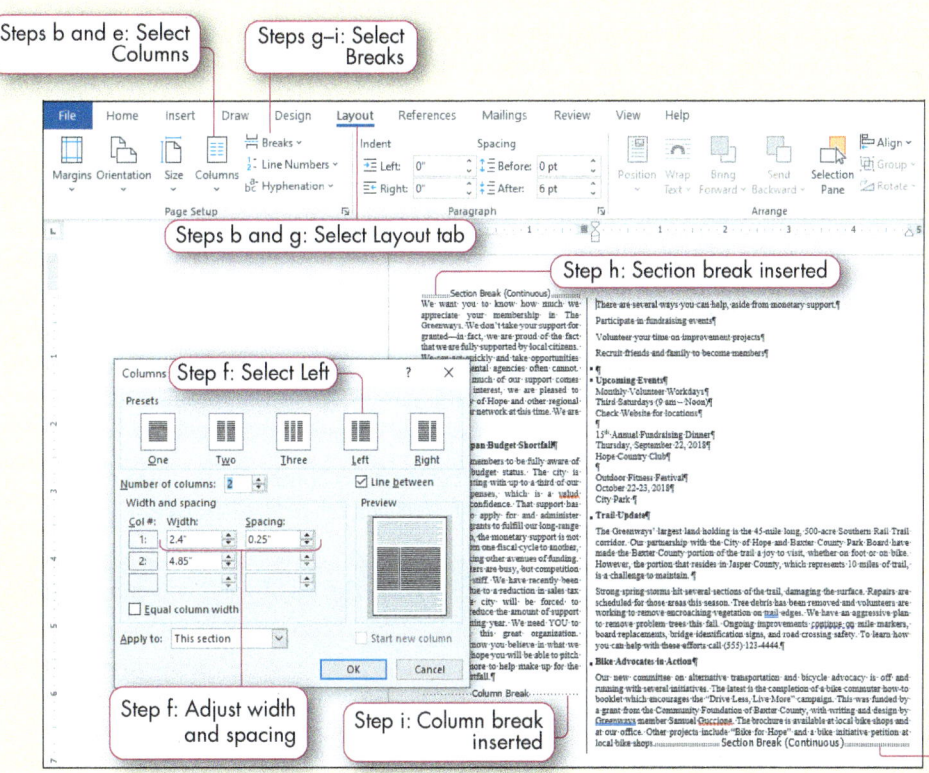

FIGURE 5.8 Format a Newsletter

a. Open *w05h1Greenways* and save it as **w05h1Greenways_LastFirst**. Ensure that non-printing characters are displayed.

> **TROUBLESHOOTING:** If you make any major mistakes in this exercise, you can close the file, open *w05h1Greenways* again and then start this exercise over.

b. Ensure that the insertion point is at the top of the document and click the **Layout tab**. Click **Columns** in the Page Setup group and select **Two**.

The text of the newsletter displays in two columns. The column width for each column and the spacing between columns is determined automatically.

c. Click the **View tab** and view the document as **One Page** in the Zoom group.

The one-page view of the document shows two columns, although the left column is significantly longer than the right. You will adjust the column lengths later.

d. Click the **Layout tab** and change the margins to **Narrow**.

Because the newsletter is a bit lengthy, smaller margins provide more working space within the document.

e. Click **Columns** in the Page Setup group and select **More Columns** to display the Columns dialog box.

f. Click **Left** in the Presets section and click to select the **Line between check box** to display a line between the columns. Click in the **Width box** beside Col # 1 and type **2.4**. Change the spacing to **0.25**. Ensure that Equal column width is deselected. Click **OK**.

The left column is narrower than the right, and a vertical line displays as a column separator.

g. Click the **View tab** and click **100%** in the Zoom group. Place the insertion point at the end of the document (after the words *local bike shops* in the right column). Click the **Layout tab**. Click **Breaks** in the Page Setup group. Select **Continuous** under Section Breaks.

Inserting a continuous section break at the end of the document ensures more even distribution of columns.

h. Place the insertion point at the beginning of the document. Click **Breaks** in the Page Setup group and click **Continuous** under Section Breaks.

A double dotted line displays, indicating that a section break occurs at the top of the left column in the document. Adding a continuous section break enables you to format the area of the document that precedes the section break differently from the section that follows it, as might be necessary if you add a masthead.

i. Place the insertion point before the second to last paragraph in the left column, beginning with *There are several ways you can help*. Click **Breaks** in the Page Setup group and click **Column**.

You insert a column break so that the list of ways you can help is not divided between columns.

The title of your newsletter is a critical element, as it is most likely the first thing a reader will view. You decide to insert a masthead to identify the newsletter. To ensure that the title displays properly as one column, you type the title before the previously inserted section break at the top of the page. Refer to Figure 5.9 as you complete Step 2.

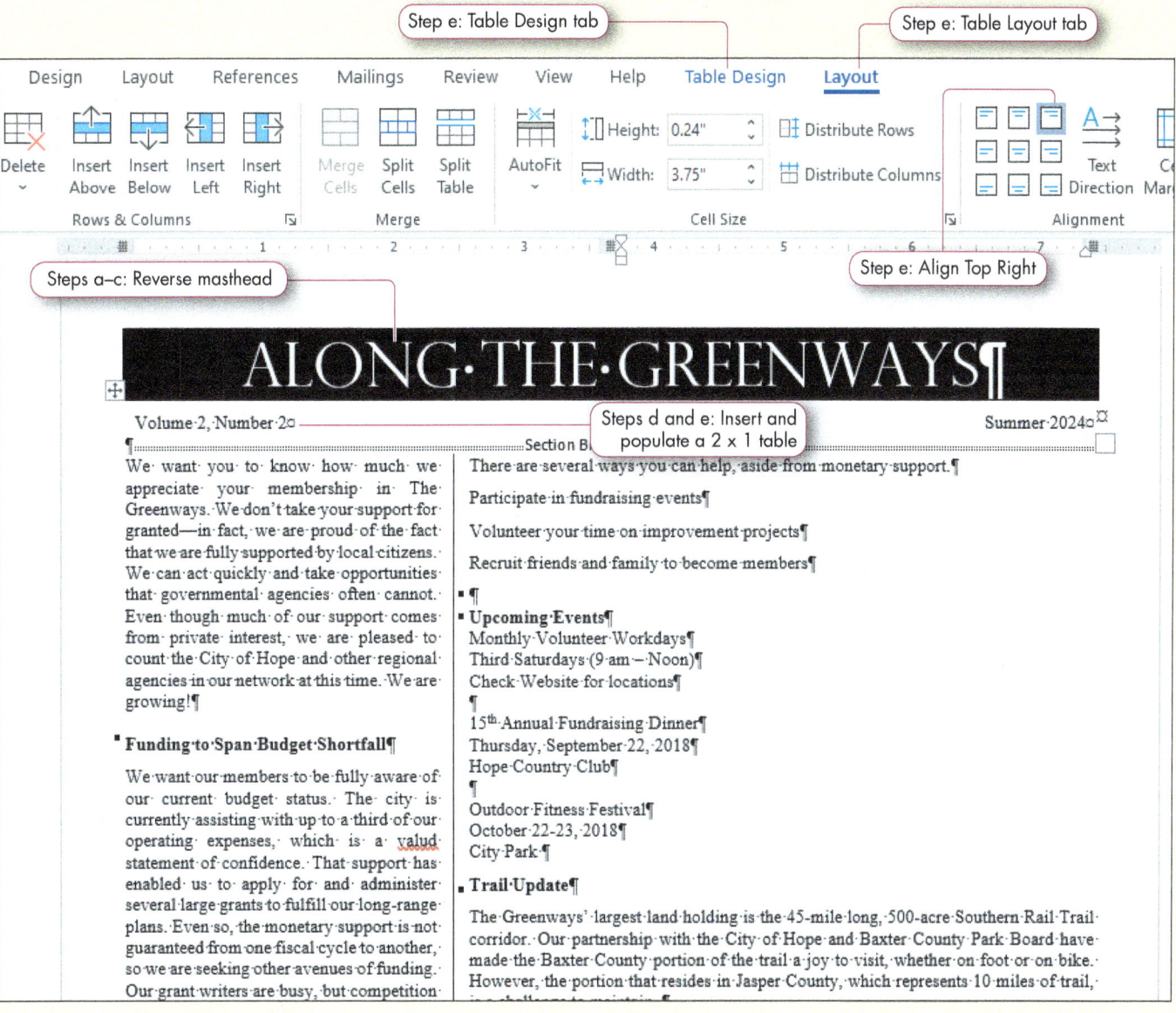

FIGURE 5.9 Create a Masthead

a. Place the insertion point to the top of the page (before the section break), click **Columns** in the Page Setup group, and then select **One**.

The section break extends across the top of the document, creating one column at the top of the page. Information you type there will not be split into two columns like the text in the section below the break.

b. Type **Along the Greenways** and press **Enter** twice. Select the text you just typed and center it across the width of the page. Change the font of the selected text to **Perpetua Titling MT** and adjust the font size to **33**. Do not deselect the heading.

The large heading is the masthead for the newsletter.

c. Click the **Borders arrow** in the Paragraph group on the Home tab and select **Borders and Shading**. Click the **Shading tab**, click the **Style arrow**, and then select **Solid (100%)**. Ensure that Paragraph displays in the Apply to box and click **OK**.

The masthead displays white text on a black background, creating a reverse masthead.

d. Click to the left of the section break just below the masthead. Using the Table command on the Insert tab, insert a **2 × 1 table**.

A table displays below the masthead and above the section break. The table includes two columns and one row.

e. Edit the table as follows:

- Type **Volume 2, Number 2** in the left cell.
- Type **Summer 2024** in the right cell.
- Click the **Table Layout tab**. Click **Align Top Right** in the Alignment group to right align content in the last cell.
- Select the entire row. Click the **Layout tab** (not the Table Layout tab) and change Spacing Before to **6 pt**.
- Click the **Table Design tab**, click the **Borders arrow** in the Borders group, and then select **No Border**.

The border is removed, although with nonprinting characters being displayed, you will see some indication that the text is in a table arrangement. When nonprinting characters are toggled off, the text will look well aligned but will not have borders.

STEP 3 ## CREATE A DROP CAP

A drop cap is often applied to the first paragraph of a document or article. In this case, you format a paragraph with a drop cap to enhance the newsletter. You also format the document with bullets to further identify topics of interest. Refer to Figure 5.10 as you complete Step 3.

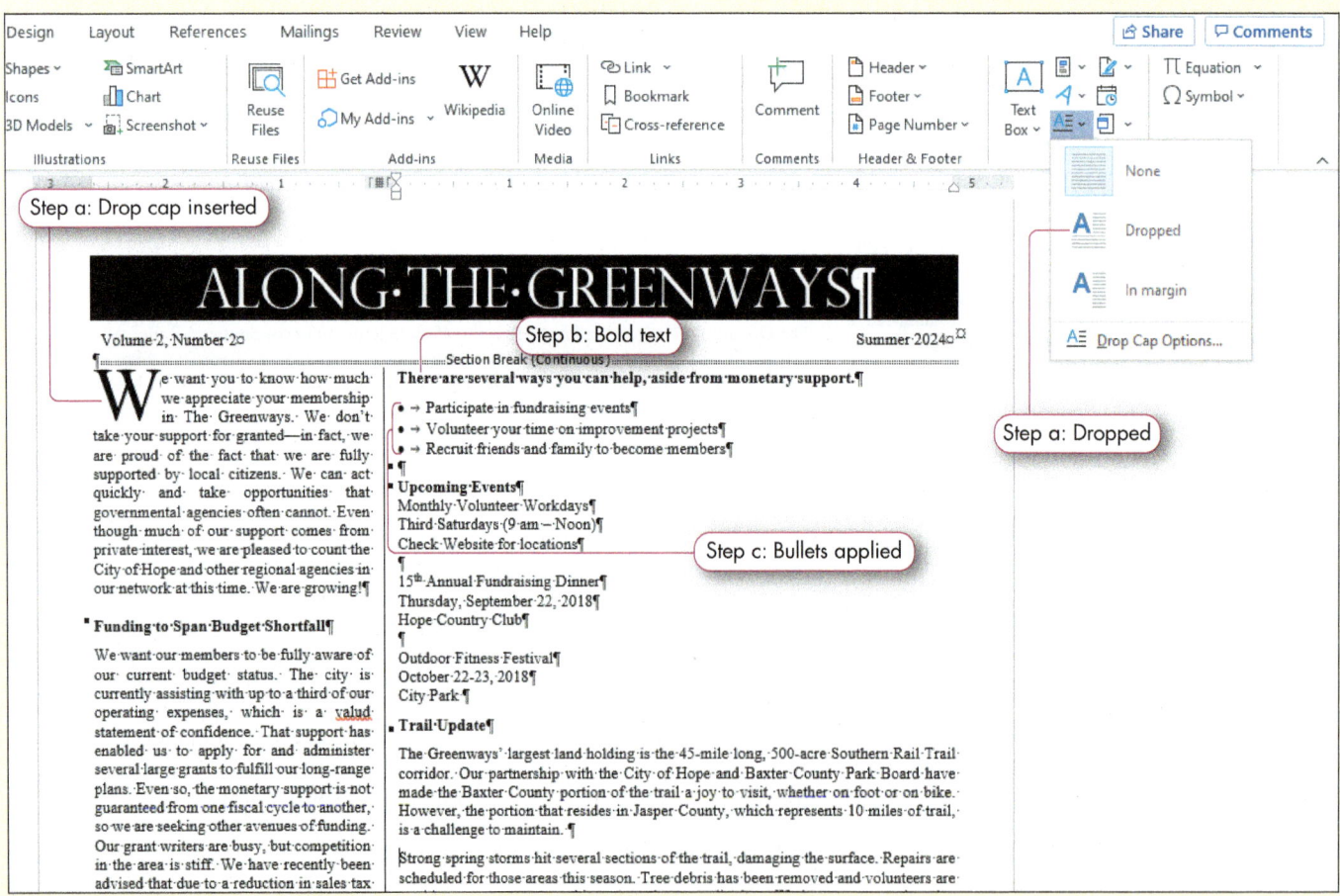

FIGURE 5.10 Create a Drop Cap

a. Place the insertion point at the left of the first letter in the first paragraph (beginning with *We want you to know*). Click the **Insert tab**, click **Drop Cap** in the Text group, and then select **Dropped**. Click anywhere outside the drop cap frame.

A drop cap object is added beside the paragraph.

b. Select the first sentence at the top of the right column, beginning with *There are several ways you can help.* **Bold** the selection.

c. Select the next three paragraphs, beginning with *Participate in fundraising events* and ending with *Recruit friends and family to become members.* Click **Bullets** in the Paragraph group on the Home tab. Click **Decrease Indent** in the Paragraph group to align the bullets with the left edge of the column. Click the **Layout tab** and remove any paragraph spacing from the bulleted paragraphs.

STEP 4 COPY AND LINK OBJECTS FROM OTHER FILES

An Excel worksheet that contains first-quarter income sources is to be added to the newsletter; however, changes to the worksheet might be necessary in the future. You decide to insert the information with a link to the original file so that when data is updated in the worksheet, it is reflected in the document. Refer to Figure 5.11 as you complete Step 4.

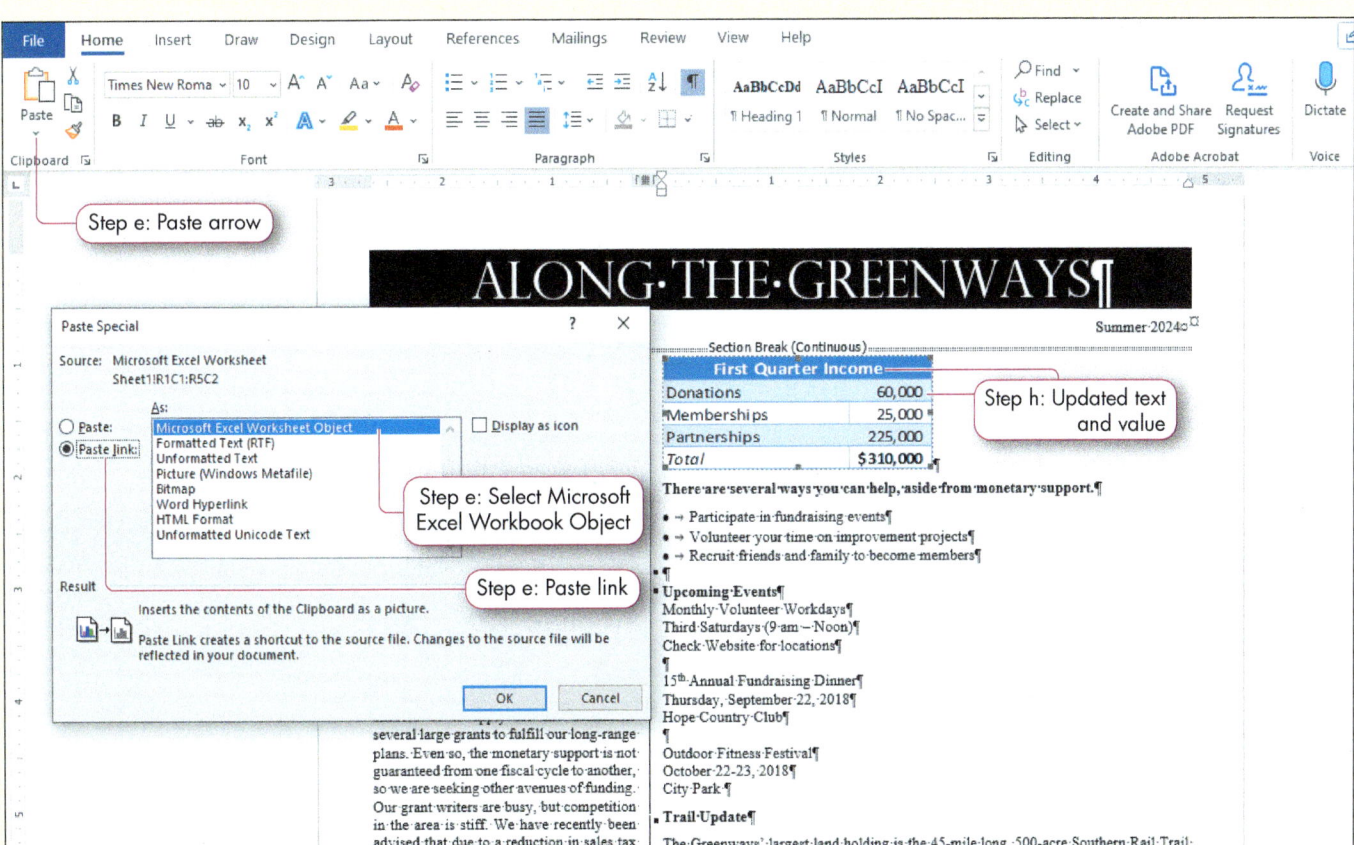

FIGURE 5.11 Link an Object

a. Start Excel. Open *w05h1Budget.xlsx*, and save it as **w05h1Budget_LastFirst**.

b. Drag to select cells A1 through B5 in the Excel worksheet.

c. Click **Copy** in the Clipboard group on the Home tab.

A moving border displays around the selection, indicating it has been copied to the Clipboard.

d. Click the **Word icon** on the Windows taskbar to return to the Word document. Place the insertion point before the heading *There are several ways you can help, aside from monetary support*. Press **Enter**. Click before the newly inserted blank paragraph.

e. Click the **Home tab**. Click the **Paste arrow** in the Clipboard group. Select **Paste Special** to display the Paste Special dialog box. In the *As* list, click **Microsoft Excel Worksheet Object**. Click **Paste link** and click **OK**.

> A link to the Excel worksheet is created so that if the Excel content changes, the same content in the Word document is updated to reflect the change.

f. Click the **Excel icon** on the Windows taskbar to return to the worksheet. Press **Esc** to deselect the cells. Click **cell A1**, type **First Quarter Income**, replacing *By the Numbers*, and then press **Enter**. Click **cell B2**, type **60000**, and then press **Enter**.

> Even though you do not type a comma, Excel automatically places a comma in the number.

g. Save the workbook and exit Excel.

h. Return to the Word document. Right-click the Excel worksheet object and select **Update Link**.

> The linked object reflects the changes you made in the Excel workbook.

> **MAC TROUBLESHOOTING:** If the update from the link does not occur, skip Step h and proceed to Step i.

i. Save the document.

STEP 5 ▶ CREATE A PULL QUOTE OR SIDEBAR

You create a pull quote to draw attention to a statement of interest to newsletter readers. Refer to Figure 5.12 as you complete Step 5.

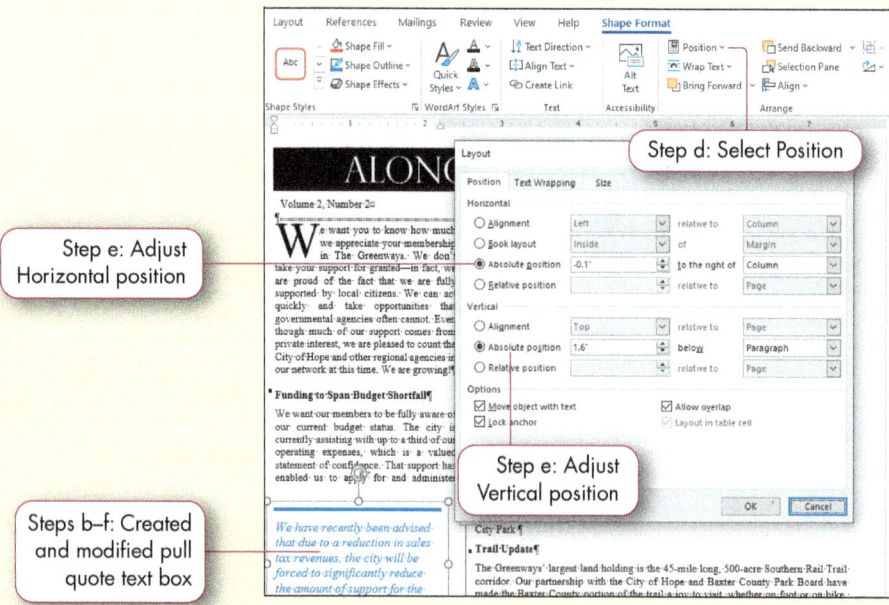

FIGURE 5.12 Create a Pull Quote

a. Select the sixth sentence in the Funding to Span Budget Shortfall section: *We have recently been advised that due to a reduction in sales tax revenues, the city will be forced to significantly reduce the amount of support for the upcoming year.* (Include the period.) Click **Copy** in the Clipboard group to copy the selected text.

b. Click before the *Funding to Span Budget Shortfall* heading. Click the **Insert tab**, click **Text Box** in the Text group, and then select **Austin Quote** in the gallery.

MAC TROUBLESHOOTING: You will not see a gallery of text box designs. Instead, choose to draw a text box, placing it in the left column near the Funding to Span Budget Shortfall heading. Paste the copied sentence in the text box. Size the text box at 1.5" high and 2.4" wide. Select Square text wrapping. Proceed to Step d to position the text box.

---

c. Click the **Home tab**, click the **Paste arrow** in the Clipboard group, and then select **Keep Text Only** (fourth option in the top row).

The text you cut earlier displays in the text box, although the text box is poorly positioned on the page.

d. Click the **Shape Format tab**, click **Position** in the Arrange group, and then select **More Layout Options**.

e. Click **Absolute position** in the Horizontal section and change the value in the adjacent box to **-0.1**. The value should be to the right of **Column**. Ensure that Absolute position in the Vertical section is selected, and change the value in the adjacent box to **1.6**. The value should be below **Paragraph**. Click to select **Lock anchor** and click **OK**.

You lock the anchor so that the text box will stay in the precise position in the document (unless you cut or move it later).

f. Change the width in the Size group to **2.4**.

The pull quote fits within the left column.

g. Check the document for spelling errors. The misspelled word *valud* should be corrected to *valued*. No names are misspelled. Ignore any grammatical or refinement errors.

Two spelling mistakes should be corrected.

h. Save the document. Keep the document open if you plan to continue with the next Hands-On Exercise. If not, close the document and exit Word. This file will be submitted to your instructor at the end of the last Hands-On Exercise.

Publish Online

For most students, utilizing online resources is as much a part of the education process as are books and instructors. Conducting academic and work-related research, completing assignments, and connecting with others is possible through the network of networks that comprises the Internet. In fact, the Internet undergirds much of life and work as we know it, providing access to a wealth of information, entertainment, and communication.

The *World Wide Web (WWW)*, or simply the Web, is a very large subset of the Internet, consisting of special types of documents known as *webpages*. Any document that displays on the World Wide Web is a webpage, typically formatted in *Hypertext Markup Language (HTML)* which is specialized code that tells a Web browser how to display text and images on a page. It also facilitates the use of hyperlinks, which enable access to other webpages or other areas or resources within the current website or document. One or more webpages comprise a website, sharing a common purpose and organizational identity. Microsoft Word includes the option to save a document in HTML format so that it can be used as a webpage.

With a bit of expertise in using Word, you can create webpages as part of an overall website design. However, more specialized website design apps are much better suited than Word for overall website design and management. In fact, professional Web designers are much more apt to code websites using HTML, CSS, or JavaScript—which are programming languages that produce code to support interactive websites. At this point, over half of all Web design is conducted using website building services or apps that enable a designer to work with tools to develop an attractive website, with the website service producing the underlying code.

Even so, Word is an attractive option if the goal is to quickly share a document online as a webpage. Such an online document can contain hyperlinks to access content in other areas, and can be designed with banners, background color, and varying styles. If not the best option for overall website design and management, Word is an excellent alternative if the focus is more on single webpages that originate from Word documents.

Word supports Web design in several ways. The approach described in this chapter centers on designing a webpage and saving it in .html (or .mht) format, as described later. Word also includes a feature whereby you can export a document as a blog post for sites such as WordPress. Finally, more experienced Web programmers can use Word as a text editor to house specific HTML code, although a text-editing app such as NotePad serves the same purpose and is often more accessible than Word for many people.

In this section, you will learn to create a webpage using Word. You will learn to develop a page with appropriate formatting, hyperlinks and bookmarks, and save it in a format for online access. You will also explore Word's built-in option of transforming a Word document into a Sway page, which is a Microsoft app used to produce interactive documents and presentations.

Build a Webpage

Building a webpage with Word requires only a few steps, primarily that of saving it appropriately so that underlying web code can be developed. For someone with a good grasp of page design and the use of such objects as SmartArt, tables, and pictures in the overall plan of a document, a webpage can appear much more professionally designed than a simple Word document that has been translated into Web code. With those tools and more in hand, you can organize and design page elements, add images, and enhance a document intended for online access with visual elements. Consider organizing page information with heading styles, enhancing banners with WordArt, and applying text formatting for visual appeal and ease of access.

Hypertext Markup Language (HTML) is a universal formatting language with the purpose of presenting webpages in a web browser, such as Microsoft Edge or Google Chrome. Although there are other coding formats, Word documents intended for Web display always utilize HTML or MHT code. MHT (MIME Hypertext Markup Language) is a specialized webpage archive format that stores HTML code and all linked resources in a single file.

> **TIP: UNDERSTAND MHT FORMAT**
> MIME (Multipurpose Internet Mail Extension) is a specification for the format of non-text email attachments, designed to be sent over the Internet. It allows such items as audio, video, and graphics to be sent through email. Building on that consolidation of items into a single attachment, the MHT (MIME HTML) webpage option utilized by Word archives online content into a single file that can be shared and viewed in a browser.

The HTML format consists of a set of codes (or tags) that are assigned to the content of a document, describing how the document is to display when viewed in a browser. The MHT format is very similar, differing primarily in the way webpage resources are bundled with the Word document. At one time, Web designers were required to be proficient in HTML coding. However, Word and other software options simplify the development of webpages so that knowledge of specific programming code is not required. Having saved a Word document as an .html or .mht document, you can view the code when you open the Word webpage in a browser, right-click the document, and then click View page source.

If you plan to use Word to develop a webpage, you can begin from a blank document or a webpage template. At least initially, you will treat the document just as any other, typing text and adjusting formatting—even inserting objects such as SmartArt and WordArt. When a document is ready to be saved for online access, you will change the file type to one of several Word options that prepare a document as a webpage.

> **TIP: POST TO A BLOG**
> To share a Word document to a blog, perhaps to a WordPress site, click the File tab, click Share, and then select Post to Blog. Click Post to Blog and then follow any suggestions for registering for a blog account if you do not already have one.

STEP 1 ▸ ## Save a Document as a Webpage

A webpage created from a Word document is actually more than one entity. Along with the single document that you design, Word will save all supporting assets, such as images, and other resource files that are necessary for rendering the saved webpage online as it also creates a set of codes to represent the document. The point is that when a Word document is converted into a webpage file, it becomes a bit bulkier than a simple text-based document, even if that is how it displays onscreen. Depending upon which webpage format you choose to use when saving a document, the set of accompanying files is either bundled with the document as a single file or placed in a separate folder that accompanies the Word document. Table 5.1 summarizes three choices that are available when you save a Word document as a webpage.

TABLE 5.1 Webpage File Types

File Type	Description
Web Page (.htm; .html)	Saves a Word document, converting the page to HTML format. Certain Word features that are not supported by the Web page environment are not shown, so the end result may not be precisely as intended. Any supporting images are saved in a separate subfolder which must accompany the HTML code. This results in a good approximation of a document, albeit in a large file size.
Single File Web Page (.mht; .mhtml)	Saves a Word document and all supporting images and resources in the same file, in MHT format. The result is a large file, combining the size of the document and all supporting files; therefore, it is often not the best choice for a webpage where space is a concern. This format also does not coordinate well with the Microsoft Edge browser. An advantage is that it is self-contained, with no need for an auxiliary folder of supporting resources.
Web Page, Filtered (.htm; .html)	Preserves document content and formatting, but removes much of the unnecessary HTML code, resulting in a smaller file size than other formats. The result is faster page loading time, but with some Word formatting features, such as bullets and numbering, not converted to the webpage. For simple display where formatting is not the primary concern, this format is a good choice.

> **TIP: NAME WEBPAGE FILES**
> When giving a Word document an HTML filename, you must follow certain rules and you should consider best practices. A good filename should be short and easy to understand by website visitors but lengthy enough to convey the page's purpose. It should also be easy to remember. Avoid cryptic names and those with mixed case. All lowercase is preferable. Consider separating words in the filename with hyphens, as that may make it easier for search engines to locate the page. As for specific rules, you must avoid special characters, sticking with letters, numbers, hyphens, underscores, and periods. Do not use spaces in a webpage filename.

Word has what many designers consider an annoying tendency to include unnecessary HTML codes and tags that add even more to the bulk. A simple one-page Word document, translated into HTML code, is likely to include thousands of lines of code. Although much of that code is superfluous and not active, the extra lines and bulk can yield a webpage that is a bit slow to load in a browser. For that reason, you will want to consider how best to save a document as a webpage, because you have several options—Web Page, Single File Web Page, or Web Page, Filtered. The file type you choose depends on how closely you want the webpage to mirror the document. In addition, if file size is a concern, you may want to select a file type that minimizes the space required.

As described in Table 5.1, there are two options for saving a document as a webpage that result in an HTM (or HTML) file—Web Page, Filtered and Web Page. Both HTM and HTML are file extensions that designate a file saved in Hypertext Markup Language, with the only difference being that the HTM extension works in operating systems and servers that do not accept four-letter extensions. The Single File Web Page option saves a document in MHT (or MHTML) type, resulting in a single webpage file. Because the .mht extension is not yet a standard among all browsers, you might find that opening the same file in different browsers could yield different results. In fact, some browsers provide no support for opening MHT files at all.

Most experts agree that the Web Page, Filtered approach results in a webpage that is likely to load more quickly on various browsers than would the other two choices. Of course, the purpose and ultimate destination of a webpage would certainly help make the determination of which file format to choose.

The difference between HTML and MHT file formats is that MHT files hold images and other associated media resources in a single file, whereas HTML only holds the text content of a page. Any images shown in HTML files are actually references to local or online images, which will load when the file is displayed. You can view an MHT file offline because all files are stored in a single file.

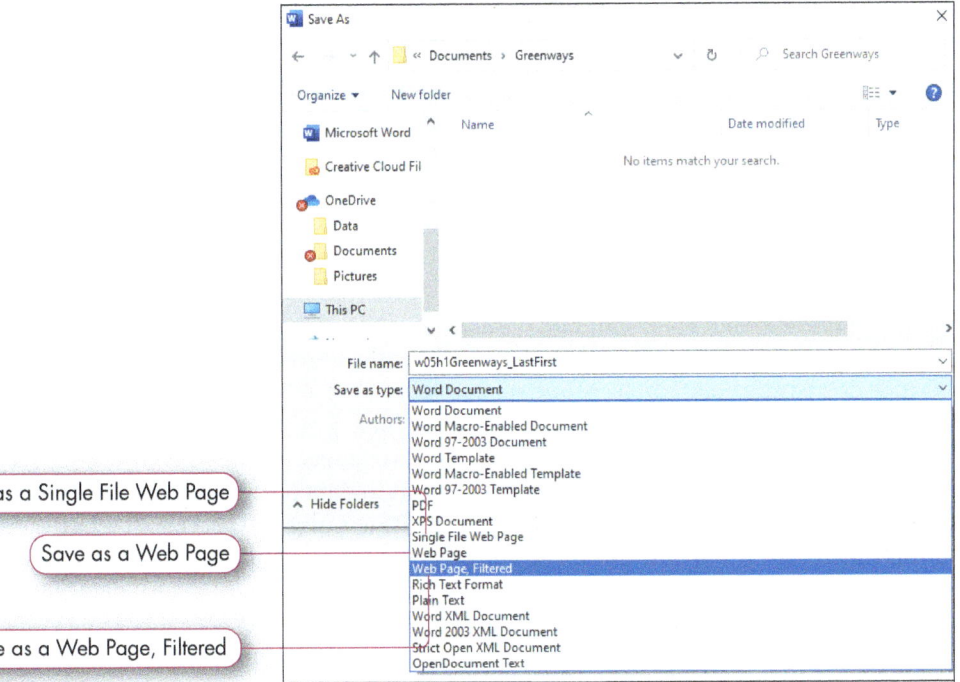

FIGURE 5.13 Save a Word Document as a Webpage

STEP 2 ## Apply a Theme and Background Color to a Webpage

Depending upon a webpage's purpose, it might be made more appealing by adding design elements such as background images, bullets, numbering, lines, and other graphical features. Varying color and fonts could make a page more readable. You should consider the use of Word themes which coordinate color and fonts. Select Themes from the Document Formatting group on the Design tab, as shown in Figure 5.14. In addition, so that a resulting webpage is clearly delineated in sections, be sure to format any headings in hierarchical styles, using Heading 1, Heading 2, and so forth.

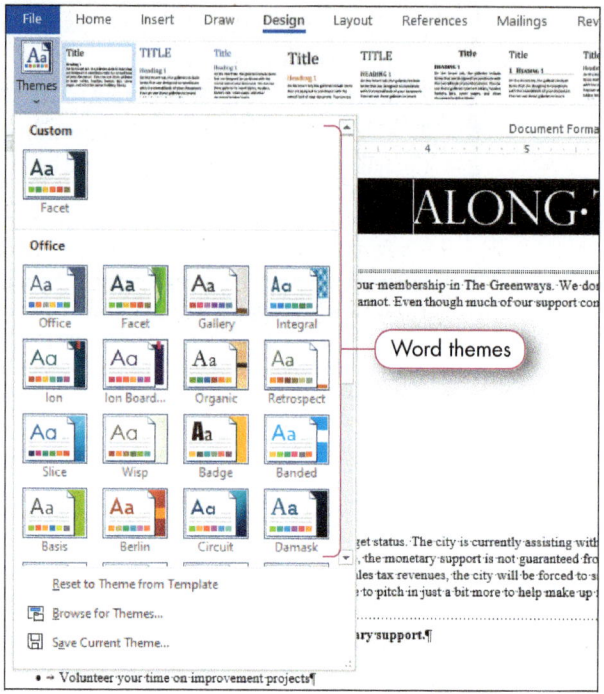

FIGURE 5.14 Apply a Theme to a Webpage

Themes assign color and font combinations to elements of a webpage, such as text, numbers, and borders. They do not automatically add a background to the webpage, but they do identify color choices that are available for use. A **background** is a color, design, image, or watermark that displays behind text in a document or on a webpage. A colored background adds visual enhancement to a webpage, filling what would otherwise be white space. A background suggests attention to detail and can help present a polished page effect. Select a background color from Page Color in the Page Background group on the Design tab. Point to any theme color to see a Live Preview, clicking to select an option.

For a broader selection of colors, click More Colors (after selecting Page Color on the Design tab). In the Colors dialog box, you can choose from various standard colors or you can choose to create a custom color mix. Using Fill Effects, you might choose to apply a gradient, texture, pattern, or picture background. Be aware that patterns or pictures used as a background are easily blurred or tiled during presentation, creating a visually distracting view—not at all what you most likely intended.

Insert Bookmarks in a Webpage or Document

Most webpages contain **hyperlinks**, typically called links, to other webpages or to other locations within the same document or website. At a user level, the terms *link* and *hyperlink* are interchangeable. In fact, Word makes no distinction between the two.

Whatever you choose to call it, a ***link*** is an active part of a document or webpage that initiates movement to another area when clicked. (If choosing a link in a document, as opposed to a webpage, you must hold Ctrl and then click the link.) If within a document, a link directs to a bookmark. If within a webpage, a link (more often called *hyperlink* in the context of online material) directs to another online location or URL.

A webpage often occupies more space than what can be displayed on a single browser page. It is not at all unusual to scroll through page contents to view those that are offscreen. However, where appropriate, you might consider simplifying the process of moving to offscreen areas by including links to other locations in the same document. A ***bookmark*** is used to mark a location to which a link can point. It is actually an electronic marker for a specific location, facilitating movement to that area from a clicked link. Regardless of whether a document is housed locally or has been saved as a webpage, the concept of working with links and bookmarks remains the same.

You might use a bookmark to facilitate movement among various locations of an FAQ (Frequently Asked Questions) page. Clicking a question link produces the corresponding location of an answer in another area, made possible by a bookmark identifying the answer's placement. Whether that link produces corresponding movement in an offline Word document or in a Word webpage, the technique is the same.

HOW TO

Create a bookmark:

1. Place the insertion point where the bookmark should be. Click the Insert tab and select Bookmark in the Links group.
2. The Bookmark dialog box displays, as shown in Figure 5.15. Type the name of the bookmark in the Bookmark name box and click Add.
3. Click OK.

A bookmark name must begin with a letter. It can include both numbers and letters but not spaces. If a bookmark includes separate words, use an underscore to connect the words. For example, a bookmark to a dog kennel area of a pet supplies document could be called dog_kennel. The name does not show in the document but serves as an internal marker to which a link can direct.

TIP: REMOVE BOOKMARKS AND LINKS IN A DOCUMENT
To remove a link, right-click the link in a document and choose from various options, including removing or editing the link. When a link is removed, the link text remains, but the action of directing elsewhere is no longer in effect. To remove a bookmark, click the Insert tab and click Bookmark in the Links group. In the Bookmark dialog box, select a bookmark and then choose to remove it. Note that you can also click Go To if you want to move directly to a selected bookmark in the document.

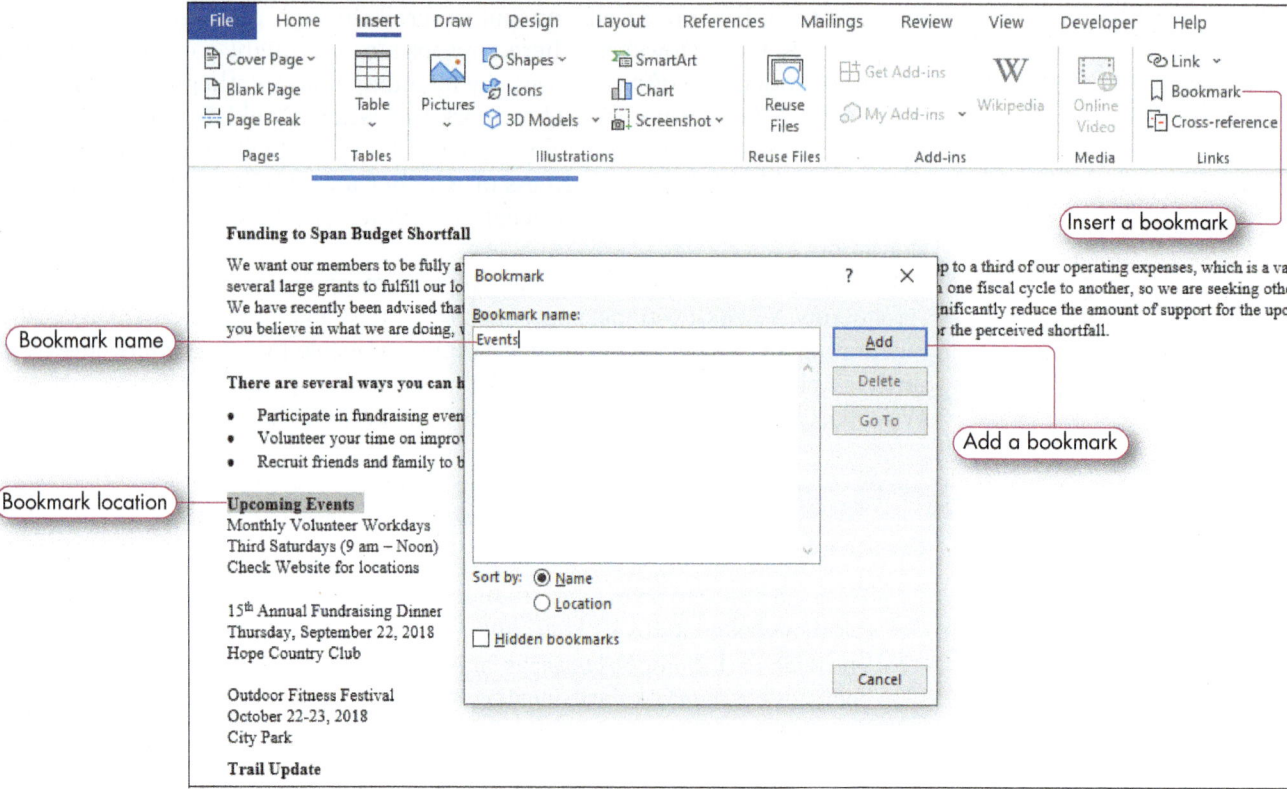

FIGURE 5.15 Create a Bookmark

STEP 3 Insert Hyperlinks in a Webpage or Document

Any object can include a hyperlink, including text, graphics, tables, charts, or shapes. For example, consider a webpage you might create that summarizes a recent visit you made to several national parks. You include a few pictures of places you toured and activities enjoyed, including an image of a lakeside lodge where you spent several days. The picture can be configured to include a hyperlink that, when clicked, directs a website visitor to the lodge website.

To create a link to another location (most often to a bookmark in an open document or to another online), select the text or object that is to contain the link. Click the Insert tab and click Link in the Links group. In the *Link to* pane of the Insert Hyperlink dialog box, select Existing File or Web Page (to link to another URL) or click Place in This Document (to link to a bookmark in the current document). See Figure 5.16 for those options and others that enable linking to a new document or to an email address.

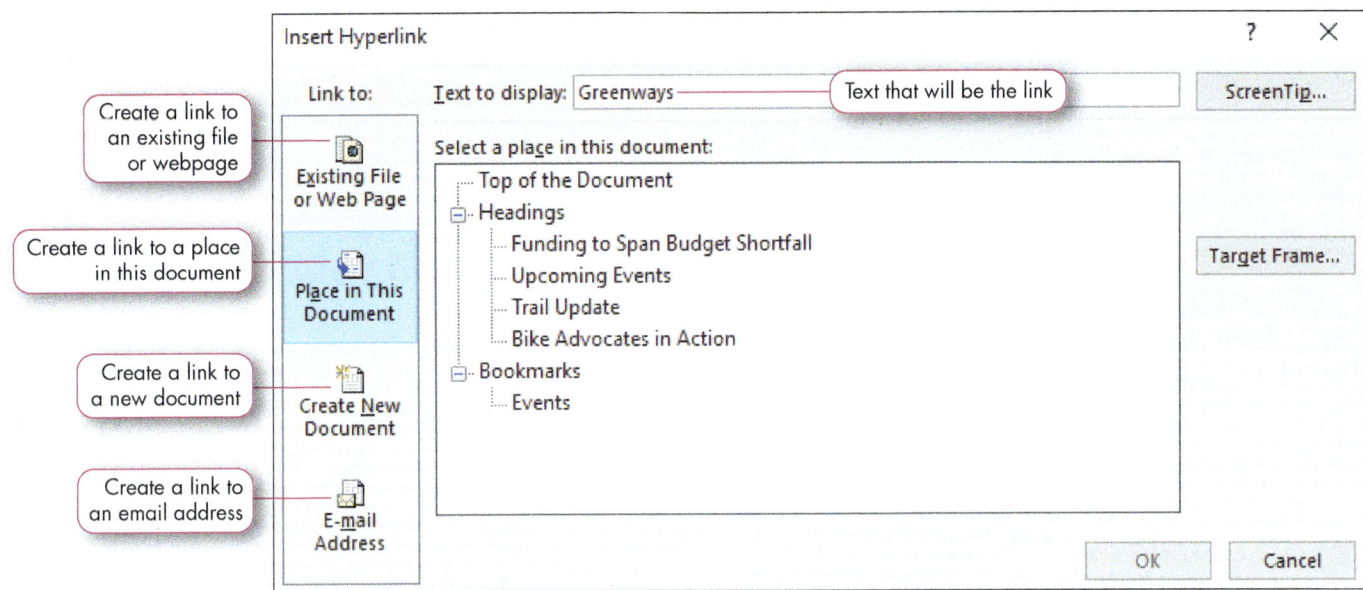

FIGURE 5.16 Create a Link

Publish a Webpage

After finalizing one or more pages for a website, it is important to preview the material before publishing it online. That way, you can get a good idea of how the webpage will look. Remember, though, that depending upon the file type and its coordination with various browsers, the final product might vary somewhat. Having prepared a document and previewed how it will look online, you will publish it to a Web server.

STEP 4 Preview and Publish a Webpage

To get a quick idea of how the page would look online, click the View tab and select Web Layout in the Views group. At any point, change to another view to continue editing, or you can edit within the Web Layout view.

You can also preview the document through Word's Web Page Preview feature which is an option not included on the ribbon by default. Although you can customize the ribbon to include Web Page Preview, a simpler approach might be to add it to the Quick Access Toolbar (QAT). That way, it is readily available but can also be removed with little effort if you find you no longer need it. Click Customize Quick Access Toolbar (the arrow at the right side of the QAT) and select More Commands. Click the *Choose commands from* arrow and select Commands Not in the Ribbon. Scroll through commands, click Web Page Preview, and click Add. Click OK. The QAT will then include a Web Page Preview selection. You might find it helpful to periodically click Web Page Preview to view a document under development.

Finally, you will save a document destined for the Web, selecting an appropriate web file type. Having saved the file, you will want to view it in your default browser. Locate and double-click the file in File Explorer to open it in a browser. You can then confirm that it shows as you want it to and displays the correct content. To check its view in another browser, right-click the file in File Explorer, click Open With, and select the browser (see Figure 5.17).

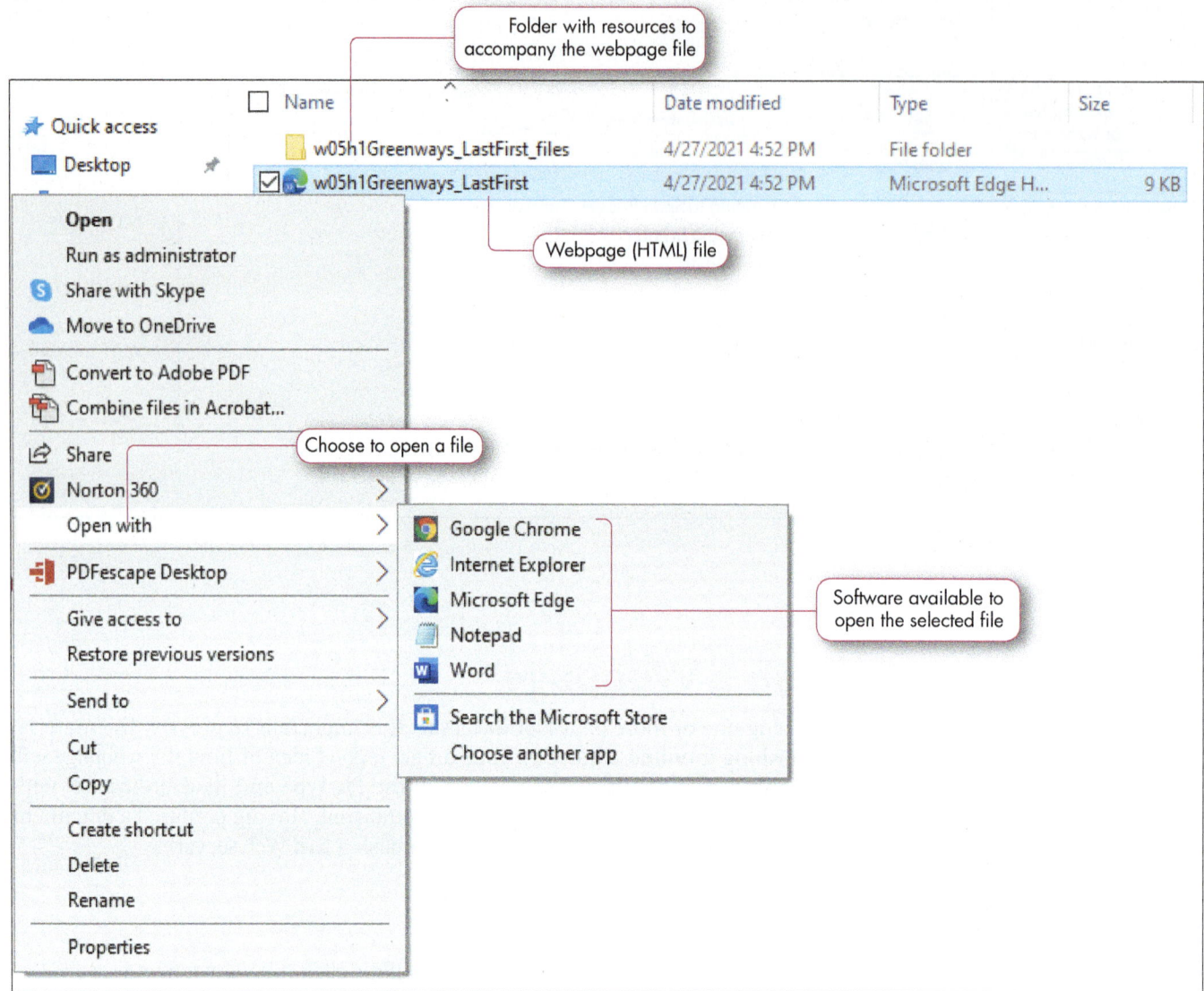

FIGURE 5.17 Open a Webpage from File Explorer

To make a Word webpage available online, you must save or publish it to a Web server, which is a computer system that hosts webpages so that they are available for viewing. Those systems are typically owned by companies that make space available for individuals at an annual or monthly price. Of course, you may be employed with an organization that affords Web server space, or your school might make space available to students. The options are many, but you do need to secure some form of online storage and display before a Word webpage can be uploaded. Depending upon the Web service you select, you might find it easiest to upload pages to the server using File Transfer Protocol (FTP), a process that both uploads and downloads files online.

Transform a Word Document into a Sway Webpage

Sway is a Microsoft app that can be used to create and share interactive reports, personal stories, and presentations, among other things. Basically an online publishing service, Sway can convert a document into a webpage that adjusts its look to accommodate various devices such as a smartphone or a tablet. The resulting document is housed in the cloud on Microsoft's Sway service. As such, the document does not occupy a webpage that you can manage; however, if the goal is to share a well-designed online approximation of a document that you created, then using Sway could be a very attractive option.

Although you can convert a Word document to a Sway page from within the Sway app, the most straightforward approach is to push an open Word document to Sway by clicking the File tab and clicking Transform. Select a style or accept the default, and then click Transform. In seconds, the document is shown in a restyled format, ready for sharing online. Before calling it done, however, you can edit or design the text by clicking Edit (see Figure 5.18). The transformed document is shown in Storyline mode (see Figure 5.19), which enables you to change the text and work with blocks of content, also called content cards. You can find tutorials from Microsoft and other online resources with information on how to edit text and add elements to content cards, such as media and interactive features.

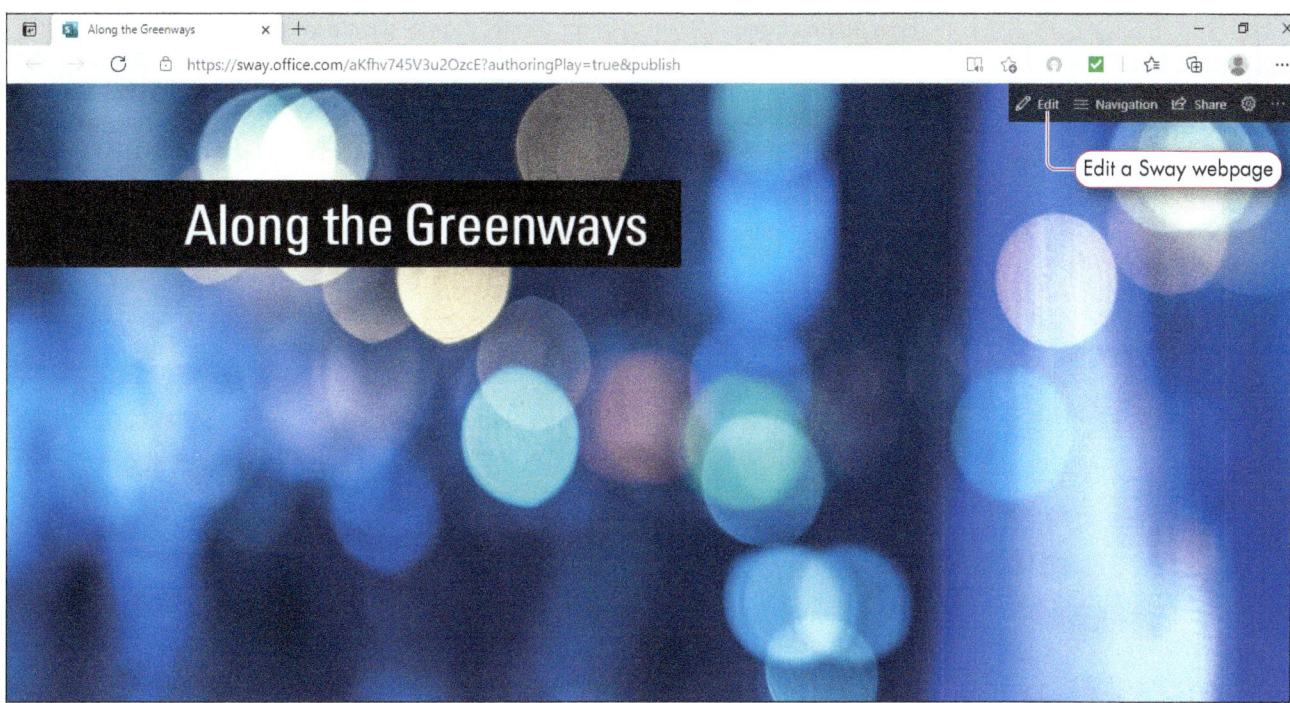

FIGURE 5.18 Edit a Sway Webpage

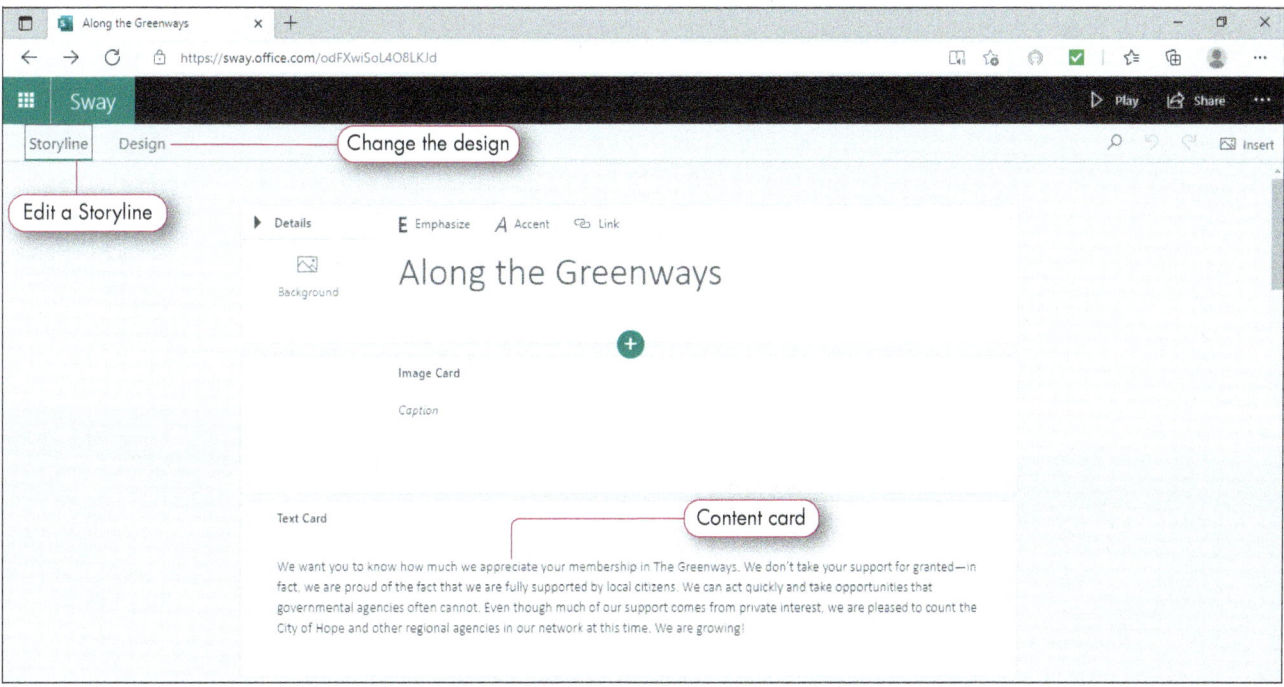

FIGURE 5.19 Sway Page Storyline

Click the Design tab and then click Styles to adjust the view and customize fonts and colors. To sample a random collection of formatting, click Remix—repeatedly, to cycle through various possibilities. Click Storyline to return to a view where text editing can occur. When the Sway document is complete, you can click Share in the top right corner to send out a link (or simply copy the URL for distribution).

TIP: USE THE SWAY APP

Although you can transform a Word document into a Sway webpage from within Word, you can instead begin building Web content by using the Sway app. You will select from starting a new blank Sway, starting from a document, or starting with a Sway template. To access the Sway app, visit http://office.com and log in to your Microsoft account. Click the App launcher in the top left corner and select Sway. If you intend to transform a document into Sway, click Start from a document and browse to the document. When the document opens in Sway, you can select a theme and modify the content. Even so, if the goal is transforming an existing document to Sway, you will most likely find it easier to use the Transform option on the File tab to begin that project. Not only is that process more straightforward, but a theme is applied before the document is transformed, unlike in the app, where you select a theme after a document is uploaded. (Sway is not available for a Mac.)

Critical Thinking

4. Describe how you might decide whether to publish a Word document by saving it in webpage format and uploading it to a server or to transform it to a Sway document. *p. 382*

5. Describe the webpage type you might choose if you were more concerned with minimizing file size than with preserving all Word formatting features. *p. 376*

6. Explain why it is more important for an end user to be able to identify a link in a document than it would be for the user to identify a bookmark. *p. 379*

Hands-On Exercises

MyLab IT HOE2 Sim Training

Watch the Video for this Hands-On Exercise!

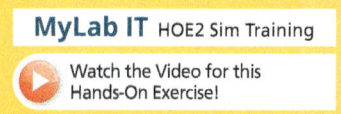

Skills covered: Save a Document as a Webpage • Apply a Theme and Background Color to a Webpage • Insert Hyperlinks in a Webpage or Document • Preview and Publish a Webpage

2 Publish Online

The Greenways newsletter is complete. Not only is it to be available in printed form, but you will also prepare it for display online, formatting it with a theme and fonts and including links and bookmarks.

STEP 1 SAVE A DOCUMENT AS A WEBPAGE

As a webpage document, the Greenways newsletter will be shared with others who have an interest in supporting the nonprofit. As you begin to design the online version, you first save it as a webpage, selecting an appropriate file type. Refer to Figure 5.20 as you complete Step 1.

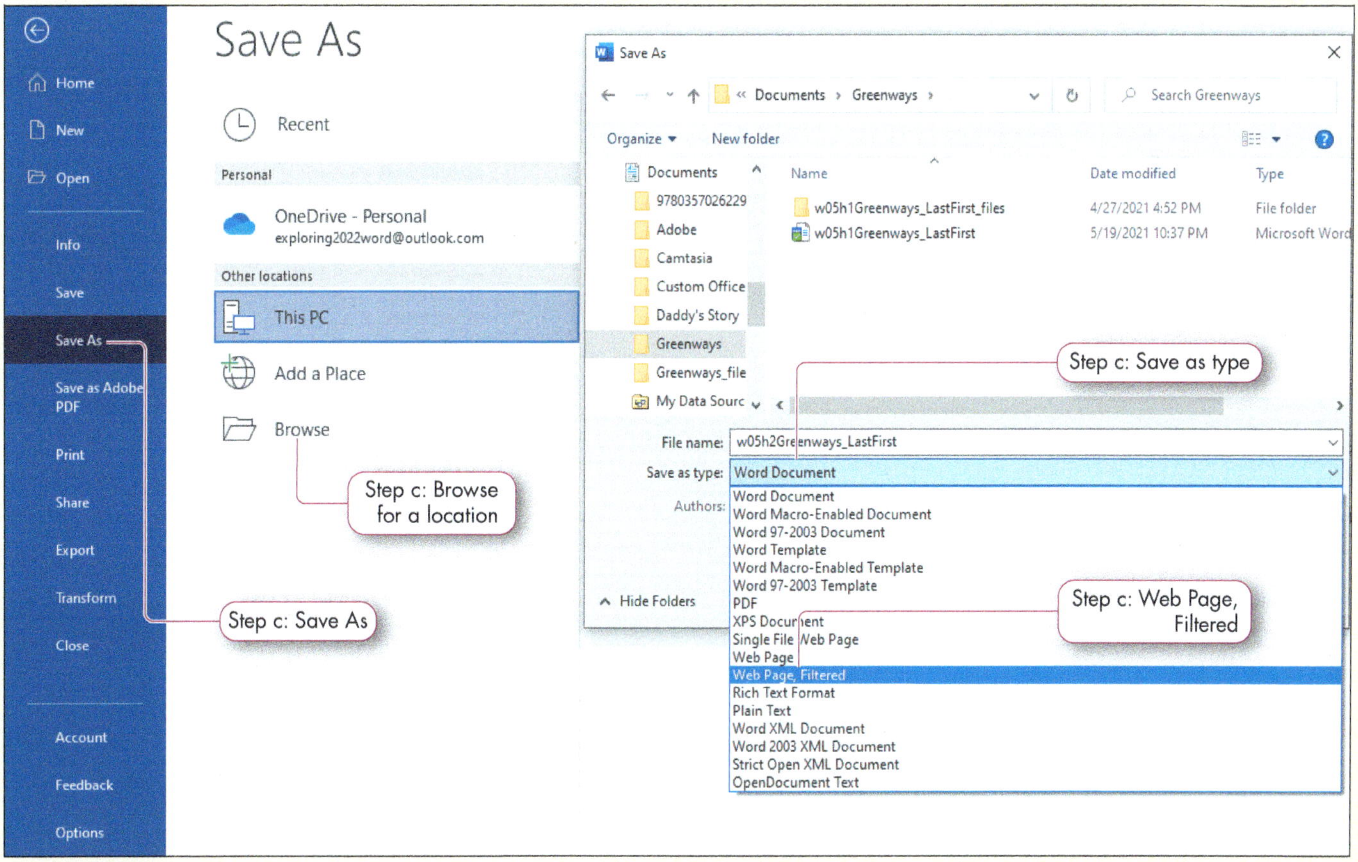

FIGURE 5.20 Save a Document as a Webpage

a. Open *w05h1Greenways_LastFirst* if you closed it after the previous exercise. Ensure that nonprinting characters are displayed. Click **Yes** when asked whether to update links.

b. Click the **View tab** and select **Web Layout** in the Views group. Right-click **Volume 2, Number 2** in the second line of the document. Click **Table Properties**. Click **Center** to center the table horizontally. Click **OK**.

Viewing the document in Web Layout view, you get an idea of how it will look online. You can still edit the document, which you do by centering the table with the volume information.

c. Click the **File tab** and click **Save As**. Click **Browse** and navigate to the location where you save student files. Click the **Save as type arrow** and select **Web Page, Filtered**. Save the file as **w05h2Greenways_LastFirst**, changing h1 to h2. Click **Change Title**. Type **Greenways News** in the Page title box and click **OK**. Click **Save**. When apprised that some Office features might be lost in the translation, click **Yes**.

> **MAC TROUBLESHOOTING:** Click the File menu, click Properties, and click Summary to change the title.

APPLY A THEME AND BACKGROUND COLOR TO A DOCUMENT

A webpage can be designed with color and font settings that increase its readability and appeal. In this case, you will apply a theme and add a background color. In addition, you will modify the font so that it is more attractive in the Web version of the document. Refer to Figure 5.21 as you complete Step 2.

FIGURE 5.21 Apply a Theme and Background Color

a. Click the **Design tab** and click **Themes** in the Document Formatting group. Select **Facet**. Click **Fonts** and select **Arial Black–Arial**. Click **Colors** and select **Aspect**.

> **TROUBLESHOOTING:** Theme fonts are not in alphabetical order so you must scroll through other selections to locate Arial Black-Arial.

b. Click **Page Color** in the Page Background group. Select **Orange, Accent 1, Lighter 80%**.

Selecting a light-colored background yields a more attractive webpage.

c. Click the **Home tab**. Format *Trail Update* and *Bike Advocates in Action* in **Title style** with a font size of **20**.

You format heading lines to give them more definition on the webpage.

d. Save the document, clicking **Yes** when advised that some Office features may be lost.

Visitors to the webpage should be able to go to areas of interest by clicking links that you will insert. Specifically, you create a link to the schedule of upcoming events and you also link to an external webpage. Refer to Figure 5.22 as you complete Step 3.

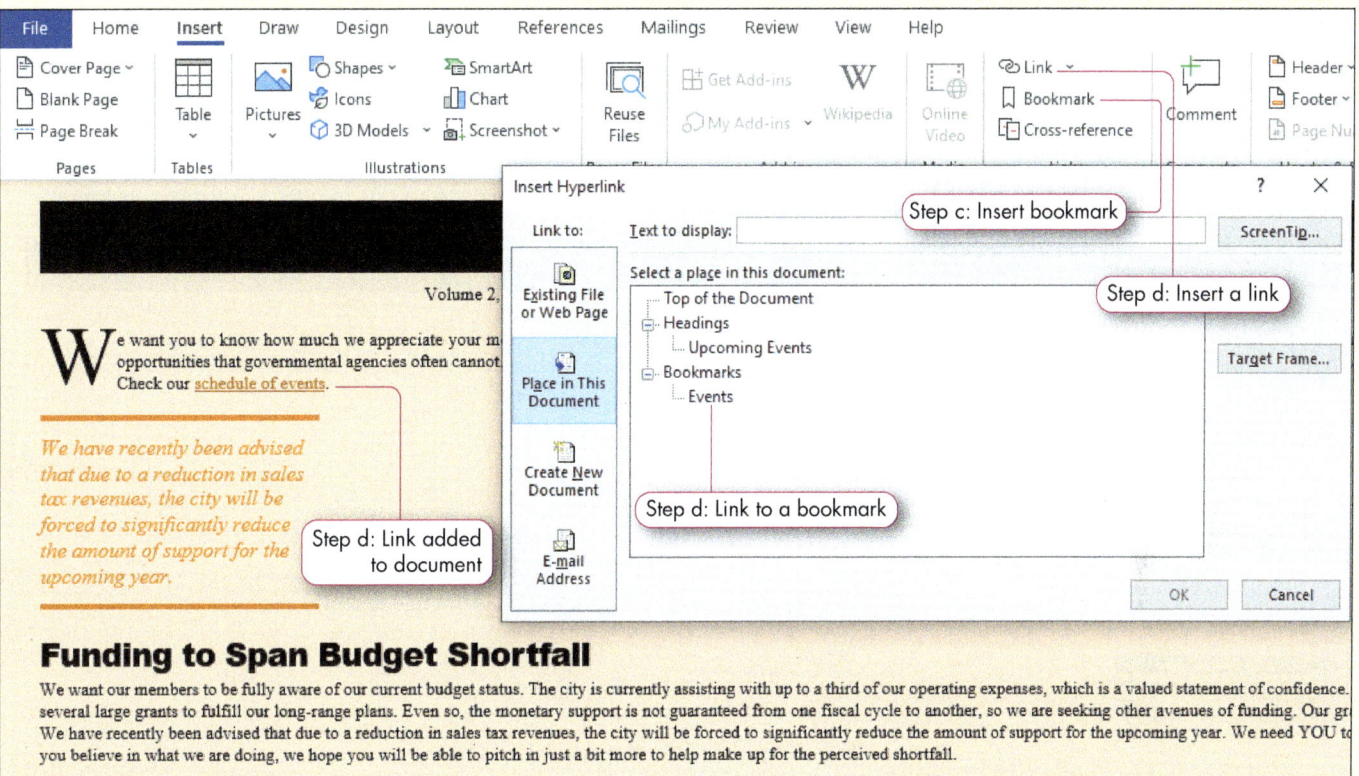

FIGURE 5.22 Insert a Link

a. Drag to select **Bike for Hope** in the last sentence of the document. Click the **Insert tab** and click **Link** in the Links group. Click **Existing File or Web Page** in the Link to area. Type **http://pearson.com** in the Address bar of the Insert Hyperlink dialog box. Click **OK**.

You insert a link to an existing webpage so that when you point to the words *Bike for Hope* and press Ctrl+Click the webpage is accessed. Although http://pearson.com is not related to the newsletter, you use the Web address as a sample to which to link.

> **TROUBLESHOOTING:** If a list of recent items displays when you click Link instead of the Insert Hyperlink dialog box, you clicked the Link arrow instead of Link.

b. Click after the last sentence in the first body paragraph, *We are growing!*. Press **spacebar** and type **Check our schedule of events.** (Include the period.)

c. Select **Upcoming Events** near the middle of the document. Click **Bookmark** in the Links group. Type **Events** in the Bookmark name box and click **Add**.

You add a bookmark to the Upcoming Events section so that any links to a list of events can be directed there.

d. Select **schedule of events** at the end of the first body paragraph. Click **Link** in the Links group. Click **Place in This Document** in the Link to area. Click **Events** under *Bookmarks* in the right pane of the dialog box. Click **OK**.

e. Point to the linked *schedule of events* text, hold **Ctrl** and click the text. (On a Mac, click the link.)

   The insertion point moves to the Upcoming Events section.

   f. Save the document, clicking **Yes** when advised that some Office features may be lost.

STEP 4 ## PREVIEW AND PUBLISH A WEBPAGE

Before publishing a webpage, you should preview it as it will display. You customize the Quick Access Toolbar to include a Web Page Preview option so you can check the document. Refer to Figure 5.23 as you complete Step 4.

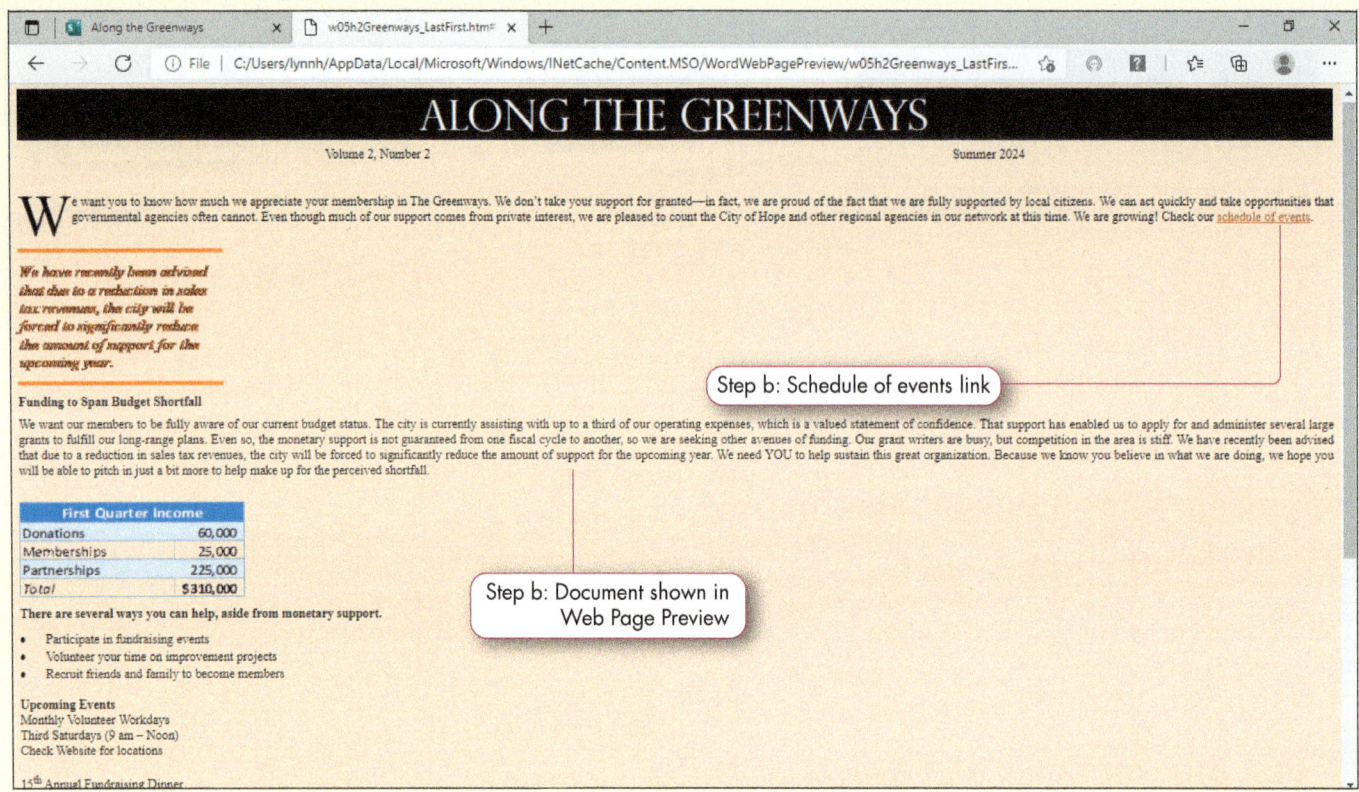

FIGURE 5.23 Preview a Webpage

   a. Click **Customize Quick Access Toolbar** (the arrow at the right side of the QAT) and click **More Commands**. Click the **Choose commands from arrow** and select **Commands Not in the Ribbon**. Scroll through the alphabetized list and click **Web Page Preview**. Click **Add**. Click **OK**.

   The Web Page Preview option is added to the Quick Access Toolbar.

   b. Click **Web Page Preview** on the QAT. Click **Yes** to update links, and indicate a browser to use, if asked. Click the **schedule of events link** in the first body paragraph.

   The Word document displays as it will when published. Clicking the schedule of events link moves to the previously bookmarked Upcoming Events section.

   > **TROUBLESHOOTING:** If the webpage is not shown in the browser you are using, proceed to Step d.

c. Click the **Bike for Hope** link near the end of the document.

The linked website, www.pearson.com, is displayed.

d. Close all open browser windows.

e. Right-click **Web Page Preview** on the Quick Access Toolbar and click **Remove from Quick Access Toolbar**.

As you may be working in a school computer lab, you remove the Web Page Preview option from the QAT.

f. Save the document, click **Yes** when advised that Office features may be lost, and close the document. You will submit this file to your instructor at the end of the last Hands-On Exercise.

Forms

A *form* is a document designed to collect data. You are likely to work with forms on a daily basis, in both print and electronic format. For example, you might open an account with an online retailer by visiting a website and providing information, or perhaps you complete a printed patient information form when you see a dentist for the first time. People often complete job applications in online format; you might even have applied for entry to a university by completing a form on the university website.

Microsoft Word includes design features that enable you to create well-structured forms that can be completed electronically or on paper. If designed to be completed on paper, a form would include formatting, labels, and blank spaces for writing or typing data. An online form, developed for data entry in electronic format, contains the same features as printed forms. In addition, an electronic form contains areas in which a user can type or otherwise indicate selections. Such a form can be designed to accept only certain types of input in restricted areas of the form. Figure 5.24 displays a completed form that is an invoice for placemats.

FIGURE 5.24 Completed Form

In this section, you will create an electronic form that includes features that enhance the data entry process. You will learn to insert and customize content controls, perform calculations in a form, and restrict editing of the document to areas of variable data.

Create an Electronic Form

When creating a form, regardless of whether it is intended for electronic or printed data entry, you define the standard layout, structure, and formatting of the document. If the form is designed for electronic data entry, you often establish settings to enable a user to enter data in specific places while preventing data entry or editing in others. Figure 5.25 shows a blank form that includes areas designed for data entry. Those areas are shown as blocks, referred to as *fields* or *content controls*.

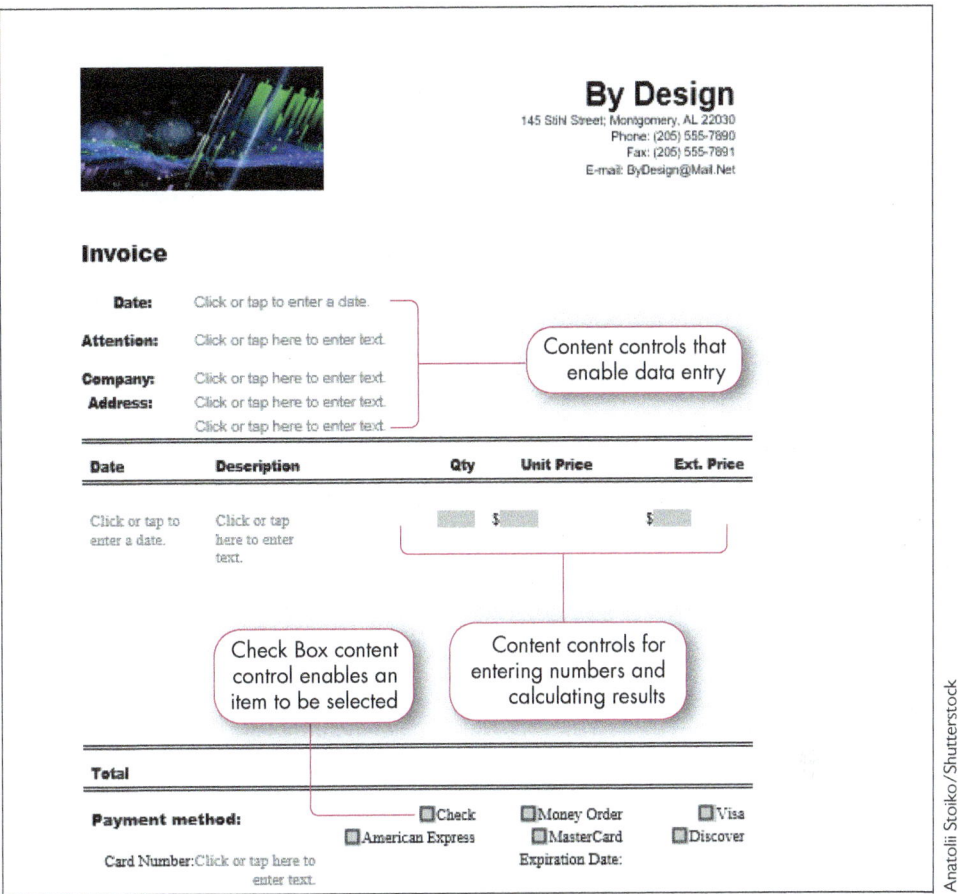

FIGURE 5.25 Form Design

The Developer tab includes options that enable you to create a form. Although the Developer tab does not display by default on the ribbon, you can customize the ribbon to include it. Right-click an empty space on the ribbon and select Customize the Ribbon. Select the Developer check box under Customize the Ribbon on the right side to include the tab on the ribbon. Alternately, you can select Options from the File tab, click Customize Ribbon in the Word Options dialog box, and ensure that the Developer tab is selected from the options on the right side of the dialog box.

> **MAC TIP: DISPLAYING THE DEVELOPER TAB**
> Select Preferences from the Word menu and click Ribbon & Toolbar (under Authoring and Proofing Tools). Select the Developer check box in the Customize the Ribbon section.

Understand Content Controls

If your intent is to develop a form for use online, you will insert **content controls**. A content control provides a location for user interaction, just as a paper form would include blanks to be filled in. Content controls display prompts such as drop-down lists, date pickers, text boxes, and check boxes, shown in Figure 5.26. (Not all of these controls are available when working with a Mac.)

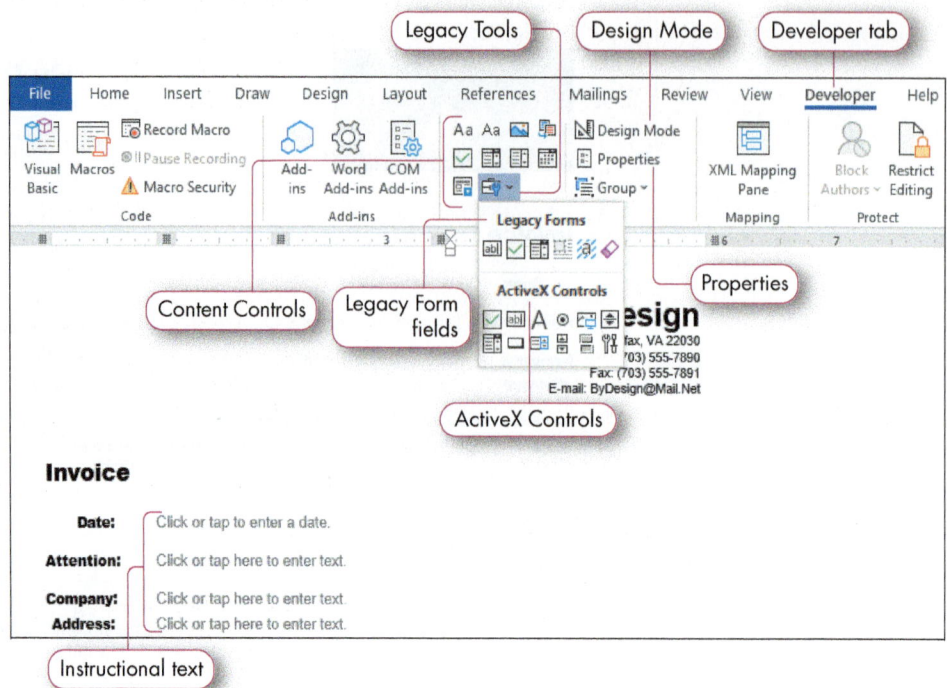

FIGURE 5.26 Use Content Controls

A **Rich Text content control** is often used to insert formatted text, images, and tables. The content control is useful when entering a large amount of text, as well. Conversely, a **Plain Text content control** enables data entry of a small amount of text that is readable by any text or file editor. Other items, such as images and tables, cannot be included.

A **Check Box content control**, as the name implies, consists of a box that is selected or deselected to represent a preference or condition. For example, you might check *Yes* or *No* to indicate that you are or are not above the age of 18. You can customize check box form fields to be selected by default or to remain deselected. You can also specify the size of a check box.

A **Drop-Down List content control** provides several options to choose from. A drop-down list is typically designed to display when you click an arrow. From that point, you select one option from the drop-down list. The selected option displays on the form.

A **Combo Box content control** combines a text box with a list box so that a user may choose from items displayed in a drop-down box or can type an entry instead of selecting from the list.

The **Date Picker content control** displays a calendar from which a user can select a date. When entering data into a form that includes a Date Picker content control, you can select a Today option, facilitating quick selection of the current date. When designing a form, you can select from several date formats in the Properties dialog box, such as 3/2/2024 or 2-Mar-24.

MAC TIP: USING CONTENT CONTROLS

The Mac version of Word only includes three types of controls, a Text Box, Check Box, and Combo Box. Use the Text Box control instead of a Rich Text Content Control, Plain Text Content Control, or Date Picker Content Control. Then select Options to customize the format. Similarly, use the Combo Box control instead of a Drop-Down List Content Control, choosing Options to indicate selections.

In addition to the content controls described previously, you can also select from a small collection of Legacy Tools in the Controls group on the Developer tab (refer to Figure 5.26). Although **Legacy Tools** were originally developed in versions of Word prior to 2007, the Legacy form field selections can still be effectively used in form development today. In fact, forms are often developed using a combination of content controls and Legacy Tools because each type has unique characteristics that contribute to form design. For example, the Text Form Field content control, which is located in the Legacy

Tools collection, is often included in forms that require numeric calculations as that field type is well suited for the purpose. In short, the choice of field type is dependent on the purpose of the form under development, but you can certainly choose from both content controls and Legacy fields if you understand the purposes and limitations of each.

> **TIP: USING ACTIVEX CONTROLS**
> ActiveX controls are available in the Legacy Tools collection, designed specifically for online forms although they can be used in other documents. ActiveX controls are useful when you need more flexible design requirements than those provided by other content controls. They are also beneficial when some type of response to user interaction is required. For example, you might include an ActiveX control in an online form so that different actions can be taken depending on which choice a user selects from a drop-down list. Or perhaps you choose to query a database to refill a combo box with items when a user clicks a button. Even so, Microsoft Edge does not support the inclusion of ActiveX controls, suggesting that the need for ActiveX controls has been significantly reduced by modern Web standards that are more interoperable across browsers.

STEP 1 ## Insert Content Controls

As you develop a form, you work in Design Mode, accessible as an option on the Developer tab (refer to Figure 5.26). *Design Mode* enables you to select control fields, positioning them in a document so you can make any necessary modifications to their layout or options. Design Mode is a toggle command; click it once to activate the feature and click it again to deactivate it. Having activated Design Mode, place the insertion point where you want to insert a content control and select an option from the Controls group. The Properties command enables you to customize a content control within a form. If you find it necessary to remove a content control, right-click the control and click Remove Content Control.

As a form designer, you should insert fields in the order in which they should be completed by a user. A user may complete an electronic form by clicking from field to field or by pressing Tab. Tab order is determined by how form fields were created, so a user who is completing form data by tabbing from one field to another automatically progresses through fields in the order in which they were placed. Once a form is designed, the tab order is not evident and is time-consuming to modify. With that in mind, it is critical that you consider the way you intend users to work through a form before you create it.

> **TIP: COLOR A CONTENT CONTROL**
> You can change the color of a content control to add emphasis to the control or to adhere to your organization's color theme. To modify the color of a content control, select the control to be colored and ensure Design Mode is selected in the Control group on the Developer tab. Click Properties. Click the Color icon in the Content Control Properties dialog box and select a color.

> **TIP: MAKING A FORM ACCESSIBLE TO ALL**
> As with any document, it is important that a form is accessible to users, even those with low vision or other disabilities. You can add help text to Legacy fields in a form; text that is added will display on the status bar (if that option is selected as help text is created) or read by an assistive screen reader, if one is in use, as a user begins to complete the form. To add help text to a Legacy field, select the field and ensure that Design Mode is active. Click Properties and click Add Help Text.

When you insert a content control, the field displays instructional text, as shown in Figure 5.26. For example, having inserted a Rich Text content control, the field displays *Click or tap here to enter text*, which provides direction to a person completing the form. Suppose the content control is placed beside a *Company Name* label, which implies that the content control should contain a company name. You can change the field's instructional text, perhaps displaying *Enter company name* in the field, clearly defining the field's intended contents. To change instructional text in a field, select an inserted field and ensure that Design Mode is active. Edit the placeholder text and format it.

Perform Calculations with Content Control Data

A form can include fields that automatically calculate or update numeric values. The update can be set to occur when an area is clicked or upon exiting a form. For example, you might design a form to automatically calculate sales tax or total price when a user enters the cost of an item. If you intend to use formulas in a form, consider using a Word table for form design rather than text that is arranged otherwise. It simplifies the alignment of values. In addition, the use of Text Form Fields (available in the Legacy Tools collection on the Developer tab) is recommended when a form is collecting numeric data or completing a calculation. A Text Form Field enables you to define contents as numeric or as a calculation, in addition to various text formats. As you define properties for a Text Form Field, you will select from a Type list that includes Regular text, Number, Calculation, and others.

When defining the properties of a Text Form Field that has been inserted in a form and that is to represent numeric data, select the field and then click Properties in the Controls group on the Developer tab (refer to Figure 5.26). At that point, select Number as the data type and consider the assignment of a default value, as shown in Figure 5.27. For example, the inclusion of a Quantity field for an item that is most often purchased in units of 1 might be described with a default value of 1. Although the quantity can be changed by a user who is completing the form, the default value would often negate the need to do so, as it is most likely the choice that would be made anyway.

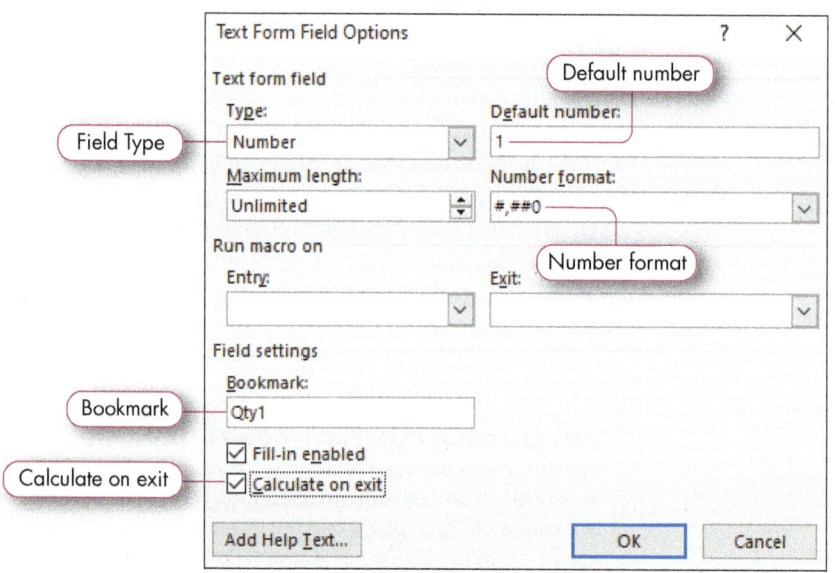

FIGURE 5.27 Form Field Properties

If the value in the Quantity field is to be included in a calculation in the form, you would also assign a bookmark name to the field. The bookmark name should uniquely describe the field so that it can be referred to in a calculation or other operation. Suppose the form has several rows, with each row including a Quantity field that is summarized in a calculation on the same row. Because each Quantity field occupies a different row, each one should be uniquely named—perhaps Qty1 for the first row's field, Qty2 for the second row, and so forth.

When defining the properties of a Text Form Field that is to be used as a calculation, perhaps to summarize a column of numbers or to multiply others, you would select Calculation as the data type. A field that has been defined as a calculation must include a formula or function as an expression, similar to the way formulas and functions can be included in a Word table. However, instead of using cell references in a calculation, as would be done in a Word table, a content control uses bookmarks. For example, having included a content control with the bookmark of *Qty1*, and another with the bookmark of *Price1*, you can insert a content control as a calculation with the expression *=Qty1*Price1*, resulting in the amount owed. To total a column of values, a content control that is defined as a calculation might include a function of *=sum(above)*.

HOW TO

Include a calculation in a form:

1. Insert a Text Form Field (available in the Legacy Forms group of the Legacy Tools collection in the Controls group) where applicable in a form to collect numeric data. Such data includes values like Quantity on Hand or Price—values that are not calculated, but simply entered.

2. Select a field that is to contain numeric data and click Properties in the Controls group. Click the Type arrow in the dialog box and select Number. Include an optional default value and assign a bookmark name if the value is to be used in a calculation. A bookmark name cannot contain spaces. Select Calculate on exit (refer to Figure 5.27).

3. Insert a Text Form Field to serve as a calculation. For example, you might insert a Sales field to multiply Quantity1 by Price1, which are previously created and bookmarked fields.

4. Click Properties in the Controls group (with the calculating field selected). Click the Type arrow and select Calculation.

5. Type a formula in the Expression box, beginning with an equal sign (for example, =Quantity1*Price1).

6. Click the Number format arrow and select a result format. Optionally, enter a bookmark name for the calculation.

TIP: USING IMMERSIVE READER

Documents that are intended for distribution, including forms, should be available to all readers, even those with limited reading skills or a disability such as dyslexia. Those who are to complete a form you designed can use Word's Immersive Reader to make the form, or any document, more accessible. Including the option to have a form read aloud or using a modified page color that is more visible to those who have low vision could greatly enhance a form's accessibility in many cases. Immersive Reader is available on the View tab in the Immersive group. Tools include an option to have a document read aloud, broken into syllables, with increased text spacing, or with modified column width and page color. The language used is the default language of the operating system. Not all tools are available in all languages; for example, text spacing is not supported by languages with complex or connected scripts, such as Arabic.

Enable Form Protection

The typical process in developing a form involves designing form content, including labels and controls for variable data, and then saving the document. Because you design a form to be a starting point for data entry, you may want to protect all or part of the form, enabling changes to occur only where user input is required. For example, a user would only be allowed to type data in locations that vary, such as when entering a name or selecting an option. Even as users enter data in certain controls, you might also want to protect those controls so they cannot be inadvertently deleted. You can protect a form's content with a password, providing access only when the password is entered. Be careful when using a password, though, because if you forget it, you will not be able to update the fields.

Protect Individual Content Controls

When designing a form for others to use, it is important to protect some areas from change while enabling data entry in others. For example, you would want to enable users to type a last name in the Last Name box, but not to modify the label *Last Name* that precedes the box.

A form is usually composed of several fields designed to accept user input. Those fields, or controls, can be locked in several ways. Typically, you want to enable data entry in a field while ensuring that the field itself cannot be deleted. In other words, you want a user to be able to change the content of the field but not to remove the field. In rare cases, you might want to ensure that a user cannot change the contents of a field. For example, a field containing sales tax is not something that will be modified often, so you could protect the field contents from change. Options to lock fields in those ways are only available for newer content controls, but are not included in properties of Legacy fields. As a developer, you can lock a selected field when you click Properties in the Controls group on the Developer tab and select an option from the Locking section of the dialog box. You can prohibit the removal of a content control, and you can ensure that the contents of a field cannot be edited.

STEP 3 ## Protect an Entire Form

To protect an entire form so that only variable data can be entered by a user, click Restrict Editing in the Protect group on the Developer tab. Select *Allow only this type of editing in the document* from the Restrict Editing pane, shown in Figure 5.28, and click the arrow below. Select an editing type and click the command to begin enforcing protection. Enter and confirm a password, or click OK to bypass password protection. Unless absolutely necessary, you should consider not assigning a password because if you forget it the form will be unavailable for future editing. To remove protection from a form, click Restrict Editing to display the Restrict Editing pane if it is not already shown, and choose to stop protection, entering a password if required.

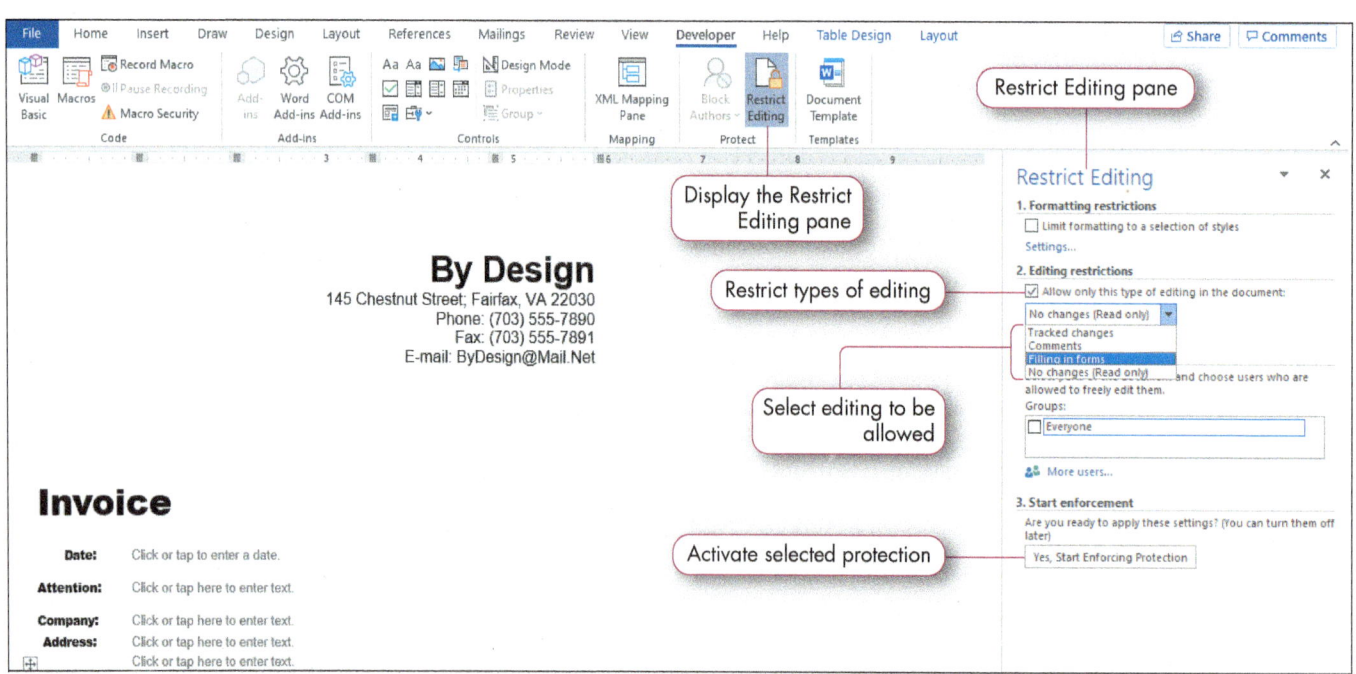

FIGURE 5.28 Restrict Editing in a Form

STEP 4 ## Complete an Electronic Form

After an electronic form is created and protected, you can begin to use it. The form can be opened in Word, and then the user can navigate the form and input the requested data. To do so, press Tab or click to move from one field to another. Some controls, such as Drop-Down Lists or Combo Boxes, may require that you click an arrow to display a list from which you make a selection.

Critical Thinking

7. Describe considerations required in developing a form that will be printed versus a form that will be accessed digitally. *p. 390*

8. Explain the purpose of using a bookmark when creating a field that is to be used in a calculation. *p. 394*

9. Describe areas of a form that are typically protected and provide rationale for such protection. *p. 396*

Hands-On Exercises

MyLab IT HOE3 Sim Training

Watch the Video for this Hands-On Exercise!

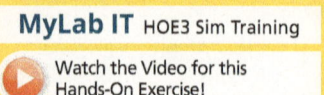

Skills covered: Insert Content Controls • Perform Calculations with Content Control Data • Protect an Entire Form • Complete an Electronic Form

3 Forms

Ms. Allen asks you to update and automate an invoice form for the Greenways retail store. Items of apparel as well as accessories with the Greenways logo are sold to businesses and individuals, along with other souvenirs. Such sales help the nonprofit achieve its goals of preserving green spaces in the area. You begin by inserting content controls and using automated calculations to summarize numeric data. When the form is complete, you protect the content and structure of the form so that only certain areas can be modified. Finally, you enter data in the newly completed form.

STEP 1 INSERT CONTENT CONTROLS

You are given a document to use as a starting point in developing an invoice form. You insert form controls for customer name, address, and sales date in the document. Refer to Figure 5.29 as you complete Step 1.

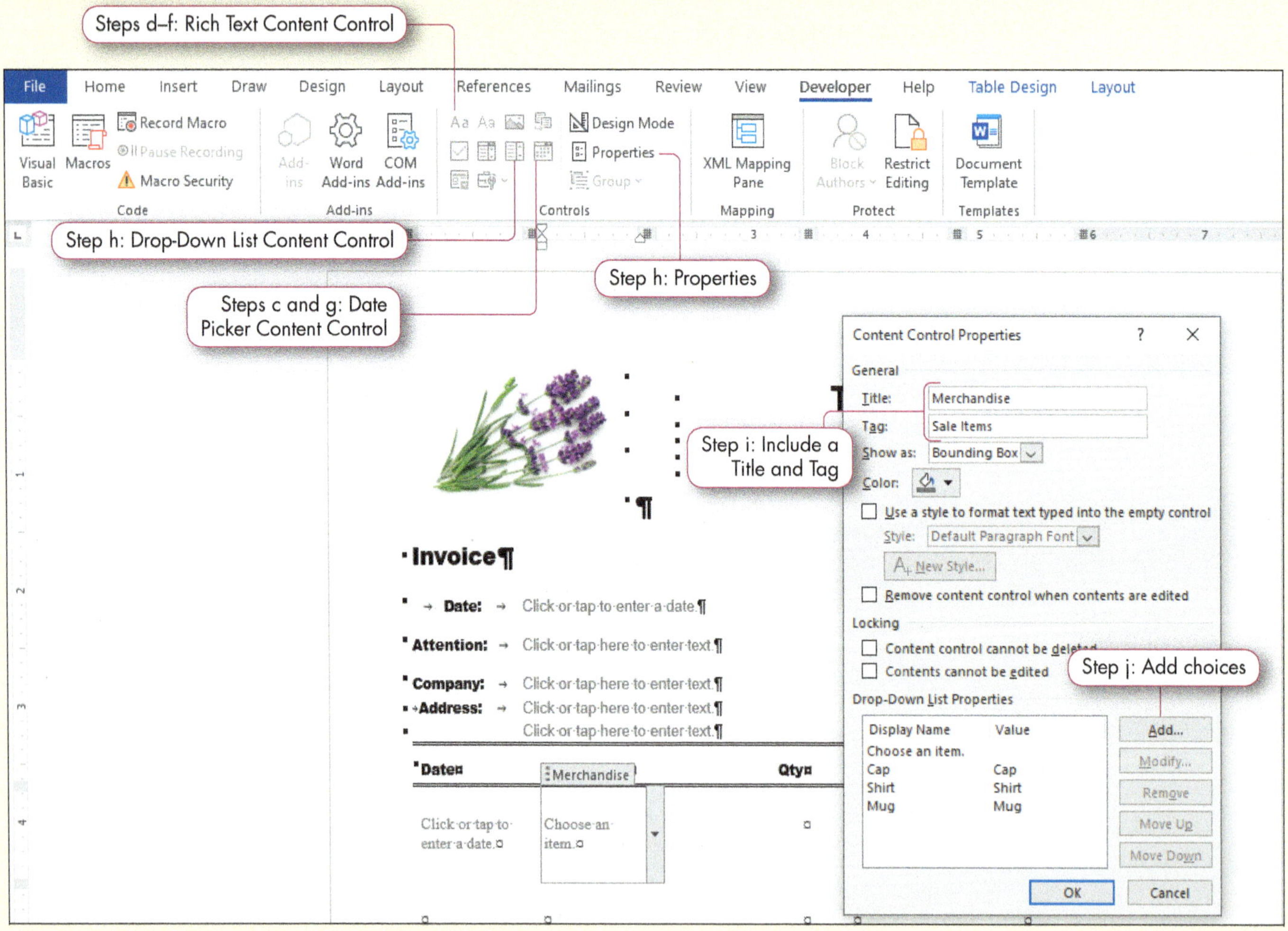

FIGURE 5.29 Insert Content Controls

a. Right-click a blank area of the ribbon and click **Customize the Ribbon**. Select the **Developer option** in the right pane (or confirm that it is already selected) and click **OK**.

> **MAC TROUBLESHOOTING:** To display the Developer tab, click Word and select Preferences. Click Ribbon & Toolbar. Select Developer and click Save.

b. Open *w05h3GreenwaysInvoice.docx* and save the document as **w05h3Greenways Invoice_LastFirst**. Ensure that nonprinting characters are displayed. Click the **View tab** and change the view to **Print Layout**.

c. Click before the paragraph mark after *Date:*. Click the **Developer tab**. Click **Date Picker Content Control** in the Controls group.

The control for choosing a date displays with a light border and the text *Click or tap to enter a date*.

> **MAC TROUBLESHOOTING:** To insert a content control for a date, click Text Box on the Developer tab. Click Options. In the Text Form Field Options dialog box, click the Type arrow and select Date. Click the Date format arrow and select a date format (m/d/yy). Click OK.

d. Click before the paragraph mark after *Attention:*. Click **Rich Text Content Control** in the Controls group.

The control for entering text displays with a light border and the text *Click or tap here to enter text*.

> **MAC TROUBLESHOOTING:** To insert a content control for text, click Text Box on the Developer tab.

e. Repeat the process described in Step d to insert Rich Text content controls after *Company:* and *Address:*.

f. Click before the paragraph mark below *Address*. Click **Rich Text Content Control** in the Controls group.

You insert another text control for the City, State, and Zip code portions of the address.

g. Click the first blank cell on the second row of the table, below *Date*. Click **Date Picker Content Control** from the Controls group. Click the next cell on the right, below *Description*.

> **MAC TROUBLESHOOTING:** To insert a content control for a date, click Text Box on the Developer tab. Click Options. In the Text Form Field Options dialog box, click the Type arrow and select Date. Click the Date format arrow and select a date format (m/d/yy). Click OK.

h. Click **Drop-Down List Content Control** in the Controls group. Click **Properties** in the Controls group to display the Content Control Properties dialog box.

Users will select from a predefined list of products when selecting this control.

> **MAC TROUBLESHOOTING:** To insert a list of items, click Combo Box. Click Options. Change the bookmark name to Items. With the insertion point in the Drop-down item box, proceed to Step j.

i. Type **Merchandise** in the Title box. Type **Sale Items** in the Tag box.

Although the inclusion of a Title and Tag is optional, the Merchandise text that you include as a Title will display in a tab attached to the control in the Word document. It serves as an identifier of the type of data you will be selecting from if you click the arrow beside the content control. Including text as a Tag—Sale Items, in this case—provides access to the control if its data ever needs to be collected within a computer program (or otherwise located and identified).

j. Click **Add** in the Drop-Down List Properties section to display the Add Choice dialog box. Type **Cap** in the Display Name box and click **OK**.

> **MAC TROUBLESHOOTING:** Type Cap in the Drop-down item box and click +.

k. Repeat the process in Step j to add two more types of merchandise: **Shirt** and **Mug**.

l. Click **OK**. Save the document.

STEP 2 PERFORM CALCULATIONS WITH CONTENT CONTROL DATA

The next section of the invoice reflects the quantity, unit price, and amount paid for products. Because these content controls are numeric, you identify them as such when you insert the content controls and modify their properties. In doing so, you make them available for use in a calculation. You include a content control, identified as a calculation, to determine amount paid, and you include a total to sum the total amount paid. Refer to Figure 5.30 as you complete Step 2.

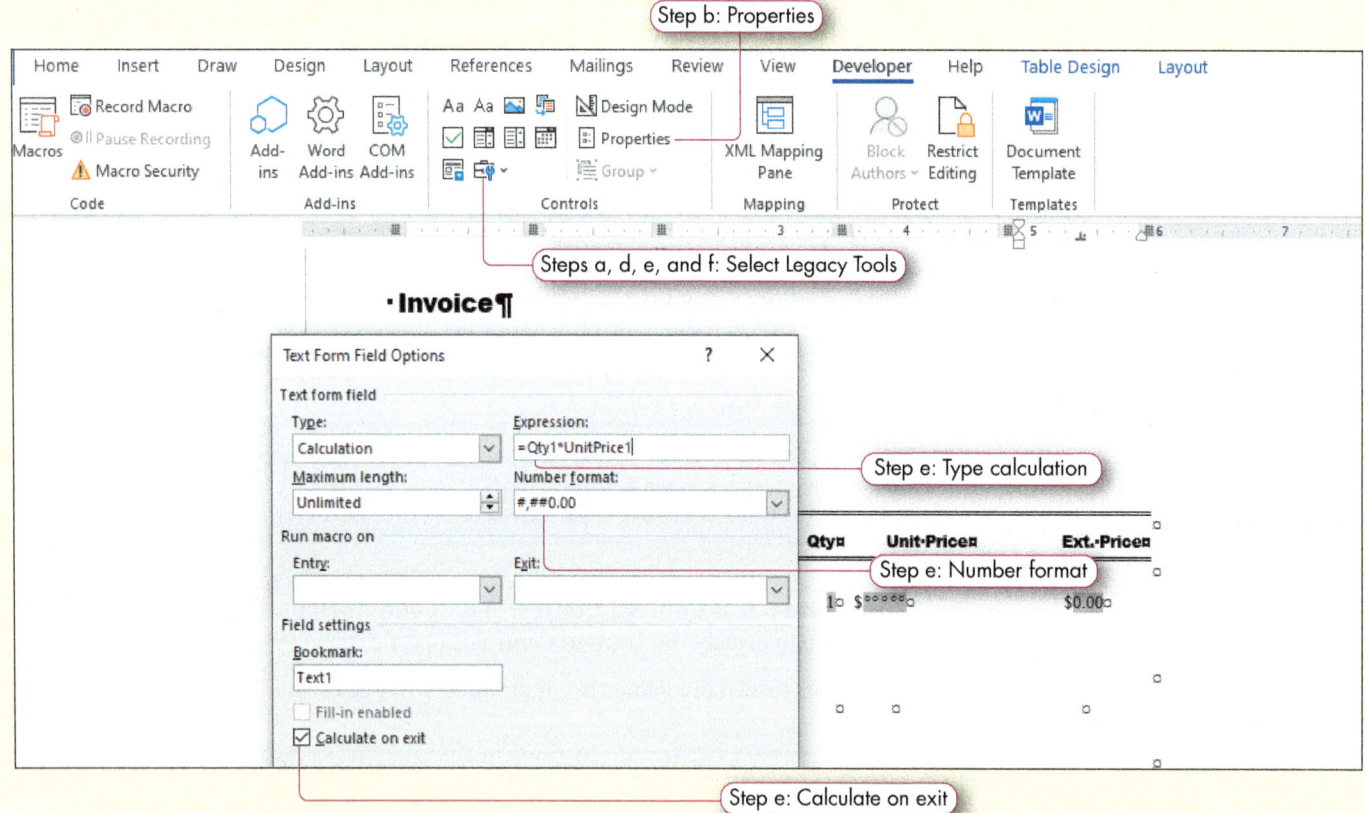

FIGURE 5.30 Perform Calculations

a. Click the cell below *Qty*. Click **Legacy Tools** in the Controls group and click **Text Form Field** in the *Legacy Forms* section. (On a Mac, click Text Box.)

A Text Form Field, which is included in the Legacy Tools collection, is used when a form is to include numeric data, especially if it is to be used in a calculation. You can specify that the field is to only contain numbers and you can also identify it as a calculation.

b. Click **Properties** (on a Mac, click Options) in the Controls group. Click the **Type arrow** and select **Number**. Type **1** in the *Default number* box.

Because the value in the field is expected to most often be 1, setting it as a default value should minimize typing required of a user entering form data.

c. Click in the **Bookmark box**, remove any existing text, and then type **Qty1**. Ensure that there is no space between *Qty* and *1*. Click to select the **Calculate on exit check box** and click **OK**.

Assigning a bookmark name to the field ensures that it can be used in a subsequent calculation. You select *Calculate on exit* to ensure that calculations are updated after values are entered.

d. Click after the dollar sign in the cell below *Unit Price*. Click **Legacy Tools** in the Controls group and select **Text Form Field** in the Legacy Forms section. (On a Mac, click Text Box.) Click **Properties**. (On a Mac, click Options.) Click the **Type arrow** and select **Number**. Click the **Number format arrow**, and select **#,##0.00**. Remove any existing text and type **UnitPrice1** in the Bookmark box. Ensure that there is no space between *UnitPrice* and *1*. Click to select the **Calculate on exit check box** and confirm that *Fill-in enabled* is selected. Click **OK**.

The selected number format ensures that the result is shown with a comma if needed and two places to the right of the decimal place.

e. Click after the dollar sign in the cell below *Ext. Price* and click **Legacy Tools** in the Controls group. Click **Text Form Field**. (On a Mac, click Text Box.) Click **Properties** (on a Mac, click Options) and change the type to **Calculation**. Type **Qty1*UnitPrice1** after the equal sign in the Expression box. Select the number format **#,##0.00** in the Number format list. Click to select the **Calculate on exit check box**. Click **OK**.

The equal sign in the Expression box indicates that a formula is to follow. The formula multiplies the value in the Qty1 field by the value of the UnitPrice1 field. Because you assigned bookmark names to the fields, you can use the bookmark names in the formula.

f. Click the far-right cell on the *Total* row, at the bottom of the *Ext. Price* column. Click **Legacy Tools** in the Controls group and click **Text Form Field**. (On a Mac, click Text Box.) Right-click the new shaded field and select **Properties**. Change the type to **Calculation**. Type **sum(above)** after the equal sign in the Expression box. Select the number format **$#,##0.00;($#,##0.00)**. Click **OK**.

You use the sum(above) function to total all values in the Ext. Price column. The result displays as a dollar value with two decimal places. Negative values are reflected in parentheses.

g. Save the document.

Your changes to the invoice form are almost complete. You add a check box for the type of payment so that a user can easily indicate a method of payment. You protect the form to enable only those edits that are necessary. That way, the only changes that can be made are to those areas that are meant to collect variable data. Refer to Figure 5.31 as you complete Step 3.

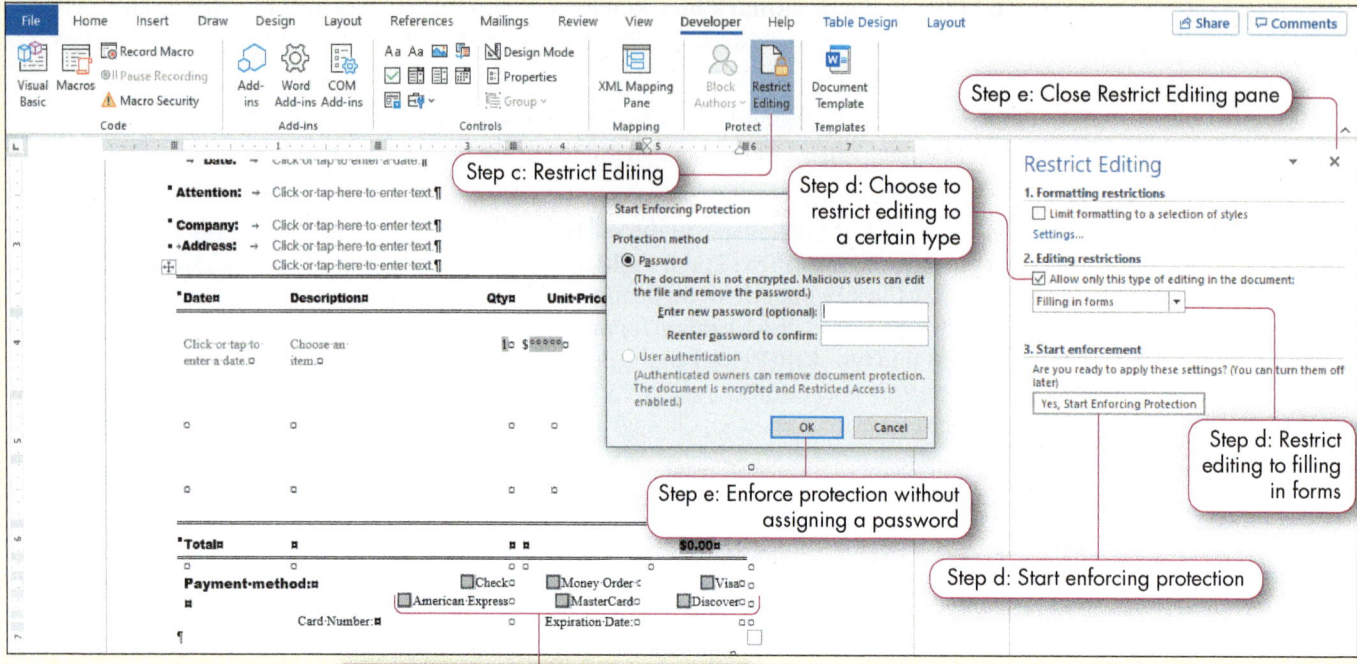

FIGURE 5.31 Protect a Form

a. Click before *Check* in the *Payment method* section near the bottom of the form. Click **Legacy Tools** and click **Check Box Form Field** in the *Legacy Forms* section. Be sure to select the Check Box control from the Legacy Forms collection, not the ActiveX Controls.

This action inserts a check box at the left of the *Check* payment method section. A user can select the check box if paying by check. You choose to insert a Legacy Tools Check Box Form Field instead of a Check Box Content Control. Although either choice results in a check box, the Legacy Tools check box is available for data entry only when the form is protected, as described in Step d.

b. Click before *Money Order*, click **Legacy Tools**, and then click **Check Box Form Field** in the *Legacy Forms* section. Add a Check Box Form Field for *Visa*, *American Express*, *MasterCard*, and *Discover*.

c. Click **Restrict Editing** in the Protect group.

The Restrict Editing pane displays.

> **MAC TROUBLESHOOTING:** Click Protect Form and proceed to Step 4.

d. Click to select **Allow only this type of editing in the document**, which displays in the *Editing restrictions* section. Click the arrow in the box below this option and select **Filling in forms**. Click **Yes, Start Enforcing Protection**.

> **TROUBLESHOOTING:** If selections in the Restrict Editing pane are grayed out, click Design Mode in the Controls group to toggle the selection.

e. Click **OK** to close the Password dialog box without setting a password. Close the Restrict Editing pane.

The only areas in the document that are available for editing are the content controls. Therefore, a user can fill in the form but cannot change other text.

f. Save the document.

To test the electronic form, you enter fictional data into the form to ensure that calculations work correctly. Refer to Figure 5.32 as you complete Step 4.

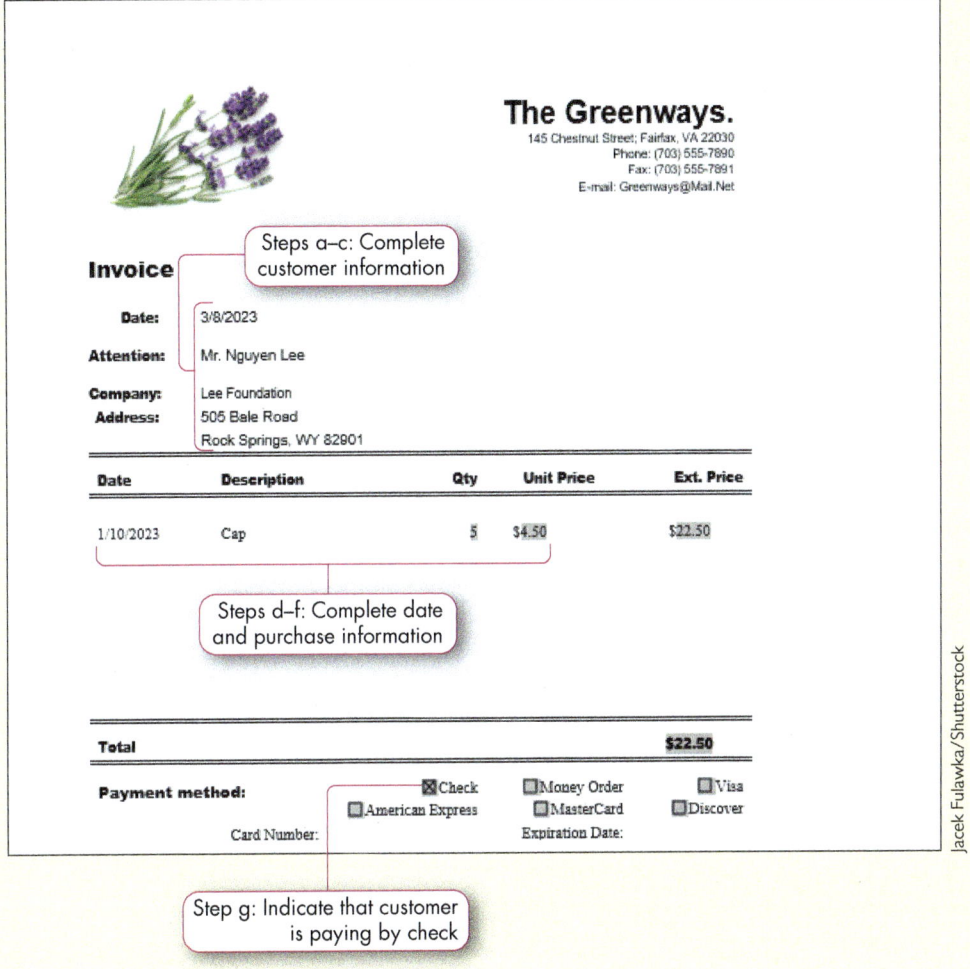

FIGURE 5.32 Complete a Form

a. Click the words *Click or tap to enter a date* near the top of the document and click the arrow. Select **Today**. (On a Mac, type today's date in the mm/dd/yyyy format.)

b. Click the words **Click or tap here to enter text**, beside *Attention*, and type **Mr. Nguyen Lee**. Press **down arrow** to move to the next field in the column.

c. Type **Lee Foundation** and press **down arrow**. Type **505 Bale Road** and press the **down arrow**. Type **Rock Springs, WY 82901** and press the **down arrow**.

d. Click the **date arrow** and select **January 10** of the current year. (On a Mac, type the date in the mm/dd/yyyy format.)

e. Click **Choose an item** on the second row of the table under *Description*, click the arrow, and select **Cap**.

f. Double-click **1** in the *Qty* field on row 1, type **5** and then press **Tab**. Type **4.50** and press **Tab**.

When you tab beyond the *Unit price* field, the Ext. Price and Total fields automatically calculate.

g. Click the check box beside *Check*.

The customer is paying by check.

h. Save and close the document. Exit Word. Based on your instructor's directions, submit:

w05h1Greenways_LastFirst
w05h2Greenways_LastFirst.html
w05h3GreenwaysInvoice_LastFirst

Chapter Objectives Review

After reading this chapter, you have accomplished the following objectives:

1. Design a newsletter.

- **Develop overall document layout:** Good design helps convey a message effectively. Envisioning a grid, in which a document page is divided into columns, can help achieve design excellence.
- **Apply and modify column layout:** As is often the case with newsletters, text can be arranged in multiple columns. Columns can be modified in size and placement.

2. Apply design features.

- **Create a masthead:** A masthead displays at the top of a document, serving as a title. A masthead is often formatted in a one-column format and in a larger or more colorful font to draw attention to the purpose of the newsletter.
- **Create a drop cap:** A drop cap is a capital letter formatted in a font size larger than the body text. Drop caps are used to draw attention and add style to a newsletter or article.
- **Copy and link objects from other files:** A Word document can include either embedded or linked objects from other files, making it possible to refer to that content from within the document.
- **Create a pull quote or sidebar:** Both a pull quote and a sidebar are often included in a text box within a newsletter, drawing attention to important information.

3. Build a webpage.

- **Save a document as a webpage:** A Word document can be saved as a webpage. Several file types are available, based on HTML or MHTML format.
- **Apply a theme and background color to a webpage:** Applying a theme and a background to a Word webpage document enhances consistency and promotes a polished online appearance.
- **Insert bookmarks in a webpage or document:** A bookmark provides a location to which a link can direct. It is a named area, although the name does not display in the document text.

- **Insert hyperlinks in a webpage or document:** A hyperlink, or link, is a selected object or text that directs movement to another position within the same document or to another webpage, among other destinations.

4. Publish a webpage.

- **Preview and publish a webpage:** Before publishing a webpage, you should preview it as it would display online. You can use Web Layout view or you can use Word's Web Page Preview option. To publish a webpage, you will work with an online server.
- **Transform a Word document into a Sway webpage:** Sway is a Microsoft app that enables you to transform a Word document into a webpage, selecting from built-in design themes and formatting.

5. Create an electronic form.

- **Understand content controls:** Content controls provide placeholders in a document for variable data that a user will supply. Various types of content controls are available.
- **Insert content controls:** Content controls are inserted in a Word document to comprise a form or a collection of areas of variable data.
- **Perform calculations with content control data:** Forms are often designed to include form fields that automatically calculate results based on the content of other fields.

6. Enable form protection.

- **Protect individual content controls:** You can apply properties to a selected form field, protecting it against deletion or modification.
- **Protect an entire form:** A form is often designed so that fields are available for data entry, but all other content is protected.
- **Complete an electronic form:** A form is designed for data entry. Upon completion, a form template is available for use electronically or in print.

Key Terms Matching

Match the key terms with their definitions. Write the key term letter by the appropriate numbered definition.

a. Background
b. Bookmark
c. Check Box content control
d. Combo Box content control
e. Content control
f. Date Picker content control
g. Design Mode
h. Drop cap
i. Drop-Down List content control
j. Embedding

k. Form
l. Hyperlink
m. Hypertext Markup Language (HTML)
n. Legacy Tools
o. Masthead
p. Object Linking and Embedding (OLE)
q. Plain Text content control
r. Rich Text content control
s. Webpage
t. World Wide Web (WWW)

1. _____ Combines a text box with a list box so that a user may choose from items displayed in a drop-down box or can type an entry instead of selecting from the list. **p. 392**

2. _____ Enables data entry of a small amount of text that is readable by any text or file editor, but does not allow entry of other items, such as images and tables. **p. 392**

3. _____ Displays a calendar from which a user can select a date. **p. 392**

4. _____ The identifying information at the top of a newsletter. **p. 362**

5. _____ Enables data entry of formatted text, images, and tables. **p. 392**

6. _____ Consists of a box that is checked or unchecked to represent a preference or condition. **p. 392**

7. _____ A block on a form that provides a location for user interaction, just as a paper document would include blanks to be filled in. **p. 391**

8. _____ A process that brings an object or data from another application or file into a document without retaining a connection to the source data. **p. 363**

9. _____ A named electronic marker for a specific location within a document. **p. 379**

10. _____ A very large capital letter at the beginning of a paragraph. **p. 363**

11. _____ Displays a list of several options from which a user can choose. **p. 392**

12. _____ Specialized documents found on the World Wide Web. **p. 374**

13. _____ Item that enables access to other webpages or other areas or resources within the current website or document. **p. 378**

14. _____ A color, design, image, or watermark that displays behind text in a document or on a webpage. **p. 378**

15. _____ Setting that enables you to select control fields, positioning them in a document so you can make any necessary modifications to their layout or options. **p. 393**

16. _____ Specialized code that tells a Web browser how to display text and images on a page. **p. 374**

17. _____ An online document that is designed to collect data. **p. 390**

18. _____ The feature that enables you to insert and link objects from different applications into a Word document. **p. 363**

19. _____ Collection of controls that were originally developed in versions of Word prior to 2007. **p. 392**

20. _____ A very large subset of the Internet. **p. 374**

Multiple Choice

1. Which of the following is a file type that includes a folder with resources related to a Word document that is saved as a webpage?
   (a) Word Web
   (b) Single Web Page
   (c) PDF
   (d) Web Page, Filtered

2. What color combination comprises a reverse masthead?
   (a) Light text on a clear background
   (b) Dark text on a clear background
   (c) Dark text on a light background
   (d) Light text on a dark background

3. What must you keep in mind when creating a password to provide access to restricted areas of a form?
   (a) A password cannot be deleted after it is set.
   (b) If you forget the password, the form is permanently unavailable.
   (c) You must identify a password that is approved by the IRM.
   (d) A password cannot be changed after it has been established.

4. Which of the following balances columns so that each column contains approximately the same amount of text?
   (a) Insert a Continuous section break at the end of the last column.
   (b) Insert a page break at the end of the last column.
   (c) Manually set column lengths in the Columns dialog box.
   (d) Press Enter until the text lines up at the bottom of each column.

5. Which type of content control enables a user to select from a list of options or type an option that might not be on the list?
   (a) Drop-Down List content control
   (b) Rich Text content control
   (c) Combo Box content control
   (d) Form field

6. As related to form design, what is a content control used for?
   (a) Restricting editing to specific areas of a form
   (b) Enabling a document to be saved as a template
   (c) Providing a placeholder for variable data that a user will supply
   (d) Identifying one or more people who can edit all or specific parts of a restricted document

7. What is a pull quote?
   (a) A type of reverse masthead
   (b) A phrase or sentence taken from an article to emphasize a key point
   (c) A section of text that is linked from one text box to the next
   (d) A phrase that is usually formatted as a WordArt object

8. Why would you consider changing a field's instructional text?
   (a) To more clearly define a field's intended contents
   (b) So that you can modify the field type
   (c) To ensure that a field can be included in a calculation
   (d) To ensure that the field is accessible to all

9. Which of the following processes inserts content from an Excel worksheet in a way that updates the Excel content in the Word document when the worksheet data changes (and when you update the item)?
   (a) Embedding
   (b) Copying and inserting
   (c) Linking
   (d) Find and replace

10. Which of the following differentiates publishing a Word document as a webpage on a server and transforming a Word document into a Sway document?
    (a) Using Sway, you do not actually manage a website, as the webpage is housed in the cloud on a Microsoft server.
    (b) Using Sway, you do not have access to themes or design settings.
    (c) You have more file type options when you save a document as a Sway webpage.
    (d) You cannot preview a Word document as a webpage, although that feature is available with a Sway webpage.

Practice Exercises

1 Real Estate Appraisal

You are a real estate appraiser who estimates the value of residential homes. At the end of each week, you must submit a report to your supervisor of the properties you appraised during the past seven days. You decide to create a form that you can fill out quickly, even while you are on location with your laptop or tablet. You have a document containing a table for the information, which you decide to automate using form fields. Refer to Figure 5.33 as you complete this exercise.

Real Estate Appraisal Tracking Report

Completed by: Student Name
Week ending: 4/29/2023

Address	City	State	Zip	Appraised Value	Date
1387 E. Main St.	Choose an item.	NH	Choose an item.	$129,900.00	4/29/2023
8977 N. Fremont Ave.	Choose an item.	NH	Choose an item.	$229,000.00	4/28/2023
14 Willings Way	Choose an item.	NH	Choose an item.	$258,000.00	4/28/2023
Click or tap here to enter text.	Choose an item.	NH	Choose an item.		Click or tap to enter a date.
			Total Value of Appraisals	$616,900.00	

FIGURE 5.33 Real Estate Appraisal Form

a. Open *w05p1Appraisal* and save the file as **w05p1Appraisal_LastFirst**. Ensure that nonprinting characters are displayed. Right-click an empty area on the ribbon and select **Customize the Ribbon**. Select **Developer** in the right pane, unless it is already selected. Click **OK**.

> **MAC TROUBLESHOOTING:** Select Preferences from the Word menu and click Ribbon & Toolbar (under Authoring and Proofing Tools). Select the Developer check box in the Customize the Ribbon section.

b. Click before the paragraph mark after *Completed by* (after the two spaces). Click the **Developer tab** and click **Rich Text Content Control** in the Controls group. (On a Mac, click Text Box.)

c. Click before the paragraph mark after *Week ending* (after the two spaces). Click **Date Picker Content Control** in the Controls group. Insert a Date Picker content control in each cell in the *Date* column in the table (excluding the Total Value of Appraisals row). Row height will automatically adjust in each of the four rows affected.

> **MAC TROUBLESHOOTING:** Click Text Box. Click Options. In the Text Form Field Options box, click the Type arrow and select Date. Click the Date format arrow and select a date format (m/d/yy). Click OK.

d. Click the first cell in the second row of the table (the *Address* column). Click **Rich Text Content Control** in the Controls group. (On a Mac, click Text Box.) Insert Rich Text content controls in each of the remaining cells in the *Address* column (excluding the Total Value of Appraisals row).

e. Click the second cell in the second row of the table (the *City* column). Click **Drop-Down List Content Control** in the Controls group. Populate the drop-down list as follows:
   • Click **Properties** in the Controls group.
   • Type **City** in the Title box. Type **Address** in the Tag box.
   • Click **Add** in the Content Control Properties dialog box. Type **Amherst**. (Do not include a period.) Click **OK**.
   • Click **Add**. Type **Epping**. Click **OK**.
   • Continue the process to add two more cities—**Mount Vernon** and **Nashua**. Click **OK** to close the dialog box.

> **MAC TROUBLESHOOTING:** Click Combo Box. Click Options. Change the bookmark name to Address. With the insertion point in the Drop-down item box, type Amherst and click +. Repeat the process to add other cities.

f. Add a Drop-Down List Content Control for each of the remaining three rows in the *City* column (excluding the Total Value of Appraisals row). Each row in the City column should be formatted as described in Step e.

g. Click the third cell in the second row of the table (the *State* column). Type **NH**. Repeat the state abbreviation in each of the remaining three rows of the State column (excluding the Total Value of Appraisals row).

h. Click the fourth cell in the second row of the table (the *Zip* column). Click **Drop-Down List Content Control** in the Controls group. Click **Properties** in the Controls group. Populate the drop-down list as follows:
   • Type **Zip** in both the Title and Tag box.
   • Click **Add** in the Content Control Properties dialog box. Type **03031**. Click **OK**.
   • Click **Add**. Type **03042**. Click **OK**.
   • Add two additional zip codes, **03057** and **03060**.

> **MAC TROUBLESHOOTING:** Click Combo Box. Click Options. Change the bookmark name to Zip. With the insertion point in the Drop-down item box, type 03031 and click +. Repeat the process to add other zip codes.

i. Repeat the process of adding a Drop-Down List content control for each of the remaining three cells in the *Zip* column (excluding the Total Value of Appraisals row), populating each with the data described in Step h.

j. Click the fifth cell in the second row of the table (the *Appraised Value* column). Click **Legacy Tools** in the Controls group and select **Text Form Field**. (On a Mac, click Text Box.) Format the field as follows:
  - Click **Properties** (on a Mac, click Options) in the Controls group.
  - Select **Number** as the type and select a Number format of **$#,##0.00;($#,##0.00)**.
  - Select **Calculate on exit**. Click **OK**.

k. Place a Text Form Field in each of the remaining three cells in the Appraised Value column (excluding the Total Value of Appraisals row) and format each as described in Step j.

l. Click in the second column of the last row (the *Appraised Value* column). Click **Legacy Tools** in the Controls group and select **Text Form Field**. (On a Mac, click Text Box.) Format the field as follows:
  - Click **Properties** (on a Mac, click Options) in the Controls group.
  - Select **Calculation** as the type and select a Number format of **$#,##0.00;($#,##0.00)**.
  - Click after the equal sign in the Expression box and type **sum(above)**. Select **Calculate on exit**. Click **OK**.

m. Click **Restrict Editing** in the Protect group on the Developer tab. Protect the form as follows:
  - Select **Allow only this type of editing in the document:**
  - Click the arrow beside *No changes (Read only)* and click **Filling in forms**.
  - Click **Yes, Start Enforcing Protection**.
  - Click **OK** without typing a password.

> **MAC TROUBLESHOOTING:** Click Protect Form. Skip all bulleted items above.

n. Complete the form with the following information:
  - Type your name in the **Completed by control**.
  - Select **Today** in the control for *Week ending*. (If using a Mac, type today's date in the mm/dd/yyyy format.)
  - Type the following information into the first three table rows.

Address	City	State	Zip	Appraised Value	Date
1387 E. Main St.	Epping	NH	03042	129,900	Today
8977 N. Fremont Ave.	Nashua	NH	03060	229,000	Yesterday's Date
14 Willings Way	Mount Vernon	NH	03057	258,000	Yesterday's Date

o. Click a value outside the current cell (in the Appraised Value column) to update the total value. Click **Stop Protection** in the Restrict Editing pane. Close the Restrict Editing pane.

> **MAC TROUBLESHOOTING:** Click Protect Form to toggle off the setting.

p. Save and close the file. Exit Word. Based on your instructor's directions, submit: w05p1Appraisal_LastFirst

Your family owns a small realty firm, TA Realty, in the lake district of North Carolina. Many of your clients seek rental homes or condos on the lakes, so you specialize in promotion of that type of property. A local publication is accepting one-page flyers from businesses in the area, so you plan to prepare a page to promote the rental of lake property. You use Word to design a flyer containing columns and objects that are formatted attractively. Saving the document as a webpage, in addition, you prepare the flyer for display online. Refer to Figure 5.34 as you complete this exercise.

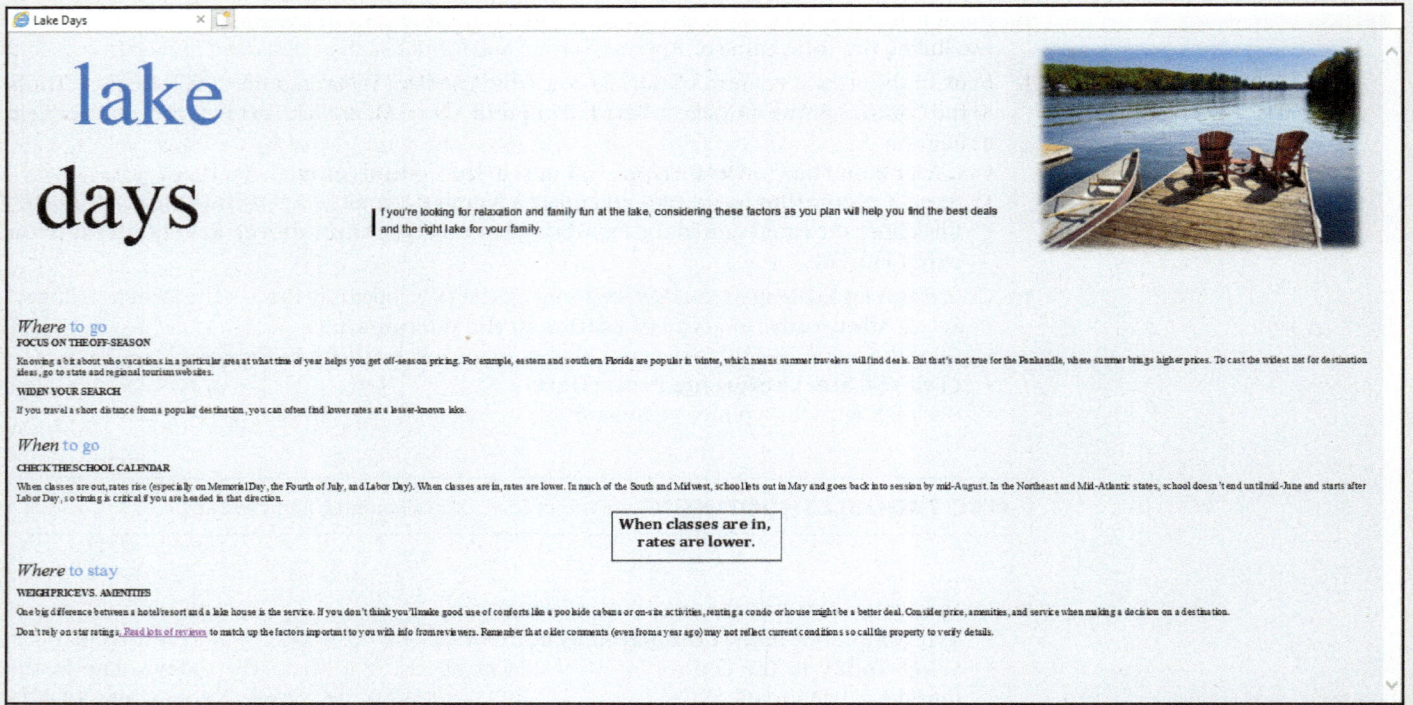

FIGURE 5.34 Lake Days Website

a. Open *w05p2Lake* and save the document as **w05p2Lake_LastFirst**. Ensure that nonprinting characters are displayed.

b. Ensure the insertion point is at the beginning of the document. Insert *w05p2Lake.jpg*. Change the width to **4.5"** and apply the **Soft Edge Rectangle picture style**. Click **Position** in the Arrange group on the Picture Format tab and select **Position in Top Right with Square Text Wrapping**.

c. Click the **Insert tab** and click **Text Box** in the Text group. Click **Draw Text Box** and click at the first paragraph mark at the top of the page. Change the text box height to **3.5** and the width to **4.5**. Click the **Layout tab** and remove any paragraph spacing.

d. Type **lake** in the text box, press **Enter**, and then type **days**. Correct the word *lake* so that the first letter is in lowercase. Change the font size of text in the text box to **90** and change the font to **Times New Roman**.

e. Click before the word *lake* and press **Tab**. Select the word *lake* and change the font color to **Orange, Accent 2, Darker 25%** (row 5, column 6). Click the **Shape Format tab**, click **Shape Fill** in the Shape Styles group, and then select **No Fill**. Click **Shape Outline** and select **No Outline**. Click **Position** in the Arrange group and select **Position in Top Center with Square Text Wrapping**.

f. Select all of the text below the first body paragraph, beginning with *Where to go* and ending at the end of the document. Click the **Layout tab**, click **Columns**, and then select **Three**.

g. Click before the words *Where to stay* in the second column. Click **Breaks** in the Page Setup group and click **Column**. Click before the words *When to go* near the end of the first column or at the top of the second column. Insert a column break.

h. Select the word **Where** in the heading line of the first column. Click the **Home tab**. Double-click **Format Painter** in the Clipboard group. Double-click the word **When** in the heading at the top of the second column and double-click the word **Where** in the heading at the top of the third column. Press **Esc**.

i. Select the words **to go** in the heading line of the first column. Double-click **Format Painter** in the Clipboard group. Drag to paint the format on the words *to go* in the heading at the top of the second column. Drag to paint the format on the words *to stay* in the heading at the top of the third column. Press **Esc**.

j. Bold the subheadings **FOCUS ON THE OFF-SEASON, WIDEN YOUR SEARCH, CHECK THE SCHOOL CALENDAR**, and **WEIGH PRICE VS. AMENITIES**. Deselect any selected text.

k. Click before the first body paragraph, beginning with *If you're looking for relaxation*. Click the **Insert tab** and click **Add a Drop Cap** in the Text group. Select **Drop Cap Options**. Click **Dropped**. Adjust the *Lines to drop* setting to **2**. Click **OK**.

l. Click **Text Box** in the Text group, and then click **Draw Text Box**. Click anywhere in the first column to place the text box. Change the height in the Size group on the Shape Format tab to **0.7** and adjust the width to **2.3**.

m. Copy the second sentence in the middle column, *When classes are in, rates are lower*. Paste the copied sentence in the text box. Center text in the text box. Change font size to **16**. **Bold** the text in the shape, including the period.

n. Change the text box font to **Cambria**. Drag the text box to position it immediately below the Column break indicator in the middle column. Click the **Shape Format tab**. Click **Align** in the Arrange group and select **Align Center**.

o. Check spelling and correct any errors. Ignore any grammatical or refinement errors. Click the **View tab** and select **One Page** in the Zoom group. If the document spans two pages, with the second page blank, remove any extra paragraph marks to return to only one page. Return the view to **100%**. Save the document.

p. Select **Web Layout** in the Views group, adjusting the view to 100% if necessary. Adjust formatting as follows:
- Click the **Design tab** and click **Page Color** in the Page Background group. Select **Gold, Accent 4, Lighter 80%** (row 2, column 8).
- Click **Themes** and select **Wisp**. Click **Colors** and select **Blue Warm**.
- Select the text box containing the sentence, click the **Shape Format tab**, click **Shape Fill**, and select **No Fill**.

q. Scroll to the last paragraph on the page and select the text *Read lots of reviews* in the second to last sentence. Create a hyperlink as follows:
- Click the **Insert tab**. Click **Link** (not the Link arrow) in the Links group.
- Ensure that *Existing File or Web Page* is selected. Type **https://tripadvisor.com** in the Address box. Click **OK**. Point to the link, hold **Ctrl**, and click the link. (On a Mac, click the link.) A browser window should open to the Tripadvisor page. Close the browser.

r. Click the **File tab** and click **Save As**. Save the file as a Word Document with the filename **w05p2Lake_LastFirst**.

s. Click the **File tab** and click **Save As**. Click **Browse** and ensure that the save location is what you use for student files. Change the filename to **w05p2LakeWeb_LastFirst**. Click **Save as type** and select **Single File Web Page**. Click **Change Title**. Type **Lake Days** and click **OK**. Click **Save**.

> **MAC TROUBLESHOOTING:** Click the File menu, click Properties, and click Summary to change the title.

t. Close the document. Exit Word. Based on your instructor's directions, submit:
w05p2LakeWeb_LastFirst.mhtml
w05p2Lake_LastFirst

Mid-Level Exercises

1 Response Team

MyLab IT **Grader**

You are a volunteer with the American Response Team, a global disaster response organization. Your primary responsibility is the development of various publications for print and online access. This project involves the development of a two-page document summarizing the organization's efforts at worldwide disaster relief. You start with a webpage document that was previously begun, although you will modify it to include additional formatting and links. You will then save it as a Word document.

a. Navigate to *w05m1Response.mhtml* in your student files and double-click the file to open it in a browser. Scroll through the document to view its contents. Close the browser window.

b. Open Word. Open *w05m1Response.mhtml* from your student files. Ensure that the view is Print Layout. Ensure that nonprinting characters are displayed.

c. Select all text from the *Preparing for Disaster* heading (not the text with a check mark) through the paragraph near the end of page 2, ending in *www.artdisastercenter.org*. Do not select the Section Break indicator and do not select the text box. Format the selected text in two columns with a line between. Do not deselect the text.

d. Change the font of all selected text to **Bookman Old Style 14 pt**.

e. Remove the background color from the document. Select the *Preparing for Disaster* heading that precedes the first body paragraph on page 1 (not the heading with the checkmark before). Insert a bookmark titled **Preparation**. Add bookmarks to other headings as follows. Be sure to add the bookmark to a heading, not a checkmarked item.

Text	Bookmark
Strengthening Communities	Communities
Response Readiness	Response
Developing a Worldwide Disaster Preparedness Center	Worldwide

f. Select the first checked item on page 1, *Preparing for Disaster*. Insert a link to the Preparation bookmark in the same document. Insert links for all other checked items on page 1, using the corresponding items in the table above as destination bookmarks.

g. Save the document with the filename **w05m1Response_LastFirst**, changing the file type to **Word Document**.

h. Point to the *Response Readiness* link on page 1, press and hold **Ctrl**, and click the link. (On a Mac, click the link.) The insertion point should be moved to the corresponding bookmark. Draw a small text box in the paragraph below the *Response Readiness* heading. Size the text box to a height of **0.8** and a width of **2.9**. Change text wrapping to **Square** and align the text box in the middle and in the center of the page.

i. Copy the first sentence in the Response Readiness section, *ART and its Star Partners are everywhere disaster strikes.* Paste the copied sentence in the text box. Change the font color of text in the text box to **Green, Accent 6, Darker 25%** and bold the text.

j. Insert a drop cap before the first body paragraph in the columned arrangement on page 1, beginning with *Global trends such as rapid population*. Select **Drop Cap Options** and click **Dropped**. Select **2** as the number of lines to drop.

> **MAC TROUBLESHOOTING:** Click the Format menu, select Drop Cap, and then click Dropped.

k. Click after the last paragraph in the Strengthening Communities section on page 2, ending in *preparedness of our community inspires us*. Press **Enter**. Link to another file as follows:
- Open the Excel workbook *w05m1Partners* and save it as **w05m1Partners_LastFirst**. Drag to select **cells A1 through C8**. Copy the selected cells.

- Return to the Word document. Click the **Paste arrow** in the Clipboard group on the Home tab and select **Paste Special**. Paste the link, selecting **Microsoft Excel Worksheet Object**.
- Return to the Excel workbook. Click **cell A7**. Type **CPR Basic Certification** and press **Enter**.
- Save and close the Excel workbook.
- Return to the Word document, right-click the inserted Excel worksheet and update the link. The Excel worksheet in the Word document should show the updated CPR heading.

l. Format all subheadings, *Preparing for Disaster, Strengthening Communities, Response Readiness,* and *Developing a Worldwide Disaster Preparedness Center* as bold, with a font color of Green, Accent 6, Darker 50%.

m. View the document in **Multiple Pages**. Note the heading at the bottom of the left column on the last page. Click before the heading, *Developing a Worldwide Disaster Preparedness Center* and insert a column break.

n. Save and close the document. Exit Word. Based on your instructor's directions, submit: w05m1Response_LastFirst

The O'Neal Society is a student campus group that is affiliated with the Admissions Office. Students who are selected for the Society are considered leaders who exemplify the best characteristics of scholarship and dedication. They serve as campus guides and are always present at home football games to serve as hosts and to collect money to help support the two live lion mascots. O'Neal Society students are assigned to various student captains, who manage scheduling and attendance at ball games. To assist in that task, you are developing a monthly schedule of captain assignments and the number of Lion banks that should be available for each game. The schedule is maintained as a Word form so that others can complete it as needed. By protecting the document from unnecessary editing, you assure that it is available in good form when needed.

a. Open *w05m2Assignments* and save the file as a **w05m2Assignments_LastFirst**. Ensure that nonprinting characters are displayed and that the Developer tab is displayed on the ribbon.

b. Insert a **Rich Text Content Control** in each cell in the first column of the *Fall 2023* table, from rows 2 through 6 (under the *Captain* heading). Insert a **Date Picker Content Control** in rows 2 through 6 of the second column (under the *Date* heading). (On a Mac, insert a Text Box for both the Captain and Date columns.)

c. Insert a **Combo Box Content Control** in rows 2 through 6 of the third column (under the *Flag Colors* heading). Values to add are **Purple, Gold, Crimson**, and **White**. It is not necessary to add a Title or Tag.

d. Insert a **Text Form Field** (from Legacy Tools) in rows 2 through 6 of the last column. The type is **Number**. There is no need to specify a number format. Be sure the field calculates on exit.

e. Add a row at the end of the table. Type **TOTAL** in the third cell on the new row. In the next cell on the same row, insert a **Text Form Field** (from Legacy Tools). The type is **Calculation**. The expression is **=sum(above)**. There is no need to specify a number format. Be sure the field calculates on exit.

f. Restrict editing to filling in forms. Start protection but do not apply a password. (On a Mac, click Protect Form.)

g. Click in the first cell of the second row of the *Fall 2023* table and type **Nazma Lee**. Text may be underlined. The date is **9/16/2023**. Flag color is **Gold**. Lion banks needed is **14**.

h. Complete the next two rows as shown below. Note that because the color of Blue is not included in the drop-down list that is presented, you must type it.

Mia Vest	9/23/2023	Purple	12
Clark Johnston	9/30/2023	Blue	15

i. Click the last cell on row 6 (immediately above the total) to force the total to recalculate. Stop protection. If text is underlined, select the entire table and remove the underline formatting.

j. Place the insertion point at the end of the document, on the second page. Open the *w05m2Captains* Excel workbook and save it as **w05m2Captains_LastFirst. S**elect **cells A1 through C5**. Copy the selection. Return to the Word document and paste the selection to the end of the Word document, creating a link to the Microsoft Excel Worksheet Object.

k. Return to the Excel workbook showing a list of the team captains. Jean Baxter cannot serve as a team captain so you will replace her. Change *Jean Baxter* to **Adrian Angelo** in the worksheet. Save the workbook and close it. Update the link in the Word document.

l. Change the background page color to **Blue, Accent 1, Lighter 80%**.

m. Save the document and close it. Exit Word. Based on your instructor's directions, submit: w05m2Assignments_LastFirst

Running Case

New Castle County Technical Services

New Castle County Technical Services (NCCTS) provides technical support for companies in the greater New Castle County, Delaware, area. NCCTS has been asked to participate in a technology fair at a local university. The fair is open to students and community members, many of whom are potential clients for New Castle's data and network solutions. You have been asked to take a rough draft of information related to data recovery solutions and use Word to create an attractive multi-page informational handout. You also plan to add a form that can be completed electronically to the flyer. That way, area businesses who already have an interest in your company can consider working with you to help make sure the job fair is a success—and they will have the added benefit of attracting qualified candidates for job opportunities. Finally, you will protect the document so that only certain changes can be made.

a. Open *w05r1NewCastle* and save it as **w05r1NewCastle_LastFirst**. Ensure that nonprinting characters are shown and that the Developer tab is included on the ribbon.

b. Select the first heading on page 1 (*New Castle County Technical Services*). Change the font to **Times New Roman** and change the font size to **24**. Bold the heading.

c. Click the **Borders arrow** in the Paragraph group on the Home tab and select **Borders and Shading**. Click the **Shading tab**. Click the **Style arrow** and select **Solid (100%).**

d. Select most text on page 1 and part of page 2, beginning with the first body paragraph (*At New Castle, we recover data…*) and ending before the heading *Preserving Data for the Life of Your Company*. Change the font to **Rockwell 12 pt**. For all the selected text, adjust paragraph spacing to **6 pt Before** and ensure that spacing **After** is **0 pt**.

e. Insert a page break before the heading near the bottom of page 2, *Preserving Data for the Life of Your Company*. Click before the first letter in the first body paragraph on page 3, *W*, and insert a drop cap, selecting **Dropped**.

> **MAC TROUBLESHOOTING:** Click the Format menu, select Drop Cap, and then click Dropped.

f. Select the sentence at the end of page 1, *We understand the importance of your company data and we'll do everything we can to retrieve your lost data*. Copy the selection. Scroll to page 5 and insert a text box, selecting **Austin Quote**. Paste the copied text in the text box.

> **MAC TROUBLESHOOTING:** Draw a text box anywhere on page 5, sizing it at 1.1" in height and 3.8" in width.

g. Drag the text box to position it under the last paragraph in the right column, above the page break. With the text box selected, click **Position** on the on the Shape Format tab in the Arrange group and select **More Layout Options**. Adjust the Horizontal absolute position to **4.4** to the right of Page and adjust the Vertical absolute position to **1.2** below Paragraph.

h. Check the spelling, correcting any spelling and grammatical mistakes. The words *cost effective* should be hyphenated. Ignore all other refinement concerns.

i. Scroll to the last page of the document. Insert a **Rich Text Content Control** after *Contact Name*, *Company*, *Phone*, and *Email*. Ensure that the content control is placed after the space that follows each item.

j. Click in the first cell on row 2, under the *Table Size Requested* heading and insert a **Drop-Down List Content Control**. (On a Mac, insert a Combo Box control.) Open Properties and add a Title of **Table**, with a Tag of **Size**. Add the following options: **8x3**, **5x3**, and **Standard Round**. Ensure that the content control cannot be deleted.

k. Click in the second cell on row 2, under the *Cost/Table* heading. Insert a **Text Form Field** from the Legacy Tools collection. Ensure that the type is **Number** and the default value is **125**. Change the bookmark to **Cost1** and ensure that it calculates on exit. You do not need to specify a number format.

l. Click in the third cell on row 2, under the *NCCTS Discount* heading. Insert a **Text Form Field** from the Legacy Tools collection. Ensure that the type is **Number** and the default value is **15**. Change the bookmark to **Discount1** and ensure that it calculates on exit. You do not need to specify a number format.

m. Click in the fourth cell on row 2, under the *Total* heading. Insert a **Text Form Field** from the Legacy Tools collection. The type should be **Calculation** and the formula should subtract the NCCTS discount from the table cost (use bookmark names in the calculation). The number format should be **$#,##0.00;($#,##0.00).**

n. Click in the fifth cell on row 2, under the *Need Setup Assistance* heading. Insert a **Drop-Down List Content Control** (on a Mac, insert a Combo Box content control and disregard the title and tag), with a title of **Setup** and a tag of **Setup**. Add two values, **Yes** and **No**.

o. Apply a table design of **Grid Table 6 Colorful** (row 6, column 1 under Grid Tables). Select row 1 and apply **Align Center alignment**.

p. Display the Restrict Editing pane and allow only filling in of forms. (On a Mac, click Protect Form.) Start protection but do not assign a password.

q. Click in the first cell of the second row and select a table size of **8x3**. Click the **Need Setup Assistance control** in the last cell on the second row and select **No**.

r. Click the control beside *Contact Name* and type your first and last names. Click the control beside *Company* and type **Dryden Services**. Add a phone number of **601-555-3330**. Add an email address of **ddsinc@outlook.com**. Stop protection and close the Restrict Editing pane.

s. Save and close the document. Exit Word. Based on your instructor's directions, submit: w05r1NewCastle_LastFirst

Disaster Recovery

University Funding

You are an editor for the university newspaper, assigned with covering press releases coming from the university president's office. Recently the president gave a State of the University address in which he outlined funding challenges facing the university. You have a rough draft of notes from the address that you will modify and prepare for posting online. In so doing, you will include appropriate formatting and a content control as follows:

- Open *w05d1Funding*.
- Check the document for spelling and grammatical errors.
- Include a drop cap in the first body paragraph.
- Format the title as an attractive masthead.
- Select University of Northwest Colorado in the first paragraph and create a link to the home page of your school or university (or to a favorite university).
- Include a content control following *Proofread?* on the last page making it possible to select *Yes* or *No*.
- Include a content control following *Date* on the last page where the date of proofreading can be indicated.
- Add a page color and adjust the theme as you see fit to ensure an attractive webpage.
   Save the document as a Single File Web Page, naming the file **w05d1Funding_LastFirst**. View the document in a browser to check for appearance. Close the document. Exit Word. Based on your instructor's directions, submit: w05d1Funding_LastFirst.mht

Cumulative Exercise

Dental Spotlight

As a student studying to become a dental hygienist, you are enrolled in a pediatric dentistry class. As a class requirement, you will develop an article spotlighting good dental health for children. The article should be designed to display well in both print and online form. In addition, you will include a form for use in reserving space for several upcoming workshops. You will use Word to format the article so that it is attractive and informative.

Create a Masthead, Create a Drop Cap, and Apply and Modify Column Layout

As a newsletter heading, you modify text as a masthead, employing the use of reverse formatting so that light text displays on a dark background. A drop cap adds interest, and you format selected text in two columns to improve the document's appearance and readability.

1. Open *w05c1Dental* and save it as **w05c1Dental_LastFirst**. Ensure that nonprinting characters are displayed.

2. Select the first line, *Dental News Spotlight*, bold and center the line, and change the font size to **20**. Shade the first line, selecting a color of **Red**. Change the font color of the heading to **White, Background 1**.

3. Apply a drop cap to the first line of the first body paragraph, beginning with *You know regular brushing*. The drop cap should be formatted with the **Dropped** option, but should occupy only 2 lines.

4. Scroll to page 4 and select the first two body paragraphs, beginning with *In celebration of*, and ending with *on making dental health fun*. Format the selection in two columns.

Create a Pull Quote or Sidebar and Copy and Link Objects from Other Files

A pull quote restates the importance of good dental health. A list of presenters for the scheduled workshops is available in an Excel worksheet that you insert and link to. That way, if any of the presenters or workshops change, the updates will show in the linked worksheet.

5. Select and copy the last sentence in the second body paragraph on page 1, *Good dental habits are critical for a lifetime of confidence and overall health*.

6. Draw a text box before the page break on page 3. Change the height to **0.9** and the width to **4**. Paste the copied sentence in the text box.

7. Change the font of text in the text box to **Perpetua Titling MT** and change the font size to **14**. Center the text. Apply a shape fill of **Blue, Accent 1, Lighter 80%**. The text will show in all caps.

8. Align the text box in the center of the page horizontally. Check the document for spelling and grammatical errors. No names are misspelled and the word *age* is used correctly. Ignore any other refinement concerns.

9. Scroll to page 4 and click the second blank paragraph under the two-columned text. Open the *w05c1Presenters* Excel workbook and save it as **w05c1Presenters_LastFirst**. Select **cells A1 through C6** and copy the selection.

10. Paste the selection in the Word document, choosing to paste a link to a Microsoft Excel Worksheet Object.

11. Return to the Excel workbook and change *Dr. Wainwright Collins* to **Dr. Hansford Hill**. Press **Enter** after making the name change. Save and close the workbook. Update the worksheet object in the Word document.

Apply a Theme and Background to a Webpage, Insert Bookmarks in a Webpage or Document, Insert Hyperlinks in a Webpage or Document

Because the document will also be published as a webpage later, you change the view to Web Layout to get an idea of how it will look. Changing the theme and background modifies the appearance, and you insert bookmarks and links to facilitate movement within the document.

12. Apply the **Badge theme** and change the theme colors to **Median**.

13. Scroll to page 1 and click the paragraph mark before the paragraph with red font color, beginning with *Since most children*. Insert a bookmark titled **Brush**. Click the paragraph mark before the next paragraph, with green font color, and insert a bookmark titled **Bottle**. Insert bookmarks on succeeding paragraphs as follows:

Location	Bookmark Title
Page 2, blue paragraph	Dentist
Page 2, purple paragraph	Healthy
Page 2, light brown paragraph	Cavities
Page 3, brown paragraph	Fluoride
Page 3, red paragraph	Sports

14. Scroll to page 1, select text in the first numbered item, **Letting kids brush alone.** Insert a link to the **Brush** bookmark in the current document. Insert links for other numbered items as follows:

Link	Bookmark
Putting baby to bed with a bottle	Bottle
Not seeing a dentist soon enough	Dentist
Offering "healthy" foods	Healthy
Thinking cavities are no big deal	Cavities
Not using fluoride	Fluoride
Loading up on sports drinks	Sports

15. Change the view to **Web Layout.** Point to any link near the top of the document, press and hold Ctrl, and click. Scroll back to the top of the document and note the different link color, indicating that the link has been clicked.

16. Change the page color to **Gray, Accent 6, Lighter 80%.** Change the view to **Print Layout.** Remove the hyperlink from the email address in the right column on page 4.

Insert Content Controls, Protect Individual Content Controls, Protect an Entire Form, Complete an Electronic Form

A worksheet, with content controls, is included so that tickets can be reserved for workshop sessions.

17. Scroll to page 4 and click the third column of the third row in the Dental Health Today table (under the *Number of Tickets*) heading. Insert a **Text Form Field** from the Legacy Tools option. Adjust the properties of the content control to show a Number with a default value of **1.** Center the content control.

18. Insert a Text Form Field for the remaining two rows in the Number of Tickets column, applying the same properties as for the first. Center each content control in the column.

19. Click before the paragraph mark that follows *Name (First and Last:)* on the same page. Insert a **Rich Text Content Control.** (On a Mac, insert a Text Box.) Adjust the properties to ensure that the content control cannot be deleted.

20. Insert a **Rich Text Content Control** beside the next two items, *Email Contact:* and *Phone:.* Adjust the properties of each to ensure that the content control cannot be deleted.

21. Insert a **Drop-Down List Content Control** beside the last line, *How Did You Hear About the Workshops?* (On a Mac, insert a Combo Box control.) Leave the Tag and Title blank and add the following choices:

   Dental Health Newsletter
   Social Media
   Dentist Office
   Other

22. Restrict editing to filling in forms only. (On a Mac, click Protect Form.) Enforce protection without assigning a password.

23. Complete the form, selecting 2 tickets to each of the workshops. Type **Jacob Ashwander** beside *Name (First and Last)*, **jashwander@centuryinc.net** beside *Email*, **307-555-0003** beside *Phone*, and select **Social Media** as the way you heard about the workshops.

24. Stop protection and close the Restrict Editing pane.

25. Save and close the document. Exit Word. Based on your instructor's directions, submit: w05c1Dental_LastFirst

LEARNING OUTCOMES

You will demonstrate how to manage and automate a document using templates, building blocks, themes, and macros.

You will also explore protecting a document with a password and editing restrictions.

OBJECTIVES & SKILLS: After you read this chapter, you will be able to:

CASE STUDY | Rose Designs

Cassie Artman purchased Rose Designs, a retail establishment specializing in landscaping and gardening supplies. Cassie wants to take the company to the next level by automating some of the resources the company uses. One of the first projects she assigns to you, her technology coordinator, is to create a sales invoice that salespeople can fill out quickly while taking phone or online orders. The invoice will be automated where appropriate to simplify the billing process. After the invoice form is complete, including customized theme settings, you will distribute it for review by others, ultimately consolidating all edits into a single document. With each sale, you will include an informational document spotlighting an available service or product. As you prepare the document, you will explore formatting and editing restrictions that ensure only necessary edits, and you learn to apply password protection to allow authorized access only.

CHAPTER 6

Creation, Automation, and Protection

NDAB Creativity/Shutterstock

FIGURE 6.1 Rose Designs Documents

CASE STUDY | Rose Designs

Starting Files	Files to Be Submitted	MyLab IT HOE Grader
Invoice (red design) template w06h1Memo w06h1Rose_Edited w06h1Logo.jpg w06h3Tulip	w06h2Rose_LastFirst.dotm w06h3Tulip_LastFirst	

MyLab IT Grader: This project is available as a Hands-On Exercise project in MyLab IT.

Document Creation

It is not always necessary to begin a document from a blank page. If a document is a common design or a type that is generic in nature, such as an employment cover letter, you are likely to find a template that can jump-start the process. A template is a predesigned file that is formatted appropriately for a specific purpose and that might also include content that can be modified to personalize the document. Some templates are designed with themes or layouts, including graphics and page design elements that streamline document creation. While a good selection of templates is included in Word, others are available from Office.com.

If a document type or format is one that is used frequently but is not available in Word's template library, you can save it as a template, making the pattern available for reuse by yourself or others. The collection of templates available through Word includes those that are generic to a large population, whereas a template that you create and save is more likely focused on a particular industry or company—perhaps even for a unique purpose in your personal correspondence or recordkeeping.

A template is typically geared to an entire document, such as a business letter or résumé. Reusable blocks of a smaller amount of predefined text, like a letterhead, cover page, company logo, or watermark, can be created and saved as building blocks, saving time in recreating those elements each time they are needed. A building block is inserted into an existing document so that there is no need to type or design its content more than once.

Not only can you customize documents with specific templates and building blocks, but you can also personalize a document with theme selections, including colors and fonts. Having modified a group of colors or fonts, you can save them as a custom set to which you can refer later in subsequent documents.

In this section, you will create and save a Word document as a template, making it available as a pattern for similar documents. Visiting Word's collection of templates, you will learn to search and download a predesigned template. You will modify a document's theme selections and you will explore the process of locating and creating building blocks that can be reused to automate and streamline repetitive tasks. In addition, you will explore viewing multiple documents in a split-screen arrangement, adjusting the view for optimal effectiveness. Using Word's Compare and Combine features, you will learn to review documents for differences and combine all or part of one document into another.

Select and Create a Template

If a document you intend to create is a type that is frequently used by others, you might search for a template that can serve as a starting point. Such would be the case if you were beginning a business letter, memo, report, résumé, agenda, calendar, brochure, or checklist. Even such items as APA-style reports and itineraries are available in template form. With a template as a launch point, creating a professional document can be a bit simpler, and almost certainly less time consuming.

As you select or create a template, you will consider generic wording that is designed to be modified or replaced by a template user. Areas intended to contain images or graphics that will vary among users are often set apart in a template. Such sections of variable data are called placeholders. By definition, a ***placeholder*** is a field or block of text that you personalize by typing text or perhaps inserting an image (see Figure 6.2). For example, a template for a family reunion flyer might include a placeholder where you type the date of the reunion, as well as a placeholder for a map image, providing directions to the locale. A placeholder is typically populated with filler text that will be replaced as you type or insert text. A newsletter template is often composed of several columns of meaningless text whose sole purpose is to fill the space until it is replaced. Not only does such filler text occupy space, but it serves as a visual display of font formatting as well as typography and layout.

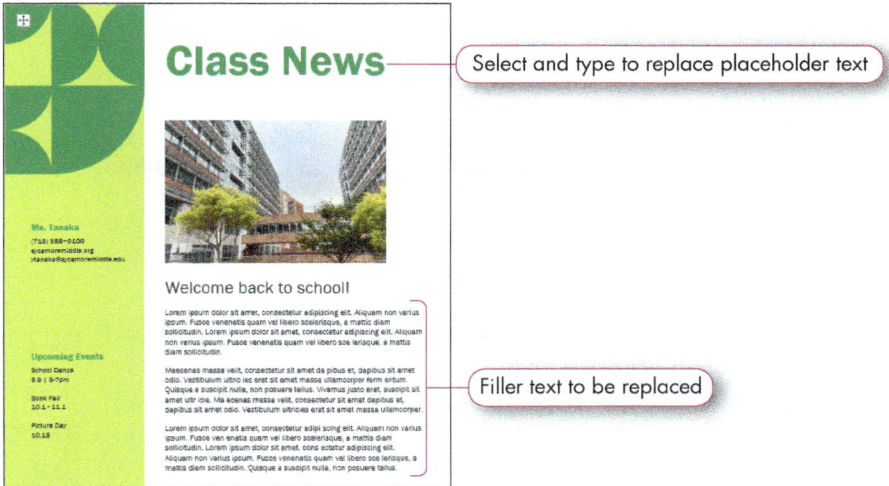

FIGURE 6.2 Use a Template

Download a Template

When you launch Word and click New, a variety of installed templates are displayed (see Figure 6.3). If Word is already open, you can access the installed templates from the New selection on the File tab. Although common templates are shown, you might not see what you are looking for in the list. In that case, you can search for a template by typing one or more key terms in the Search box in the New window.

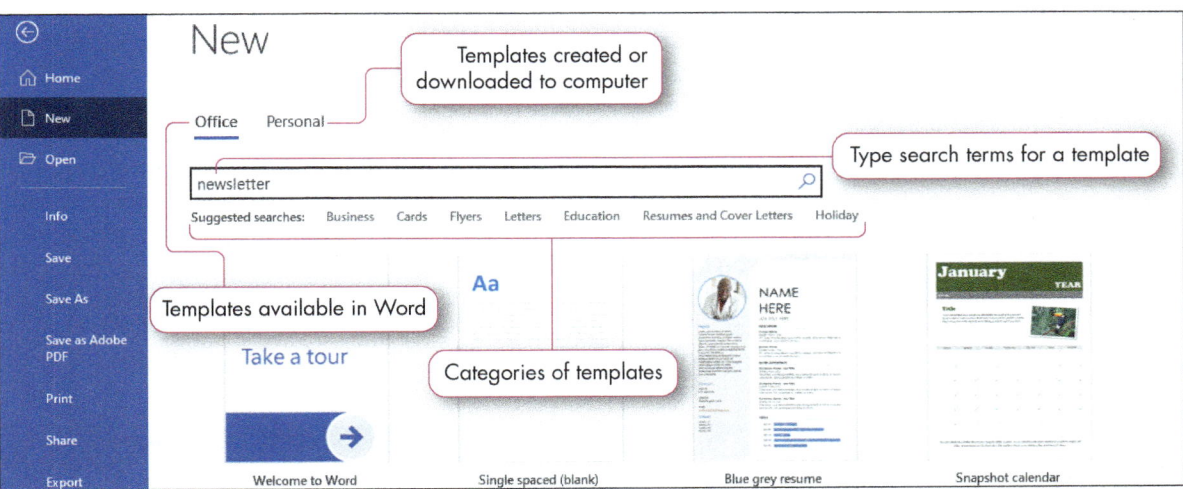

FIGURE 6.3 Select a Document Template

Having located a template, download it by clicking Create (see Figure 6.4). At that point, you can modify the template file, including personal information or design features. The downloaded and modified document is then saved as a Word document, with a .docx extension, unless you specify otherwise.

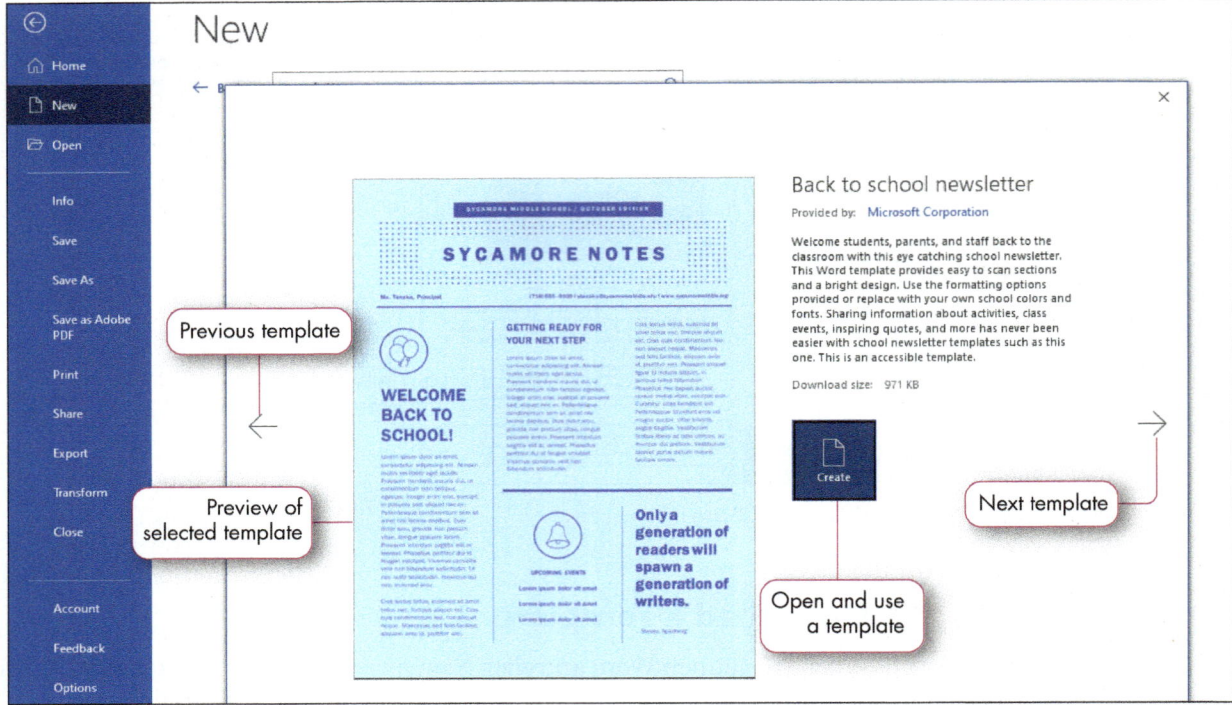

FIGURE 6.4 Preview and Select a Template

Save a Document as a Template

If you create or use the same document frequently or if you are creating a document for others to use and modify with only minor updates each time, you can save the document as a template, optionally inserting placeholders for variable information. A document that is saved as a template includes a filename with a .dotx or .dotm file extension. As described later in this chapter, the .dotm file type is reserved for a document that contains one or more macros.

When you save a document as a template, Word automatically saves the template to a default location for templates, which is the Custom Office Templates subfolder of the Documents folder in File Explorer. A saved template is also available on the Personal tab when you begin a new document (refer to Figure 6.3). You can instead specify a location on your own hard drive, portable storage device, or OneDrive account by navigating to the folder of your choice as you save the template. Be aware that templates saved in other locations do not display in the Custom Office Templates folder.

HOW TO

Save a document as a template:

1. Open a document.
2. Click the File tab.
3. Click Save As and click Browse.
4. Change the *Save as type* to Word Template (see Figure 6.5). (On a Mac, select Save as Template.)
5. Click Save (to save to the Custom Office Templates folder), or navigate to another folder and click Save.

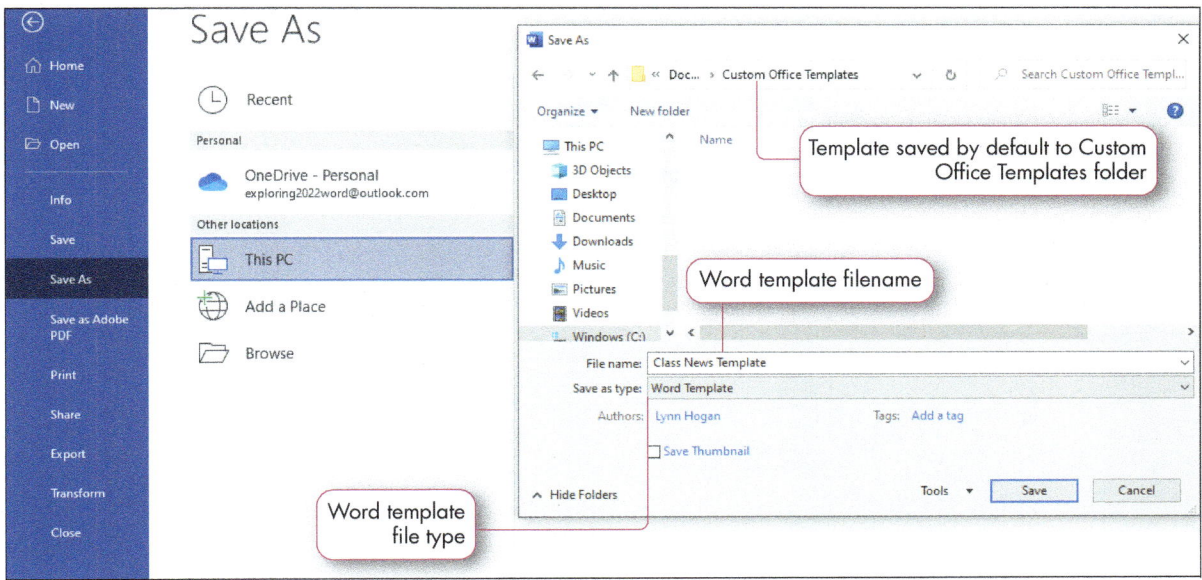

FIGURE 6.5 Save as a Word Template

Use Building Blocks

Predefined items, like tables, lists, headers, and text boxes—basically any data or graphic element that you plan to reuse—can be saved as a ***building block*** so that it is available for placement in any document. Although you might not be aware of it, you have most likely worked with several building blocks that are built into a typical Word installation. Such items as cover pages, watermarks, bibliographies, and tables of contents are considered building blocks, accessible through corresponding galleries of selections.

The terms *Quick Parts* and *building blocks* are often used interchangeably, as both refer to document elements that can be reused. More specifically, ***Quick Parts*** is often used to refer to a selection on the ribbon (in the Text group on the Insert tab) that provides access to categories of building blocks, whereas a building block is the actual item that is being reused. In addition to types mentioned previously, other building blocks include document properties, fields (page number, for example), and ***AutoText*** (a document element that is composed of text or graphics, such as a logo or contract disclaimer, typically created and saved by an individual Word user).

Building blocks are available for preview and selection through the Building Blocks Organizer, shown when you click Quick Parts in the Text group on the Insert tab (see Figure 6.6). The extensive list is organized by galleries, including Bibliographies, Cover Pages, Equations, Footers, Headers, Page Numbers, Table of Contents, Tables, Text Boxes, and Watermarks. Click any of the building blocks in the Building Blocks Organizer to see a preview and a description of the item. In addition, you can edit properties, delete an entry, or insert a selected building block into an open document.

> **MAC TIP: ACCESS BUILDING BLOCKS**
> The Building Blocks Organizer is not available. However, you can access predefined building blocks from individual galleries such as Cover Page, Table of Contents, Watermarks, and so on. You can also use AutoText, available when you click the Insert tab and AutoText, to create a building block.

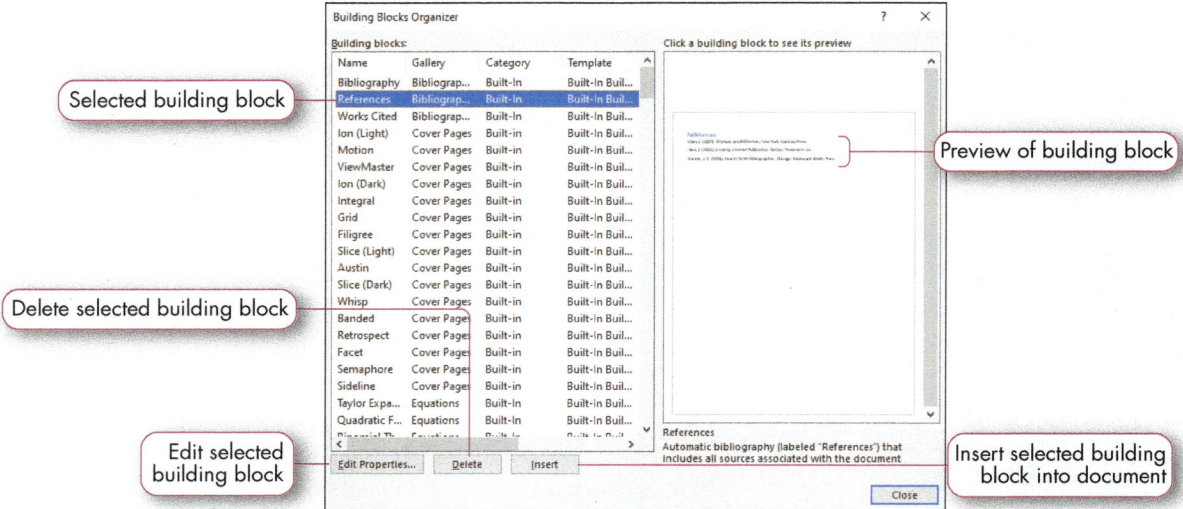

FIGURE 6.6 Building Blocks Organizer

Create and Insert a Building Block

In addition to a predefined set of building blocks created by Microsoft, such as watermarks or equations, you may find that you frequently use personalized document content. Perhaps a logo, specially formatted header or footer, or unique tables are to be saved for reuse. Such document elements are referred to as AutoText building blocks.

When you create a new building block, you can assign it to any gallery, usually placing it according to its purpose. For example, a cover page that is often used for company correspondence could be saved in the Cover Pages gallery. A building block with no particular gallery assignment, such as a standard contract clause or a lengthy distribution list, could be saved in the AutoText gallery or Quick Part gallery, as an item that is available for reuse. A slight difference between an item saved to the AutoText gallery and one saved to the Quick Part gallery is that AutoText is placed in the Normal document template, while a Quick Part entry is saved to the Building Blocks template. For a typical user, the template choice matters little; a power user who plans to share building blocks or transfer them from one system to another is more concerned with specific templates in which building blocks are saved, as accessibility and overwriting concerns are considered.

> **TIP: PLACE A BUILDING BLOCK IN THE CURRENT TEMPLATE**
> Building blocks are saved to a template—typically either the Normal template or Building Blocks template. If you are creating a personal template—a file saved as a Word Template or Word Macro-Enabled Template—you can indicate that a custom building block is saved to that template only, making it available to all documents based on the template.

Regardless of where you plan to house a building block entry, the process of creating it begins when you create and then select the text or graphic item. For example, if a header is to be saved for reuse, you should first design the header and then select it. Click Quick Parts in the Text group on the Insert tab and select Save Selection to Quick Part Gallery. The Create New Building Block dialog box displays, as shown in Figure 6.7, which is where you name, classify, describe, and control the placement of the new building block, including selecting the gallery to which you want to save the building block entry.

> **TIP: PLACE A BUILDING BLOCK IN THE AUTOTEXT GALLERY**
> Each building block is housed in one of several available galleries. The AutoText gallery is often used for custom building blocks such as a disclaimer or letterhead. A quick way to save a selection to the AutoText gallery is to click the Insert tab, click Quick Parts, and select Save Selection to AutoText Gallery. Provide a name for the building block and accept or change the default settings in the Create New Building Block dialog box (see Figure 6.7).

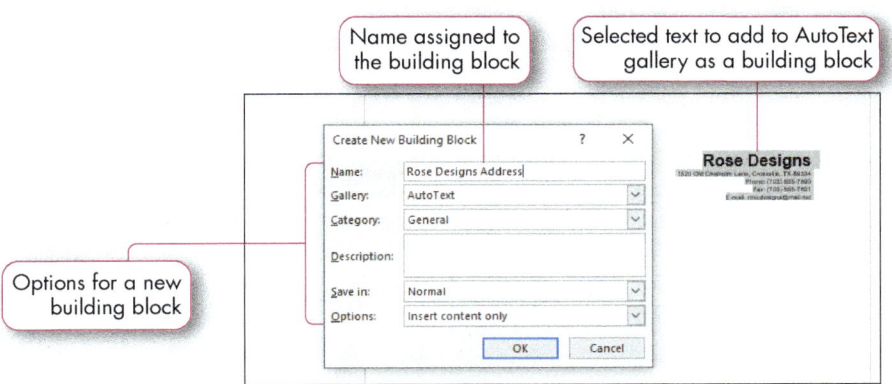

FIGURE 6.7 Create a New Building Block

Options in the Create New Building Block dialog box enable you to document an item being created.

- **Name:** Assign a unique name that describes the building block being saved, preferably one that is easily associated with its content.
- **Gallery:** Select the gallery in which to store the building block. Unless the item is clearly associated with an existing gallery, such as a footer or company watermark where you might select the Footers gallery or Watermarks gallery, you should save it to either the AutoText or Quick Part gallery.
- **Category:** Select the General category or create your own category to identify your company, department, or project so that related building blocks are organized by purpose or organization.
- **Description:** Type a short description of the building block. The description will display in the Building Blocks Organizer when the building block is previewed.
- **Save in:** Select a template in which to save the building block. Building blocks saved in the Quick Part gallery are saved in the default Building Block template (Building Blocks.dotx), whereas AutoText entries are saved by default in the Normal.dotm template. Both of those templates are global, in that items stored there are available to other documents. If a building block is to be shared with others, you should consider saving it in a separate template. Unless you are concerned with high-level template organization or sharing with others, however, you should accept the default template for the building block being saved.
- **Options:** Choose one of the following three options:
  ○ Insert content only.
  ○ Insert content in its own paragraph (even if it is placed in the middle of an existing paragraph).
  ○ Insert content in its own page (places a page break before and after the building block).

Prior to inserting a building block into a document, place the insertion point where you want the building block to be located. Then click Quick Parts in the Text group on the Insert tab. You can either select AutoText and select the specific AutoText entry or select Building Blocks Organizer. To more quickly locate a building block, click a column heading in the Building Blocks Organizer to sort the list. Select a building block and click Insert to place it in an open document. Alternatively, as mentioned earlier, many building blocks are already located in existing galleries, such as cover pages and tables of contents. To insert any of these, click the item from the relevant gallery.

Customize Theme Settings

When you create a new blank document, it is automatically formatted with the default Office document theme. If you are considering a change in document theme, you can choose another from the Themes group on the Design tab. Each theme contains subsets of colors, font selections, spacing, and effects, making it possible to customize those items within a single theme. In fact, Word contains multiple color schemes, font combinations, and theme effects that result in hundreds of available theme customizations.

STEP 3 ▸ Customize Theme Colors

Theme colors are sets of coordinated colors for current text, background, accents, and hyperlinks. Selecting from color combinations associated with a document theme, you can change the overall hue. As shown in Figure 6.8, each theme includes a wide range of color themes. You can also create a custom theme color set encompassing color combinations for the four text/background colors, six accent colors, and two hyperlink colors included in a document theme.

HOW TO

Create a custom set of theme colors:

1. Click the Design tab.
2. Click Colors in the Document Formatting group.
3. Select Customize Colors at the bottom of the gallery to modify the colors in the current theme.
4. Select colors for the text/background, accents, and hyperlinks in the Create New Theme Colors dialog box.
5. Type a custom theme color name in the Name box.
6. Click Save. The new color theme is placed into effect in the current document and displays at the top of the theme color gallery.

MAC TIP: CUSTOMIZE COLORS

Although you cannot use Word to customize theme colors, you can customize colors and save them as a custom theme in PowerPoint. They are then available in a Word document. Access a saved theme when you click Themes on the Home tab and then, under Custom, select a theme that was created in PowerPoint.

TIP: REMOVE A CUSTOM SETTING

To delete a set of custom colors or fonts, display the Colors gallery or Fonts gallery, right-click the item to be removed, and click Delete. Accept the deletion.

FIGURE 6.8 View and Customize Theme Colors

Customize Theme Fonts

Theme fonts contain a coordinating heading and body text font for each different theme. You can view fonts used in a selected theme when you click Fonts in the Document Formatting group on the Design tab, as shown in Figure 6.9. Theme fonts display at the top of the font list when you click the Font arrow on the Home tab or on the Mini toolbar. As with theme colors, you can change the document text by choosing a new font set with a predefined font type. You can also create a customized theme font set.

HOW TO

Create a custom theme font:

1. Click the Design tab.
2. Click Fonts in the Document Formatting group and select Customize Fonts.
3. Click the Heading font arrow to select a preferred font for all headings.
4. Click the Body font arrow to select a font for body text.
5. Type a custom theme font name in the Name box.
6. Click Save. The new font theme is placed into effect in the current document and displays at the top of the theme font gallery.

MAC TIP: CUSTOMIZE FONTS

Although you cannot use Word to customize fonts, you can customize fonts and save them as a custom theme in PowerPoint. They are then available in a Word document. Access a saved theme when you click Themes on the Home tab and then, under Custom, select a theme that was created in PowerPoint.

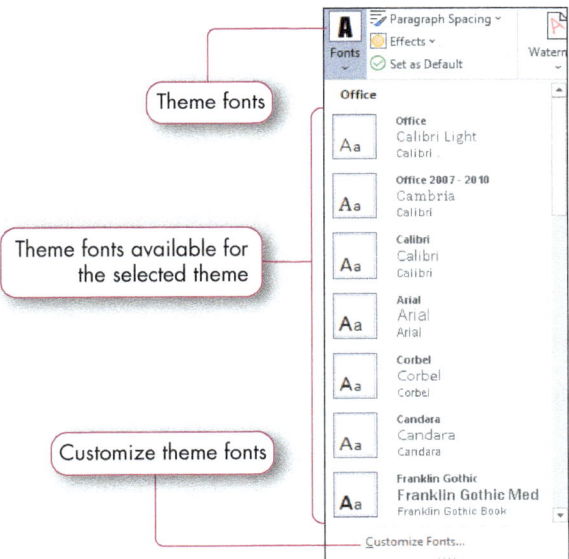

FIGURE 6.9 View and Customize Theme Fonts

Apply Theme Effects

Theme effects include lines, fill, and 3-D effects, such as shadows, glows, and borders. When you apply a theme effect, the selection affects objects such as shapes, SmartArt, and graphics. Unlike theme colors and theme fonts, you cannot customize the set of theme effects, but you can choose and apply a theme effect from the built-in sets and then save it to your own document theme. When a shape or object is created, the theme effect is reflected in the styles gallery for the selected object on the object's format tab.

Click Effects in the Document Formatting group on the Design tab to view sets of available effects, shown in Figure 6.10. Each diagram includes three shapes—a circle, rectangle, and arrow. The circle indicates line weight, the rectangle represents bevels and shadows applied to an object, and the arrow shows gradient fill effects.

> **MAC TIP: THEME EFFECTS**
> Theme effects are not available.

Theme effects →

Effects available for selected theme (Office) →

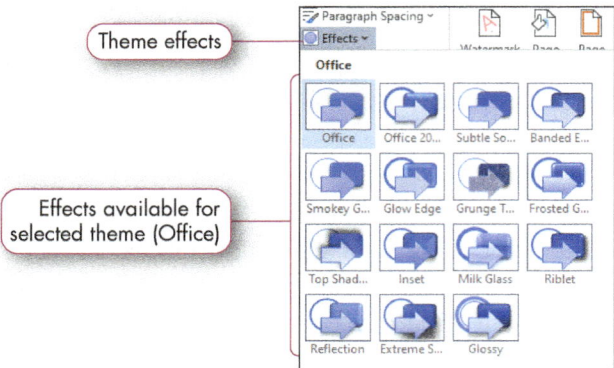

FIGURE 6.10 View and Apply Theme Effects

Save a Custom Theme

Customized settings, including theme colors and theme fonts, can collectively comprise a custom theme that you create and name. Themes are saved with a .thmx extension in the Templates folder in the subfolder Document Themes.

> **HOW TO**
>
> **Save selected theme elements to a custom theme:**
>
> 1. Click the Design tab, select a theme, and incorporate color and font settings into a custom collection.
> 2. Click Themes in the Document Formatting group.
> 3. Select Save Current Theme at the bottom of the gallery, name the new theme, and save it.

Compare and Combine Documents

Using Word, you can work with multiple documents at the same time, combining all or part of several documents as well as viewing documents beside one another. As you combine two or more documents, it is possible to indicate which portions to keep or omit. Or you might want to collapse several documents into one. Perhaps several people have edited individual copies of a single document, and upon the return of those documents, you intend to compare changes before consolidating all into one iteration. Finally, your goal may be to view two documents in a side-by-side arrangement as you visually compare the two.

STEP 4 View Documents Side by Side

The **Side by Side view** enables you to display two versions of the same document on the same screen. This feature is useful when you want to compare an original to a revised document or when you want to cut or copy content from one document and paste it to another. When the documents display side by side, synchronous scrolling is active by default. **Synchronous scrolling** enables you to scroll through both documents at the same time using either of the two scroll bars. If you want to scroll through each document independently, click Synchronous Scrolling in the Window group on the View tab to toggle it off, and use the respective scroll bars to navigate through each document.

To view two documents side by side, you must have both documents open. The View Side by Side command is grayed if only one document is open. When multiple documents are open, click View Side by Side in the Window group on the View tab; the Word window splits to display each document, as shown in Figure 6.11. If you have more than two documents open, when you click View Side by Side, the Compare Side by Side dialog box displays so you can select which document to show beside the active document.

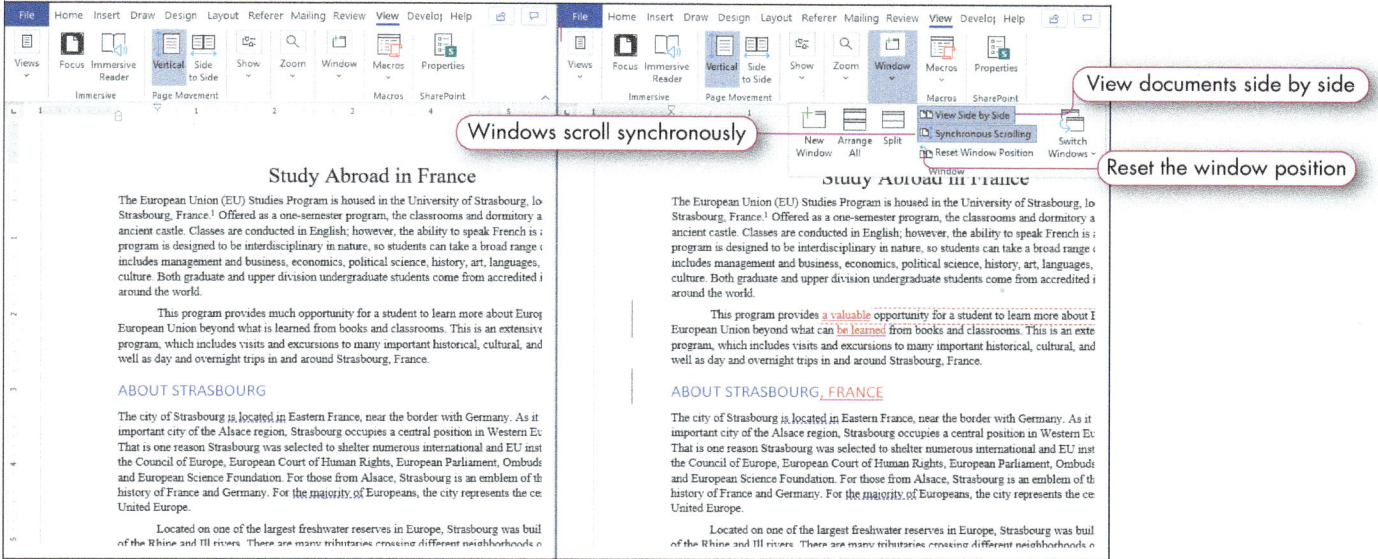

FIGURE 6.11 View Documents Side by Side

While in Side by Side view, you can resize and reposition document windows so that they share the screen equally. To reset document windows to the original side-by-side viewing size, click Reset Window Position in the Window group on the View tab. To close the Side by Side view, click View Side by Side to toggle it off. The document that contains the insertion point when you close the Side by Side view will display as the active document.

> **MAC TIP: SIDE BY SIDE VIEW**
> View Side by Side and Synchronous Scrolling are not available.

STEP 5 Consolidate Documents

Consolidating documents involves merging multiple documents into one. Although the reasons for consolidating documents are varied, the methods of completing that task are few, when working with Word. The first step is usually to compare documents and select components to merge. Often, that involves determining differences, perhaps noting where changes have occurred between document versions. Even if consolidation is not the ultimate goal, you might find it necessary to compare documents simply to see if changes were made.

Legal blacklining is a way to compare two documents while displaying changes made. The process compares two documents, showing what has changed between them in a new third document (if you make that selection). Legal blacklining is popular in the legal profession, enabling comparison of versions of documents or contracts while also tracking the progress of a manuscript or document component. Word's *Compare* feature uses the process of legal blacklining to evaluate the contents of two versions of a document for a line-by-line comparison, displaying a merged version with markup and tracked changes showing the differences between them.

To compare two documents, click Compare in the Compare group on the Review tab. Select Compare. Documents do not have to be open for the comparison to occur. At its base level, the Compare Documents dialog box enables you to select the two documents to evaluate. Click More in the dialog box to select from settings that refine the comparison process, as shown in Figure 6.12. You can select items to compare and indicate whether changes shown should be at the word or character level. Changes can be shown in the original document, the revised document, or a new document.

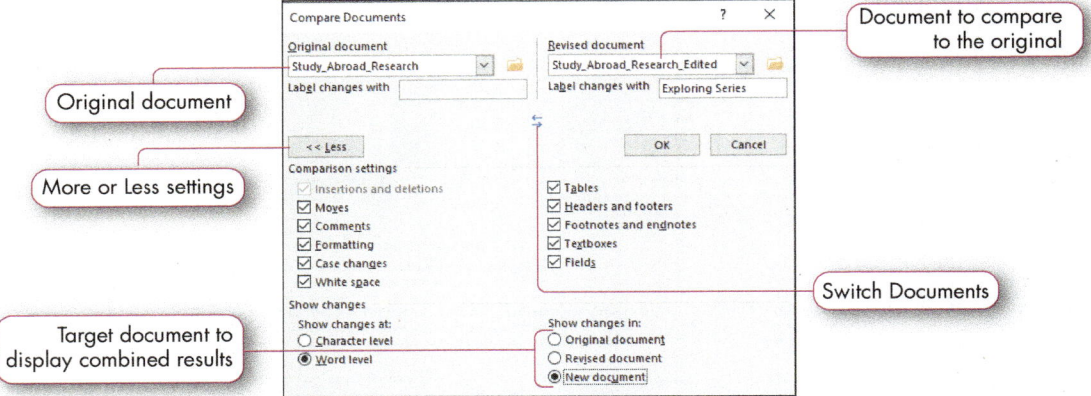

FIGURE 6.12 Compare Documents Dialog Box

Comparing two documents is informative. However, if the goal is to combine multiple documents, you can use Word's **Combine** feature to integrate all changes into a single document. Similar to comparing documents, the Combine Documents dialog box contains the same set of options. If you do not want to modify the original documents, you should combine the changes into a new document.

To combine two documents, click Compare in the Compare group on the Review tab and select Combine. With the same set of options described in the Compare process, you can indicate what should be combined, whether revisions should be selected at the word or character level, and whether to combine changes into an existing or new document.

MAC TIP: COMPARE AND COMBINE

Compare two versions of a document to see how they differ or merge two versions, combining content into a single document. In both cases, open one of the two versions. To compare two versions, click Tools on the menu, point to Track Changes and click Compare. To combine two versions, click Combine Documents on the Tools menu. In both cases, browse to locate the original document and the revised version.

Critical Thinking

1. Describe circumstances in which it would be advantageous to download a template rather than develop a document from scratch. *p. 422*

2. Describe similarities between templates and building blocks, also providing rationale on choosing one over the other for various document purposes. *p. 425*

3. Provide an example of when you might choose to compare two documents without combining them, as well as an example of when you would both compare and combine two documents. *p. 431*

Hands-On Exercises

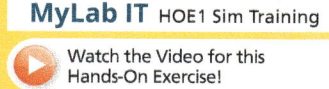
1 Document Creation

Cassie asks you to update and automate an invoice form so that it is easier to use. Because you do not already have an invoice form on file, you will search Word's template library for one that is suitable. Having settled on a form, you will consider customizing theme selections and will compare multiple versions of the form after others have reviewed it.

STEP 1 DOWNLOAD A TEMPLATE AND SAVE A DOCUMENT AS A TEMPLATE

You identify an invoice template that can be modified to suit your purposes so you download it from Word's library of templates. Refer to Figure 6.13 as you complete Step 1.

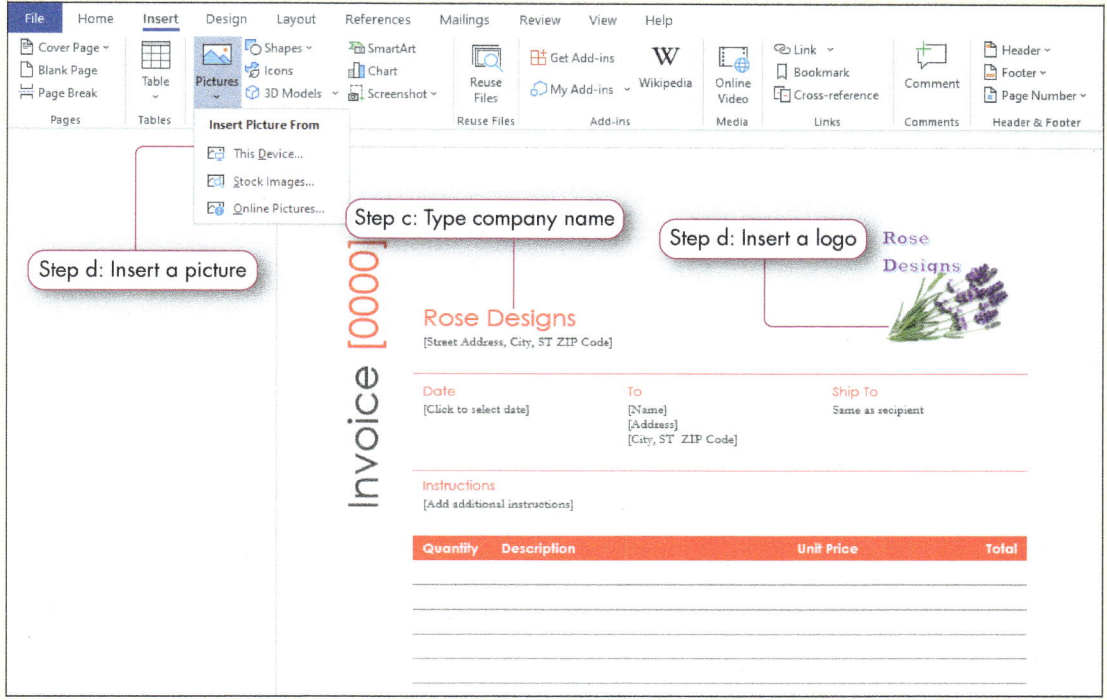

FIGURE 6.13 Select and Download an Invoice Template

a. Start Word. Click **New**.

The New tab displays a list of available templates.

> **MAC TROUBLESHOOTING:** Click the File menu and select New from Template.

b. Type **invoice** in the *Search for online templates* box and press **Enter**. In the New pane, scroll down to locate and click the **Invoice (Red design)** template. Click **Create**.

> **TROUBLESHOOTING:** If you do not find the template, open *w06h1Invoice.dotx* from the student data files.

A download window displays briefly and the Invoice (Red design) template opens as a new document.

c. Click the **Company placeholder** at the top left side of the invoice and type **Rose Designs**.

d. Click the **replace with Logo placeholder**. Click the **Insert tab**, click **Pictures** in the Illustrations group, and select **This Device**. Navigate to the student data files and double-click *w06h1Logo.jpg*.

A company logo, saved as a picture file, is inserted on the invoice.

e. Click the **File tab** and click **Save As**. Click **Browse**. Change the file name to **w06h1Rose_LastFirst**. Click the **Save as type arrow** and select **Word Template**. Navigate to the location where you save your student files. Click **Save**.

Although Word saves templates to the default Custom Office Templates subfolder in the Documents folder, you change the save location to another. When you save this document as a template, you can open it later, complete the invoice for a sale, and save the completed document as a Word document without altering the original invoice template.

STEP 2 ## CREATE AND INSERT A BUILDING BLOCK

As you continue to develop an invoice form, you create an AutoText building block containing the company address. It will remain available for use in any document that requires the one-line company address. Refer to Figure 6.14 as you complete Step 2.

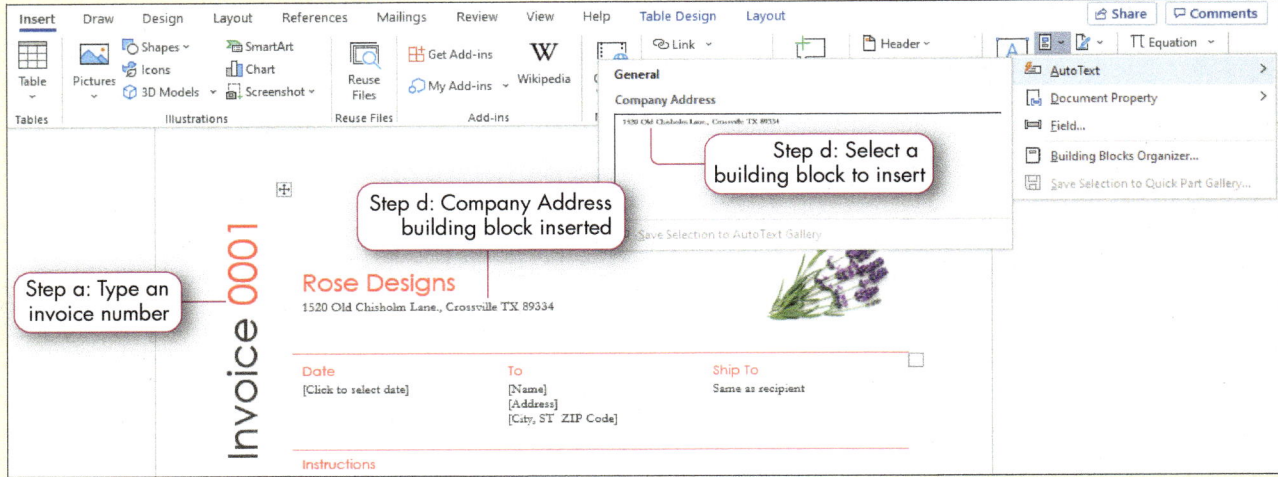

FIGURE 6.14 Insert a Custom Building Block

a. Ensure that nonprinting characters are shown. Click the **Invoice Number placeholder** at the top left side of the invoice and type **0001**.

The filler text in the Invoice Number placeholder is replaced with the number you type.

b. Open *w06h1Memo*. Select the address line shown in the middle of the memo, beginning with *1520 Old Chisholm Lane*.

You select the company address so that it can be saved as a custom building block.

c. Create a custom building block for the company address as follows:

- Click the **Insert tab**. Click **Quick Parts** in the Text group, point to **AutoText**, and then click **Save Selection to AutoText Gallery**.
- Type **Company Address** in the Name box of the Create a Building Block dialog box. The Gallery is AutoText and the Category is General. In the Description box, type **This is a one-line address for Rose Designs.** (Include the period.) Ensure that the template is Normal, and that *Insert content only* is selected. Click **OK**. Close w06h1Memo without saving the document.

> **MAC TROUBLESHOOTING:** Click Insert on the menubar, point to AutoText, click Auto-text. and click Add. Close w06h1Memo.

> **TROUBLESHOOTING:** If asked whether to redefine the building block, click Yes. That may happen if a previous student using the same computer did not delete the building block.

d. Click the **Street Address placeholder** under the company name at the top left side of the invoice template. Click the **Insert Tab**, click **Quick Parts** in the Text group, point to **AutoText**, and select **Company Address**.

> **TROUBLESHOOTING:** If a hard return is placed after the company address line, click before the hard return and press Delete to remove it.

The Company Address AutoText building block is inserted in the invoice.

> **MAC TROUBLESHOOTING:** Click Insert on the menubar, point to AutoText, and click Autotext. Select the company address and click Insert.

e. Click **Quick Parts** and click **Building Blocks Organizer**. Ensure that Company Address is selected, click **Delete**, and click **Yes**. Click **Close**.

Because you may be working in a school computer lab, you delete the building block from the list of building blocks.

> **MAC TROUBLESHOOTING:** Click Insert on the menubar, point to AutoText, and click Autotext. Select the company address and click Delete..

f. Save the template.

STEP 3 ## CUSTOMIZE THEME COLORS AND CUSTOMIZE THEME FONTS

The red theme of the invoice does not coordinate well with the purple shade of the company logo, so you customize theme colors to more closely match the logo. In addition, you customize the theme font selection so that the print is crisp and legible. Refer to Figure 6.15 as you complete Step 3.

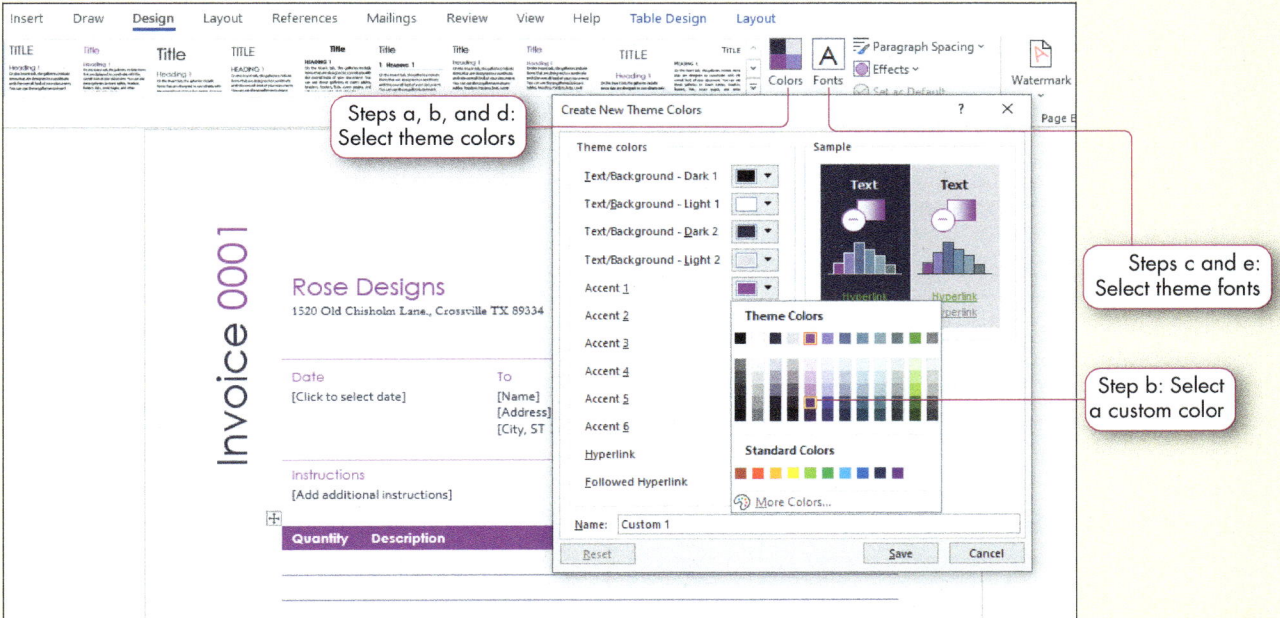

FIGURE 6.15 Customize Theme Colors and Fonts

a. Click the **Design tab**, click **Themes** in the Document Formatting group, and change the theme to **Facet**. Click **Colors** in the Document Formatting group and select **Violet**.

You change theme colors to a violet shade that more closely coordinates with the company logo.

b. Click **Colors** and select **Customize Colors**. Click the **Accent 1 arrow** and select **Lavender, Accent 1, Darker 25%** (row 5, column 5). Type **Invoice Colors** in the Name box, replacing any existing name. Click **Save**.

A deeper shade of purple provides more contrast.

c. Click **Fonts** in the Document Formatting group and select **Customize fonts**. Click the **Heading font arrow** and select **Century Gothic**. Click the **Body font arrow** and select **Corbel**. Type **Invoice Fonts** in the Name box. Click **Save**.

A sans serif font selection for both heading and body text is legible, uncluttered, and easy to read.

d. Click **Colors** in the Document Formatting group. Right-click **Invoice Colors**, shown at the top of the list, and click **Delete**. Click **Yes**.

Because you may be working in a school computer lab, you delete the custom set of colors you created.

e. Click **Fonts** in the Document Formatting group. Right-click **Invoice Fonts**, shown at the top of the list, and click **Delete**. Click **Yes**.

Because you may be working in a school computer lab, you delete the custom set of fonts you created.

f. Save the template.

STEP 4 VIEW DOCUMENTS SIDE BY SIDE

Before completing the invoice template, you asked for input from another colleague. He returned the edited document for your consideration. You view the original invoice side by side with the edited version for a quick visual comparison. Refer to Figure 6.16 as you complete Step 4.

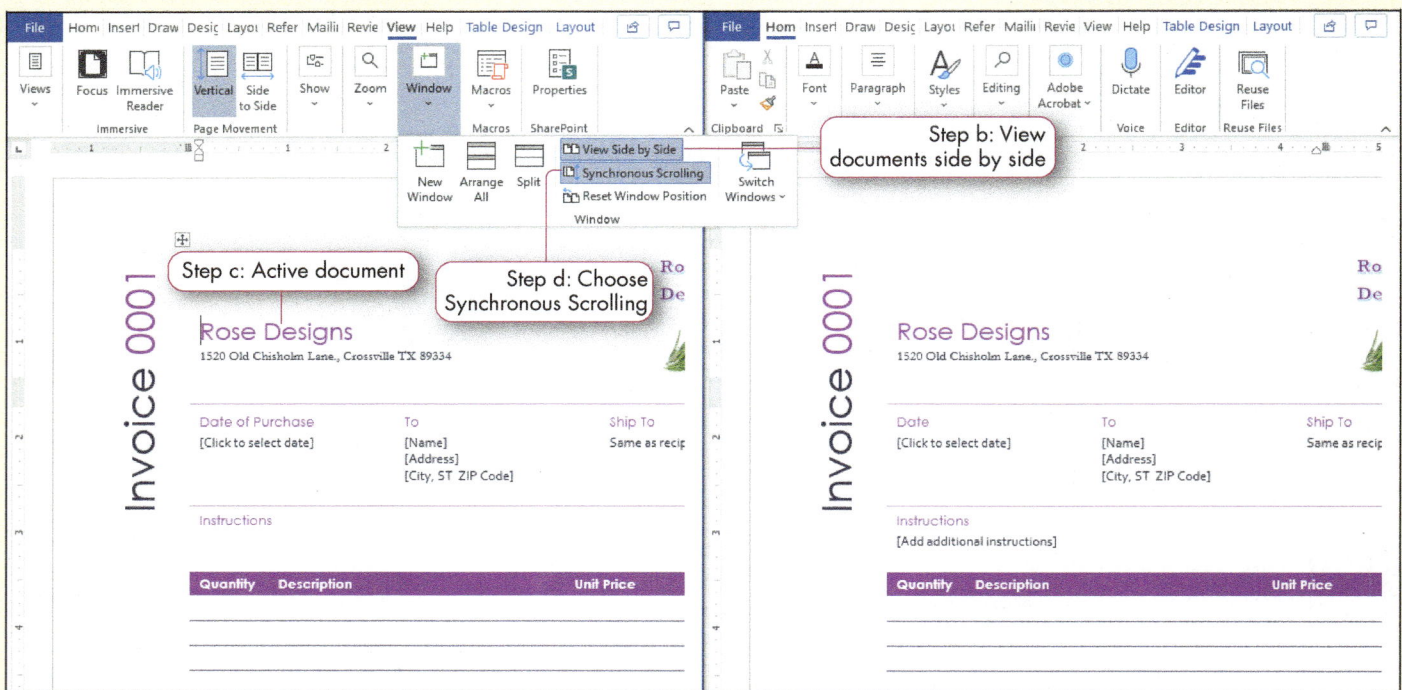

FIGURE 6.16 View Documents Side by Side

a. Open *w06h1Rose_Edited*. (Ensure that you open the document from within Word, not from File Explorer.)

b. Click the **View tab** and click **View Side by Side** in the Window group.

Two windows display, containing the contents of each file. The two documents are very similar, although you may notice a few minor differences. Because w06h1Rose_Edited is the last document that you opened, it is the active window. In the Window group of the active window, when you click Window, you see Synchronous Scrolling highlighted to indicate the setting is on. As you scroll in one document, the other will also scroll.

> **TROUBLESHOOTING:** If the view of one or both documents is insufficient, you can resize a window. Drag a border of the window until the size is acceptable.

c. Click the **active document** and click the **arrow** at the bottom of the vertical scroll bar several times to scroll to the bottom of the invoice in both windows.

Both documents scroll at the same time.

d. Click **Synchronous Scrolling** in the Window group in the active document to turn the toggle off.

Note that Synchronous Scrolling is no longer highlighted. Now you can scroll through each document individually.

STEP 5 CONSOLIDATE DOCUMENTS

You agree with one of the edits on the returned invoice, but choose to reject another. By comparing the documents and combining all edits into the original document, you are able to incorporate the accepted change and save the completed template. Refer to Figure 6.17 as you complete Step 5.

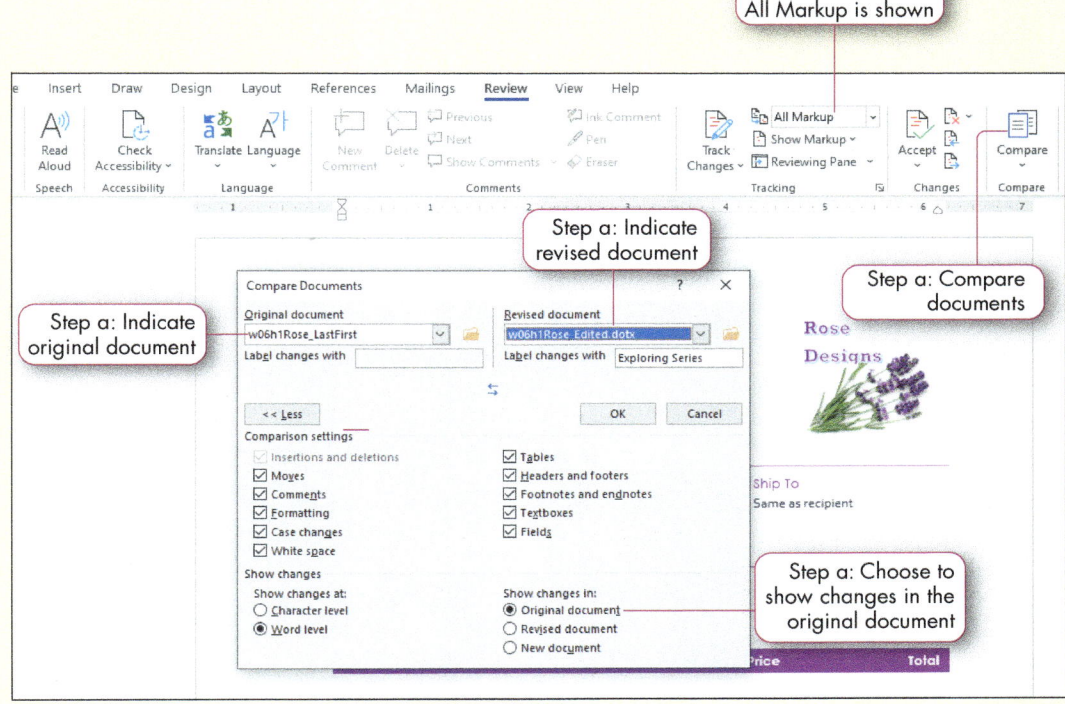

FIGURE 6.17 Compare Documents

a. Click the **Review tab** (in either of the side-by-side documents). Click **Compare**. Select **Compare**. Complete the dialog box as follows:

- Click the **Original document arrow**, scroll through any selections shown, and click **w06h1Rose_LastFirst**.
- Click the **Revised document arrow**, scroll through any selections shown, and click **w06h1_Rose_Edited**.
- Click **More** (unless the dialog box is already expanded). Select **Original document** in the *Show changes in* area. Click **OK**.

Any differences between the two invoice versions are shown in the original document.

b. Close w06h1Rose_Edited (the one with no revision marks shown). Maximize w06h1Rose_LastFirst if it does not show in full size.

c. Ensure that All Markup in the Tracking group on the Review tab is selected.

Note, among the changes that were made, the addition of *of Purchase* to the Date line, and the deletion of the bracketed words *Add additional instructions*. You will reject the first change but keep the second.

d. Click the **colored underlined words** *of purchase* in the Date line. Click the **Reject and Move to Next arrow** in the Changes group on the Review tab.

You determine that the addition of the words *of purchase* are redundant because the document is a sales invoice, so you reject that change. The second change, however, clarifies what is expected so you accept that.

e. Click the **Accept arrow** in the Changes group and click **Accept All Changes and Stop Tracking**.

f. Save the template. Keep the template open if you plan to continue with the next Hands-On Exercise. If not, close the template, and exit Word.

Macros

As you work with Word, you might find yourself repeating tasks, such as applying the same border within various sections of the same document. Even routine editing and formatting can become a repetitive task. Word's Macro feature enables you to automate such tasks. A **_macro_** is a set of instructions, or a program, that you group together as a single command to execute a series of keystrokes. Automating frequently executed tasks can save a great deal of time. However, because a macro is code that could be misused by those intent on causing mischief, it is also important to understand the security risks associated with macros and the protection that is available from Microsoft.

In this section, you will learn to create, run, and modify a macro and test it for accuracy. You will explore the inherent security risks associated with the use of macros and identify methods of counteracting those risks.

Create a Macro

If the set of steps you follow are routine and easily replicated, you can create a macro by recording the steps and providing a name for the macro so you can access it again. That way, you can repeat the task by running the macro. Before creating a macro, identify the job you want to record and rehearse the steps you will follow to accomplish it. Doing so helps you create (record) the macro successfully the first time.

STEP 1 ▶ ### Record a Macro

When you record a macro, Word saves a series of keystrokes and command selections, converting them into coded statements that can be referred to by a group name. Recording a macro is similar to recording video or audio. You turn the recorder on by selecting Record Macro, which is a command located either in the Macros group on the View tab or in the Code group on the Developer tab, as shown in Figure 6.18. To show the Developer tab on the ribbon, click the File tab and click Options. Click Customize Ribbon.

Ensure that Main Tabs shows under Customize the Ribbon, and select Developer, if it is not already selected. The Developer tab is helpful for creating and editing macros, as well as for creating and editing forms, as it includes options for inserting check boxes and other content controls.

> **TIP: USE THE STATUS BAR TO RECORD A MACRO**
> You can record a macro by clicking the button on the Word status bar (shown if the Macro Recording setting is selected on the Word status bar or if you have previously recorded a macro in Word). To customize Word so that you can record a macro by selecting from the status bar, right-click the status bar and click Macro Recording. While you are recording the macro, the command changes to Stop Recording, which you click when you have completed all the steps for the macro.

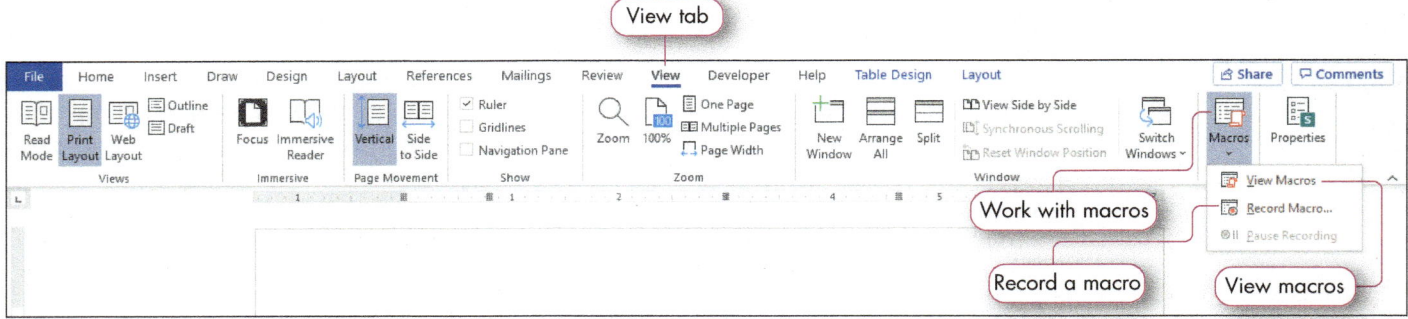

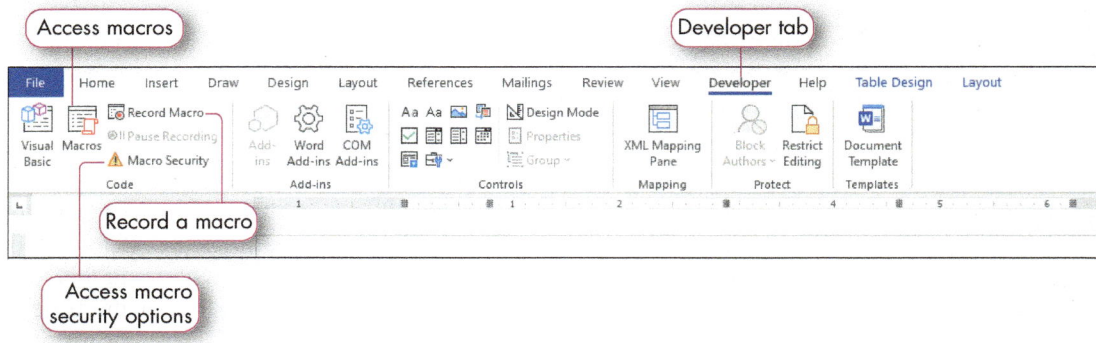

FIGURE 6.18 Use the Developer and View Tabs

When you begin to record a macro, the Record Macro dialog box opens, as shown in Figure 6.19. In the Record Macro dialog box, name the macro. A macro name must begin with a letter and must not contain any spaces or unusual characters. The length can be up to 80 characters, and the name must not conflict with any reserved commands or keywords such as Print, Save, Copy, or Paste. You can use letters, numbers, and underscores in a macro name, but periods are disallowed. Make the name as descriptive as possible so its purpose will be obvious when you want to run it again.

You can assign the macro to a button that can be placed on the Quick Access Toolbar, or you can assign a macro to a keyboard combination. Both options are available in the Record Macro dialog box.

You also use the Record Macro dialog box to indicate where the macro will be stored—either in the current document only or within the Normal template that is available to all Word documents. By default, Word will assign the macro to the Normal template. If, instead, you want the macro to only be housed within the current document, you must make that selection.

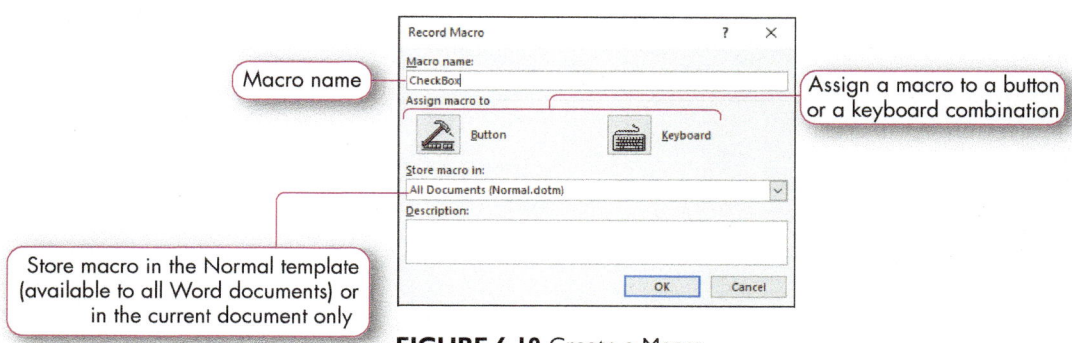

FIGURE 6.19 Create a Macro

Record a macro:

1. Click Record Macro in the Code group on the Developer tab (or choose to record a macro from the Macros selection on the View tab).

2. Type a macro name.

3. Choose how you want to store the macro, either in the Normal template or the current document only.

4. Type a description (optional).

5. Choose to assign the macro to the Quick Access Toolbar (see Figure 6.20), a keyboard combination (see Figure 6.21), or add it to the list of macros.

6. Model the task you are recording by clicking commands or pressing keys for each step.

7. Click Stop Recording. You can also click Pause Recording to interrupt the recording temporarily and click Resume Recorder when you are ready to continue.

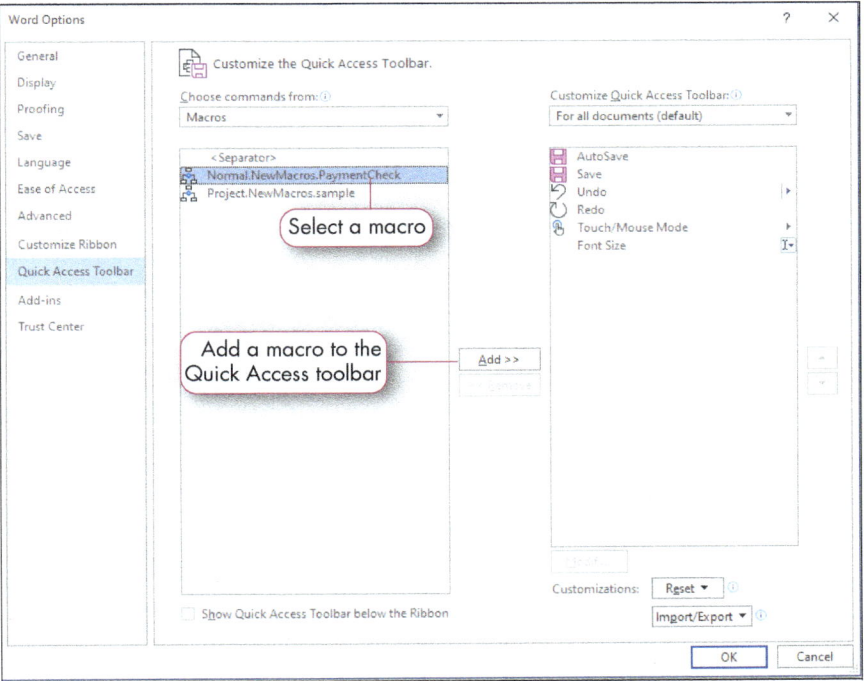

FIGURE 6.20 Assign a Macro to a Quick Access Toolbar Button

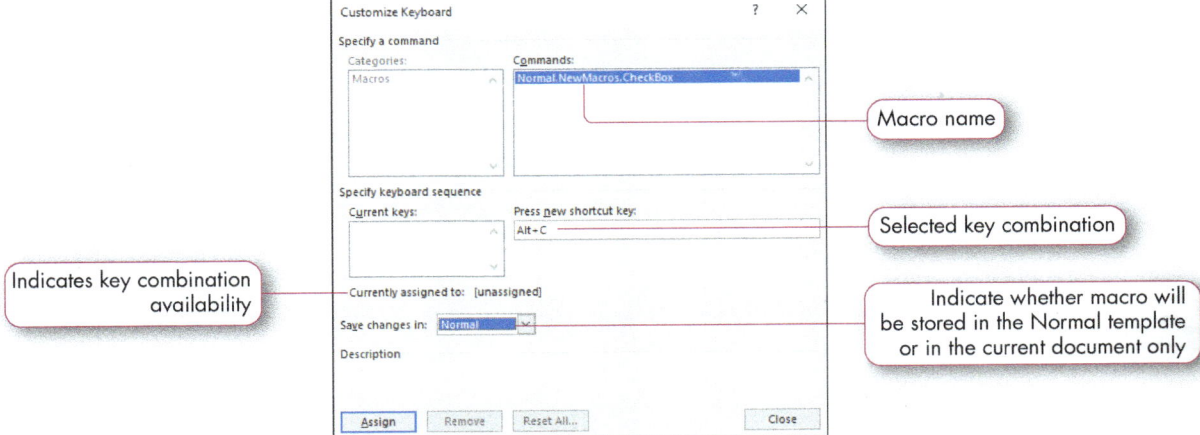

FIGURE 6.21 Assign a Macro to a Keyboard Combination

Before beginning the process of recording a macro, you should save the document. As you model an activity for a macro, the pointer assumes the appearance of a tape used in a tape recorder. Word records everything—every keystroke and click of the mouse (including any errors and corrections to errors). For this reason, you do not want to perform any unnecessary actions while recording a macro. Practice the process, perhaps even recording keystrokes on paper, before recording it as a macro so you are less likely to make mistakes.

If you make mistakes as you are recording, you can stop the process and re-record the macro or modify the macro code in VBA, which is addressed in the Modify a Macro section of this chapter. If you choose to re-record a macro, you can delete a faulty macro. To do so, open the Macro dialog box by clicking Macros in the Code group on the Developer tab, select a macro to remove, and then click Delete (see Figure 6.22). At that point, you can begin the recording process again. You can also run or edit a macro from the Macros dialog box.

Run a Macro

Having recorded a macro, you will run it to see if the macro performs the intended process. When a macro is tested and finalized, it is available to run at any time. Run a macro by placing the insertion point in the document where the macro is to begin and then clicking the macro button on the Quick Access Toolbar or pressing the specific key combination that you assigned to the macro. Alternatively, if a button or keyboard combination was not assigned, the Macros dialog box, shown in Figure 6.22, includes an option to run a selected macro. When you run a macro, Word processes the series of commands and keystrokes saved in the macro.

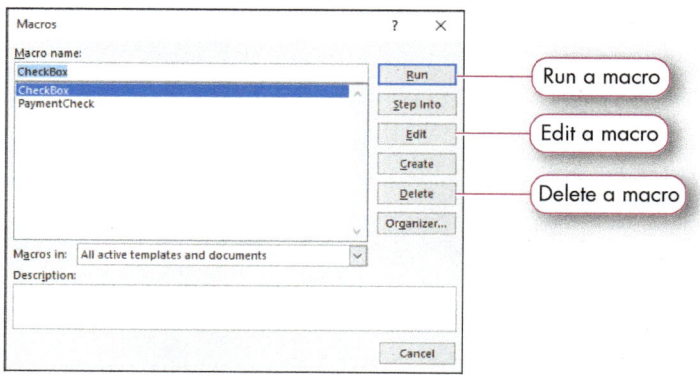

FIGURE 6.22 Manage Macros

STEP 2 ## Modify a Macro

If you test a macro and find that it does not work as intended, you might find it more effective to modify the macro than to re-record it in its entirety, especially if only a slight change is necessary. Or perhaps the document affected by the macro has changed in such a way that the macro should be modified to ensure that it runs correctly. You might even find it necessary to create a new macro that is a modification of an existing macro. In any of these situations, you can access the code that the macro instructions are based on and edit them to generate the intended result.

Macro instructions are written in ***Visual Basic for Applications (VBA)***, a subset of the Visual Basic programming language that is built into Microsoft Office. Fortunately, you do not have to be a programmer to use VBA, but it does help to be familiar with VBA code when editing a macro. As you record a macro, your actions are coded in a VBA application. The code, shown as a series of programming statements, can be accessed in the Visual Basic Editor (see Figure 6.23). If you are even slightly familiar with Visual Basic, you can make

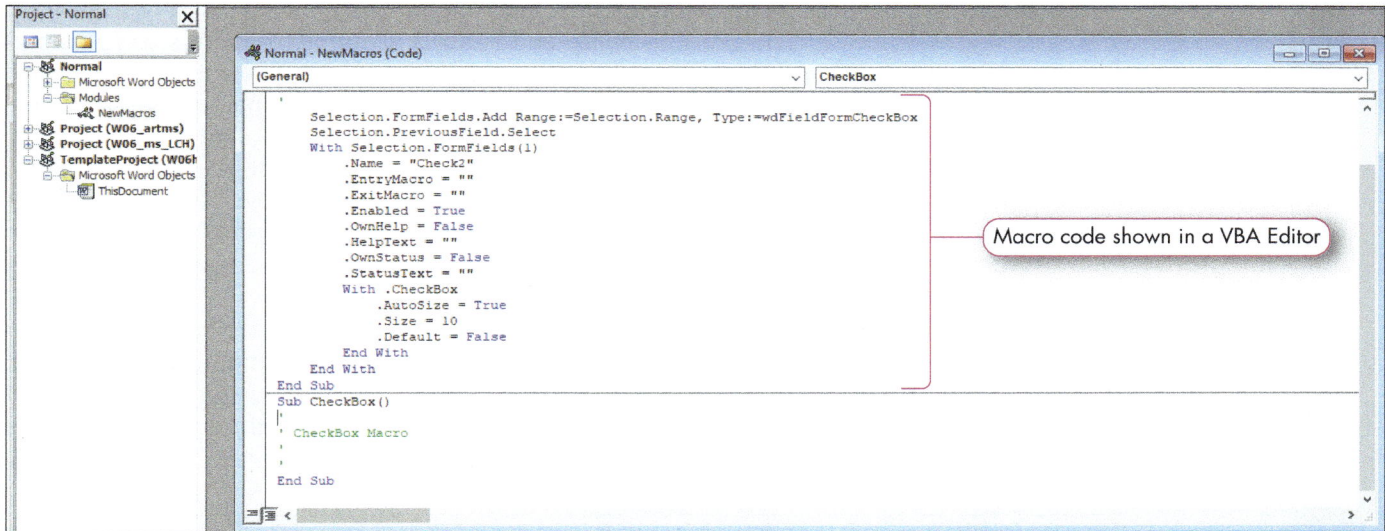

FIGURE 6.23 Macro VBA Code

minor adjustments to the code to modify a macro. To modify a macro, open the Macros dialog box, select a macro to edit, and then click Edit (refer to Figure 6.22). Make the necessary modifications to the macro and then close all open VBA windows. After editing a macro in this manner, you should run the macro again to ensure that it works as intended.

When you save a document that you have created that includes macros, you should save it as a Word Macro-Enabled Document file type, which adds the .docm extension to the filename. By saving the file as a .docm file, the availability of macros included in the document is ensured. If a document that contains a macro is not saved as macro-enabled, the macros will not be saved and will need to be rerecorded.

Understand Macro Security

Like a macro, a malicious program, such as a virus, is a series of coded steps. Because macros can contain malicious coding that, when run, can infect your system, macro security is of great importance in the Office environment. Especially when you download Word material from online sources or as an email attachment, you are at risk for transferring a malicious macro to your computer. Fortunately, you can use Word settings to protect your computer from malicious macros.

Work with Security Settings

When you download a Word document from an email attachment or an online source, a malicious virus could be hiding in a macro, disabling your system. For that reason, Microsoft has added strong usability and security features to address any document containing macros, regardless of whether a macro is actually malicious. The level of threat posed by a macro cannot be determined ahead of time, so macro security is applied to all documents containing macros.

When you open a document that contains macros, you will see a yellow message bar below the ribbon with a security warning and an Enable Content option (see Figure 6.24). If you are sure the document is from a reliable source, click Enable Content. Doing so makes the file a trusted document, and when you open it again you will not see the same warning.

Although in most cases Word's high security setting is desirable, at times you may want to modify it. For example, if you plan to transfer a file containing a macro between computers, or if the source of a macro is one that you trust, you can override the strict security setting so you can avoid having to enable content when the document is opened. Microsoft's Trust Center, which contains security settings that you should not modify

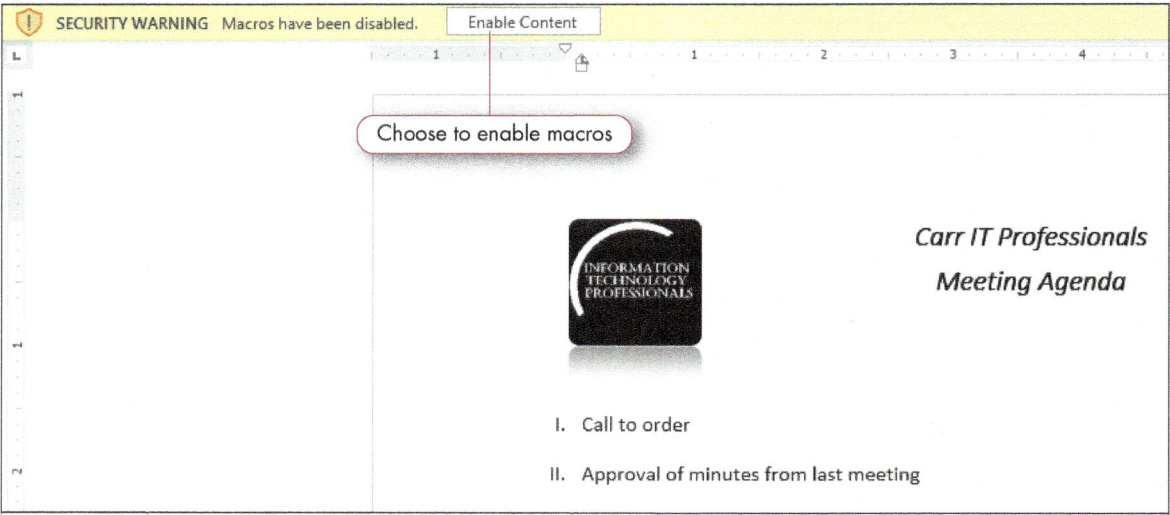

FIGURE 6.24 Document with Macros Disabled

without good cause, is accessible in Word when you click File, Options, Trust Center, and Trust Center Settings. It is also available when you click Macro Security in the Code group on the Developer tab. Security options are shown in Figure 6.25. Keep in mind that security settings might not be available to you in a company or school, as the system administrator might have locked them. Table 6.1 describes Trust Center settings.

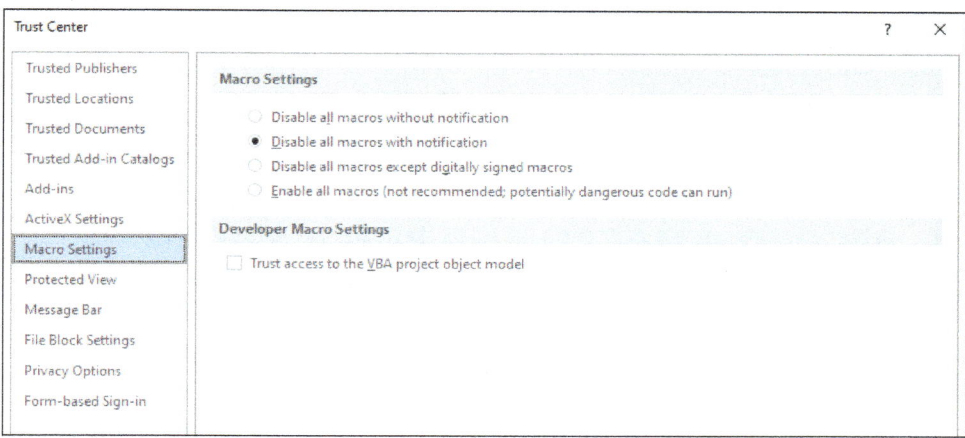

FIGURE 6.25 Use the Trust Center

TABLE 6.1	**Trust Center Settings**
Macro Setting	**Description**
Disable all macros without notification	All macros and security alerts are disabled.
Disable all macros with notification	This is the default setting. All macros are disabled, but you are alerted when a document contains a macro. You can enable macros on a case-by-case basis.
Disable all macros except digitally signed macros	This setting works similarly to *Disable all macros with notification*; however, it enables macros to run if they are digitally signed by a trusted publisher. If you have not included the publisher in your trusted list, you will be alerted. The alert enables you to allow a macro or to include a publisher in your trusted list. All unsigned macros are disabled, and you will not see an alert.
Enable all macros (not recommended; potentially dangerous code can run)	This setting enables all macros to run regardless of their authenticity or signature. This option is not recommended because it exposes your computer to potential attacks by viruses.
Trust access to the VBA project object model	This setting is for use by developers only.

> **MAC TIP: MACRO SECURITY**
> To access Security & Privacy settings, click the Word menu, and then click Preferences. You can choose one of the following levels of Macro security:
> - Disable all macros without notification
> - Disable all macros with notification
> - Enable all macros (not recommended; potentially dangerous code can run)

Critical Thinking

4. Discuss how you would determine that a process should be automated through a macro. *p. 439*

5. Explain why it is a good idea to save a document before running a macro. *p. 442*

6. Explain why enhanced security is necessary for documents that contain macros. *p. 444*

Hands-On Exercises

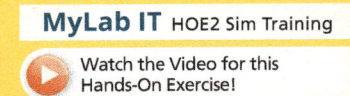
Skills covered: Record a Macro • Run a Macro • Modify a Macro

2 Macros

Your position at Rose Designs requires that you create forms frequently. As you work with the invoice form, you decide to automate the task of creating a check box for each payment method with a macro. After creating and testing the macro, you use the Visual Basic Editor to make a slight modification. Finally, you test the macro one last time before calling it final.

STEP 1 RECORD A MACRO AND RUN A MACRO

You create a macro to insert a check box and change the property settings for that form control. Automating the process saves time because there are several check boxes to insert, and ensures consistency. You begin the process of recording a macro to insert check boxes by assigning the macro to the current document. Refer to Figure 6.26 as you complete Step 1.

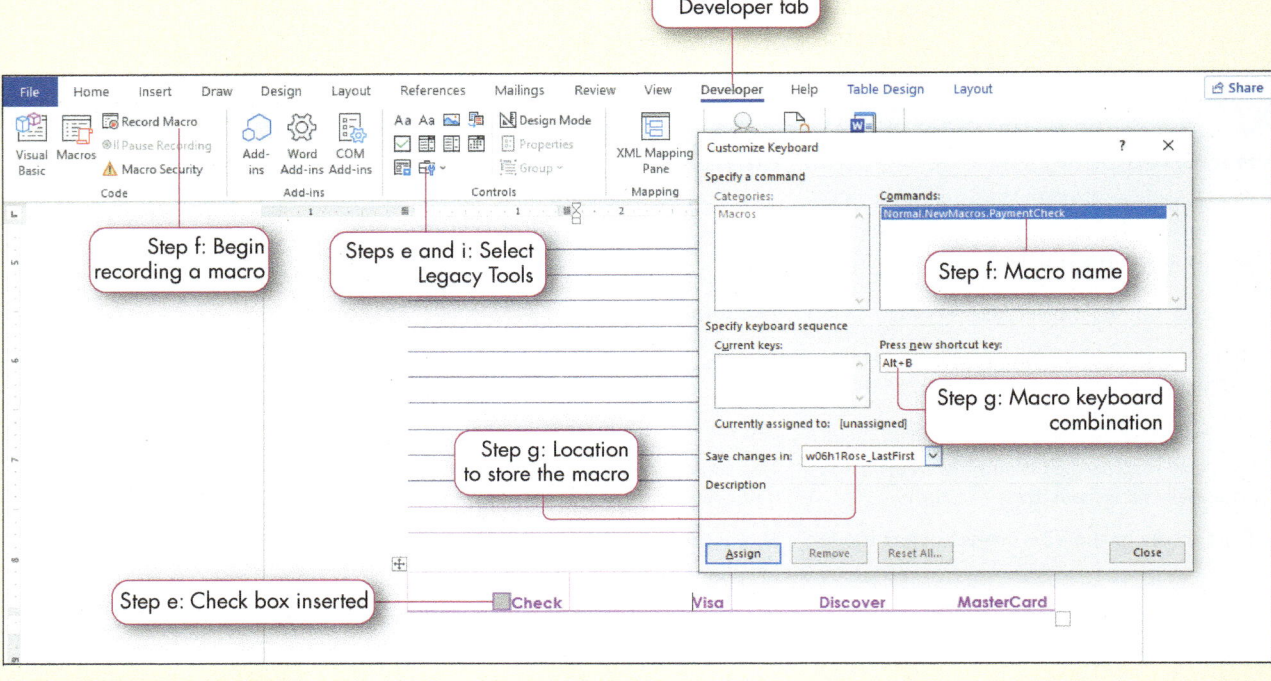

FIGURE 6.26 Record a Macro

a. Open *w06h1Rose_LastFirst* if you closed it at the end of the last exercise. Save the file as **w06h2Rose_LastFirst**, changing the file type to **Word Macro-Enabled Template**. Ensure that it is saved with your student files.

You save the file as a template that can include macros.

b. Click after *Thank you for your business!* near the end of the invoice form and press **Enter**. Insert a **4x1 Table**. Type **Check** in the first cell, **Visa** in the second, **Discover** in the third, and **MasterCard** in the fourth.

A one-row table summarizes payment methods.

c. Apply a table style of **Grid Table 1 Light – Accent 1** (row 1, column 2 under Grid Tables).

d. Click the **File tab** and click **Options**. Click **Customize Ribbon**. Select **Developer** in the Main Tabs section (unless it is already selected).

The Developer tab is shown on the ribbon.

e. Place the insertion point to the left of the *Check* payment method in the table. Click the **Developer tab** and click **Legacy Tools** in the Controls group. Select **Check Box Form Field** in the Legacy Forms section (on a Mac, select the Checkbox form control).

You select from the Legacy Tools collection, developed for use in earlier versions of Word but still available and effective when used in fillable forms.

> **TROUBLESHOOTING:** If bounded boxes display beside template text rather than a single check box, perhaps pushing the table onto the next page, you selected the Check Box control from ActiveX Controls instead of the Legacy Forms section. Click Undo on the Quick Access Toolbar and repeat Step e.

f. Click to the left of the *Visa* payment method in the second cell of the table. Click **Record Macro** in the Code group. Type **PaymentCheck** in the Macro name box. Click the **Store macro in arrow** and select **Documents Based On w06h2Rose_LastFirst**.

The Record Macro dialog box displays so that you can name the macro before you record it.

g. Click **Keyboard**. Press **Alt+b** (on a Mac, press option+control+b). Ensure that changes are saved in **w06h2Rose_LastFirst**.

h. Click **Assign** and click **Close**.

Word assigns the keyboard shortcut Alt+b to the PaymentCheck macro. The pointer resembles an arrow with an attached recorder. Any mouse or keyboard action will be recorded until the recording is stopped.

i. Click **Legacy Tools** in the Controls group and select **Check Box Form Field** in the Legacy Forms section. Click **Properties** in the Controls group. Select **Checked** in the default value section of the dialog box. Click **OK**.

You insert a Check Box control beside the Visa payment method and ensure that it is checked by default. That is because most of the payments you receive are through Visa, so it is most likely that it will be checked each time.

> **MAC TROUBLESHOOTING:** Select a Checkbox form field, click Options, select Ticked, and click OK.

> **TROUBLESHOOTING:** If you click something unintentionally or find yourself off track, click Stop Recording in the Code group. Close the document without saving, open *w06h2Rose_LastFirst*, and begin this step again.

j. Click **Stop Recording** in the Code group.

You can also click the square icon on the left side of the status bar to stop recording.

k. Save the document. Place the insertion point at the left of the *Discover* payment method. Click **Macros** in the Code group. Ensure that the macro related to PaymentCheck is selected. Click **Run**.

Having recorded a macro to insert a check box on the Rose Designs invoice, you run the macro to test it. Word runs the macro and inserts a Check Box control that is checked beside Discover.

> **TROUBLESHOOTING:** If the macro does not place a checked checkbox beside the payment method, delete any checkboxes that might have been added, click Macros in the Code group on the Developer tab, select the PaymentCheck macro, click Delete (on a Mac, click the minus sign), and click Yes. Repeat Steps f–j, beginning with the insertion point to the left of MasterCard.

l. Assign a button on the Quick Access Toolbar for the PaymentCheck macro as follows:

- Click the **File tab** and click **Options**. Click **Quick Access Toolbar**.
- Click the **Customize Quick Access Toolbar arrow** at the top right of the dialog box and select **For w06h2Rose_LastFirst**.

- Click the **Choose commands from arrow** and click **Macros**. Select the **Project.NewMacros.PaymentCheck macro**, click **Add**, and then click **Modify**. Click a solid blue square button (or a button of your choice), click **OK**, and then click **OK** again.

You assign a button to the PaymentCheck macro so that it is available on the Quick Access Toolbar.

> **MAC TROUBLESHOOTING:** Click the Word menu and select Preferences. Click Ribbon & Toolbar and click Quick Access Toolbar. Click the *Choose commands from* arrow and click Macros. Select the PaymentCheck macro and click the right arrow to add to the Customize Quick Access Toolbar pane. Click Save and close the Word Preferences dialog box. Note that optional buttons are not available on the Mac. When you add a macro to the Quick Access Toolbar, it assigns a generic button.

> **TROUBLESHOOTING:** If you are working in a school computer lab, you may not be able to modify the Quick Access Toolbar by adding the macro button.

m. Place the insertion point at the left of the *MasterCard* payment method. Press **Alt+b** or click the **macro button** on the Quick Access Toolbar.

Word runs the macro again and inserts a Check Box control that is checked next to the MasterCard payment method.

n. Save the template but do not close it.

STEP 2 ▶ MODIFY A MACRO

The Rose Designs invoice is near completion. The macro works well, but because you want all payment methods to be available (unchecked) on the template, you need to ensure that check boxes are not checked by default. Rather than delete each check box control and begin again, you modify the macro using the Visual Basic Editor. Then you run the macro again to replace the incorrectly checked boxes. Refer to Figure 6.27 as you complete Step 2.

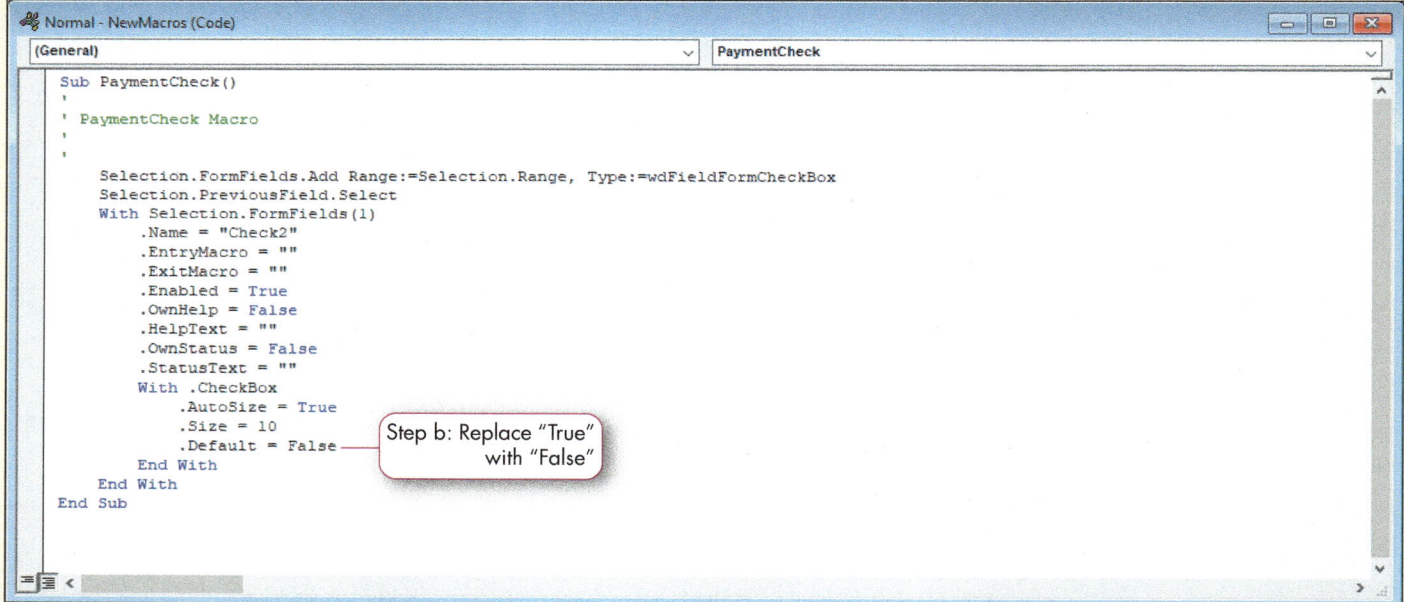

FIGURE 6.27 Modify a Macro

a. Click **Macros** in the Code group. Ensure that **PaymentCheck** is selected and click **Edit**.

The Visual Basic Editor program opens so that you can edit the programming statements.

b. Delete the word **True** at the end of the statement *.Default = True* and replace it with the word **False**.

You modify the Default statement near the end of the code, which shows a True value; this causes the box to display as checked. By changing the value to False, the box displays without a check.

> **TROUBLESHOOTING:** Do not delete any other part of the Default statement or any other programming statements. If you do, the macro may not run correctly. If you accidentally delete programming statements, refer to Figure 6.27 to retype them, and edit the Default statement again.

c. Close all open Visual Basic windows so that the change is saved and you return to the Word document.

You are ready to run the macro again to test the revised macro. Then you will run it repeatedly to replace the checked boxes with boxes that are not checked.

d. Drag to select the checked box beside *Visa* (or click at the left of the check box and press Shift+→) to select the checked box.

e. Click the **View tab**, click the **Macros arrow** in the Macros group, and then select **View Macros**.

The Macros dialog box displays so that you can run a macro.

f. Ensure that **PaymentCheck** is selected in the Macro name box and click **Run**.

The checked box is replaced by a box that does not display as checked.

g. Select the checked box that displays beside *Discover* and press **Alt+b** (or click the macro button on the Quick Access Toolbar).

h. Run the PaymentCheck macro to ensure that an unchecked box displays beside *MasterCard*.

i. Save and close w06h2Rose_LastFirst.dotm. You will submit this file to your instructor at the end of the last Hands-On Exercise. Keep Word open if you plan to continue with the next Hands-On Exercise.

Document Protection

As you work with documents containing confidential information, you may want to protect those documents from unauthorized access. In other situations, you might want to store reference documents, such as policies and procedures, on an organization's network for others to read but not change. To assist in such situations, Word provides tools that enable you to protect documents on many levels.

In this section, you will learn to protect documents against unauthorized access, as well as changes to formatting or content. You will also learn to mark a document as final and set passwords.

Apply Document Restrictions

Word enables you to focus on the preparation and formatting of documents of all sorts. Some documents, such as contracts or other binding agreements, will undoubtedly contain text that should not be changed once the document is considered final. Other documents may contain formatting that should not be altered. Word includes features that enable you to finalize a document so that it cannot be changed. In addition, you can limit access to formatting features so that others cannot alter styles. You can use these restrictive features independently or in combination. Occasionally, you will want to enable editing by a select few while protecting a document from changes by others. Using Word, you can protect a document in a variety of ways.

STEP 1 Mark a Document as Final

When you want to share a document with others but do not want them to make any changes, you create a read-only file. A read-only file lets recipients read but not change a document unless they remove the read-only status. Word provides a Mark as Final feature that enables you to designate a document as a read-only file. A document that has been marked as final is identified by a Final property on the status bar, as shown in Figure 6.28. The designation effectively identifies the document as a final copy, not a draft. The Mark as Final feature is found on the File tab in the Info section. (On a Mac, use Always Open Read-Only on the Review tab to mark a document as final.) When marked as final, editing and proofing marks do not display; all commands in the ribbon are grayed out; and the document cannot be modified unless the read-only status is removed. Click Edit Anyway, shown in Figure 6.28, to remove read-only status and edit a document.

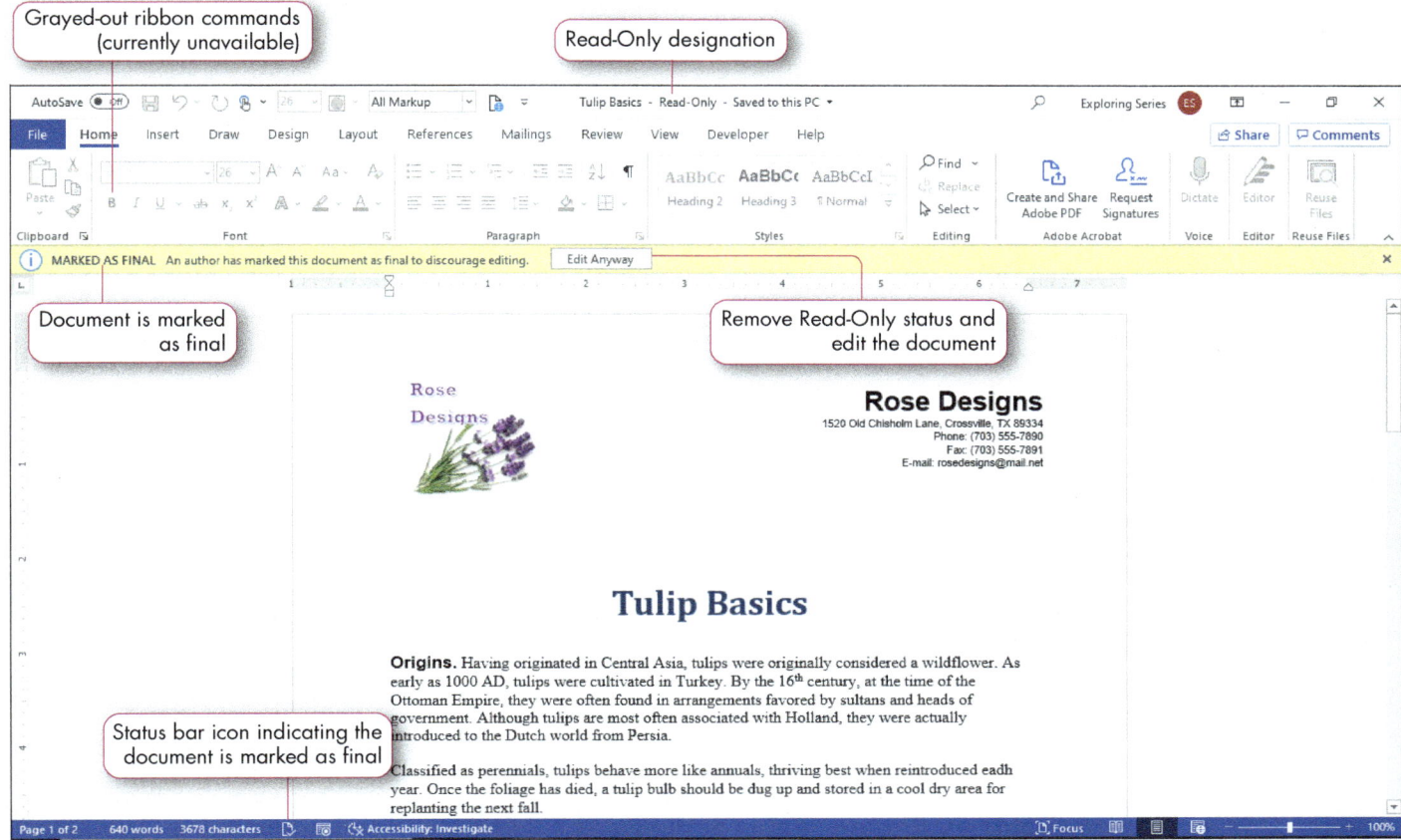

FIGURE 6.28 Mark a Document as Final

Marking a document as final is not a security feature, as anyone who receives an electronic copy of the file can choose to edit the file by removing the read-only status from the file. Marking a document as final simply advises that the file should only be modified under allowable conditions.

> **TIP: ASK READERS TO OPT-IN TO EDITING**
> Instead of marking a document as final so that it automatically opens with a Read-Only designation, you can ask a reader to choose whether to open a document as read-only. Click the File tab, click Info, and click Protect Document. Select Always Open Read-Only and save the file. Before the document is opened, a reader must respond to a prompt: *The author would like you to open this as read-only, unless you need to make changes. Open as read-only?* Responding *Yes* or *No* dictates the form in which the document opens.

Because the Mark as Final setting can be bypassed by anyone, you should consider using the Restrict Editing command for document security, including preventing changes to a document. The Restrict Editing pane, shown in Figure 6.29, includes an option to apply a read-only setting to an open document. To open the Restrict Editing pane, do one of the following:

- Click Restrict Editing in the Protect group on either the Developer tab or the Review tab.
- Click Info from the File tab, click Protect Document, and then click Restrict Editing.

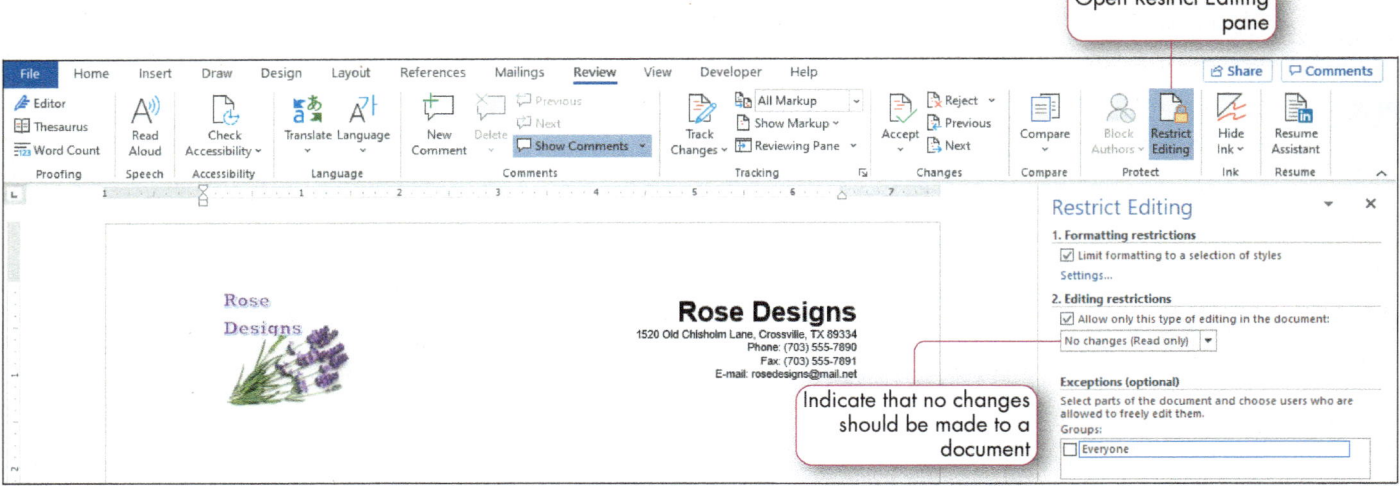

FIGURE 6.29 Restrict Editing in a Document

STEP 2   ## Set Formatting Restrictions

An organization may prefer to use certain styles and formatting, ensuring consistency among company documents. Some styles may even be unique to the organization. As such, it is likely that document formatting in some company documents should not be changed, intentionally or otherwise. As a document designer, you can limit the availability of styles, allowing others access to only a select few (if any) styles. For example, if you restrict the Heading 3 style, then no one can apply that style in the current document. To ensure that styles cannot be modified, you set *formatting restrictions* on documents. When you apply formatting restrictions, you identify styles that are available, restricting access to all others, as shown in Figure 6.30.

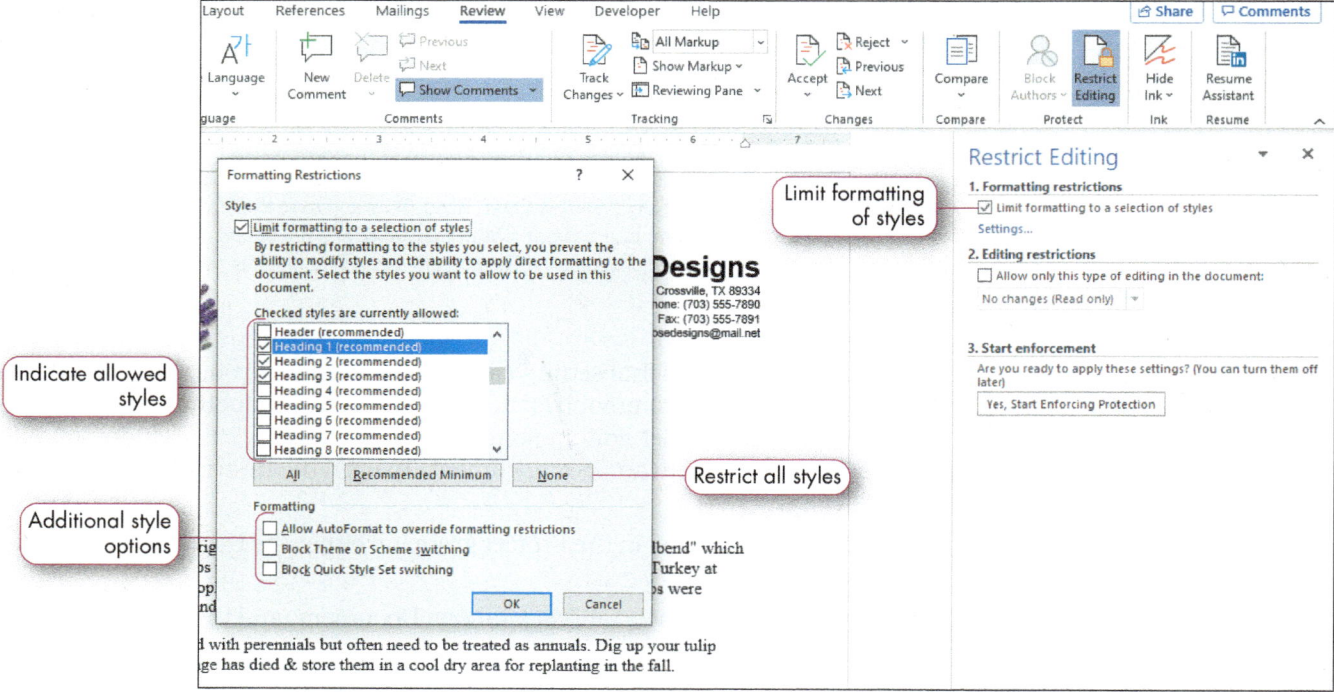

FIGURE 6.30 Limit Styles

Apply formatting restrictions:

1. Open the Restrict Editing pane and click the *Limit formatting to a selection of styles* check box to select it.
2. Click Settings and deselect any styles in the dialog box that should be restricted.
3. Apply other restrictions or allowances, as shown in Figure 6.30. Click OK to close the dialog box.
4. Click *Yes, Start Enforcing Protection* and enter a password (or click OK to bypass the password setting). If a password is entered, you must confirm it by typing it again.

> **MAC TIP: RESTRICT EDITING**
> Restrict Editing to apply formatting restrictions is not an option.

STEP 3 ▶ Set Editing Restrictions and Exceptions

Word enables you to set several levels of editing restrictions, limiting the types of changes that can be made to a document. For example, if you want to track changes a user makes to a document, even if the user neglects to activate Track Changes, you can ensure that the Track Changes feature is always active. Doing so keeps you apprised of changes made to collaborative documents. You can limit users to inserting comments without changing document content, or restrict data entry to areas of variable data in a form. To apply editing restrictions, display the Restrict Editing pane and click the *Allow only this type of editing in the document* check box to select it. Select a restriction as described in Table 6.2 and click Yes, Start Enforcing Protection.

TABLE 6.2	Editing Restrictions
Restriction Type	**Description**
Tracked changes	Enables the Track Changes feature automatically and marks the document with any changes made.
Comments	Enables users to add comments to the document but prohibits other changes.
Filling in forms	Enables users to fill in variable data on a form but prohibits other changes.
No changes (Read only)	Prohibits all changes to a document.

Even though a document is identified as a read-only file, you can extend editing privileges to a select group of individuals. A **user exception** is one or more persons who can edit all or specific parts of a restricted document. For example, you might want all team members to edit only a certain section of a collaborative document. You can create an exception by enabling users to edit that section only. It is possible to create various user exceptions throughout a document by enabling some individuals to edit certain text, while enforcing editing restrictions for others. Word color-codes text for which you create different user exceptions.

HOW TO

Apply user exceptions to document restrictions:

1. Open the Restrict Editing pane. Click the Editing restrictions check box to select it and indicate the editing to allow.
2. Select text that should be made available for editing to a select group of people. Click the Everyone check box to select it (refer to Figure 6.29), or click More users to open the Add Users dialog box where you can add user names, domains, or email addresses for the individuals you want to add, separated by semicolons. Click OK.
3. Click Yes, Start Enforcing Protection and enter a password (or click OK to bypass the password setting).

TIP: USING INFORMATION RIGHTS MANAGEMENT SERVICE

You can use Microsoft's Information Rights Management (IRM) service to restrict permission to document content to only those people who have been authorized through the service. IRM enables you to set permissions so that only intended recipients can edit the document content to which they are granted access. By using IRM, you can specify different users and the types of permissions granted to them, effectively enforcing corporate policy related to dissemination of confidential or proprietary content. To use the service, Microsoft Windows Rights Management Services (RMS) Client software must be installed.

You typically apply restrictions when a document is considered complete. Even so, you may occasionally want to make changes to a document that has been restricted. In that case, you must remove editing restrictions, applying them again after changes are complete. To remove editing restrictions, click Stop Protection in the Restrict Editing pane, entering a password if required.

Work with Passwords

For documents that are highly confidential or that contain sensitive information, you can set a password to limit access. A password is also recommended when you store a document on a network drive but want to restrict access to only those who are approved to view the document. In any situation where a document must be protected and made available to only a few, you should consider assigning a password, but be advised that once a password is set, you must remember it, as there is no way to retrieve the password and the file will become permanently unavailable if the correct password is not provided. A password can include letters, numbers, and symbols; a strong password uses a combination of all three. A document password is case-sensitive, so it can, and should, include both uppercase and lowercase letters.

STEP 4 ▶ ## Set a Password

You can set a password in several ways in Word, and you can indicate the type of protection a password applies. A ***password*** can protect an entire document so that no one can open the document without the proper password, or you can require a password to open the file for editing while enabling anyone to open a read-only copy of the document.

You can restrict access to an entire document in a couple of ways, either through a simple password or through encryption. Although the end result appears to be the same, the underlying principle is very different. Assigning a password to prevent users from modifying a document is like locking important papers in a safe, granting access only to those who know the combination. Encrypting contents of a document, however, is akin to shredding the important papers before locking them in a safe. A password still grants access, but the shredded bits must be put back together behind the scenes before the document is displayed for editing. In either case, through encryption or the use of a simple password, a user is still required to enter a password before access is granted. The strongest protection is through encryption, but a secure password is sufficient for most documents.

HOW TO

Create a password that encrypts and protects an entire document:

1. Click the File tab and ensure that Info is selected.
2. Click Protect Document.
3. Click Encrypt with a Password, type a password, and then click OK.
4. Retype the password to confirm and click OK.

Create a password that protects an entire document without encryption:

1. Click the File tab and click Save As.
2. Click Browse and navigate to the save location, opening the Save As dialog box.
3. Click Tools (at the left of the Save button as shown in Figure 6.31) and click General Options.
4. Type a password in the *Password to open* box. Click OK, confirm the password, and click OK again.
5. Click Save.

Create a password to open a document:

1. Click the Review tab and click Protect Document in the Protect group.
2. Click in the *Set a password to open this document* box and type a password.
3. Click OK, confirm the password, and click OK.

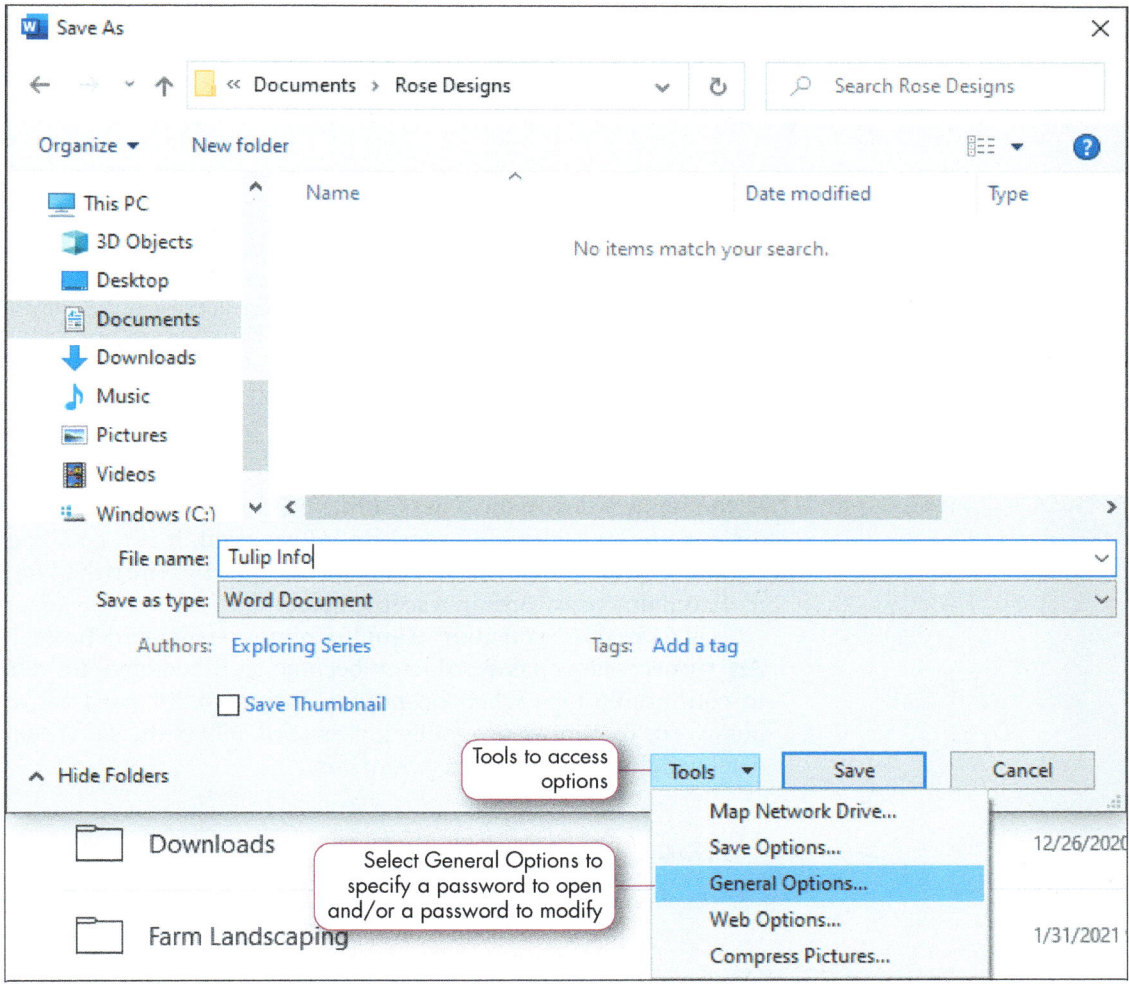

FIGURE 6.31 Save with a Password

You may want to enable some users to open and edit a document, while others should be restricted to read-only access. Unlike marking a document as final, protecting a document with a password that specifies whether a user can modify or only read a document is a more specific way to ensure appropriate access.

HOW TO

Enable anyone to open a read-only copy of a document, but require a password to modify contents:

1. Click the File tab and click Save As.
2. Click Browse and navigate to the save location, opening the Save As dialog box.
3. Click Tools (at the left of the Save button) and click General Options.
4. Click in the *Password to modify* box and type a password. Click OK, confirm the password, and then click OK again.
5. Click Save.

MAC HOW TO

Create a password to modify document contents:

1. Click the Review tab and click Protect Document in the Protect group.
2. Click in the *Set a password to modify this document* box and type a password.
3. Click OK, confirm the password, and then click OK.

TIP: USE A PASSWORD

When saving a document, you can include both a password to open and another password to modify, which provides another level of protection. If the second password is not known, a user can click Read Only to view the file and can then edit the document but cannot save the document with changes in the same location from which it was opened. The document can be edited and saved in a different location but can only be opened again if the initial password to open the document is known.

Modify or Delete a Password

If you know a document's password, you can change or delete it at any time. Especially for documents containing sensitive information, it is a good idea to change passwords periodically. Of course, the use of passwords carries the risk of forgetting them, so be sure to record any passwords in a secure place.

On occasion, you may want to remove password protection from a document. An unnecessary password can become cumbersome to remember and annoying to continually type when opening a document. Or perhaps you want to change the password. To remove or modify a password, follow the same steps you took to set it, but delete or change it in the password box.

Critical Thinking

7. Explain why an organization might restrict editing to a selection of styles, allowing some while disallowing others. *p. 452*

8. Provide rationale for marking a document as final, especially since doing so does not actually keep a user from editing the document. *p. 451*

Hands-On Exercises

MyLab IT HOE3 Sim Training

Watch the Video for this Hands-On Exercise!

Skills covered: Mark a Document as Final • Set Formatting Restrictions • Set Editing Restrictions and Exceptions • Set a Password • Modify or Delete a Password

3 Document Protection

The management of Rose Designs has decided to include printed information related to an item or service provided by the company with each sale. The spotlighted item will change each month, with this month's being that of tulip bulbs. You have received a draft document with suggested changes that you have now incorporated. You mark the document as final while also setting formatting restrictions, applying editing exceptions, and setting a password.

STEP 1 MARK A DOCUMENT AS FINAL

The document has been reviewed by several people and you are satisfied that this is the final version, so you mark it as final. Refer to Figure 6.32 as you complete Step 1.

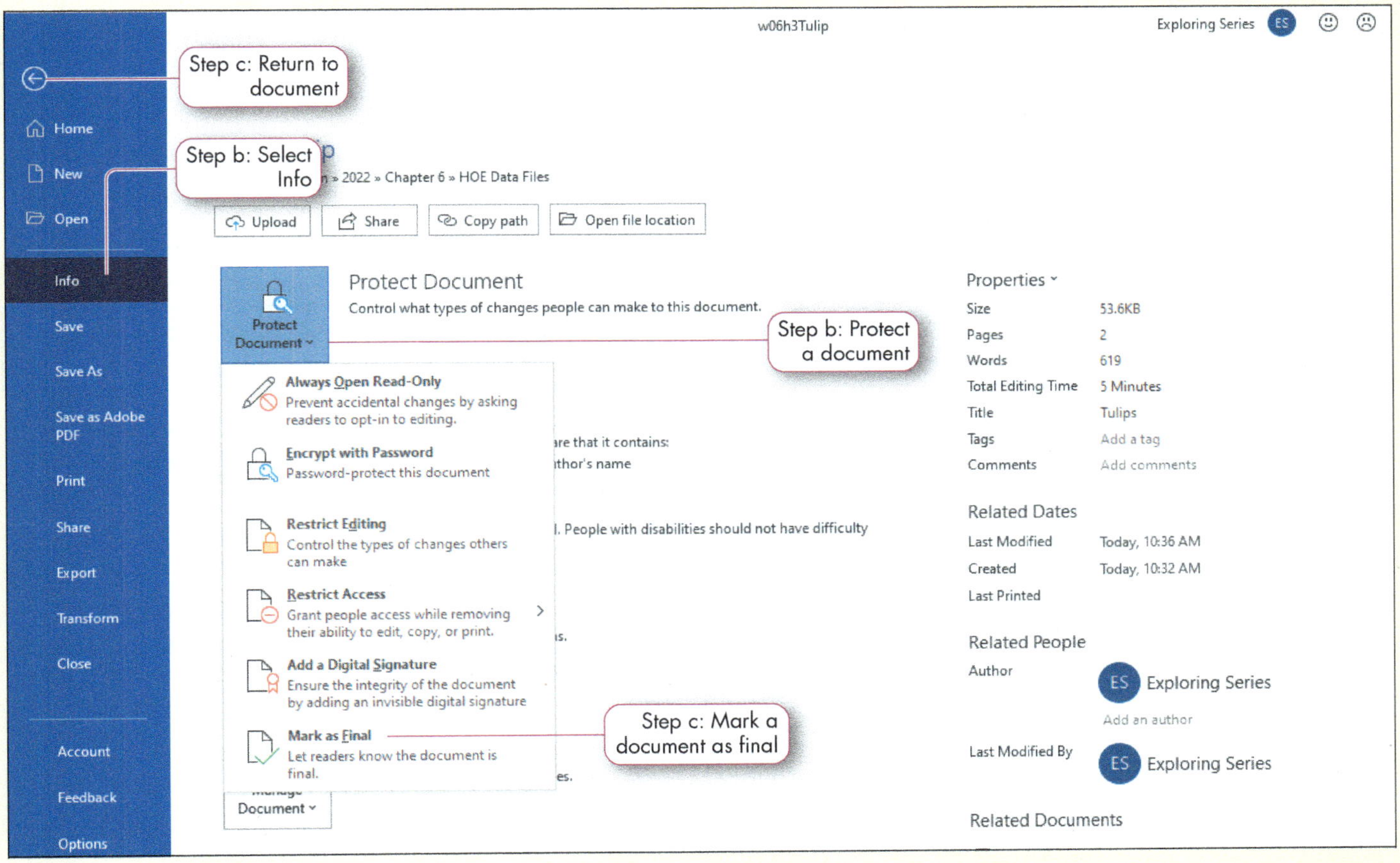

FIGURE 6.32 Mark a Document as Final

a. Open *w06h3Tulip* and save it as **w06h3Tulip_LastFirst**.

b. Click the **File tab**, click **Info**, and then click **Protect Document.**

c. Click **Mark as Final**. Click **OK**. Click **OK** again. Click **Back**.

The yellow bar at the top of the document advises that the document has been marked as final.

> **MAC TROUBLESHOOTING:** Select Always Open Read-Only on the Review tab in the Protect group.

SET FORMATTING RESTRICTIONS

You are now ready to send the tulip information to the marketing manager so she can review the document and provide suggestions. However, you want to restrict editing to changes in styles. Refer to Figure 6.33 as you complete Step 2.

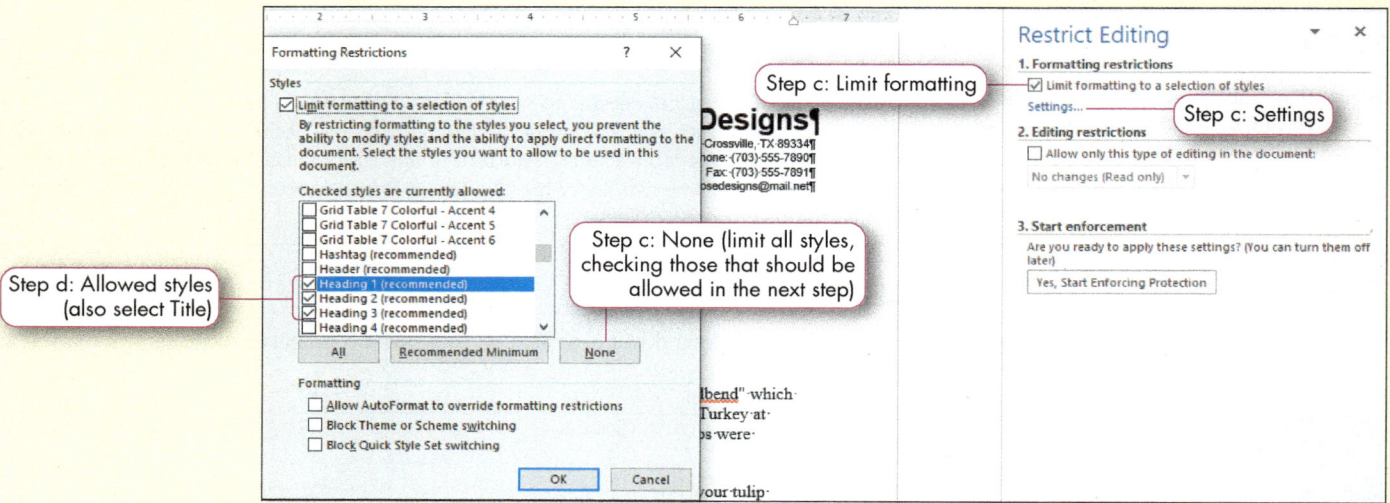

FIGURE 6.33 Limit Formatting

a. Click **Edit Anyway** in the yellow bar at the top of the document.

b. Click the **Review tab** and click **Restrict Editing** in the Protect group to display the Restrict Editing pane.

> **MAC TROUBLESHOOTING:** Read through this step and proceed to Step 3, as Restrict Editing is not available. Contact your instructor for further direction.

c. Click the **Limit formatting to a selection of styles** check box in the Restrict Editing pane to select it. Click **Settings** to display the Formatting Restrictions dialog box. Click **None**. Do not click OK.

You remove the allowance that all styles can be changed, effectively restricting a user from changing any styles.

d. Scroll through the list of styles and select **Heading 1 (recommended), Heading 2 (recommended), Heading 3 (recommended)**, and **Title (recommended)**. Click **OK**. Click **No** in the Microsoft Word dialog box that asks if you want to remove styles that are not allowed.

After removing all styles from the list that can be edited, you return access to selected styles.

e. Click **Yes, Start Enforcing Protection** in the Restrict Editing pane. Click **OK** to refrain from setting a password.

f. Click the **Home tab**.

Most commands on the Home tab are grayed out, indicating that the document is restricted against formatting changes. The only styles shown in the Styles group are those that are currently available.

g. Place the insertion point in the title *Tulip Basics* and click **Title** in the Styles group. (If Title is not shown, click More in the Styles group.)

Word enables you to apply a different style if that style was enabled when you edited restrictions; however, you cannot change character or paragraph formatting.

h. Save the document.

SET EDITING RESTRICTIONS AND EXCEPTIONS

You want the company botanist to review the tulip information for accuracy. You use features to restrict the document to the insertion of comments only. Refer to Figure 6.34 as you complete Step 3.

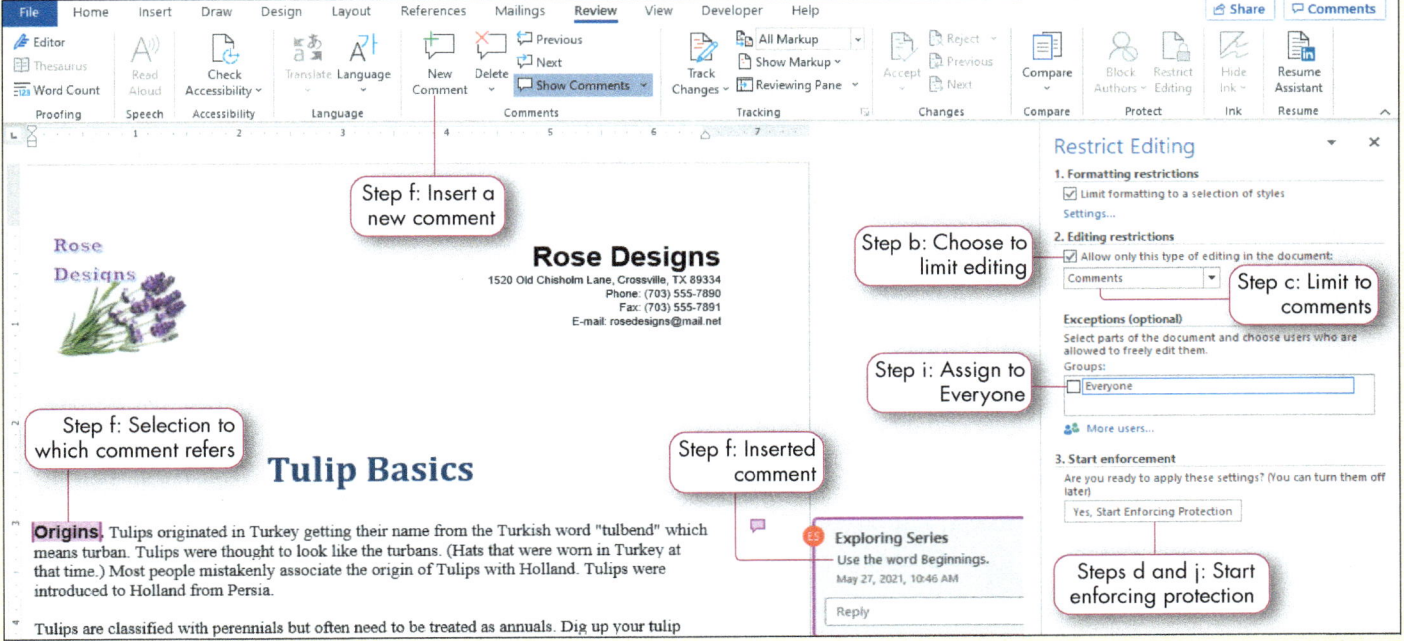

FIGURE 6.34 Limit Editing to Comments

a. Click **Stop Protection**, which displays at the bottom of the Restrict Editing pane.

The formatting restriction is removed so that the entire document can be edited.

b. Click the **Allow only this type of editing in the document** check box in the *Editing restrictions* section of the Restrict Editing pane to select it.

The Editing restrictions arrow is available so that you can specify the type of editing to restrict. Additionally, an Exceptions (optional) section displays on the pane so that you can apply user exceptions to the editing restrictions.

c. Click the **Editing restrictions arrow**, which displays *No changes (Read only)*, and click **Comments**.

> **MAC TROUBLESHOOTING:** Click the Review tab and click Protect Document in the Protect group. Click the *Protect document for* check box to select it. Click Comments. Click OK. Skip to Step e.

d. Click **Yes, Start Enforcing Protection**. Click **OK** to bypass the step of adding a password.

The only change allowed is that of placing comments. Formatting restrictions are also in place once again.

e. Select the word **Origins** at the beginning of the first body paragraph and press **Delete**.

You cannot delete the text. The status bar displays the message *You can't make this change because the selection is locked*. The Restrict Editing pane now displays buttons to show document regions you can edit. However, because you restricted editing to comments only, no regions are available for editing.

f. Click the **Review tab**. Click **New Comment** in the Comments group and type **Use the word Beginnings.** (Include the period.) Click **Post comment**.

The editing restrictions allow you to insert a comment.

g. Close the Comments pane. Click **Stop Protection** in the Restrict Editing pane. Confirm that check boxes for Formatting restrictions and Editing restrictions in the Restrict Editing pane are selected.

h. Select the two body paragraphs near the middle of the first page, beginning with *Planting* and ending with *5 to 6 inches apart*.

i. Click the check box beside **Everyone** in the *Exceptions (optional)* section of the Restrict Editing pane to select it. Deselect the text.

> **TROUBLESHOOTING:** If you are unable to click the check box for *Everyone* in the *Exceptions (optional)* section of the Restrict Editing pane, make sure you have first selected text in the document.

Although you indicated earlier that the only change allowed is the addition of comments, you select a set of paragraphs and apply a user exception so that those paragraphs can be edited. The paragraphs you selected display with a light gray background, indicating that a user exception is applied to them.

j. Click **Yes, Start Enforcing Protection**. Click **OK** to bypass the selection of a password.

k. Select the first body paragraph in the document, beginning with *Origins*. Press **Delete**.

You cannot delete the paragraph because it is not included in the user exception and is protected against editing.

l. Click anywhere in the second paragraph of the available text (shaded light yellow to indicate that it is available). The paragraph begins with *Tulips prefer soil with reasonable*. Click the **Home tab** and select **Heading 1** from the Styles group. (If Heading 1 is not shown, click More in the Styles group.) Close the Restrict Editing pane.

Word enables this editing because you are a part of *Everyone* included in the user exception for the heading. You can use that particular style because it is allowed in the formatting restrictions.

m. Save the document.

SET A PASSWORD AND MODIFY OR DELETE A PASSWORD

The document is complete and ready for distribution. To protect against unauthorized access you set a password, ensuring that only those who should be allowed to modify the document are granted access. Refer to Figure 6.35 as you complete Step 4.

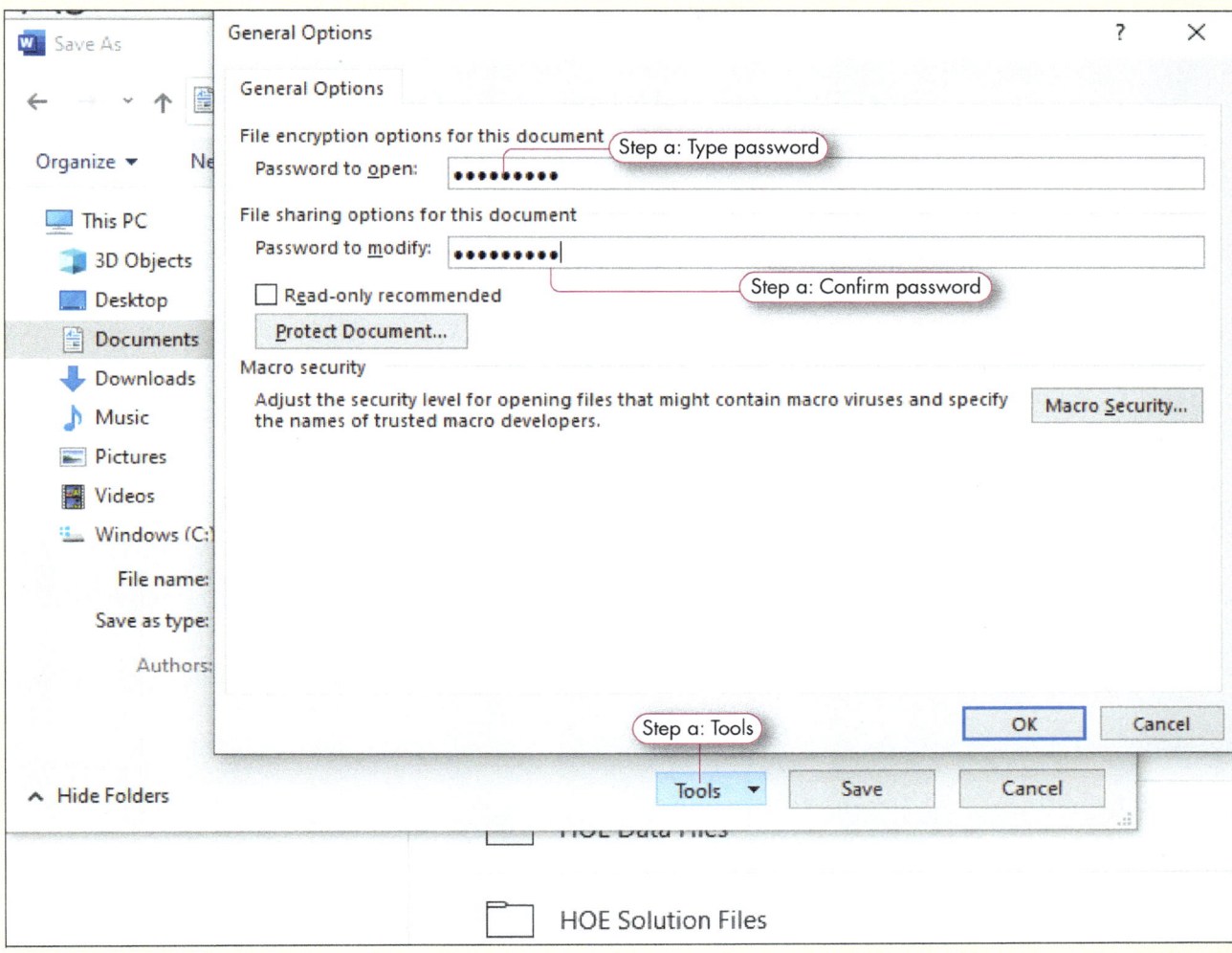

FIGURE 6.35 Set and Modify a Password

a. Click the **File tab** and click **Save As**. Click **Browse** and navigate to the location where you save your student files. Click **Tools** (near the bottom of the Save As dialog box). Click **General Options**. With the insertion point in the *Password to open* box, type **Expl0r!ng** and click **OK**. Confirm the password and click **OK**. Save and close the document. If asked whether you want to replace the document, respond affirmatively.

> **MAC TROUBLESHOOTING:** Click the Review tab and click Protect Document in the Protect group. Click *Set a password to modify this document*. Type Expl0r!ng in the password box. Click OK. Confirm the password and click OK. Close the document.

b. Open **w06h3Tulip_LastFirst**, type **Expl0r!ng** in the password box, and then click **OK**.

Having supplied the password, you are able to open the document.

c. Repeat Step a, but instead of typing in the *Password to open* box, delete all characters (shown as solid round dots). Click **OK**. Save and close the document.

You have removed the password.

d. Open **w06h3Tulip_LastFirst**. Click the **File tab** and click **Info**. Click **Protect Document**. Click **Encrypt with Password**. Type **Expl0r!ng** in the Encrypt Document box and click **OK**. Confirm the password. Save and close the document.

> **MAC TROUBLESHOOTING:** Contact your instructor for further information, as Encrypt with Password is not available.

e. Open **w06h3Tulip_LastFirst**. Type **Expl0r!ng** in the Password box and click **OK**.

The document opens after you supply the password.

f. Click the **File tab** and click **Info**. Click **Protect Document**. Click **Encrypt with Password.** Delete all characters (shown as solid round dots). Click **OK**.

g. Save and close the document. Exit Word. Based on your instructor's directions, submit:
w06h2Rose_LastFirst.dotm
w06h3Tulip_LastFirst

Chapter Objectives Review

After reading this chapter, you have accomplished the following objectives:

1. Select and create a template.

- **Download a template:** Use a Word template to create documents such as letters, memos, reports, résumés, agendas, calendars, brochures, and checklists. Templates are available to download from the File tab or when you first open Word.

- **Save a document as a template:** Save a document that you use frequently, with only minor modifications, as a template. Word saves templates with an extension of .dotx.

2. Use building blocks.

- **Create and insert a building block:** A building block is text or a graphic that you plan to reuse, such as a logo, disclaimer, or header. Building blocks are listed in the Building Blocks Organizer.

3. Customize theme settings.

- **Customize theme colors:** Various sets of theme colors are included in a design theme. To create a custom color theme, you can modify colors in the current theme and save the set with a new name.

- **Customize theme fonts:** Various sets of theme fonts are included in a design theme. To create a custom font set, you can modify font selections in the current theme and save the set with a new name.

- **Apply theme effects:** Theme effects are related to lines and fills, such as shadowing, glows, and borders. Although you cannot create a custom set of theme effects, you can choose from built-in sets.

- **Save a custom theme:** Having chosen theme colors, theme fonts, and theme effects, you can save changes as a custom theme, resulting in a file with an extension of .thmx.

4. Compare and combine documents.

- **View documents side by side:** Compare two documents when you view them side by side. You can scroll them in sync or independently from one another.

- **Consolidate documents:** Word's Compare and Combine features make it possible to evaluate the contents of multiple documents, noting differences, while also integrating changes from multiple documents into one.

5. Create a macro.

- **Record a macro:** A macro is a series of actions that can be recorded and assigned a name. Later, the steps can be repeated by running the macro.

- **Run a macro:** Word enables you to refer to a macro by name or to invoke it by a keyboard combination or button (depending on how it was created) so that the tasks included are repeated.

- **Modify a macro:** After a macro is created, you can modify it by adjusting its underlying code.

6. Understand macro security.

- **Work with security settings:** As a coded set of steps, a macro has the potential of being used as a vehicle for viruses and malicious software. Microsoft's Trust Center provides security settings that lessen the risk of damage from the use of macros in a document.

7. Apply document restrictions.

- **Mark a document as final:** The Mark as Final command enables you to create a read-only file, with the status property set to Final. This is a helpful command for communicating to other people that the document is not a draft but a completed and final version.

- **Set formatting restrictions:** You can set formatting restrictions to allow or disallow various document formatting features related to styles.

- **Set editing restrictions and exceptions:** Editing restrictions specify conditions for users to modify a document, such as disallowing all restrictions except for comments, or the completion of form fields. Exceptions for individuals or groups can be made, so editing can occur in selected areas of a document.

8. Work with passwords.

- **Set a password:** You can control access to a document by setting a password. A password can be used to protect the entire document from unauthorized access or to control access for modification.

- **Modify or delete a password:** After a password is created, you can change it or delete it.

Key Terms Matching

Match the key terms with their definitions. Write the key term letter by the appropriate numbered definition.

a. AutoText
b. Building block
c. Combine
d. Compare
e. Formatting restriction
f. Legal blacklining
g. Macro
h. Password
i. Placeholder

j. Quick Parts
k. Side by Side view
l. Synchronous scrolling
m. Theme colors
n. Theme effects
o. Theme fonts
p. User exception
q. Visual Basic for Applications (VBA)

1. _____ The process of comparing two documents, showing what has changed between them in a new third document. **p. 431**

2. _____ Provides a location for entry of various types of variable data. **p. 422**

3. _____ Feature that uses the process of legal blacklining to evaluate the contents of two versions of a document for a line-by-line comparison. **p. 431**

4. _____ Theme options that include lines, fill, and 3D collections, such as shadows, glows, and borders. **p. 429**

5. _____ Enables you to move through the view of two documents at the same time using either of the two scroll bars. **p. 430**

6. _____ Feature shown on the ribbon, and also a Building Block gallery, that provides access to categories of building blocks. **p. 425**

7. _____ Collections of a coordinating heading and body text font for each different theme. **p. 429**

8. _____ Records a set of instructions that executes a specific task. **p. 439**

9. _____ Feature that integrates all changes between multiple documents into a single document. **p. 432**

10. _____ Represents a macro in programming code. **p. 443**

11. _____ Comprises an individual or group that is allowed to edit all or specific parts of a restricted document. **p. 453**

12. _____ A document element that is composed of text or graphics, such as a logo or contract disclaimer, typically created and saved by an individual Word user. **p. 425**

13. _____ A series of characters designed to protect a document from unauthorized access or to limit modification of a document. **p. 454**

14. _____ Sets of coordinated colors for current text, background, accents, and hyperlinks. **p. 428**

15. _____ A predefined item, like a table, list, header, and text box, that you plan to reuse. **p. 425**

16. _____ A setting that limits the types of styles users can apply in a document. **p. 452**

17. _____ A feature that enables you to view two documents side by side on the same screen. **p. 430**

Multiple Choice

1. What must you consider when creating a password to secure a document from unauthorized access?
   (a) A password cannot be deleted after it is set.
   (b) If you forget the password, the document will be permanently unavailable.
   (c) You must identify a password that is approved by the IRM.
   (d) A password cannot be changed after it has been established.

2. Why might you occasionally choose to modify Word's security settings related to opening a document that includes macros?
   (a) So that a document can be copied to an external disk drive or to online storage
   (b) So that a setting, such as theme colors, can be changed
   (c) So that if you trust the source of a macro you do not need to enable the document each time you open it
   (d) So that the document can be used repeatedly for data entry

3. Which feature enables you to integrate all changes from multiple documents into a single document?
   (a) Side by Side view
   (b) Compare
   (c) Combine
   (d) Consolidate

4. What does the Mark as Final feature do?
   (a) It enables you to designate a document as a read-only file.
   (b) It makes it possible to include a macro in the document.
   (c) It enables you to protect the document with a password.
   (d) It requires the use of Windows Rights Management Services (RMS) Client software.

5. Which of the following features would ensure that a customized cover page designed for reuse is available for inclusion in other documents?
   (a) The Quick Parts theme
   (b) Building blocks
   (c) Combine
   (d) Encryption

6. What is the difference between a file type that includes a .dotx extension and one that includes .dotm?
   (a) A .dotm file is reserved for a document that is protected by a password, whereas a .dotx file has no password assigned to it.
   (b) A .dotx file includes modified theme colors; a .dotm file is configured with the default Office theme.
   (c) A .dotx file is a downloaded template file, whereas a .dotm file is a template file that has been created by a user.
   (d) A .dotm file is reserved for a document that contains one or more macros, whereas a .dotx file indicates that a document is a template.

7. How would you indicate that a document is intended for read-only access?
   (a) Click the File tab, click Info, and protect a document by marking it as final.
   (b) Click the View tab, click Restrict Editing, and choose the Exclude command in the Restrict Editing pane.
   (c) Click the Developer tab, click Macro Security, and select Read-Only in the Trust Center.
   (d) Click the View tab, click Restrict Editing, and mark the document as final.

8. Which of the following is the least appropriate advice to give to someone who wants to learn how to create and run macros?
   (a) Decide what you want the macro to accomplish.
   (b) List the sequence of tasks you want to perform prior to recording the macro.
   (c) Change your macro security settings to enable all macros all the time.
   (d) Practice completing the steps before actually recording the macro.

9. Which two ribbon tabs include commands that enable you to record and modify macros?
   (a) Developer and Review
   (b) Home and Developer
   (c) View and Design
   (d) Developer and View

10. In which of the following areas would you modify Word's security settings related to macros?
    (a) Restrict Editing pane
    (b) Protect Center
    (c) Code group on the Developer tab
    (d) Encryption Center

1 Dinner to Go

You and a college friend have opened a new business, Dinner to Go: a service for busy people who want home-cooked meals. Your company contracts to provide biweekly, monthly, or special occasion meals with fresh ingredients prepared and served in private homes. Your personal chef service is marketed as a timesaver for busy professionals who value family time and want to avoid drive-thru meals. With various levels of service, you are prepared to assume the tasks of menu planning and grocery shopping as well as meal preparation. You have prepared a document that describes the company and its services to potential clients; however, you plan to update it with current services, plans, and prices. You will create a macro to apply heading formats. When the document is complete, you will mark it as final, and you will protect areas of the form to prevent editing. Refer to Figure 6.36 as you complete this exercise.

Dinner to Go (dinner@dtg.net)

Dinner to Go

Tired of always wondering what to put together for dinner? Tired of feeling guilty about the drive-thru meals you often serve your family? Tired of menu planning, or the lack thereof? We have your answer—**Dinner to Go**. The name says it all. We will step in at whatever level you need, preparing dinner as often as you require it, using only the freshest ingredients. And the best part is, we prepare it in your own kitchen and serve it family style so you and yours can enjoy precious time spent together enjoying a home-cooked meal.

Dinner to Go has been in business for over 5 years. It is one of only a few such services in this community, but we know it's the best. Our reputation for attention to detail, delicious and wholesome meals, and various service plans ensures that we are your solution for meal planning. Check our online reviews at dinnertable.org and blueribbonmeals.net. Then contact us for an estimate or for more information.

Our commitment to your satisfaction is guaranteed. The following list of services attest to the breadth of our commitment to excellence—anywhere from an occasional special occasion meal to weekly dinner planning. You can contact us online at www.dinnertogo.tishomingo.com or simply sign and return this document to us for a complimentary estimate within five (5) business days.

Dinner Services
In-home meals are prepared by at least two of our employees, all of whom are trained chefs and nutritionists. When you contract with us for menu planning and grocery shopping, we arrive at your home with everything necessary to create an over-the-top dinner for your family. If you prefer, you can purchase groceries that are on hand when our chefs arrive. Of course, our employees are bonded, insured, and trustworthy, as they will require access to your kitchen area for meal preparation.

Special Occasion Meals
Family reunions, holiday meals, and any special occasion calls for a special touch when it comes to food. We specialize in preparing meals of any size for any gathering. Talk with us about your next gathering. We'd love to be a part.

Service Plans
We are sure you would like to have a home cooked meal as often as possible for your family. We also know that it's not possible to work outside the home and still make that happen as often as you would like. You may not need a meal every day, but how about twice a week, or once every couple of weeks? One of our service plans is sure to meet your needs and your budget. Just let us know how we can help.

Meal Charges
Please visit www.dinnertogo.tishomingo.com for a complete listing of plans and charges. The truth is that we are flexible enough to work with you in determining what will be best for you

Page 1 of 2

Dinner to Go (dinner@dtg.net)
and your family. Of course, we do honor long-term commitments with a reduced rate, but are just as happy to provide only occasional support when life gets too busy! Because each family requires a different level of service, be assured that if you do not find a service plan at our online site that meets your needs, we will be glad to design one especially for you. We provide free consultation and you are under no obligation to sign on with our meal service. All we ask is that you give us a try.

Dinner to Go
8734 North National Ave.
Tishomingo, GA 38101

Page 2 of 2

FIGURE 6.36 Dinner to Go Document

a. Open *w06p1Dinner*. Click the **File tab** and click **Save**. Click **Browse**. Change the filename to **w06p1Dinner_LastFirst** and ensure that the file type is **Word Macro-Enabled Document**. Ensure that nonprinting characters display.

b. Ensure that the Developer tab displays on the ribbon. If it does not, click the **File tab**, click **Options**, click **Customize Ribbon**, and then check **Developer** in the right pane. Click **OK**.

c. Record a macro by completing the following steps:
   • Click before the heading *Dinner Services* on the first page.
   • Click the **Developer tab** and click **Record Macro** in the Code group.
   • Type **Heading** in the Macro name box.
   • Click the **Store macro in arrow**.
   • Click **w06p1Dinner_LastFirst (document)**.

- Click **Keyboard** to display the Customize Keyboard dialog box.
- Press **Alt+h** to assign that keystroke combination to the macro (on a Mac, press command+option+h).
- Click the **Save changes in arrow**, click **w06p1Dinner_LastFirst**, and then click **Assign**.
- Click **Close** to return to the document, where the macro recording symbol displays with the pointer. You are now recording the macro.
- Click the **Home tab**, click the **Borders arrow**, and then select **Borders and Shading**.
- Click the **Shading tab**. Click the **Style arrow**, click **Solid (100%)**, and then click **OK**.
- Click **Stop Recording** on the status bar (or click the Developer tab and click Stop Recording).

d. Click before the heading *Special Occasion Meals* on the first page. Press **Alt+h** to run the macro and apply the reverse effect to the heading. Similarly, run the macro on the headings *Service Plans* and *Meal Charges*.

> **TROUBLESHOOTING:** If the macro does not shade headings as intended, click Macros in the Code group on the Developer tab, select the Heading macro, click Delete and click Yes. Repeat Step c.

e. Select the last three lines in the document, containing the company name and address. Click the **Shading arrow** in the Paragraph group on the Home tab and select **Blue, Accent 1, Lighter 80%** (row 2, column 5).

f. Click the **Design tab**, click **Themes**, and select **Retrospect**. Click **Colors** in the Document Formatting group and select **Orange**.

g. Click **Colors** in the Document Formatting group and click **Customize Colors**. Click the **Accent 1 arrow** and select **Orange, Accent 2, Darker 25%** (row 5, column 6). Change the name in the Name box to **Marketing** and click **Save**.

> **MAC TROUBLESHOOTING:** Proceed to Step h without customizing colors.

h. Create a logo building block as follows:
- Click at the end of the document and press **Enter**. Click the **Insert tab**, click **Icons** in the Illustrations group, and type **Fork** in the search box. Select the icon shown at the top of the document in Figure 6.36 (although the icon will be shown in a black color). Click **Insert**.

> **TROUBLESHOOTING:** Select a similar icon, or image, if the one shown in Figure 6.36 is not available.

- Ensure that the object is selected and that the Graphics Format tab is selected. Click **Graphics Fill** in the Graphics Styles group and select **Orange, Accent 2, Darker 25%** (row 5, column 6).
- Click **Layout Options** at the right side of the logo and select **Square** (row 1, column 1 under With Text Wrapping). Close Layout Options but do not deselect the object.
- Click the **Insert tab**. Click **Quick Parts** in the Text group, point to **AutoText**, and select **Save Selection to AutoText Gallery**. Type **Logo** in the Name box and click **OK** to accept all defaults.

> **MAC TROUBLESHOOTING:** Save the selection as an AutoText entry when you click Insert on the menubar point to AutoText, click Auto-text, and complete the process.

> **TROUBLESHOOTING:** If asked whether to redefine the building block, click Yes. That may happen if a previous student using the same computer did not delete the building block.

i. Scroll to the top of the document and click the blank paragraph that follows *Dinner to Go*. Click **Quick Parts** in the Text group and click **Building Blocks Organizer**. Click **Logo**. Click **Insert**. Scroll to the bottom of the document, select the logo, and press **Delete** to remove it from that location.

j. Edit a current macro as follows:

- Click the **Developer tab**, click **Macros** in the Code group, click **Insert_Header**, and click **Edit**.
- Click before @dtg.net in the line of VBA code that reads *Selection.TypeText Text:="Dinner to Go (dinnertogo@dtg.net)"*.
- Backspace to remove the characters *togo* in the email address so that the email address is *dinner@dtg.net*.
- Close all open Visual Basic for Applications windows, returning to the document.

k. Double-click in the header area (top margin) of the current page. Press **Alt+i** to run the Insert_Header macro, inserting text in the header. The email address is modified as a result of modifying the macro. Click **Close Header and Footer** on the Header & Footer tab.

l. Click the **Review tab** and click **Restrict Editing** in the Protect group. Select **Allow only this type of editing in the document**, click the **Editing restrictions arrow**, and click **Comments**.

> **MAC TROUBLESHOOTING:** The Restrict Editing pane is not available. Click the Review tab and click Protect Document in the Protect group. Click the *Protect document for* check box to select it. Click Comments. Click OK.

m. Scroll to the *Meal Charges* section near the end of the document and triple-click the first body paragraph under the heading, beginning with *Please visit www.dinnertogo.tishomingo.com* to select the entire paragraph. Select **Everyone** in the *Exceptions (optional)* section of the Restrict Editing pane. Click **Yes, Start Enforcing Protection**, and click **OK** to enforce protection without assigning a password. The selected paragraph is shaded and open for editing by anyone, but only comments are allowed in other areas. Click outside the selected paragraph to deselect it.

> **MAC TROUBLESHOOTING:** Skip Step m and proceed to Step n (without changing *Tishomingo* to *Belmont*), as it is not possible to set a user exception.

n. Change the word *us* in the second-to-last sentence of the shaded paragraph in the *Meal Charges* section to **our meal service**. Select the word **Tishomingo** in the address box and change it to **Belmont**. The change is not possible because with the exception of one paragraph, the document is protected from editing.

o. Click **Stop Protection** in the Restrict Editing pane. Click the **Editing restrictions arrow** in the Restrict Editing pane and click **No changes (Read only)**. Enforce protection without providing a password. Close the Restrict Editing pane.

> **MAC TROUBLESHOOTING:** Click Always Open Read-Only in the Protect group on the Review tab.

p. Click the **File tab** and click **Info**. Click **Protect Document**. Click **Encrypt with Password**. Type **Expl0r!ng**. (Do not include the period.) Click **OK**. Type the password again and click **OK**. Click **Save**. Close the document.

> **MAC TROUBLESHOOTING:** Read through but skip Steps p-s as setting an encrypted password is not available and the Restrict Editing pane is not open.

q. Start Word. Open **w06p1Dinner_LastFirst**, supplying a password of **Expl0r!ng**. (Do not include the period.)

r. Click the **Developer tab** and click **Restrict Editing** in the Protect group. Click **Stop Protection**.

s. Click the **File tab** and click **Info**. Click **Protect Document**. Click **Encrypt with Password**. Press **Delete** repeatedly to remove the password. Click **OK**. Click **Back** to return to the document. Close the Restrict Editing pane.

t. Click the **Insert tab** and click **Quick Parts** in the Text group. Click **Building Blocks Organizer**. Select **Logo** in the Building Blocks Organizer dialog box, click **Delete**, and click **Yes**. Click **Close**.

> **MAC TROUBLESHOOTING:** Delete the AutoText entry by clicking Insert on the menubar, AutoText, and Auto-text. Select the item to delete and click Delete.

u. Click the **Design tab** and click **Colors** in the Document Formatting group. Right-click **Marketing** and click **Delete**. Click **Yes**.

v. Check for any spelling or grammatical errors, ignoring any punctuation (grammar) concerns.

w. Save and close the document. Exit Word. Based on your instructor's directions, submit: w06p1Dinner_LastFirst.docm

2 Kayak Fishing Blog

You and a friend, both avid bass fishers, have recently discovered the pleasure of kayak bass fishing. In fact, you have both joined the National Kayak Fishing Association, and are planning to participate in as many tournaments as possible. You are starting a blog on kayak fishing to introduce others to the sport. As the blog is a joint effort, you and your friend will collaborate on most blog posts; you will ensure that the final result of every post includes comments from both contributors. As the first blog entry, you are describing the sport and explaining why it has such appeal. You will start with a Word document, developing a pattern for future blog posts, and will save the first blog as a template. In so doing, for the first effort, you will combine entries from both blog partners, and ensure that it is attractive by working with document themes. Finally, you will restrict editing where necessary to finalize the template. Refer to Figure 6.37 as you complete this exercise.

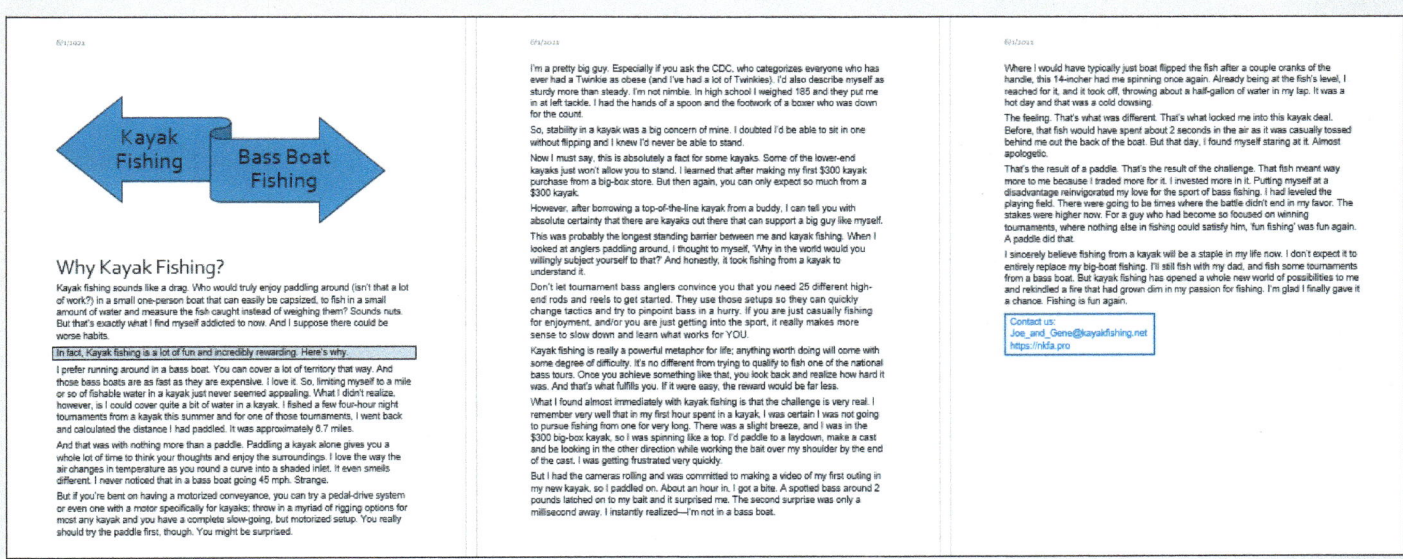

FIGURE 6.37 Kayak Fishing Blog

a. Open *w06p2Kayak*. Click the **File tab** and click **Save**. Click **Browse**. Change the filename to **w06p2Kayak_LastFirst** and change the file type to **Word Macro-Enabled Template**. Change the location to where you save your student files and click **Save**. Click **OK** to upgrade the document to a newer version. Ensure that nonprinting characters display.

b. Ensure that the Developer tab displays on the ribbon. If it does not, click the **File tab**, click **Options**, click **Customize Ribbon**, and then check **Developer** in the right pane. Click **OK**.

c. Open *w06p2Kayak2* and scroll to the last page. Click the text box containing the contact information to select it. Ensure that the entire text box is selected. Click the **Insert tab** and click **Quick Parts**. Point to **AutoText** and click **Save Selection to AutoText Gallery**. Type **Kayak Fishing Contact** in the Name box in the Create New Building Block dialog box. Click **OK**. Close w06p2Kayak2 without saving.

d. Click the **Design tab**, click **Themes**, and click **Banded**. Click **Colors** in the Document Formatting group and select **Blue Warm**. Click **Effects** in the Document Formatting group and select **Glow Edge**.

e. Click **Colors** in the Document Formatting group and click **Customize Colors**. Click the **Text/Background - Light 1 arrow** and select **Light Blue, Text 2, Darker 90%** (row 6, column 4). Click in the **Name box** and type **Kayak Blog**. Click **Save**.

> **MAC TROUBLESHOOTING:** Proceed to Step f without customizing theme colors.

f. Click **Page Borders** in the Page Background group, select **Box**, change the color to **Blue-Gray, Accent 1** (row 1, column 5), and change the line width to **1 pt**. Click **OK**.

g. Record a macro in the template as follows:
- Click the **Developer tab** and click **Record Macro** in the Code group.
- Type **Date_Header** in the Name box and click the **Store macro in: arrow**. Select **Documents Based On w06p2Kayak_LastFirst**.
- Click **Keyboard** and press **Alt+h**. Click **Assign** and click **Close** (on a Mac, press command+option+h).
- Click the **Insert tab** and click **Header** in the Header & Footer group. Click **Edit Header**.
- Click **Date & Time** in the Insert group. With the first option selected, showing the date as *month/day/year*, ensure that **Update automatically** is selected, and click **OK**.
- Click **Close Header and Footer** in the Close group.
- Click the **Stop Recording button** on the status bar.

> **TROUBLESHOOTING:** If you make any mistakes in naming or recording the macro, click Macros in the Code group on the Developer tab, select the macro, and click Delete. Click Yes. Repeat Step g.

h. Double-click in the header area (top margin) and delete the date. Click **Close Header and Footer** in the Close group. Run the macro by pressing **Alt+h**.

> **TROUBLESHOOTING:** If the macro does not place the date correctly in the header, refer to the previous Troubleshooting to delete the macro and repeat Steps g and h.

i. Click at the end of the document and press **Enter**. Click the **Insert tab**, click **Quick Parts**, click **Building Blocks Organizer**, and click **Kayak Fishing Contact**. Click **Insert**. The contact information text box is shown in the color of the current theme.

> **MAC TROUBLESHOOTING:** Click the Insert tab, point to AutoText, and click Auto-text.

j. Save the document but do not close it. Place the insertion point before the first body paragraph on page 1, beginning with *Kayak fishing sounds like*. Open *w06p2Kayak2* from your student files. Click the **View tab** and click **View Side by Side** in the Window group. Note the difference in the logo color. Scroll through the documents, noting various formatting and color differences. Close w06p2Kayak2 (the document with the orange logo).

> **MAC TROUBLESHOOTING:** Viewing documents side by side is not available.

k. Compare two documents as follows:

- Click the **Review tab**, click **Compare**, and then click **Compare**.
- Click the **Original document arrow** and click **Browse**. Navigate to the location of *w06p2Kayak_LastFirst.dotm* and double-click the file.
- Click the **Revised document arrow** and click **Browse**. Locate and double-click *w06p2Kayak2*.
- Click **More** (unless the dialog box is already expanded), select **Original document** in the *Show changes in:* section, and click **OK**.
- Click the **Display for Review arrow** in the Tracking group and click **Simple Markup** (unless it is already selected). Click any **revision mark**, shown as a vertical line, at the left side of the document to view changes. Click the **revision mark** again to collapse the view.
- Click the **Accept arrow** in the Changes group and click **Accept All Changes and Stop Tracking**.

l. Click the **Design tab**. Click **Colors** in the Document Formatting group. Right-click the custom set of colors titled **Kayak Blog**. Click **Delete**. Click **Yes**. Click the **Insert tab**, click **Quick Parts**, and click **Building Blocks Organizer**. Click **Kayak Fishing Contact** and click **Delete**. Click **Yes** to confirm the deletion. Click **Close**. You delete the custom set of colors, as well as the Kayak Fishing Contact building block, as you may be working in an open computer lab.

> **MAC TROUBLESHOOTING:** Read through this step and proceed to Step n as Restrict Editing is not available.

m. Click the **Developer tab** and click **Restrict Editing** in the Protect group. Select **Limit formatting to a selection of styles** in the Formatting restrictions section. Click **Settings**. Click **None** to deselect all styles. Scroll through the styles list and select **Title (recommended)**. Click **OK**. Click **No** when asked whether you want to remove styles that are not allowed. Click **Yes, Start Enforcing Protection**. Click **OK** to bypass a password.

n. Ensure that the insertion point is at the beginning of the first body paragraph on page 1. Press **Enter**. Click the newly inserted blank paragraph above the first body paragraph. Click the **Home tab**. Note that the only style, other than Normal, in the Styles group is Title. Click **Title**. Type **Why Kayak Fishing?** (Include the question mark.)

> **MAC TROUBLESHOOTING:** Click Always Open Read-Only in the Protect group on the Review tab.

o. Click **Stop Protection** in the Restrict Editing pane. Close the Restrict Editing pane. Click the **File tab**, click **Info**, click **Protect Document**, and then click **Always Open Read-Only**. Click **Save**.

p. Close the template. Exit Word. Based on your instructor's directions, submit: w06p2Kayak_LastFirst.dotm

Mid-Level Exercises

1 River City Media

MyLab IT Grader

You are an intern for a media services company that specializes in marketing of all types, including website development and various types of printed material. Much of your time is dedicated to promoting the firm through print, using Word to generate such items as newsletters, flyers, and mailings. Your current project is the development of a newsletter template to be used for this and subsequent printings. Basic features, such as titles, headings, and even font selection will be consistently applied by using the template you are developing. Where possible, macros will automate routine tasks and the document will be protected from unnecessary editing. Word's themes gallery, with supporting color, font, and effect choices, ensures an attractive and color-coordinated effort.

a. Open *w06m1Media* and save the file as **w06m1Media_LastFirst**, selecting a file type of **Word Macro-Enabled Template**. Ensure that the template is saved with your student files instead of the Custom Office Templates folder. Ensure that nonprinting characters are displayed and that the Developer tab is shown on the ribbon.

b. Click before the second body paragraph on page 1, beginning with *We at River City Media*. Open the Building Blocks Organizer, scroll to the Text Boxes gallery and select the **Grid Quote** building block. Insert it in the document.

c. Use the Align command in the Arrange group on the Shape Format tab to align the text box in the center and also in the middle (ensuring that Align to Margin is first selected). Copy the last sentence in the first body paragraph, *Trust us to take your marketing to the next level*, and paste it in the text box, replacing existing text. Be sure to include the period when copying the sentence.

d. Select a design theme of **Organic**. Create a Custom Font with a Heading font of **Franklin Gothic Medium** and a Body font of **Franklin Gothic Book**. Name the customized font set **Newsletter Font**.

> **MAC TROUBLESHOOTING:** Proceed to Step e without customizing theme fonts.

e. Adjust the font size of text in the text box to **18**. Change text box height to **1.4**. Choose a Shape Effect of **Bevel**, and select **Round** (row 1, column 1 under Bevel).

f. View the current document template (w06p1Media_LastFirst) and a revised version (*w06p1Media_Combine*) side by side. Scroll through both documents in sync, noting the differences in formatting and/or content. Close w06m1Media_Combine (the one without the text box on page 1).

> **MAC TROUBLESHOOTING:** Viewing documents side by side is not available.

g. Combine the original document (w06m1Media_LastFirst) and the revised version (w06m1Media_Combine) so that all changes are collected in the original document. Ensure that All Markup is shown in the newly combined document and scroll through, noting changes. Correct the first sentence of the second body paragraph so that it begins *We at River City Media excel in just one thing*. Accept all changes and stop tracking.

h. Record a macro that is stored in the current document only. The macro should be named **Insert_Watermark**, assigned to a key combination of **Alt+w**. (On a Mac, select another keyboard combination.) The steps to record follow:
   - Click the **Design tab**.
   - Click **Watermark** in the Page Background group.
   - Click **Custom Watermark**. Click **Text watermark**.
   - Double-click *ASAP* in the Text box to select it and press **Delete**.
   - Type **For Approval**.
   - Click **Apply**. Click **Close**. Click the **Developer tab** and click **Stop Recording** in the Code group.

> **TROUBLESHOOTING:** If you make any mistakes in naming or recording the macro, click Macros in the Code group on the Developer tab, select the macro, and click Delete. Click Yes. Repeat Step h.

i. Click **Undo** to remove the watermark. Run the macro to ensure that it works as intended. You might receive an error message, indicating that an entry is out of range. If so, click **End** to remove the error message and ensure that the insertion point is located within the document.

j. Modify the macro as follows:
- Click **Macros** in the Code group on the Developer tab.
- Select **Insert_Watermark** and click **Edit**.
- Select and remove the line of code that reads **Selection.ShapeRange.Name = "PowerPlusWaterMarkObject#########"** (where # is shown as a variable number).
- Close all open VBA windows.

k. Run the **Insert_Watermark** macro again to confirm that it works well.

l. Delete the customized font set, **Newsletter Font**.

m. Open the Restrict Editing pane and limit changes to **Comments only**. Apply a user exception to let everyone edit the newsletter heading, *River City Media*. Enforce protection without assigning a password. Close the Restrict Editing pane.

> **MAC TROUBLESHOOTING:** User exceptions are not available. Click the Review tab and click Protect Document in the Protect group. Click the *Protect document for* check box to select it. Click Comments. Click OK.

n. Click the **File tab** and click **Info**. Protect the document by marking it as final. The document will be automatically saved during that process.

o. Close the file. Do not save changes to Building Blocks, if asked. Exit Word. Based on your instructor's directions, submit:
w06m1Media_LastFirst.dotm

2 Personal Letterhead

As a designer of handcrafted items, you are starting an online business. You will be corresponding with potential clients, both electronically and in print, and you want your creative talent to be evident, not only in the products you deliver but in the branding of all that you do—including your personal stationery. You will begin with a Word template, modifying it to suit your style and color choices. The document will be saved as a template so that it can be used repeatedly, ensuring consistency and minimal effort on your part. When the template is complete, you will protect it appropriately so that the letterhead is not inadvertently modified.

a. Start Word. Click **New**. Use the search term **Letterhead** to search for a template. Choose the *Personal Letterhead* template. If you do not find the template, open *w06m2Letterhead.dotx* from your student files. Save the template as **w06m2Letterhead_LastFirst**, choosing a file type of **Word Template**. Ensure that the template is saved in your student files (not in the Custom Office Templates folder). Ensure that nonprinting characters are displayed and that the Developer tab is shown on the ribbon.

b. Change the document theme to **Parallax**. Customize theme colors, changing Accent 2 to **Blue, Accent 1**. Name the custom color setting **Letterhead**. Customize the theme fonts, changing Heading font to **Lucida Sans**. Name the custom font setting **Letterhead**.

> **MAC TROUBLESHOOTING:** Proceed to Step c without customizing fonts or colors.

c. Create a building block as follows:
- Double-click in the footer area. Select the bird banner.
- Click the **Insert tab** and click **Quick Parts** in the Text group. Click **Save Selection to Quick Part Gallery** (On a Mac, insert AutoText instead of Quick Parts.)
- Type **Bird_Banner** in the Name box. Ensure that **w06m2Letterhead_LastFirst** is shown as the template to which the building block will be saved. Click the **Options arrow** and select **Insert content in its own paragraph**. Click **OK**.

d. Double-click the left margin of the header area and insert the **Bird_Banner** building block. Close the header.

e. Open **w06m2Letterhead_Combine**. View *w06m2Letterhead_LastFirst.dotx* and *w06m2Letterhead_Combine* (located in the student files) side by side, noting any differences. Close w06m2Letterhead_Combine (the document without the banner in the header).

f. Compare *w06m2Letterhead_LastFirst* (original document) and *w06m2Letterhead_Combine* (revised document), showing changes in the original document. Accept all changes and stop tracking. Ensure that the banner remains in the header area of the original document. If it does not, use the Building Blocks Organizer to insert the Bird_Banner building block at the left margin of the header.

g. Click *Your Name* at the top left side of the document to select the placeholder. Type **Denise Hanna**.

h. Point to *Denise Hanna* and click the **Table Move handle** in the top left corner of the table that comprises the letterhead. Change the table design to **List Table 1 Light – Accent 1** (row 1, column 2 under List Tables). Deselect the table.

i. Click the **Design tab**, click **Colors** in the Document Formatting groups, right-click **Letterhead**, and delete the custom theme colors. Similarly, delete the **Letterhead custom theme fonts**. You delete the custom settings because you may be working in a computer lab.

j. Open the Restrict Editing pane. Apply editing restrictions so that the document is marked as **No changes (Read only)**.

> **MAC TROUBLESHOOTING:** The Restrict Editing pane is not available.

k. Select the body of the letterhead template, excluding the letterhead at the top of the document. Apply a user exception to the selected text so that everyone can edit that part of the letter. The letterhead at the top of the document remains protected. Enforce protection without applying a password. Close the Restrict Editing pane.

> **MAC TROUBLESHOOTING:** User exceptions are not available.

l. Click the **File tab**, click **Info**, and protect the document with an encrypted password of **Expl0r!ng**. (Do not include the period.) Save and close the template.

m. Start Word. Open *w06m2Letterhead_LastFirst.dotx*. Supply a password of **Expl0r!ng**. (Do not include the period.) Change the address in the letterhead to **2087** instead of 2086. The change is not allowed because the user exception was not applied to the letterhead area. Change the words *Warm Regards* in the closing to **Sincerely**. Ensure that the comma following the closing remains in place. The change is allowed because the body of the letter is included in the user exception.

> **MAC TROUBLESHOOTING:** Do not change the address in the letterhead, as a user exception was not applied.

n. Click the **File tab** and click **Info**. Click **Protect Document** and click **Encrypt with Password**. Remove the password and click **OK**.

o. Save and close the template. Exit Word. Based on your instructor's directions, submit: w06m2Letterhead_LastFirst.dotx

New Castle County Technical Services

New Castle County Technical Services is continuing its outreach by collaborating with a local community college on a job fair at which area employers staff tables to promote their business and encourage applicants. The newsletter used at the recent technology fair is the perfect vehicle to generate interest in the upcoming job fair, so you plan to modify it slightly to ensure an attractive and informative document. Because you plan to develop additional newsletters in the future, you save the current document as a template and restrict editing to areas that may change.

a. Open *w06r1NewCastle*. Save the document as a Word Macro-Enabled Template with the name **w06r1NewCastle_LastFirst**. Specify the filename and file type first, and then ensure that the template is saved with your student files (not in the Custom Office Templates folder). Ensure that nonprinting characters are displayed and that the Developer tab is included on the ribbon.

b. Use the Compare feature to compare the contents of the open template (the original document) with *w06r1NewCastle2* (the revised document), showing all changes in the original document. Ensure that All Markup is shown. Scroll through the document, noting the various formatting changes. Accept all changes and stop tracking.

c. Select the **New Castle County Technical Services** WordArt heading at the top of the document and save the selection to the Quick Part gallery. Name the building block **New Castle Heading**. Ensure that the building block is saved in the current template. Accept all other default settings.

d. Scroll to page 4 and insert a new blank paragraph above the heading *Preserving Data for the Life of Your Company*. Click the blank paragraph. Insert the **New Castle Heading** building block. Delete the blank paragraph following the heading. Select the WordArt title, *New Castle County Technical Services*, at the top of page 4 and change the font size to **24**. Drag the WordArt object to visually center it horizontally.

e. Change the document theme to **Organic**. Scroll to the bottom of page 4 so that the SmartArt diagram is shown. Click **Effects** in the Document Formatting group and apply the **Reflection** effect. Note the slight change in the SmartArt diagram as a result of the choice of theme effects.

f. Create a customized set of theme fonts, selecting **Arial Black** for the Heading font and **Arial Narrow** for the Body font. Name the set **Promotion**.

> **MAC TROUBLESHOOTING:** Proceed to Step h without customizing fonts or saving theme settings.

g. Click **Themes** on the Design tab. Save the current theme settings as **w06r1NewCastleTheme**.

> **TROUBLESHOOTING:** If asked whether to replace the theme, click Yes. That happens if another student at the same computer previously saved the theme.

h. Move to page 1 of the document and click at the left of the word *Locally* in the first bulleted item. Record a macro, assigning the name **BulletFormat**. Store changes in **Documents Based On w06r1NewCastle_LastFirst** and assign a keyboard combination of **Alt+b**. (On a Mac, select another keyboard combination.) Changes should be saved in **w06r1NewCastle_LastFirst**.

i. The macro should follow these steps:
   - Click the **Home tab**.
   - Click the **Bullets arrow**.
   - Click the **black checkmark** (or choose a clear round bullet if the checkmark is not shown).
   - Click the **Bullets arrow** and click **Define New Bullet**.
   - Click **Font**. Click the **Font color arrow**. Click **Red** (column 2 in Standard Colors).
   - Click **OK**. Click **OK**.
   - Click the **Developer tab** and stop recording.

j. Click **Decrease Indent** in the Paragraph group to move the bulleted items back to the left margin. Edit the VBA code for the BulletFormat macro so that the color is Blue instead of Red. You will find the coded instruction near the end of the VBA code in the line that reads *Color = wdColorRed*. Change the word *Red* in that instruction to **Blue**. (Do not type the period.)

k. Ensure that the insertion point is placed before the word *Locally* in the first bulleted item. Run the macro to ensure that all bullets on page 1 are modified to blue.

l. Scroll to page 5 and click before the first bulleted item, beginning with *When was the last time your IT staff*. Run the BulletFormat macro, adding the blue checkmark to all bulleted items.

m. Open the Restrict Editing pane. Restrict editing to **Comments**. Select all text that is shown in two columns, beginning on page 4 and extending through the end of the document. Create a user exception so that selected text remains available. Enforce protection without assigning a password. Close the Restrict Editing pane. Deselect the columned text.

n. Scroll to page 4 and change the percentage in the second body paragraph in the left column from *60%* to **65%**. On the same page, change the word *company* in the first sentence of the first paragraph to **business**. The change is not allowed because it is not in the area that is open for editing. Close the Restrict Editing pane.

o. Save and close the template. Exit Word. Based upon your instructor's directions, submit:
w06r1NewCastle_LastFirst.dotm
w06r1NewCastleTheme.thmx

Disaster Recovery

Cognitive Creativity

As an economics major, you are finalizing a research paper on the topic of cognitive creativity. Because you were temporarily using another computer and without access to online resources, you edited a copy of the paper that now must be combined with the original so that all edits are included. For purposes of this class, you are not bound by the requirements of a writing style, so you are free to explore various theme colors and fonts. In addition, you will automate the inclusion of a personalized header and will choose a building block from Word's Building Blocks Organizer. Specifically, ensure that the following items are in place before submitting the paper:

- Open *w06d1Cognitive* and save the document as **w06d1Cognitive_LastFirst**. The file type should be Word Macro-Enabled Document.
- Compare *w06d1Cognitive_LastFirst* (the original document) with *w06d1Cognitive_Combine* (the revised document), saving all changes in the original document. Accept all changes and stop tracking.
- Change the document theme to **Organic** and select any subset of theme colors.
- Click before *The irrationality of humans* near the top of the document and record a macro called **BulletPoint**. Do not assign the macro to a key combination or button. Store the macro in the current document only. The macro should place a bullet of your choice, colored in anything other than black, decreasing the indent of the bulleted item so that it begins at the left margin.
- Run the BulletPoint macro to place the same bullet beside the remaining two lines that should be bulleted (below the first).
- Include a cover page, selecting from the built-in set of cover page building blocks (shown in the Pages group on the Insert tab) or from a cover page template shown as a result of a search for online templates.
- Modify the cover page to include at a minimum the report title and your name. The design of other areas, if any, is up to you.
- Mark the document as final so that it is shown as a Read only file.
- Save and close the file. Exit Word. Based on your instructor's directions, submit: w06d1Cognitive_LastFirst.docm

Cumulative Exercise

Company Agenda

You are an employee with Carr IT Professionals, charged with promotional activities such as coordinating involvement in local job fairs and university events. Each month, you and other company employees meet to coordinate the month's activities and to determine future direction. For each of those monthly meetings, you prepare an agenda. A template is perfect for that task, as it saves design time and provides a consistent pattern. You locate and modify an agenda template and modify it to include appropriate formatting, theme colors, and building blocks. So that the agenda is not inadvertently modified, you limit editing. Where automation through macros is helpful, you consider that task as well.

Download and Save a Word Template and Create and Insert a Building Block

As most meetings of company staff are short and to the point, you choose to prepare a succinct agenda with a set number of items that can be addressed. Using a template provided by Microsoft, you personalize the document with a bit of company information and save it as a template file for use each month.

1. Open a new blank document. Conduct a search for online templates using the key term **Agenda**. Download the **Formal meeting agenda template** and save it as a **Word Macro-Enabled Template** named **w06c1AgendaTemplate_LastFirst**. Upgrade to the newest version, if asked. If you cannot locate the agenda, open *w06c1Agenda.dotx* from the student files.

2. Insert an unformatted footer (click the **Insert tab**, **Footer**, and **Edit Footer**) and type **Carr IT Professionals**. (Do not type the period.) Click **Insert Alignment Tab** in the Position group on the Header & Footer tab. Select **Right** and click **OK**. Type **http://carr.it/info.net**. (Do not type the period.) Press **Enter**. Type **Your Business is Our Business** and italicize the second footer line. Right-click the **hyperlink** in the footer and click **Remove Hyperlink**.

3. Select the footer text and create a Quick Part building block, ensuring that the building block is available to all documents based on the current template. Name it **Agenda_Footer**. Close the footer.

4. Open the Building Blocks Organizer and scroll to locate **Agenda_Footer**. (The building block is located in the Quick Part gallery.) Edit the building block properties, including a Description of **This footer is designed for use on all company agenda documents**. (Include the period.) Click **Yes** when asked if you want to redefine the building block entry.

5. Replace the words *Company/Department Name* in the first paragraph with **Carr IT Professionals**. (Do not type the period.) Click at the left of *Carr IT Professionals* and insert *w06c1Logo.png*. Resize the logo to a height of **1** and choose a position of **Position in Top Left with Square Text Wrapping**.

6. Delete the three paragraphs under the heading lines, beginning with *Type of Meeting* and ending with *Names of Invitees*.

Consolidate Documents and Customize Theme Colors

Because the company's administrative assistant is very involved in preparing and distributing documents related to company activities, you ask him for help in proofing the agenda template before it is final. He has made a few changes and has sent to you an electronic copy of the updated agenda. To save time, you will combine the two documents, resulting in one that you can then add finishing touches to, including adjusting theme colors.

7. Open *w06c1Agenda_Combine*. View the two versions of the agenda side by side, noting any obvious differences. Close w06c1Agenda_Combine.

8. Save **w06c1Agenda_LastFirst**. Compare w06c1Agenda_LastFirst (the original document) and w06c1Agenda_Combine (the revised document), saving all changes in the original document.

9. Note the deletion of the *Roll Call item* and the addition of *Upcoming Events*, both of which you agree with. Change the view to **No Markup** to view the document as it will display if you accept changes. Accept all changes and stop tracking.

10. Change the document theme to **Retrospect**. Add a Box page border in **Orange, Accent 1**, with a width of **1 pt**. Customize theme colors, selecting **Accent 1** of **Green, Accent 6 - Darker 25%** (row 5, column 10). Name the custom theme colors **Carr_Colors**.

> **MAC TROUBLESHOOTING:** Proceed to Step 11 without customizing colors.

11. Select the logo in the top left corner and adjust the color to **Black and White: 25%** in the Recolor section (row 1, column 5). Change the picture style to **Reflected Rounded Rectangle**.

12. Save the template.

Record, Run, and Modify a Macro

For some meetings, the agenda might be printed on different-sized paper with custom margins, so you create a macro to make that adjustment. Having created the macro, you modify the VBA code to change the left margin slightly, resulting in an attractive modified agenda.

13. Record a macro titled **Custom_Page**. The macro should be stored in the current template. You will not assign the macro to either a button or a keyboard combination.

14. Design the macro by completing the following steps.
    - Click the **Layout tab**. Click the **Dialog Box Launcher** in the Page Setup group.
    - Click the **Paper tab**.
    - Click the **Paper Size arrow** and click **Executive**.
    - Click the **Margins tab**.
    - Click the **Left down arrow** twice to change the Left margin to **1**. Click the **Right down arrow** twice to change the Right margin to **1**. Click **OK**.
    - Stop recording.

15. Edit the macro to change the line of VBA code that reads *.LeftMargin = InchesToPoints(1)* to **.LeftMargin = InchesToPoints(1.5)** so that the left margin is adjusted.

16. Click **Macros** in the Code group on the Developer tab, select **Custom_Page** and click **Run** to run the macro and adjust the paper size and margins.

17. Click the **Layout tab**. Click the **Page Setup tab**, click **Paper**, and then choose **Letter**. Having tested the macro, you return the template to its original size.

18. Save the template.

Work with Security Settings, Mark a Document as Final, Set Editing Restrictions and Exceptions, Set a Password, and Modify or Delete a Password

With the template nearing completion, you will restrict editing to only those areas that should be open to change. In addition, you explore setting a password, ultimately removing the password when you decide against it.

19. Click the **Developer tab** and click **Macro Security** in the Code group. Note that all macros are disabled with notification. As this is the preferred setting, click **Cancel** without making changes.

20. Click the **Design tab**. Click **Colors** in the Document Formatting group. Right-click **Carr_Colors** and select **Delete**. Confirm the deletion. (Because you may be working in a computer lab, you delete the set of custom colors.)

21. Open the Restrict Editing pane. Mark the document as final by restricting editing to **No changes (Read only)**.

22. Set a user exception so that everyone can change any part of the *New Business* section. Enforce protection without assigning a password. Close the Restrict Editing pane.

> **MAC TROUBLESHOOTING:** Skip this step and proceed to Step 23 as Restrict Editing is not available.

23. Click the **File tab** and protect the document with an encrypting password of **Expl0r!ng**. (Do not include the period.) Confirm the password, save, and close the document.

24. Start Word. Open **w06c1Agenda_LastFirst.dotm**, supplying a password of **Expl0r!ng**. (Do not include the period.) Enable content, if requested.

25. Change item *IV* to read **New business to consider**. (Do not type the period.)

26. Modify the password that you created in step 23, removing the password.

27. Save and close the template. Exit Word. Based on your instructor's directions, submit: w06c1Agenda_LastFirst.dotm

Microsoft Office 2021 Specialist Word

Online Appendix materials can be found in the Student Resources located at **www.pearsonhighered.com/exploring**.

MOS Obj #	MOS Objective	Exploring Chapter	Exploring Section Heading
1.	**Manage Documents**		
1.1	**Navigate within documents**		
1.1.1	Search for text	**Chapter 1**: Introduction to Word	Find and Replace Document Content
1.1.2	Link to locations within documents	**Chapter 5**: Document Publications	Insert Hyperlinks in a Webpage or Document
1.1.3	Move to specific locations and objects in documents	**Chapter 5**: Document Publications	Insert Bookmarks in a Webpage or Document
1.1.4	Show and hide formatting symbols and hidden text	**Chapter 1**: Introduction to Word	Create a Document
1.2	**Format documents**		
1.2.1	Set up document pages	**Chapter 1**: Introduction to Word Common Features	Modify a Document Change the Page Layout
1.2.2	Apply style sets	**Chapter 1**: Introduction to Word	Select and Modify Styles
1.2.3	Insert and modify headers and footers	Common Features	Create Headers and Footers
1.2.4	Configure page background elements	**Chapter 1**: Introduction to Word	Configure Page Background Elements
1.3	**Save and share documents**		
1.3.1	Save documents in alternative file formats	**Chapter 1**: Introduction to Word	Save in Alternative File Formats
1.3.2	Modify basic document properties	**Chapter 1**: Introduction to Word	Modify Document Properties
1.3.3	Modify print settings	**Chapter 1**: Introduction to Word	Select Print Options
1.3.4	Share documents electronically	**Chapter 4**: Research and Collaboration	Share Documents Collaborate with Word and Word for the web
1.4	**Inspect documents for issues**		
1.4.1	Locate and remove hidden properties and personal information	**Chapter 1**: Introduction to Word	Run the Document Inspector
1.4.2	Locate and correct accessibility issues	**Chapter 1**: Introduction to Word	Ensure Document Accessibility
1.4.3	Locate and correct compatibility issues	**Chapter 1**: Introduction to Word	Ensure Document Compatibility
2.	**Insert and Format Text, Paragraphs, and Sections**		
2.1	**Insert text and paragraphs**		
2.1.1	Find and replace text	**Chapter 1**: Introduction to Word	Find and Replace Text
2.1.2	Insert symbols and special characters	**Chapter 2**: Document Presentation	Insert Symbols and Special Characters
2.2	**Format text and paragraphs**		
2.2.1	Apply text effects	**Chapter 2**: Document Presentation	Change Text Appearance
2.2.2	Apply formatting by using Format Painter	Common Features	Use Screen Tips

MOS Obj #	MOS Objective	Exploring Chapter	Exploring Section Heading
2.2.3	Set line and paragraph spacing and indentation	**Chapter 2:** Document Presentation	Select Line and Paragraph Spacing Select Indents
2.2.4	Apply built-in styles to text	**Chapter 2:** Document Presentation	Apply and Modify Styles
2.2.5	Clear formatting	**Chapter 2:** Document Presentation	Change Text Appearance

2.3 Create and configure document sections

MOS Obj #	MOS Objective	Exploring Chapter	Exploring Section Heading
2.3.1	Format text in multiple columns	**Chapter 1:** Introduction to Word	Format Text into Columns
2.3.2	Insert page, section, and column breaks	**Chapter 1:** Introduction to Word	Work with Sections
2.3.3	Change page setup options for a section	**Chapter 1:** Introduction to Word	Work with Sections

3. Manage Tables and Lists

3.1 Create tables

MOS Obj #	MOS Objective	Exploring Chapter	Exploring Section Heading
3.1.1	Convert text to tables	**Chapter 3:** Document Productivity	Convert Text to a Table and Convert a Table to Text
3.1.2	Convert tables to text	**Chapter 3:** Document Productivity	Convert Text to a Table and Convert a Table to Text
3.1.3	Create tables by specifying rows and columns	**Chapter 3:** Document Productivity	Create or Draw a Table

3.2 Modify tables

MOS Obj #	MOS Objective	Exploring Chapter	Exploring Section Heading
3.2.1	Sort table data	**Chapter 3:** Document Productivity	Sort Data in a Table
3.2.2	Configure cell margins and spacing	**Chapter 3:** Document Productivity	Format Table Text
3.2.3	Merge and split cells	**Chapter 3:** Document Productivity	Merge and Split Cells
3.2.4	Resize tables, rows, and columns	**Chapter 3:** Document Productivity	Change Row Height and Column Width
3.2.5	Split tables	Online Appendix	Online Appendix
3.2.6	Configure a repeating row header	**Chapter 3:** Document Productivity	Sort Data in a Table

3.3 Create and modify lists

MOS Obj #	MOS Objective	Exploring Chapter	Exploring Section Heading
3.3.1	Format paragraphs as numbered and bulleted lists	**Chapter 2:** Document Presentation	Create Bulleted and Numbered Lists
3.3.2	Change bullet characters and number formats	**Chapter 2:** Document Presentation	Create Bulleted and Numbered Lists
3.3.3	Define custom bullet characters and number formats	**Chapter 2:** Document Presentation	Create Bulleted and Numbered Lists
3.3.4	Increase and decrease list levels	**Chapter 2:** Document Presentation	Create Bulleted and Numbered Lists
3.3.5	Restart and continue list numbering	**Chapter 2:** Document Presentation	Create Bulleted and Numbered Lists
3.3.6	Set starting number values	**Chapter 2:** Document Presentation	Create Bulleted and Numbered Lists

MOS Obj #	MOS Objective	Exploring Chapter	Exploring Section Heading
4.	**Create and Manage References**		
4.1	**Create and manage reference elements**		
4.1.1	Insert footnotes and endnotes	**Chapter 4**: Research and Collaboration	Create Footnotes and Endnotes
4.1.2	Modify footnote and endnote properties	**Chapter 4**: Research and Collaboration	Create Footnotes and Endnotes
4.1.3	Create and modify bibliography citations sources	**Chapter 4**: Research and Collaboration	Create a Source and Include a Citation
4.1.4	Insert citations for bibliographies	**Chapter 4**: Research and Collaboration	Create a Source and Include a Citation
4.2	**Create and manage reference tables**		
4.2.1	Insert tables of contents	**Chapter 4**: Research and Collaboration	Create a Table of Contents
4.2.2	Customize tables of contents	**Chapter 4**: Research and Collaboration	Create a Table of Contents
4.2.3	Insert bibliographies	**Chapter 4**: Research and Collaboration	Create a Bibliography
5.	**Insert and Format Graphic Elements**		
5.1	**Insert illustrations and text boxes**		
5.1.1	Insert shapes	**Chapter 2**: Document Presentation	Insert a Shape
5.1.2	Insert pictures	**Chapter 2**: Document Presentation	Insert a Picture
5.1.3	Insert 3D models	**Chapter 2**: Document Presentation	Insert a 3D Model
5.1.4	Insert SmartArt graphics	**Chapter 2**: Document Presentation	Insert SmartArt
5.1.5	Insert screenshots and screen clippings	**Chapter 2**: Document Presentation	Insert a Screenshot
5.1.6	Insert text boxes	**Chapter 2**: Document Presentation	Insert a Text Box
5.2	**Format illustrations and text boxes**		
5.2.1	Apply artistic effects	**Chapter 2**: Document Presentation	Format an Object
5.2.2	Apply picture effects and picture styles	**Chapter 2**: Document Presentation	Format an Object
5.2.3	Remove picture backgrounds	**Chapter 2**: Document Presentation	Format an Object
5.2.4	Format graphic elements	**Chapter 2**: Document Presentation	Format an Object
5.2.5	Format SmartArt graphics	**Chapter 2**: Document Presentation	Format an Object
5.2.6	Format 3D models	**Chapter 2**: Document Presentation	Format an Object

MOS Obj #	MOS Objective	Exploring Chapter	Exploring Section Heading
5.3	**Add text to graphic elements**		
5.3.1	Add and modify text in text boxes	**Chapter 2**: Document Presentation	Format an Object
5.3.2	Add and modify text in shapes	**Chapter 2**: Document Presentation	Format an Object
5.3.3	Add and modify SmartArt graphic content	**Chapter 2**: Document Presentation	Insert SmartArt
5.4	**Modify graphic elements**		
5.4.1	Position objects	**Chapter 2**: Document Presentation	Resize and Position an Object
5.4.2	Wrap text around objects	**Chapter 2**: Document Presentation	Resize and Position an Object
5.4.3	Add alternative text to objects for accessibility	**Chapter 2**: Document Presentation	Format an Object
6.	**Manage Document Collaboration**		
6.1	**Add and manage comments**		
6.1.1	Add comments	**Chapter 4**: Research and Collaboration	Add a Comment
6.1.2	Review and reply to comments	**Chapter 4**: Research and Collaboration	View Comments Reply to Comments
6.1.3	Resolve comments	**Chapter 4**: Research and Collaboration	View Comments Reply to Comments
6.1.4	Delete comments	**Chapter 4**: Research and Collaboration	Add a Comment
6.2	**Manage change tracking**		
6.2.1	Track changes	**Chapter 4**: Research and Collaboration	Use Track Changes
6.2.2	Review tracked changes	**Chapter 4**: Research and Collaboration	Use Track Changes
6.2.3	Accept and reject tracked changes	**Chapter 4**: Research and Collaboration	Accept Changes
6.2.4	Lock and unlock change tracking	**Chapter 4**: Research and Collaboration	Track Changes

MOS Obj #	MOS Objective	Exploring Chapter	Exploring Section Heading
I.	**Manage Document Options and Settings**		
1.1	**Manage documents and templates**		
1.1.1	Modify existing document templates	**Chapter 6:** Document Management	Download a Template
1.1.2	Manage document versions	**Chapter 6:** Document Management	Compare and Combine Documents
1.1.3	Compare and combine multiple documents	**Chapter 6:** Document Management	Compare and Combine Documents
1.1.4	Link to external document content	**Chapter 5:** Document Publications	Copy and Link Objects from Other Files
1.1.5	Enable macros in a document	**Chapter 6:** Document Management	Record a Macro
1.1.6	Customize the Quick Access toolbar	Common Features	Use and Customize the Quick Access Toolbar
1.1.7	Display hidden ribbon tabs	**Chapter 5:** Document Publications	Create an Electronic Form
1.1.8	Change the Normal template default font	Online Appendix	Online Appendix
1.2	**Prepare documents for collaboration**		
1.2.1	Restrict editing	**Chapter 5:** Document Publications	Enable Form Protection
1.2.2	Protect documents by using passwords	**Chapter 6:** Document Management	Set a Password
1.3	**Use and configure language options**		
1.3.1	Configure editing and display languages	**Chapter 1:** Introduction to Word	Use Language and Translation Features
1.3.2	Use language-specific features	**Chapter 1:** Introduction to Word	Use Language and Translation Features
2.	**Use Andvanced Editing and Formatting Features**		
2.1	**Find, replace, and paste document content**		
2.1.1	Find and replace text by using wildcards and special characters	Online Appendix	Online Appendix
2.1.2	Find and replace formatting and styles	Online Appendix	Online Appendix
2.1.3	Apply Paste Options	Online Appendix	Online Appendix
2.2	**Configure paragraph layout options**		
2.2.1	Configure hyphenation and line numbers	Online Appendix	Online Appendix
2.2.2	Set paragraph pagination options	Online Appendix	Online Appendix

MOS Obj #	MOS Objective	Exploring Chapter	Exploring Section Heading
2.3	**Create and manage styles**		
2.3.1	Create paragraph and character styles	**Chapter 1:** Introduction to Word	Select and Modify Styles
2.3.2	Modify existing styles	**Chapter 1:** Introduction to Word	Select and Modify Styles
2.3.3	Copy styles to other documents or templates	Online Appendix	Online Appendix

3. Create Custom Document Elements

3.1	**Create and modify building blocks**		
3.1.1	Create QuickParts	**Chapter 6:** Document Management	Create and Insert a Building Block
3.1.2	Manage building blocks	**Chapter 6:** Document Management	Create and Insert a Building Block
3.2	**Create custom design elments**		
3.2.1	Create custom color sets	**Chapter 6:** Document Management	Customize Theme Colors
3.2.2	Create custom fonts sets	**Chapter 6:** Document Management	Customize Theme Fonts
3.2.3	Create custom themes	**Chapter 6:** Document Management	Save a Custom Theme
3.2.4	Create custom style sets	Online Appendix	Online Appendix
3.3	**Create and manage indexes**		
3.3.1	Mark index entries	**Chapter 4:** Research and Collaboration	Create an Index
3.3.2	Create indexes	**Chapter 4:** Research and Collaboration	Create an Index
3.3.3	Update indexes	**Chapter 4:** Research and Collaboration	Create an Index
3.4	**Create and manage tables of figures**		
3.4.1	Insert figure and table captions	**Chapter 3:** Document Productivity	Include a Table Caption
3.4.2	Configure caption properties	**Chapter 3:** Document Productivity	Include a Table Caption
3.4.3	Insert and modify a table of figures	**Chapter 4:** Research and Collaboration	Manage a Table of Figures

4. Use Advanced Word Features

4.1	**Manage forms, fields, and controls**		
4.1.1	Add custom fields	**Chapter 5:** Document Publications	Insert Content Controls
4.1.2	Modify field properties	**Chapter 5:** Document Publications	Insert Content Controls
4.1.3	Insert standard content controls	**Chapter 5:** Document Publications	Insert Content Controls
4.1.4	Configure standard content controls	**Chapter 5:** Document Publications	Insert Content Controls

MOS Obj #	MOS Objective	Exploring Chapter	Exploring Section Heading
4.2	**Create and modify macros**		
4.2.1	Record simple macros	**Chapter 6:** Document Management	Record a Macro
4.2.2	Name simple macros	**Chapter 6:** Document Management	Record a Macro
4.2.3	Edit simple macros	**Chapter 6:** Document Management	Modify a Macro
4.2.4	Copy macros to other documents or templates	Online Appendix	Online Appendix
4.3	**Perform mail merges**		
4.3.1	Manage recipient lists	**Chapter 3:** Document Productivity	Edit a Data Source
4.3.2	Insert merged fields	**Chapter 3:** Document Productivity	Insert Merge Fields
4.3.3	Preview merge results	**Chapter 3:** Document Productivity	Complete a Merge
4.3.4	Create merged documents, labels, and envelopes	**Chapter 3:** Document Productivity	Insert Merge Fields

Glossary

@mention Directs a chat or conversation to a specific individual, group, or channel in Microsoft Teams.

Accessibility Checker A feature that locates elements in a document that might cause difficulty for people with disabilities to read.

Activity feed A summary of all activities within a Microsoft Teams channel.

Alignment The positioning of the text relative to the margins.

Alignment guide A horizontal or vertical green bar that displays as you move an object, assisting with aligning the object with text or with another object.

All Markup A markup view that shows the document with all the revisions, markups, and comments using the formats predefined in Track Changes options.

American Psychological Association (APA) A writing style established by the American Psychological Association with rules and conventions for documenting sources and organizing a research paper (used primarily in business and the social sciences).

App An application that adds additional functionality to Microsoft Teams.

Application software Programs used to complete tasks such as email, gaming, and social networking as well as word processing, presentations, and spreadsheets.

Argument A positional reference contained within parentheses in a function such as a cell reference or value, required to complete a function and produce output.

AutoCorrect A feature that automatically corrects standard spelling and word usage errors as they are typed.

AutoRecover A feature that enables Word to recover a previous version of a document.

AutoSave A feature that saves files every few seconds if those files are housed on OneDrive, OneDrive for Business, or SharePoint Online.

AutoText A type of building block to store text or graphics that will be reused, such as a standard contract clause or a long distribution list.

Background A color, design, image, or watermark that displays behind text in a document or on a webpage.

Bibliography A list of sources consulted by an author during research for a paper.

Bookmark A feature that provides an electronic marker for a specific location in a document, enabling the user to go to that location quickly.

Border Lines that display at the top, bottom, left, or right of a paragraph, a page, a table, or an image.

Border Painter A feature that enables you to choose border formatting and click on any table border to apply the formatting.

Breakout room A feature in Microsoft Teams that enables meeting participants to be divided into smaller groups.

Building block A predefined block of text for standardized content that can be placed in any document.

Bulleted list A list of points that is not sequential; each point is typically identified by a graphic element that itemizes and separates bulleted items.

Caption A descriptive title for a table.

Cell The intersection of a column and row in a Word table, PowerPoint table, or Excel worksheet.

Center alignment A setting that positions text horizontally in the center of a line, with an equal distance from both the left and right margins.

Channel A section within a team that relates to a specific department, project, or topic.

Chat A form of communication like a text or instant message used in Microsoft Teams.

Check Box content control A form element that consists of a box that can be checked or unchecked.

Chicago Writing Style A writing style established by the University of Chicago with rules and conventions for preparing an academic paper for publication.

Citation A brief, parenthetical reference placed at the end of a sentence or paragraph that directs a reader to a source of information you used.

Clipboard An area of memory reserved to temporarily hold selections that have been cut or copied that enables you to paste the selections.

Column A format that separates document text into side-by-side vertical blocks, often used in newsletters.

Combine A feature that integrates all changes from multiple authors or documents into one single document.

Combo Box content control A content control that combines a text box with a list box, so that a user may choose from items displayed in a drop-down box or can type an entry instead of selecting from the list.

Command A button or area within a group that you click to perform tasks.

Command box Used to search for and access almost anything within a team.

Comment A note, annotation, or additional information to the author or another reader about the content of a document.

Comment balloon A feature that displays as a boxed note in the margin and, when selected, highlights the text to which the comment is applied.

Compare A feature that evaluates the contents of two versions of a document side by side for a line-by-line comparison and displays a merged version with markup and tracked changes showing the differences between them.

Compressed (zipped) folder A folder that uses less storage space and can be transferred or shared more easily.

Connector A type of app that offers frequently updated content.

Content control A form element that displays prompts such as drop-down lists, date pickers, text boxes, and check boxes so that users can quickly fill out electronic forms.

Contextual tab A tab that contains a group of commands related to the selected object.

Copy A command used to duplicate a selection from the original location and place a copy in the Office Clipboard.

Cover page The first page of a report, including the report title, author, and other identifying information.

Crop The process of trimming edges that you do not want to display.

Cropping handle Location on the top, bottom, left, right, or any corner of a selected image that can be dragged to remove a portion of the image.

Current List A list that includes all citation sources you use in the current document.

Cut A command used to remove a selection from the original location and place it in the Office Clipboard.

Data source A list of information that is merged with a main document during a mail merge procedure.

Date Picker content control A form element that displays a calendar that can be used to select a date.

Design Mode The setting that enables users to view, insert, and modify content controls.

Desktop The main workspace for the operating system.

Desktop publishing A process that uses software, such as Word, to design commercial-quality printed material.

Dialog box A box that provides access to more precise, but less frequently used, commands.

Dialog Box Launcher A button that when clicked opens a corresponding dialog box.

Dock A feature of macOS desktop used to access frequently used apps, files, and folders.

Document Inspector A feature that checks for and removes certain hidden and personal information from a document.

Document property Data element that is saved with a document but does not display in the document as it is shown onscreen or is printed.

Document theme A unified set of design elements, including font style, color, and special effects, that is applied to an entire document.

Draft view A view that shows a great deal of document space but no margins, headers, footers, or other special features.

Drop cap A very large capital letter at the beginning of a paragraph.

Drop-Down List content control A form element that enables choices from one of several existing entries.

Embed A process that brings an object or data from another application or file into a document, enabling the object to be edited without changing the source.

Endnote A citation that displays at the end of a document.

Field An item of information in a data source record.

File Explorer A Windows app that is used to manage folders and files across various storage locations.

File management An organizational structure for contents stored on a computer.

File tab A tab on the ribbon that contains commands that do things "to" a file rather than "in" a file.

Finder A macOS app that is used to manage apps, folders, and files across various storage locations.

First line indent A setting that marks the location to indent only the first line in a paragraph.

Font A combination of typeface and type style.

Footer Information that displays at the bottom of a document page.

Footnote A citation that displays at the bottom of a page.

Form A document designed to collect data.

Form letter A document used in a mail merge process including standard text that is personalized with recipient information.

Format Painter A feature that enables you to quickly and easily copy all formatting from one area to another in Word, PowerPoint, and Excel.

Formatting The process of modifying text by changing font and paragraph characteristics.

Formatting restriction A setting that limits the types of styles users can apply in a document.

Formula A combination of cell references, operators, values, and/or functions used to perform a calculation.

Function A predefined computation that simplifies creating a complex calculation and produces a result based on inputs known as arguments.

Gallery An Office feature that displays additional formatting and design choices. An area in Word which provides additional text styles. In Excel, the gallery provides a choice of chart styles, and in Power Point, the gallery provides transitions.

Group (Common Features) A subset of a tab that organizes similar tasks together.

Group (Word) The process of combining selected objects so they display as a single object.

Hanging indent A setting that aligns the first line of a paragraph at the left margin, indenting remaining lines in the paragraph.

Header An area with one or more lines of information at the top of each page.

Header row The first row in a data source that contains labels describing the data in rows beneath.

Hyperlink An electronic marker that points to a different location within the same document using a bookmark, opens another document, or displays a different webpage in a browser.

Hypertext Markup Language (HTML) A universal formatting instructional language that describes how a document displays when viewed in a browser.

Indent A setting associated with how part of a paragraph is distanced from the margin.

Index An alphabetical listing of topics covered in a document, along with the page numbers on which the topic is discussed.

Insert Control An indicator that displays between rows or columns in a table, enabling you to insert one or more rows or columns.

Insertion point A blinking bar that indicates where text that you next type will display.

Jump List A list of program-specific shortcuts to recently opened files, the program name, and pinning options.

Justified alignment A setting that spreads text evenly between the left and right margins, so that text begins at the left margin and ends uniformly at the right margin.

Keyboard shortcut A combination of two or more keys pressed together to initiate a software command.

Layer The process of placing one object on top of another.

Leaders The series of dots or hyphens that leads the reader's eye across the page to connect two columns of information.

Left alignment A setting that begins text evenly at the left margin, with a ragged right edge.

Left indent A setting that positions all text in a paragraph at an equal distance from the left margin.

Legacy Tools A set of controls that is accessible by both current and earlier Word versions.

Legal blacklining A way to compare two documents and to display the changes between the two documents.

Line spacing The vertical space between lines in a paragraph.

Link An active part of a document or webpage that initiates movement to another area when clicked.

Linking The process of importing an object from another application so that the object retains a connection to the file that contains the original data.

Live Layout A feature that enables you to watch text flow around an object as you move it, so you can position the object exactly as you want it.

Live Preview An Office feature that provides a preview of the results of a selection when you point to an option in a list or gallery. Using Live Preview, you can experiment with settings before making a final choice.

macOS The operating system that runs on Apple desktop and laptop computers.

Macro A set of instructions that executes a specific task or series of keystrokes; often used to automate repetitive tasks using only a button click or keyboard combination.

Mail Merge A process that combines content from a main document and a data source.

Main document A document that contains the information that stays the same for all recipients in a mail merge.

Margin The area of blank space that displays to the left, right, top, and bottom of a document or worksheet.

Markup A feature to help customize how tracked changes are displayed in a document.

Master List A database of all citation sources created in Word on a particular computer.

Masthead The identifying information at the top of a newsletter or other periodical.

Meeting A get-together in real time with others to share audio, video, and screen content.

Merge field An item that serves as a placeholder for the variable data that will be inserted into the main document during a mail merge procedure.

Microsoft 365 A productivity software suite including a set of software applications, each one specializing in a particular type of output.

Microsoft Access A relational database management system in which you can record and link data, query databases, and create forms and reports.

Microsoft Excel An application that makes it easy to organize records, financial transactions, and business information in the form of worksheets.

Microsoft PowerPoint An application that enables you to create dynamic presentations to inform groups and persuade audiences.

Microsoft Teams A Microsoft application that facilitates communication and collaboration in real time between groups of individuals in different locations.

Microsoft Word A word processing software application used to produce all sorts of documents, including memos, newsletters, forms, tables, and brochures.

Mini Toolbar A toolbar that provides access to the most common formatting selections, such as adding bold or italic or changing font type or color. Unlike the Quick Access Toolbar, the Mini toolbar is not customizable.

Modern Language Association (MLA) A writing style established by the Modern Language Association, with rules and conventions for preparing research papers (used primarily in the area of humanities).

No Markup A markup view that provides a completely clean view of a document, temporarily hiding all comments and revisions, and displays the document as it would if all changes were applied and does not show any of the markups or comments.

Numbered list A list that sequences items by displaying a successive number beside each item.

Object An item, such as a picture or text box, that can be individually selected and manipulated in a document.

Object Linking and Embedding (OLE) A feature in Microsoft Office that enables you to insert an object into a presentation either as an embedded or linked object.

Office An online suite of Microsoft 365 applications that are available through a OneDrive account.

OneDrive Microsoft's cloud storage system. Saving files to OneDrive enables them to sync across all Windows devices and to be accessible from any Internet-connected device.

Order of operations A set of rules that controls the sequence in which arithmetic operations are performed. Also called the *order of precedence*.

Outline view A structural view of a document that can be collapsed or expanded as necessary.

Page orientation The orientation of a page for viewing. Portrait orientation is when a page is taller than wider. Landscape orientation is when a page is wider than taller.

Paragraph spacing The amount of space before or after a paragraph.

Password A series of characters designed to protect a document from unauthorized access or to limit modification of a document.

Paste A command used to place a cut or copied selection into another location.

PDF Reflow A Word feature that converts a PDF document into an editable Word document.

Picture A graphic file that is retrieved from storage media or the Internet and placed in an Office project.

Pin A command used to add a tile to the Start menu.

Placeholder A field or block of text used to determine the position of objects in a document.

Plagiarizing The act of using and documenting the works of another as one's own.

Plain Text content control A form element that enables all types of data entry but prohibits formatting.

Portable Document Format (PDF) A file type that was created for exchanging documents independent of software applications and operating system environments.

PowerPoint Live A content-sharing method that enables Microsoft Teams meeting participants to view a PowerPoint presentation at their own pace.

Print Layout view A view that closely resembles the way a document will look when printed.

Pull quote A phrase or sentence taken from an article to emphasize a key point.

Quick access A feature of File Explorer that contains shortcuts to files and folders used most often.

Quick Access Toolbar A feature that provides one-click access to commonly executed tasks. It is hidden by default but displays under the ribbon when activated.

Quick Parts A feature on the ribbon, and also a Building Block gallery, that provides access to categories of building blocks.

Range A group of adjacent or contiguous cells in a worksheet. A range can be adjacent cells in a column (such as C5:C10) or row (such as A6:H6), or a rectangular group of cells (such as G5:H10).

Read Mode A view in which text reflows automatically between columns to make it easier to read.

Real-time co-authoring A Word feature that shows several authors simultaneously editing the document in Word or Word for the web.

Record A group of related fields representing one entity, such as data for one person, place, event, or concept.

Revision mark A mark that indicates where text is added, deleted, or formatted while the Track Changes feature is active.

Ribbon The command center of Office applications. It is the long bar located just beneath the title bar, containing tabs, groups, and commands.

Rich Text content control A control that is often used to insert formatted text, images, and tables.

Right alignment A setting that begins text evenly at the right margin, with a ragged left edge.

Right indent A setting that positions all text in a paragraph at an equal distance from the right margin.

Sans serif font A font that does not contain a thin line or extension at the top and bottom of the primary strokes on characters.

Screenshot A picture of a device display.

ScreenTip A small message box that displays when you place the pointer over a command button. The purpose of the command, short descriptive text, or keyboard shortcut if applicable will display in the box.

Search A feature used to search the computer for programs, folders, files, and Web searches.

Search box A box, located on the title bar of any application window, that enables you to search for help and information about a command or task you want to perform and presents you with a shortcut directly to that command.

Section A part of a document that contains its own page format settings, such as those for margins, columns, and orientation.

Serif font A font that contains a thin line or extension at the top and bottom of the primary strokes on characters.

Shading A background color that displays behind text in a paragraph, page, or table element.

Shape A geometric or non-geometric object, such as a rectangle or an arrow, used to create an illustration or highlight information.

Shortcut menu A menu that provides choices related to the selection or area at which you right-click.

Side by Side view A feature that enables you to display two documents side by side on the same screen.

Sidebar Supplementary text that displays along the side of a document.

Simple Markup A Word feature that simplifies the display of comments and revision marks, resulting in a clean, uncluttered look.

Sizing handle A series of dots on the outside border of a selected object, enabling the user to adjust the height and width of the object.

SmartArt A visual representation of information that can be created to effectively communicate a list, process, or relationship.

SmartArt Text pane A pane that displays beside a SmartArt diagram, enabling you to enter text.

Snap Assist A feature in Windows used to place windows to either side of the screen.

Snap layout A Windows 11 feature that provides options for open windows as to how they can be arranged on the screen.

Source A publication, person, or media item that is consulted in the preparation of a paper and given credit.

Start menu Provides main access to all programs and features on the Windows computer.

Status bar A bar located at the bottom of the program window that contains information relative to the open file. It also includes tools for changing the view of the file and for changing the zoom size of onscreen file contents.

Style A named collection of formatting characteristics that can be applied to text or paragraphs.

Style manual A guide to a writing style outlining required rules and conventions related to the preparation of papers.

Style set Predefined combinations of font, style, color, and font size that can be applied to selected text.

Stylistic set Embedded appearance options that enable subtle changes in style, character appearance, and other settings.

Symbol A character or graphic not normally included on a keyboard.

Synchronous scrolling A feature that enables you to scroll through two documents at the same time using either of the two scroll bars.

System software The essential software that a computer needs to function. System software includes the operating system and utility programs.

Tab Located on the ribbon, each tab is designed to appear much like a tab on a file folder, with the active tab highlighted.

Tab selector The small box at the leftmost edge of the horizontal ruler.

Tab stop A marker on the horizontal ruler specifying the location where the insertion point stops after Tab is pressed to align text in a document.

Table A grid of columns and rows that organizes data.

Table alignment The horizontal position of a table between the left and right margins.

Table of contents A page that lists headings in the order in which they display in a document and the page numbers on which the entries begin.

Table style A named collection of color, font, and border designs that can be applied to a table.

Tag A data element or metadata that is added as a document property. Tags help in indexing and searching.

Task view A view that provides a single view of all open windows.

Taskbar A feature of the Windows desktop that provides quick access to commonly used programs or settings.

Team A collection of people, conversations, files, and tools in Microsoft Teams.

Template A predesigned file that contains preformatted text and/or graphics such as a theme and layout and may include content that can be modified.

Text box A rectangular object that contains text and that can display in any location within a document; if text changes, the box dimensions automatically adjust to accommodate.

Text wrapping The way text flows around an image.

Theme A collection of design choices that includes colors, fonts, and special effects used to give a consistent look to a document, workbook, presentation, or database form or report.

Theme color A feature that represents coordinated colors for the current text and background, accents, and hyperlinks.

Theme effect A feature that includes lines or fill effects to incorporate into a document theme.

Theme font A feature that contains a coordinating heading and body text font.

Thesaurus A tool used to quickly find a synonym (a word with the same meaning as another) for a selected word.

Three-part indent marker An icon located at the left side of the ruler that enables you to set a left indent, a hanging indent, or a first line indent.

Tile A feature on the Start menu that is a shortcut to launch a program or open a folder in Windows.

Title bar The long bar at the top of each window that displays the name of the folder, file, or program displayed in the open window and the application in which you are working.

Toggle command A button that acts somewhat like light switches that you can turn on and off. You select the command to turn it on and then select it again to turn it off.

Track Changes A Word feature that monitors all additions, deletions, and formatting changes you make in a document.

Turabian writing style A writing style that originated as a subset of Chicago.

Ungroup A process that divides a combined single object into individual objects that comprise it.

User exception An individual or group that can edit all or specific parts of a restricted document.

View The various ways a file can display on the screen.

Virtual desktop A way to group windows together on separate desktops.

Visual Basic for Applications (VBA) A programming language that is built into Office and used to code and edit macros.

Watermark Text or graphics that display behind text.

Web Layout view A view that displays the way a document will look when posted on the Internet.

Webpage Any document that displays on the World Wide Web.

Whiteboard A feature that enables users to work collaboratively on a shared canvas.

Windows The Microsoft operating system that is available for desktops, laptops, and tablet computers.

Word for the web An online component of Office consisting of a Web-based version of Word with sufficient capabilities to enable you to edit and format a document online.

Word processing software A computer application, such as Microsoft Word, used primarily with text to create, edit, and format documents.

Word wrap The feature that automatically moves words to the next line if they do not fit on the current line.

WordArt A feature that modifies text to include special effects, such as color, shadow, gradient, and 3D appearance.

Works Cited A list of sources cited by an author in his or her work.

World Wide Web (WWW) A very large subset of the Internet that stores webpage documents.

Writing style Provides a set of rules that results in standardized documents that present citations in the same manner and that include the same general page characteristics.

Zoom slider A feature that displays at the far-right side of the status bar. It is used to increase or decrease the magnification of the file.

Index